CONTEMPORARY IMMIGRATION IN AMERICA

CONTEMPORARY IMMIGRATION IN AMERICA

A State-by-State Encyclopedia

VOLUME 1

ALABAMA–MISSOURI

Kathleen R. Arnold, Editor

 **GREENWOOD**

AN IMPRINT OF ABC-CLIO, LLC
Santa Barbara, California • Denver, Colorado • Oxford, England

Copyright © 2015 by ABC-CLIO, LLC

Library of Congress Cataloging-in-Publication Data

Contemporary immigration in America : a state-by-state encyclopedia /
   Kathleen R. Arnold, editor.
     pages cm
   Includes bibliographical references and index.
   ISBN 978-0-313-39917-6 (hard copy : alk. paper) — ISBN 978-0-313-39918-3 (ebook)
1. United States—Emigration and immigration—Encyclopedias.
2. Immigrants—United States—Encyclopedias.   I. Arnold, Kathleen R., 1966– editor.
   JV6465.C745   2014
   304.8'73003—dc23   2014039672

ISBN: 978-0-313-39917-6
EISBN: 978-0-313-39918-3

19 18 17 16 15   1 2 3 4 5

This book is also available on the World Wide Web as an eBook.
Visit www.abc-clio.com for details.

Greenwood
An Imprint of ABC-CLIO, LLC

ABC-CLIO, LLC
130 Cremona Drive, P.O. Box 1911
Santa Barbara, California 93116–1911

This book is printed on acid-free paper ∞

Manufactured in the United States of America

CONTENTS

VOLUME 2

INTRODUCTION

Contemporary Immigration in America: A State-by-State Encyclopedia is a two-volume reference work aimed at a broad audience, including secondary school students through graduate students and researchers, as well as journalists and the general public. The encyclopedia is written in an accessible manner with each state chapter including a historical timeline, which covers the entire history of the state; topical essays that provide more in-depth discussion of important immigration events, issues, legislation, or topics in the state; and descriptions of notable figures or groups that have been or are involving themselves in state immigration issues. Each chapter concludes with a bibliography listing important print and electronic information resources to aid anyone researching state and local immigration history and political issues. The term "contemporary," as discussed later, indicates that the encyclopedia is on the postwar period, from 1945 to the present. The focus on state and local issues is both relatively unique—most treatments of immigration cover national trends and issues and federal policies—and absolutely significant, given the recent power that states have had to determine immigration policy. However, even before these powers were granted to the states, focusing on state and local immigration issues and policies from the postwar period to the present brings attention to the diversity of immigration settlement in each area and to the programs—particularly guest worker schemes and refugee resettlement—that have significantly contributed to the history of each state but are often ignored or treated in isolation in the mainstream literature on immigration. Moreover, the specific development of each state shapes a distinctive context of reception for new immigrants. For example, Utah's history as a place of refuge for Mormons has not only shaped policies more oriented toward families and less toward individuals but has also brought these policies—which could be deemed "conservative" or "traditional"—very close to what more progressive immigrant activists and policymakers want. Another interesting example is Idaho, which has the highest concentration of Basque residents and Basque descendents in the world, outside of their Spanish state. Interestingly, both Utah and Idaho have been active in recent immigration policies and debates, even though the two states have relatively low numbers of immigrants. Finally, while each chapter is uniform in format, each author or set of authors has written their chapters from different methodological perspectives, focusing on different issues, and logically, analyzing groups specific to that region. As I state below, each chapter should serve as a good starting point for more in-depth research, and this encyclopedia is one of the few projects that have compiled this information in one resource, allowing for state-by-state comparisons.

The subject of immigration in the United States is particularly interesting not only because it has been a controversial topic since at least the 1990s but also because of the way it brings together what is often conceptually divided. For example, issues of immigration not only pertain to foreign residents but also help to define citizenship. However, the shaping of political inclusion goes beyond formal policies and is also produced by norms about alienage, race, economic class, "model minorities," and gender. Debates and assumptions about immigrants not only identify "in groups" and "out groups" within the foreign population but also target American-born minorities, intersecting with gender and class (see Shah 1997, 8, 38, 191–95; Morrison 1994, 97–100). For these reasons, the subject of immigration brings together a number of academic disciplines—it links public policy experts to international relations theorists, scholars of American politics and government to political theorists and legal theorists, and experts on economic globalization to feminist and race theorists of American politics. Recent changes in state and local immigration further highlight the degree to which immigration is a complex and interdisciplinary subject.

These recent changes and the broader relationship between state and local immigration policy are the particular focus of this encyclopedia; this relationship has become especially controversial since at least the 1990s (in recent times, anyway). Lurking behind the tension between the federal government and the states' implementation of immigration policy is far more than would appear: changes in politico-economic policy (a turn to a neoliberal framework); the greater participation of immigrant workers in urban economies, including the feminization of labor; and the greater polarization of wealth that has occurred in recent decades. This is a particularly interesting moment to investigate these relationships because the conflicts between the federal government and state and local policies highlight deficiencies in other areas (outside of immigration, strictly speaking), including access to medical care and overburdened emergency services; inadequate policing; major cutbacks in public education; the scaling back of the social safety net; and higher unemployment and a more insecure job market for the majority of workers. While certain immigrant groups have been blamed for all of these domestic issues, the federal government has sought to walk a middle road: both tightening the border and increasing detention and deportation as major policy tools while continuing to look away as industries hire undocumented immigrants across the United States. The effect is not to deter undocumented entry and undocumented residency so much as to make the lives and political status of these individuals more precarious. The Postville, Iowa, raid of a kosher meat processing plant in 2008 is an example of the tension between economic exploitation and political precariousness (see Camayd-Freixas 2008; "The Shame of Postville, Iowa" *New York Times* 2008)

In response to what is perhaps rightly viewed as a contradictory set of policies, some states have recently implemented policies that are even harsher, more punitive, and often more overtly ethnically or racially oriented than federal law. (For the opposite view, see Schuck 2007.) Clearly, the fact that certain religious institutions, neighborhoods, and cities have chosen to establish sanctuary areas for immigrants is proof that local institutions are not always harsh toward immigrants. Nevertheless, sanctuary areas have highly precarious legal standing and the numbers of these sites are not particularly high. Many of these states are moving toward offering, or currently do offer in-state tuition at state colleges and universities for resident undocumented children. More recently, many of these states have also attempted to opt out of the Secure Communities Program because it has been deemed a failure, often targeting the wrong people. All of these moves indicate sympathy toward immigrants and the desire to ensure more legal avenues for immigrants to regularize their status, rather than detaining or jailing them.

The difficulty in this matter is complex and includes the basic fact that the federal government has traditionally had purview over immigration policy due to its plenary power (see Bosniak 2006; Hernández 2008; Kanstroom 2007; Varsanyi 2008). Plenary power is the exclusive authority of Congress and the executive to make decisions on matters of immigration, without limits or judicial review. Congressional and executive authority in this sphere is linked to broader notions of sovereignty and territorial control, of which immigration is one important aspect. Thus, immigration is regulated by "Congress's plenary, or absolute power to regulate immigration as part of its authority over foreign relations, in the same realm as declaring war and making treaties" (Ngai 2006, 293; see also Bosniak 2006, 50–51, 53). In essence, this power allows the federal government to treat foreigners as rightless. However, up until the 1990s, "local and state governments were almost wholly excluded from this policy realm" and thus were paradoxically required to recognize the "personhood" of immigrants and, therefore, as individuals having constitutional rights (Varsanyi 2008, 878). Nevertheless, in the 1990s, the passage of three laws shifted this power dynamic, leading to "partial devolution": the Anti-terrorism and Effective Death Penalty Act, the Illegal Immigration Reform and Immigrant Responsibility Act, and the Personal Responsibility and Work Opportunity Reconciliation Act (see Varsanyi 2008, 878 and Fix and Tumlin 1997; some have called this "the new federalism"—see Edwards 2010 and Schapiro 2010). Among other things, these acts allow states to draw a more rigid distinction between citizen and foreigner and permit various forms of discrimination, both economic (see Fix and Tumlin 1997) and racial (see Varsanyi 2008). Working, legal residents and the poor in general, including poor children, are also at greater risk of increased poverty and malnutrition as a result of these measures. Nevertheless, these changes have also led to decreased state latitude in dealing with undocumented immigrants and severe restrictions on providing sanctuary spaces (see Fix and Tumlin 1997).

As several states have argued in the past, when they have a disproportionate number of immigrants crossing their borders, whether legally or "illegally," federal policy is inadequate to deal with these massive influxes. Although claims that new immigrants tend to settle more in certain states (e.g., California and Arizona) than in others are true, these statements often presuppose a class orientation. States and local areas are worried about individuals who are called "labor immigrants" (see Portes and Rumbaut 2006) rather than professional foreign workers—that perhaps speaks to broader worries about the economic trends I have identified earlier. In the context of economic recession and the greater polarization of incomes, labor immigrants have often been blamed for depressing wages, "stealing" welfare, and "stealing" jobs (see Arnold 2008; Arnold 2011). However, with a changing job market and a more neoliberal orientation, these dynamics are perhaps different today: there is less job security at all class and employment levels; there is greater difficulty in attaining adequate healthcare; there is less mobility within companies; and a service economy has led to more labor intensity, combined with increased geographical and physical isolation. Saskia Sassen also compellingly argues that working class jobs have been increasingly devalued as unskilled and viewed in gendered and racist terms that lead to the greater invisibility of workers (Sassen 1998). State and local authorities have responded to claims about the purported economic threat of immigrants by ensuring that even knowingly renting an apartment to an undocumented immigrant can be actionable; attempting to prevent the establishment of hiring halls for day-laborers and restricting the use of public space for the same reason; and enacting English-only laws (see Preston 2011; see also Sandoval and Tambini 2004; Crenshaw 1991).

However, to complicate matters, some of the states that are introducing incredibly strict legislation—like Missouri, as of this writing—have little to no immigration activity. As Blank notes, "Missouri is projected to have less than 1 percent of the nation's 12 million illegal immigrants" (Blank 2008; see also Preston 2008). Moreover, there is some evidence that immigration policy has been shaped by private companies who have done so to reap economic gain (Sullivan 2010). And so the argument about disproportionate burdens cannot really explain what has been a 15-year backlash against immigration. Alternatively, states like Alabama have enacted laws that have effectively placed them in a bind: the state relies heavily on undocumented immigrant labor in its agricultural sector but, nevertheless, enacted policies that have "scared" immigrants away (see Robertson 2011, October 3). Even with a case such as Arizona (see Archibold 2010; Savage 2011), where the number of authorized and undocumented entrants is probably higher than in many other areas of the country, the discourse of an immigration "problem" and various states of emergency that have purportedly resulted from this problem must be tied to broader issues in these areas, including economic instability, unemployment, an unequal educational system, and inadequate healthcare. The charges that immigrants have "caused" these issues could be challenged, even if immigrants are certainly implicated in these crises. Beyond these claims of unfair burdens that immigrants purportedly create is the issue of democracy—should immigrants be treated as political equals with constitutional rights?

The unique aspects of plenary power have meant that foreigners on U.S. soil can be treated according to radically different standards than citizens; devolution only means that the same treatment is carried out at state and local levels. At best, this may indicate a sort of second-class status that can change with naturalization (the application for and acceptance to citizenship). At worst, it can mean immigrants—at least certain sectors of the immigrant population—can be subjected to a range of policies and procedures that are violations of human rights norms. This treatment includes internment in the mass detention system; the suspension of habeas corpus rights, in some cases; and the controversial use of deportation as a major tool of immigration policy since the mid-1990s (see Dow 2004; Kanstroom 2007). Even when foreigners are legal residents or citizens, their citizen rights can be revoked or suspended (Kanstroom 2007). Because of this, some immigrant families and communities can feel threatened: they could lose their residency, mixed-status families could be pulled apart, and economic and educational gains could be lost. On the other hand, since the Obama administration took office in 2009, there has been greater use of judicial discretion to allow individuals to remain in the United States and perhaps regularize their status. The Obama administration also introduced Deferred Action for Childhood Arrivals in 2012, attempting to help long-term resident immigrants who are undocumented because they arrived with their parents.

The education of the children of undocumented immigrants poses one such dilemma of democracy. According to the majority ruling in *Plyler v. Doe* (1982), children of undocumented immigrants have been permitted to attend public schools, from kindergarten through high school (see *"Plyler v. Doe"*). To avoid creating a class of second-class citizens, it was ruled that these children have not broken the law and should be given opportunities to be educated and gain a civic education. The Texas statute that was being challenged in this case was deemed unconstitutional because it discriminated against a group who could be classified as "persons"; therefore, it violated the Fourteenth Amendment and, thus, went against the equal protection clause of this amendment. Although this decision has remained controversial, it has ensured that these children have had access to public education. It also went beyond the formal definition of citizenship and broadened the political community to include resident foreigners. Nevertheless, the children of undocumented entrants are not guaranteed the right to pursue post-secondary education and so this access has been continuously debated. In the recent assertion of their sovereignty, some states, such as Texas, have chosen to allow the children of undocumented immigrants to attend colleges and community colleges. Other states have not only attempted to bar access to post-secondary institutions but have also tried to challenge the terms of *Plyler*. South Carolina, for example, has blocked all access to universities (see Associated Press, 2009). States that have placed prohibitions on access to higher education have done so because they have interpreted the Illegal Immigration Reform and Immigrant Responsibility Act (IIRIRA 1996) of 1996 as barring undocumented students from certain provisions of higher education (and, as stated, in certain cases, the states have barred them from access to colleges and universities altogether) (see Varsanyi 2008). The Development, Relief, and Education for Alien Minors (DREAM) Act could resolve these issues by introducing a plan for these young adults to not only participate in higher education or military service but also to make their status more "regular" by becoming permanent legal residents. The act would also supplant Section 505 of IIRIRA, ensuring that states could provide full access to tuition benefits and other benefits of higher education (see U.S. Citizenship and Immigration Services 1996). This act could end the fragmentation of an immigrant's political status, which has occurred with partial devolution and, thus, could shape a more positive and consistent basis of political belonging for resident foreigners. All of these plans have also been criticized for placing very high burdens on immigrants to pursue legal status, including lengthy waits and hidden costs (particularly lawyer's fees) (see Gonzales 2014).

Contemporary Immigration in America: A State-by-State Encyclopedia covers many of these issues and much more, including English-only laws, lesbian and gay politics, refugee placement, labor issues, detention centers, and the ongoing debate about educating the children of undocumented immigrants beyond secondary level education with the DREAM Act as the representative legislation for those who believe these children should be able to continue with their education. Each author has expertise in these issues and many have, additionally, studied transnational families and the effects of globalization on local areas (and vice versa). Each state chapter provides a chronology that begins with the foundation of the United States (and in some cases, the colonial era) up through the present. The remainder of the chapter covers immigration from the postwar period to the present. As Monica Varsanyi has stated in her work regarding state and local immigration policies, there is a need for more scholarly and research attention regarding state and local policies and norms. Quite a lot of the literature on immigration focuses on federal policy and power dynamics (see Varsanyi 2010). Exploring state and local policies and issues, this encyclopedia aims to fill this gap and to also contribute to establishing a history of recent historical dynamics that help to explain current norms, policies, and debates in a richer historical context. Although the term "contemporary," when designating U.S. immigration, usually means from 1965 on, we have chosen the postwar period as a starting point for these chapters for several reasons.

First, paying attention to this time period brings a focus on to what is often conceived of as a time of very low immigration and thus, of little interest. However, this era is fascinating in terms of learning how Cold War norms shaped immigration policies and particularly the relationship between the United States and Mexico. The Bracero Program was developed during World War II and officially lasted up until 1964—this program should be considered as an important part of this history, for example. Various refugee groups were also allowed entry as a result of war but others were denied entry (see Shanks 2001). Racial quotas remained until 1965 but were now interpreted in Cold War terms and thus given more political meaning. The 1965 Hart–Celler Act eliminated the racial bias of the old system but maintained the quota system and, correspondingly, low entry numbers. It also provided for family reunification, which unintentionally led to a significant increase in immigrants from certain areas but no marked increases from older immigrant groups. If contemporary immigration has undergone major changes since 1965, it is not because the act was entirely radical in its design.

Since 1965, a lot has changed. The urban areas of the United States have had significant demographic changes as a result of the family reunification provision of the 1965 Act (Sassen 1998, 35–37). Immigrant-sending countries have also changed, reflecting how family reunification was used by newer immigrants and underutilized by older immigrant groups. Additionally, as discussed earlier, the economy has changed in significant ways, ensuring that even when unemployment is high, that working class immigrants will find jobs (Sassen 1998, 45–49). By the 1980s, the initial signs of a backlash against immigration had emerged, culminating in the Immigration and Control Reform Act of 1986 and the legislation of the 1990s identified earlier (see Nevins 2002). This legislation reflected some significant concerns, including a fear of domestic terrorism, "illegal" immigrants taking jobs, the increasing role of drugs in American urban areas, and the desire to reform the welfare state. The legislation from the mid-1990s arguably instituted a sort of revolution in the approach to immigrants, even if this revolution had been culminating. The United States went from a system that had begun to use detention and deportation as immigration policy tools in very minor ways to using them as a significant policy tool, as legitimated by the Antiterrorism and Effective Death Penalty Act of 1996, which provided for a system of *mass* detention and deportation (see Dow 2004; Kanstroom 2007). This act and the provisions of the war on drugs have significantly altered the terms upon which the border is treated; it has turned several minor crimes into deportable offenses post facto and has created an atmosphere of fear in certain immigrant communities. Although several prominent immigrant researchers have argued that undocumented immigration is difficult at the border, but often easier once the person has gotten in, the provisions of this 1996 law have certainly changed the terms upon which all immigrants—including those who have naturalized—can operate in politico-economic space. The threat of detention and deportation, combined with the notion that families will be geographically split up if they have mixed immigration status, challenges the notion that the United States is lax about immigration and/or that immigrants today have unqualified benefits, even if they are undocumented. In fact, the context of reception for many immigrant groups has become harsher.

Although backlashes against immigrants—which are often against poorer immigrants—often wax and wane, the events of September 11, 2001, ensured that the anti-immigrant backlash of the 1990s continued for far longer than it probably would have. Immediately after the attacks, individuals from the Middle East and/or of the Muslim faith were immediately under suspicion (see Akram and Johnson 2002; Verdeja 2002). Refugee numbers were also relatively low because of increasingly stringent government policies (see Schoenholtz 2005; Schrag et al. 2010). By 2006, debates had turned back to the original targets—lower-income immigrants from Central America and Mexico. The time period between 2006 and 2008 can now be thought of as a new period of heightened backlash, with the added provisions that, since the mid-1990s, states have had more legislative and governmental latitude in determining the lives of immigrants.

Today, we are living with the legacy of the 1965 Act, which at best, had aimed at abolishing any racial quotas (and thus eugenic presuppositions) from immigration policy and equalizing our relations with all sending countries. We also live with a changed economy and a different, perhaps fragmenting relationship between states and the federal government. This fragmentation, in turn, ensures that the political status of immigrants is much more ambiguous today. Detention centers are now established institutions in many states and the DREAM Act is still being debated. This encyclopedia fills an important gap in the literature on immigration by providing both historical and current information about state and local immigration, from policy making to everyday life. Hopefully, it will help inform readers about these important debates and consider the most democratic means to deal with the immigration issue—if, indeed, there really is an issue.

A note on the chapters: a variety of authors have contributed to these volumes and each contributor has written about immigration history and policies in a different way. I would like to note that certain sources, including Center for Immigration, FAIR, and NumbersUSA, which are mentioned in some state essays, are considered biased by other scholars and researchers. Readers should approach this subject with a critical eye and use these state essays as beginning reference points.

Finally, thank you to my contributors and to John Wagner at ABC-CLIO for their patience in the production of this project. I dedicate this work to my daughter Hannah.

WORKS CITED

Akram, Susan, and Kevin R. Johnson. "Migration and Regulation Goes Local: The Role of States in U.S. Immigration Policy: Race, Civil Rights, and Immigration Law after September 11, 2001: The Targeting of Arabs and Muslims." *New York University Annual Survey of American Law* 58, no. 295 (2002). http://papers.ssrn.com/sol3/papers.cfm?abstract_id=365261. Accessed March 17, 2014.

Archibold, Randal C. "Arizona Enacts Stringent New Law on Immigration." *New York Times*, April 23, 2010. http://www.nytimes.com/2010/04/24/us/politics/24immig.html. Accessed April 1, 2014.

Arnold, Kathleen R. *America's New Working Class*. College Station: Penn State University Press, 2008.

Arnold, Kathleen R. *American Immigration after 1996: The Shifting Ground of Political Inclusion*. College Station: Penn State University Press, 2011.

Associated Press. "College Board Wants More Help for Illegal Immigrants." *USA Today*, July 22, 2009. http://usatoday30.usatoday.com/news/washington/2009-04-21-college-board-immigrants_N.htm. Accessed April 1, 2014.

Blank, Chris. "Missouri Immigration Restrictions Take Effect in 2009." *Missourian*, December 30, 2008. http://www.columbiamissourian.com/stories/2008/12/30/missouri-immigration-restrictions-take-effect-2009/. Accessed April 1, 2014.

Bosniak, Linda. *The Citizen and the Alien*. Princeton, NJ: Princeton University Press, 2006.

Camayd-Freixas, Erik. Statement of Dr. Erik Camayd-Freixas. Federally Certified Interpreter at the U.S. District Court for the Northern District of Iowa Regarding a Hearing on "The Arrest, Prosecution, and Conviction of 297 Undocumented Workers in Postville, Iowa, from May 12 to 22, 2008." Before the Subcommittee on Immigration, Citizenship, Refugees, Border Security and International Law. July 24, 2008. http://judiciary.house.gov/hearings/pdf/Camayd-Freixas080724.pdf. Accessed April 1 2014.

Crenshaw, Kimberlé. "Mapping the Margins: Intersectionality, Identity, Politics, and Violence against Women of Color." *Stanford Law Review* 43, no. 6 (July 1991): 1241–299.

Dow, Mark. *American Gulag: Inside U.S. Immigration Prisons.* Los Angeles and Berkeley: University of California Press, 2004.

Edwards, James R. Jr. "Federalism Lives!" Center for Immigration website, April 14, 2010. http://www.cis.org/edwards/federalism-arizona. Accessed April 1, 2014.

Fix, Michael E., and Karen C. Tumlin. "Welfare Reform and the Devolution of Immigrant Policy." New Federalism: Issues and Options for States, No. A-15. Urban Institute website, October 1, 1997. http://www.urban.org/publications/307045.html. Accessed April 1, 2014.

García Hernández, César Cuauhtémoc. "No Human Being Is Illegal." *Monthly Review*, June 2008. http://www.monthlyreview.org/080616garcia.php. Accessed April 1, 2014.

Gonzales, Alfonso. *Reform without Justice: Latino Migrant Politics and the Homeland Security State.* New York: Oxford University Press, 2014.

IIRIRA (Illegal Immigration Reform and Immigrant Responsibility Act). U.S. Citizenship and Immigration Services, September, 1996. http://www.uscis.gov/ilink/docView/PUBLAW/HTML/PUBLAW/0–0–0–10948.html . Accessed March 28, 2014.

Kanstroom, Daniel. *Deportation Nation.* Cambridge, MA: Harvard University Press, 2007.

Morrison, Toni. "On the Backs of Blacks." In Nicolaus Mills, ed. *Arguing Immigration.* New York: Simon and Schuster, Touchstone Books, 1994, pp. 97—100.

Nevins, Joseph. *Operation Gatekeeper: The Rise of the "Illegal Alien" and the Making of the U.S.-Mexico Boundary.* New York and London: Routledge, 2002.

Ngai, Mae M. "No Human Being Is Illegal." *Women's Studies Quarterly* 34, no 3/4 *Envy* (Fall–Winter 2006): 291–95.

"*Plyler v. Doe.*" Legal Information Institute, Cornell University Law School. http://www.law.cornell.edu/supct/html/historics/USSC_CR_0457_0202_ZO.html. Accessed April 1, 2014.

Portes, Alejandro, and Rubén Rumbaut. *Immigrant America.* 3rd ed. Berkeley and Los Angeles: University of California Press, 2006.

Preston, Julia. "In Reversal, Courts Uphold Local Immigration Laws." *New York Times*, February 10, 2008. http://www.nytimes.com/2008/02/10/us/10immig.html. Accessed April 1, 2014.

Preston, Julia. "In Alabama, a Harsh Bill for Residents Here Illegally." *New York Times*, June 3, 2011. http://www.nytimes.com/2011/06/04/us/04immig.html?_r=1. Accessed April 1, 2014.

Robertson, Campbell. "After Ruling, Hispanics Flee an Alabama Town." *New York Times*, October 3, 2011. http://www.nytimes.com/2011/10/04/us/after-ruling-hispanics-flee-an-alabama-town.html?scp=7&sq=alabama%20law&st=cse.   Accessed   April 1, 2014.

Robertson, Campbell. "Alabama Immigration Law's Critics Question Target." *New York Times*, October 27, 2011. http://www.nytimes.com/2011/10/28/us/alabama-immigration-laws-critics-question-target.html?_r=1&scp=1&sq=alabama%20immigration%20law&st=cse. Accessed April 1, 2014.

Sandoval, Carlos, and Catherine Tambini, directors. *POV: Farmingville.* Farmingville, 2004.

Sassen, Saskia. *Globalization and Its Discontents: Essays on the New Mobility of People and Money.* New York: New Press, 1998.

Savage, David G. "Arizona Appeals Immigration Ruling to Supreme Court." *Sacramento Bee*, August 13, 2011. http://articles.latimes.com/2011/aug/11/nation/la-na-court-immigration-20110811. Accessed April 1, 2014.

Schapiro, Robert. "Immigration Federalism: Red and Blue." *Concurring Opinions: the Law, the Universe, and Everything*, May 13, 2010. http://www.concurringopinions.com/archives/2010/05/immigration-federalism-red-and-blue.html. Accessed April 1, 2014.

Schoenholtz, Andrew I. "Refugee Protection in the United States Post-September 11." *Columbia Human Rights Law Review* 36, no. 2 (2005): 323–64.

Schrag, Philip G., Andrew Schoenholtz, Jaya Ramji-Nogales, and James P. Dombach. "Rejecting Refugees: Homeland Security's Administration of the One-Year Bar to Asylum." *William and Mary Law Review* 52, no. 3 (2010): 651–804.

Schuck, Peter S. "Taking Immigration Federalism Seriously." *The Forum* 7, no. 3, Article 4, (2007). http://www.bepress.com/forum/vol7/iss3/art4. Accessed April 1, 2014.

Shah, Sonia, ed. *Dragon Ladies: Asian American Feminists Breathe Fire*. Boston: South End Press, 1997.

"The Shame of Postville, Iowa." *New York Times*, July 13, 2008, "Week in Review," p. 11.

Shanks, Cheryl. *Immigration and Politics of American Sovereignty, 1890–1990*. Ann Arbor: University of Michigan Press, 2001.

Sullivan, Laura. "Prison Economics Help Drive Arizona Immigration Law." National Public Radio website, October 28, 2010. http://www.npr.org/templates/story/story.php?storyId=130833741. Accessed April 1, 2014.

Varsanyi, Monica W. "Rescaling the 'Alien,' Rescaling Personhood: Neoliberalism, Immigration, and the State." *Annals of the Association of American Geographers* 98, no. 4 (2008): 877–96.

Varsanyi, Monica, ed. *Taking Local Control: Immigration Policy Activism in U.S. Cities and States*. Palo Alto, CA: Stanford University Press, 2010.

Verdeja, Ernesto. "Law, Terrorism, and the Plenary Power Doctrine: Limiting Alien Rights." *Constellations* 9, no. 1 (2002): 89–97.

1

ALABAMA

William P. Kladky

CHRONOLOGY

1519	Spanish explorer Alonso Álvarez de Piñeda (1494–1520) travels the Gulf of Mexico from Florida to Mexico, including Mobile Bay.
1528–1536	Spaniard Pánfilo de Narváez (1478–1528) fails to set up a colony on the Florida Gulf Coast.
1539–1541	Hernando de Soto (1496–1542) explores the Southeast, meeting Chief Tuskaloosa in the Battle of Maubila in southwestern Alabama.
1702	The brothers Pierre Le Moyne d'Iberville (1661–1706) and Jean-Baptiste Le Moyne de Bienville (1680–1767) establish the French fort and settlement of Fort Louis de la Mobile, 27 miles north of Mobile Bay along the Mobile River.
1704	King Louis XIV (1638–1715) pays the passage and dowries for 25 women to travel from France on *The Pelican* to Louisiana to become wives of the colonists. Known as cassette girls, another group arrives in Louisiana in 1728.
1721	The *Africane* sails to Mobile harbor with a cargo of 120 slaves, only half of those who boarded in Guinea in French West Africa.
1724	The French Code Noir is extended from French West Indies to the French North American colonies, thus institutionalizing slavery in the Mobile area.
1756–1763	After the Seven Years' War (known as the French and Indian War in North America) is won by Great Britain, France cedes its claims east of the Mississippi River to the British and its claims west of the river to Spain.

1780	The Spanish capture Mobile area during the American Revolution.
1783	At the conclusion of the Treaty of Paris ending the American Revolution, Great Britain, in a treaty with Spain, cedes West and East Florida to the Spanish.
1797–1799	A survey verifies the claims of the United States that its southern boundary with Spanish West Florida is at the 31st parallel. Ellicott's Stone is placed 26 miles north of Mobile in 1799 to mark the boundary.
1798	Georgia's western land claims, including Alabama, are organized into the Mississippi Territory.
1799	The United States takes possession of Fort St. Stephens from the Spanish, its first land holding in Alabama.
1802	Georgia formally cedes its western claims in return for the establishment of its southern boundary at the 31st parallel.
1803–1811	The Federal Road is built connecting Georgia and Fort Stoddert, a military post 29 miles north of Mobile. Immigrant settlers from South Carolina and Georgia use it to move to Alabama.
1805–1806	White settlers begin moving into former Native American lands in western (Choctaw) and northern (Chickasaw and Cherokee) Alabama.
1813	The United States annexes West Florida, from the Pearl River to the Perdido River, from Spain. The Spanish surrender Mobile area to American forces.
1814	Under the Treaty of Fort Jackson, 23 million acres of Creek territory are ceded to the United States, opening up about half of Alabama to white settlement.
1817	The Alabama Territory is created when the U.S. Congress permits the division of the Mississippi Territory.
1819	U.S. president James Monroe (1758–1831) signs the Alabama enabling act, and Alabama becomes the 22nd state.
1830s	Irish Catholic immigration increases sharply because of the plunging price of Atlantic voyages.
1830	The Indian Removal Bill is approved by Congress. In subsequent land cession treaties between the United States and each of the American Indian peoples in Alabama, the tribes cede their remaining lands east of the Mississippi in exchange for western lands.
1832	Alabama's first railroad, the Tuscumbia Railway, opens, running two miles from Tuscumbia Landing to Tuscumbia.
1837	Part of the Second Creek War (Seminole War), the Battle of Hobdy's Bridge is the last Indian battle in Alabama.
1838	The Alabama Indians are moved to the western lands via the "Trail of Tears."
1840s	Germans immigrate to the state in sufficient numbers to support the formation of their own military units. Many settle in Mobile, the

	leading port of entry, and others pass through the city during their journeys to interior destinations.
1869	Several hundred Chinese arrive to work on the Alabama-Chattanooga Railroad and in cotton mills.
1871	Birmingham is founded, evolving into the center of the southern iron and steel industry and drawing many immigrants.
1890s	Immigration to Birmingham, which had from its beginning attracted immigrants and migrants, speeds up. The largest foreign-born groupings are the Germans, Irish, English, Russians, and Italians.
1900	Only 14,592 (0.8 percent) of Alabama's population of 1,828,697 are foreign-born: 3,634 from Germany, 2,347 from England, 1,792 from Ireland, 862 from Italy, 617 from Canada, 539 from France, and 468 from Russia.
1919	As large numbers of immigrants from eastern and southern Europe come to Alabama after World War I, long-term residents react negatively to the new immigrants' differences; this reaction puts pressure on the state to pass an anti-Catholic law requiring daily prayer readings in the public schools. The Ku Klux Klan is also formed.
1930	The state's population reaches 2,646,248, including 15,615 foreign-born: 2,140 from Italy; 2,114 from Germany; 1,760 from England; 968 from Greece; 902 from Canada; 556 from Poland; and 466 from France.
1960	Alabama's population of 3,266,740 includes 2,611 persons of Asian origin; 485 Mexicans; 288 Chinese; and 127 Filipinos.
1970s	Latinos (2.8 percent of the metro population) and Asians (1.2 percent) begin arriving in numbers to work in Birmingham's expanding service industry or in construction and move into the middle suburbs.
1990	Alabama's voters overwhelmingly pass a constitutional amendment making English the state's official language.
2010	The U.S. Census finds that Alabama has the second-highest growth in Latino/a population, with many of these immigrants arriving since 2000.
2011	The Alabama Legislature passes House Bill (HB) 56, the state's version of Arizona's strict anti-immigrant law, Senate Bill 1070; unlike other such laws, HB 56 includes provisions aimed at education.

HISTORICAL OVERVIEW

PRE-1800

The American Indian tribes living in Alabama at the time of first European contact were the Iroquoian-speaking Cherokee, and the Muskogean-speaking Alabama (Alibamu), Chickasaw, Choctaw, Creek, Koasati, and Mobile. The Spanish

De Soto and his men crossing the Tombigbee River on rafts, during an early exploration of Alabama Territory. This illustration originally appeared in *The Life, Travels and Adventures of Ferdinand de Soto, Discoverer of the Mississippi* by Lambert A. Wilmer. Philadelphia: J.T. Lloyd, 1858, 441. (Library of Congress)

were the first Europeans to enter Alabama, which they named "La Florida." The 1528 expedition by Pánfilo de Narváez (1478–1528) may have traveled in southern Alabama. The first documented European visit was by Spanish explorer Hernando de Soto (1496/1497–1542) who explored the Coosa, Alabama, and Tombigbee rivers in 1539.

As in much of the New World, the Spanish were soon joined and rivaled by the English and the French. Claiming the entire region north of the Gulf of Mexico, including the territory of Alabama in the Province of Carolina, King Charles II of England made land grants in the area to some of his favorites in 1663 and 1665. As early as 1687, English traders from Carolina traveled around the Alabama River.

In 1702, Pierre Le Moyne d'Iberville (1661–1706) and his brother Jean-Baptiste Le Moyne de Bienville (1680–1767) established the French fort and settlement of Fort Louis de la Mobile, north of Mobile Bay along the Mobile River as the capital of New France, or *Louisiane* (Louisiana). After abandoning Fort Louis to floods in 1711, they rebuilt Fort Conde on a bluff. This fort was Mobile's beginning, the first permanent European settlement in Alabama. Soon other French settlers followed. The first French "cassette girls" arrived in 1704. King Louis XIV (1638–1715) paid for the passage and dowries for 25 young orphaned women to travel from France on *The Pelican* to Louisiana to become wives of the colonists, including some in Alabama. Other cassette girls arrived in 1728. They got their name because the French government provided each with a *cassette* or trunk and a set of clothes.

Several immigrants from Canada arrived soon afterward to begin a successful fur trade with the Choctaw, Creek, and Cherokee tribes. Based in Mobile, their trade flourished as far away as Tennessee. They had little competition because most Spaniards were interested only in gold.

Only 500 people had come to the French colony by 1716. It really flourished when the colony was turned over to the Mississippi Company, a speculative venture by financier John Law (1671–1729). A national bank was chartered, and settlers began to arrive by the boatload in Mobile, Biloxi, and New Orleans. Many indigo and rice plantations were started after the first load of slaves came in 1719.

In 1721, French slave ships began to arrive in Alabama, usually carrying blacks from West Africa. Mortality rates on the passage were very high. Many Africans were first shipped to a Caribbean island, where they were "prepared" for the regime of slavery. An even larger rush of slave importation began at the end of the eighteenth century when Alabama was a U.S. territory. Eli Whitney's invention of the cotton gin in 1793 led to a flourishing of cotton agriculture in Alabama in the early nineteenth century. Slavery became the essential element in the state's biggest industry, producing a demand for slave labor. The port of Mobile was the largest slave trading center. Although the U.S. Congress outlawed the international slave trade after 1808, some importation of slaves continued.

In their rivalry for local domination in the eighteenth century, the English and the French each tried to ally with the American Indian tribes. The French set up the military posts at Fort Toulouse, near the intersection of the Coosa and Tallapoosa rivers, and Fort Tombecbe on the Tombigbee River. A part of northern Alabama was within the land grant for the colony of Georgia that the English government made to James E. Oglethorpe (1696–1785) and his associates in 1732. In 1739, Oglethorpe signed a treaty with the Creek Indians west of the Chattahoochee River.

French occupation of Alabama ended with the 1763 Treaty of Paris, which concluded the French and Indian War (1754–1763). Britain then controlled the area between the Chattahoochee and the Mississippi rivers, and the part of Alabama south of the 31st parallel. The area north of the 31st parallel became a part of the "Illinois Country," which the English Crown reserved for the American Indians. In 1767, the border of the West Florida province was moved north to 32° 28' N latitude. By the 1783 Treaty of Versailles, Britain ceded West Florida to Spain.

Immediately afterward, traders and trappers arrived from British Georgia. The British set up trading posts across the territory, making Mobile the center of trading. Most posts were in Washington, Baldwin, and Clarke counties, and near Muscle Shoals and Montgomery. When Spain temporarily took control of the area in 1780, the outposts were temporarily shut down. The outbreak of the Revolutionary War in 1776 drove a few hundred British sympathizers from Georgia to settle in the Alabama-Tombigbee River Basin.

Under the Treaty of Madrid, Spain ceded the area east of the Mississippi between 31° N and 32° 28' N to the United States in 1795. Three years later, the U.S. Congress designated this district as the Mississippi Territory. A 12- to 14-mile strip near the northern boundary of Alabama and Mississippi was claimed by South Carolina, but it renounced this claim to the federal government in 1787.

More American Indian land was obtained for white settlement by the Yazoo land scandal. Beginning in 1785, Georgia pressed its claim to Alabama and

Mississippi, claiming all land to the Mississippi River between the 31st and 35th parallels. In 1795, a corrupt Georgia legislator was bribed to sell off 35 million acres of American Indian land (known as the Yazoo territory). By the time voters had elected a less corrupt legislature and the deal was discovered, much of the land had already been sold to white settlers. In 1802, the federal government finally resolved the mess when it induced Georgia to abandon its claims in exchange for a payment of $1.25 million. Legal challenges to Georgia's attempt to repeal the sale were decided by the U.S. Supreme Court's landmark *Fletcher v. Peck* decision in 1810. In one of the first instances of the Court overturning a state law, the Court held that the land sales could not be retroactively canceled.

A 1797–1799 survey verified the claims of the United States that its southern boundary with Spanish West Florida was at the 31st parallel. Ellicott's Stone was placed 26 miles north of Mobile in 1799 to mark the boundary. In 1799, the United States also took possession of Fort St. Stephens from the Spanish, making it the first U.S. land in Alabama.

Nineteenth Century

In 1804, the boundaries of the Mississippi Territory were extended to include all of the Georgia purchased north to the Tennessee line. The Alabama portion of the Mississippi Territory grew from 6,422 whites and 2,624 slaves in 1810 to 99,198 whites and 47,665 slaves in 1820—an increase of 137,817 persons, or 1400.4 percent over the decade.

During the period between 1803 and 1811, the Federal Road was built connecting Milledgeville, Georgia, and Fort Stoddert, an American military post located 29 miles north of Mobile. The road was formerly a Creek horse trail through the Tennessee and Alabama river basins. Settlers from South Carolina and Georgia used it to travel to Alabama. Conflict between the settlers and American Indian tribes led to the American Indians giving up even more land. In 1805, the Chickasaw ceded some land in northern Alabama to the United States. Soon afterward, the Cherokee and the Choctaw also gave up some of their claims in the southwestern part of the state.

In 1812, the U.S. Congress added the Mobile District of West Florida to the Mississippi Territory, which was divided in 1817, with the western part becoming the state of Mississippi and the eastern part becoming the Alabama Territory. American settlers flocked in, mostly from Georgia and the Carolinas. The settlers' great lust for land intensified conflict with the American Indians. Encouraged by the British after the War of 1812 began, the Shawnee chief Tecumseh (1768–1813) tried to forge an American Indian alliance of resistance to American settlement. Under the Treaty of Fort Jackson, which ended the 1813–1814 Creek War, the Creeks, Red Sticks, and tribes neutral during the conflict ceded about three-fifths of Alabama to the United States. After the 1816 cessions by the Cherokee, Chickasaw, and Choctaw, only about a quarter of Alabama was occupied by the American Indians. There was trouble when white settlers rushed into the lands before the time fixed by the treaty. Finally, U.S. troops were sent to enforce the treaty's provisions. The troops were also helpful in ensuring that the Creeks lived up to their agreement.

On December 14, 1819, Alabama was admitted to the Union as the 22nd state. The 1820 Federal Census found that Alabama's population was 144,317, of which 96,245 were white and 48,082 were African American, with 47,449 of the latter being slaves and 633 being free. The population essentially doubled in the 1820s to 309,527, an increase of 114.5 percent. Some 99 percent of the population lived in rural areas. Those farms and plantations along rivers and streams with flatboat transportation to downriver markers flourished. Most new arrivals were from nearby states and territories.

The 1830 Indian Removal Act and the 1832 Treaty of Cusseta accelerated the displacement of the southeastern tribes, including the Creek, Cherokee, Choctaw, Chickasaw, and Seminole. President Andrew Jackson (1767–1845) refused to enforce the government's past treaties or to protect the American Indians from aggressive, violent white settlers. The result was to encourage Alabama and Mississippi to adopt extreme states' rights position regarding American Indian tribes. Even before more American Indians moved during the period between 1834 and 1837, settlers flocked to the area. Soon, even the Cherokee in Alabama's northeast were ejected. The Cherokees had become successful farmers, with a newspaper, orchards, large farms, herds of cattle, and black slaves.

Throughout this period, the settlement in Alabama was facilitated and dependent upon its various waterways. The Mobile, Birmingham, and Montgomery all flourished because of their nearness to navigable water. Many immigrants soon arrived in search of opportunities. Many settled at Cahaba, then the state capital. Selma began to grow at this time, enhanced by a ferry service that was set up across the Alabama River to Cahaba. The 1830s was also a period of Irish immigration, economic difficulties, and intergroup conflict. Irish Catholic immigration increased sharply because of the plunging price of Atlantic voyages.

Nat Turner's 1831 slave rebellion in Virginia inspired Alabama to enact an anti-immigration law in 1832; the law forbade the importation of potentially disruptive slaves. But there were violations. The last known shipment of African slaves into Alabama was in 1860, when the *Clotilde* arrived in Mobile Bay with 116 Africans from several different tribes, including the Tarkbar tribe of Tamale, Ghana. Because the federal authorities intervened, the Africans brought on the *Clotilde* could not be legally enslaved; however, they were treated as chattel. When freed, the Africans settled at Magazine Point, three miles north of Mobile, and called their community "Africatown."

In 1844, a Jewish merchant from Bavaria came to Mobile, where he began selling various wares with a wagon rather than a backpack. Other merchants soon arrived to serve the expanding population. The strong national immigration surge in the 1840s and 1850s definitely impacted Alabama. Political unrest and agricultural disasters had driven many to leave Europe, and they were poorer and more Catholic than previous arrivals. Germans immigrated to the state in sufficient numbers by the 1840s to support the formation of their own military units. Many Germans settled in Mobile, the state's leading port of entry, and others passed the port on their way to interior destinations.

A plank (wooden) road began to be built in Alabama in 1849. This roadbed was eventually abandoned, after it was realized the planks warped in the winter and were attacked by boring insects and dry rot in the summer. Stagecoach lines arose, with three carrying passengers and mail by 1840. By 1850, the state's population had jumped to 771,623, including 342,844 slaves and 2,265 free blacks.

By 1860, Alabama's population reached nearly 1 million (964,201). The white population was 54.6 percent, and the rural population held steady at 94.9 percent. The 435,000 enslaved blacks comprised 45 percent of the state's population. The 1860 Census found only 160 Native Americans. Mobile had 1,276 German residents, and 1,325 Germans lived elsewhere in the state.

In 1861, Alabama seceded from the Union to join the Confederate States of America. During the Civil War, about 10,000 slaves escaped and joined the Union army, along with 2,700 white men. The state's population remained the same during the 1860s, as the expected growth was neutralized by death and emigration. Sufficient Jewish immigrants had arrived in Mobile by 1861 for a Jewish women's benevolence society to be formed. They organized religious worship, provided assistance to the poor, and housed new arrivals.

After the Civil War, plantation owners and other businesses across the country became interested in enticing Chinese workers because they were "docile and thrifty" (Zolberg 2006, 183–84).It was often claimed that the Chinese would work for starvation wages and not complain no matter how noxious the work environment was. As a counter-narrative to this sort of claim, one should consider that societal forms of racism combined with exclusionary immigration policies made the Chinese more vulnerable, thus constraining their bargaining power in the marketplace. When they could, they were one of the most organized groups in litigating injustices up to the Supreme Court level, but this was only in response to a myriad of repressive measures. In Alabama, several hundred Chinese were recruited to work on the Alabama-Chattanooga Railroad and in cotton mills in 1869. From then on, Chinese immigration was opposed by the U.S. labor movement, which demanded exclusion.

After National Reconstruction concluded in 1877, the state began an industrial and building boom. Many schools were built, along with numerous other infrastructure improvements. In 1871, land promoters founded Birmingham at the junction of the Alabama and Chattanooga and South and North Railroads, which were still under construction. The site was also very close to significant deposits of iron ore, coal, and limestone—the three principal raw materials used in making steel. The name of England's principal industrial city was chosen to advertise the Alabama city as an iron and steel production center.

According to the 1880 U.S. Census, Alabama's population exceeded 1 million for the first time, leaping an impressive 26.6 percent since 1870. Almost all—94.6 percent—lived in rural areas. Despite this population growth, only 9,734 were foreign-born: 3,238 were born in Germany; 2,966 in Ireland; 1,004 in England; 442 in France; 426 in Scotland; 143 in Sweden and Norway; and 4 in China.

The state's industrial development continued throughout the 1880s and 1890s. To lessen the dependence upon black labor, companies promoted immigration to fill the new jobs. This produced a temporary immigration increase. The 1890 Census discovered that 18.7 percent of the state's mining workers were foreign-born, with most from England, Scotland, Ireland, Holland, and Italy.

Immigration to Birmingham, which had from its beginning attracted immigrants and migrants, sped up in the 1890s. First- and second-generation immigrants constituted 13.4 percent of the city's population by 1890. The largest foreign-born groupings were the Germans, Irish, English, Russians, and Italians. By 1902, German immigration was strong enough to support a German language newspaper, *The Birmingham Courier*. There was a great increase in Italian immigration after 1890, and Italians became the largest group by 1910. However, the overall percentage of the foreign-born reduced steadily after 1890 by a significant increase in white migration from other southern states. The foreign-born declined to 17.5 percent in 1910 and to 15.1 percent in 1920. Most immigrants came for jobs in the coal, iron, and steel industries. These numerous foreign-born immigrants made Birmingham a "city of churches" (Harris 1977, 36–37), including many Roman Catholic (38.0 percent of white church membership), Greek Orthodox (1.4 percent), Protestant (51.5 percent), and Jewish (1.8 percent) places of worship. Immigrants formed self-protection and support groups, with some, like the German-American Union and the Irish Democratic Club, becoming politically powerful.

1900–1950

In 1900, 45 percent of Alabama's population of 1,828,697 was African American. Only 14,592 were foreign-born: 3,634 were born in Germany; 2,347 in England; 1,792 in Ireland; 862 in Italy; 617 in Canada; 539 in France; and 468 in Russia. Still mostly farmers, some 88.1 percent of the population lived in rural areas. Alabama, along with most other southern states, had less than 1 percent of newcomers or foreign-born in 1910.

Birmingham continued to grow. The city's Jewish population had increased from 20 in 1878 to 1,400 in 1905. Blast furnaces, such as the Ensley Works of the Tennessee Coal, Iron and Railroad Company (TCI, made the city an important center for iron production). Despite housing overcrowding and cholera outbreaks, Birmingham's population leaped from 38,000 to 132,000 during the decade between 1900 and 1910, attracting both rural white and black migrants.

Beginning in 1911, a serious public effort was finally made to provide all-weather roads across the state with the establishment of the State Highway Department. Road construction was further enabled by an expansion in federal funds to Alabama for this purpose after 1921.

The anti-Catholic movement that had begun nationally around 1910 grew stronger after World War I. In Alabama, the movement was strong because a large number of immigrants from eastern and southern Europe came to Alabama after the war. In Fairfield, over 5,000 Italians had settled, drawn by jobs at TCI. The competition for jobs inflamed simmering tensions, such as the long-term residents' negative reaction to the new immigrants' Roman Catholicism and very different cultural traditions. In response, the state passed an anti-Catholic measure in 1919, which required daily prayer readings in the public schools. A more noxious response was the rise of the Ku Klux Klan, which had a membership of approximately 18,000 in Birmingham, which had only 32,000 registered voters in 1924.

By the 1920s, Birmingham was the 19th-largest city in the United States and contained over 30 percent of Alabama's population. Heavy industry and mining were the basis of the city's economy. Because of low transportation and labor costs, the city became the largest and cheapest foundry iron-producing center. By 1915, about one-quarter of the nation's foundry pig iron was produced in Birmingham.

Alabama grew rapidly during the 1900–1920 period, with a population increase of some 28.4 percent to 2,348,174. The number of foreign-born remained miniscule, with 2,732 born in Italy; 2,427 in Germany; 1,942 in England; 1,582 in Russia; 915 in Greece; 892 in Canada; 809 in Ireland; 616 in France; and 583 in Austria. By 1930, the state's population reached 2,646,248. Of the 15,615 foreign-born, 2,140 were born in Italy; 2,114 in Germany; 1,760 in England; 968 in Greece; 902 in Canada; 556 in Poland; and 466 in France. The state was slowly urbanizing, with 71.9 percent of the population still living in rural areas.

From 1910 to 1940, tens of thousands of blacks migrated north from Alabama in the Great Migration to seek jobs, education, and freedom from overt racism and lynching. The state's rate of population growth dropped from 20.8 percent in 1900 and 16.9 percent in 1910 to 9.8 percent in 1920, reflecting the impact of this out-migration.

In 1940, Birmingham was the industrial center of the South and had a population of 267,583. Mobile's population had grown to 78,720 and the capital of Montgomery had a population of 78,084. Cotton and corn were the leading agricultural products, and woven cotton goods and blast-furnace products were the leading industries.

ALABAMA'S RECENT IMMIGRATION HISTORY

Until very recently, Alabama has continued its history of failing to attract a large immigrant population. Its experience has been very similar to Louisiana and Mississippi, the other states in what is sometimes called the Deep South Triad, which have not done as well as other states in the otherwise booming New South. Alabama consistently was one of the lowest five states regarding the percentage of foreign-born population in its total population during the period between 1950 and 2010. In 1950, Alabama's 0.4 percent tied for 47th position. In 1970, its 0.5 percent was tied for 48th position. The state's percentage never exceeded 2.0 percent until 2000, when it had only the 44th lowest percentage of foreign-born.

As of the 1950 Census, Alabama's population exceeded 3 million for the first time at 3,061,743. Its black population had decreased 0.3 percent since 1940 to 979,617. There were only 13,286 foreign-born persons over 21 years of age in the state, which was a miniscule 0.4 percent of the population. In 1960, on the eve of important civil rights battles, 30 percent of Alabama's population of 3,266,740 was African American. Some 2,611 persons were of Asian origin, while 485 were Mexican, 288 were Chinese, and 127 were Filipino. For the first time, more Alabamians lived in urban (51.7 percent) than rural (48.3 percent) areas.

The population boom that occurred when many Northerners moved to the South and the Southwest in the years after 1960 largely bypassed historic port cities like New Orleans, Biloxi, and Mobile, which have experienced little demographic and economic growth by comparison. The state's population has continued to rise, just not at the atmospheric rates of some other areas. By 1980, Alabama's population had risen to 3,894,000, a 19.2 percent increase since 1960. Most of the increase was white; the black population had only risen 1.6 percent. The urban population share jumped to 60 percent. The 1990 Census found Alabama's growing population exceeded 4 million at 4,040,587. Continuing its urbanization trend, some 60.4 percent of the state's population now lived in urban areas. Many traditional auto production states, like Michigan, Indiana, and Ohio, lost thousands of jobs in the automotive industry to states like Alabama, stimulating the population gains.

Throughout this period, Alabama's rate of international migration varied considerably. In 1981–1982, it declined 4.9 per 1,000 compared to a national 2.2 percent increase. But, beginning in 2005, the state's rate increased steadily, from

8.0 in 2005–2006, another 4.9 percent in 2006–2007, and another 3.5 percent in 2008–2009. All of these rates for Alabama slightly exceeded the national average for those years.

Alabama's immigrants have mainly been Latino/as, whose population increased significantly after the mid-1990s. During that decade, like the other southern states, Alabama's Latino/a population grew significantly, at a rate of 156.4 percent. Alabama's Asian population climbed as well, but not at the significant rates seen for Latino/as, surging 29.5 percent during the 1990s. By 2000, the state's population of 4,447,100 included 45,349 Latino/as, or 1.0 percent. The black population also increased to 1,138,726, representing a 26 percent gain since 1970. Only 3.3 percent (131,712) of the state's population spoke another language besides English, with 34.8 percent speaking English not well or not at all. Of course, studies that consider time in the United States as a significant variable show almost 100 percent language acquisition.

The national Second Great Migration, during which blacks moved from southern states to the North and to the West, was reversed during the 1996–2007 period when migrants from the Black Belt moved to more traditional southern metropolitan areas, such as New Orleans, Birmingham, and Jackson. In the period between 2000 and 2008, in-migration rates slowed but continue to be substantial in southern states, ranging from Alabama's low of 11.4 percent. The state did have significant personal income growth between 2001 and 2003. Alabama's 8.1 percent increase was the second highest in the South and well above the 5 percent national average.

Between 2005 and 2013, Alabama became a new immigrant destination. Reasons given for this change include the impact of the Immigration Reform and Control Act of 1986, which legalized 2.3 million undocumented Mexican immigrants; a recession in California that froze employment; and increasing U.S.–Mexican border enforcement at heavily utilized crossings that pushed immigrants to use more remote locations and try opportunities in areas beyond California. Simultaneously, southern industrial reorganization (e.g., beef-processing plants that relocated in rural areas) has created a need for low-skilled, low-wage labor unmet by local labor pools.

There have been some signs that at least part of Alabama is becoming more welcoming to immigrants. Birmingham has become a very diverse community. It has developed "ethnoburbs," suburban multiethnic clusters of residential areas and business districts in large American metro areas in which no one ethnic minority group is a majority. Beginning in the 1970s, Latinos (2.8 percent of the metro population) and Asians (1.2 percent) began arriving in numbers to work in Birmingham's expanding service industry or in construction. Many of these immigrants have moved into the so-called middle-ring suburbs. There remains, though, a sharp residential separation between Birmingham's blacks (28 percent of the metro population) and whites (68 percent) that corresponds somewhat to the area's ridge and valley topography.

Moreover, a number of organizations have arisen to help the new arrivals to adjust to life in Alabama, much as their predecessors did in earlier centuries. For example, the Hispanic Interest Coalition of Alabama is "dedicated to the social, civic, and economic integration of Hispanic families and individuals in Alabama" (Winders 2011, 600).

TOPICAL ESSAYS

BEASON-HAMMON ALABAMA TAXPAYER AND CITIZEN PROTECTION ACT (HOUSE BILL 56)

Alabama's recent anti-undocumented immigrant activities have not been unprecedented in the state's history. As earlier described, an immigrant surge in 1980 brought state action and in 1990 Alabama's voters overwhelmingly passed a constitutional amendment that made English the state's official language. The state's transportation department subsequently began to administer state driver's license tests only in English. In 1996, in *Alexander v. Sandoval,* a Mexican Spanish-speaking immigrant brought a suit against the state arguing that the English-only policy violated Title VI of the Civil Rights Act of 1964 because it was discriminatory. The U.S. District Court and 11th Circuit Court of Appeals consequently ruled that Alabama had to stop giving the written exam only in English because it discriminated against non-English-speaking residents.

The increase in immigration since the 1990s again stirred anti-immigrant feelings. This is somewhat surprising because today a mere 120,000 of the estimated 11 million undocumented U.S. immigrants live in Alabama, and comprise just 2.5 percent of the state's population. Only a third of the state's 34,000 Latino children are undocumented, and they are less than 1 percent of Alabama's students. What has perhaps caused the eruption of anti-immigrant action is the suddenness of the immigration increase, combined with ethnic and racial bias. The state's undocumented population is estimated to have doubled since 2005, and the 2010 U.S. Census found that Alabama had the second-highest growth of Latino population in the nation since 2000. Alabama's 208 percent increase from 24,629 to 75,830 was the seventh-highest rate of increase in Latino/a population during the 1990s. Also, many of the new arrivals have a low level of education, low English literacy, are from many different parts of Mexico, and are disproportionately male. For example, Jefferson County had at least 200 men for every 100 women. The sight of so many Latino men working jobs that theoretically might go to American-born workers has also stimulated much negative reaction. The county's Latino/a employment increase of 267.1 percent dwarfs the comparatively paltry 1.3 percent increase in non-Latino/a employment.

Alabama, at an average annual 1.6 percent employment increase, was the only southern state that lagged behind the nation (1.8 percent) in adding jobs. This may indicate that the new Latino/a arrivals posed a serious threat for jobs. However, the new immigrants mostly took jobs in manufacturing (30.4 percent compared to 17.6 percent of non-Latino/a whites) and construction (10.5 percent compared to 8.2). In 2000, some 20 percent of Jefferson County Latino/as were employed in construction.

Regardless, Alabama's state government has taken several strong, controversial steps to combat undocumented immigration. Alabama is one of the three states that has been working with the U.S. Department of Homeland Security to arrest undocumented immigrants if they are discovered during routine police work. In 2011, Alabama passed a voter ID law similar to several other states. Then the state became one of five states to pass a version of Arizona's strict anti-immigrant Senate Bill 1070, but, unlike other states, Alabama included provisions aimed at education. The Beason-Hammon Alabama Taxpayer and Citizen Protection Act (House Bill [HB] 56)—considered the toughest of the anti-immigration statutes—includes a provision giving police new authority to question an immigrant's legal status, puts employment and business restrictions on undocumented immigrants, and authorizes checking the immigration status of criminal suspects and public school students. The last action is particularly controversial because Alabama is only the third state in 30 years to require public schools to ask about schoolchildren's immigration status.

Reaction to the passage of HB 56 immediately was very negative. The U.S. Justice Department sued to enjoin the law's enforcement, arguing that federal immigration law preempted the Alabama law. The 11th Circuit Court subsequently held that most of the challenged provisions, for example, criminalizing an undocumented immigrant's failure to complete or carry registration documents, were illegal because of the U.S. Supreme Court's decision in *Arizona v. United States* (2012). However, the court upheld Alabama's requirement that police investigate the immigration status of detainees and arrestees. In a companion case brought by private plaintiffs, the 11th Circuit Court also ruled that part of the Alabama law requiring schools to collect data about students' immigration status violated equal protection.

To critics, HB 56 has aspects of Alabama's segregationist past, with some accusing the law of targeting Latino/as, calling it the "new Jim Crow" (Barker 2011, 4). Bishop William Willimon of the North Alabama Conference of Baptists called the bill an embarrassment and argued that it was motivated by "intimidation and meanness" (Allen 2011, 15–18). The Southern Poverty Law Center, during a Montgomery protest, said, "It has set Alabama back at least 20 years" (RNS 2011, 19).Some Alabama educators predicted that the rate at which Latino/a students are held back a grade will be four times what it was in 2010. "A child who is in

Opponents of Alabama's immigration law gather for a rally outside the statehouse in Montgomery, Alabama, on February 14, 2012. The groups were calling for the repeal of HB 56, which has been considered one of the harshest anti-immigration laws in the country. (AP Photo/Dave Martin)

fear cannot learn, and that is what we are dealing with," said one longtime principal (Maxwell 2012, 9).

Despite this opposition, a statewide opinion poll of likely Alabama voters recently found wide support for HB 56. Some 75 percent of Alabama voters supported it, with 52 percent of voters saying they "strongly support" the law. Only 24 percent opposed HB 56, and just 18 percent thought that HB 56 "will harm Alabama's economy by depriving businesses of workers they need," whereas 59 percent believed that it "will free-up jobs for other Alabama workers and will save the state money on services for illegal immigrants" (Edwards 2011, 8). One commentator approvingly opined that the law was benefiting state taxpayers and causing more undocumented immigrants to "self-deport" (PR Newswire 2012).

Two years later, in 2013, HB 56 had not done what it was supposed to—drive undocumented Latino/a immigrants from the state and free the factory jobs for natives. Many immigrants have left, but native Alabamians have not been hired because employers instead have been hiring refugees. Although Alabama's unemployment rate has fallen to 8.5 percent since HB 56 was enacted, this has occurred because the labor force shrank. In 2013, a number of Alabama politicians, business owners, and citizens concluded that HB 56 is too strict and is hurting the state's reputation as a place to do business. In 2012, the state proposed to amend HB 56 to "clarify the law's scope, bring some disputed provisions in line with federal law and reduce unnecessary burdens on legal residents and businesses," according to the governor (Associated Press 2012, 5). It remains to be seen whether Alabama will continue to fight immigration as it has in the past years, or whether it will somewhat embrace diversity as much as the rest of the country has.

NOTABLE GROUPS

Somos Tuskaloosa

In 2011, Gwendolyn Ferreti and Rev. Fred Hammond began a group called "Somos Tuskaloosa," which has been rewarded for fostering positive and constructive change in the wake of Alabama HB56 and a tornado that left significant damage in Tuscaloosa. Like some of the best immigrant grassroots organizations in this country, this group educates immigrants regarding laws and policies that may affect them and gives them some legal training. The group's mission is to advance social justice and to fight racism.

BIBLIOGRAPHY

Alabama Writers Program Workers. *Alabama: A Guide to the Deep South*. New York: Hastings House, 1941.

Allen, Bob. "Church Leaders Challenge Alabama's Immigration Law." *Christian Century* 128 (2011): 15–18.

Ambinakudige, Shrinidhi, Domenico Parisi, and Steven M. Grice. "An Analysis of Differential Migration Patterns in the Black Belt and the New South." *Southeastern Geographer* 52 (2012): 146–63.

Associated Press. "Suit Requests Data on Ala. Immigration." *Education Week* 32 (2012): 5.

Barbieri, Magali, and Nadine Ouellette. "The Demography of Canada and the United States from the 1980s to the 2000s: A Summary of Changes and a Statistical Assessment." *Population* 67 (2012): 177–280.

Barker, Cyril Josh. "Southern Racist Immigration Laws Cause Labor Disruption." *New York Amsterdam News*, November 24, 2011, 4.

Bland, Richard L. "Alabama in 1848: As Described by Traugott Bromme." *Alabama Review* 61 (2008): 48–60.

Bogie, Donald W., and Danny E. Harrison. "An Examination of Population Changes in Alabama's Black Belt Counties: 1960–1970 and 1970–1980." *Sociological Spectrum* 2 (1982): 351–65.

Carter, Ted. "Alabama Says Immigration Reform Costly, Mississippi Calls It Moneymaker." *Mississippi Business Journal Regional Business News*, March 5, 2012. http://msbusiness.com/businessblog/2012/03/05/alabama-says-immigration-reform-costly-ms-calls-it-moneymaker/. Accessed March 17, 2013.

Christensen, Stephanie. "The Great Migration, 1915–1960." Blackpast.org. 2013. http://www.blackpast.org/?q=aah/great-migration-1915–1960. Accessed March 17, 2013.

Dwoskin, Elizabeth. "Alabama Rethinks Its Harsh Immigration Law." *Bloomberg Businessweek* 4256 (2011): 34–36.

Easton, Paul. "School Attrition through Enforcement: Title VI Disparate Impact and Verification of Student Immigration Status." *Boston College Law Review* 54 (2013): 313–52.

Edwards, James R. Jr., "Alabama Sees Self-Deportations Rise." *Human Events* 67 (2011): 8.

Elliott, James R., and Marcel Ionescu. "Postwar Immigration to the Deep South Triad: What Can a Peripheral Region Tell Us about Immigrant Settlement and Employment?" *Sociological Spectrum* 23 (2003): 159–80.

Farmer, Frank L., and Zola K. Moon. "An Empirical Note on the Social and Geographic Correlates of Mexican Migration to the Southern United States." *Journal of Rural Social Sciences* 26 (2011): 52–73.

Fleming, Walter L. "Reorganization of the Industrial System in Alabama after the Civil War." *American Journal of Sociology* 10 (January 1905): 473–500.

Gibson, Campbell, and Kay Jung. *Historical Census Statistics on the Foreign-Born Population of the United States: 1850–2000.* Population Division, Working Paper No. 81. Washington, DC: U.S. Census Bureau, 2006.

Grow, Brian. "Aliens: A Little Less Alienated." *Businessweek*, May 9, 2004, 62–64. http://www.businessweek.com/stories/2004–05–09/aliens-a-little-less-alienated. Accessed March 17, 2013.

Harris, Carl V. *Political Power in Birmingham, 1871–1921.* Knoxville: University of Tennessee Press, 1977.

Higham, John. *Strangers in the Land: Patterns of American Nativism 1860–1925.* New Brunswick, NJ: Rutgers University Press, 1955.

Johnson, Kevin R. "Sweet Home Alabama? Immigration and Civil Rights in the 'New' South." *Stanford Law Review Online* 64 (2011): 22–28.

Kochhar, Rakesh, Roberto Suro, and Sonya Tafoya. "The New Latino South: The Context and Consequences of Rapid Population Growth." Pew Hispanic Center, July 26, 2005. http://pewhispanic.org/files/reports/50.pdf. Accessed July 30, 2014.

Love, Jeremy B. "Alabama Introduces the Immigration Debate to Its Classrooms." *Human Rights* 38 (2011): 7.

Lowery, Charles. "The Great Migration to the Mississippi Territory, 1798–1819." *Mississippi History Now*, 2012. http://mshistorynow.mdah.state.ms.us/articles/169/the-great-migration-to-the-mississippi-territory-1798–1819. Accessed March 17, 2013.

Massey, Douglas S., and Chiara Capoferro. "The Changing Diversification of American Immigration." In Douglas S. Massey, ed. *New Faces in New Places: The Changing Geography of American Immigration,* Chapter 2. New York: Russell Sage Foundation, 2008, pp. 25–50.

Maxwell, Lesli A. "Immigration Law Casts Shadow over Schooling in Alabama." *Education Week* 31 (2012): 8.

Maxwell, Lesli A., and Mark Walsh. "Ala. Blocked from Asking about Students' Citizenship Status." *Education Week* 32 (2012): 6.

McDaniel, Paul N., and Anita I. Drever. "Ethnic Enclave or International Corridor? Immigrant Businesses in a New South City." *Southeastern Geographer* 49 (2009): 3–23.

Murphy, Pat. "Most of Tough Alabama Immigration Law Unenforceable, Rules 11th Circuit." *Lawyers USA Regional Business News*, August 27, 2012.

Nadel, Stanley. "German Jews in America." In Stephen P. Norwood and Eunice G. Pollack, eds. *Encyclopedia of American Jewish History*. Santa Barbara, CA: ABC-CLIO, 2008, pp. 24–36.

Newkirk, Margaret, and Gigi Douban. "In Alabama, Legal Immigrants Wanted for Dirty Jobs." Businessweek.com, October 4, 2012, 2. http://www.businessweek.com/articles/2012–10–04/in-alabama-legal-immigrants-wanted-for-dirty-jobs.   Accessed March 17, 2013.

PR Newswire. "New Alabama Opinion Poll Shows Broad Support for State Immigration Enforcement Law." *PR Newswire US*, March 19, 2012. http://www.prnewswire.com/news-releases/new-alabama-opinion-poll-shows-broad-support-for-state-immigration-enforcement-law-143363536.html.   Accessed March 17, 2013.

Puga, Kristina. "Immigrant Group in Alabama Wins National Prize for Creating Positive Change." NBC Latino website. June 5, 2013. http://nbclatino.com/2013/06/05/immigrant-group-in-alabama-wins-national-prize-for-creating-positive-change.   Accessed July 4, 2013.

Reyes, Paul. "Help Not Wanted." *Mother Jones* 37 (2012): 24.

RNS, "Alabama Immigration Law Called Nation's 'Meanest'." *Christian Century* 128 (2011): 19–318.

Rogers, William Warren, Robert David Ward, Leah Rawls Atkins, and Wayne Flynt. *Alabama: The History of a Deep South State*. Tuscaloosa: University of Alabama Press, 1994.

Rogoff, Leonard. "Jews in the South." In Stephen P. Norwood and Eunice G. Pollack, eds. *Encyclopedia of American Jewish History*. Santa Barbara, CA: ABC-CLIO, 2008, pp. 145–49.

Schmid, Carol. "Immigration and Asian and Hispanic Minorities in the New South: An Exploration of History, Attitudes, and Demographic Trends." *Sociological Spectrum* 23 (2003): 129–57.

Smith, H.A., and O.J. Furseth. *Latinos in the New South: Transformations of Place*. Farnham, UK: Ashgate Publishing, Ltd., 2006.

Swanton, John R. *The Indian Tribes of North America*. Bureau of American Ethnology Bulletin 145. Washington, DC: U.S. Government Printing Office, 1953.

Wickham, DeWayne. "GOP Political Fears Shape Alabama Immigration Law." *USA Today*, November 8, 2011, 07a.

Wilentz, Sean. *The Rise of American Democracy*. New York: W. W. Norton & Company, 2005.

Winders, Jamie. "Representing the Immigrant: Social Movements, Political Discourse, and Immigration in the U.S. South." *Southeastern Geographer* 51 (2011): 596–614.

Zolberg, Aristide R. *A Nation by Design: Immigration Policy in the Fashioning of America*. New York: Russell Sage Foundation, 2006.

2

ALASKA

John T. Radzilowski

CHRONOLOGY

1741	Russian explorers have first contact with Alaska.
1760s	Russian fur traders make regular trips to the Aleutian Islands and nearby areas. They encounter indigenous groups such as Aleut, Yupik, and Alutiiq. The Russian Empire claims Alaska as its colony.
1790s	The Russian government consolidates fur trading operations under the name of the Russian American Company. Because of reports of abuse and exploitation of native Alaskans, particularly the Aleut, the government intervenes to protect these individuals. The Russian Orthodox Church aids in these efforts and protects individuals of mixed Russian and indigenous descent. Father Ioann Veniaminov (later St. Innocent of Alaska) leads this effort, learning indigenous languages, restricting alcohol consumption, and opening schools.
1800	The Russians move their capital from Kodiak to Sitka. The Tlingit and Haida, two indigenous groups, challenge this effort.
1804	The Tlingit successfully block the Russians from establishing a post at Sitka and so the Russians send another expedition to try again. They come to a compromise that limits Russian exploitation of resources.
Mid-1800s	Russians face logistical difficulties in maintaining a distant colony and encounter economic competition from the Americans and the British.

1867	The Russians sell Alaska to the United States for $7.2 million.
1878	Chinese workers are hired in canneries in Alaska. Tlingit individuals protest their arrival because of the threat to their jobs.
1880s	Commercial fishing is developed in southeast Alaska. Despite the prevalence of scientific racism at this time, indigenous groups are hired over outsiders because they are considered more reliable workers. Unfortunately, European diseases, such as small pox, lead to the decline of the indigenous groups. Mainland workers—especially immigrants—are increasingly hired.
1880	The first significant gold strike is linked to three immigrants: an Irish individual, a French Canadian, and a German.
1886	White miners force 80 Chinese workers from the Treadwell mine near Juneau onto ships.
1898	Three Swedish immigrants inaugurate the Nome gold rush.
1900	Chinese immigrants are the dominant ethnic workers in canneries. Within the next decade, their numbers decline. Japanese briefly take their place.
1902	An Italian prospector starts the Fairbanks gold rush.
1910s	Filipinos begin to arrive and work in canneries.
1920s	An influx of Mexicans, who mostly leave by the 1930s, begins. Filipinos begin to replace the Mexican workers in salmon-packing. Filipinos come to be known as "Alaskeros."
1920s and 1930s	Because of a restrictive and eugenic immigration policy on the U.S. mainland, indigenous Alaskan groups are once again hired in fishing and other natural resource extraction industries. Norwegians also come to work as fishermen and in canneries and as loggers. Russian Old Believers arrive in central Alaska. Some Italian immigrants also arrive to work in canneries and on fishing boats. Filipinos could enter the United States freely until 1934.
1940s	Filipinos arrive in greater numbers and begin to settle in Anchorage. Many move to central Alaska because they are affiliated with the U.S. Military in some way.
1942	The 220 Japanese individuals living in southeast Alaska are expelled from the state as a result of Executive Order 9066.
Postwar period	Little significant immigration to Alaska except for Filipinos is seen.
1980s	Filipinos are still an important immigrant population.
1990s	Filipinos continue to arrive, often because of family reunification.
2004	The Spanish language becomes the most commonly spoken non-English language in Alaska (it had been Yupik).
2012	Alaska has had temporary seasonal foreign migrant work for decades, particularly on ships. These immigrants include individuals from the Philippines, Mexico, Poland, Turkey, and Romania. Koreans and Vietnamese have established small communities in Anchorage.

HISTORICAL OVERVIEW

RUSSIAN ALASKA

Alaska is the largest and least densely populated state in the United States. Its total land area is bigger than the states of Texas, California, and Montana combined, while its population is only 722,000, ahead of only North Dakota, Vermont, and Wyoming. Approximately two-thirds of its population is located within 50 miles of its largest city, Anchorage. Due to its low population, natural resource-based extractive economy, pre-statehood peculiarities, and recent settlement, historical literature on Alaska is in its infancy and literature on immigrants is nearly nonexistent. Thus, the state's immigration and migration history remains virtually unknown, despite the fact that Alaska has long attracted immigrants and continues to do so.

Russian explorers first sighted Alaska in 1741 and by the 1760s Russian fur traders were making regular forays to Aleutian Islands and areas of the mainland along the southwest coast. The Russian Empire laid claim to Alaska as its only noncontiguous colony. The first people the Russians encountered were primarily Aleut, Yupik, and Alutiiq groups. The Aleuts, in particular, were subjected to brutal treatment by the Russian fur traders, who were often freelancers working under a variety of chartered corporations. The early fur traders themselves were a diverse range of men, including ethnic Russians and other Slavic subject peoples, Cossacks, Buryat and other Siberian natives, and men of mixed heritage. By the 1790s, the Russian government forced the consolidation of all fur trading operations under the Russian American Company (which would eventually become a quasi-state company). At the same time, it began to regulate the treatment of native Alaskans and curb the worst of the abuses. A crucial part of this was the introduction of the Russian Orthodox Church. Under the able leadership of Father Ioann Veniaminov (later St. Innocent of Alaska), the church became the advocate for the protection of native Alaskans and the growing Creole population of mixed Russian and native ancestry. Veniaminov learned several native languages, curbed the liquor trade, opened schools, developed written forms of native languages, translated religious texts, and taught skills such as carpentry.

In 1800, facing the growing British, Spanish, and American competition, the Russians tried to move their capital from Kodiak to Sitka in southeast Alaska. Unlike the relatively dispersed and isolated peoples of western Alaska, the native groups they encountered here—primarily the Tlingit and Haida—were highly organized, sophisticated, and well-armed nations already experienced in dealing with Europeans. After an initial effort to establish a post at Sitka was wiped out by the Tlingit, a major Russian expedition had to be sent to recapture the site in 1804. The result was a wary truce in which Russian rights to exploit local resources were limited.

Russia's American colony never proved economically viable. This was due to the tortuous logistics of trying to supply Alaska from European Russia and the difficulty in getting furs and walrus ivory back home in a timely manner. The relatively poor relations with native Alaskans further hurt the colony. Groups like the Tlingit and Haida maintained lively trading relations with the Hudson's Bay Company and with American and British whalers, undercutting Russia's ability to successfully barter for furs. Russia's growing rivalry with Britain in the mid-nineteenth century and its inability to potentially defend the colony in the face of British naval power, made it increasingly clear that the Alaskan venture was untenable. In 1867, the Russians sold Alaska to the United States for $7.2 million.

Probably at no point under the Russian colonial era did the European population of the colony top 1,000, and during most times, it was probably far less. The mainstay of the Russian American Company, the Alaskan Creoles, also made up the overwhelming majority of adherents of Russian Orthodoxy. Following the American takeover, the white population of Alaska actually declined, although precise numbers are impossible to ascertain.

AMERICAN ALASKA AND DEVELOPMENT OF AN EXTRACTIVE ECONOMY

The early decades of American rule are best described as "benign neglect." The new U.S. possession had no laws and, outside of the outpost at Sitka, no government presence beyond occasional visits by naval ships. Economic activity that might have attracted immigrants to Alaska was virtually nonexistent.

This situation slowly began to change in the 1880s. The growing market for preserved food led commercial fishing companies to move canning operations from California and Washington to southeast Alaska to take advantage of the colossal runs of Pacific salmon found in the region's streams and rivers. This change marked the beginning of the territory's modern economy, which was and continues to be based on natural resource extraction. Aptly described by historian Steven Haycox as "the American colony," Alaska exports raw materials—mainly seafood, timber, oil, and minerals, which are unprocessed or minimally processed—and imports finished products, including some made with Alaskan-sourced raw materials (see Haycox 2002). This fact has led to an economy that is highly dependent on international commodity markets and the vagaries of business decisions made by corporations outside the state, especially those from Seattle. As a result, Alaska's demand for workers and its draw for immigrants have often fluctuated wildly and have been and continue to be influenced by the need for seasonal and temporary labor.

Salmon fishing and packing was the first big industry to use large numbers of immigrant workers. Initially, the industry sought to employ the native peoples of the southeast panhandle: Tlingit, Haida, and Tsimshian. In the racial taxonomy of the late nineteenth century, outsiders considered these well-established coastal peoples to be more reliable than their counterparts from the mainland United States. One San Francisco company even briefly featured a native-looking family in modern clothes in their advertisements. The attraction of cannery work often resulted in local migration as natives vacated older villages to move closer to cannery sites.

Nevertheless, the native groups of the southeast coast did not provide a real solution to the growing demand for cannery workers and, thus, from the beginning canneries were importing immigrant workers. Most native families viewed cannery work as merely a supplement to their subsistence economy. It provided some additional income to their fishing, hunting, and gathering, allowing them to purchase trade goods or amass wealth for potlatches. Thus, wage labor was only viewed as a welcome but temporary expedient to fulfill specific short-term goals. Additionally, the population of Alaska natives available in the southeast region was limited. In the mid- and later nineteenth century, European diseases such as small pox hit these groups hard, reducing overall numbers and forcing additional consolidation of villages. Finally, the canneries had little control over a workforce that could, if it wished, walk off the job and fill winter larders with the region's abundant natural food supply.

The solution was to import immigrants from the West Coast via a system of short-term contract labor. Canneries contracted with foremen, who were usually better established or more ruthless members of the immigrant communities. They, in turn, recruited their co-ethnics, receiving a fee per head and sometimes kickbacks from the recruits if jobs were scarce. Recruiters supplied crews ranging in numbers between 50 and 150 men and guaranteed to pack a set amount of salmon during the season. As a result of this contract system, immigrant laborers flooded north and the percentage of Alaskan natives in canneries dropped from a majority at the start of the industry to 18 percent by 1904. In the 1920s and 1930s, the number of Native Alaskans in the canneries increased once again due to the restrictive immigration laws enacted in the early 1920s (see Buchholdt 1996, 52).

Chinese workers from San Francisco and Seattle were the first large immigrant group to be recruited for the canneries. The first Chinese laborers came to Alaska by 1878. Facing increasing discrimination, violence, and immigration restrictions, the advent of large-scale salmon packing provided a steady if not seasonal source of employment for Chinese immigrants. Sparsely populated Alaska provided a working environment without the danger of a massive white backlash and, despite the difficulties, the Chinese were soon the dominant ethnic group in the canneries, making up at least 40 percent of the entire workforce by 1900. So ubiquitous were the Chinese as fish packers, that when a Seattle inventor devised a machine to automatically gut and clean salmon in 1903, it was dubbed the "iron chink."

A salmon cannery about 20 miles south of Ketchikan, Alaska, in the Tongass National Forest, between ca. 1900 and ca. 1930. The salmon industry has been and continues to be a major source of employment in this state. (Library of Congress)

The initial arrival of Chinese workers was resented by Native Alaskans. When a group of 18 Chinese workers arrived in Sitka in 1878 to manufacture cans, the local Tlingit rioted against the potential threat to their jobs and the coming of yet another foreign group to their lands. A government report noted:

> As soon as the Chinamen were descried a general howl arose, and the wildest excitement was manifested. Before the lines were made fast, runners started for the village, and the whole beach suddenly became in instant commotion. Old and young, lame, halt, and blind, all started pell-mell for the "heathen Chinee."
>
> Annah Hoots, the war chief, made a most inflammatory speech to the young bucks, to the effect that the Chinamen should not be permitted to land. . . . The situation was critical and I firmly believe had the Chinamen landed before a proper understanding was had every man of them would have been ruthlessly murdered. . . . [T]he point of controversy was that the Chinese had been imported to catch the fish and that the Indians were half naked and hungry, deserved the employment by right, and they would fight before they would permit any such infringement upon their reserved rights. It was their country and John Chinaman should not come. . . . Mr. Hunter very frankly explained . . . that it was his intention to buy all the fish from the Indians; that the Chinamen were brought along to make tin cans, and when they had finished the cans they would be sent away. Furthermore, if the Indians would learn to make cans, no more Chinamen should be employed. (Price 1990, 50)

Initial resistance to Chinese labor by Native Alaskans does not appear to have been sustained. The expansion of the salmon-packing industry opened up new opportunities for Alaskan natives but also needed additional labor inputs. By the 1890s, Chinese were the largest group in salmon-packing. Most appear to have been recruited from Seattle and San Francisco. Because canneries were often in isolated locations, distant from towns and villages, the cannery workers had little chance to interact with local populations, native or otherwise. This isolation was a crucial feature of the experience of immigrant workers in the canneries. Workers were not only isolated from locals but were also isolated from one another. Surveys of early twentieth-century censuses indicate that the many small and often temporary canneries scattered across southeast Alaska were mono-ethnic. Whether through design or by the nature of recruitment based on ethnic ties, each small cannery appeared to be dominated by a single group.

In the first decade of the twentieth century, the number of Chinese workers in salmon-packing began to decline. Not only did canneries begin to recruit large groups of other immigrants, but it also appears that Chinese immigrants on the West Coast were increasingly finding economic opportunities closer to home. Work in the canneries appears to have been a temporary option that allowed most immigrants an opportunity to meet immediate economic goals. In the 1900s, Japanese immigrants became a significant labor force in the industry. The Japanese role in the industry was fairly brief compared to the Chinese, as the overall number of Japanese remained smaller thanks to fast imposition of restrictions on immigrant flows from Japan. Due to the seasonal nature of the salmon industry and their limited economic goals, Chinese and Japanese immigrants left a fairly small impact on the state, though small numbers of both groups stayed in some towns, occasionally opening small businesses. In spite of their small numbers, racial restrictions on Asian immigrants did exist in many communities in the early twentieth century, sometimes resulting in small, segregated residential enclaves. Alaska's remaining Japanese residents, totaling 220, nearly all from southeast Alaska, were expelled in 1942 as part of President Franklin D. Roosevelt's national Executive Order 9066. Only about 80 returned after World War II.

Chinese and Japanese were not the only groups to arrive during this period. In the years just before and during the Mexican Revolution, several thousand Mexican immigrants arrived in southeast Alaska to work in the canneries. Like the Japanese, this first wave of Mexican immigrants was a temporary phenomenon. By the early 1920s, the number of Mexicans working in Alaska began to decline, becoming a negligible presence by the early 1930s. While a Mexican American community emerged in Alaska in the late twentieth century, it had no connection to this early wave of Mexicans.

European immigrant groups were also a significant factor in salmon fishing. Norwegians and Norwegian Americans followed the route of the Great Northern Railroad out of Midwestern Scandinavian communities to Seattle and from there north to Alaska, working on the railroad and in the burgeoning logging industry.

Norwegians appear to have been independent fishermen but quite a few served as foremen in canneries, as loggers, and on purse seiners (boats that fish with nets) in Alaskan waters. Finns and Swedes were also important in logging, mining, and fishing. Italian immigrants were also a visible presence in the industry, working both on fishing boats and in canneries. According to the records of the Alaska Packers' Association, crews of gill netters working in Alaskan waters between the 1910s and the 1950s were dominated by Italians. It is likely that many lived the remainder of the year in Italian communities in the Bay Area, though a scattering of Italians did settle in Alaska's coastal communities and some found work in the canneries as well. South Slavic immigrants, particularly Croatians and Serbs, also worked in the canneries in significant numbers during short periods. For many immigrants, the salmon industry provided a short-term option for labor. The hardships of cannery work and isolation from established ethnic enclaves limited the attraction of permanently working in Alaska.

ALASKEROS

The most sustained immigrant group in Alaska's history has been Filipinos. The first Filipinos arrived in the 1910s to work in canneries. By the early 1920s, they were replacing Mexicans in salmon-packing and were probably the largest single immigrant group in the state. Unlike many of the groups that had entered the canneries, the Filipinos became an enduring feature of the salmon industry. Although many Filipinos in Alaska, known as "Alaskeros," would be temporary workers like their Chinese or Mexican counterparts, some Filipinos, unlike the other ethnic groups in the canneries, would also settle with their families and establish a permanent presence in Alaska. The first Filipino communities in the state included Ketchikan and Juneau in the southeast panhandle and Kodiak in southwest Alaska. Later, Anchorage would develop as the state's biggest Filipino enclave with smaller communities arising in Fairbanks, Valdez, and Kenai. Filipino dominance in the cannery workforce continued throughout the late twentieth century. In a 1978 study of five large processing plants in Alaska, three had a workforce that was over 90 percent Filipino, while a fourth estimated the Filipino component of its work force at close to 80 percent. Significantly, none of the processors surveyed in the study had more than two Filipinos serving as foremen.

Early Filipino workers were recruited from the West Coast on the contract system much like their Chinese and Japanese counterparts, though some contractors brought workers directly from the Philippines. Unlike Chinese or Japanese, Filipinos were free to come to the United States until 1934. Some of the workers were students at American colleges and universities. One article noted that, "the Filipinos, needing money to go to school, often without a cent, [are] eager to take advantage of the opportunity to go off during the summer months when schools and colleges are closed, to earn a substantial part of their keep for the winter months" (Buchholdt 1996, 50).

Despite the advantages offered by Alaska canneries, the work was difficult and workers were often exploited both by the packing companies and by the contractors, who were often their co-ethnics. According to historian Theresa Buchholdt, "contractors made their profits on the difference between the actual labor cost and the estimated cost" (Buchholdt 1996, 50). The average wage for a cannery worker was about $25 a month in the 1900s, $35 a month by the 1910s, and $65 prior to full unionization in the mid-1930s. As a result, contractors pushed their workers to greater speed as every can packed over and above what had been estimated at the start of the season meant more money for the contractors. Since many workers did not speak English well, the workers were highly dependent on the contractors whose relationship with the canneries and greater knowledge of American conditions gave them an advantage. Workers had to buy their equipment, such as rubber boots, from company stores at high prices. They received meal tickets for food but were served an unending diet of fish. Any additional food also had to be purchased from company stores. The poor working conditions and low pay led to efforts to unionize the industry. In Washington and Alaska, Filipinos were at the forefront of organizing the salmon industry by the 1930s, which resulted in a gradual increase in wages.

Despite the hardships associated with cannery work, the industry continued to attract Filipinos in the decades following World War II. Although more and more Filipinos would come for other jobs as time went on, canneries remained the number one draw. Most Filipinos in Alaska did improve their income and supported their families. In one survey in the late 1970s, 76 percent reported an overall improvement in their standard of living. Although large-scale immigration from the Philippines remained relatively low throughout the 1960s and 1970s, the state continued to attract new Alaskeros directly from the old country. A few were still recruited by agencies but up to 40 percent came to join family or marry spouses who were already U.S. citizens.

Although the early Alaskero communities were based around the salmon industry, the growth of the Filipino community in Anchorage, the state's largest city, was more complex. Anchorage's rapid growth during and after World War II was initially fueled by government spending on the military and related infrastructure. In the 1940s, the city's population mushroomed from about 3,000 to about 47,000 by the end of decade. The Cold War threat from the Soviet Union necessitated the siting of major army and air force installations in Alaska, and Anchorage and, to a lesser extent, Fairbanks were the main beneficiaries. Many Filipinos came to central Alaska during this period as employees of the U.S.

military, as members of the armed services themselves, or as spouses or children of servicemen. Anchorage's Filipino community thus had a somewhat different profile than more blue-collar communities like Ketchikan or Juneau. Anchorage Alaskeros were more likely to be educated and many of them worked in technical or even white-collar jobs.

Alaskeros founded several mainly social and cultural community organizations in the state. Despite the relative size of the Filipino population in some communities, there has been little effort at political organization. Immigration from the Philippines continues to be a factor in Alaska, and as of 2010, Tagalog was the third-most frequently spoken non-English language in the state. Other Filipino languages had only a limited presence (see Table 1). Nevertheless, the long association of Alaskeros with fish-processing work seems to be coming to a gradual end as new groups, such as Mexicans, continue to come to the state and as Filipinos gain increasing access to higher education and white-collar jobs.

THE MINING FRONTIER AND OTHER MIGRATIONS

Individual immigrants played an important early role in Alaska's famed mining history. The state's first major gold strike in 1880 was attributed to three immigrants: one Irish, one French Canadian, and one German. The French Canadian immigrant, Joe Juneau, lent his name to the city that grew up near the gold mine and later became Alaska's capital. Three Swedish immigrants, dubbed "the Three Lucky Swedes," started the Nome gold rush in 1898, while the 1902 Fairbanks gold rush was started by an Italian prospector. Of those coming through Alaska to the famous Klondike goldfields of the Yukon, about one-third of them were foreign-born, not counting Canadians. The majority were from northern and western Europe. Chinese immigrants also arrived to work on the gold mines, though their presence was short-lived due to hostility and violence from white miners. In 1886, a mob of white miners forced 80 Chinese workers from the Treadwell mine near Juneau onto two small ships and sent them south. Similar incidents happened on a smaller scale at other gold mining sites.

As copper and other minerals were discovered in the state and the focus of mining shifted from individual prospectors to a large-scale, capital-intensive industry, the number of immigrants increased. The population of mining districts in the early twentieth century averaged around one-third immigrants. Irish, Swedes, and Finns predominated but a significant number of Italians, Serbs, Croatians, Montenegrins, Slovaks, Hungarians, Poles, Russians, and Greeks were also present. Many of these immigrants likely had experience in hard rock mining in the Lower 48. The arrival of many South Slavs also helped revitalize the Orthodox Church in communities like Juneau, which had two Serbian societies by World War I. The

Table 1   Non-English Languages Spoken at Home: Alaska,
2000–2010 (Alaska Native Languages Highlighted)

Language	Number of Speakers
Spanish	22,649
Yupik	18,950
All Filipino languages	9,600
Tagalog only	8,935
Inupik	7,203
Korean	4,370
German	3,575
Russian	2,950
Eskimo	2,156
French	2,145
Athabascan	1,493
Aleut	1,261
Samoan	1,185
Tlingit	1,141
Japanese	1,390
Lao	1,135
Chinese (Mandarin)	1,130
Kuchin	1,093
Vietnamese	755
Thai	740
Hmong (Miao) dialects	710
Italian	520
Polish	495
Ilocano	450

number of immigrants in Alaskan mines declined after World War I due to restrictions on immigration from eastern and southern Europe and the gradual playing out of some of the state's most productive ore fields.

Other industries attracted some immigrants as well. A short-lived effort to introduce reindeer herding in Alaska was based on the skills of Sami immigrants from Norway and Finland. A variety of ethnic farming colonies were attempted in Alaska to attract Icelandic, Norwegian, and Swedish immigrants, all of which came to naught. Although a 1930s New Deal project to settle impoverished farm families from the Midwest in Alaska's Matanuska Valley did bring some immigrants, the only really sustained agricultural colony for immigrants was a migration of Russian Old Believers to central Alaska in the 1920s and 1930s. The Old Believers came primarily from existing settlements in Oregon, but some were recent arrivals from the Soviet Union, fleeing communist persecution. Today, the small Old Believer communities, though sharply split between those who accept the legitimacy of priests and those who do not, continues to be a visible presence in central Alaska.

RECENT TRENDS IN IMMIGRATION TO ALASKA

Following the completion of the Trans-Alaska Oil Pipeline in 1977, the basic outlines of the state's economy remained based almost completely on natural resource extraction. Tourism has proved to be the only growth industry of any significance since the 1980s. During the 1980s and 1990s, periodical lowering of oil prices and gradual declining of North Slope production put a brake on economic growth and the number of jobs available to immigrants. Following the terrorist attacks of September 11, 2001, and the subsequent conflicts in the Middle East and the growth in world demand for oil, Alaska's economy has seen modest growth. As a result, Alaska has not been a major destination for the new wave of immigrants from Latin America, Asia, Africa, and the former Soviet bloc that arrived on American shores in the 1980s, 1990s, and 2000s. Filipinos remained an important exception. The prevalence of existing family ties and the familiar migration pattern to Alaska have ensured a continuing trickle of Filipino immigrants, some of whom are semipermanent residents who expect to return home at some future date.

Although largely outside of the major job-related migration patterns of Mexican immigrants, Alaska has begun to attract a Mexican immigrant population that, relative to the size of the state's population, is significant. As of 2004, Spanish overtook Yupik as the most commonly spoken non-English language in Alaska and cable systems in Anchorage and Juneau began to feature Spanish language networks (see Table 2). The state is now the destination for enough Mexican nationals that the Mexican government opened a consulate in Anchorage. By contrast, to date, Filipino immigrants are only served by an honorary consul in Juneau and most consular functions are handled by Filipino missions on the West Coast (see Table 2). Most Mexicans in Alaska are working in fish-processing, construction, and oil, with Anchorage and Juneau appearing to have the largest communities. The exact proportion of Mexicans to Mexican Americans is unclear given the small numbers and seasonal nature of the work.

Seasonal immigration continues to be a feature of the Alaskan economy (see Table 3) due to the demands of the seafood and tourism industries. Many workers arrive for the summer months and then go elsewhere. Although Filipinos and Mexicans remain the largest groups in onshore seafood-processing, over the past

Table 2   Foreign Consular Offices in Alaska

Foreign Consular Offices in Anchorage

Consulates	Honorary Consulates
Canada	France
Norway	Britain
Japan	Poland
Korea	Czech Republic
Italy	Germany
Finland	
Mexico	

Foreign Consular Offices in Juneau

Consulate	Honorary Consulate
Canada	Philippines

Foreign Consular Offices in Fairbanks

Consulate	Honorary Consulate
Canada	n/a

decade, processors have set up "student" work program where foreign college students from countries such as Poland, Turkey, or Romania arrive to work in the plants. These jobs, sometimes arranged by middlemen, are often highly exploitative, with the students required to pay their own travel expenses. Food and housing are poor and sometimes dangerous. Workers are also at the mercy of the plant production schedules, sometimes working long hours, other times not working (and not getting paid) when slowdowns occur, and permanent workers get what hours are to be had. Other temporary student workers have turned up in various parts of the tourism industry, working at resorts and restaurants.

The large cruise ship companies that ply the waters of southeast and south-central Alaska have also created a niche for temporary workers. Crews of the cruise ships are often not U.S. citizens and, because the ships are often registered overseas, U.S. immigration laws do not apply. Filipinos are among the most visible but crews can be from as far afield as Russia, South Africa, and Southeast Asia. Onshore, the cruise ship lines encourage franchise businesses that sell jewelry and souvenirs to tourists (often getting a kickback per visitor to the franchise). Store operators spend part of the year in Alaska and part in the Caribbean or other tourist hubs served by the same lines. Some are natives of the Caribbean, but American Indians are also prominent. Last, the companies recruit large numbers of drivers and guides. The majority of these are U.S. citizens from the Lower 48, with an apparent preference for Mormons because their

Table 3   Nonimmigrant Admissions by Selected Category of Admission, Listing Alaska as State of Destination: FY 2010

Total	Tourists/Business Travelers		Students/ Exchange visitors	Temporary Workers and Families	Diplomats and Other Representatives	Others	Unknown
	Visa Waiver	Others					
116,789	85,204	20,693	5,492	2,743	650	11,130	877

employers assume that they will not drink alcohol or get in legal trouble while in Alaska.

The greater Anchorage area continues to attract many of the immigrants who come to Alaska. Because Anchorage is the state's largest city and the hub of the oil industry, many of immigrants to the city are educated and entrepreneurial. Korean and Vietnamese immigrants have created modest communities in Anchorage and are well represented among small business owners and operators. Typically, the state gains between 1,500 and 2,000 immigrant admissions per year (see Table 4), but not all those remain permanently in the state. Beyond Anchorage, some of the smaller communities do attract clusters of immigrants who are noticeable because they stand out from the rest of the population. The southwest Alaskan town of Bethel, which is isolated from the main road network in the state, has become home to Albanian and Korean immigrants who drive taxis, making Bethel the town with the highest number of taxis per capita in the United States. The immigrant drivers serve both visitors and senior citizens who lack cars.

Ethnically, people of northern and western European ancestry remain the largest groups in the state (see Tables 5 and 6). Native Alaskans and American Indians are the second largest racial group in Alaska, amounting to just over 14 percent of the population, though they constitute the majority in many smaller communities. Alaska also has a large mixed race population, which at over 7 percent of state inhabitants exceeds the national average for persons of mixed race. The majority are mixed white-Alaskan native or white Asian, though intermarriage between Alaska natives and Filipinos is not uncommon.

The prospects for the state continuing to attract immigrants in equal or greater numbers compared to the past decade depend on the health of the state's extractive industries, which are primarily oil and seafood. Parts of the state attract an ongoing number of nonimmigrant migrants from the rest of the United States. Some come to Alaska for skilled positions that the state's workforce cannot fill; others seek the mystique of America's "Last Frontier" as portrayed on television reality shows and in movies and books. The same factors attract immigrants from overseas as well. The state's ability to develop a less cyclical and less resource-dependent economy have largely come to naught due to the vast

Table 4   Persons Obtaining Permanent Legal
Residence Status: Alaska, 2001–2010

2001	1,389
2002	1,557
2003	1,188
2004	1,261
2005	1,524
2006	1,554
2007	1,617
2008	1,534
2009	1,608
2010	1,703

Table 5   Alaska, Major Ethnic Groups: 2010

	Group	Number
1	German	130,862
2	Irish	78,413
3	British/English	67,464
4	Eskimo	54,761
5	French/French-Canadian	35,551
6	Scottish/Scots-Irish	29,619
7	Norwegian	27,444
8	Italian	23,845
9	Black/African American	23,263
10	Tlingit and Haida	22,365
11	Mexican	21,642
12	Filipino	19,394
13	Polish	19,243
14	Athabascan	18,838
15	Swedish	17,602
16	Aleut	16,978
17	Dutch	13,853
18	Russian	10,027
19	Welsh	5,920
20	Finnish	5,796
21	Danish	5,282

Source: U.S. Census, American Community Survey, 1 Year
Estimates (Ancestry), 2010; Idem, 2000 Summary File 1, 2007.

distances involved and the cost for shipping between Alaska and the Lower 48. Absent some change in Alaska's economic structure, the number of immigrants seeking to make the state home is likely to remain modest.

Table 6   Alaska Racial Groups and Persons of Hispanic/Latino Origin: 2010

Group	Number	Percentage
White	473,576	66.7
American Indian/Alaskan Native	104,871	14.8
Two or More Races	51,875	7.3
Hispanic or Latino	39,249	5.5
Asian	38,135	5.4
Black/African American	23,263	3.3
Native Hawaiian or Pacific Islander	7,409	1.0

Source: U.S. Census, Profile of General Population and Housing Characteristics, 2010 (Alaska), table DP-1.

Senator Mark Begich, D-Alaska, speaks on Capitol Hill in Washington, D.C., on March 28, 2012. (AP Photo/Jacquelyn Martin)

NOTABLE FIGURES

Mark Begich (1962–)

U.S. senator Mark Begich (D-Alaska) has consistently advocated for immigrants' rights consistent with the moderate approach taken by his party and that of key Republican legislators who are open to immigration. Begich voted for the failed Development, Relief, and Education for Alien Minors Act in 2010 and supports current (as of 2013) reform, including increased border security and allowing a more definitive legal path to citizenship for immigrants. Because of his support for immigration reform, the anti-immigration group NumbersUSA began taking out ads in the Alaskan media arguing that any path to naturalization for undocumented workers is "amnesty" and accusing Begich of a "plan to give Alaska jobs to foreign workers" (Christiansen 2013). Although the ads do not discourage voting for Begich, they have racial undertones and incorrectly assess the economic impact that support for this sort of legislation would have. Against these assertions, it could be argued that Begich's advocacy for immigration reform simply reflects the rich diversity of Alaska and its immigrant heritage.

BIBLIOGRAPHY

Advincula, Anthony. "Cold? Yes. Isolated? Sure. But Alaska's Filipinos Thrive." *New America Media*, 2010. http://newamericamedia.org/2010/10/despite-isolation-filipinos-thrive-in-alaska.php. Accessed February 25, 2014.

Alaska State Historical Library. *Alaska Packers' Association Records, 1891–1970*. Juneau, AK: Microfiche.

Black, Lydia T. *Russians in Alaska, 1732–1867*. Fairbanks: University of Alaska Press, 2004.

Buchholdt, Thelma. *Filipinos in Alaska, 1788–1958*. Anchorage: Aboriginal Press, 1996.

Christiansen, Scott. "Begich Attacked by Anti-Immigration Group." *Anchorage Press*, April 11, 2013. http://www.anchoragepress.com/news/begich-attacked-by-anti-immigration-group/article_afcf07ba-a2fb-11e2–92b2–0019bb2963f4.html. Accessed June 23, 2013.

Dotson, Bob. "Town Clings to Customs despite External Influences." msnbc, September 19, 2008. http://today.msnbc.msn.com/id/26574964/ns/today-today_news/t/town-clings-customs-despite-external-influences/. Accessed February 25, 2014.

Espinosa, Henni. "*Filipinos File Class Action Lawsuit vs. Alaska*." abs-cbn news, July 8, 2011. http://www.abs-cbnnews.com/global-filipino/07/08/11/filipinos-file-class-action-lawsuit-vs-alaska. Accessed February 25, 2014.

Filipino-American Society of Juneau. http://filamalaska.org/. Accessed February 25, 2014

Filipino Community of Anchorage. www.filipinocommunityofanchoragealaskainc.org. Accessed February 25, 2014.

The Filipino Community Incorporated. www.filcomalaska.org/. Accessed February 25, 2014.

Haycox, Steven. *Alaska: An American Colony*. Seattle: University of Washington Press, 2002.

Johnson, Vanessa. "Mexicans in Alaska: The Last Immigration Frontier." *Newspaper Tree* [El Paso], September 12, 2008. http://www.newspapertree.com/culture/2847-mexicans-in-alaska-the-last-immigration-frontier. Accessed February 25, 2014.

"Korean Church Planter Takes Gospel to Alaska's Capital." *Baptist Press*, January 19, 2012. http://www.bpnews.net/printerfriendly.asp?ID=36990. Accessed February 25, 2014.

Krause, Aurel. *The Tlingit Indians: Results of a Trip to the Northwest Coast of America and the Bering Straits*. Translated by Erna Gunther. Seattle: University of Washington Press, 1956.

Liljebad, Sue Ellen. "Filipino Alaska: A Heritage." Alaska Historical Commission, Department of Education, State of Alaska, 1981. Microfiche manuscript, Alaska State Historical Library.

Liljebad, Sue Ellen. "Filipinos and the Alaska Salmon Industry." *Alaska in Perspective* 1, no. 2 (1978): 1–9.

Loshbaugh, Shana. "Ceremony, Gift Celebrate History of Russian Village." *Peninsula Clarion* [Kenai], April 16, 2000. http://peninsulaclarion.com/stories/041600/new_041600new0030001.shtml. Accessed February 25, 2014.

Lutz, John. "After the Fur Trade: The Aboriginal Labouring Class of British Columbia, 1849–1890." In Brian D. Palmer, and Joan Sangster, eds. *Labouring Canada: Class, Gender, and Race in Canadian Working-Class History*. Don Mills, Ontario: Oxford University Press, 2008, pp. 17–34.

"Nikolaevsk." http://www.usgennet.org/usa/ak/state/nikolaevsk.html. Accessed February 25, 2014.

Norris, Frank. "North to Alaska: An Overview of Immigrants to Alaska, 1867–1945." Alaska Historical Commission Studies in History, No. 121, June 1984. Microfiche manuscript, Alaska State Historical Library.

O'Malley, Julia. "Lunch Service Sees Increasing Number of Koreans." *Ketchikan Daily News*, December 10, 2007, 3.

Price, Robert E. *The Great Father in Alaska: The Case of the Tlingit and Haida Salmon Fishery*. Douglas, AK: First Street Press, 1990.

Salazar, Leticia. "Filipino Migration to Alaska." Alaska Historical Commission, Studies in History, No. 10, 1979. Microfiche manuscript, Alaska State Historical Library.

Stanton, William J. "The Purpose and Source of Seasonal Migration to Alaska." *Economic Geography* 31, no. 2 (April 1955): 138–48.

Tizon, Tomas Alex. "America's Taxi Capital: Bethel, Alaska." *Los Angeles Times*, November 30, 2007. http://www.latimes.com/news/nationworld/nation/la-na-taxicabs30 nov30,0,6941400.story. Accessed February 25, 2014.

U.S. Bureau of the Census. "The American Community—Asians." American Community Survey Reports, February 2007. http://www.census.gov/prod/2007pubs/acs-05.pdf. Accessed February 25, 2014.

U.S. Department of Homeland Security, Office of Immigration Statistics. *Immigration Yearbook 2010.* Washington, DC: Government Printing Office, 2010.

Volz, Matthew. "Wandering Old Believers Find a Home in Alaska." *Moscow Times,* July 20, 2004. http://www.themoscowtimes.com/news/article/wandering-old-believers-find-a-home-in-alaska/229533.html. Accessed February 25, 2014.

3

ARIZONA

Amy Lively

CHRONOLOGY

1853 (**December 31**)	The United States and Mexico agree to the Gadsden Purchase, giving the United States territory that becomes the southern regions of Arizona and New Mexico. This purchase leads to an influx into the area of Chinese immigrants seeking work as laborers on the construction of the southern transcontinental railroad.
1877	Army Scout Ed Schieffelin discovers silver in the hills of the San Pedro Valley in southern Arizona. He calls his claim "Tombstone," drawing immigrants from Europe to work on the mines. As Tombstone grows, Chinese and Mexican immigrants provide laundry, construction, and food services.
1885	Hachiro Onuki, a Japanese immigrant, arrives in Arizona and changes his name to Hutcheon Ohnick. He becomes a naturalized U.S. citizen and is a partner in Phoenix's first electricity and gas plant.
1898	The arrival of railroad service marks the end of Globe's frontier era and the beginning of its heyday as a mining community. Globe's population swells as immigrants from Italy, Ireland, Mexico, and areas of Eastern Europe descend on the town to work in the nearby copper mines.
1901	The territorial government passes a law forbidding "Caucasians" from marrying Chinese and African American immigrants.
1903 (June 1)	A group of miners, primarily comprising Mexican immigrants, Italian immigrants, and Mexican Americans, goes on strike in Clifton.

	The dispute begins after the Detroit Copper Mining Company of Arizona and the Arizona Copper Company cut wages to comply with the territorial government's new eight-hour workday law. The strike ends when massive flooding devastates the region, killing over 50 people, and the community is placed under martial law.
1910	The Mexican Revolution begins and many Mexicans flee to safety in Tucson. By the end of the decade, Tucson's Mexican population increases over 75 percent.
1917	Arizona passes the Alien Land Law. Directed primarily at Chinese immigrants, the law prohibits anyone who is not a U.S. citizen from buying land in the state. The law is declared unconstitutional in 1947.
1931	Construction of the Hoover Dam at the Arizona–Nevada border begins. Chinese laborers are forbidden from working on the construction of the dam.
1942 (July 23)	In response to a nationwide labor shortage, President Franklin Roosevelt signs an executive order legalizing the temporary migration of Mexican laborers into the United States. Workers in Arizona that arrive via the "Bracero Program" primarily work in fields harvesting fruit, vegetables, and cotton. The program is officially terminated in 1964.
1946 (September 22)	Mexican miners, who recently returned from World War II, go on strike against Phelps Dodge in Clifton-Morenci in eastern Arizona. Phelps Dodge gives in to the demands of the miners 104 days later, agreeing to offer Mexicans the same pay, benefits, and opportunity for promotion as Anglo workers.
1946 (November 5)	Chinese immigrant, Wing F. Ong, is elected to the Arizona House of Representatives, making him the first Chinese American to serve as a legislator in U.S. history.
1954 (July)	The Immigration and Naturalization Service initiates a deportation program in the Southwest, informally known as "Operation Wetback," in which both immigrants and Mexican American citizens are detained and deported back to Mexico.
1959	Judge Herbert F. Krucker overturns the state's anti-miscegenation law, requiring the clerk of Pima County to recognize the marriages of five interracial couples, including that of Japanese American Henry Oyama and Mary Ann Jordan.
1968	Tucson's small Chinatown, dating back to the nineteenth century, is demolished as part of the city's urban renewal plan. Researchers discover the Ying On Compound, a small community of working-class elderly Chinese men, still residing there.
1972 (May)	The United Farm Workers, led by Cesar Chavez, starts a petition to force a recall election for Governor Jack Williams, who signs a bill

making it illegal for farmworkers to strike or boycott during harvest season. Although the attempt to recall Williams fails, thousands of Mexicans and Navajos become registered voters in Arizona for the first time.

1974 (November 5) Mexican immigrant Raul H. Castro becomes the first Latino elected governor of Arizona.

1980 (July 5–6) A professional human smuggler, or "coyote," abandons 26 Salvadoran immigrants in the sweltering heat near Organ Pipe Cactus National Monument. Thirteen of the immigrants are found dead from heat exposure and dehydration.

1990 Arizona's population of undocumented immigrants is estimated at 268,700.

1992 (November 3) Joe Arpaio is elected Maricopa's county sheriff. In 2008, he initiates crime suppression sweeps in predominantly Latino neighborhoods, targeting undocumented immigrants.

1994 (August 8) Cesar Chavez is posthumously awarded the Presidential Medal of Freedom by President Bill Clinton.

2002 Mexican immigrants in Arizona account for $4 billion in purchasing power.

2003 (May) Fourth-generation Mexican American Arturo Moreno, a native of Tucson, is the first Latino to own a Major League Baseball team when he purchases the Anaheim Angels for $183 million.

2004 The state's population of undocumented immigrants grows to approximately 830,900.

2004 (November 2) Proposition 200 is passed by Arizona voters, requiring proof of citizenship to register to vote or apply for public benefits. The law is overturned by the U.S. Ninth Circuit Court of Appeals in 2010, although the provision requiring voter identification at the polls is upheld.

2010 (April 23) Governor Jan Brewer signs Senate Bill (SB) 1070 into law, making it a crime to be in Arizona without legal authorization and requiring law enforcement to question and detain individuals suspected of being undocumented immigrants.

2010 (July 6) The federal government sues the State of Arizona over SB 1070, claiming that the law usurps federal authority over immigration laws.

2010 (July 28) One day before SB 1070 is due to take effect, U.S. district judge Susan Bolton blocks key elements of the bill with a temporary injunction.

2011 (February 10) Governor Jan Brewer files a counter lawsuit against the federal government for failure to control the Arizona–Mexico border and failure to enforce federal immigration laws.

2011 (April 12) The U.S. Ninth Circuit Court of Appeals upholds the block on SB 1070.

HISTORICAL OVERVIEW

POST–WORLD WAR II TO THE PRESENT

Immigration in Arizona has been inextricably tied to Mexico. Certainly other countries, particularly Asian nations, are represented in Arizona's immigrant population. However, the shared 362-mile border between Arizona and Mexico, the influence of Mexican culture on Arizona—especially in the state's central and southern regions—and the economic relationship between Arizona and Mexico make Mexico the focal point of Arizona's immigration past and present.

In many ways, Arizona at the end of World War II was a vastly different state than when the war began. No longer could Arizona be considered simply an agricultural and copper mining state. Aerospace and electronics manufacturing took the lead in contributing to Arizona's economy and provided employment opportunities that attracted residents to the state's largest cities, Phoenix and Tucson. The citrus groves that at one time separated Phoenix from outlying communities, such as Scottsdale, Tempe, and Mesa, disappeared, forming the beginning of a vast metropolitan area.

Yet, even as Phoenix grew, agriculture in the state's rural areas was still part of the local economy and Mexican laborers could find work in the fields, often picking cotton or sugar beets. After the war ended, Arizona continued to benefit from the largest guest worker program in the history of the United States. The Mexican Labor Program, informally known as the Bracero Program, was the result of a bilateral agreement between Mexico and the United States and an attempt to regulate the migration of job-seeking Mexicans into the United States. American growers encouraged Mexican labor, although many circumvented the Bracero Program to avoid having to pay a minimum wage. Nonetheless, between 1942, when President Franklin Roosevelt signed the executive order that launched the program, and 1964, when the program officially ended, over 300,000 skilled Mexican laborers served as *braceros* in the United States.

Prior to World War II, Mexican labor was also prevalent in the state's copper mines. Many Mexican Americans left their jobs to serve in the war; but when they returned, they found that their status and achievements in the military did not change their status in Arizona. Returning Mexican war veterans in the mining community of Clifton-Morenci in eastern Arizona found segregated restaurants and unequal wages for the same work. When mining giant Phelps Dodge refused to accommodate the request of Mexican American workers for equal pay for equal work, the workers went on strike on September 22, 1946. After 104 days, Phelps Dodge gave in to the union demands and agreed to pay, benefits, and opportunities for promotions equal to those of Anglo workers.

Despite the labor victory in the mines, the manufacturing jobs that began to appear in Arizona were not open to Mexicans or African Americans. Jim Crow laws existed in Phoenix in the 1940s and 1950s and defense plants and manufacturing companies, such as Motorola, hired only Anglos. Some Phoenix restaurant owners hung "Whites Only" signs in their windows. Little distinction was made between legal Mexican immigrants, undocumented Mexican immigrants, and Mexican American citizens, some of whom descended from families that have been in Arizona for generations. Little credence was also given to those Mexicans who considered themselves to be white and avoided associating with the Civil Rights Movement that was beginning to take shape in the African American community.

The flow of Mexicans across the border into Arizona, both legally and illegally, roused nativist fears that were already brewing in the state and the nation in the 1950s. The federal government instituted a deportation program in 1954, which aimed at rounding up Mexicans in the southwest and sending them to Mexico. Operation Wetback, as the program was known, was led by the commissioner of the Immigration and Naturalization Service (INS), Joseph Swing. Barrios in Arizona, California, and Texas, were targeted and both Mexican American citizens and undocumented Mexican immigrants were detained and deported. Many other Mexicans fled south across the border out of fear of the INS sweeps. While the program was short-lived due to lack of continued funding—it began in July 1954 and ended in the fall of that year—the INS claimed to have deported over 1 million Mexican immigrants, although there was no evidence to support this number.

While Operation Wetback temporarily halted immigration from Mexico, neither Operation Wetback nor the end of the Bracero Program in 1964 signaled the end of Mexican immigration into Arizona. A poor economy in Mexico and the availability of work in the United States has kept Arizona growers supplied with cheap Mexican labor. Some growers sponsored former *braceros* who received their "green cards" after applying for U.S. citizenship, but most employers simply hired undocumented workers whenever work was available. Without a legal guest worker policy to replace the Bracero Program, the flow of undocumented immigrants from Mexico into Arizona continued for decades.

Chinese immigrants have had a presence in the state, dating back to the late 1800s when Chinese laborers worked on the Southern Pacific Railroad or in the mines, often in more dangerous duty and for lower wages than Mexican workers. Some Chinese immigrants opted to stay in the state when work on the railroad was complete and they typically remained in Tucson, although others moved north to Phoenix. Some Chinese came to Phoenix or Tucson after arriving at Angel Island, the immigration processing center near San Francisco, and discovered that opportunities for Chinese were more favorable in Arizona. It was common for a Chinese family to open a grocery store in the lower socioeconomic areas of a city and live in the back of the store. Both Phoenix and Tucson had areas near downtown designated as Chinatown in the first half of the twentieth century, but neither of the districts remains today.

The postwar era brought changes for Phoenix's Chinese immigrants. Many Chinese families still operated grocery stores, but after the war there was a migration away from the Latino and African American neighborhoods of South Phoenix. The city's boundary was moving north and the Chinese moved with it. By 1950, there were 200 Chinese grocers in Phoenix, which was twice the number of the previous decade. Independent grocers, whether owned by Chinese immigrants or not, declined soon after this period, facing stiff competition from chain supermarkets that began to move into the Phoenix area. One of those grocers, Wing F. Ong, became an immigration attorney and a politician. In 1946, he was elected to the Arizona House of Representatives, becoming the first Chinese American in U.S. history to serve in a state legislature; he was elected to the Arizona State Senate in 1966.

Substantial changes in federal immigration law came with the Immigration Act of 1965. Immigration quotas based on national origin were equalized. While a cap of 120,000 immigrants from the Western Hemisphere and 170,000 from the Eastern Hemisphere was implemented, family members of immigrants already legally in the United States were allowed to bypass those caps. This provision resulted in a tremendous influx of immigrants from non-European nations. Between 1971 and 2002, over 7 million immigrants entered the United States from Asia and over 5 million from Mexico. However, the act did not limit undocumented immigration from Mexico. Those who were not spouses, children, or parents of U.S. citizens were subject to the Western Hemisphere cap, but the poor Mexican economy continued to drive immigrants north into Arizona, even if it meant crossing the brutal heat of the desert or paying human smugglers, or "coyotes."

The United Farm Workers (UFW) was a visible element in the Arizona political scene in the early 1970s. Arizona's native, Cesar Chavez, co-founded the organization to provide a method for farmworkers to organize and fight for better wages and working conditions. However, Chavez's native state denied farm labor the right to organize in May 1972 when, 45 minutes after it was passed by the legislature, Arizona governor Jack Williams signed a bill sponsored by agri-business that made it illegal for workers to strike or boycott during harvest season.

Chavez challenged Williams. Besides starting a hunger strike, he organized an effort to recall the governor. The UFW registered over 100,000 new voters, many of whom were Mexican Americans and Navajos who had never voted before, and collected over 168,000 signatures on recall petitions. While the attorney general of Arizona stopped the recall election, the newly enfranchised voters made their presence felt at the polls in state elections to come. Four Mexican Americans and two Navajos were elected to the state legislature in 1972, and two years later, Democrat and Mexican immigrant Raul Hector Castro became the first Latino to be elected governor of Arizona.

The Udall Center at the University of Arizona has estimated that in 1980 approximately 180,000 undocumented immigrants entered Arizona. That number grew to 850,000 in 2000. The center contends that the primary reason for immigration remained constant from the nineteenth century to the twenty-first century—employment opportunity. Mexicans, more than any other immigrant group, can earn more money in the United States than they can in their home country. The Udall Center also points out that as the American population ages, the ability of Americans to do labor-intensive work in industries such as agriculture and construction has declined, offering employment opportunities to able-bodied immigrants. However, without a legal system to adequately process the number of Mexican immigrants seeking work in Arizona, combined with a willingness of employers to hire workers illegally, the state's population of undocumented immigrants dramatically increased.

Undocumented Mexican workers are typically paid in cash and do not usually have bank accounts or pay income taxes, making their contributions to the state's economy difficult to quantify. The contribution of Arizona's legal Mexican immigrant population is clearer. They contribute billions of dollars to the local economy. In 2002, Mexican immigrants accounted for $4 billion in purchasing power in Arizona and generated almost $60 million in bank fees by sending money back to family members in Mexico. A 2003 study by Thunderbird, The American Graduate School of International Management, concluded that the relationship between Mexico and Arizona, taking into account commerce, investments, and tourism, is worth $8 billion each year to Arizona and $5.5 billion to Mexico.

Between 2000 and 2008, Arizona's undocumented immigrant population swelled by 70 percent. In 2008, Maricopa county sheriff Joe Arpaio, who has served as sheriff of Arizona's most populated county since 1992, responded to this increase by instituting crime suppression sweeps in Phoenix's predominantly Latino neighborhoods. Arpaio openly stated that his deputies looked for undocumented immigrants in these sweeps and by 2010 they had made approximately 1,000 arrests, typically for minor offenses. Approximately 70 percent of those arrested were undocumented immigrants.

By 2010, Latinos comprised 30 percent of the state's population, although they made up less than 12 percent of Arizona's registered voters. The majority of the state's lawmakers were Republicans and they supported tough immigration laws, such as Senate Bill (SB) 1070. Arizona shot into the national spotlight in April 2010 with the passage of SB 1070, which was touted as the toughest anti-illegal immigration bill in the country. Citing lack of action by the federal government and growing concern about Mexican drug cartel crime spilling over the state's borders, Governor Jan Brewer signed the bill on April 23, 2010, sparking a firestorm of controversy. The key element of the law required anyone suspected by law enforcement of being in the state illegally to produce federal documents confirming their legal right to be in the country. Supporters hailed the bill as a much-needed step toward securing the border, while critics argued that the bill would lead to racial profiling. The bill was stalled by a preliminary injunction from U.S. district court judge Susan Bolton. The injunction was upheld in April 2011 and Brewer vowed that the state would appeal to the Supreme Court.

While the debate over immigration from Mexico rages on, both legal and undocumented immigration into Arizona from Asia has increased. In 2009, the Border Patrol in Tucson reported 281 undocumented immigrants from China were detained between October 1 and December 31. Chinese immigrants paid up to $40,000 to smugglers to transport them over the Mexican border, compared to the $1,500 to $3,000 that Mexican immigrants paid. As with Mexicans, Chinese immigrants go to Arizona seeking better jobs and better educational opportunities. The overall population of Asian Americans in Arizona doubled to 176,695 between 2000 and 2010, making it the fastest-growing immigrant population in the state during the first decade of the twenty-first century.

TOPICAL ESSAYS

Senate Bill 1070

SB 1070, sponsored by Republican senator Russell Pearce, was passed by the Arizona Senate on April 19, 2010. The bill made it a misdemeanor for undocumented immigrants to be in the state and required local law enforcement to ask for documentation if an individual who was suspected of being in the state illegally. SB 1070 also permitted lawsuits against local government if it was believed that local and federal immigration laws were not being enforced. Governor Jan Brewer, a Republican who assumed the office when Democrat Janet Napolitano was picked by President Barack Obama to be the secretary of Homeland Security in 2009, had the choice of vetoing the bill, doing nothing and simply allowing it to become law, or signing it. With hundreds of protestors gathering around the State Capitol building in Phoenix, Brewer signed SB 1070 on April 23, citing concerns about growing border violence and the lack of action by the federal government to protect the state.

The bill immediately sparked local and national controversy as critics argued that it would lead to racial profiling, since the bill did not define how a law enforcement official would be able to suspect an individual of being in Arizona illegally. There were also concerns from cities, towns, and businesses about the economic ramifications of the bill, such as the possible loss of tourism or business partnerships. The Arizona Hotel and Lodging Association reported that in the first week after Brewer signed SB 1070, 19 meetings and conferences were canceled specifically because of the bill, resulting in a loss of approximately $6 million.

Some said that Major League Baseball should move the All-Star Game, scheduled to be held in Phoenix in July 2011, and some players openly questioned whether or not they would attend. Arizona congressman Raul Grijalva, a Democrat, called for a boycott against the state. Supporters of the bill argued that since the federal government had not adequately protected the border, and since violent crime at the border, particularly at the hands of Mexican drug cartels, was on the rise, the governor was forced to take action to protect the state.

The bill was due to take effect on July 29, 2010, 90 days after the end of the last legislative session. However, the Obama administration indicated in mid-June that it would contest the law, stating that it is unconstitutional for states rather than the federal government to set immigration policy. The Justice Department filed a lawsuit in federal court in Phoenix, just one of a series of lawsuits that included suits by the cities of Tucson and Flagstaff, the American Civil Liberties Union, and the Mexican American Legal Defense and Educational Fund. The state of Arizona countersued in federal court in February 2011, citing the federal government's failure to protect the citizens of Arizona.

In 2011, flanked by Arizona attorney general Tom Horne, left, Arizona governor Jan Brewer explains why she thinks the controversial anti-immigration law (particularly targeting the undocumented)—SB 1070—which was partially enjoined by the Ninth Circuit Court, will be reinstated when the U.S. Supreme Court hears Arizona's appeal in its next session. Brewer has been widely criticized by immigration advocates for her stance on this issue. (Rick D. Elia/Corbis)

The day before SB 1070 was scheduled to take effect, U.S. district judge Susan Bolton issued a preliminary injunction that blocked the key components of the bill, including requirements that immigrants carry federal immigration documents, provisions that would make it illegal for undocumented immigrants to perform day labor, and authority for law enforcement officers to question a person suspected of being in the state illegally. Bolton cited concerns that law enforcement would wrongfully arrest legal citizens and that legal citizens would have an undue burden to prove their citizenship. Bolton also stated that it was likely that federal laws already in existence would take precedence over the proposed state law. The state appealed the injunction, but, in April 2011, the U.S. Court of Appeals for the Ninth Circuit upheld the injunction. On May 9, 2011, Brewer announced that the state would appeal to the Supreme Court.

NOTABLE FIGURES

Joe Arpaio (1932–)

Massachusetts native Joe Arpaio, who served as a Drug Enforcement Agency (DEA) agent for 25 years before leading the Arizona branch of the DEA, was elected sheriff of Maricopa County in 1992. Maricopa County is the home of more than half of the state's residents, including the Phoenix metropolitan area. He was reelected in 1996, 2000, 2004, 2008, and 2012.

Known for instituting policies such as requiring inmates of county jails to wear pink underwear, housing inmates in tents throughout the year, limiting them to two meals per day to save costs, and reviving the use of chain gangs, Arpaio was also a central figure in Arizona's immigration debate. A vocal opponent of undocumented immigration, Arpaio has facilitated crime suppression sweeps, more commonly known as "immigration sweeps" throughout Maricopa County, targeting specific neighborhoods in search of undocumented immigrants. Critics of the actions have accused Arpaio of racial profiling and, in 2009, the Department of Homeland Security removed the sheriff's authority to arrest suspected undocumented immigrants solely because of their immigration status. Undeterred, Arpaio continued the sweeps, stating that he is enforcing Arizona's trespassing laws.

The U.S. Department of Justice launched an investigation into Arpaio's jail policies and immigration sweeps in 2009, and then sued him in September 2010 to compel him to release documents related to the investigation and to provide access to employees and facilities. The investigation focused on whether or not Arpaio violated the civil rights of inmates and those targeted in his immigration sweeps.

Arpaio was an ardent supporter of SB 1070, the controversial bill signed by Governor Jan Brewer in 2010 that would make it a crime to be in Arizona without the proper documentation confirming one's legal right to be in the state. Arpaio, stating that he did not understand why the bill was controversial, simply stated that it was a crime to be in Arizona illegally and that the law should be enforced. Days before the law was due to go into effect, Arpaio threatened to arrest and detain anyone causing a civil disturbance while protesting the law, although U.S. district judge Susan Bolton blocked the key elements of SB 1070, preventing it from taking effect as planned.

Sheriff Arpaio and the Maricopa County Sheriff's Office became the subjects of multiple legal battles and personnel scandals in 2010. In January of that year, a federal grand jury in Phoenix was empanelled to investigate charges that Arpaio used his office to bring legal charges against his political enemies. The Sheriff's Office was the subject of a six-month investigation led by Pinal County sheriff Paul Babeu in late 2010. The investigation came as the result of allegations of corruption in the Sheriff's Office, including operating an illegal slush fund and targeting political enemies. Soon after the findings were released in April 2011, two of Arpaio's top deputies, Dave Hendershott and Larry Black, were forced to resign.

County budget officials also reported, in April 2011, that the Sheriff's Office misspent nearly $100 million over the previous eight years, which the Sheriff's Office blamed on an error in the bookkeeping system. In May 2011, critics of Arpaio, including Maricopa County supervisor Mary Rose Wilcox, demanded that Arpaio resign, stating that he was unfit to serve, and calling on the federal government to place the Sheriff's Office in receivership. Arpaio stated that he would never resign.

RAUL CASTRO (1916–)

Raul H. Castro was born June 12, 1916, in Cananea, Sonora, a border town in northern Mexico. His father, Francisco, was a miner and his mother, Rosario, was a midwife. Castro's parents legally immigrated to southern Arizona with Castro and his 12 siblings when Castro was a young child. Castro earned a teaching degree at Northern Arizona University in Flagstaff in 1939, paying his tuition by working as a waiter and plucking chickens. The same year that Castro graduated from college, he became a naturalized citizen but was unable to find work other than manual labor due to his Mexican heritage.

Castro's entry into politics came after he went to law school at the University of Arizona in Tucson and started his law practice there, eventually becoming deputy county attorney in 1951. Like many Latinos of that era, Castro was unhappy with the discrimination that existed, particularly in employment opportunities and in the educational system. This unhappiness led to his decision to run for the Pima County attorney position. Despite the fact that he was given little chance for victory

Arizona's Raul Hector Castro takes the oath of office on October 26, 1964, as U.S. ambassador to El Salvador. Castro, shown here, was born in Mexico and became a U.S. citizen in 1939. He also served as a judge in the Arizona Superior Court and currently resides in Tucson. (Bettmann/Corbis)

and even his own brothers did not vote for him, Castro won the 1954 election by the slim margin of 65 votes.

While on a campaign stop in Tucson, Lyndon Johnson met Castro. In 1964, President Johnson appointed him U.S. ambassador to El Salvador. Castro then served as ambassador to Bolivia in 1968 before returning to Tucson in 1969 after Johnson left office. Castro missed politics and became the Democratic nominee for governor in 1970, but lost to the incumbent, Republican Jack Williams. Castro ran for governor again in 1974 on a platform that, in part, emphasized developing partnerships with Mexico and introducing bilingual education in schools. The race against the Republican nominee, Russell Williams, was too close to call until the day after the election, November 5, when Castro declared victory. The Mexican immigrant became the first—and only—Latino governor of Arizona by 4,100 votes.

Castro did not complete his term as governor because he was appointed ambassador to Argentina in 1977 by President Jimmy Carter. Not all in the Latino community were happy that Castro accepted the appointment, but Castro felt that it was his duty to serve his country when the president called and that his duty extended beyond just the desires of Latinos. Castro returned to Tucson after Carter's presidential term ended in 1981, and he eventually moved south to the Arizona border town of Nogales, where he practiced law until his retirement in 2004. The Raul H. Castro Institute, located at the downtown campus of Phoenix College, is named for him and was launched by Democratic governor Janet Napolitano in 2006, with the mission of improving the quality of life in the Latino community by impacting policy decisions in health and human services, education, civic participation, and leadership.

WING F. ONG (1904–1977)

When Wing F. Ong arrived in San Francisco from Canton, China, with his family in 1918, he was 14 years old. He did not know English, but Chinese children were prohibited from attending public school in San Francisco, making it difficult to learn the language. Ong contacted a family in Phoenix, who assured him he could attend school there and so he moved to Phoenix and, at 15 years old, enrolled in grammar school, which he attended for three years while working in a family restaurant, sleeping in its basement at night. By the time he enrolled in high school three years later, he was fluent in English.

After graduating from high school, Ong enrolled in the University of Arizona and in the summer worked as a houseboy for Governor Thomas Campbell. His relationship with Campbell not only led to an interest in politics but also was beneficial when Ong, his wife, and his infant son were detained in San Francisco years later after a visit back to their homeland. A phone call to Campbell from

Angel Island, the West Coast immigration processing center, led to the immediate release of the Ong family.

Asian immigrants did not enter politics in the United States in the 1940s, but Ong's relationship with Campbell and the treatment he received in San Francisco led to his interest in holding public office. Now a grocer and a married father of four children, Ong ran for the State House of Representatives in 1944, but lost by 17 votes. At that point, he felt that he should have a better understanding of law if he wanted to help create it, so he earned his law degree from the University of Arizona in Tucson, where he was a classmate of Barry Goldwater. At the age of 36, Ong was one of only eight Chinese American lawyers in the United States.

Ong again ran for the Arizona House of Representatives again in 1946 and this time he won, becoming the first Chinese American to serve as a state legislator in the nation's history. He served two terms in the House of Representatives before focusing his attention on immigration law, particularly for Chinese immigrants upon their arrival in San Francisco. Arizona governor Sam Goddard appointed Ong as goodwill ambassador to China in 1965. Ong was elected to the Arizona State Senate in 1966, where he served one term. Ong died in 1977.

BIBLIOGRAPHY

August, Jack L. "Wing F. Ong and the American Dream in Phoenix." *Arizona Food Industry Journal* (November 2008). http://afmaaz.org/Journal/2008 percent20Journals/November percent202008.pdf. Accessed February 25, 2014.

Busby, Mark, ed. *The Southwest: The Greenwood Encyclopedia of American Regional Cultures*. Westport, CT: Greenwood Press, 2004.

Castro, Raul H., and Jack L. August Jr. *Adversity Is My Angel*. Fort Worth: Texas Christian University Press, 2009.

Ceasar, Stephen. "In Arizona, a Stream of Illegal Immigrants from China." *New York Times*, January 22, 2010. http://www.nytimes.com/2010/01/23/us/23smuggle.html. Accessed February 25, 2014.

Daniels, Roger. "The Immigration Act of 1965." America.gov Archive, April 2, 2008. http://www.america.gov/. Accessed February 25, 2014.

"Economic Impact of Mexico-Arizona Relationship." Thunderbird, the American Graduate School of International Management, May 2011. http://www.ime.gob.mx/investigaciones/aportaciones/arizona.pdf. Accessed February 25, 2014.

Fox News Latino. "Arpaio's Office Accused of Misusing $99 Million." April 14, 2011. http://latino.foxnews.com/latino/news/2011/04/14/arpaios-office-accused-misusing-million/. Accessed February 25, 2014.

Gans, Judith. "Immigrants in Arizona: Fiscal and Economic Impacts." University of Arizona Udall Center for Studies in Public Policy. June 2008. http://udallcenter.arizona.edu/immigration/publications/impactofimmigrants08.pdf. Accessed February 25, 2014.

Garcia, Juan Ramon. *Operation Wetback: The Mass Deportation of Mexican Undocumented Workers in 1954*. Westport, CT: Greenwood Press, 1980.

Gonzalez, Daniel. "Arizona's Asian Population Now Fastest-Growing in State." *Arizona Republic*, May 16, 2011. http://www.azcentral.com/news/articles/2011/05/16/20110516arizona-asian-population-growth.html. Accessed February 25, 2014.

Gorman, Ann. "Arizona Sheriff Launches 17th Immigration Sweep." *Los Angeles Times*, July 30, 2010. http://articles.latimes.com/2010/jul/30/nation/la-na-arizona-immigration-raids-20100730. Accessed February 25, 2014.

Hernandez, Kelly Lytle. "Mexican Immigration to the United States 1900–1999." Annenberg Foundation, n.d. http://www.learner.org/courses/amerhistory/pdf/Mexican_Immigration_L-One.pdf. Accessed February 25, 2014.

"Illegal Immigration to the United States: Causes and Policy Solutions." University of Arizona Udall Center for Studies in Public Policy, February 2007. http://udallcenter.arizona.edu/immigration/publications/fact_sheet_no_3_illegal_immigration.pdf. Accessed February 25, 2014.

James, Randy. "Sheriff Joe Arpaio." *Time*, October 13, 2009. http://www.time.com/time/nation/article/0,8599,1929920,00.html. Accessed February 25, 2014.

KGUN9. "Critics Call for Resignation of Sheriff Arpaio." May 12, 2011. http://www.kgun9.com/story/14637086/critics-demand-sheriff-arpaio resign?clienttype=printable. Accessed February 25, 2014.

Lacey, Marc. "Justice Dept. Sues Sheriff Joe Arpaio Over Bias Investigation." *New York Times*, September 2, 2010. http://www.nytimes.com/2010/09/03/us/03sheriff.html. Accessed February 25, 2014.

"Mexican Immigrants in the United States, 2008." Pew Research Center Publications, April 15, 2009. http://pewresearch.org/pubs/1191/mexican-immigrants-in-america-largest-group. Accessed February 25, 2014.

"The Official Bracero Agreement." The Farmworkers Website. http://www.farmworkers.org/bpaccord.html. Accessed February 25, 2014.

PBS. "Becoming American: The Chinese Experience. 'Portrait, by Jack Ong'." 2003. http://www.pbs.org/becomingamerican/portraits/portrait.php?id=26. Accessed February 25, 2014.

"The Promise of Gold Mountain: Tucson's Chinese Heritage." University of Arizona. http://parentseyes.arizona.edu/promise/. Accessed February 25, 2014.

Rau, Alia Beard, and Michael Kiefer. "SB 1070 Block Upheld." *Arizona Republic*, April 12, 2011. http://www.azcentral.com/arizonarepublic/news/articles/2011/04/12/20110412xgr-1070ruling0412.html. Accessed February 25, 2014.

Riccardi, Nicholas. "Grand Jury Investigating Sheriff Joe Arpaio of Arizona." *Los Angeles Times*, January 9, 2010. http://articles.latimes.com/2010/jan/09/nation/la-na-arpaio9-2010jan09. Accessed February 25, 2014.

Shaw, Randy. *Beyond the Fields: Cesar Chavez, the UFW and the Struggle for Justice in the 21st Century*. Berkeley and Los Angeles: University of California Press, 2008.

Sheridan, Thomas E. *Arizona: A History*. Tucson: University of Arizona Press, 1995.

United Farm Workers. "History of Sí Se Puede." http://www.ufw.org/_board.php?mode=view&b_code=cc_his_research&b_no=5970&page=1&field=&key=&n=30. Accessed February 25, 2014.

Watanabe, Teresa, Anna Gorman, and Nicholas Riccardi. "Arizona's Crackdown on Illegal Migrants Feels Familiar." *Los Angeles Times,* April 16, 2010. http://articles.latimes.com/2010/apr/16/local/la-me-arizona17–2010apr17. Accessed February 25, 2014.

Wingett, Yvonne. "Ex-Gov. Castro Recalls Beating Odds." *Arizona Republic,* May 21, 2011. http://www.pc.maricopa.edu/data/GlobalFiles/file/rci/AZ percent20Republic percent20Raul percent20Castro-1.pdf. Accessed February 25, 2014.

Wingett, Yvonne, J.J. Hensley, and Michael Kiefer. "Sheriff Joe Arpaio Sued by Justice Department in Civil Rights Probe." *Arizona Republic,* September 3, 2010. http://www.azcentral.com/news/articles/2010/09/02/20100902joe-arpaio-sued-by-justice-department-brk-02-ON.html. Accessed February 25, 2014.

Ye Hee Lee, Michelle. "More Asian Americans Run for Arizona Office." *Arizona Republic,* September 19, 2010. http://www.azcentral.com/news/election/azelections/articles/2010/09/19/20100919asian-americans-arizona-politics.html. Accessed February 25, 2014.

4

ARKANSAS

William P. Kladky

CHRONOLOGY

1541	Spanish conqueror Hernando de Soto (1496–1542) leads the first European expedition to Arkansas.
1673	Jesuit Father Jacques Marquette, S.J. (1637–1675) and Louis Jolliet (1645–1700) travel to the mouth of the Arkansas River and visit Quapaw villages.
1681	Robert La Salle (1643–1687) arrives to search for the Mississippi's mouth and to claim the river area for New France. French settlement in the area begins.
1682	René-Robert Cavelier (1643–1687), sieur de La Salle, claims the Mississippi Valley for King Louis XIV of France, calling it "Louisiana."
1686	*La Poste d'Akancas* (Arkansas Post) is established by La Salle's lieutenant, Italian mercenary soldier Henri de Tonti (1649–1704) as a trading post.
1720	The "Mississippi Bubble" financial scam of Scottish banker John Law (1671–1729) collapses, ending his efforts to entice settlers to emigrate from Germany to begin an agricultural settlement at Arkansas Post.
1731	Louisiana, including present-day Arkansas, becomes a royal colony of France.
1740	Cotton agriculture is introduced to the area by Jean-Baptiste Le Moyne de Bienville (1680–1767), governor of Louisiana. As a result, immigration increases.

1762	As a result of the Treaty of Fontainebleau (Paris) ending the Seven Years' War, France cedes most of its North American possessions to Britain. A separate, secret treaty gives parts of Louisiana (including Arkansas) west of the Mississippi River to Spain.
1766	The first Spanish governor, Antonio de Ulloa (1716–1795), arrives facing opposition. A trickle of Spanish settlers follows.
1780s	Anglo settlers come to Arkansas, forcing the Native Americans living there to move westward to Oklahoma.
1800	French and Spanish diplomats sign the secret treaty of San Ildefonso, returning Louisiana (including Arkansas) to French control.
1803	American diplomats James Monroe (1758–1831) and Robert Livingston (1746–1813) negotiate to purchase New Orleans, to ensure continued American shipping rights on the Mississippi. The French government offers them all of Louisiana, for $15 million. Thus, Arkansas becomes part of the United States.
1804	President Thomas Jefferson (1743–1826) approves an Act of Congress dividing the newly acquired former French colony into the Territory of Orleans and the District of Louisiana (which includes Arkansas).
1812	President James Madison (1751–1836) approves an act setting aside 6 million acres of land (including Arkansas land) to be used as bounty lands for soldiers enlisting to fight the British, or for those displaced by the New Madrid earthquake. The War of 1812 veterans are promised 160-acre tracts of land.
1812	Congress creates the Missouri Territory, which includes Arkansas.
1813	"Arkansas County"—current-day Arkansas—is created by the Missouri Legislature.
1818	Arkansas County is divided into Clark, Hempstead, and Pulaski counties. The Quapaw are forced to give most of their land south of the Arkansas River to the United States.
1819	President James Monroe signs an Act of Congress creating the Territory of Arkansas. The first territorial legislature meets at Arkansas Post.
1820	General Andrew Jackson signs a treaty with the Choctaw nation granting the Choctaw lands in western Arkansas.
1830s and 1840s	Early migrants to Arkansas include French soldiers and Germans.
1836	Arkansas becomes the 25th state of the Union on June 15; James Conway (1798–1855) is elected its first governor.
1850s	Chinese immigrants, primarily from Canton province in southern China, Hong Kong, and Taiwan, begin to come to Arkansas.
1853	Arkansas's first railroad, the Arkansas Central, is chartered by the state legislature.
1860s and 1870s	During the Reconstruction era, Arkansas makes a formal, organized effort to encourage immigration.

1861	Arkansas is admitted to the Confederate States of America. A divided Arkansas sends 50,000 troops to the Confederate army and 15,000 troops to the Union army.
1865	The Unionist government at Little Rock becomes the sole constituted authority of the state.
1868	Because of Ku Klux Klan violence, 13 counties are put under martial law.
1870s and 1880s	The state experiences an immigration wave. German, Polish, Italian, and Japanese immigrants begin arriving, driven by political oppression and prejudice in their home countries as well as economic opportunities in Arkansas. Chinese immigrants are brought in by the Arkansas Valley Immigration Company to work in the cotton fields. Slovaks purchase land in Prairie County, and a number of Bohemian and Russian immigrants also come to settle. Coal mining opportunities draw Eastern and Central European immigrants.
1874	Republicans Elijah Baxter (1849–1939) and Joseph Brooks (1821–1877) each claim the governorship. President Ulysses Grant recognizes Baxter as the lawful governor.
1877	President Grant signs an act establishing the Hot Springs Reservation (Hot Springs National Park).
1891	The Separate Coach Law, segregating blacks and whites on trains and trams, is enacted as the state's first "Jim Crow" law.
1906	Diamonds are discovered in Pike County, the first deposit to be found in the United States. Some settlers follow.
1917	About 72,000 Arkansans serve during World War I, with 2,000 fatalities, mainly from disease and accidents.
1920s	Greek immigrants begin to arrive, primarily moving to the Little Rock area.
1921	Oil is discovered near Smackover.
1925	The state Supreme Court rules in *Brickhouse v. Hill* that state constitutional amendments 7, 8 and 9 (initiative and referendum, woman suffrage, and an enlarged Supreme Court) are legal.
1932	Hattie O.W. Caraway (1878–1950), named in 1931 to fill out the Senate term of her deceased husband, Thaddeus H. Caraway (1871–1931), is elected, becoming the first woman elected to the U.S. Senate.
1942	Internment camps for West Coast Japanese Americans are established near Jerome and Rohwer.
1948	Decorated former marine Sidney P. McMath is elected governor on a reform platform. He appoints African Americans to state boards for the first time since Reconstruction; he also promotes highway construction and encourages industrial development.
1957	The Little Rock schools are forcibly desegregated by the federal government.

1966	Winthrop P. Rockefeller (1912–1973) is elected governor, Arkansas's first Republican governor since 1874. He actively promotes migration and immigration.
1970	Dale L. Bumpers (1925–) of Charleston is elected governor, who promises to rid Arkansas of "the old machine and the money machine."
1974	Bumpers successfully challenges Senator J. William Fulbright in the Democratic primary and wins election to the U.S. Senate. David H. Pryor (1934–) of Camden is elected governor. University of Arkansas Law School professor William J. Clinton (1946–) loses his race for the Third Congressional District seat.
1976	Clinton is elected attorney-general, advocating victim compensation, the rights of the elderly, tough ethics laws for public officials, and tighter oversight of utilities, and opposing the 25-cent pay phone call.
1978	Attorney General Clinton is elected governor.
1980	Arkansas is ranked in the top five states in percentage of population over the age of 65, due to the "Retiree Movement." The federal government tells Governor Clinton that Camp Chaffee will house 120,000 Cuban "freedom flotilla" refugees.
1991	Lt. Gov. Jim Guy Tucker (1943–) becomes acting governor in Clinton's absence on campaign for the presidency.
1992	Clinton is elected the 42nd president of the United States. Lt. Gov. Tucker becomes governor.
1994	Tucker is elected governor, and Sharon Priest becomes the first woman to be elected to the office of Arkansas secretary of state.
2000–2005	Arkansas has the fourth-fastest-growing immigrant population and fastest-growing Latino population (48 percent) of any state.
2002	Bentonville-based Wal-Mart is identified as the world's largest corporation.
2007–2012	Anti-immigrant protests occur in the state.

HISTORICAL OVERVIEW

BEGINNINGS

Arkansas got its name from early French explorers, who called it "Akansea," a phonetic spelling of the Illinois Indian word for the "People of the South Wind," now called the Quapaw, who are descendants of migrants down the Mississippi River. The modern spelling came from early French usage and the *Arkansas Gazette*. In 1881, the name's pronunciation officially was set by the general assembly after scholarly investigation.

Beginning around 11,700 BCE, the first indigenous peoples inhabited the area now known as Arkansas after crossing today's Bering Strait, formerly Beringia. The first people in modern-day Arkansas likely hunted woolly mammoths by running them off cliffs or using clovis points. These early peoples of Arkansas likely lived in base camps and departed on hunting trips for months at a time. Further warming led to the beginnings of agriculture in Arkansas around 650 BCE. Burial mounds, surviving today in places such as Parkin Archeological State Park and Toltec Mounds Archeological State Park, become common in northeast Arkansas. The Quapaw, Caddo, and Osage Nations lived in Arkansas prior to the westward movement of peoples from the East.

The great Mississippi River, the state's meandering eastern boundary, enabled European discovery and settlement of Arkansas. In 1541, the Spanish explorer Hernando de Soto became the first European to visit the state. In 1673, the French explorers Jacques Marquette (1637–1675) and Louis Jolliet (1645–ca. 1700) reached the mouth of the Arkansas River. Robert La Salle (1643–1687) came in 1681 to search for the Mississippi's mouth and to claim the river area for New France. La Salle and Henri de Tonti (1649–1704) claimed the river in 1682. The French colonization of the Mississippi Valley ended with the later destruction of Fort St. Louis by the Iroquois in 1691.

The first settlement in the state was Arkansas Post, founded in 1686 by Henri de Tonti. The Post disbanded in 1699 and was reestablished in 1721 as a trade and fur trapper center. The accompanying French settlers mingled and intermarried with Quapaw natives. A moratorium on furs by Canada sunk the Post's economy and many settlers moved. Later, Scottish banker John Law (1671–1729) tried to entice settlers to emigrate from Germany to start an agriculture settlement at Arkansas Post but failed when his "Mississippi Bubble" financial scam collapsed in 1720. Maintained because of its Mississippi River importance, the Post was relocated several times. In 1727, Father Paul de Posson reported that the Post had a French population of 30.

In 1762, the secret treaty of Fontainebleau gave Spain the Louisiana Territory, including Arkansas, in exchange for Florida. The first Spanish governor, Antonio de Ulloa (1716–1795), arrived in 1766 but faced much opposition from existing settlers. Some Spanish settlers arrived at this time. In 1783, the sole Arkansas battle during the American Revolutionary War occurred with a siege of the Post by the British, assisted by the Choctaw and Chicksaw Indians. In 1800, the Post's population was an estimated 400, with about 14 percent being Scotch Irish. During this time, Indians displaced from east of the Mississippi entered Arkansas. Especially after the War of 1812, when veterans of the conflict were promised 160-acre tracts land, white settlers arrived in increasing numbers and eventually forced the Arkansas Indians to move west into what would become Oklahoma.

THE LOUISIANA PURCHASE AND TERRITORIAL STATUS

Arkansas became a Spanish possession after the U.S. Revolutionary War ended in 1783. The Spanish sought to encourage settlement but were understandably ambivalent about allowing American immigrants. Napoleon Bonaparte's defeat of Spain meant that Louisiana, including Arkansas, became a French possession under the Third Treaty of San Ildefonso, which was concluded in 1800. Napoleon subsequently sold Louisiana to the United States, which doubled in size as a result of the Louisiana Purchase. The already uneasy relationship between settlers and American Indians was completely overturned by the resulting rush of new settlers.

President Thomas Jefferson then initiated the Lewis and Clark Expedition to find the nation's new northern boundary, and the Dunbar Hunter Expedition, led by William Dunbar (1750–1810), explored the new southern boundary. In the process, the Dunbar group explored central Arkansas.

Arkansas became a territory after the Territory of Missouri applied for U.S. statehood on March 2, 1819, as a slave state. Missouri's admission threatened to upset the delicate balance between slave and free states. The new territory of Arkansas was carved out of that portion of the Missouri Territory that lay south of the 36°30' north parallel, except the Missouri Bootheel. New York representative John Taylor (1784–1854) proposed an amendment, banning slavery in the new territory, to the Arkansas Enabling Act. This attempt to ban slavery was soundly defeated, but a proposal for gradual emancipation lingered unresolved until Speaker of the House Henry Clay (1777–1852) killed Taylor's amendment and thus enabled Arkansas to become slave territory.

The new Arkansas Territory had a population of over 14,000, excluding American Indians, and its capital was Arkansas Post. Its lands included Arkansas and Oklahoma, with the exception of the western Oklahoma panhandle. The added Oklahoma lands became Indian Territory by 1828, leaving the current boundary of Arkansas. After French workmen came from a failed colony at New Biloxi in 1720, the Arkansas Post received a steady stream of immigrants until the mid-1800s. The Post included the commandant and his family, priests, soldiers, hunters and fur traders, African American slaves, Native Americans, and merchants. A significant migration of settlers, including many slaveholders, moved into the territory. Families immigrated to Arkansas from Appalachia (mainly Tennessee, Kentucky, and North Carolina). Whites from Mississippi, Alabama, and Georgia also came to farm. Most of the plantation owners moved to the Delta part of the state, and utilized numerous slaves on their large lots. As a result of all this movement, the population more than doubled every decade after the 1820s.

Early immigration to Arkansas was mostly to the north and west. In 1830, about 68 percent of the population and 61 percent of the black slaves lived in the highland sections of Arkansas. Most settlers started small self-sufficient farms, producing grain, cattle, and hogs. The northwest parts of the territory were not cotton farmers, and that area had a black slave population of only 2 percent at this time. Later, the swamps were drained to allow large-scale cotton production. The wealthy planters in the southeastern section of the territory supported slavery to secure enough manual labor to harvest cotton.

With the population surge, the sizable Native American population was soon pushed elsewhere. The Quapaw signed an 1818 treaty—which was reneged upon by the United States in 1819—giving up their hunting lands except for 32 million acres along the Arkansas River. The Osage signed a treaty to leave in 1825. Fort Smith, Arkansas, and Fort Gibson, Oklahoma, were established by the federal government to keep peace between the fighting American Indians and the en- croaching settlers. With settlers demanding the Quapaws's fertile lands around the Arkansas River, the federal government forced the Quapaw and the Caddo onto a reservation in Louisiana in the 1820s.

With the indigenous groups gone and land cheap and fertile, immigration quickened with the high demand for land. Settlers previously had little incentive to explore Arkansas's wilderness as long as cheap, plentiful lands were available in other areas. Once these lands were full, the migrants came for many reasons: for adventure, to join family and friends, to get land, and for work. Early migrants included French soldiers and Germans. German Swiss and Italian immigrants began the Arkansas winemaking industry in the 1820s and 1830s. Encouraging settlement, the state and federal government sold public lands for as little as $1.25 per acre. The Arkansas "Donation Law" of 1840 gave tax-forfeited lands to more prosperous settlers. In 1850, the state sold swamp and river-overflow land for 50 cents an acre if the buyer agreed to build levees to stabilize the parcel. Over 3 mil- lion acres had been sold by 1859.

On the negative side, the poor transportation system kept the level of migration somewhat low. The rivers and waterways were a primary means of travel at this time. Later, roads and then railroads were built after the Civil War. As the low- lands were cleared and broken for cotton, the black slave population grew from 1,617 in 1820 to 20,000 in 1840. Jewish immigrants came to the state as early as 1825, trickling in from Germany and Central Europe to escape political oppres- sion. They established small communities in Little Rock, Fort Smith, Pine Bluff, Batesville, and other areas.

STATEHOOD

In the 1830s, Germans began coming to Arkansas. By 1833, Arkansas's popula- tion exceeded 40,000 and it became eligible for statehood. The question of becom- ing a state was first raised by National Republican Benjamin Desha (1790–1835) in 1831 in the *Little Rock Arkansas Advocate*. Many Democrats thought the taxa- tion to fund a state government would be too burdensome. The applications of

Michigan and Arkansas were first denied by congressional Whigs because the prospective states were dominated by Democrats, but both Arkansas and Michigan developed state constitutions despite the ruling.

After significant debate over slavery and representation, the U.S. Congress approved the Arkansas Constitution after a 25-hour session. President Andrew Jackson (1767–1845) signed the bill creating the State of Arkansas on June 15, 1836. In the 1820s, the Swiss, coming by way of Kentucky, began to immigrate to Arkansas and purchased land for settlement. They were attracted by the Missouri Pacific Railroad's advertisements for fertile delta lands in Phillips County for settlement at low prices. Most settled around Barton and Hicks, and farmed, constructed railroad cross ties, and sold cords of wood to the railroad company. During the 1830s, Arkansas plantation owners utilized eastern capital to import some 15,000 black slaves, with most coming from western Africa.

After the end of the Mexican War in 1848, thousands of Arkansans migrated to Texas, while others went to California in 1849 to participate in the gold rush. Because of an 1859 law requiring free blacks to leave the state by the end of the year or risk being enslaved, Arkansas's free black population fell from 682 in 1858 to 144 in 1860. After the 1840s, Chinese immigrants—primarily from Canton province in Southern China, Hong Kong, and Taiwan—began to arrival in Arkansas. They were hired as railroad workers, cooks, launderers, grain farmers, fruit growers, tide-land drainers, and miners.

As of 1860, Arkansas really was a frontier. Some 95 percent of the state's 324,335 Anglos were born in the United States, with 97 percent of those born in the South. The foreign-born population included 1,312 Irish; 1,143 Germans; and some others. Most of the state was unimproved, with no banks, canals, or decent roads. The state had only 28 miles of railroad track state, compared to Michigan's 799 miles. Little Rock's population was only 3,727. Baptist circuit riders and some Methodist missionaries brought the Gospel to the state.

The black slave population in 1860 was approximately 111,115. Most were concentrated in the eastern and southeastern sections of the state, with relatively few elsewhere. For example, the 1860 black slave population of northwestern Benton County was 384 out of a total county population of 9,306, whereas southeastern Chicot County had 7,512 slaves out of a total population of 9,234. African Americans were a majority in six counties and slaveholders constituted but 3.5 percent of the white population in 1860. However, the planter class dominated the state, and the idea of secession was popular. The state's voters supported secession by a vote of 27,472 to 15,826 in special state election held on March 4, 1861. Arkansas formally seceded from the Union on May 6, 1861. During the Civil War, many small battles were fought in Arkansas. The northwestern section of the state suffered the most battle damage.

THE POST–CIVIL WAR PERIOD

During the Reconstruction era of the late 1860s and early 1870s, Arkansas made a formal, organized effort to encourage immigration. State legislation was enacted promoting immigration, and immigration societies were formed. The state's population did increase during this period, but few foreign immigrants arrived. Arkansas did attract some African American immigration, which was promoted by the state's Office of State Lands and Migration. Under the leadership of an African American, William H. Grey, the Office of State Lands and Migration described the state as a new Africa. Although Reconstruction was not as bad in Arkansas as in some other southern states, whites definitely reasserted their control, as in other southern state governments. Onerous labor and property reforms (such as sharecropping and tenant farming) were enacted and rigorously enforced. In the upland regions, the few blacks who lived there left. As a result, several Arkansas towns became "sundown towns," where African Americans were prevented by local residents from settling. The Arkansas Democratic Party fought Reconstruction by consolidating its power to prevent alliances between African Americans and poor whites. Several laws were passed to do this: a literacy test for voter registration was enacted in 1891 and in 1892 a constitutional amendment was passed imposing a poll tax and residency restrictions. The result of these measures was the virtually disenfranchisement of blacks and poor whites.

After Reconstruction, the same immigrant wave that brought millions to the United States also brought thousands to Arkansas. Many Germans immigrated to Arkansas during the 1870s and 1880s. They mainly came for religious freedom and for better economic conditions. Railroad companies and local newspapers played an important role in encouraging their move, as did the German Immigration Aid Society of Little Rock, which praised Arkansas's rich soil and abundant minerals. Most Germans came to the Arkansas River Valley between Little Rock and Fort Smith. The settlers lived in such towns as Stuttgart, Althiemer, Engelburg, Imboden, Ulm, Fort Smith, Jonesboro, and Pocahontas.

In 1877, Polish immigrants began to arrive in Arkansas, driven by political oppression and prejudice in their home region. They established the town of Marche in Pulaski County. Count Timothy von Choinski of Posen, Poland, purchased 11,000 acres from the Little Rock and Fort Smith Railroad Company located in Pope, Conway, Faulkner, and Pulaski counties. By 1878, over 200 Polish families had immigrated, mainly from the Posen, Galicia, and Silesia provinces in Poland. Descendants of the original founders still live around Marche, off Highway 65 in Pulaski County.

In the 1870s and 1880s, Chinese immigrants were brought in by the Arkansas Valley Immigration Company to work on the cotton fields of Lincoln, Jefferson, and Pulaski counties. Because the Chinese were contracted for less than five years and were paid wages and the cost of their passage, some believed this as a post-Reconstruction way to "punish the Negro for having abandoned the control of his master" (Department of Arkansas Heritage 2012). Eventually, a number of the Chinese immigrants became small businessmen in the Delta region.

As a result of all this immigration, the state grew rapidly during this period, from 484,471 in 1870 to 802,525 in 1880 (an increase of 65.6 percent), and to 1,113,775 in 1890. Railroads, seeking buyers for the lands they have acquired through government grants, were especially active in encouraging immigration after Reconstruction. Later immigrants included Italians and, in the early 1900s, Germans.

Small Jewish communities also grew; Jewish merchants with economic connections to Memphis, St. Louis, Cincinnati, and other cities moved to Arkansas seeking business opportunities. Anti-Semitism and legal restrictions in their home countries stimulated a small number of Jews to immigrate to Arkansas from Poland and Latvia. In the late 1880s, Japanese immigration to Arkansas started as part of an effort by the Arkansas Valley Immigration Company to bring Chinese immigrants to replace protesting black labor. These Asian immigrants were young, from rural areas, and worked as cheap labor on farms, railroads, mines, and canneries. This effort was frustrated by the national Chinese Exclusion Act of 1882.

Additional Central European immigrants settled in Prairie County between Hazen (in Prairie County) and Stuttgart (Arkansas County) in the 1890s. The Slovak Colonization Society purchased land in Prairie County and moved 50 families to Arkansas to farm. They found Slovaktown, which later changed its name to Slovak, in Prairie County. Around this time, a number of Bohemian and Russian immigrants also came to settle.

In 1890, Austin Corbin brought a group of Italian families to Chicot and Lonoke counties in southeastern Arkansas to grow and harvest cotton. This was part of a plan to replace African American tenant farmers, who have migrated to northern cities. By 1897, nearly 1,000 Italians had arrived. They mostly lived on Sunnyside, a plantation farmed by other immigrants and African Americans. Unfortunately, many Italians died of malaria, amid the unsanitary water, substandard housing, and inadequate and expensive medical care. Many of the Italian immigrants left within five years to settle in other parts of the state, such as Pine Bluff, the Little Italy and New Dixie areas of Perry County, and Tontitown in northwestern Arkansas. In northwestern Arkansas, Pietro Bandini, an Italian priest, came to help foreign immigrants from being exploited. Several Sunnyside out-migrants founded Tontitown, and Italian immigrants from Sicily came to Helena in the late 1800s.

During this time, coal mining opportunities in western Arkansas drew a number of Eastern and Central European immigrants, who worked in Coal Hill and west of Clarksville. The Little Rock and Fort Smith Railroad Company also recruited European workers for the mines. Slavic workers were brought in to break a strike leading to the 1915 Jamestown War (also called the Wheelbarrow Strike). These immigrants frequently did not bring their families and they left as soon as they made some money to take back to their homelands.

One of the largest permanent immigrant groups was the Germans, with several groups arriving during the 1870s and 1880s under the guidance of Catholic religious organizations such as St. Benedict's Colony. By the end of 1878, 150 families had settled in Arkansas. Coming from Germany, Alsace-Lorraine, Switzerland, and Poland, they were recruited by a Catholic priest, in partnership with the Little Rock and Fort Smith Railroad Company. The railroad offered them inexpensive land in the Arkansas River Valley.

The mission of St. Joseph was established by German, Swiss, and French immigrants at Morrilton in Conway County, with other missions established in Conway in Faulkner County. Other immigrant settlements were at Russellville, Clarksville, and many small towns along the river and railroad.

Early Twentieth Century

In 1900, the African American population of Arkansas was 366,984, about 28 percent of the state's total population. But since blacks could not vote and could

Immigrant workers weighing in cotton in Pulaski County, Arkansas, October, 1935. (Library of Congress)

not serve on juries, they were excluded from the political process. The black population peaked in 1910 at 30 percent, but then fell steadily to only 16 percent in 1980.

Road construction in the state finally began to occur in earnest in the new century. About 100 miles were paved by 1915. Delays were frequent because the high costs of paving were prohibitive for local governments.

Greek immigrants began to arrive at this time, mainly moving to the Little Rock area. In the late 1920s, the Greek community in Little Rock numbered more than 200. By the 1940s, another 30 Greek families have moved to the Fort Smith area, where many were involved in the restaurant business supporting the military personnel stationed at what is now Fort Chaffee. Pockets of Greek immigrants also appeared in Pine Bluff and Hot Springs (Garland County).

In 1915, the town of Little Italy was founded by several Italian immigrants who had first settled in Chicago and Michigan's Upper Peninsula around 1900. Attracted by the Ouachita Mountains, which reminded them of their Italian mountainous villages, they initially named their town Alta Villa and began to clear the rocky soil to begin wine cultivation. When the town grew, its name was Americanized to "Little Italy." Their wineries supplied bootleg wine during Prohibition (1919–1933) but also expanded into legally selling grapes to food stores in the area and other regions. Hundreds of acres were cultivated by the end of Prohibition. Today, despite a population of fewer than 100, the town has four bonded wineries, which now yearly bottle thousands of gallons of port and claret wine.

Economic growth surged in Arkansas during the 1920s, which stimulated a rise in immigration. Mineral production in the state was aided by the increased utilization of bauxite in war-related processes. However, beginning with the Great Depression and the attendant agricultural crisis of the 1930s, Arkansas's population declined. Immigration fell to practically nothing. Much of the state's farm population left for the industrial cities of the Midwest and the East and West Coasts. In the 1930s, Arkansas had an out-migration of over 128,000. Many were African Americans, who moved mainly to the large cities of the Midwest. Some 5,000 blacks moved to Memphis, 10,000 to St. Louis, and 12,000 to Chicago. The growth in industrial jobs in the North and Midwest had attracted many African Americans from the South, who left for a better quality of life. Agricultural changes also meant that farmworkers were not needed in as great a number. As a result, thousands left Arkansas. During World War II, blacks also migrated to California, where good jobs were expanding in defense industries.

Industrialization, urbanization, and modernization did not come to Arkansas until after the Depression of the 1930s. The plantation system remained dominant, retarding the state's economic development. This system was reinforced when the state became a major rice producer. The temporary cotton boom inspired by World War I spread prosperity but merely postponed the inevitable demise of King Cotton. The price of cotton began falling in the late

1920s, with floods further reducing production, and the Depression forced many into poverty.

During the late 1930s and 1940s, many Arkansan farmers left the state. With few jobs available in Arkansas, many left for employment in cities in other states. Some 416,117 left during the 1940s alone. Only 19 of the state's 75 counties had population growth during the 1940s, and they were already the most populous. Agriculture in Arkansas temporarily was saved by the New Deal. Its subsidies allowed many white and black farmers to return to self-sufficiency. Afterward, however, cotton and row crop agriculture were abandoned, and two-thirds of Arkansas farms ceased production.

1945 TO THE PRESENT

Arkansas's population losses in the 1940s continued in the 1950s. The virtual demise of the family farm led to the state losing approximately 44 percent of its population by 1960. The net loss from migration totaled 919,000 between 1940 and 1970. Arkansas slowly industrialized and the loss in farm employment meant that jobs simply were not available. The continuing high birth rate kept the state from experiencing even larger declines. The state's population declined 8.4 percent during 1940–1960.

Some of these economic and population trends began to change in the 1960s. As the nation's Sunbelt gained population, the state also had a net in-migration. In 1970, Arkansas's population reached 1,923,295, a 7.6 percent increase since 1960. During the 1970s, the state's population began to grow rapidly.

Arkansas played a central role in an early stage of the civil rights movement. In one of the first major cases of the civil rights era, the U.S. Supreme Court ruled in *Brown v. Topeka Board of Education* (1954) that segregated schools were unconstitutional. In 1957, Governor Orval E. Faubus deployed the Arkansas National Guard to support the segregationists, but backed down after a federal judge granted an injunction from the U.S. Department of Justice. After white mobs rioted when the nine black students sought to attend all-white Little Rock Central High School in 1957, President Dwight D. Eisenhower (1890–1969) deployed the 101st Airborne Division to Little Rock and federalized the Arkansas National Guard to protect the students and ensure their safe passage to school.

By the end of the Faubus administration, the public mood had changed. Winthrop Rockefeller (1912–1973), who served as governor from 1966 to 1970, was devoted to bringing industry into his adopted state and building a strong Republican Party in one of the nation's most Democratic states. Rockefeller was the first Republican governor since Reconstruction; he helped give the state a new image so it could better attract more industries and residents.

Between 1970 and 1980, the state gained 180,000 residents through migration, as the Ozarks became one of the fastest growing rural areas in the United States. Most of the new residents had migrated from other states. Industrial development quickened, as Arkansas factories produced bicycles, rubber goods, blue jeans, and much more. For example, Baxter County's growth in one five-year period in the 1970s was 111 percent. This prosperity also brought environmental pollution and suburban sprawl.

The 1980 state population was 2,286,435, mostly living in rural areas and small towns. The population of Little Rock was 158,461, but most other cities were below 70,000. A study found that half the population lived on farms or towns with populations under 2,500. Technological advances allowed rice farmers operating as cooperatives to prosper, with a surge in jobs in the Stuttgart area.

During the recession of the early 1980s, the state experienced a small net decline of 2,000 in migration. As conditions improved and migrants came for jobs, net migration from 1985 to 1990 amounted to a gain of nearly 36,600. Unfortunately, the economic good times ended in the late 1980s and unemployment in Arkansas rose above the national average to 12.3 percent, while immigration dipped below other states' experiences. Still badly trailing the rest of the nation, Arkansas was still in 49th place for per capita income and support for public education during this period.

Between 1990 and 1998, Arkansas had net gains of 106,000 in domestic migration and 9,000 in international migration. During 1993–1994, Arkansas received 94,000 in-migrants, primarily from the South and Midwest. Out-migrants mostly went to the same regions. In 1998, 914 immigrants came to the state. Between 1990 and 1998, the state's overall population increased by 8 percent. In the 1995–2000 period, 252,100 people moved into the state and 209,984 moved out, for a net gain of 42,116, 2,496 of whom were aged 65 or over. The state's immigrant population nearly tripled from 25,000 to 74,000 during the 1990s. Between 2000 and 2005, the state was tied for fourth in the nation with a 37 percent foreign-born growth rate.

Recently, changing racial attitudes and growth in jobs have created a new migration of African Americans back to metropolitan areas in the developing South, especially to knowledge industry jobs in Georgia, North Carolina, and Texas. Arkansas has gained population as a result. Arkansas's 2011 population was estimated by the census to be 2,937,979, with 80.1 percent white, 15.6 percent black, 1.3 percent Asian, and 0.9 percent American Indian. Of this population, 81.9 percent had graduated from high school and 19.1 percent had a college degree.

TOPICAL ESSAYS

Forced Immigrants and the New Immigrants

Arkansas has had many forced immigrants. During World War II, the federal government moved many people of Japanese ancestry into relocation camps. Two camps in the state operated from 1942 to 1945, with 16,000 internees. Most internees left when they were freed. During 1975–1976, Fort Chaffee hosted more than 50,000 Vietnam War refugees, providing them medical care and relocating them to permanent housing. Many Vietnamese and Laotians settled in Arkansas. During 1980–1982, over 19,000 Cuban refugees known as "Mariel boat people" were relocated to Fort Chaffee. Many found family and sponsors elsewhere, and almost none remained in the state after their release.

New immigrants made the state's diverse population even more varied. Although few in number, Chinese Americans in Arkansas were very active. They formed the Chinese Association during World War II to aid the war effort. Aided by the Immigration and Nationality Act of 1965, many Chinese escaping from the Chinese mainland settled in the urban parts of the state. Marshall Islanders migrated from the Pacific to Springdale, Arkansas, in the late 1990s in search of employment. Primarily, they moved to northwest Arkansas to work in the chicken plants and other factories. There were an estimated 6,000 Marshall Islanders in Springdale in 2009. Hindu immigrants from India arrived in the mid-1950s.

Between 1990 and 2008, Arkansas, typical of the southeastern United States, had significant economic expansion along with record-high immigration. One of the reasons was that Latinos (including those who are both documented and undocumented) were moving to more rural areas with less established Latino communities because of the lower cost of living, especially housing.

Arkansas had the fourth fastest-growing immigrant population and fastest-growing Latino population (48 percent) compared to any state during the 2000–2005 period. The state had only about 100,000 immigrants, a tiny 4 percent of the state's total population. However, the population of immigrants in Arkansas is growing much faster than the national average. Like other southeastern new-growth states, Arkansas had a greater share of recently arrived Mexican and other Latin American immigrants. The state's foreign-born population was heavily Latino, with Mexico and other Latin American countries contributing some two-thirds of the state's immigrants in 2005. According to the U.S. Citizenship and Immigration Services (USCIS), some 27,000 undocumented immigrants resided in Arkansas in 2000, a rise of 400 percent from the USCIS estimate in 1996.

A 2007 study by the Winthrop Rockefeller Foundation found that half of Arkansas immigrants were undocumented, with most coming to the state for work. The 81 percent employment rate in 2000 for undocumented males was higher than that for legal immigrants, naturalized citizens, or native-born men. Much of the foreign-born population was in western Arkansas (e.g., Springdale, Rogers, Fayetteville, and Fort Smith), while a substantial number were in the Little Rock metropolitan area. Benton, Washington, Sebastian, and Pulaski counties had 63 percent of Arkansas's immigrant population. The same study found that Mexican and Central American immigrants were less educated than the native-born, but European and Asian immigrants were better educated than the American-born.

ANTI-IMMIGRANT PROTESTS SINCE 2007

Since 2007, immigration to Arkansas has been so strong that Mexico opened a diplomatic office in downtown Little Rock in 2010. This surge in documented and undocumented Latino immigrants to the state has stimulated both positive and negative reactions. The governor ordered state troopers to "get tougher" on undocumented immigrants. When the neighboring states of Missouri and Oklahoma passed restrictive anti-immigrant laws, similar statutes were introduced in Arkansas.

In contrast, in 2007, the Arkansas Friendship Coalition was formed to advocate that states should follow federal immigration laws instead of making their own. Members included several of Arkansas's largest companies—Tyson Foods (meat-processing), Alltel, (wireless), and Stephens (investment)—and ministers, civic leaders, and the local American Civil Liberties Union (ACLU). The coalition argues that the state depends upon immigrants and benefits from a strong immigrant population increase. There now are many immigrants in the state. According to the U.S. Census Bureau, 6 percent of the state's population lived in immigrant households in 2010, with some 60 percent (compared to a national average of 54 percent) aged 20–45. Their lower educational levels mean they do not have the better-paying jobs, but a recent report estimated that the annual revenue from Arkansas's manufacturing industry would be $1.4 billion lower without immigrant labor.

Despite this impressive economic data, Arkansas witnessed strong anti-immigrant protests beginning in 2004. Possible explanations for this include the fact that most of the state's immigrant population has arrived in the past 15 years, with 56 percent of the state's 2005 foreign-born population coming in 1995 or later, compared to the nation's 40 percent average. Additionally, a higher proportion of the state's immigrants have come from Latin America (67 to 49 percent), a much higher percentage of Arkansas's immigrants are undocumented (51 versus 29 percent nationally), and a lower share is naturalized (23 versus 32 percent).

In 2010, an Arkansas group known for opposing undocumented immigration began pushing for state legislation similar to Arizona's strict illegal immigration law. "Secure Arkansas" collected signatures for a ballot proposal that would amend the Arkansas Constitution to deny state services to most undocumented immigrants. In 2010, the measure advocated by Secure Arkansas also did not collect enough signatures for the ballot. The amendment would have banned most undocumented immigrants from receiving state benefits but would not have applied to children under 14 years of age. Sponsors of the measure submitted approximately 78,000 signatures for the 2010 ballot, but only 67,542 were valid.

U.S. representative Tim Griffin, R-Arkansas, speaks at the Republican Party of Arkansas state convention in Hot Springs, Arkansas, on July 19, 2014. Griffin is an advocate of strengthening the border and blames President Obama for recent waves of unaccompanied minor children. (AP Photo/Danny Johnston)

There were both positive and negative reactions to immigrants in Arkansas in 2012. In 2011, U.S. representative Tim Griffin, R-Little Rock, in accusing the Obama administration of selectively prosecuting immigration cases, cited a memo issued by the U.S. Department of Homeland Security to provide staff with guidance on "prosecutorial discretion" to focus its resources on the agency's enforcement priorities. The Arkansas Illegal Immigrant Benefits Ban Amendment did not make the 2012 Arkansas state ballot as an initiated constitutional amendment. In 2012, the Arkansas chapter of the ACLU criticized the 90-day extension of an immigration enforcement program in Benton and Washington counties.

NOTABLE GROUP

Arkansas United Community Coalition

The Arkansas United Community Coalition is based in Fayetteville, Arkansas, and was established in 2010. Mireyah Rieth is the executive director. This group provides services and education to immigrants, including legal education and advocacy regarding districting issues that pertain to ethnic minorities. The coalition aims to effect positive change in communities.

BIBLIOGRAPHY

Arkansas Department of Parks and Tourism. "History & Heritage." 2012. http://www.arkansas.com/things-to-do/history-heritage/. Accessed February 25, 2014.

Arkansas Friendship Coalition. "Introduction." 2012. http://www.arfriendshipcoalition.org/. Accessed February 25, 2014.

Arkansas History Commission. "Arkansas History Questions and Answers." 2011. http://www.ark-ives.com/pdfs/ArkQ-A.pdf. Accessed February 25, 2014.

Arnold, Morris S. *Colonial Arkansas, 1686–1804: A Social and Cultural History.* Fayetteville: University of Arkansas Press, 1991.

Arnold, Morris S., Thomas A. DeBlack, George Sabo III, and Jeannie M. Whayne. *Arkansas: A Narrative History.* Fayetteville: University of Arkansas Press, 2002.

Ashmore, Harry S. *Arkansas: A Bicentennial History.* New York: W. W. Norton & Company, 1978.

Ballotpedia.org. 2012. "Arkansas Illegal Immigrant Benefits Ban Amendment (2012)." http://ballotpedia.org/wiki/index.php/Arkansas_Illegal_Immigrant_Benefits_Ban_Amendment_(2012). Accessed February 25, 2014.

Balogh, George W. "Immigration." *Encyclopedia of Arkansas History and Culture.* 2011. http://www.encyclopediaofarkansas.net/encyclopedia/entry-detail.aspx?entryID=5034. Accessed February 25, 2014.

Berry, Terry. "Hunter-Dunbar Expedition." *Encyclopedia of Arkansas.* The Butler Center. 2011. http://www.encyclopediaofarkansas.net/encyclopedia/entrydetail.aspx?search=1&entryID=2205. Accessed February 2014.

Capps, Randolph, Everett Henderson, John D. Kasarda, James H. Johnson Jr., Stephen J. Appold, Derrek L. Croney, Donald J. Hernandez, and Michael E. Fix. "A Profile of Immigrants in Arkansas." Washington, DC: Urban Institute, 2007. http://www.urban.org/publications/411441.html. Accessed February 2014.

City-data.com. "Arkansas—Migration." 2012. http://www.city-data.com/states/Arkansas-Migration.html. Accessed February 25, 2014.

Department of Arkansas Heritage. "Discover Arkansas History." 2012. http://www.arkansasheritage.com/discover/default.aspx. Accessed February 25, 2014.

Dorer, Chris. "Little Italy (Pulaski and Perry Counties)." *Encyclopedia of Arkansas History and Culture.* 2010. http://www.encyclopediaofarkansas.net/encyclopedia/entry-detail.aspx?entryID=5513. Accessed February 25, 2014.

Early, Ann M. "Indian Mounds." *Encyclopedia of Arkansas.* The Butler Center, 2011. http://www.encyclopediaofarkansas.net/encyclopedia/entry-detail.aspx?entryID=573. Accessed February 25. 2014.

"Illegal, but Useful: Where Would Arkansas Be without Immigrants?" *The Economist,* November 1, 2007. http://www.economist.com/node/10064271. Accessed February 25, 2014.

Johnson, William R. "Prelude to the Missouri Compromise: A New York Congressman's Effort to Exclude Slavery from Arkansas Territory." *Arkansas Historical Quarterly* 24 (Spring, 1965): 47–66.

Key, Joseph. "Quapaw." *Encyclopedia of Arkansas*. The Butler Center, December 16, 2011. http://www.encyclopediaofarkansas.net/encyclopedia/entry-detail.aspx?search=1&entryID=550. Accessed February 25, 2014.

Lancaster, Guy. "Wineries." *Encyclopedia of Arkansas*. The Butler Center, 2012. http://www.encyclopediaofarkansas.net/encyclopedia/entry-detail.aspx?entryID=1171. Accessed February 25, 2014.

Lyon, John. "Illegal Immigration Foes Want Arkansas to Emulate Arizona." *Arkansas News*, April 27, 2010. http://arkansasnews.com/2010/04/27/illegal-immigration-foes-want-arkansas-to-emulate-arizona/. Accessed February 25, 2014.

NWA Online. "Secure Arkansas Seeks Signatures for Petition." 2010. http://www.nwaonline.com/news/2010/apr/14/secure-arkansas-seeks-signatures-petition/. Accessed February 25, 2014.

Rockoff, Stuart. "Jews." *Encyclopedia of Arkansas History and Culture*. 2011. http://www.encyclopediaofarkansas.net/encyclopedia/entry-detail.aspx?entryID=2297. Accessed February 25, 2014.

Sabo, George, III. "Origins: Ice Age Migrations 28,000—11,500 B.C." *Indians of Arkansas*, 2008. http://arkarcheology.uark.edu/indiansofarkansas/index.html?pageName=Ice percent20Age percent20Migrations. Accessed February 25, 2014.

Tucker, David M. *Arkansas: A People and Their Reputation*. Memphis: Memphis State University Press, 1985.

U.S. Bureau of the Census. *Arkansas Quick Links*. Washington, DC: U.S. Government Printing Office, 2012. http://quickfacts.census.gov/qfd/states/05000lk.html. Accessed February 25, 2014.

U.S. Bureau of the Census. *Selected Place of Birth and Migration Statistics: 1990*. Washington, DC: U.S. Government Printing Office, 1995.

U.S. Bureau of the Census. *State & County QuickFacts*. Washington, DC: U.S. Government Printing Office, 2012. http://quickfacts.census.gov/qfd/states/05000.html. Accessed February 25, 2014.

United States Citizenship and Immigration Services (USCIS). "Immigration to Arkansas." 2012. http://www.usimmigrationsupport.org/arkansas.html. Accessed February 25, 2014.

Urban, Peter. "Arkansas Immigration Advocates Slam House GOP over Anti-Dream Vote." *Arkansas News*, June 6, 2013. http://arkansasnews.com/sections/news/arkansas-immigration-advocates-slam-house-gop-over-anti-dream-vote.html. Accessed July 10, 2013.

Urban, Peter. "Griffin Grills Homeland Security Chief on Immigration Policy." *Arkansas News*, October 26, 2011. http://arkansasnews.com/2011/10/26/griffin-grills-homeland-security-chief-on-immigration-policy/print/. Accessed February 25, 2014.

Watkins, Beverly. "Efforts to Encourage Immigration to Arkansas, 1865–1874." *Arkansas Historical Quarterly* 38 (March 1979): 32–62.

Williams, C. Fred. "Contemporary Arkansas." In C. Fred Williams, S. Charles Bolton, Carl H. Moneyhon, and LeRoy T. Williams, eds. *A Documentary History of Arkansas*. Fayetteville: University of Arkansas Press, 1984, pp. 241–318.

Williams, C. Fred. "Modern Arkansas, 1900 to 1954." In C. Fred Williams, S. Charles Bolton, Carl H. Moneyhon, and LeRoy T. Williams, eds. *A Documentary History of Arkansas*. Fayetteville: University of Arkansas Press, 1984, pp. 159–240.

Winthrop Rockefeller Foundation. *A Profile of Immigrants in Arkansas*. Washington, DC: Urban Institute, 2007.

Wood, Ron. "ACLU Denounces Extension of Immigration Enforcement Program." NWA-online.com, 2012. http://uspolitics.einnews.com/article/119780242. Accessed February 25, 2014.

5

CALIFORNIA

Anthony Rama Maravillas

CHRONOLOGY

40,000–10,000 BCE	Native Americans immigrate to California.
1492 CE	At the time of Columbus's first voyage to the Americas, there are about 300,000 American Indians inhabiting California.
1542	The Spanish navigator Juan Rodríguez Cabrillo commands two small ships that make landfall in San Diego Bay.
1602	The Spanish explorer Sebastian Vizcaíno and his crew sail along the California coast as far north as Cape Mendocino.
1697–1769	The Spanish Crown government declines to further explore and colonize California.
1775	Spanish sailors discover the mouth of the San Francisco Bay, the "Golden Gate."
1781	*Pobladores*, colonists from Mexico, first settle in Los Angeles.
1824	The Mexican Empire, having gained its independence from Spain, declares both Alta and Baja California to be its territories.
1826–1827	The first appearance of Americans in California, who had made the crossing over the Sierra Nevada Mountains, catalyzes an influx of immigrants from the United States.
1846–1847	American soldiers and émigrés succeed in gaining control of Monterey, Sonoma, Yerba Buena, and Los Angeles, completing the military conquest of Mexican California.
1848–1850	A "Gold Rush" in the mountains east of Sacramento moves thousands to immigrate to California; its residents ratify a state constitution and elect representatives; California becomes a U.S. state in September 1850.

1869	Sacramento's Central Pacific Railroad completes the first intercontinental rail line as its workers meet those of the Union Pacific at Promontory Summit, Utah.
1882	The Chinese Exclusion Act bars future Chinese immigrants from entering the United States.
1906	The massive San Francisco earthquake registers 8.3 on the Richter scale.
1906	Japanese school children in San Francisco are forced to attend segregated schools.
1910	Rumors of the overweening and illegal influence of the Central Pacific Railroad in all facets of public life are rife; the reformer Hiram Johnson is elected governor.
1914	San Diego becomes home-base for the new U.S. Navy Pacific Fleet.
1924	The Immigration Act proscribes further Japanese immigration.
1930	As the effects of the worldwide Great Depression begin to threaten workers' jobs, incomes, and standards of living, immigrant Filipinos and Mexican farmworkers join to strike against reductions in their wages in the Imperial Valley.
1936–1937	First the San Francisco Bay Bridge and then the Golden Gate Bridge are completed.
1941	World War II begins as the American territory of Hawai'i is attacked by Japanese military forces.
1942	U.S. president Franklin Delano Roosevelt issues Executive Order 9066, which mandates the internment of all Japanese aliens and Japanese Americans in California and elsewhere.
1943	The "Zoot Suit Riots" between young Latino *Pachucos* and U.S. military servicemen occur in Los Angeles.
1954	Former California governor Earl Warren is selected as U.S. Supreme Court chief justice by U.S. president Dwight D. Eisenhower.
1955	Walt Disney opens his "Disneyland" theme park in suburban Orange County.
1960	Governor Pat Brown unveils his master plan for Higher Education that makes college education available to more Californians than ever before.
1965	The "long hot summers" of urban battles between African Americans and police begin with the Watts Riots in Los Angeles.
1965	The Immigration Act of 1965 inadvertently allows greater Asian and Latin American immigration to California through a provision for family reunification.
1965–1970	The national Grape Strike is staged by the United Farm Workers led by San Jose resident César Chávez.
1976	The first sales of Steve Jobs and Steve Wozniak's Apple I computer occur.

1978	The U.S. anti-tax revolt movement begins when California voters pass Proposition 13.
1989	The Loma Prieta earthquake occurs during the "Bay Bridge World Series" between the San Francisco Giants and the Oakland Athletics.
1992	The "Los Angeles Riots," stemming from the acquittal of the officers charged in the Rodney King beating, occur; the riots illuminate tension not only between African Americans and the Los Angeles police but also between different ethnic groups. On the one hand, the riots lead to attacks on some Korean store owners; on the other hand, the riots create solidarity between different ethnic groups in affected neighborhoods.
1994	Proposition 187, which denies any benefits to undocumented immigrants, is passed by voters; it is quickly deemed unconstitutional and is repealed.
2003	Governor Gray Davis is recalled by the state's electorate and replaced by former Hollywood actor Arnold Schwarzenegger, a conservative on immigration issues and particularly working-class immigrants.
2005	Los Angeles mayor Antonio Villaraigosa is elected as the city's first Latino chief executive since 1872.
2006	Mass protests on behalf of immigrant rights and the rights of the undocumented occur in Los Angeles and San Francisco; these protests are among the largest of many occurring across the United States and are some of the best-attended protests since 1960s civil rights protests.
2010	Former governor Jerry Brown, who previously held the office from 1975 to 1983, is reelected governor as Californians suffer the job losses, falling home prices, and general malaise caused by the 2008 global financial crisis and the Great Recession of 2007–2009.

HISTORICAL OVERVIEW

1940–1980

The people of the United States experienced World War II (1941–1945) in many dramatic ways. For one, this war entailed the mass mobilization of millions of American men and women who were to fight its battles. Second, on the home front, massive industrial production and full employment were necessitated by this conflict. Of all the U.S. states, California was the most irrevocably transformed by World War II.

The defense industries needed to arm the millions of the nation's military forces fighting the war were well established in the Golden State. As a result, millions of new Californians, drawn from various corners of the country, were needed to work

Former members of the 442nd Regimental Combat Team and the 100th Regiment turn shovels of earth during the groundbreaking ceremony for the Go for Broke Monument on April 5, 1998, in Los Angeles, California. The memorial honors those Japanese Americans who fought in World War II while their families remained locked up in internment camps at home. (AP Photo/Keith Skehon)

in those busy factories and workshops. A total of 500,000 people moved to the San Francisco Bay area to work in defense-related jobs between 1940 and 1944, and of these 160,000 were in-state migrants. The millions of G.I.s who trained in or were transshipped through the Golden State at military facilities, such as the P-38 warplane training base at Ontario's Latimer Field and the troop processing post at Camp Stoneman in Pittsburg, added to this influx.

The U.S. effort to prevail in World War II turned out to be a blessing for California. In 1942, a U.S. Naval Air Station was built in Los Alamitos, and the Marine Corps constructed its premier air station in El Toro. The same year, the navy transformed San Francisco Bay area's Treasure Island into an important base for its Pacific Theater-bound sailors. Oakland, Richmond, Alameda, and Vallejo formed the nucleus of the West Coast's wartime shipbuilding industry. By 1943, those East Bay cities produced 35 percent of the nation's total output of new warships and transports. The federal contracts involved in outfitting the nation's armed forces also put millions of taxpayer dollars in the bank accounts of hundreds of ancillary industries throughout California.

The Cold War that succeeded the "hot" World War II ensured that the federal largesse of the 1940s continued into the 1980s. Federal defense contracts with California companies, along with the annual active duty military and civilian Department of Defense payrolls pumped $50 billion into the Golden State between 1950 and 1960. Los Angeles, in particular, benefited from this cash infusion. In 1959, that city's workers earned 61 percent of the total defense spending in California; as a result, the population of Los Angeles increased by about 1 million, from 1.5 million in 1940 to 2.5 million in 1960. That same year in Orange County, 31,000 Californians labored directly in defense-related industries, including 10,000 at Hughes Aircraft and the same number at Autonetics in Anaheim. In Northern California, Oakland's Cold War-era boosters sought to sell that city and the rest of the East Bay as a good investment. A 1945–1955 publicity campaign among eastern and Midwestern investors interpreted the entire Oakland/East Bay region as an "Industrial Garden." Critical to that campaign were the region's single family California ranch and bungalow homes, small factories, and large industrial complexes that would facilitate lucrative economic growth and ensure social stability. War, whether of the "cold" or "hot" variety, turned out to be quite promising for California.

The post–World War II era inaugurated other significant changes in California. President Dwight D. Eisenhower successfully lobbied Congress to pass the Interstate Highway Act of 1956. It financed the construction of a total of 42,500 miles of highways nationally; among these were a series of freeways in the Los Angeles area. There, over 700 miles of roads made up the main transportation network for a region whose people, scattered in dozens of suburbs, largely eschewed public transport. That situation was a sea change from their predecessors of the 1920s who enjoyed an electric interurban railway that once included more than 1,100 miles of track. The trend toward the private automobile facilitated by the expansion of California's highways even affected its people's religiosity. In 1955, Rev. Robert Schuller of the Reformed Church of America began his ministry by utilizing an otherwise empty drive-in theater in Orange. On Saturday mornings that year, Schuller preached from atop the cinema's Snack Bar, while his congregants listened in, using the speakers that were placed at every parking space.

Californians contributed to a postwar conservative resurgence that challenged the hegemony of the Democratic Party-led New Deal political consensus that had been the rule since 1933. While this insurgency may have been more of an expression of popular discontent with some of President Harry Truman's policies, a generation of influential Republican politicians was elected in 1946 that included two famous Californians: U.S. senator William F. Knowland and U.S. representative Richard Nixon. Nixon, a native of Yorba Linda and a Whittier resident, was a political novice, who, despite being a Quaker, was a U.S. Navy veteran. He won his seat by upsetting the incumbent, the New Deal liberal Jerry Voorhis, in the 12th District, east of Los Angeles, in a particularly contentious and controversial race. Nixon, thereby, initiated a political ascent that eventually culminated in his election to the presidency in 1968, making him the first native Californian to hold that office.

The postwar years also saw California lead the way in challenging the Jim Crow racial segregation policies and customs that marred the nation's democracy. While Dr. Martin Luther King Jr. and his confederates were crucial in toppling de jure and institutionalized discrimination in the Deep South starting in 1955, court cases initiated in the Golden State in the 1940s may have actually begun the national Civil Rights Movement.

In January 1948, the U.S. Supreme Court decided in *Oyama v. the State of California* that the state's Alien Land Laws were unconstitutional. These California laws denied the Japanese *Issei* immigrant generation, which was forbidden U.S. citizenship by law, equal protection by preventing them from passing property to their children.

Another landmark case, *Mendez v. Westminster*, was first brought in 1945 by a Mexican American asparagus farmer against the Westminster School District in Orange County. It involved future U.S. Supreme Court justices Thurgood Marshall and Earl Warren. These two later figured prominently in the 1954 *Brown v. Board of Education* decision. It struck down the Court's 1896 "separate but equal" ruling that condoned racial segregation in the public schools.

Mendez simply wanted to have his children attend the local "American" 17th St. School instead of the resource-poor, underfunded Hoover School, which was reserved for the area's Mexican American schoolchildren. Sensing an opportunity to further its goal of desegregating the country's schools, the National Association for the Advancement of Colored People dispatched Marshall, who then filed an amicus brief in support of Mendez. As it turned out, the California Ninth Circuit Court of Appeals ruled in Mendez's favor in April 1947, arguing that Mexican American school children should not be relegated to segregated schools. Of even greater importance was the fact that Governor Warren concluded from this case that it was time to end official support for segregation in California's schools. As the chief justice of the U.S. Supreme Court, this decision influenced Warren's thinking in *Brown* and other cases concerning Americans' personal and civil rights from 1954 to his retirement in 1969.

The national post–World War II affluence impacted California's colleges and universities. In 1900, only 7 percent of the nation's college-age students attended institutions of higher learning; in the 1930s, 14 percent did so; in 1961, that number increased to 38 percent. Thus, by the 1960s, waves of undergraduates, pushed along by rising family incomes, were able to afford to pursue college educations. California governor Pat Brown's Higher Education Act of 1960, which mandated greater public financial support for the state's colleges, helped this phenomenon along.

The greater diversity of the student bodies of California's universities presented challenges to the 1950s-era policies of the schools' leaders. For example, at the state's flagship campus—the University of California at Berkeley—school president Clark Kerr and his administrators believed that a culture of the "life of the mind" and teaching should rule on campus. They also were convinced that they, as the embodiment of the university, should act as their students' mentors and chaperones. However, challenges to Kerr's rules began in the fall of 1964 term.

What became known as the Free Speech Movement started in early October 1964 with a 36-hour standoff as hundreds of students prevented the Berkeley police from jailing a visiting political activist. This incident was followed by the organization of a governing body, the "Free Speech Movement," which held the First Amendment as its defining ethic. In November, students staged a sit-in at Sproul Hall, resulting in the arrests of 773 Berkeley undergraduate and graduate students. Finally, much to Kerr's chagrin, over two-thirds of the over 900 professors present at an Academic Senate meeting in early December passed a resolution endorsing the Free Speech Movement's positions on campus speech and advocacy, thereby effectively capping off the student uprising with some faculty activism. This semester-long insurgency was the first campaign waged by America's 1960s "counter-culture," a broadside fired at the "establishment's" norms and mores, which were being challenged not only in California but in the rest of America, too.

As attested to by U. C. Berkeley's Free Speech Movement, the 1960s and the 1970s were momentous years for Californians. The students, however, were not the only actors on the state's figurative stage; its workers also engaged in the general societal upheaval that characterized this 20-year period.

More than 5,000 of California's agricultural workers staged a five-year boycott of the state's grape growers beginning in September 1965. This event made César Chávez, the leader of the United Farm Workers Association (UFWA), nationally known. Together with another small union, the Agricultural Workers Organizing Committee (AWOC), mostly made up of hundreds of Filipino *Manong* laborers, Chavez's UFWA wanted to expose to the public the California's grape growers' abuses of their workforce.

The Filipino farm laborers originally opposed the Californian growers' decision to pay them $1.25 an hour, which was lower than the $1.45 paid to Mexican "guest workers" brought in under the Bracero Program. The Filipinos' agenda of a living wage and better working conditions was soon shared by the Mexican Americans of UFWA. Chávez acted as the spokesperson and most visible leader from among a group of leaders, which included the Filipino labor activist Larry

Itliong and Latina activist Dolores Huerta. Chávez advocated Gandhian nonviolent direct action, a tactic that was invaluable against their formidable opponents, the politically connected, wealthy growers. Although the boycott continued until 1970, AWOC and UFWA won their first contract in negotiations with the Schenley Corporation, one of the richest grape-growing companies, in April 1966. This success may have been prompted in part by the tremendous amount of national attention paid to the 300-mile walk staged the previous month by the two unions from Delano, in the heart of grape country, to the state capitol in Sacramento.

The student activism that was given such impetus by the Free Speech Movement was augmented by the onset of the Vietnam Conflict (1959–1973). The federal government joined in this societal change with President Lyndon B. Johnson's "War on Poverty," which funded programs and agencies on behalf of the nation's poor, such as Head Start and the Office of Economic Opportunity. In California's 1966 gubernatorial race, Ronald Reagan, a former Hollywood actor, ran as a conservative Republican who opposed the Democrats' efforts to reshape society. Reagan appealed to some of the state's conservative white voters who were alarmed by developments such as the Watts Riot of 1965, the Black Panthers militants' call for "Black Power," and the U. C. Berkeley protestors, whom Reagan dismissed as "beatniks, radicals, and filthy-speech advocates." In response, California's voters threw out incumbent governor Pat Brown and elected Reagan by almost 1 million votes. Although Reagan's policies were often inadequate to handle some of the state's biggest problems, his two terms as governor were relatively unremarkable in terms of major change.

In the 1970s, Californians once again reiterated their state's preeminence by initiating the anti-tax revolt that culminated in the passage of Proposition 13 at the polls in June 1978. Proposition 13 was the creation of 75-year-old political conservative Howard Jarvis. Long a foe of the liberal activist governments fostered by the New Deal, Jarvis claimed California's major problem was that its citizens were overtaxed. The solution, which coincidentally comported with Jarvis's goal of weakening all levels of government by decreasing their revenues, was to lead successful tax revolts across the United States. In fact, this happened. Because a majority of the state's voters supported Proposition 13, property taxes, tied to rising assessments, were frozen at relatively low amounts for millions of California homeowners. Subsequently, this caused funding shortfalls for various public services, such as the police and fire departments, libraries, and schools. Pleased with their lower tax bills, this movement caused many Californians to now support the anti-"Big Government" plank of the national Republican Party. The cascade of middle- and working-class California voters, who had formerly supported Democrats, when joined by millions of similar voters in the other states, helped propel Governor Reagan to the American presidency in the 1980 election. Reagan, thus, became the second Californian in the White House.

1980S TO THE PRESENT

California's past few decades, perhaps in keeping with the spirit of the "sizzling" 1960s, were also turbulent. Federal attempts to come to grips with the extra-legal immigration that originated mostly in California's Latin American neighbors have marked California politics since the late 1980s. The Immigration and Nationality Act of 1965, which equalized the national quota system and sought to reunify families split by immigration, helped to make the state more racially diverse. It facilitated, in particular, the legal movement of families from Asia and Latin America to California. As a growing backlash against immigration developed, the Immigration Reform and Control Act (IRCA) of November 1986 presented the opportunity of "amnesty," or "legalization," for some undocumented immigrants who had been in the state continuously since January 1982. Also, it offered the same deal to seasonal farmworkers who had been lawfully employed for at least 90 days in the previous year up to May 1986. The Omnibus Immigration Act of 1990 built on its predecessor by increasing the quota of legitimate immigrants. Predictably, there was blowback in the form of nativist sentiments as expressed in California's Proposition 187 in November 1994. Approved by a majority of the voters, it denied undocumented immigrants access to the state's schools and medical clinics. The provisions of this proposition were later deemed unconstitutional. Some important subsequent laws were enacted in Propositions 209 (1996) and 227 (1998), which appeared to be aimed squarely at the state's Latino population.

The first few years of the twenty-first century presented Californians with new challenges. First, there was a bifurcated national economy on which the top income-earners had steadily accrued most of the wealth created by America's workers and consumers since 1980, while the vast majority muddled along with wages and benefits stagnant in real terms since the mid-1970s. Second, Californians, along with millions of other Americans, had been compelled to rely on credit cards, home equity lines of credit, and a series of economic bubbles to finance their cost of living. This situation came to a head when a financial "meltdown" finally occurred between early 2007 and the last months of 2008. Many U.S. banks suffered tremendous losses when millions of their gimmicky "sub-prime" (interest rate) mortgages failed. These losses nearly plunged California, the United States, and many of its foreign trading partners into another Great Depression. The lingering effects of the Great Recession of 2007–2009 for Californians include an unemployment rate of over 10 percent, the loss of innumerable foreclosed homes and accompanying equity, the abrupt disappearance of long-saved wealth, and postponed retirements. Finally, there has been much uncertainty, and some anxiety, concerning the very nature of California's society as time passes. As undeniable demographic changes develop in the 2010s, the old non-Latino, white-dominated California is disappearing. In the early twenty-first century, ethnic minorities, particularly Latinos, possess consistently higher birth rates than those of the state's whites. The future for the Golden State's inhabitants will be interesting indeed.

TOPICAL ESSAYS

THE EFFECT OF STATE AND NATIONAL LEGISLATION ON CALIFORNIA'S POSTWAR IMMIGRATION

Immigration is one crucial cornerstone of the long-term collective prosperity that the people of California have enjoyed for generations now. Indeed, their state is the most populous and the wealthiest among its peers, which has been true since the end of World War II in 1945. The primary reason for California's dynamism is not the fruits of its considerable agribusinesses that feed the nation, the defense industries that have employed thousands for decades, or the many information technology firms that together are known globally as "Silicon Valley." The secret to California's success is its inhabitants: the over 30 million-strong Californians. Their labor, genius, and productivity make their home state so rich and distinctive. Crucial to this is the constant inclusion of resourceful, would-be Californians who bring skills, creativity, and strong work ethics. Altogether, these disparate peoples create a multiethnic California, a nation-state that is the entire world in miniature.

Historically, several important laws passed by the U.S. Congress and California's own legislature have impacted the movement of people to the Golden State. A serious review will be undertaken here, because these various immigration laws have helped to shape California's society. First, the specific provisions of those laws will be scrutinized. Second, the ways in which such laws have affected the state's people will be examined.

An immigration wave originating in various regions of the world affected the United States beginning in the 1880s and continued up to the outbreak of World War I in 1914. To gain some greater discretion regarding who was to enter and reside in the country, and in response to pressure from nativist groups, the federal government enacted a number of restrictive immigration laws. These were made official in 1917, 1921, 1924, and, most critical of all for California, 1927.

The 1927 immigration law, titled the "National Origins Act," was actually the culmination of the earlier acts. It set quotas for a certain period of about 153,700 new immigrants: 43 percent were to be welcomed from the United Kingdom, 17 percent from Germany, and 12 percent from Ireland. There was no provision for arrivals from Asian countries. In sum, these laws severely limited immigration from Europe, ended the influx of Asians, but yet had little influence on the inflow of Latin Americans. This result was problematic for California because it naturally drew newcomers from the Asian nations, most of them the workers needed for its variegated economy. The flip side of this is that Latin Americans, who had long provided California with a readily available and relatively cheap source of labor, were conveniently ignored by the politicians who crafted the original bill.

In 1952, amid the tension of the Cold War, Congress enacted the Immigration and Nationality Act, which upheld the quotas of the 1927 law. These quotas were overturned by the Immigration and Nationality Act of 1965, which eliminated the National Origins formula and provided for the admission of 15.53 million immigrants between 1966 and 1991. Its main provisions were the reunification of families, the call for immigrants who possessed needed skills, and the deletion of the earlier acts' provisions that prohibited the entry of Asians and Africans. Thus, these laws helped "darken" and diversify American society by encouraging the arrival of ethnic groups not previously welcomed. A look around many California cities will attest to the effectiveness of this clause. Along those lines, the Refugee Act of 1980 was enacted to regulate the inflow of immigrants created by the conclusion of the long Vietnam War, many of whom settled in southern California. The Immigration Act of 1990 was built on the 1965 law by approving an additional 1.88 million new arrivals for the 1992–1993 period.

The Reagan administration worked with Congress to ensure the passage of the IRCA of 1986. It provided amnesty and the "legalization" of their status for those undocumented aliens who had resided in the United States since January 1982. The same offer was made to seasonal farm laborers who had been lawfully employed in the United States for at least 90 days prior to May 1986. IRCA also mandated sanctions against U.S. employers who had consistently contracted with undocumented immigrants. Finally, this law provided for an expanded guest-worker program. Many undocumented immigrants who had traveled to live and work in the Golden State benefited from its guarantees; others did not benefit from these provisions.

In 1996, Congress passed two laws that continued to significantly affect immigrants. The first was the Antiterrorism and Effective Death Penalty Act; the second was the Illegal Immigration Reform and Immigrant Responsibility Act. Both reflected the anti-immigrant attitudes popular at that time. Significantly, greater discretion was placed in the hands of Immigration and Naturalization Service (INS) agents who could now determine the suitability of certain immigrants, decide whether detention was necessary for certain asylum-seekers, and judge, without much oversight, which individuals were to be turned back at their initial point of entry to the United States. More broadly, these acts established a mass detention and deportation system. As a result, because California shares a long border with Mexico, INS agents stationed from San Diego to the Arizona state line were, in some cases, able to determine arbitrarily those who could legally enter the country and those who could be barred.

The Patriot Act of 2001 was enacted during the "War on Terror" that was initiated by the September 11, 2001, terrorist attacks on New York City and Washington,

D.C. Kathleen R. Arnold argues that, like the preceding IRCA and the two 1996 immigration laws, the Patriot Act was hostile in intent and actually founded upon a national anti-immigrant groundswell that had become apparent in the 1990s. This sentiment was manifested in California by a series of anti-immigrant and anti-Latino "propositions," such as Propositions 187, 209, and 229, which were potential laws put on the ballot by citizens who had effectively bypassed the normal legislative process. In the name of national security, the Patriot Act facilitated enhanced surveillance of immigrants by the authorities by relaxing the procedural safeguards that guarantee individuals' civil rights. The Patriot Act was furthered in this regard by permitting outright racial profiling by public officials throughout the country. The Patriot Act also enabled the relatively quick deportation of immigrants from countries such as Cape Verde, Jamaica, Haiti, and Mexico (Arnold 2011, 38).

In analyzing the manner in which these laws have shaped and transformed California, we can begin with an examination of a law, enacted during the country's first few decades of existence, which has determined the nature of American society itself for many years. Any interpretation of a particularly crucial provision of the Naturalization Act of 1790 would hold that the United States is destined to be a "white man's country." In its original wording, this law expressly restricted American citizenship to "free whites" who had resided in the country for at least two years. Thus, by omitting any mention of African American slaves, indentured servants, free blacks, and, in fact, any other racial groups, this law had the effect of making only whites from Europe eligible to be American citizens. Had this law remained as it was first drafted, the multiethnic California of the present would never have developed, except perhaps as some stratified, apartheid state. Fortunately, activists-citizens took matters in their many hands and changed the course of the state's history.

The official obstacles that prohibited citizenship for non-European immigrants become apparent during the mid- and late nineteenth century when thousands of Chinese immigrated to the United States in search of jobs and other economic opportunities. With the 1790 Naturalization Act as a precedent, Congress passed the Chinese Exclusion Act of 1882, which, among other things, indisputably barred these non-whites from ever becoming citizens. Those Chinese men already in the United States were destined neither to return home to their families nor bring their wives and families to the United States. Instead many of these Asian trailblazers became "Lo Wah Kiu," lonely and elderly overseas Chinese.

The Japanese, South Asian, and Filipino immigrants who began to arrive by the 1880s faced the same barriers to full citizenship in their adopted home country. Restricted to manual labor and low wages, like the Chinese pioneers, all of them were treated in California as unwelcome sojourners. Moreover, because the majority of the Filipinos and Sikh Indians were men, many in the pre–World War II era were destined to live their lives in the United States as unwilling bachelors.

Like the Chinese who had preceded them, these Japanese, Sikhs, and Filipinos founded whole neighborhoods in Los Angeles, the Imperial Valley, Yuba County, and Stockton in which they hoped to live and commiserate with their ethnic kin.

The saving grace for these Asian immigrants who sought to own land, homes, and businesses was the Fourteenth Amendment. It automatically made their U.S.-born offspring citizens. By putting the titles of their properties in the names of their citizen-children in the pre-World War II period, Asian resident aliens effectively skirted the four California Alien Land laws passed between 1913 and 1927, which forbade land ownership by aliens ineligible for citizenship. After this practice was challenged by the authorities, the U.S. Supreme Court ruled in the 1948 case *Oyama v. the State of California* that California's Alien Land laws actually denied the immigrant generation of Japanese, the *Issei*, equal protection. Consequently, those discriminatory laws were rendered moot and were gradually not enforced by state government officials. Despite such progress, the advance toward full citizenship for Asian Americans was a slow and painful process throughout the twentieth century.

Another step in gaining civil equity for Asians in the United States was taken in the early 1950s. In the post–World War II era, groups such as the Japanese American Citizens League and some of the Nisei U.S. Army veterans pressured Congress to rescind the racial restrictions of the 1790 Naturalization Act. Japanese American veterans, such as those of the U.S. military's most decorated unit of World War II, the 442nd Regiment, lobbied the federal government to reward their parents' efforts of raising such accomplished patriot-warriors by officially putting them on the road to naturalization. This Congress finally did in the Immigration and Nationality Act of 1952, which permanently rescinded the racial and national origins criteria mandated in the 1790 act (by equalizing country quotas).

For the past 160 years, a group of immigrants whose ancestors had long roots in the state had come to work and live in California. These are the Mexicans whose fellow nationals had historically settled in California for many years. Kevin Starr claims that Latino California existed roughly between 1769, when the Spanish Crown began to dispatch colonists directly from Mexico, to 1850, when, after being acquired by the United States after the U.S.–Mexican War, California became a state (Starr 2005, 80). During the twentieth century, many Mexicans were drawn to California and other U.S. states by the Bracero Program (1942–1964), which was initiated during World War II.

By 1947, about 200,000 *braceros* contributed to the American war effort by planting, tending, and harvesting crops in a total of 21 states. However critical their work was, the *braceros* could never become either U.S. residents or citizens because, as per the terms of the *Bracero* treaty, they were required to eventually return to Mexico. Nonetheless, some of them stayed in the United States, either legally or illegally, as one stream within a river of undocumented Mexican immigrants.

In the postwar era, many Mexicans were driven to immigrate to California, and elsewhere in the country, by both poverty and hope. But some have had difficulty naturalizing: about 30 percent of California's Mexican population was made up of non-citizens according to U.S. Census figures released in 2006. In 2011, undocumented Mexicans were estimated to number around 6.5 million out of a total of perhaps 11 million undocumented immigrants in the entire country.

Deteriorating economic conditions in Mexico over the past few decades have rendered millions in its working class jobless. Thus, in the past several years millions of that nation's poorest crossed without documents into the United States; in doing so, they cross deserts, used tunnels dug beneath border fences and checkpoints, and contracted with human smugglers. Once in the United States, these undocumented immigrants responded to word-of-mouth recruitment for jobs that would pay wages which allow them to support themselves and also remit cash to relatives at home. In California, these immigrants tended to work in labor-intensive industries, such as manufacturing, food-processing, agriculture, landscaping, and construction, and also in the restaurant and hospitality businesses.

Some opponents of undocumented Mexican immigrants have accused them of deliberately timing their pregnancies so that their children would be born in the United States. According to the Fourteenth Amendment, such youngsters are, by virtue of the location of their births, American citizens. They are what some critics dismiss as "Anchor Babies," a controversial phrase that has recently been deemed a slur on the parents and the children by the *American Heritage Dictionary*. One criticism of the Anchor Babies stereotype is that they are but tools of a strategy designed to at least guarantee citizenship and all its benefits to the progeny of de facto lawbreakers, if not to enable their undocumented parents to become citizens through the family reunification provision of the 1965 Immigration and Nationality Act. Nevertheless, others argue that this simplifies a complex set of decisions and situations, if indeed there are "anchor babies."

Currently, the nation's elected leadership wrangles over what is perceived as the illegitimate movement between Mexico and the United States. The 1986 IRCA is one past attempt to come to grips with this alleged dilemma. Some contemporary political leaders suggest long electrified fences, alligator-filled moats, and additional National Guardsmen and Border Patrol agents and "aviation assets" as solutions. However, the reality is that the numbers of undocumented crossings have precipitously dropped since the peak recorded in 2000. In 2010, the Border Patrol reported 447,731 arrests. Compare this to the over 1.6 million people captured by the border authorities in 2000, and it can be argued that fewer of them are motivated to make this risky move. Diminished work opportunities in a weakened U.S. economy, stricter border controls, and more job prospects at home may have actually given many in Mexico a pause to reconsider the arduous trek to "El

Norte." In fact, some of those undocumented trekkers apprehended in 2010 were undocumented Mexican immigrants who, after having already been established in the United States, were simply making return trips following arrests and deportation by the U.S. Immigration and Customs Enforcement agency. Of course, focusing exclusively on individual crossings by Mexicans ignores broad-scale "pull" factors from the United States, including North American Free Trade Agreement provisions, word-of-mouth recruitment in various industries, and neoliberal policies in both countries that demand and yet prohibit worker mobility.

Another group who entered California in the post–World War II period were themselves products of that epic conflagration. The war required about 16 million American military servicemen and women, most of them between the ages of 18 and 30, to wage war in far-flung places. As young people often do, they flirted with, romanced, and even married foreign women and men in those countries where they were assigned. Their spouses were the famous "War Brides," and the lesser-known "War Grooms." One estimate of the total number of such war-facilitated marriages, which occurred between 1942, when the first U.S. troops landed in Britain and Australia, and 1952, when the numerical restrictions of the Asiatic Barred Zone were lifted, is about 1 million.

The War Brides Act was the immigration law that allowed a massive influx of foreign spouses following the end of the war in 1945. It was approved by Congress on December 28, 1945, three months after the end of World War II. Effective for eight years, this law made possible the legal entry of about 700,000 foreign spouses of U.S. military personnel by explicitly classifying them as non-quota immigrants.

Despite many initial hardships, the war spouses traveled to the United States, where many have lived the rest of their lives. Hildegard Gibbs, originally from Munich, Germany, first settled in a public housing project in Richmond in 1947. She remembers marveling at the many consumer goods available in the United States, and then bemoaning her own family's lack of money. In 1949, Betty Arrieta, the president of the British Brides Club in Oakland, helped arrange the chartering of an entire Transocean Company DC-4 to transport 44 war brides, 16 children, and 12 babies for a visit to relatives in Britain (Shukert and Scibetta 1988, 227–51). Gregoria Fangonilo and Pacita Partolan Caballes were Filipinas who had married Filipino American G.I.s who had participated in the U.S. offensive to liberate the Philippines from Japanese military occupation. Both Fangonilo and Cabelles were able to immigrate to the United States in 1947 under the War Brides Act, and each settled into long-lasting marriages with their husbands in Palo Alto (Houle 2007, 84–88). In the aftermath of a terrible global conflict, war spouses, such as the women discussed earlier, each immigrated to California. In the 60 and more years since, they have contributed their talents, energies, and, in the case of those who had children, genes to that diverse pool of humanity that comprised the state's society.

Other immigrants have been admitted to California in the postwar era. These include those who have been affected directly by this nation's wars abroad. Thus, today there are Californians who hail from Vietnam and the other Southeast Asian countries that were devastated by the eight-year Vietnam Conflict that was officially declared by the United States in March 1965. The Golden State also hosts more recent immigrants who are refugees of an even longer American war in Afghanistan, which began in October 2001 and continues as of 2014. The former Taliban rulers of Afghanistan are thought to have supported and given sanctuary to the Al Qaeda terrorists who staged the September 11, 2001 attacks on the United States.

By 1985, over 245,000 Vietnamese; 218,000 Laotians; and 160,000 Cambodians had come to the United States. All told, by 1990, about 1.5 million people from the former Indochina region had legally immigrated to the United States. The 1980 Refugee Act accommodated the movement of these peoples. Although the U.S. government had planned to settle them throughout the country, almost 50 percent of the Vietnamese now live in southern California, mostly in such Orange County cities as Westminster and Garden Grove. The first generation, having arrived without much wealth, initially appeared to be a traditional disadvantaged minority needing public aid, not the vaunted "model minority" that other Asians have been touted as being (Daniels 2002, 369). Some research indicates that if refugees have fled particularly dangerous circumstances, they will often have more post-traumatic issues and thus need more help than others. Regardless, the term "model minority" is often argued to be another form of racial stereotyping, used to "discipline" other minorities; at the very least, it is politically charged and hierarchical.

There were approximately 240,000 Afghan refugees in the United States as of 2007. In the years since the U.S. military and the North Atlantic Treaty Organization allies invaded Afghanistan to eradicate its Taliban rulers, about 60,000 Afghans have settled in the San Francisco Bay area. The majority there reside in the East Bay town of Fremont. After many years of conflict, the date from the 1979–1989 Cold War proxy fight between armies of the Soviet Union and the U.S.–supported Muslim *Mujahideen* through to the present conflict, life in California has been a respite for those Afghans who were able to get to the United States. However, California's Afghans have experienced some problems with their neighbors. Following the September 11 terror attacks, some experienced or were threatened with violence simply because of their Muslim faith, which is popularly associated with the perpetrators of those certain events. In the United States, various Afghans have also been troubled by the lack of employment, the loss of the status once enjoyed at home, and other culture-based issues. Like the Vietnamese, California's Afghans will have to work diligently to create their own niche within the multicultural American society.

Immigration has enriched and invigorated California's society for many decades now. The strong backs and wills of those who, despite the many obstacles and trials, have been able to make their way to the Golden State to stay ensured that this state's people will never collectively accede to mediocrity. While there are multiple impediments to actually gaining residency in California, they are not merely logistical or financial. For one, there are the various immigration laws that have been put into place by the federal government to regulate the process and the very individuals who have sought to make the United States and California, in particular, their new home. These laws have not always been fair and evenhanded toward all immigrants. American immigration laws have been carefully negotiated at times, such as when the *Issei* gradually pushed their way to naturalization in late 1940s, and vehemently contested, as in the case of nation-wide protests held by thousands of undocumented Latino immigrants and their supporters on May 1, 2006. In all instances, the main goal of these and the other would-be Americans who have encountered the formidable barrier of U.S. federal immigration laws is simply a fair and legitimate opportunity to become legal U.S. residents, if not full-fledged citizens.

Elliot Robert Barkan, the eminent historian of U.S. immigration, once wrote that migration, the act of moving from one region or country to another, "involves the choices and actions of individual men and women and their families" (Barkan 1996, 4). In fact, the evidence shows that it is California, the state of both important ideas and of aspirations, which many of these itinerant decision makers choose. Accordingly, these immigrants then act so that they could one day literally arrive at their goal. Hence, the Golden State can rightly be called the destination of choice for a significant percentage of the world's people.

NOTABLE FIGURES

Cesar Chavez (1927–1993)

Although Cesar Chavez was born in Arizona, his childhood experiences as a migrant farmworker in California and his famous campaign against grape farmers in California make him one of the most notable figures who fought on behalf of migrant workers and, more generally, individuals of Mexican descent. He exposed poor working conditions, low pay, and maltreatment of farmworkers, helping to raise standards for agricultural labor. The organization he founded with Dolores Huerta, the UFWA, continues to fight on behalf of immigrant agricultural workers today.

BIBLIOGRAPHY

Arnold, Kathleen R. *American Immigration after 1996*. University Park, PA: Penn State Press, 2011.

Barkan, Elliott Robert. *And Still They Come, Immigrants and American Society 1920s to 1990s*. Arlington Heights, IL: Harlan Davidson, 1996.

Burner, David. *Making Peace with the Sixties*. Princeton, NJ: Princeton University Press, 1996.

Cave, Damien. "Crossing over, and over." *The New York Times*, October 3, 2011, 1 and 6.

Cooper, Helene. "Arizona Sees a Boom in Voting-Age Hispanics." *The New York Times*, December 2, 2011, A19.

"Crying Wolf." *The Economist*, November 19, 2011, 31–32.

Daniels, Roger. *Coming to America*. New York: Harper Perennial, 2002.

Hayes-Batista, David E. *La Nueva California, Latinos in the Golden State*. Berkeley: University of California Press: 2004.

Houle, Michelle E., ed. *The Filipinos*. Detroit: Greenhaven Press, 2007.

Jackson, Kenneth T. *Crabgrass Frontier, the Suburbanization of the United States*. New York: Oxford University Press, 1985.

La Botz, Dan. *Cesar Chavez and La Causa*. New York: Pearson Longman, 2006.

Liptak, Adam. "Court to Weigh Arizona Statute on Immigration." *The New York Times*, December 13, 2011, A1 and A3.

MacLachlan, Colin M., and William H. Beezley. *El Gran Pueblo, a History of Greater Mexico*. Upper Saddle River, NJ: Prentice Hall, 2004.

Maravillas, Anthony Rama. "Nixon in Nixonland." *Southern California Quarterly* 84 (Summer 2002): 169–81.

McGirr, Lisa. *Suburban Warriors: The Rise of the New American Right*. Princeton, NJ: Princeton University Press, 2002.

"Moving Out, on and Back." *The Economist*, August 27, 2011, 51.

Perlstein, Rick. *Nixonland*. New York: Scribner, 2008.

Preston, Julia. "Anchor Baby: A Term Redefined as a Slur." *The New York Times*, December 9, 2011, A17.

Schaller, Michael. *Reckoning with Reagan*. New York: Oxford University Press, 1992.

Self, Robert O. *American Babylon, Race and the Struggle for Postwar Oakland*. Princeton, NJ: Princeton University Press, 2003.

Shukert, Elfrieda Berthiaume, and Barbara Smith Scibetta. *War Brides of World War II*. New York: Penguin Books, 1988.

Starr, Kevin. *California, a History*. New York: Modern Library, 2005.

Starr, Kevin. *Golden Dreams, California in an Age of Abundance, 1950–1963*. New York: Oxford University Press, 2009.

Takaki, Ronald. *A Different Mirror: A History of Multicultural America*. New York: Back Bay Books, 1998.

Takaki, Ronald. *Strangers from a Different Shore*. New York: Back Bay Books, 1998.

Tiongson, Antonio T., Edgardo V. Gutierrez, and Ricardo V. Gutierrez. *Positively No Filipinos Allowed*. Philadelphia: Temple University Press, 2006.

Wilson, James. *The Earth Shall Weep, a History of Native America*. New York: The Grove Press, 1998.

6

COLORADO

Gayle Kathleen Berardi

CHRONOLOGY

1–1299 CE	Advent of great prehistoric cliff-dwelling civilization in southwestern Colorado.
1500	Ute Indians occupy southern Rocky Mountain area making the Native Americans the oldest continuous residents of Colorado.
1682	French explorer Robert de La Salle appropriates for France all of the area now known as Colorado, east of the Rocky Mountains.
1760s	Spanish explorers enter Colorado looking for silver and gold.
1820s	Numerous Native American tribes live in the Colorado area, including the Cheyenne, Arapaho, Kiowa, Comanche, Pawnee, and Sioux.
1840s	Mexico grants lands, south of the Arkansas River and in the San Luis Valley in Colorado, to the wealthy.
1848	By the Treaty of Guadalupe Hidalgo, Mexico cedes to United States most of western Colorado, that part of the future state that had not been acquired by the Louisiana Purchase in 1803.
1851	First permanent non-Native American settlement in Colorado is founded at Conejos in the San Luis Valley.
1858	Discovery of gold deposits in Colorado brings prospectors from the East, including immigrants from numerous northern European countries.
1861	Congress establishes the Colorado Territory.
1870s	Railroads are built throughout Colorado by several immigrant groups, including Chinese, English, and German groups.

1872	A Territorial Immigration Board is created.
1876	Colorado becomes a state.
1878	A major silver strike in Leadville brings many immigrants to Colorado.
1880	Colorado population (based on U.S. Census) is 194, 327, with the foreign-born numbering 39,790. Immigrants are primarily from the German Empire, Ireland, Britain, the Austro-Hungarian Empire, Canada, and China.
1882	The Chinese Exclusion Act, the first major federal immigration law, suspends Chinese immigration for 10 years and bars Chinese in the United States from citizenship.
1882	A steel mill in Pueblo, later to become the Colorado Fuel and Iron Company, recruits immigrants to work in the mill and in coal mining camps.
1889	The Territorial Board of Immigration is replaced by Bureau of Immigration and Statistics.
1891	A gold strike in Cripple Creek brings new residents to the area to mine for gold, including many immigrants from northern Europe.
1891	The Federal Bureau of Immigration is established.
1899	The first beet sugar refinery is built in Grand Junction. Immigrants from Germany, Japan, Mexico, and northern Europe are recruited to work in the sugar beet industry.
1900	Colorado's total population is 541,483 and the foreign-born population is 91,000.
1909	The State Board of Immigration is created.
1914	A strike of coal miners in southern Colorado leads to the Ludlow Massacre, during which several miners are killed by the state militia. Most of the coal miners are immigrants recruited by the Colorado Fuel and Iron Company.
1917	The United States declares war on Germany; the war causes anti-immigrant sentiment, which culminates with the rise of the Ku Klux Klan (KKK) in Colorado.
1920	Colorado's population is 939,191 and the foreign-born number rises to 106,954. New immigrants are primarily from Italy, the Austro-Hungarian Empire, the Russian Empire, the German Empire, Britain, Ireland, and Sweden.
1921	The Quota Act limits immigrants to 3 percent of each nationality present in the United States in 1910.This provision cuts southern and eastern European immigrants to less than one-quarter of the number that arrived before World War I.
1924	The KKK secures control of the Republican Party in Colorado and elects a pro-Klan governor and U.S. senator.
1940	Colorado's population is 1,123,296 and that of the foreign-born is 71,600. Immigrants are primarily from Germany, Mexico, and Italy.

	The number of immigrants declines due to naturalization and because of restrictive immigration policies.
1941–1945	Because of World War II, there is a decline in the number of immigrants coming to Colorado as well as a rise of anti-immigrant sentiment toward Germans and Japanese.
1942	The federal government establishes Amache, an internment camp for Japanese in southeastern Colorado.
1943	The Chinese Exclusion Act is repealed.
1950s	The Bracero guest worker program brings Mexican workers to Colorado.
1952	The Immigration and Nationality Act retains country quotas (racial quotas) but justifies their continuation in Cold War terms.
1960	Colorado's population is 1,753,947 and the foreign-born population is 59,881. Immigrants are primarily from Germany, Mexico, and Italy.
1965	Federal immigration law equalizes national origin quotas and provides for family reunification, professional qualifications as the basis for entry, and broadened criteria for refugee status.
1980	Colorado's population is 2,889,733 and the foreign-born population is 114,130. Immigrants are primarily from Mexico, the Philippines, Korea, and India, with some refugees from Cuba and Vietnam.
1986	The Immigration and Reform Control Act enables some undocumented immigrants to become legal residents, while others are now more "illegal."
1990s	A booming economy draws skilled and unskilled immigrants to Colorado.
2000s	The decade sees the growth of immigrants arriving in Colorado and the rise of anti-immigrant sentiment.
2000	Colorado's population is 4,301,261 and the foreign-born number increases to 369,903. Immigrants are primarily from Mexico, Germany, and Canada.
2001	The USA Patriot Act amends the Nationality Act to broaden the scope of foreigners ineligible for admission, including the increased use of deportation due to terrorist activities, broadly defined.
2001	Representative Tom Tancredo and former Colorado governor Dick Lamm issue a joint statement about the allegedly detrimental impact of undocumented immigration on Colorado.
2002	The federal government conducts raids in Colorado at worksites looking for workers without work documents. The Air Force Academy in Colorado Springs is raided by immigration agents, who arrest 27 construction workers, landscapers, and maintenance workers.
2005	The Pew Hispanic Center estimates that between 225,000 and 275,000 undocumented immigrants live in Colorado.

2006	The Colorado state legislature, in regular and special sessions, passes 17 laws intended to identify undocumented immigrants; to limit publicly funded services and benefits; and to require all persons, regardless of citizenship or immigration status, to provide documentation for certain benefits and legal papers.
2007	The Colorado state legislature reviews immigration laws passed in 2006 for unintended consequences. New legislation clarifies earlier laws. The Colorado State Patrol's immigration-enforcement unit is formed.
2008	The Colorado state legislature creates a pilot guest worker program.
2009	Legislation to provide in-state tuition for undocumented immigrants fails in the Colorado state legislature.
2010	Colorado's population is 5,029,196 and the foreign-born number increases to 410,000. Immigrants are primarily from Mexico, Korea, and Germany.
2010	Protests against the Arizona Immigration law are held in Denver.
2011	The Colorado state legislature proposes a bill similar to the Arizona immigration law (Senate Bill [SB] 1070), but the bill fails to make it to a vote.
2011	A bill that would provide in-state tuition for undocumented immigrants fails in the Colorado state legislature. This was the fifth time such a measure had failed. A bill that would have allowed police to arrest undocumented immigrants without a warrant if law enforcement had probable cause to believe there were in the country illegally is also defeated.
2013	The legislature repeals the 2006 law (SB 90) that authorized police to communicate with federal authorities if they suspected individuals whom they had arrested were also undocumented. Undocumented students who came to the country as children are allowed in-state tuition at state colleges and universities.

HISTORICAL OVERVIEW

Colorado has a rich history of immigrants contributing to the growth of the state, especially to its economic development and cultural diversity. This history includes the settlement of this territory by various Native American tribes and the later arrival of Spanish and French explorers during the early history of the state. By the 1800s, Colorado became a ranching and farming state with a need for workers, many of whom came from eastern and Midwestern states. By the mid- to late 1800s, the state was flooded with gold seekers who hoped to strike it rich in the mountains of Colorado. Many of these individuals were either newly arrived immigrants to the United States or from families of immigrants. With the economic growth of the state, Colorado began to actively recruit immigrants to the still sparsely populated state. This effort was supported by the territorial and later state government and businesses.

RECRUITMENT OF IMMIGRANTS

In the 1800s, as with many states and territories, Colorado established an immigration board to recruit immigrants to the state. As defined in the language of the statute, the specific role of the board was to:

> adopt and put in execution such measures as will best promote and encourage immigration to the Territory, and for this purpose it shall publish and disseminate such useful information as can be obtained concerning the developed and undeveloped resources of the territory, and may provide for one of its members, or such other person as the Board may select, to attend [to] such Agricultural and Institute Fairs as may be deemed expedient for the display of the Agricultural and Mineral products of the Territory. (Colorado Territorial Assembly 1872, 137–38)

By encouraging immigrants to settle in Colorado, the legislature hoped that new laborers would work on farms and in mines, and start small businesses. In addition, the new immigrants would help Colorado achieve statehood by increasing the population, developing the natural resources, and increasing the state's tax base (all requisite criteria for becoming a state in the late 1800s). The board's five members actively recruited immigrants by creating pamphlets that were distributed in the eastern part of the United States and in Europe. The pamphlets described Colorado as having rich farm country, numerous natural resources, reliable sources of water, and a pleasant climate.

In addition to the Board of Immigration, railroads, agricultural communities, and mining companies recruited immigrants in Colorado. Railroads, for example, provided transportation to the territory and in some instances provided land for new residents. Of course, personal communication between immigrants who had arrived earlier and their family members influenced many other immigrants to settle in Colorado.

In 1889, The Territorial Board of Immigration was replaced by the Bureau of Immigration and Statistics, which functioned until 1897. It was replaced in 1909 by the State Board of Immigration. In addition to carrying on the work of the earlier board, the agency collected information about the state's resources, particularly the economic resources that would be of interest to new arrivals to Colorado. The state board actively worked with local communities to attract immigrants for specific industries.

Mexican workers, who were recruited and brought to the Arkansas Valley, Colorado, Nebraska, and Minnesota by the FSA (Farm Security Administration) to harvest and process sugar beets, under contract with the Inter-mountain Agricultural Improvement Association in May 1943. (Library of Congress)

For example, in 1860, Pueblo worked with the state board to create a description of the community that captured its best living conditions. It stated that Pueblo was:

> [a] town consisting of one store and [a] dozen houses is prettily situated on the Arkansas, (River) and with the luxuriance of verdure that surround it, would make a delightful sojourn for the ruralist. . . . Leaving the station, the road winds along the serpentine Arkansas, which looks beautiful-its banks heavily fringed with trees. Along its borders are improved farms, their crops looking very promising and the amount of land under cultivation indicating a strong faith in the richness and fertility of the soil of the extensive bottomlands of Colorado. We were surprised at the goodly character of the improvement, the number of houses, the many men employed in field labor and the amount of stock grazing in the verdant valleys. (Hogan 1990, 153)

This description helped Pueblo recruit over 30 different nationalities to work in the local steel mill and surrounding coal mining camps.

The work of the State Immigration Board eventually tended less toward recruitment of immigrants and more toward a statistical board. Over time, businesses became more important in the direct recruitment of immigrants in Colorado.

IMMIGRANTS IN THE UNITED STATES AND COLORADO

Beginning in the 1880s, part of Colorado's population growth was directly related to the dramatic increase of immigration to the United States. Many of the arriving immigrants traveled to the West to meet family members or to pursue the "American Dream" in the gold fields, in new manufacturing jobs, and in small businesses. Between 1870 and 1880, more than 2.8 million immigrants arrived in the United States. Between 1880 and 1890, 5.2 million immigrants arrived and, in 1890, 3.7 million immigrants arrived.

At the beginning of this period, immigrants arrived from familiar locales. About 50 percent were from Ireland or the German Empire. In 1883, 193,000 immigrants were of German origin and 81,000 were from Ireland. These countries of origin began to change by the end of the 1880s. Traditionally designated as "new immigration," this shift brought millions of people from the south and east of Europe to the mines, mills, and factories in the United States. In the early 1900s, around 75 percent of the 448,000 immigrants were from Italy, the Russian Empire, or Austria-Hungary. In 1907, 1.2 million entered the United States, with 285,000 from Italy; 258,000 from Russia; and 338,000 from the Hapsburg monarchy. Thus, between 1880 and 1920, 23.5 million immigrants arrived in the United States. Of these new immigrants, in the 1890s, over 70 percent were men and boys aged 14 to 45; after 1908, women and children arrived in large numbers to join their relatives. Most of the new arrivals were farmers, uneducated and with little money. Earlier immigrants, the "old immigrants," viewed these more recent immigrants as poor, illiterate, and unlikely to adapt to American life. They were seen as speaking different languages, dressing oddly, and practicing strange religions.

In the 1900s, this open door policy changed to reflect the rise of nativist sentiment in the United States. Colorado was not isolated from this anti-immigrant feeling as seen by the rise of the KKK and its involvement in state politics. It was successful in influencing the election of the mayor of Denver (Stapleton in 1923) and the governor of Colorado (Morley in 1924).

Under Governor Morley's leadership, the state legislature proposed measures to exclude certain immigrants from the state and to make it illegal to use wine for sacramental purposes. The latter law specifically targeted Catholic immigrants from southern Europe. Nonetheless, the number of immigrants in Colorado continued to increase. By 1900, 91,000 foreign-born were living in Colorado, and by 1910 the number increased to 110,000. Not only had the size of the population increased but so had the diversity. Where previous immigrants were primarily from German states, northern Europe, and Canada, their numbers now included Slovaks, Slovenians, Croatians, Russians, Mexicans, Japanese, Chinese, and Greeks.

However, after World War I the number of foreign-born began to drop, and by 1940 it was around 71,600. This drop was due to discrimination against German immigrants and the passage of the Quota Act of 1921. This act limited immigrants to 3 percent of each nationality present in the United States in 1910. This cut the percentage of immigrants living in the United States and in Colorado. In the aftermath of World War II, there was also a decline in German and Japanese immigration.

During the 1940s, with a predicted labor shortage due to World War II, Colorado participated in the federal Bracero Program. This program brought Mexicans to Colorado to work as farm laborers. Many of these workers returned to Mexico after the expiration of their work visa. The truly significant increase in the number of Mexicans and other immigrants in Colorado would not occur until the passage of the 1965 Immigration Act. This act equalized national origin quotas and gave preference to those with family ties in the United States and those with needed skills. By 1980, the number of immigrants in Colorado reached 114,130. During this time, most immigrants came from Mexico, the Philippines, Korea, and India.

Between 1980 and 2000, the immigrant population grew significantly. With this increase, immigration, which previously had been viewed primarily as a federal issue, now became a state concern. This change in view occurred for three major reasons. First, the 2000 census showed that Colorado was and is becoming a new destination state for immigrants (legal and undocumented). In 2006, the foreign-born population in Colorado was 489,496 or 10.3 percent of the population. Of this number, it was estimated that 3 percent were undocumented immigrants. With this population change, Colorado ranked 16th in the United States for its foreign-born population. The foreign-born were primarily from Mexico (52 percent), Asia (18 percent), and Europe (14 percent). And finally, the census also showed that the increase in foreign-born living in Colorado from 1990 to 2000 was 205 percent. Coloradans were becoming aware of the presence of immigrants by their number, new residential patterns, and the rise of ethnic stores and restaurants.

Second, in 1999, Tom Tancredo was elected to Congress from Colorado's Sixth Congressional District (south and west of Denver). As an ardent supporter of restricting undocumented immigration to the United States, Tancredo's sense of urgency had not been heard in the state since the early 1900s. One impact of his rhetoric was to elevate residents' expectations about what Congress should do in reforming immigration policy. The central expectation was that local and state concerns and needs would be addressed by a national policy. When this did not occur, Coloradans, as in other states, looked to state initiatives and legislation to address their perceived concerns.

Finally, post-September 11, 2001, immigration became intertwined with the issue of terrorism. This viewpoint was expressed in Colorado by callers in radio talk shows, in editorials in newspapers, and by messages to state legislators. This concern led to the development of multiple immigration law proposals to be considered by the Colorado state legislature in 2006. With the passage of several of these laws (see Topical Essay section on Colorado's state immigration laws later),

Colorado became known as having the toughest immigration laws in the United States. Following the legislation, there was a drop in the number of both undocumented and legal immigrants coming to the state. However, it is not clear that the legislation was the direct cause of this drop. At the same time as the laws were passed, the state suffered a downturn in the economy that may have had an impact on all workers.

Today, even though the arrival of immigrants has slowed, Colorado is still considered a designation state for immigrants. This can be seen in the 2010 census, which found 410,000 foreign-born living in Colorado. The dramatic increase that occurred in the 1990s did not continue into the 2000s primarily because of the economic recession that began in 2007. But other factors, such as anti-immigrant sentiment and stricter immigration laws, played a role in this development.

TOPICAL ESSAYS

THE CHALLENGES AND CONSEQUENCES OF COLORADO'S IMMIGRATION LAWS

Colorado has a long history of approaching the issue of immigration from a state perspective. For example, beginning in the late 1800s, the territory of Colorado established a Board of Immigration to encourage and oversee the arrival of immigrants in the state. However, it was not until recently, in 2006, that the Colorado State General Assembly became actively involved in addressing immigration issues. Leaders in the House and Senate were determined to pass laws that would result in Colorado having the toughest immigration policy in the United States.

During the 2006 session, legislators proposed several bills, but it was not until the special summer session (2006) that numerous bills were passed that led to Colorado being considered one of the toughest states on undocumented immigrants. With the increased awareness by Coloradans of immigrants in their communities, pressure was put on state legislators to do what the federal government apparently would not do—pass immigration laws that would discourage undocumented immigrants from coming to the state.

In 2006, the Colorado General Assembly, controlled by Democrats for the first time in 44 years, responded to constituents' concerns by proposing 17 bills and 3 resolutions that broadly addressed immigration. The "citizen" legislature, which meets once a year for 120 days (January to May), passed seven laws and one joint resolution. The passage of the measures was seen as a compromise by Republicans, who demanded bills that would have a greater impact on undocumented immigrants. In particular, Republicans wanted to restrict state benefits that they felt undocumented immigrants were receiving and that were being paid for by state tax dollars. In addition, it was clear that the Democratic leadership felt the urgency to address immigration at least with a very public introduction of bills with the knowledge that in all likelihood the bills would be killed in committee.

Colorado Senate president Joan Fitz-Gerald, D-Golden, right, makes a point while Colorado Speaker of the House Andrew Romanoff, D-Denver, listens during a news conference over an immigration ballot issue in the state capitol in Denver on June 20, 2006. (AP Photo/David Zalubowski)

The attempt to express the sentiment of citizens could be seen in several of the bills and in the joint resolution. For example, SB 90 proposed that there would be no sanctuary for undocumented immigrants in any Colorado city. However, it did not provide for anything that did not already exist in federal law. Importantly, for legislators and citizens, the bill captured a growing concern in Colorado that many cities, in particular Denver, Aspen, and Vail, were not complying with federal laws and thus were becoming known as a "sanctuary" for immigrants. The resolution expressed the view of many legislators that it was necessary to gain the support of fellow westerners on the issue of immigration. It was hoped that other western governors would push their legislators to pattern their immigration proposals after the ones passed by Colorado. The bills that did pass addressed numerous issues, such as human trafficking, human smuggling, and fraudulent work documents.

The following brief description of passed bills and the joint resolution summarizes the 2006 immigration legislation:

- No Sanctuary for Undocumented Immigrants—Prohibits local government from passing an ordinance to bar police from cooperating with federal officials in reporting undocumented immigrants.

- Fraudulent Work Documents—Prohibits the manufacture of phony work documents; sets civil and criminal penalties.
- Human Smuggling—Makes smuggling a class III felony.
- Human Trafficking—Makes trafficking a class III felony.
- Smuggling Enforcement—Creates a new division in the Colorado State Patrol to address human smuggling and trafficking.
- Secure Documents Implementation Audit—Requires the state auditor to study the implementation of the 2003 Secure and Verifiable Identity Document Act and requires agencies to accept only "secure" ID documents; rules out Mexico's Matricula Consular IDs.
- Public Contracts with Companies Employing Undocumented Workers—Prohibits state and local governments from contracting or subcontracting with any businesses that employ undocumented workers; creates a tip line to report suspected companies.
- Comprehensive National Immigration Policy—Joint Resolution—Endorses the Western Governors' Association resolution, which supports a temporary guest worker program; opposes blanket amnesty; and calls for sanctions against employers that hire undocumented immigrants.

The Defend Colorado Now Initiative

At the same time that the legislature was contemplating immigration legislation, a citizen's group was attempting to get an immigration initiative on the ballot. The proposed amendment to the state constitution was spearheaded by Defend Colorado Now (DCN) and asked voters in its ballot title:

> Shall there be an amendment to the Colorado constitution concerning the restriction of non-emergency government services to certain persons who are lawfully present in the United States, and, in connection therewith, restricting the provision of non-emergency services by the State and local governments to United States citizens and aliens lawfully present in the United States, except as mandated by federal law; and providing for the implementation and enforcement of this restriction? (Colorado Secretary of State 2008)

Similar to initiatives in other states, it attempted to restrict nonemergency services to undocumented immigrants. The initiative was originally filed in 2003 by Representative Tom Tancredo but did not make the ballot because there were not enough signatures collected to put it on the ballot. The DCN tried again in 2006 and received approval from the Colorado Title Setting Board on January 4. The board ruled that the initiative met the constitutional requirement that the measure did not address multiple issues. However, on June 12, the Colorado Supreme Court, in a 4–2 ruling, stated that the initiative contained numerous subjects and would not be on the November ballot. Governor Bill Owens (R) expressed his displeasure with the Supreme Court's ruling and his desire for a rehearing before the Court. In a press conference, Owens called the ruling "inconsistent, inappropriate and arrogant" (Owens June 13, 2006). He urged the Supreme Court to reconsider its ruling and was supported by Attorney General John Suthers, who said he would file for reconsideration. Owens threatened to call a special session of the legislature if the Court did not act in a timely fashion and reverse its decision. On June 26, the Colorado Supreme Court denied the petition for a rehearing and, on June 29, the governor called a special session.

The 2006 Colorado General Assembly Special Session

The contentious events leading up to the special session made it unlikely that action would be taken to place the initiative on the November ballot or that bills addressing other immigration concerns would be passed. The perceived urgency of the session was underlined when Governor Owens threatened to call additional sessions if action was not taken to his satisfaction.

The Democrats responded to the call for a special session with criticism of Governor Owens's past efforts on immigration laws. Senate president Joan Fitz-Gerald (D) stated, "Illegal immigration is not a new problem. Bill Owens has been Governor since 1999 and he's had a Republican House and Senate and they've done nothing. And now all of a sudden in three days in a special session we're going to solve this? No. Their party is in charge of the U.S. Congress and that is the prime mover and shaker on immigration issues" (Bartels 2006).

A Remedy from Outside the Legislature

Going into a divisive session, help in resolving the deadlock came from an unlikely individual; someone outside of the legislature and with ties to DCN. Former Colorado governor Richard Lamm, an outspoken critic of undocumented immigration and of federal immigration policy and a supporter of the DCN ballot initiative, began working to find a compromise to the constitutional measure before the legislature. Lamm later described his effort as turning from a "Constitutional to a Legislative Approach" (Lamm July 1, 2006).Helping him with this approach was former Denver mayor Federico Peña. Peña had expressed concern over the lack of sanctions against employers of undocumented immigrants and a desire for national immigration reform. What seemed to bring Lamm and Peña together was their desire to have national legislation that would address their multiple concerns about immigration. If the national government would not act, they held, the responsibility would fall to the states. However, the legislature would only be able to pass significant legislation if a compromise could be found.

Relying on a recently passed Georgia law, Lamm and Peña put together measures that included restrictions on who could get public benefits coupled with a stringent verification system. The measures also included penalties for employers of undocumented immigrants. Lamm characterized this action, which seemed disloyal to DCN supporters, as a move to get more accomplished in July through the passage of laws, than waiting for a vote on the initiative in November. As Lamm explained:

> Should we merely ask to put our initiative back on the ballot? That seemed inadequate to me. Why not go directly to legislation preventing illegal aliens from getting benefits, plus a secure method of verifying that applicants for public benefits were legal? Why not get in July most or all of what we were seeking next November? If we went the ballot route, we would still need implementation legislation next January (as required by the initiative), which probably would not pass until May of 2007. WHY WAIT? Strike while the politics favor our cause! (Lamm July 1, 2006)

The third partner in supporting the legislative route was Governor Owens. He agreed to sign legislation if it addressed the main issues of the initiative. With this compromise, the legislative session produced 34 measures; 22 were postponed, 2 were referred to voters, and 10 bills were signed into law by Governor Owens. The following is a summary of the passed bills and referenda:

- Services for Communicable Diseases—Exempts from any prohibition of services to undocumented immigrants for care of communicable diseases.
- Restrictions on Defined Public Benefits (House Bill [HB] 1023)—Requires state agencies and local governments to verify the lawful presence in the United States of any person 18 years or older who applies for public benefits; sets forth a list of documents that can be used to verify legal presence in the United States.
- Eligibility for Economic Development Incentives—Requires employers seeking economic development incentive awards to verify that they do not employ undocumented immigrants.
- Deny Business Permits for Illegal Aliens—Requires denial of permits or revocation of such permits if a person is in the United States illegally.
- Withhold State Tax for Services—Requires employers who pay contractors who fail to provide a correct taxpayer ID number to withhold state income taxes at the full rate.
- Employer Fines for Fraudulent Documents—Requires all Colorado employers to attest to verification of legal work status of all employees.
- Undocumented Alien Labor Tax Deduction: Referendum—Refers to voters a measure to prohibit businesses from claiming wages paid to illegal immigrants as a deductible expense (passed November 2006).
- Immigration Extortion—Includes criminal extortion to extend to those who threatened someone who is reporting the immigration status of an individual.

- Illegal Immigration Costs Reimbursement—Directs the attorney general to recover costs from federal government for state costs associated with undocumented immigration.
- Attorney General to Initiate Immigration Lawsuit: Referendum K—Refers to voters a measure to direct the Colorado attorney general to sue the federal government to demand enforcement of federal immigration laws (passed November 2006).
- Voting by Persons Not Entitled to Vote—Makes it illegal for anyone to vote if they are not entitled to vote.
- Involuntary Servitude—Creates a new class III felony for coercing anyone to work with or without pay, by threatening to take actions that would result in that person's incarceration or deportation from the United States.

After the five-day session ended, both Democrats and Republicans declared that Colorado now had the toughest immigration policy in the country. Further, the governor stated that the new laws would mean that 1 million people receiving state aid would have to verify their citizenship and, of these, 50,000 undocumented immigrants would be removed from these programs (Owens July 11, 2006).The DCN director, Fred Elbel, declared the session a success, even though he restated his regret that Coloradans did not get a chance to vote on the initiative.

However, not everyone saw the session as a success. Bob Beauprez, a Republican candidate for the governor's office stated: "I'll give the legislature and the Governor credit for taking some little baby steps toward this problem. There's a whole lot more to be done" (Kelderman 2006). Even Owens agreed with this point when he said, "The Legislature failed to enact commonsense solutions in several areas that require real and necessary reform . . . the biggest disappointment is that the initiative isn't on the November ballot" (Migoya 2006).

The Colorado Legislation: An Example for Other States

With praise coming from many citizens, interest groups, and other states, the Colorado General Assembly was optimistic that the implementation of the legislation would go smoothly. The implementation costs were estimated to be around $1 million but it was hoped that this would be offset by savings from not providing services to undocumented immigrants.

Many of the laws took effect on August 1, 2006, with the remainder on January 1, 2007. HB 1023, which denied certain social service benefits to undocumented immigrants, was the law that was most anticipated by supporters and watched by government agencies for challenges and unintended consequences. Initially, the numerous provisions of the law caused confusion among government agencies that had a short period of time to comply. Causing additional problems was the fact that the legislature had passed more than 15 related immigration laws since the spring 2006 session and many of them overlapped or had contrary provisions.

In particular, it was not known if HB1023 would cover all licenses issued by the state. This included over 600,000 licenses issued for professionals ranging from plumbers and electricians to doctors. Clarification was required from the Colorado attorney general to determine which licenses were to be covered under an earlier law. However, at the same time, the attorney general ruled that some documents not usually deemed licenses would be covered by the law. Certain authorizations for citizen business actions would also fall under this classification. These problems were acknowledged by Governor Owens's spokesperson who stated, "[T]his is not an easy process . . . there will be unforeseen situations and there will be bumps in the road" (Kim 2006).

Types of Documents

The difficulty in implementing the laws fell to the agencies that needed to create new rules to put the laws into effect. This was especially problematic for the implementation of HB1023. State agencies on August 1 had to issue rules addressing the question of which type of documents would be acceptable to prove legal residency in the United States. For example, the Department of Revenue added documents to those provided for in the legislation (Colorado driver's license, ID card, tribal document, and military ID). The new documents included a U.S. passport and a birth certificate.

Colorado director of revenue Michael Cooke also had to shift resources and personnel to centers statewide and open an annex next to the state capitol in Denver. In preparing for the implementation of the law (HB 1023), it was clear that both government agencies and businesses were unsure how much it would cost and how the laws would impact them.

The difficulty for citizens was the possibility that the documents needed to obtain licenses and other legal documents (such as a death certificate) would be unavailable. This was particularly true for the elderly who may not have had a birth certificate and could not easily obtain one. This would also be particularly ironic for some Native Americans who found themselves without birth certificates to prove their U.S. citizenship.

The rules also caused problems when multiple documents were needed. For many, this was just an inconvenience; for others, it made it impossible to get licenses or benefits. This situation did in fact occur right after the legislation was put into effect. However, the "individuals" affected were not always those who were expected to feel the impact of the law. For example, on August 6, two race horses were denied access to race at Arapahoe Park near Denver because the owners had to show they had legal residence in the United States. Previously, owners and out-of-state jockeys had been able to show licenses from other states. According to the director of Colorado's Division of Racing, "We had some problems getting someone with the right information about what to do; it was unexpected" (Migoya August 10, 2006).

The law also brought back into place a requirement that automobile dealers check the identification of a car buyer. This check needed to be done if the car would be registered in Colorado. However, the implementation of the law led many dealers to check everyone buying a car, and, because of this, it was reported that some buyers had gone to other states. According to the Colorado Independent Auto Dealers Association, a few dealerships that relied on customers from Mexico had to consider closing.

Months after the passage of HB1023, Colorado Senate president Joan Fitz-Gerald declared she was concerned that undocumented immigrants, as well as legal residents of Colorado, were being denied public benefits due to the lack of documents. Fitz-Gerald described the agencies as overzealous in their implementation: "They're going beyond the intent of the law. I wanted to see what the issues are out there. I suspect they're all related to HB 1023" (Washington 2006). Fitz-Gerald was joined by human rights activists who declared that the new immigration laws had unintended consequences, such as legal residents not seeking public services that they were entitled to receive.

Cost of Implementing the Laws

One of the central arguments heard in the immigration debate that led to the 2006 special session was that undocumented immigrants were costing the state millions of dollars in public benefits. This notion led to the proposed amendment to the state constitution and HB 1023. What was not presented to legislators was the exact cost of the public benefits (i.e., empirical proof for this claim). Rather, estimates were suggested by proponents and opponents of the measures. In addition, when HB 1023 was passed, there was only a rough estimate of the cost to the state for implementation of the law and other related laws.

Following the special session, the Joint Budget Committee asked each state department to report how much money had been spent in implementing HB 1023 and to report any savings. The report showed that 18 departments had added $2.03 million in costs and reported no savings. In addition, no department could report if any undocumented immigrants were being denied state services. Responding to the report, Senator Abel Tapia, chair of the Joint Budget Committee, declared, "We're finding very few departments where these bills have a major effect . . . I thought it was a waste of money when we were doing it, but I don't think the general public believed that the state wasn't spending money on illegal immigrants" (Couch 2007). Legislators were disgruntled that the governor had not made the information available before the special session. However, some legislators did not accept the report; they called for additional studies, noting that the data had been manipulated for ideological purposes.

Examples of the compliance costs as found in the study were:

Health Care	87,287
Human Services	173,000
Labor and Employment	374,828
Regulatory	378,107
Revenue	372,533
(Couch 2007)	

At the same time that the report was released, the attorney general requested $50,000 to conduct a lawsuit against the federal government as mandated by Referendum K, which directed the attorney general to sue the federal government to demand enforcement of federal immigration laws. This money was requested even though the attorney general stated it would be a futile effort, which turned out to be the case when the attorney general later dropped the lawsuit.

While the legislators and the governor sparred over this issue, the national news had taken notice. Numerous articles analyzed the often-heard statement that Colorado had passed the toughest immigration laws in the United States and was saving the state money. However, many legislators and citizens agreed with Joan Lunden when she reported that, "Coloradans discovered that it was spending millions of dollars to enforce the law (HB 1023) that saved virtually nothing because federal law already prohibits illegal immigrants from getting welfare" (Lunden 2006).

In 2013, with greater representation by Democrats sympathetic to state immigrants, anti-immigration policies were challenged. SB 90, the policy allowing police to communicate with federal authorities regarding an arrestee's immigration status, was repealed because it was argued that the measure created a threatening atmosphere for all immigrants, regardless of legal status, including raising fears of racial profiling and of being wrongfully detained. In the same year, a policy passed that allowed the children of undocumented parents to pay in-state tuition at state universities and colleges.

Impact on the Availability of Labor

One of the most common reasons given to support tough immigration laws in the post-9/11 decade was that undocumented immigrants were allegedly taking jobs away from legal residents and citizens. This argument was part of the speeches Representative Tancredo gave throughout Colorado. This concern was captured in a speech in 2003, when he stated:

Undocumented immigrants are low-skilled and willing to work for low wages. When President Bush said that every willing worker should go to a willing employer, I asked

> him if he really believed that. When he did, I responded that we have willing workers (Americans) who cannot get jobs because they have been taken by illegals at low wages. (Tancredo, Colorado State University-Pueblo 2004)

This sentiment was seized upon by state legislators and was reflected in the floor and committee debates.

If the intent of the legislation was to discourage undocumented immigrants from coming to Colorado, the laws were successful. As soon as the special session ended, immigrants inside and outside Colorado described the state as "unfriendly" to immigrants and held that it should be avoided. This was the advice given to legal immigrants as well.

The result was that fewer immigrant laborers came to Colorado during the 2006 and 2007 agricultural season. This decrease had an impact on fruit and vegetable crops in Colorado. In particular, the labor shortage meant that there were not enough workers to pick fruit and vegetables as they ripened. Based on anecdotal evidence, it was estimated that 40 percent of the fruit crop was not picked and that the vegetable crop did not fare much better. Related to this, 2007 was the first year in decades that seed crops were not planted on the western slope of Colorado.

Although the numbers were debatable, the fact that workers were needed was not. This led to resorting to an old practice as a response to the unintended consequences of the legislation from the special session. A representative from southern Colorado proposed that prisoners be used to pick crops on a trial basis. The pilot program, run by the Department of Corrections, placed low-risk prisoners in the southeastern part of Colorado. The inmates were paid about 60 cents a day. Farmers were required to pay the Department of Corrections for transportation and security.

Representative Dorothy Butcher (D-Pueblo), in proposing the program, expressed concern that 50 percent of immigrant laborers were unlikely to return to the farms around Pueblo and, thus, the prisoner program would provide a much-needed workforce. Many farmers endorsed the plan and said that offering higher wages to local laborers had not provided enough of an incentive to entice workers to the fields. The Department of Corrections endorsed the program, saying it would provide skills and a work ethic for the inmates.

Opponents of the program criticized it as being reminiscent of chain gangs and forced labor. For example, Julian Ross of the Colorado Immigrant Rights Coalition argued:

> Many immigrants are leaving Colorado for other states that will actually embrace their contributions as good citizens and hard workers. This exodus from Colorado has profound negative consequences on our economy and the very fabric of our society. (Frosch 2007)

A similar sentiment was expressed by Christie Donner, the executive director of the Colorado Criminal Justice Reform Coalition, who stated:

> This feels like the re-invention of the plantation. You have a captive labor force essentially working for their room and board in order to benefit the employer. This isn't a job training program. It's an exploitation program. (Frosch 2007)

Response by Subsequent Legislative Sessions

It is clear that the results from this wave of anti-immigration legislation led to numerous challenges and unintended consequences. But were the goals of the legislation met? In many ways, it was too early to say because detailed analysis had not been conducted by the legislature or state departments. However, one goal that had been met, at least temporarily, was the discouragement of undocumented immigrants from coming into the state. This may have been due to the legislation as well as the downturn in the economy.

In addition, the laws forced all residents to find documents that would enable them to receive licenses and other government documents. For example, lost birth certificates had been replaced and social security cards were found. Rules were in place that helped Coloradans understand what was needed to prove their citizenship or legal residency.

But even with these successes, it was recognized by Coloradans and members of the legislature that these laws were limited measures and that it was the role of the federal government to provide leadership and reform in the area of immigration policy. Perhaps this was why the 2007 legislative session did not follow the special session with significant immigrant legislation. Rather the legislature had to step back and evaluate the impact of the 2006 legislation.

With that, the only major proposal of the 2008 session was to establish a liaison office with Mexico to aid Mexicans in getting visas to work in Colorado. In essence, the bill (HB 1325) proposed a program that would help the federal government issue worker visas. Senator Abel Tapia (D-Pueblo) explained, "All we're doing is trying to expedite the (federal) visas. What we have found is the visa process is filled with a lot of stumbling blocks, bureaucratic sidetracks. It is very, very hard to get through" (Ashby February 3, 2007). Under the plan, Colorado would bring up to 1,000 workers with an additional 1,000 for five years. The visas would not lead to citizenship and would ensure that the workers return to Mexico after the 10-month visa expired and 20 percent of their wages would be withheld and returned only after they returned to Mexico. Some would argue that the latter provision is a form of debt peonage, which the United States had sought to eradicate in the late nineteenth century. The bill also called for adding three new positions in the Department of Labor and Employment who would process the applications. The bill had the support of numerous labor and farm organizations, such as the

Colorado Farm Bureau and the Rocky Mountain Farmers Union. The proposal received mixed responses from both Republicans and Democrats. Many feared it would create unwanted red tape and bureaucratic overlap with the federal government. A small minority worried this plan was exploitative and reminiscent of older, bound labor arrangements. In 2012, the bill was reviewed, and, in 2013, numerous challenges to these provisions were introduced.

Conclusion

The immigration laws passed by the Colorado General Assembly in 2006 were the accumulated result of intense lobbying by citizens, interests groups, and the governor. After many months of debates and proposals, the legislature was successful in passing immigration laws that tackled some of the concerns expressed by critics of federal immigration policy. However, the desire for tougher laws led to the special session in which significant legislation was passed. The legislation restricted access to undocumented immigrants for certain social services, demanded that specific documents be used to obtain licenses and services, and covered other areas such as human trafficking.

The legislation, while achieving the goal of making Colorado unattractive to many undocumented and legal immigrants, resulted in numerous challenging and unintended consequences. These consequences ranged from labor shortages in the agricultural area, confusion over which documents were acceptable for services, and inequitable application of new rules to increasing the state's cost for implementation of the laws without any significant cost savings. These factors, in turn, led the Colorado legislature to reevaluate its role in passing immigration laws that historically had been the purview of the U.S. Congress. Unfortunately, this was not accompanied by a review of the consequences of the 2006 laws. The legislature has moved from describing Colorado as having the toughest immigration laws in the United States to a state that must work with the federal government to address citizen concerns over immigration. As noted above, strong anti-immigration measures were challenged in 2013 after these harsher measures were found to be overreaching in their aims. Thus, the future of Colorado immigration policy will depend on the legislature taking the necessary efforts to reform past laws and insure future laws do not have the multiple unintended consequences that have plagued the laws from the 2006 regular and special sessions.

NOTABLE GROUPS

COLORADO IMMIGRANT RIGHTS COALITION

The Colorado Immigrant Rights Coalition is an umbrella organization encompassing the whole state that includes student groups, business interests, community organizations, and religious groups. This broad-based coalition was founded in 2002 to advocate on behalf of all immigrants and refugees in the state. Its missions is to create a more open context of reception for resident foreigners of all ages and it is committed to the application of human rights principles in policy, education, and law enforcement, among other areas. The coalition also develops links between longer-term civic groups and newer immigrants. Among its accomplishments, this coalition has worked to challenge policies that create a chilling effect on immigrant rights, including helping to pass the 2013 Community and Law Enforcement Trust Act (which repealed SB 90); aiding passage of the ASSET bill in 2013 (which provided for undocumented resident college students to pay in-state tuition where applicable); helping eligible students to use Deferred Action for Childhood Arrivals (the Deferred Action program of 2012–2013) to get legal work or a driver's license; and co-founding the "Ya Es Hora Colorado" to help approximately 2,000 legal permanent residents to become citizens.

BIBLIOGRAPHY

Abbot, Carl, Stephen J. Leonard, and Thomas J. Noel. *Colorado: A History of the Centennial State*. Boulder: University Press of Colorado, 2005.

Acuña, Salvador. Consultant to the Colorado Trust Immigration Integration Project. Personal Interview, 2007.

Ashby, Charles. "Senators to Unveil Farm Workers Bill." *The Pueblo Chieftain*, February 3, 2007.

Ashby, Charles. "Visa Changes No Help for Labor Shortage." *The Pueblo Chieftain*, February 9, 2007.

Bartels, Lynn. "Dems Suspect Owens of Political Moves." *Rocky Mountain News*, June 29, 2006. http://www.highbeam.com/doc/1G1-147592001.html. Accessed July 31, 2014.

Berardi, Gayle. *The Social and Political Impacts of Immigration in the Development of Pueblo, Colorado: 1880–1920*. Unpublished Paper, 2002.

Colorado Immigrant Rights Coalition Website. "Mission, Principles and Goals" and "History." n.d. http://coloradoimmigrant.org/. Accessed February 2, 2014.

Colorado Secretary of State. "Ballot Title DCN Initiative." 2008. http://www.elections.colorado.gov/www/2005–2006percent20 Initiatives. Accessed March 2, 2014.

Colorado Secretary of State. "Colorado Title Board Initiatives." 2006. http://www.elections.colorado.gov.www/2005–2006. Accessed March 2, 2014.

Colorado Territorial Assembly. *General Laws, Private Acts, Joint Resolutions and Memorials Passed at the Ninth Session of the Legislative Assembly of the Territory of Colorado*. Denver: Colorado Territorial Assembly, 1872.

Couch, Mark. "Colorado Immigration Law Falls Short of Goal." *The Denver Post*, January 25, 2007. http://www/denverpost.com/ci. Accessed March 2, 2014.

Defend Colorado Now. "Initiative Language." November, 2006. http://www.defendcoloradonow.org/amendment. Accessed March 2, 2014.

Faiola, Anthony. " Immigrant Policies Diverge." *The Washington Post*, October 15, 2007. http://www/washingtonpost.com/immigrant policies. Accessed March 2, 2014.

Frosch, Dan. "Inmates Will Replace Migrants in Colorado Fields." *The New York Times*, March 4, 2007. http:/www.nytimes.com/2007/03/04/Us/04prisoners. Accessed March 2, 2014.

Hogan, Richard. *Class and Community in Frontier Colorado*. Lawrence: University Press of Kansas, 1990.

Kelderman, Kri. "Colorado Election in National Spotlight." Stateline.org. August 1, 2006. http://www.stateline.org/live/details.Accessed March 2, 2014.

Kim, Myung Oak. "Immigration Law Cast Wide Net." *Rocky Mountain News*, July 29, 2006. http://www.rockymountainnews.com/news/2006/july/29/immigration.   Accessed March 2, 2014.

Kottke, Lenna. "Local Nonprofit Faces Complications Meeting Requirements." 2007. index.cfm/user/specialtransit. Accessed March 2, 2014.

Lamm, Richard, and Gary Imhoff. *The Immigration Time Bomb: The Fragmenting of America*. New York: Truman Alley Books/E.P. Dutton, 1985.

Lamm, Richard. "Open Letter from Dick Lamm to Defend Colorado Now." Defend Colorado Now Website. July 1, 2006. http://www.defendcoloradonow.org/legislation/letter_lamm_2006jul01.html. Accessed March 2, 2014.

Lamm, Richard. *Two Wands, One Nation: An Essay on Race and Community in America*. New York: Fulcrum Publishing, 2006.

Lunden, Jennifer. "Immigration Remains a Hot Topic in 2008—Interview by Liane Hansen." December, 30, 2006. New York: Weekend Edition-National Public Radio. http://www.npr.org/templates/story/story.php?storyId=17703675. Accessed March 2, 2014.

Migoya, David. "Laws on Illegal Immigrants Bring Glitches." *The Denver Post*, August 10, 2006, A-1, Section 1A.

Migoya, David. "New Era of Immigration." *The Denver Post*, August 1, 2006, A-1, Section 1A.

Owens, Bill. Press Conference, Denver, Colorado, June 13, 2006.

Owens, Bill. Press Conference, Denver, Colorado, July 11, 2006.

Reid, T. R. "In Colorado, a Deal on Immigration Bills: GOP Angered as Issue Won't Go to Voters." *The Washington Post*, July 12, 2006. http://www.washingtonpost.com. Accessed March 2, 2014.

Straayer, John A. *The Colorado General Assembly*. Boulder: University Press of Colorado, 2006.

Tancredo, Tom, Representative. Immigration Presentation given at CSU-Pueblo, Colorado, 2004.

U.S. Census Bureau. "Report on Immigration in U.S. States." 2006. http://.censusbureau/gov/immigration/state. Accessed March 2, 2014.

Vock, Daniel. "With Feds Stuck, States Take on Immigration." December 6, 2007. http://www.hstoday.us/channels/dodnational-defense/single-article-page/with-feds-stuck-states-take-on-immigration/4733820c658e3071d9e0c06c42ac8c52.html. Accessed March 2, 2014.

Washington, April M. "Immigration Law under Security: Public Benefits Rules Are 'Overzealously' Enforced, Senators Say." *Rocky Mountain News*, December 8, 2006. http:/rockymountiannews.com/news/2006/dec/08/immigration. Accessed March 2, 2014.

7

CONNECTICUT

Anne Gebelein

CHRONOLOGY

1614	The first Europeans, Dutch, and English explorers and traders, arrive in Connecticut and find complex Native American societies, many aligned in confederacies. Their tribal names still grace common places in the state: for example, Quinnipiac, Hammonasset, and Tunxis. Native Americans gave Connecticut its name; "Quinnehtukqut" (beside the long tidal river) is an Algonquian term used to designate the area along what is today the Connecticut River.
1633	English and Dutch establish fortified trading posts—the Dutch in what is today Hartford, the English in what would become Windsor. English Puritans leave Massachusetts to establish the first permanent settlements of European immigrants in Connecticut, in Windsor, and in Wethersfield the following year.
1633	A devastating smallpox epidemic ravages Native American populations.
1636	English settlers in Windsor, Wethersfield, and Hartford unite to create the Colony of Connecticut.
1637	European immigrants launch their first attack on native inhabitants in the Pequot War. Native women and children are divided among English troops, with some of the captives sold as slaves in the West Indies.
1639	The Colony of Connecticut establishes the Fundamental Orders, or the first state constitution, an act that gives Connecticut its nickname of "The Constitution State."

1639	The oldest existing document of slavery in Connecticut is a record from this year of a Dutch commissary in Hartford, Gysbert Op Dyck, who "by accident or otherwise, killed a negro boy, Louis Berbice, from Dutch Guiana, belonging to him."
1640s	New England begins to trade with the West Indies, a relationship in which colonies like Connecticut supply colonies like Barbados with food, livestock, and lumber in exchange for sugar, molasses, and rum. With the molasses, New England makes its own rum, which it then sells to African communities, who then send slaves to the West Indies in a triangular trade that brings a flow of traders and slaves from the West Indies to New England.
1643	Slavery is legalized in Connecticut through the articles of the New England Federation.
1665	The New Haven Colony, formed in 1638, is absorbed by the Connecticut Colony.
1675–1676	King Philip's War pits English against Native Americans and ends the latter's ability to live traditional tribal lives in southern New England. American Indians who surrender in Connecticut before the end of the war are dispersed among English families to serve them; 188 prisoners of war are sold into slavery by Massachusetts leaders.
1730	Census reports 700 blacks out of a total population of 38,000. While in the 1700s the average household has one or two servants, these are not necessarily slaves. Servitude is a nebulous condition that often allows for freedom after a number of years of service and is not limited to blacks. People of African descent are crucial, however, to the economic development of New England, providing much needed labor in maritime industries, in clearing land, and in farming, as slaves and servants. A number gain their freedom, become tradesmen, and later pass their trades down to their free children and grandchildren.
1776	At the time of the Revolution, it is estimated that approximately 96 percent of Connecticut's population is of English heritage and between 2 and 3 percent is of African heritage.
1777–1783	Approximately 400 Connecticut blacks serve in the Revolutionary War, many gaining their freedom with their salaries and others benefiting from their owners' sudden generosity when celebrating the end of the war.
1780–1840	Approximately 750,000 residents migrate out of the state in search of arable land, since the state's supply is exhausted by the 1760s. The state's total population only increases 5 percent during this time.
1784	Gradual Emancipation Act is passed and later amended in 1797, decreeing that all children born of slaves are to be liberated at age 21.
1820s	Irish immigrants begin to arrive in Connecticut. They help build the Farmington and Enfield canals, and later the New Haven and

Hartford railroads. They establish Hartford's Catholic Church of the Most Holy Trinity in 1830.

1833   Prudence Crandall (1803–1890), the state's official heroine, opens her Canterbury school to African American girls.

1839   The Cuban slave ship *Amistad* arrives in New Haven harbor, commandeered by mutinous Africans resisting their enslavement. Their ensuing trial and return to Africa galvanizes the abolitionist movement in the state.

1840   Bavarian Jews establish Congregation Mishkan Israel in New Haven, and in 1843, they establish Hartford's Beth Israel. Germans begin to immigrate to the state in significant numbers in the early nineteenth century, many of them Jews. French and Canadians are also migrating to Connecticut but in smaller numbers.

1847   G. Fox and Co., a department store, is opened in Hartford by Gerson Fox (1811–1880), perhaps Connecticut's most successful German Jewish immigrant.

1848   All slavery is outlawed in Connecticut, although freed blacks enjoy few of the benefits their white counterparts do. They develop parallel but separate political and social customs, among them, electing their own "African governors."

1850s   Significant numbers of Irish immigrants arrive in Connecticut fleeing the potato famine; by 1860, there are 55,500.

1852   Litchfield-native Harriet Beecher Stowe (1811–1896) publishes *Uncle Tom's Cabin*, which has tremendous impact on the country's view of slavery and inspires abolitionists everywhere.

1854   Yung Wing (1828–1912) becomes the first Chinese student to graduate from an American University. He later orchestrates the arrival and studies of 120 other Chinese males in the state. Wang donates 1,237 volumes of Chinese books to Yale and convinces the university to hire its first professor of Chinese studies, planting the seeds for Yale's worldwide prominence in East Asian studies today. Later, he lobbies against the Chinese Exclusion Act of 1882, which only Connecticut and Massachusetts do not ratify.

1860   Over 8,000 Germans, of a variety of religions, are recorded as living in the state. Between British, Irish, Scottish, Germans, and small numbers of other groups, approximately one-quarter of Connecticut's residents are foreign-born or first-generation Americans.

1861   With the start of the Civil War, Connecticut industry provides the Union war effort with Samuel Colt's revolvers and Charles Goodyear's rubber. Connecticut's manufacturing of weapons, military wagons, rubber ponchos and boots, uniforms, and steamships makes Hartford the richest city in the country during the 1860s. This manufacturing boom employs blacks and whites in factories in Hartford, New Haven, Collinsville, and the like, although preference is given to European immigrants. Blacks form two regiments, serve in the Civil War, and are feted by Governor Buckingham when they return home in 1865.

1868   Connecticut schools become integrated by law.

1874–1891   Mark Twain publishes his most famous works in Hartford, among them *Tom Sawyer* and the *Adventures of Huckleberry Finn*.

1890   The state census of this year offers the categories of white (733,438), African American (12,302), American Indian (228), Chinese (272), Japanese (18), Filipino, and all other (no data for either).

1890–1910   Massive numbers of Europeans arrive on Connecticut shores, in addition to English and Scottish immigration paths that are already constant since 1800. Christians from Italy, Ireland, and Poland and Jews from Lithuania and Russia flee economic and political instability. Large numbers of mostly Christian Slavs, but also Jews and other ethnic groups, leave the Austro-Hungarian Empire in search of better economic opportunity. French Canadians arrive to work in textile communities in southeastern Connecticut.

1910   About 30 percent of the state's population is recorded as foreign-born.

1910–1930   Connecticut's African American population doubles as black southerners move north in the Great Migration, pulled by the industrial labor vacuum created by war and the American exclusion laws (1921–1924), which shut off European immigration, and pushed by boll weevil infestations that destroyed southern crops. By 1930, more southern-born blacks are living in Connecticut than northern-born blacks. New Haven also records over 400 foreign-born blacks in 1930, most from the West Indies. The collapse of the sugarcane industry in the West Indies drives blacks of all classes from the Antilles. For decades, African American teenage boys from the South also migrate to Connecticut tobacco fields in the summers to work, among them Martin Luther King.

1920   Connecticut records show 80,000 Italian residents, up from 100 in 1870. Polish residents number 46,623. By 1920, the Irish control the Connecticut Democratic Party. By 1920, Greater Hartford's Jewish population numbers 18,000 and Eastern European Jews outnumber Germans by five to one. Increasing numbers of Catholics and Jews mean higher birth rates, different values, and unpredictable loyalties, which cause increasing tension between Yankee Protestants and immigrant newcomers.

1922–1924   The Ku Klux Klan stages a series of rallies and enjoys record membership of men who are anti-immigrant, anti-Jewish, and anti-Catholic; the organization claims 18,000 members statewide.

1933   Blacks and Jews celebrate the payoff of their combined lobbying, the passage of the Civil Rights Law, which outlaws racial discrimination in the state.

1940–1945	The dramatic rise in the aviation industry in the 1920s, leading to the rapid growth of Pratt and Whitney Company, Sikorsky Aircraft, Hamilton Standard, United Aircraft, and Chance Vought Company, meaning that Connecticut labor is in high demand during World War II. About 130,000 new workers migrate to the state.
1946–1964	During this period of the Puerto Rican Great Migration, Puerto Ricans are invited to work in factories in cities like Bridgeport and Waterbury and in Willimantic's textile mills as part of the U.S. government's strategy of alleviating poverty during Operation Bootstrap. Tens of thousands of citizens leave the island, many settling in New York and Connecticut.
1950	The West Indian Social Club of Hartford is formed by Caribbean men who had migrated to Connecticut to fill agricultural labor shortages during World War II under the Acme Program.
1950–1970	State population increases from 2 to 3 million, caused by the baby boom and great numbers of job seekers continuing to move into the state. Overcrowding, the G.I. Bill, and the suburbanization of Connecticut companies lead thousands out of urban centers and into suburbs. The non-white population doubles between 1950 and 1960, from 53,000 to 107,000.
1952	The first Puerto Ricans are flown to Connecticut to work in tobacco farming. They remain an important presence in migrant farmwork in the 2000s.
1960	The state census of this year offers the categories of white (2,423,816), Negro (107,449), American Indian (923), Chinese (865), Japanese (653), Filipino (726), and all others (802). Of the Chinese, 280 live in Storrs/Mansfield, home of the University of Connecticut (UConn), and the majority of Filipinos are in the Groton/New London area in maritime industries. In the 1960s, 80,000 Hispanics migrate to the state, although there is not yet a category for them on the census.
1965	The Immigration Act of 1965 ends the quota system that privileges immigrants whose ethnic composition matched proportionally to those residents already in the United States. This change dramatically shifts Latin American and Asian immigration to the United States and Connecticut sees large increases in the number of Filipinos and Hispanics.
1967–1969	Riots break out across the state over inequalities between minorities and whites. In response to these expressions of deep need, Puerto Rican activists create La Casa de Puerto Rico, which leads to the formation of TAINO Housing and the Hispanic Health Council.
1970	Italians (56,604), Canadians (32,331), and Polish (24,120) are the largest foreign-born groups residing in Connecticut. Vietnamese, Russians, and Cubans arrive as political refugees.

1972	La Escuelita, a bilingual, bicultural school, is founded by Puerto Rican activists in response to the national Bilingual Education Act of 1968.
1975	Dr. Henry C. Lee joins the University of New Haven, where he creates the Forensic Sciences Program. Dr. Lee later achieves worldwide fame for his expertise in the field.
1980	The National Refugee Act of 1980 changes the nature of refugees accepted into the United States from those fleeing communism to those at greatest risk of persecution for their race, ethnicity, nationality, religion, political views, or social group. Catholic Charities, Integrated Refugee & Immigrant Services (IRIS), and other agencies in Connecticut are designated as receiving agencies, and they help settle Bosnian and Afghani refugees in the 1990s, and, in the 2000s, Iraqi, Somali Bantu, and Burmese Karen refugees.
1980	The numbers of Asians and Pacific Islanders on the census reach 18,970, the two largest groups being Asian Indians and Chinese. They are a mix of small business owners, industry and academic specialists, and unskilled laborers.
1980	The Chinese Cultural Center of Hartford is founded.
1981	The state's first black mayor, Thirman Milner, is elected in Hartford.
1985	American Thread Company of Willimantic moves to North Carolina and later to Mexico. Its move marks the end of 150 years of the textile industry's dominance in the region and the tens of thousands of jobs it provided immigrants. At its height in the early twentieth century, it was the largest factory in Connecticut and the largest thread mill in the country. Its move puts thousands of Puerto Ricans in Willimantic out of work.
2001	Eddie Perez is elected Hartford's first Latino mayor.
2006	A city police officer lures 11 Ecuadoran day laborers in Danbury into a van by posing as an employer and turns them over to waiting Immigration and Customs Enforcement agents. The arrest causes outrage in Connecticut communities, and Yale Law School agrees to represent the "Danbury 11." Danbury settles with the Ecuadorans in 2011 and pays them $400,000 in damages, the biggest settlement in the history of civil rights actions regarding day laborers.
2007	The city of New Haven creates a new identity card that allows its residents to obtain bank accounts and city privileges. Anti-immigrant forces decry it as a means for the undocumented to have greater mobility; city officials respond that it helps keep its residents safe.
2010	Connecticut census data shows that of 3,574,097 residents, blacks represent 10.1 percent, American Indians 0.3 percent, Asians 3.8 percent, Latinos/as 13.4 percent (Puerto Ricans 7.1 percent), biracials 2.6 percent, and white non-Hispanics 71.2 percent.

2010	The West Indian Social Club of Hartford, the largest organization of its kind, celebrates 60 years of serving the West Indian community.
2011	Blue Hills, Connecticut, a community that overlaps sections of Hartford and Bloomfield, is listed as the U.S. community with the largest percentage of inhabitants of Jamaican ancestry (23.9 percent).
2011	Connecticut becomes the 13th state to pass an in-state tuition bill, allowing children who grew up in the state but whose parents migrated without documentation, to attend institutions of higher learning at in-state resident tuition rates, rather than at the more costly foreigner rate.

HISTORICAL OVERVIEW

The proper tracking of immigrants has always been a challenge, since the national categories that census takers use have changed over time and are imprecise, as can be seen with terms like "Hispanic" and "black." Are Afro-Brazilian immigrants black? Are they Hispanic? Are Maya-Quiche Indians from Guatemala Hispanics? Are they Native American? On the island today, 75 percent of Puerto Ricans consider themselves white; many have historically answered "white" when given a U.S. Census survey, since the term "Hispanic" (in itself problematic) did not appear until the 1970s. A challenge to tracking immigration within Connecticut is that the state has had more diverse migratory patterns than other states: immigrants come from all parts of the world, and no one group dominates among the foreign-born. While there are pockets of immigrants from countries all over the world—for example, Iranians in Farmington, Ghanaians in Manchester, Lebanese and Cape Verdeans in Waterbury, Israelis in Stamford and West Hartford, and Lithuanians in New London. Because addressing all immigrant groups faithfully would require a book, this chapter will focus more generally on the categories used by the U.S. Census to organize diverse peoples and mention points of interest within the groups. Given the complex phenomenon of immigration in Connecticut and the imprecise census terminology, it is important to consider a combination of census data, historical record, and personal narratives to accurately represent the waves of foreigners who have come to call the Nutmeg State their home.

BLACKS

Africans first came to Connecticut in significant numbers in the 1640s, brought by English and Dutch from the West Indies or in direct trade with western African tribes. By 1730, they represented 700 of a total population of 38,000, and by the Revolutionary War, their numbers were significant enough to send 400 men to fight for the country's freedom as well as their own. Many purchased their freedom from servitude and learned trades, which they passed on to their progeny; eventually, all were released from bondage through the Gradual Emancipation Act of 1784 or the state's 1848 law outlawing all slavery. African Americans in Connecticut also sent two regiments to fight in the Civil War; however, abolitionist's sympathies quickly evaporated after freedom was won, and blacks were forced to live separate lives from European Americans, attending their own churches, schools, and theaters, and even electing their own "African governors" in yearly festivals. These parallel universes existed throughout the nineteenth and early twentieth centuries and were very much in place when new waves of blacks arrived in Connecticut starting in 1910. By 1900, African Americans in Connecticut were overwhelmingly urban, largely because they were denied housing in areas desirable to whites, who had no interest in integration. They were also blocked from good factory and clerical jobs and were limited to manual labor, farming, and domestic work. In the poorer neighborhoods of cities like New Haven and Hartford, West Indians and southern blacks arrived to meet African Americans whose ancestors could be traced back almost 300 years in Connecticut towns. These new blacks came principally to work in tobacco.

Tobacco had been an important crop in Connecticut since Native Americans cultivated it along the banks of the Connecticut River, and it has drawn multiple populations to the state. Although there was an enormous wave of European immigration to the United States during the years between 1890 and 1910, immigration dropped dramatically during World War I, and the Johnson Quota and Johnson-Reed Acts of 1921 and 1924 placed new limits on European immigration. Europeans working in tobacco quickly shifted to factory work to support the war effort. The labor vacuum drew African Americans up from the South, part of the Great Migration of blacks who were escaping Jim Crow segregation and underemployment because of boll weevil infestations of crops and canceled orders for cotton goods due to the war. Blacks also migrated in search of better educational opportunities and better treatment. The African American population in Connecticut doubled between 1910 and 1930, in part because the National League on Urban Coalition worked with tobacco farmers to recruit southern blacks, and other industries followed their example. Many of the first workers were teenage boys brought up by teachers and community members to earn summer employment, who later returned to Connecticut as professional adults. During the Great Migration, 400,000 blacks traveled north between 1916 and 1917, and during those same two years, Hartford's black population rose from 1,500 to 4,000. Southern blacks quickly outnumbered northern ones. New Haven also recorded over 400 foreign-born blacks in 1930, most from the West Indies. The collapse of the sugarcane industry in the West Indies drove blacks of all classes from the Antilles, and many followed traditional migratory paths from the West Indies to Connecticut that were established in the 1600s. In addition,

Jamaicans had a long history of working for the United States, first as "swallow workers" when slavery was abolished and plantations needed farm hands, and later when the U.S. government recruited over 90,000 Jamaicans to work on the Panama Canal.

These migrants and foreigners had no choice but to enter African American neighborhoods—regardless of whether they were welcome in these neighborhoods—since, as blacks, they were excluded from all others. During World War II, new waves of Jamaicans arrived in Connecticut under the Acme Program to fill needed labor shortages, particularly in tobacco. In 1950, they established the West Indian Social Club in Hartford, which continued to be a vital resource for the West Indian communities of the state 60 years later. While the G.I. Bill, the suburbanization of Connecticut companies, and overcrowding in cities led to whites moving to the suburbs in record numbers, restrictive covenants on properties in towns like West Hartford prohibited blacks from buying suburban homes. Blacks were only allowed to live in certain neighborhoods if they were domestics serving whites in those areas. As they were still restricted in educational and job opportunities at mid-century, blacks occupied larger and larger parts of cities whose tax bases continued to dwindle given the increasingly lower socioeconomic status of its residents. The number of blacks in the state doubled again in the 1950s and 1960s, partly because the mechanization of farming in the South put blacks out of work, and because of increasing terrorism by white supremacists in response to the Civil Rights Movement. West Indians continued to move to the state to join their families or to work as migrant farm and tobacco workers. Slowly but surely during the 1970s and 1980s, African Americans in cities like Hartford, Waterbury, Bridgeport, and New Haven assumed leadership roles in federal and local governments, after having learned important leadership skills from their work in the Civil Rights Movement, and benefiting from changes in legislation. In addition, short-lived race riots between 1967 and 1969 brought attention to the fact that young blacks had energy and talent that needed to be channeled and developed. With the support of Affirmative Action, the National Association for the Advancement of Colored People, the Urban League, the Connecticut Commission on Civil Rights, and greater social service networks and active recruitment, increasing numbers of blacks achieved higher education goals, becoming teachers, police officers, firefighters, and government officials.

In the 2010s, people of African descent continue to face challenges in Connecticut regarding public education, de facto segregation, and housing. However, in the 1990s and 2000s, African Americans finally broke out of cities and into the suburbs, moving to Hamden, Bloomfield, and Windsor in significant numbers. They have also heavily influenced the social service and government sectors of certain regional economies. Black immigrants continue to seek out the neighborhoods of African Americans, often to join their family members. Blue Hills,

Connecticut, a community that overlapped sections of Hartford and Bloomfield, was in 2011 ranked as the U.S. community with the largest percentage of inhabitants of Jamaican ancestry (23.9 percent).

While many blacks in the 2010s claim West Indian ancestry, not all are Jamaican. For example, of the 16,000 blacks in Stamford in 2013, over 6,300 claimed West Indian roots, but over 3,000 claimed to speak a language other than English at home. Many of these were black Cubans, Puerto Ricans, or Haitians. Haitians began migrating to the New York area in large numbers shortly after François Duvalier became president in 1957, and eventually spread east to Stamford and Bridgeport. The first waves were skilled professionals and later ones more mixed regarding their socioeconomic status. Numbers of Haitians also worked in Connecticut farms, particularly Franklin's Mushroom Farm.

Small numbers of non-English-speaking blacks who appeared in the 2010 Census were also Africans; currently 3.6 percent of the foreign-born in Connecticut are from the African continent. Many have come to Connecticut from countries as diverse as Uganda and Egypt to work as professionals or to study; others are Somali Bantus brought here as refugees by Catholic Charities in Hartford and IRIS in New Haven. The Bantus tend to work in unskilled labor positions or to further migrate to join Maine's large Bantu population. Most African immigrants are relative newcomers to the state.

Blacks in the 2010 Census numbered 362,296 or 10.1 percent of the state's population. Biracial (black and white) residents numbered 24,786 or 0.7 percent. It is also important to mention that a significant number of Jamaicans live part of each year in Connecticut as migrant workers, returning home each November to tend to their own crops. About 20,000 migrant workers have spent each growing season in the state working on over 400 farms and nurseries. The majority of them are from Jamaica or Puerto Rico, and many have lived part of every year in towns like Windsor or Enfield for over three decades. Smaller numbers are migrant or seasonal workers from Guatemala and Mexico, most of whom migrated into the state in the 1990s and 2000s.

ASIANS

While there was evidence of Chinese moving to Connecticut as early as the 1850s, Asians did not arrive in Connecticut in large numbers until after World War II. Filipinos were among the first to form a significant community. The Philippines was a special case as a sending country because it was a U.S. territory from 1898 until World War II, and, consequently, many citizens began migrating to the West Coast in the first half of the century as farmworkers. Filipinos were heavily recruited by the navy, and well over 250,000 Filipinos served the United States in World War II, only to find themselves stripped of promised benefits by the Congressional Rescission Act of 1946. The War Brides Act of 1945 and Alien Fiancées and Fiancés Act of 1946 did allow Filipino women and children to follow their American husbands to the United States, and these families and Filipinos who continued to work for the navy settled in New London County to serve the Groton Naval Base and the Coast Guard. In the 1970s and 1980s, another wave of Filipinos migrated to Connecticut to help the U.S. medical establishment manage both injuries from the Vietnam War and later from the AIDS epidemic. Filipino nursing training was based on the same model the United States uses, and with their fluency in English, Filipino nurses were in high demand as foreign-born medical personnel. Filipinos represented the second-largest group of foreign-trained physicians in the country after Asian Indians; in fact, the high worldwide demand for Filipino medical expertise was part of the reason that Filipino migration has slowed in the United States in general. In Connecticut, Filipinos, currently the third-largest Asian group in the state, grew in numbers from 5,160 in 1990 to 10,019 in 2000 to 11,998 in 2010. They continued to hold a significant presence in the medical field and in defense and maritime industries in New London County and have recently begun working in the American Indian casinos as well.

Asians currently represented 3.8 percent of the total Connecticut population, although they represented 22 percent of its foreign-born. In 2010, 135,565 people in the state claimed Asian heritage, up from 83,789 in 2000 and 50,698 in 1990. Within this general category, the two largest groups were growing rapidly: Asian Indians increased from 11,112 in 1990 to 26,654 in 2000 to 46,415 in 2010. The Chinese population doubled between 1990 (11,082) and 2000 (21,216) and added another 10,000 residents in the 2010 Census. The greatest concentration of Asians is in Fairfield County, although they are spread out across the state and have created many small ethnic neighborhoods, like Filipinos and Asian Indians in New London County and Chinese in the Mansfield/Storrs area of Tolland County. Asians in Connecticut tend to be more educated than other immigrants and earn higher salaries. There are more females than males (51.5 to 45.6), which is partly due to the common practice of adopting Chinese girls. Asians configure a wide-ranging diversity of cultural, linguistic, and ethnic groups, from Pakistani to Cambodian Hmong to Japanese to Bangladeshi. Asian Indians and Chinese are the highest wage earners, and both groups first got a foothold in the Connecticut economy by opening restaurants, although most adults today are working in technical and medical fields. Many Asian groups have carved out niche markets for themselves in certain service industries: Koreans are principally small business owners, in dry-cleaning and nail salons, in particular. They have well-established networks of support that include internal lending practices to facilitate business ownership. Other successful business owners have been the Pakistanis, who have opened the franchises Edible Arrangements and Sam's Food Stores.

Southeast Asians began to arrive as refugees in the 1970s; Vietnamese, Laotians, and Cambodians were sponsored by church groups and private organizations. While many arrived with advanced degrees, their limited English skills initially led them to jobs in factories like Frito-Lay in Killingly, and in agriculture. The Franklin Mushroom Farm employed hundreds of these newcomers before it moved to Pennsylvania in 2006. The Danielson and Killingly communities in particular have reached out to Southeast Asian refugees, sponsoring many Laotian families. Increasing numbers are also settling in New Britain and Hartford. The most recent Asian group to immigrate to the state is the Burmese ethnic Karen, brought by Catholic Charities as U.S. government refugees. Many have been waiting for resettlement in refugee camps on Thailand's border for over 20 years, after the Burmese military seized their farms and drove them from the country. Taking a plane to Hartford meant not only their first view of a city, but their first ride in a plane. Southeast Asians have struggled with language, health, and educational issues, like most recent immigrants.

While Asians may be statistically more educated and wealthy than other immigrants, this fact is a bit misleading, since the wealth gap between Chinese and Indian professionals and Southeast Asian refugees is profound, and many refugees also suffer from posttraumatic stress disorder and other stress-related diseases. Since Asians are scattered throughout the state, many smaller pockets suffer from linguistic and cultural isolation. Towns must be flexible and proactive to meet their needs. A recent immigrant group to Connecticut offers a good example: Chinese from the provinces of Guangdong and Fujian have moved from New York City to New London County to work in the Mohegan and Pequot Casinos. Homeowners began to rent their houses to dozens of men at once, in a practice called "hotbedding." Citizens in Montville and Norwich have had to work creatively to ensure the health and safety of this newest wave of immigrants because they speak neither Cantonese nor Mandarin, have families to support in New York and in China, have little access to health providers who can understand them, and may sacrifice their own welfare to support families in both New York and China.

More generally, Asians bring diverse cultural practices to the state, which they freely share with others. Indians and Pakistanis have friendly games of cricket at the Windsor Cricket Club, screen Bollywood movies in Bloomfield, and offer dance classes at New Haven's Jewish Community Center. The Asian American Cultural Center at UConn Storrs has regular events for the public, as does the Chinese Cultural Center in Hartford; the Riverfront Dragonboat Festival, for example, has quickly turned into a regional favorite.

Asians are only beginning to enjoy political representation in the state. The Asian Pacific American Affairs Commission was formed in 2008 through an act of the general assembly; it comprises Asian American leaders who advise legislators of the population's needs. Three Asian Americans currently hold state legislative positions: William Tong, the first Asian American Democrat to take a district (147); Tony Hwang, a Fairfield Republican, and Dr. Prasad Srinivasan, a Glastonbury Republican.

LATINOS/AS

The earliest evidence we have of Latin American migration to the United States was shortly after the Revolutionary War, when statesmen and business-men flocked to cities like Philadelphia, New York, and Washington, D.C., to bask in the glow of a successful independence movement and organize for their own. There was a significant trade triangle between Puerto Rico, Cuba and New York, and in the 1820s and 1830s businessmen from all three created alliances and so-cial organizations that facilitated travel, investment, education, and settlement. The effects of this alliance eventually spread east to Connecticut. In 1830, the first student from Latin America enrolled at Yale University; Connecticut's first record of a Puerto Rican businessman buying a house in Bridgeport dated back to 1840. However, while small numbers of Latin Americans and members of Caribbean Spanish colonies continued to move to New England throughout the nineteenth century, they did not migrate to the area in large numbers until the mid-twentieth century.

The first to arrive remains the state's most important Spanish-speaking popu-lation today. The Jones Act of 1917 offered citizenship to Puerto Ricans and the U.S. government a new population to send to World War I. At least 18,000 partici-pated. When men from the continental United States headed for foreign shores to fight World War II, over 50,000 Puerto Ricans accompanied them. When World War II ended, U.S. government officials at last began to focus on their neglected colony, the poorest in the region since the sugarcane industry declined when the Spanish were forced out by Americans in 1898 in the Spanish-American War, and limited U.S. agricultural investment offered too few jobs. Beginning in the late 1940s, operation Bootstrap encouraged the industrialization of the island as well as ex-migration to alleviate poverty. Many of the island residents who chose to leave were offered jobs in factories in cities like Bridgeport and Waterbury and in the textile industry in Willimantic and New Haven. Tens of thousands of citi-zens left the island, many settling in New York and Connecticut during the years between 1946 and 1964, which period is now considered the Puerto Rican Great Migration. Puerto Ricans were also employed by Kofkoff Egg Farms, formerly of Hartford and currently in Lebanon, Connecticut, and many also came to Connect-icut to work in tobacco farming, the first arriving in 1952. Puerto Ricans remain an important presence in migrant farmwork in the 2010s.

In the 1940s and 1950s, factory jobs still paid living wages in the state, and Puerto Ricans in Bridgeport, Hartford, and Waterbury were able to buy homes and educate their children, who often went on to become educators and social workers. Like most newcomers, they established helping agencies like La Casa de Puerto Rico, developed relationships with local parishes and began sports leagues. Relatives sent for extended family, and between chain migration, a steady exodus from New York, and local births, the Puerto Rican population increased rapidly. The 1960 state census put their numbers at 15,247; by 1970, that figure rose to 37,603, and by 1980, 88,361 Puerto Ricans called the state home.

The 1960s brought new challenges to this expanding population. Economic conditions in cities steadily worsened. Factories first began to shut down in the 1960s, such as the brass mills in Waterbury, considered the "Big Three" employers in the region. Puerto Ricans began to organize in the mid-1960s with the help of St. Peter's Catholic Church, holding the first Puerto Rican Day Parade in Connecticut, drawing 20,000 people, an event that also encouraged voter registration. In 1965, they formed the Puerto Rican American Association of Connecticut to promote employment opportunities and voter registration, and the group began to negotiate with Mayor Nicholas Carbone. Blacks and Hispanics were inspired by the Civil Rights Movement, and young people started regional chapters of the Black Panthers and the Young Lords. Frustration over poor treatment by law enforcement and public officials led to riots (or protests) between 1967 and 1969, but, fortunately, an increasingly organized Puerto Rican community rallied to use the event to develop an identity politics that highlighted their unique needs and pushed for long-term change. In 1971, a teacher recruitment program began to operate out of the University of Hartford, and Puerto Ricans began to recruit highly skilled bilingual educators from the island to assist in the implementation of the National Bilingual Education Act of 1968. In 1972, they developed the first successful program in the state. Maria Sanchez, a local business owner and the main peacemaker during the Comanchero Riot, became the first Puerto Rican elected to office, gaining a seat on the Hartford School Board in 1973.

As Connecticut's manufacturing base slowly shrank over the next three decades and the economy increasingly shifted toward a service-sector economy, subsequent generations of islanders who arrived found fewer well-paying jobs, and natives found themselves largely shut out of quality educational systems that would allow them access to the service industries. Large cities also struggled to balance their budgets on immigrant and migrant salaries. Wages for manufacturing and farming began their slow and steady decline relative to inflation, and it is widely acknowledged by economists that those wages have been flat for 30 years. In 1985, the closing of American Thread Company of Willimantic marked the end of 150 years of the textile industry's dominance in the region, and the tens of thousands of jobs it provided newcomers. In the early twentieth century, it was the largest factory in Connecticut and the largest thread mill in the country. Its move put thousands of Puerto Ricans in Willimantic out of work.

What is remarkable about the Puerto Rican community in Connecticut is that it has risen to political power faster than any other migrant or immigrant group in the state's history. By 1991, Puerto Ricans achieved political representation in Hartford commensurate with their proportion of the city's population. In 2001, Eddie Perez became the first Puerto Rican mayor, and current mayor Pedro Cegarra, who was elected in 2010, is also Puerto Rican. Puerto Ricans now dominate the politics in the state capital and hold significant sway in Hartford's city council. They manage a network of helping agencies founded to better working and living conditions for all city residents. Puerto Ricans have grown from a few hundred in the late 1940s to 252,972 in the 2010 state census. Given that there is a total estimated Latino/a population in Connecticut of 479,087, Puerto Ricans, who comprise 52.8 percent of the state's Hispanic population, are the largest Hispanic group by far. Mexicans come in a distant second at 50,658 or 10.6 percent.

Mexicans are recent immigrants in the state. Some were recruited by Nucor Steel Connecticut in Wallingford, and others left New York in search of new opportunities, and some were drawn to work in large nurseries like Prides' Corner Farm in Lebanon or Imperial Nurseries in Granby. Still others work in small factories. Mexicans began arriving in large numbers in the late 1980s, with most originating from Puebla, and later waves from Tlaxcala, Michoacán, and other central Mexican states. Most were first generation and have yet to gain any political influence. They are mostly in urban areas, although they have a strong showing in medium-sized towns like Norwalk, Willimantic, and Wallingford.

Dominicans represent another significant Latino group in Connecticut, currently numbering 26,000. They first migrated to New York City in the mid-1960s after the United States invaded the Dominican Republic and facilitated emigration as a way to avoid social unrest. Many of those who arrived were small business owners from urban areas who transformed Washington Heights' streetscape into a bustling series of bodegas. This expertise translated to Connecticut as business owners reached beyond New York for new markets in cities like Hartford and New Haven. In addition, factory jobs attracted Dominican

Hartford Democratic mayor Eddie Perez celebrates his reelection in downtown Hartford, Connecticut, on November 6, 2007. (AP Photo/George Ruhe)

women to cities like Waterbury and Stamford, although they too became entrepreneurs, opening beauty salons, clothing stores, and child-care businesses.

Peruvians, Ecuadorans, and Brazilians are three South American immigrant groups that are growing so rapidly in the state that all three sending countries have opened consulates. The Peruvian Consulate opened its doors in 2002 and the Brazilian in 2010, both in Hartford. The Ecuadoran Consulate was established in New Haven in 2008.

Peruvians first migrated to Connecticut in the 1950s and 1960s. Most came to the state because a U.S. company went to the Ancash Mountains north of Lima to hire some local farmers, who then brought their families. The 2010 Census counted 16,424 Peruvians in the state but the consulate estimated their numbers to be closer to 28,000–30,000. Peruvians have principally settled in the cities of Hartford, Bridgeport, Norwalk, Stamford, and New Haven, and continue to recreate religious and social activities from their home country during the year in events open to the public. Peruvian Americans in the state are a mix of unskilled laborers in cleaning and construction and professionals in accounting, general medicine, odontology, teaching, and engineering. The latter have formed the Association of Peruvian-American Professionals, which has been a significant force in organizing the community and promoting cultural and professional events.

Ecuadorans have been arriving to the Nutmeg State since the 1970s, almost all from the Oriente or Eastern region, from an area called Morona-Santiago. About 80 percent of the population works in construction, cleaning, landscaping, and manual and seasonal labor. Ecuadorans have settled principally in Danbury and New Haven, and number between 23,700 and 25,000.

In 2000, Connecticut was home to 5 percent of all Brazilians in the United States, with many spilling over from the 17 percent in Massachusetts and the 10 percent in New York. They predominantly work in service occupations and construction and are concentrated in Danbury and in the Parkville section of Hartford. They have their own social outreach agency, Aliança Brasileira, and a consular office in Hartford.

Migration from Europe

While the bulk of immigrants arriving in Connecticut before World War II were Europeans fleeing poverty, contemporary migration from Europe is decreasing relative to that of other geographic regions. About 28.5 percent of Connecticut's immigrants are European, but they represent an older, shrinking population; Latin Americans and Caribbean immigrants currently represent 42 percent of the state's foreign-born, and 22 percent stem from Asia. A consideration of the state's European ethnic heritage reveals that the largest ancestries are Italian, followed by Irish, English, German, French/French Canadian, and Polish. While families continue to migrate to join relatives, particularly the Polish, centered in New Britain with an estimated 8.3 percent of the state's population, this trend is ever-diminishing. A complex series of factors have contributed to this decline, among them the elimination of quotas in the Immigration Act of 1965 that privileged immigrants whose ethnic family members were already in the United States. Increasing economic opportunities, improved social welfare programs, and the rise of the European Union have allowed more in-migration in Europe. Lastly, most generations born in the United States have only tenuous connections to distant relatives abroad, unlike newer immigrant groups.

NOTABLE FIGURES

GUIDO CALABRESI (1932–)

Judge and professor Guido Calabresi came to New Haven as a boy when his parents fled Italian fascism during World War II. He joined the Yale Law School faculty in 1959, where he became the youngest full professor in its history. He served as dean from 1985 to 1994, and is now Sterling professor emeritus. Former students include Supreme Court justices Clarence Thomas, Sonia Sotomayor, and Samuel Alito. Calabresi is currently a senior judge of the U.S. Court of Appeals for the Second Circuit, nominated by President Bill Clinton in 1994. A legal scholar, he is considered one of the founders of the field of law and economics and has published 4 books and over 100 articles.

HENRY LEE (1938–)

Dr. Henry C. Lee was born in China and raised in Taiwan. He is an expert in forensic science who has become famous for his consulting on over 8,000 law enforcement cases worldwide. His cases include the trials of O. J. Simpson and William Kennedy Smith and investigations into the deaths of Jon Benet Ramsey, Chandra Levy, and White House counsel Vincent Foster, and the kidnapping of Elizabeth Smart. He founded the Forensic Sciences Program at the University of New Haven in 1975, where he directs the Forensic Science and Research Center. He is currently the chief emeritus for Scientific Services for the State of Connecticut and has served as chief criminalist from 1979 to 2000. Dr. Lee has been the recipient of numerous medals and awards and honorary degrees. He has co-authored over 40 books and has his own television series *Trace Evidence*.

AMII OMARA-OTUNNU (1952–)

Amii Omara-Otunnu is a professor of History at the UConn. He also holds the UNESCO Chair in Human Rights and is a coordinator of UNESCO Chairs in

Human Rights in the region that comprises Israel, Western Europe, and North America. He is the founder and executive director of the Institute of Comparative Human Rights at UConn and is executive director of the UConn-African National Congress Partnership. Professor Omara-Otunnu earned degrees from Harvard University, the London School of Economics, and the University of Oxford. In June 2005, the World Affairs Council gave professor Omara-Otunnu *The Luminary Award*, which was created to honor those who have had a significant impact on global affairs.

JACQUES PÉPIN (1935–)

Jacques Pépin is an internationally renowned chef who first began cooking as an adolescent in his mother's restaurant. After working in Paris for heads of state, he came to the United States in 1959 to work at the restaurant Le Pavillon in New York City. He was then hired by Howard Johnson to develop food lines for his hotel restaurants, and after earning two degrees at Columbia University, Pépin wrote his first of over 20 cooking books. Pépin has appeared in a number of PBS series on cuisine, including one with Julia Child called *Julia and Jacques Cooking at Home* and *Jacques Pépin: Fast Food My Way*. He currently writes for *Food & Wine* magazine, teaches at Boston University, and is a dean at the French Culinary Institute in New York City. Pépin resides in Madison, Connecticut, and is a frequent guest on the *Faith Middleton Show* of NPR Connecticut.

BARBARA RICHARDS (1945–)

Dr. Barbara Richards, a former Yale professor and now professor of sociology at Housatonic Community College (HCC), and community activist, was instrumental in the passage of Connecticut's 2011 In-State Tuition Bill. Dr. Richards spent years as a full-time community organizer in New Haven, focusing on low-income and immigrant neighborhoods, before joining HCC in 1992. In addition to serving on the New Haven Board of Aldermen, she was elected by the faculty of Connecticut's 12 community colleges to the Standing Advisory Committee (SAC) of the Board of Governors for Higher Education in Connecticut. Through her work for the SAC, Dr. Richards learned to affect statewide policy issues regarding higher education; as a community college professor, she witnessed firsthand the difficulties the undocumented had in trying to afford an education. Consequently, in 2004, she began to use her community-organizing skills to change state law, which regarded long-term in-state undocumented residents as foreigners. She proposed in-state tuition rates for the children of undocumented immigrants, and worked to organize community and legislative support for six years until House Bill 6390, An Act Concerning Access to Postsecondary Education, finally passed in 2011.

Maria Sánchez (1926–1989)

Maria Sánchez (born Maria Clemencia Colón) migrated to Hartford from Puerto Rico in 1954. She became a neighborhood advocate for housing, bilingual education, and general welfare issues, a role which led her to become the first Puerto Rican to be elected to public office in Hartford. She used her small business, a newsstand store, as a meeting ground for political activism and community advocacy. Sánchez organized voter registration drives and helped establish La Casa de Puerto Rico, The Spanish American Merchants Association, and the Puerto Rican Day State Parade, among others. Her sustained fight for bilingual education led to the opening of the Ann Street School and the formation of a bilingual teacher's corp. She was a member of the Democratic Town Committee in 1969 when the Comancheros riot broke out, and she worked with city officials and the community to resolve tensions and seek long-term solutions to social unrest. Sánchez was elected to Hartford's school board in 1973, a position she held for 16 years; this position gave her the distinction of being the first Puerto Rican in office. She was also the first to be elected to the Connecticut General Assembly in 1988. The Maria Sánchez Elementary School in Hartford is dedicated to her memory.

Igor Sikorsky (1889–1972)

Igor Sikorsky was a pioneer in aviation who designed and flew the first helicopter and the first multi-engine plane. Sikorsky fled Bolshevik Russia in 1919 and eventually landed in Bridgeport, Connecticut. In 1923, a group of friends and students financed his first company, the Sikorsky Aero Engineering Company, where he built the twin-engine Sikorsky S-38 amphibian and Sikorsky S-42 "Flying Clippers." The ability of these planes to land on water allowed for the rapid development of commercial air transportation across the ocean. Launched in 1939, his helicopter VS-300 brought to life an improved version of a machine he had first imagined in his childhood, designed with rubber bands in 1901 as an 11-year-old. Sikorsky was a deeply religious man who was proud of the life-saving abilities of his helicopter. Winner of dozens of awards in the United States, France, England, and Russia, he was inducted into the Aviation Hall of Fame in 1968. He continued to work as an engineering consultant with Sikorsky until he died at age 83 in 1972.

BIBLIOGRAPHY

African Americans in Connecticut: Civil War to Civil Rights. Video. Co-production of the Connecticut Humanities Council and Connecticut Public Television, executive producers Bruce Fraser and Larry Rifkin, 1998.

Asian Pacific American Affairs Commission, Connecticut. www.cga.ct.gov/asianamerican
/commissioners.html. Accessed March 3, 2014.

Capps, Randolph, Stephen Zuckerman, Everett Henderson, Allison Cook, and Karina
Fortuny. *Immigrants in Connecticut: Labor Market Experiences and Health Care
Access*. Report of The Urban Institute, commissioned by Democracy Works,
Hartford, 2005.

City-Data.com. www.city-data.com. Accessed March 3, 2014.

Colonial Wars in Connecticut. www.colonialwarsct.org. Accessed March 3, 2014.

Connecticut History Online. www.cthistoryonline.org. Accessed March 3, 2014.

Connecticut Indian Tribes. http://www.accessgenealogy.com/native/connecticut/index.htm.
Accessed March 3, 2014.

Connecticut's Heritage Gateway. www.ctheritage.org. Accessed March 3, 2014.

Connecticut State Data Center. http://ctsdc.uconn.edu/index.html. Accessed March
3, 2014.

Connecticut State Library Website. www.cslib.org. Accessed March 3, 2014.

Cruz, José. *Identity and Power: Puerto Rican Politics and the Challenge of Ethnicity*. Philadelphia: Temple University Press, 1998.

Dr. Henry Lee Website. www.drhenrylee.com. Accessed March 3, 2014.

Fowler, William Chauncey. *The Historical Status of the Negro in Connecticut. A Paper Read
before the New Haven Colony Historical Society*. Charleston, SC: Walker, Evans &
Cogswell Co., 1901.

Fraser, Bruce. *The Land of Steady Habits: A Brief History of Connecticut*. Hartford: The Connecticut Historical Commission, 1986.

Gabany Guerrero, Tricia. "Connecticut." In Mark Overmyer-Velazquez, ed. *Latino America:
A State by State Encyclopedia*. Westport, CT: Greenwood Press, 2008, pp. 125–44.

Glasser, Ruth. *Aquí Me Quedo: Puerto Ricans in Connecticut*. Hartford: Connecticut Humanities Council, 1997.

Hartford's West Indian Social Club Website. www.westindiansocialclubinc.org. Accessed
March 3, 2014.

Hunter, Kathleen. *African-Americans in Connecticut*. Hartford, CT: State Department of Education, 2001.

Igor Sikorsky Archives. www.sikorskyarchives.com. Accessed March 3, 2014.

Jacques Pepin Website. http://www.jacquespepin.com. Accessed March 3, 2014.

Jamaican Ancestry Maps. www.epodunk.com. Accessed March 3, 2014.

Liebovitz, Liel, and Matthew Miller. *Fortunate Sons: The 120 Chinese Boys Who Came to
America, Went to School, and Revolutionized an Ancient Civilization*. New York: W.W.
Norton and Co., 2011.

Purkayastha, Bandana, ed. *Asian Americans in Connecticut Census 2000: Race, Ethnicity,
Household and Family*. Asian American Studies Institute Research Paper Series, vol.
3, no. 1. Storrs, University of Connecticut, 2004.

Rodríguez, Clara. "Puerto Ricans: Immigrants and Migrants, a Historical Perspective." Americans All, A National Education Program Publication, n.d. http://www.americansall
.com/resources/ethnic-and-cultural/9.9_Puerto_Ricans_Immigrants_and_Migrants
.pdf. Accessed March 3, 2014.

Roth, David, ed. *Connecticut History and Culture: An Historical Overview and Resource Guide for Teachers*. Hartford: The Connecticut Historical Commission, 1985.

Slavery in Connecticut. www.slavenorth.com/connecticut.htm. Accessed March 3, 2014.

State of Connecticut Official Website. www.ct.gov. Accessed March 3, 2014.

Swift, Mike. "The State's Asian Boom." August 9, 2005. www.courant.com/archives. Accessed March 3. 2014.

Torres, Andres, ed. *Latinos in New England*. Philadelphia: Temple University Press, 2006.

U.S. Census Bureau. http://factfinder2.census.gov. Accessed March 3, 2104.

Warner, Robert Austin. *New Haven Negroes: A Social History*. New York: Arno Press and the New York Times, 1940, 1968.

Windham Textile and History Museum. www.millmuseum.org. Accessed March 3, 2014.

Wood, Carlos. "Igor Sikorsky." In *Memorial Tributes, National Academy of Engineers*, Vol. 1. Washington, DC: National Academy Press, 1979. http://www.nap.edu/openbook.php?record_id=578&page=253. Accessed July 31, 2014.

8

DELAWARE

William P. Kladky

CHRONOLOGY

Pre-16th Century	Delaware is inhabited by several groups of Native Americans, including the Lenni-Lenape in the north and the Nanticoke in the south.
16th Century	Delaware's coastline is first explored by Europeans.
1609	Henry Hudson, sailing under the Dutch flag, is usually credited with Delaware's discovery.
1610	Captain Samuel Argall of Virginia names Delaware for his colony's governor, Thomas West, baron De La Warr.
1631	Dutch traders found Zwaanendael, located near Lewes, and establish an economically oriented colony.
1698	Holy Trinity Church is erected in Wilmington. It is now the oldest Protestant Church in the United States still in regular use.
1704	The representatives of the province of Pennsylvania and the lower counties begin separate meetings, one at Philadelphia, and the other at New Castle. William Penn and his heirs remain proprietors of both and appoint the same person as head of both.
1777 (August)	During the American Revolutionary War, General Sir William Howe leads a British army through Delaware en route to a victory at the Battle of Brandywine and the capture of the city of Philadelphia.
1777 (September 3)	The only true Revolutionary War engagement in Delaware is the Battle of Cooch's Bridge, fought at Cooch's Bridge in New Castle County.

1787 (December 7)   Delaware becomes the first state to ratify the Constitution of the United States and thus becomes known as "The First State."

1802   Éleuthère Irénée du Pont establishes a gunpowder mill near Wilmington. The mill begins Delaware's chemical industry, which has drawn many in-migrants and immigrants as workers.

1813   The oldest black church in the country is chartered in Delaware by the former slave, Peter Spencer, as the "Union Church of Africans." It is now known as the African Union Methodist Protestant (AUMP) Church.

1860   The U.S. Census finds that 91.7 percent of Delaware's black population, some 20,000 persons, is free.

1861 (January 3)   Despite being a slave state, Delaware votes against secession.

1897   Delaware's fourth constitution, which is still in effect, is established.

1912   The chemical industry built by the du Pont family is divided by a federal antitrust suit, but the company still is sufficiently powerful to buy control of the General Motors Corporation in the 1920s. Employment increases as a result.

1920s and 1930s   As a result of educational reforms and large-scale infrastructure improvements, Delaware's agricultural and commercial sectors boom and migrants arrive to help with the harvest.

1950s   Wilmington's population consists of a mix of the early Swedish, Finnish, Dutch, Quaker, and non-Quaker English, supplemented by French, Irish, and Scotch individuals.

1950s and 1960s   The state's population jumps over 40 percent because of a net migration of 122,000.

1971   Passage of the Coastal Zone Act (outlawing heavy industrial development and protecting wetlands and habitats) leads to Sussex County becoming a major vacationland, with a population boom and increase in migration.

1981   As a result of the state's usury laws being revised by the legislature, many large New York banks set up their legal subsidiaries in Delaware (especially in the Wilmington area).

1990s   The state's immigrant population grows by 136 percent; the largest immigrant groups are Mexicans (35 percent) and Cubans (3 percent). Other groups—Dominicans, Guatemalans, and other immigrants from Latin American countries—make up about 25 percent of this new population. As in the past, most of this immigration is concentrated in New Castle County, which is now home to approximately 70 percent of Latinos in the state.

2003   The "DART First State" public transportation system is named "Most Outstanding Public Transportation System" by the American Public Transportation Association.

2003 (September 18)   Hurricane Isabel results in declaration of 1 of only 12 presidential disaster declarations for the state.

2006	Rallies are held in Delaware and several other states for the national "Day without an Immigrant" protests.
2009 (January 20)	Delaware U.S. senator Joseph F. Biden (Democrat) becomes the 47th U.S. vice president.
2010	1,829 foreigners are naturalized in Delaware. The majority come from India (339), Mexico (127), People's Republic of China (104), and Kenya (78).
2012	Senate Bill 169 would allow undocumented students to pay tuition and fees at the in-state, resident rate at public higher education institutions and would permit all those qualified to apply for state scholarships and grants. The bill died in committee for lack of support.

HISTORICAL OVERVIEW

BEGINNINGS

Transportation has always been the most important factor in Delaware's history and land use. Where people live and what they do for a living is initially determined by rivers, then rails, later roads, and, presently, technology. The Delaware River brought the original European settlers to Delaware. For more than three centuries, it has served as a waterway connecting many Delaware towns to each other and to Philadelphia, as well as bringing many immigrants to the state.

Before the Europeans arrived, Delaware was inhabited by several American Indian tribes, including the Lenni-Lenape in the north and the Nanticoke and Assateague in the south. Henry Hudson, an English navigator for the Dutch East India Company, is credited with Delaware's discovery. During 1614–1620, Dutch ships explored the Delaware River area, calling it the "South River" (the Hudson being the "North River"). The West India Company—wielding powers that made it virtually an extension of the government—authorized settlement focusing on economic exploitation rather than colonization. To this end, Giles Hosset and Jacob Jansen purchased land from the American Indians between Cape Henlopen and Bombay Hook, which they registered on July 15, 1630. Because of a misunderstanding or jealousy over the rich fur trade, a first settlement at Lewes was massacred by the American Indians in 1632. Aside from one other clash, relations between the Dutch traders and the American Indians were peaceful.

Seeing a commercial opening, the Swedish South Company began settlement operations in the mid-1630s as the Thirty Years' War was convulsing Europe. The Swedish captain Peter Minuit purchased land from the American Indians from Bombay Hook to the Schuylkill River in Pennsylvania. In 1638, a Swedish expedition landed at "Paradise" in Delaware Bay, either at Swanendael/Zwaanendael (now Lewes) or further north. Subsequently, Peter Minuit purchased a deed from the American Indian chiefs. A fort was built and was named after Sweden's young

Workers at the Delaware Hosiery Mill in Wilmington, May 1910. (Library of Congress)

queen, Christina. The Minquas Kill was first called the Elbe, but was changed to Christina Kill, now the Christina River, flowing into the Delaware River at Wilmington.

Slaves were soon brought to the area. The first African in Delaware was Anthony, captured in 1638. Some Dutch settlers owned slaves as servants and farmworkers and the English continued this practice. Plantations needing slaves developed in Delaware's south. In the northern section, before 1700, some slaves were freed. At this early time, the split between north and south Delaware had yet to develop fully, but the "Tidewater" slave-based agricultural base of southern settlement was an indication of things to come.

In 1640, Swedish colonization expeditions began, with the first permanent group arriving in 1641, and subsequently erecting a church. Dutch and Finns joined with the Swedes as the first permanent settlers. Swedish settlement activity quickened when the Crown learned that the English had established a settlement at Varkens Kill (Salem, New Jersey) and a trading post on the Schuylkill. While the Swedes were as interested as the Dutch in the area's commercial potential, the Swedes were also more motivated to establish homes.

The European rivalry between the Dutch and the Swedes also impacted the fledgling Delaware settlements. In the early 1650s, the Dutch, firmly ensconced at New Amsterdam (New York), began to reexplore the "South River." A Dutch captain erected a fort at Sand Hook (New Castle) to control the river traffic, naming it Fort Casimir. Incidentally, he purchased the exact same land from the American Indians that they had previously sold the Swedes. The Dutch fortified the fort with settlers from New Jersey. Responding at last to the situation, the Swedish crown sent Johan Printz, who anchored at Fort Casimir on May 21, 1654, and was victorious without bloodshed.

By 1655, the Dutch were back in control, and Fort Christina was renamed Fort Casimir. After this, some of the earliest settlers included a boat of unlucky Finns who set sail before the change in power and now found themselves in enemy territory. However, the Finns were accommodated and stayed. Because of the difficulties in settlement, with disease and frequent mishaps, the Dutch pursued a policy of cooperating with the Swedish settlers, even encouraging many to settle. The population then was estimated at about 1,000. It consisted mostly of Swedes and Dutch, with a few English, Finns, and French.

But the English were also interested in Delaware. In 1664, two English war vessels took the fort at New Amstel (now known as New Castle), and sent some black slaves to the English in Maryland and Virginia. This action began a rush of English settlers from Virginia, Maryland, New Jersey, New York, and Europe. In 1672, the European war between the Dutch and England and France led to the temporary Dutch recapture of the Delaware settlements. While this control lasted only a year, the governor's formation of district courts at Upland (Chester), New Castle, and the Whorekill (Lewes) established a precedent for the county division of the future state.

With the end of the Anglo-Dutch War in 1674, the English regained the territory and established the Delaware Colony. In 1681, William Penn arrived to take possession of his province, which was formerly that of the Duke of York. Penn found Swedes, Dutch, English, Scottish, and French Protestants. Quakers soon arrived to join them. At Penn's first assembly in 1682, the eager Delaware members asked for union with Penn's province. Penn changed the names of various entities, including Sussex and Kent counties.

Because pirates, such as Blackbeard (Edward Teach), Henry Avery, William Kidd, and others, plundered the Atlantic and Delaware River coasts during 1680–1700, the colonies on the river attracted few additional settlers. This common victimhood did not, however, cause the Delaware and Pennsylvania counties to get along any better. The minor strife between the three lower counties (Delaware) and Pennsylvania intensified when Penn appointed officers for the counties without consultation. Penn commissioned a separate governor in 1692 after Delawareans left the general assembly in protest. Incompetent government by the Quakers was also an important factor in the split. In 1704, the first separate assembly was held at New Castle. The counties then conducted their affairs as a Crown Colony and were included without a name under English administrative law.

During the first half of the eighteenth century, the counties developed rapidly. Internal improvements were made, agriculture and fishery thrived, and the population increased, all enabled and supported by the strong English legal system. The economic and social movements of the early eighteenth century signaled the state's geographical division. In the north, Wilmington's active port and many jobs drew newcomers from the surrounding farms and from Europe. The southern section continued its agricultural pursuits. Immigrants to the state continued to be English, Scotch-Irish, and Welsh.

During this period, many shiploads of immigrants were unloaded at the port of New Castle. Interestingly, a number of the state's early teachers were indentured servants, such as Charles Thomson, who became the secretary to the Continental Congress. In the 1720s, it was apparently a common expression to say, "Let us go and buy a School Master" when a ship arrived. At least somewhat discerning, the assembly did forbid importing convicts from English jails or disabled paupers from poorhouses.

Originally, Willington, with 20 houses in 1735, Wilmington was renamed after William Penn's friend Spencer Compton, the Earl of Wilmington (1673–1743). The town benefited from its proximity to New Castle, for immigrants newly arrived at that port sought lodging and employment in Wilmington. On their way to Philadelphia, many stayed in Wilmington. This two-step path to Wilmington was especially true of Irish Protestant immigrants in the mid-1750s.

Despite the continuing immigration, towns in the colony remained very small. A 1756 report stated that there were 100 houses at Dover, 100 at Lewes, 250 at New Castle, and 260 at Wilmington.

From Colony to State

Under British control, the colony thrived during the latter part of the colonial period. The population increased dramatically, due both to immigration and a surplus of births over deaths. The colony continued to be aggregated with Pennsylvania for many practical and analytic purposes. In 1776, when Delaware joined the other 12 colonies in declaring independence from Britain, the new state's first constitution contained a declaration against slavery and a 1787 law freed any slave brought into the state, which had entered the union in December 1787. Delaware was one of the few states with such a provision. During the American Revolutionary War, only one small battle was fought in Delaware. British troops occupied Wilmington shortly after the nearby Battle of Brandywine on September 11, 1777. The British remained until 1778 when they left the Philadelphia area.

The first federal census in 1790 discovered that Delaware had a population of 59,096, consisting of 46,310 whites, 3,899 free blacks, and 8,887 black slaves. An indication of the colony's farming emphasis, Sussex County—the southernmost in the state—had the most population, with 800 more people than New Castle County and 1,500 more than Kent County. Most free blacks lived in Kent County, with the slaves primarily in agricultural Sussex County.

During the nineteenth century, the fishing industry flourished in Delaware, primarily in the southern section, where it drew settlers. Between 1750 and 1850, the state—especially Wilmington—was the locus of a great shipbuilding industry. This industry started when the Dutch and Swedish colonists built boats for coastline trading along the many navigable streams flowing into the Delaware River and the Chesapeake Bay. In part due to its many useful sources of water power, Delaware had the largest concentration of mill industries in the colonies. Christiana Bridge was the major shipping point for millers, and Newport sent large shipments of grain to Philadelphia. The 1780–1810 period was characterized by significant commercial development, with Wilmington specializing in the manufacture of flour, paper, carriages, furniture, iron, and cotton and Brandywine specializing in the grain trade.

The textile industry began to flourish in earnest at this time, pioneered by the Irish exiles Rowan and Jacob Broom. This industrial development led naturally to a growth in the colony's towns, as the new firms sought workers. Immigrants passed the word to their compatriots in their home country, inspiring additional immigration.

Wilmington's population doubled from 1,200 to 2,500 between 1776 and 1800. This growth was due to several factors. Largely because of the draw of the new industries and their employment opportunities, there had been a new wave of Irish immigration to Wilmington. Famines and political oppression in Ireland played a crucial "push" role. Additional immigrants came to the city because of an uprising in Santo Domingo, Dominican Republic, producing an influx of French. In 1793, refugees fleeing Philadelphia's yellow fever epidemic came to Delaware. Possibly because of its lower numbers and lower density, Wilmington had avoided this plague.

Irish immigration was extremely important during this time. Immigrating passengers often arrived at the Delaware ports of Newcastle (now New Castle) and Wilmington. During the colonial period, these ports had become stopovers for ongoing traffic to Philadelphia, especially after Pennsylvania put duties on incoming servants and established strict quarantine regulations for immigrants. Passengers instead chose Delaware for initial debarkation, going overland or by separate tender to their final destination. The port of Newcastle thus stayed twined with Philadelphia into the eighteenth century. For example, Irish ships advertised for Philadelphia (and other destinations) "by way of" Delaware for some time (Bric 2001).

By 1812, Wilmington's population hit 5,000, spurring the founding of libraries, schools, and factories. The town's shipping was hampered by the War of 1812 embargo. Shortly afterward, though, Wilmington's status as an employment destination was revived by the development of regular steamboat service to Philadelphia. New industries began to develop and the population increased. In the 1830s, Wilmington benefited from manufacturing and shipping development.

This industrial diversification happened just in time. The 1825 opening of the Erie Canal and the advent of railroads led to the decline in Delaware's flour milling industry, which could not effectively compete with western growers and millers. With so many different industries, state employment recovered, and the trend in population growth was barely affected.

During this period, a frequently used land migration route was from Philadelphia to Wilmington and then to Baltimore. There was very little migration from New York and New Jersey to Delaware, but many people went back and forth between Virginia, Delaware, Pennsylvania, and Maryland. The state's proximity to Philadelphia always inspired travel and resettlement; the gentry, for example, sent their sons there for education.

As of 1850, Delaware consisted of mostly native-born, with only 5.7 percent foreign-born; the state's population in 1850 was 91,532, including 18,073 free blacks and 2,290 black slaves. Of the state's population, 42,780 were in New Castle County, 22,816 in Kent County, and 25,093 in Sussex County. Milford on the Mispillion River and 15 miles from Chesapeake Bay was the state's fourth-largest town; by the 1850s, it specialized in shipping and shipbuilding. When railroads undermined its water shipping business, Milford's fruit-drying and iron manufacturers made up the difference.

The completion of the Delaware railroad in 1856, largely through the west center of the state, led to the creation of many villages and to the various logging ventures and other commercial developments, thus further increasing the population and enriching the southern farmlands. While the state had drawn Irish immigrants to its industrial and powder mills since the 1790s, the great Irish migration to the United States after the potato famine in the 1840s and 1850s significantly impacted Delaware. Many Irish went to Wilmington.

THE CIVIL WAR PERIOD

Delaware did not share significantly in the 1830–1860 Irish, German, and British immigration waves that mostly impacted large cities. By 1860, the state had 8.2 percent foreign-born, indicating a small immigration growth. This figure remained lower than for the nation as a whole, which had a 13.2 percent foreign-born rate at that time.

Although Delaware voted for pro-slavery candidate John C. Breckinridge (1821–1875) rather than for Abraham Lincoln (1809–1865) in the 1860 presidential election, the state did not secede. In 1860, there were only 2,000 slaves among the 22,000 blacks in the state. While Delaware was the sole slavery state where a black was legally considered free unless proven to the contrary and many slaves were freed, economic advantage played a significant role in defining freedom. Because Delaware had such a short growing season, growers calculated that it was less expensive to hire farmworkers at low wages than to maintain slaves for the entire year. Manumission also became a crafty way to get rid of slaves who were too old or sick to work. Delaware also was the home of many abolitionists who bravely fought against slavery.

In 1862, the University of Delaware got its true start with the passage of the national Morrill Act, which gave federal land to the states. The university subsequently expanded exponentially, drawing students from the United States and foreign countries. As the university expanded, so did Newark, where it was located.

Due to the prosperity Wilmington enjoyed during the Civil War, city merchants and manufacturers pushed Wilmington's residential boundaries farther westward in the form of large homes along tree-lined streets. This movement was spurred by the first horsecar line, which was initiated in 1864 along Delaware Avenue. The industrial expansion attracted workers from Italy and Poland, as well as the Ukraine.

Large-scale industrial development and transportation expansion were concentrated in Delaware's north. By 1868, Wilmington was producing more iron ships than the rest of the nation altogether. It was also rated first in gunpowder production and second in carriages and leather. In 1866, Wilmington became one of the first cities in the nation to install an electrically powered trolley system, which branched to the west and north. While this system first benefited the city of 42,000, it was later to have a mixed suburban impact. The significant German influx in the 1870s and 1880s grew large enough to prompt antagonism, mostly because of the additional skilled workers it brought into competition for the state's skilled jobs.

In the late nineteenth century, a comparative backwardness in education and farming techniques led to a decline in population in southern Delaware as other regions became more competitive and productive. The northern part of the state continued to expand. This expansion was aided by the national "good roads" movement in the early 1900s, especially in New Castle County.

1900 TO THE PRESENT

Many early nineteenth-century immigrants to the state settled in Wilmington. In 1900, the state's foreign-born percentage was 8.9, still significantly lower than the nation's 13.2 percent. But in Wilmington, in 1900, some 14 percent of its 76,508 residents were foreign-born. Some of these immigrants had been attracted by the DuPont Company's expanding industrial chemical industry, which also produced several related industries, including explosives manufacture.

By 1900, there were 4,870 Irish in Wilmington, comprising only 6 percent of its population but 38 percent of all of the city's foreign-born population, which reached its peak in 1910. The 1910 Census discovered that 15.6 percent of the city's 87,411 residents were immigrants. The older immigrants consisted of 3,000 Irish, 2,000 Germans, and 1,000 English, but were joined by 2,000 Italians, as well as a number of Poles and Russian Jews. The latest groups had been drawn by post-1880s railroad and highway construction and pushed by European wars of different types. Many Polish farmers were displaced, when their country was carved up by its powerful neighbors—Russia, Prussia, and Austria—and Russian Jews fled czarist pogroms. World War I was a great stimulus to Wilmington's blast furnaces and shipyards. Skilled workers, artisans, and the semiskilled poured into the city.

The state's development was further enhanced by the building of the DuPont Road (now U.S. 13 and U.S. 113) by Coleman du Pont (1863–1930), at his own expense in 1917. Coupled with the development of a statewide system of highways funded by the Federal Aid Highway Act in 1916, the numbers of cars and trucks in Delaware skyrocketed in the 1920s and 1930s. Delaware's agricultural and commercial sectors boomed: chickens in Sussex County and peaches, tomatoes, soybeans, and potatoes throughout the state. Migrants soon arrived to help in the fields with the harvest.

After World War I, the state continued through educational reform and large-scale infrastructure improvements. For example, Dover's population doubled between 1920 and 1950 as the expansion of government brought industry and new residents. As of 1950, over 25,000 of the state's 43,598 blacks lived in urban areas.

Despite its diversity, Wilmington's population continued its decline from its peak of 120,000 in the 1920s. Its decline was typical of other smaller mid-Atlantic cities because its manufactures were geared toward an agrarian rather than an industrial economy. But as capital goods became more valuable, steel companies, for example, changed from manufacturing steel rails to structural steel, and the small size of the city became a disadvantage in marketing to other manufacturers.

In 1950, Wilmington consisted of a mix of the early Swedish, Finnish, Dutch, Quaker, and non-Quaker English, supplemented by French, Irish, and Scotch since the mid-eighteenth century. Its population continued to decline due to urban renewal projects in the 1950s and 1960s and the riots and civil unrest that followed the 1968 assassination of the Reverend Martin Luther King Jr. An influx of Puerto Ricans (American citizens) in the 1950s and 1960s was not enough to stabilize the city's population decline.

Wilmington's population problems did not typify the state, which had its largest jump in population—slightly more than 40 percent—between 1950 and 1960. Part of this was a net gain from the migration of 122,000 people during the 1940–1970 period. While business fared well in Delaware, the state lagged behind in many social welfare indicators in the mid-1990s. Delaware's rates of teenage pregnancy and infant mortality were among the highest in the country, and its welfare benefits were lower than any nearby state except West Virginia. Other problems in the 1990s included housing shortages, urban sprawl, and pollution.

The 2000 Census found that Delaware's population increased a significant 17.6 percent from 1990, making it the 14th fastest-growing state. Symbolic of the changes in the state, Ruth Ann Minner was elected Delaware's first woman governor in 2001. She was once a receptionist. The 2010 U.S. Census found that Delaware had a population of 897,934—68.9 percent white, 21.4 percent black, 0.5 percent American Indian and Alaska Native, 3.2 percent Asian, 0.1 percent Native Hawaiian and other Pacific Islander, 3.4 percent from other races, and 2.7 percent from two or more races. Latinos/as comprised 8.2 percent of the 2010 population.

In 2011, Delaware had 57 incorporated municipalities, with populations ranging from 100 to 73,500 people. There were 13 incorporated areas in New Castle County, 18 in Kent County, 24 in Sussex County, and 2 areas were bi-county. Still the state's largest city, Wilmington continued to be a city of extreme contrasts. While the corporate part throve, the city had one of the highest per capita rates of HIV infection in the United States, with disproportionate rates of infection among African American males.

TOPICAL ESSAYS

Du Pont Road and Coastal Development

Post-war Delaware had been impacted significantly by highway development. While completed in 1917, the DuPont Road, which crossed the state at about Interstate 95, had a mixed legacy after 1945. Despite the significant economic development that had occurred since its opening, the road also contributed to the decline of the state's largest city.

The road's development was enabled by the state legislature's granting of eminent domain power to the Boulevard Commission, which was unsuccessfully fought by affected farmers. The DuPont Highway anchored what became a road system that made population expansion and suburban-exurban development possible. While Delaware continued to be an attractive immigration destination, and this stemmed in part from this economic development, Wilmington had also lost population and businesses to the rapidly growing suburban areas of New Castle County. Wilmington saw a steady decrease in industry, business, and population after World War II. A 1972 study by the University of Delaware concluded that the highway contributed to Wilmington's decline but to New Castle County's boom.

The statewide highway system also enabled the development and expansion of Delaware's coastal area. From its 1872 founding by the Rehoboth Beach Camp-Meeting Association of the Methodist Episcopal Church, Rehoboth Beach became a popular spot for out-of-state and international visitors. The American private car revolution in the 1950s and the extensive road improvements of that decade were critical elements in the development of Delaware's coastal area, as was the passage in 1971 of the state's Coastal Zone Act, which outlawed heavy industrial development in the area and protected wetlands and habitats. As a result, the coastal areas have flourished as a major vacationland and have led to population expansion and economic development in Sussex County.

Rehoboth's summer employment opportunities draw many workers from Eastern European countries and Asia. Also, since the 1990s, Rehoboth has drawn many visitors who have decided to stay and retire. Retirement communities have begun to sprout where there was grassland before. The population has increased accordingly.

Delaware Becomes America's Corporate Headquarters

Over one-fifth of all active U.S. corporations listed in Moody's *Manual* were chartered in Delaware. The Delaware Corporation Law, passed in 1899, and subsequently amended, had company-friendly provisions that have proven powerful draws. In the law's first 30 years, 84,146 businesses were incorporated in the state, resulting in 20–40 percent of all state revenue. Delaware had solidified its financial position by retaining a Court of Chancery, which had developed an expertise in stockholder and other legal suits affecting large corporations. Most other states have merged common law cases into other courts.

Wilmington became a national financial center for the credit card industry, largely due to regulations revised in 1981. The Financial Center Development Act of 1981, among other provisions, eliminated the usury laws enacted by most states, thereby removing the cap on interest rates that banks may legally charge customers. In 1986, the state adopted legislation targeted at attracting international finance and insurance companies. To profit from this, many major credit card issuers are headquartered in Wilmington.

In another move that also has attracted corporations, the Delaware legislature enacted a law in 1988 that required a would-be acquirer to capture 85 percent of a Delaware chartered corporation's stock in a single transaction or wait three years before proceeding. This law strengthened Delaware's position as a safe haven for corporate charters during an especially turbulent time filled with hostile takeovers. As a result, the city was the corporate domicile of more than 50 percent of the publicly traded companies in the United States and over 60 percent of the Fortune 500. This corporate friendliness has resulted in northern Delaware becoming a financial employment center, fueling population growth and immigration.

2003 Gay Rights Ordinance

To some extent, Delaware has been friendly to same-sex issues for some time. In 1826, the death penalty for "sodomy" was changed to a maximum of three years' solitary confinement, which was the most lenient "sodomy" prison sentence in the United States for over 100 years.

Rehoboth Beach's cultural reputation as a gay-friendly resort has led to a surge in same-sex couples as visitors and residents. This trend was enhanced when Delaware passed its gay marriage law in 2009. The state's first move in this direction was on May 19, 2003, when a sexual orientation antidiscrimination ordinance was passed for Rehoboth Beach. On May 11, 2011, the Civil Union and Equality Act of 2011 was signed by the governor. Civil unions were legal for same-gender Delawareans as of January 2012. Possibly reflecting this friendliness to same-sex relationships, the 2010 U.S. Census found that Delaware had a slightly higher percentage of same-sex households (between 0.96 and 1.75 percent) than the nation's 0.95 percent. This was also higher than other mid-Atlantic states.

In-Migration Spurs Rapid Growth

The 2010 U.S. Census found that Delaware was growing rapidly, primarily in the south. The state's population grew 14.6 percent (eighth highest in the nation) from 783,600 in 2000 to 897,934 in 2010. Most growth came in southern New Castle County and in Kent and Sussex counties, with Kent and Sussex each up between 25 and 30 percent. The state's 2010 population density of 460.8 persons per square mile also ranked eighth. The largest cities were Wilmington, 70,851; Dover, 36,047; and Newark, 31,454. Aside from Wilmington's 2.4 percent decline, the other cities gained: Dover, 12.2 percent; Newark, 10.2 percent; and Middletown, 206.3 percent. The most populous county was New Castle with 538,479 people, up 7.6 percent since 2000. Sussex's population of 197,145 represented a 25.9 percent increase, and Kent County's population increased 28.1 percent to 162,310.

Delaware has continued to attract in-migrants and immigrants because of its bright economic situation. In the 1990s, for example, the state lost 2.9 percent of its industrial employment, but this was less than any of its neighboring states. In 2008–2009, Delaware's in-migration primarily came from New Jersey

(1,975), Maryland (1,489), and Pennsylvania (1,384), with 201 people from foreign countries. Out-migration mainly went to Florida (445), North Carolina (379), and Georgia (310). From 2009 through 2010, in-migration changed to Pennsylvania (7,318), Maryland (4,969), and New York (4,251), with foreigners numbering 3,027. Out-migration was to Maryland (8,340), Pennsylvania (4,608), and Florida (3,099).

Historically, Delaware has drawn migrants from other states at steady but not spectacular rates. Between 1970 and 1990, there was a net migration of only about 25,000 and most settled in New Castle County. The waves of southern black migration during the century brought poor, uneducated blacks to Delaware and other mid-Atlantic states. Puerto Ricans and highly trained whites also were attracted by the state's vibrant industry and economy. Blacks and Latinos largely went to Wilmington, and whites went to New Castle County's suburbs.

Net domestic migration to the state between 1990 and 1998 totaled 29,000, while net international migration totaled 8,000. In 1998, Delaware admitted 1,063 foreign immigrants. The state continued to get a trickle of immigrants. In 2000, the state's 5.7 foreign-born percentage was still well below the nation's 11.1 percent. Between 1990 and 1998, the state's overall population increased 11.6 percent. In the period between 1995 and 2000, 101,461 people moved into the state and 84,078 moved out, for a net gain of 17,383, of whom 2,679 were age 65 or over.

Primarily as a consequence of this in-migration, Delaware's population is projected to grow by more than 225,000 between 2010 and 2040, an increase of 25 percent, reaching a projected population of more than 1.1 million, according to the Delaware Population Consortium. Sussex County is expected to see the largest percentage increase in population—57 percent—and to grow by almost 112,000 to 308,290 people. Kent County's population is projected to reach 204,952 by 2040, gaining nearly 45,000 for an increase of 28 percent. New Castle County is expected to grow by 13 percent over the same period, adding almost 69,000 to reach a 2040 population of 606,881.

A State of People from Out of State

Compared to national averages, the state's residents were more likely to stay or to come from a different state. Delaware had a higher than national average percentage of households that did not move, 85.9 percent and 84.6 percent, respectively, and a lower than national average percentage of movement within the same state, 10.1 percent and 12.6 percent, respectively. For moves from different states, Delaware's percentage was higher than the national average, 3.5 percent and 2.2 percent, respectively. In 2010, of the Delaware's population of 889,812 people, 90,001 moved within the state, with 30,759 inbound and 30,055 outbound, for a net change of 704.

Delaware has had a much lower percentage of population born in the state than in the country as a whole, with 48.3 percent of the state's population in-born compared to 60 percent for the nation. Only 11 states had a lower percentage in 2000. The predominant states of birth for current Delaware residents were Pennsylvania, 107,044; Maryland, 50,294; New York, 35,052; New Jersey, 31,437; and Virginia, 14,593. Some 56, 806 were born outside of the country.

Delaware's 44,898 foreign-born comprised 5.7 percent of the state's population, which was over twice the 22,275, or 3.3 percent, in 1990. The United Kingdom, Germany, India, Italy, and Canada were the main places of origin. Adding to the population increase has been the growth in naturalized citizens. In 2010, 1,829 were naturalized in Delaware. The most came from India (339), Mexico (127), People's Republic of China (104), Mexico (87), and Kenya (78).

THE NEW FACE OF IMMIGRATION TO DELAWARE

From 1990 to 2010, the state's population increased mostly due to a significant wave of immigration. Reflecting a national trend, most immigrants were Latinos. In the 1990s, the state's immigrant population grew by 136 percent. The largest immigrant groups were Puerto Ricans (37 percent), who are U.S. citizens; Mexicans (35 percent); and Cubans (3 percent). Other groups—Dominicans, Guatemalans, and other immigrants from Latin American countries—amounted to about 25 percent. As in the past, most of this immigration was concentrated in New Castle County, which is now home to approximately 70 percent of the Latinos/as in the state.

However, in a reversal of previous trends, Sussex County actually had the fastest recent Latino growth rate. This trend is credited to the employment growth in the county, especially in the agricultural sector. A recent study found that immigration of Puerto Ricans to the United States was directly responsive to economic conditions. Additionally, undocumented immigrants, particularly Mexicans, have also been immigrating to Delaware. Estimates of this group vary considerably from 13,500 to 35,000.

This new immigration has created various pressures on the state's social and economic infrastructure, and its social fabric. For example, according to Kids Count, a national and state-by-state effort to track the status of children in the United States, Latinos have the highest school dropout rates and comprise 14 percent of all dropouts in Delaware.

Response to undocumented immigration in Delaware has been mixed. In Sussex County, undocumented workers have been an important part of the workforce in the poultry, construction, and service industries. But when the influx has been significant, it has reawakened nativism. Georgetown conducted a raid of immigrant residences in 2005, probably responding to a large increase in Guatemalan and Mexican immigrants. Fifty-five men, all undocumented, were arrested. In Elsmere, where the Latino population tripled from 11.7 percent in 1990 (700) to about 33 percent in 2000, a law was proposed in 2005 that would have police ticketing anyone who could not provide proof of U.S. residency within 72 hours and would fine landlords and employers $1,000 for each undocumented person they housed or employed.

Alternatively, Delaware has been trying to join the 12 states that have made college accessible regardless of one's immigration status. In 2012, Senate Bill 169 was introduced into the legislature. The bill would have allowed undocumented students to pay tuition and fees at the in-state, resident rate at public higher education institutions, and it would have permitted all qualified individuals to apply for state scholarships and grants. The bill failed to pass. Also, the state has witnessed protests against proposed federal laws that would make undocumented immigration a felony and threaten with criminal penalties anyone who offered assistance to an undocumented immigrant. In 2006, rallies were held in Delaware and several other states for the national "Day without an Immigrant" protest. It remains to be seen if the state can successfully acclimate these new arrivals to become Delawareans, or whether they will—like so many immigrants in the past, such as those arriving at New Castle in the eighteenth century—transit through Delaware en route to other more accommodating homes.

NOTABLE GROUPS

La Esperanza

La Esperanza is a community group based in Sussex County, Delaware, that provides resources and referrals to Latino/a immigrants in education, family services, and refugee services. The group is faith based and was founded by Carmelite nuns in 1996 and local Latino/a leaders. The group helps immigrants from Mexico and Guatemala, in particular. The organization's community outreach partners with local businesses to aid economic integration and its website provides news and resources regarding immigration policy (La Esperanza homepage, n.d.).

BIBLIOGRAPHY

Bric, M. J. "Patterns of Irish Emigration to America, 1783–1800." *Eire-Ireland* 36, no.1/2 (2001): 10–28.

Brown, R. H. *Historical Geography of the United States*. New York: Harcourt, Brace and Co., 1948.

City-data.com. "Delaware—Migration." 2012. http://www.city-data.com/states/Delaware-Migration.html. Accessed March 4, 2014.

Delaware Economic Development Office. *Data Book, 2012*. Dover: State of Delaware, 2012.

Delaware Office of State Planning Coordination. *News and Updates: 2010 Census Finds 897,934 Persons in Delaware*. Dover: State of Delaware, 2012.

Delaware Office of State Planning Coordination. *News and Updates: Delaware Population Projected to Grow by 25 Percent by 2040*. Dover: State of Delaware, 2012.

Eckman, J. *Delaware: A Guide to the First State*. New York: Hastings House, 1955.

La Esperanza, La Esperanza homepage, n.d., http://www.laesperanza.org/. Accessed July 31, 2014.

Find-the-data.org. "Compare Delaware Migration." 2010. http://state-migration.findthe data.org/d/a/Delaware#. Accessed March 4, 2014.

Gibson, C., and K. Jung. *Historical Census Statistics on the Foreign-Born Population: 1850 to 2000*. Population Division, Working Paper No. 81. Washington, DC: U.S. Census Bureau, 2006.

Gibson, C., and K. Jung. *Historical Census Statistics on Population Totals by Race, 1790 to 1990, and by Hispanic Origin, 1970 to 1990, for the United States, Regions, Divisions, and States*. Population Division, Working Paper No. 76. Washington, DC: U.S. Census Bureau, 2002.

Gonzalez, G. "Immigration and Delaware." *PA Times* 31, no. 1 (2008): 5.

Harty, K. "Illegal Immigration: The Fight in Delaware." *The News Journal*, 2006. http://www.delawareonline.com/article/20060820/NEWS/608200370/Illegal-Immigration-fight-Delaware. Accessed March 4, 2014.

Hoefer, M., N. Rytina, and B. C. Baker. *Estimates of the Unauthorized Immigrant Population Residing in the United States: January 2010*. Washington, DC: Office of Immigration Statistics, Policy Directorate, U.S. Department of Homeland Security, 2011.

Hoffecker, C. E. *Delaware: A Bicentennial History*. New York: W. W. Norton, 1977.

Kolchin, P. *American Slavery: 1619–1877*. New York: Hill and Wang, 1994.

Leepson, M. "Middle Atlantic States: Fight against Stagnation." *Editorial Research Reports 1980* (1981): 245–64.

Lemon, J. T. "The Agricultural Practices of National Groups in Eighteenth-Century Southeastern Pennsylvania." In D. Ward, ed. *Geographic Perspectives on America's Past: Readings on the Historical Geography of the United States*. New York: Oxford University Press, 1979, pp. 129–47.

Livingston, G. "U.S. Birth Rate Decline Linked to Recession." 2010. http://www.pewsocial trends.org/2010/04/06/us-birth-rate-decline-linked-to-recession/. Accessed March 4, 2014.

Lofquist, D. *Same-Sex Couple Households*. American Community Survey Briefs, ACSBR/10-03. Washington, DC: U.S. Census Bureau, 2011.

Mackun, P., and S. Wilson. *Population Distribution and Change: 2000 to 2010*. 2010 Census Briefs. Washington, DC: U.S. Census Bureau, 2011.

Malone, Nolan, Kaarl F. Baluja, Joseph M. Costanzo, and Cynthia J. Davis. *The Foreign-Born Population: 2000*. Census 2000 Brief, C2KBR-34. Washington, DC: U.S. Census Bureau, 2003.

Molloy, R., C. L. Smith, and A. Wozniak. "Internal Migration in the United States." *Journal of Economic Perspectives* 25, no. 3 (2011): 173–96.

Passel, J.S., and D. Cohn. "Unauthorized Immigrant Population: National and State Trends, 2010." Pew Hispanic Center, 2011. http://pewhispanic.org/files/reports/133 .pdf. Accessed March 4, 2014.

Perry, M.J., and P.J. Mackun. *Population Change and Distribution, 1990–2000*. Census 2000 Brief, C2KBR01–2. Washington, DC: U.S. Census Bureau, 2001.

Pew Research Center. "U.S. Birth Rate Decline Linked to Recession." 2010. http://www .pewsocialtrends.org/2010/04/06/us-birth-rate-decline-linked-to-recession/. Accessed March 4, 2014.

Pieklo, J. "States Advance Tuition Equity for Undocumented Students." Care 2 News Network, 2012. http://uspolitics.einnews.com/article/92314308. Accessed March 4, 2014.

Procter, M., and B. Matuszeski. *Gritty Cities*. Philadelphia: Temple University Press, 1978.

Proximity One. "State-to-State Geographic Mobility: Migration Flows in 2009." 2012. http://proximityone.com/statemigration09.htm. Accessed March 4, 2014.

Ren, P. "Lifetime Mobility in the United States: 2010." American Community Survey Briefs, ACSBR10–07. Washington, DC: U.S. Census Bureau, 2011.

Rodriguez, H. "Review of Emotional Bridges to Puerto Rico: Migration, Return Migration, and the Struggles of Incorporation by Elizabeth M. Aranda." *Contemporary Sociology* 37, no. 1 (2008): 29–30.

Semple, E.C., and C.F. Jones. *American History and Its Geographic Conditions*. New York: Russell & Russell, 1933.

Towardequality.org. "Timeline of LGBT History in Delaware." 2012. http://www.toward equality.org/timeline.html. Accessed March 4, 2014.

Urbina, I. "National Briefing Mid-Atlantic: Protest over Immigration Proposal." *New York Times*, February 15, 2006, 20.

U.S. Census Bureau. *2010 American Community Survey 1-Year Estimates: State-to-State Migration Flows, 2010*. Washington, DC: U.S. Census Bureau, 2011.

U.S. Census Bureau. *Cumulative Estimates of the Components of Resident Population Change for Counties: April 1, 2010 to July 1, 2011*. Washington, DC: U.S. Census Bureau, 2011.

U.S. Census Bureau. *State of Residence in 2000 by State of Birth: 2000*. Census 2000 Brief, PHC-T38. Washington, DC: U.S. Census Bureau, 2005.

U.S. Department of Homeland Security. "Estimates of the Unauthorized Immigrant Population Residing in the United States: 1990 to 2000." 2003. http://www.dhs.gov /xlibrary/assets/ statistics/publications/Ill_Report_1211.pdf. Accessed March 4, 2014.

Ward, D. "The Internal Spatial Differentiation of Immigrant Residential Districts." In D. Ward, ed. *Geographic Perspectives on America's Past: Readings on the Historical Geography of the United States*. New York: Oxford University Press, 1979, pp. 335–43.

Woodard, C. *American Nations: A History of the Eleven Rival Regional Cultures of North America*. New York: Viking, 2011.

9

FLORIDA

Jessica L. Lavariega-Monforti

CHRONOLOGY

1513	Arrival of Europeans to Florida, beginning with the Spanish explorer Juan Ponce de León y Figueroa who explores and names the area; Florida is inhabited by an estimated 350,000 people belonging to a wide array of tribes.
1564–1565	René Goulaine de Laudonnière founds Fort Caroline in what is now Jacksonville in the 1560s as a haven for French Huguenots seeking religious freedom.
1565	The first documented immigrants, Spanish missionaries, arrive in St. Augustine, led by Pedro Menéndez de Avilés.
1565 (September 20)	Menéndez de Avilés attacks Fort Caroline, killing most of the French Huguenot soldiers defending it.
1567	Dominique de Gourgues recaptures the Fort Caroline settlement from the Spanish and slaughters all the Spanish defenders.
1586	Sir Francis Drake, an English sea captain and sometime pirate, pillages and burns St. Augustine.
1655	By this time, Catholic missionaries convert 26,000 members of indigenous communities.
1656	The Timucuan Rebellion against the Spaniards occurs in St. Augustine.
1659	A measles epidemic kills 10,000 indigenous and many soldiers of the garrison at St. Augustine.
1738	Black freemen settle in a buffer community north of St. Augustine, called Gracia Real de Santa Teresa de Mosé, the first free slave settlement in North America.

1740	The British and their colonies wage war repeatedly against the Spanish and capture St. Augustine.
1763	Spain trades Florida to Great Britain for control of Havana, Cuba. Almost the entire Spanish population leaves, taking along most of the remaining indigenous population to Cuba.
1763	The British divide the territory into East Florida and West Florida; East Florida is the site of the largest single importation of white settlers in the colonial period.
1763	The East Florida's non–American Indian population hovers at about 3,000.
1767	Creek Indians migrate into Florida and form the Seminole tribe.
1767	Dr. Andrew Turnbull, a Scottish doctor turned British consul, transplants around 1,500 indentured settlers from southern Europe to grow hemp, sugarcane, and indigo and to produce rum.
1771	Governor John Moultrie writes to the English Board of Trade that "[i]t has been a practice for a good while past, for negroes to run away from their Masters, and get into the Indian towns, from whence it proved very difficult to get them back." When British government officials pressure the Seminoles to return runaway slaves, they reply that they had "merely given hungry people food, and invited the slaveholders to catch the runaways themselves."
1775	Beginning of the arrival of thousands of loyalist refugees from the rebellious American colonies.
1776	Turnbull's colony collapses and the survivors flee to safety with the British authorities in St. Augustine.
1783	The Treaty of Paris ends the Revolutionary War and returns all of Florida to Spanish control, but without specifying the boundaries.
1783	Many loyalist refugees from the American colonies are deported to the Bahamas, Jamaica, and other islands of the British West Indies.
1790	Between 1790 and 1804, a few Americans from the southern states and British planters returning from the Bahamas enter Florida.
1804	The Spanish officially close East Florida to American immigration, but settlers continue to cross the Georgia–Florida border.
1810	Parts of West Florida are annexed by the proclamation of President James Madison, who claims the region as part of the Louisiana Purchase.
1810 (September 23)	British settlers, resentful of Spanish rule, rebel and establish the free and independent Republic of West Florida, which lasts for 90 days.
1812	The United States annexes the Mobile District of West Florida to the Mississippi Territory.
1817	The East Florida's non–American Indian population hovers at about 5,000.
1822	Florida becomes a territory of the United States.
1845 (March 3)	Florida is admitted to the Union as the 27th U.S. state.

1858	The Seminole Wars force all but a few Native Americans out of Florida.
1868	The state's Bureau of Immigration is established by the state constitution; the Bureau continues until 1891.
1870s	Dennis Eagan, Florida's commissioner of Lands and Immigration, engages in an advertisement campaign designed to recruit new settlers and counteract negative information that is circulating about the state.
1874	Immigration reports begin to be collected and transmitted through the Statistics Bureau of the Treasury Department.
1900	The state's African American population numbers more than 200,000, which comprises 44 percent of the total population.
1908	The organized movement to attract foreigners comes to a clear halt; an immigration convention is held by Governor Napoleon B. Broward. The governor invites all southern governors, southern mayors, newspaper editors, and other notable figures, but none of the other governors make an appearance; the convention fails to promote immigration and actually turns into an anti-immigration meeting.
1910	The total foreign-born population of the state doubles. The major population subgroups include Cubans (15,656), Germans (7,488), English (7,414), and Italians (7,413), along with appreciable numbers of Finns, Turks, Chinese, Russians, and Greeks.
1910	Anglo Democrats proceed to pass Jim Crow legislation establishing racial segregation in public facilities and transportation.
1920	Florida's population reaches 1 million.
1920–1925	Outside speculators, easy credit access for buyers, and rapidly appreciating property values lead to soaring housing prices and massive population growth in Florida.
1921–1928	A series of major hurricanes devastate Florida, contributing to economic slowdowns.
1933	Under the act of March 3, 1933, and an executive order effective August 10, 1933, the Immigration and Naturalization Service (INS) is formed.
1940	The INS is transferred from the Department of Labor to the Department of Justice.
1940s–1950s	Florida is transformed as air conditioning and the interstate highway system encourage emigration from northern states.
1940	The Jewish population in Florida reaches about 25,000; about 40,000 blacks have left Florida by this point.
1959	In-migration of Cuban exile begins.
1960–1962	James Baker, the headmaster of Havana's elite Ruston Academy, enlists Miami's archdiocese in Operation Pedro Pan, an airlift to help get children out of Cuba. When the October 1962 Cuban missile crisis terminates all flights out of Cuba, Operation Pedro Pan ends,

	but, by then, over 14,000 Cuban boys and girls aged 6 to 17 had been brought to the United States.
1961 (April 17)	U.S.-supported Cuban exiles unsuccessfully invade Cuba at the Bay of Pigs.
1962	All commercial flights from Havana to Miami are suspended.
1963	The first wave of Haitian refugees leaving Duvalier's rule arrive in South Florida; they request political asylum, which is summarily rejected by the INS and the boat is sent back to Haiti.
1965	Cuban refugee airlift begins; Cubans are admitted under special quotas. President Lyndon Johnson signs the Immigration Act, which eliminates race, creed, and nationality as a basis for admission to the United States. As soon as the old quota system is removed, non-European immigration levels rise.
1966 (November 2)	President Johnson signs into law the Cuban Adjustment Act. Any Cubans who have reached U.S. territory since January 1, 1959, will be eligible for permanent residency after two years of residency in the United States. Nearly 123,000 Cubans are able to apply immediately.
1980	About 125,000 Cubans arrive in Miami with the Mariel boatlift; 25,000 Haitians arrive as well, but the majority do not qualify for asylum.
1980	Responding to a wave of Cuban refugees coming to the United States on the *Freedom Flotilla*, the Refugee Act systematizes processes for refugees and codifies asylum status.
1982 (January 15)	The INS deports a Cuban émigré for the first time since the 1959 Revolution, saying that Andrés Rodríguez Hernández had not sufficiently proved a well-founded fear of persecution.
1990	About 154,000 Asian immigrants reside in the state.
1991	President George H. W. Bush begins using facilities at the U.S. Naval Air Station in Guantánamo, Cuba, to detain Haitians who try to flee to the United States as a result of the military coup in Haiti.
1994	The Balsero migration leads to 50,000 Cuban in-migrants.
1994	About 84,000 Colombian-origin people live in Miami-Dade County.
1999 (November 25)	On Thanksgiving Day, six-year-old Elián González is found in the Straits of Florida clinging to an inner tube. His mother has drowned, as do 11 others in the raft, as they are fleeing Cuba. Over the next six months, U.S. relations with Cuba are tested during the bitter struggle over returning the child to his father in Cuba. Cuban exiles in Miami lead the battle to keep Elián in the United States.
2000 (June 28)	Elián González and his family return to Cuba.
2003 (March 1)	The Homeland Security Act of 2002 transfers the service and benefit functions of the U.S. INS into the Department of Homeland Security and the U.S. Citizenship and Immigration Services (USCIS).
2009	Florida loses 1 percent of its population after being hit hard by the economic downturn.

HISTORICAL OVERVIEW

Despite the ebbs and flows in immigration since the 1500s, immigration on a large scale is really more of a contemporary phenomenon in the Sunshine State. For example, between 1890 and 1960, the proportion of foreign-born population ranged from 5.9 percent (1890) to 5.5 percent (1960). Between 1960 and 1990, however, Florida's immigrant population grew from 5.5 percent to 13 percent of total state population; this represented 525 percent growth in 30 years. Further, in 1950, Florida was ranked 20th among the states in population; 60 years later, it was ranked third. Where did this growth come from? Without question, Florida became the destination for many retirees from the Northeast, Midwest, and Canada, due to low tax rates and warm climate. However, a far larger proportion of newcomers have arrived from Latin American and Caribbean countries like Cuba, Haiti, Nicaragua, and Puerto Rico (sometimes via New York). Additionally, the Cuban Revolution of 1959 led to a large wave of Cuban immigration into South Florida, which transformed Miami into a major center of commerce, finance, and transportation for all of Latin America.

A Cuban soldier stands by a refugee ship at the small port of Mariel, Cuba, on April 23, 1980, as the refugees aboard wait to sail for the United States, where they hope to start new lives. Cuban president Fidel Castro agreed to let the Cubans leave the communist island aboard boats that took them to Florida. (AP Photo/Jacques Langevin)

CONTEMPORARY IMMIGRATION: CUBANS AND HAITIANS

Since 1960, there have been six major waves of immigration from Cuba to Florida, each of which has brought a unique character to the state. The early waves of Cuban exiles were of a business/professional class, including government employees, many of whom had very high levels of education. Subsequent waves have included the families of earlier arrivals. In the spring of 1980, a major immigration event was sparked as 125,000 Cubans fled Cuba by boat from the port of Mariel. These boats arrived on Miami shores, leaving the city and the state of Florida in a position of needing to process this extraordinarily large number of people within a short period of time. Tent cities were erected in the Orange Bowl and under Interstate 95, causing increasing tension in the city and among exiles being held inside the camp. These immigrants were known for the city they left behind and were called Marielitos (although the term is considered pejorative).

In the post-1980 period, immigration from Cuba to Florida slowed until the mid-1990s. During this time, Cuba was going through a "special period"—a time of extreme economic hardship as a result of losing a major trade partner with the fall of the Soviet Union. At the same time, the United States was experiencing economic growth and Florida was growing at an even faster rate. Given the long history of in-migration to the Sunshine State from Cuba and the presence of an established Cuban American community, along with economic and political upheaval in Cuba, some Cubans attempted to leave their homeland, crossing the Florida Straits by boat or raft. These rafters were known as *balseros*, and at the height of this movement there were 300–400 people arriving in Florida by raft each day without legal immigration documents. According to U.S. immigration law, Cubans represented a special case because of the political climate in their country of origin. In 1966, legislation was passed that gave Cubans special rights to enter the United States, adjusted their status to legal permanent resident, and sponsored family members abroad for immigration purposes (see the Cuban Adjustment Act of 1966). Unlike other immigrants, Cubans were not required to enter the United States at a port of entry. Also, unlike other immigrants, being a public charge did not make a Cuban ineligible to become a permanent resident.

While immigration has been deemed a federal issue since the 1930s, requiring congressional legislation to make changes, states have taken an active role in dealing with the more local consequences of immigration. For example, after years of complaints that the federal government was not doing enough, Florida sued the federal government for failing to stop undocumented immigration and tried to get governmental funds to help with the costs of undocumented immigration. Although the lawsuit was unsuccessful, the Justice Department released $18 million to Florida to assist in the Florida Immigration Initiative. In May 1996, Governor Lawton Chiles and Attorney General Janet Reno launched the Florida Immigration Initiative—a series of federal/state efforts intended to combat undocumented, uncontrolled migration into Florida. These efforts included removing criminal aliens from Florida's streets, prisons, and jails; the creation of an airport court at Miami International to expedite the removal of aliens who attempted to enter the airport; increased staffing for the Citizenship USA office to help with naturalization cases in Florida; along with other provisions. This legislation dictated that undocumented reentries were to be handled by federal prosecutors after data were released from Florida law enforcement agencies.

Further, in October 1998, Governor Chiles and INS commissioner Doris Meissner signed a landmark mass migration agreement—another first between a state and the federal government—which detailed how the federal government would assume primary responsibility for onshore response operations if migrants evaded interdiction at sea and arrived undocumented on Florida's shores. The agreement also provided for reimbursement to be made to state and local governments for any requested assistance to the federal operations. The Chiles Administration also established the Florida/Haiti Initiative in 1996 to promote democracy and help improve the health, education, government, and economy of the Caribbean nation. The initiative was designed to serve as a catalyst to mobilize material and human resources for a wide variety of needs in Haiti. Finally, in 1999, Florida requested compensation of $56 million from the federal government under the federal State Criminal Alien Assistance Program toward the incarceration of undocumented immigrants. It was subsequently determined that Florida taxpayers were responsible for $34.4 million, as the federal government only paid $21.6 million in compensation.

The federal government acted in 1996 as well. To end the influx of *balseros* from Cuban shores, President Bill Clinton and Fidel Castro agreed to tighten travel restrictions and used military intervention (via coast guard/navy) to stem the flow of rafters leaving Cuba and arriving in U.S. waters. For example, the "wet foot, dry foot" policy was the name given to a consequence of the 1995 revision of the Cuban Adjustment Act of 1966. With this policy, the Clinton administration came to an agreement with Cuba that it would stop admitting people found at sea. Since then, a Cuban caught (interdicted) on the waters between the two nations (i.e., with "wet feet") would summarily be sent home or to a third country. One who made it to shore ("dry feet") got a chance to remain in the United States, and later would qualify for expedited "legal permanent resident" status and U.S. citizenship.

In the 2010s, about 50 percent of the Cuban-origin population in the United States resides in south Florida. Cuban immigrants and their progeny have transformed the sociopolitical landscape in Florida. Some have even argued that reverse assimilation has taken place across the state as a result of their arrival and incorporation into society. Spanish is widely spoken in the southern part of the state, and Cuban American politicians have been elected to local and statewide positions. Latino immigration to the state goes beyond Cubans, however. By 1990, the proportions of Mexicans, Puerto Rican, and other Hispanics all grew more rapidly than did the Cuban exile community in the state. These various communities also settled in areas beyond Miami-Dade. For example, large populations of Puerto Ricans can be found in the Tampa and Orlando metropolitan areas, while Mexican and Central American communities have emerged in the central part of the state. There are also now sizeable Colombian, Nicaraguan, Argentinean, and Dominican populations living in Florida.

Emigration from Haiti, and other Caribbean states, continues as well. As Haiti descended into chaos following the collapse of the Duvalier dictatorship in the late 1980s, Haitians began arriving in the United States in large numbers. Up until 1990, the foreign-born population from Haiti ranked behind most foreign-born groups in terms of size. In 2008, however, the Haitian-born population was the fourth-largest immigrant group from the Caribbean basin following the foreign-born from Cuba (974,657), the Dominican Republic (771,910), and Jamaica (636,589). Florida had the largest number of foreign-born residents from Haiti (247,991, or 46.4 percent of the total Haitian-born population) in 2008, followed by New York (128,750, or 24.1 percent). Despite the political unrest in Haiti, the U.S. government had historically considered Haitians to be economic immigrants rather than political refugees like Cubans. In 1981, the Reagan administration established a policy of interdiction in the Haitian case; this involved the stopping and searching of certain vessels suspected of transporting undocumented Haitians. Many Haitians on their way to Florida by boat (without legal immigration documents) have been detained and returned to their homeland; the wet foot/dry foot policy has not applied to this group of immigrants. For example, from 1981 to 1990, over 22,000 Haitians were interdicted at sea. In 1994, after the political unrest in Haiti, the Clinton administration made a slight change in the interdiction and repatriation policies of the preceding Reagan and Bush administrations—undocumented Haitians who were interdicted could be interviewed as potential refugees. However, this change lasted only a few weeks.

In 1997, federal legislation was passed to address Haitian immigration in the form of the Haitian Refugee Immigration Fairness Act (HRIFA). The act enabled Haitians who filed asylum claims or who were paroled into the United States prior to December 31, 1995 to adjust to legal permanent residence. Over 15,000 Haitians adjusted under HRIFA. However, the discrepancy between the treatment of

Haitian and Cuban immigrants continued. Some have indicated that the differential treatment was the result of racism because most Haitians were racially black while that was not the case for most Cubans. This debate continues in the 2010s; nevertheless, significant Haitian communities have emerged and Haitian politicians have had successful bids in local elections in South Florida, where the Haitian community was concentrated.

AFRICAN AMERICANS: NATIVES AND MIGRANTS

While there is no doubt that Florida's population has changed markedly through in-migration of new groups, out-migration has had an impact as well. For instance, 40,000 African Americans moved north in earlier decades of the twentieth century during the Great Migration. By 1960, African Americans in Florida numbered 880,186, but represented only 18 percent of the state's population. This was a much smaller proportion than in 1900 when, according to the Census Bureau, they comprised 44 percent of the state's population, but numbered 231,209. Since the nineteenth century, educated black middle classes have developed in numerous cities across the state. By their leadership in Florida and other states, African Americans gained national support and passage of the Civil Rights Act of 1964 and Voting Rights Act of 1965, which protected voting for all citizens. In the years after such legislation, African Americans and other minorities in the South began to vote and participate more fully in the political process. However, the African Americans struggle for civil rights was occurring at the same time (1950s–1970s) as massive in-migration from Cuba, other parts of Latin America and the Caribbean, and northern U.S. states. This confluence of events led to relatively high tensions across the African American, Latino, and white ethnic communities in Florida; some would argue this ethnic and racial tension has continued, in a lesser form, today, and perhaps feeds into contemporary anti-immigrant sentiment.

ASIAN IMMIGRANTS AND JEWISH MIGRANTS TO THE SUNSHINE STATE

In addition to Latino and white ethnic immigrants and African American migrants, Florida has also experienced significant immigration from Asians. During the 1970s and 1980s, Asian newcomers emerged as the state's fastest-growing population; Filipino/as, Chinese, and Asian Indians were the largest subgroups within this population. Many Asian immigrants came during this time period for one of three reasons. First, U.S. military involvement in the region led to increasing numbers of war brides, military employees, and refugees—particularly in areas like Jacksonville, where military bases are located. Second, the national origin quotas put in place by federal immigration legislation were abolished in 1965 via immigration reform, thereby opening up the possibility of increased immigration via employment and skills and family reunification. Third, the economy of the Sunbelt region pulled those looking for employment to it as opposed to other U.S. locations. Since the 1960s, Asian immigrant populations have tended to settle in Florida's large metropolitan counties, such as Dade, Duval, Broward, and Pinellas. This immigration further diversified the already-changing ethno-racial composition of Florida's population.

The immigration story of Florida is as old as immigration to the "New World" yet as dynamic as any state in the United States. It is a state that has always been on the edge—balancing settled and native-born populations with ever-changing demographics as new immigrants have entered. The Spanish, French, and British were newcomers, from the perspective of indigenous populations. Then African slaves and freemen joined their ranks. A whole host of different country-of-origin groups, from Poles and Jews, to Cubans and Mexicans, to Chinese and Filipinos have followed and continued to integrate themselves into Florida's population. For example, today with about 750,000 Jews, Florida is home to the third-largest Jewish population in the country, and the numbers continue to rise. Immigrants came for many reasons. Many Cuban refugees fled their country after the Revolution, Latin American businesspeople came to expand trade, Haitian refugees were trying to escape poverty and political upheaval, and fiscal conservatives from the Frostbelt poured in at 500 a day, every day, for decades.

The Impact of Contemporary Immigration and Demographic Shifts

As a result of these myriad streams of in-migration to the state, Florida was transformed from swampland to one of the largest states in the United States over the past half century. Miami became the financial capital of much of Latin America, pushing the state to open its doors to the South. In 2008, 40 percent of all U.S. exports to Latin and South America passed through Florida. The warm weather brought the elderly from northern states, causing a need for the development of massive healthcare and insurance industries. One of the many strengths of the contemporary Florida economy lies in the medical/biotech field and laboratories. However, this population also supported the idea of low taxes, which therefore limited state-level investments in infrastructure.

Over time, the need for agricultural labor has brought blacks, Latinos, and some Asians to the orange groves, cane fields, and tomato farms. Florida produces about 75 percent of U.S. oranges and accounts for about 40 percent of the world's orange juice supply. Many of these people have transitioned into the service and tourism industries as the needs in agriculture changed or their opportunity structures allowed. Florida is the top travel destination in the world. The tourism industry has an economic impact of $57 billion on Florida's economy. In a different vein, the arrival of Jewish immigrants and migrants from northern states has diversified religion across the state, as did the entrance of Asians four decades ago. No other southern state has such a large Jewish population. Since about 2000, an average of 1,000 people move to Florida daily; all of this growth has built a strong construction industry as well.

The Future of Florida

According to the 2010 Census, Florida gained 2.8 million people since 2000—the equivalent of the entire state of Kansas. "For Florida, the main thing is it shows that growth, in spite of the recession, was solid for the decade," argued Stan Smith, state demographer with the University of Florida (Kunerth 2010). But for Florida, a state whose economy depended on the growth it had experienced historically, the population increase over the past decade was the lowest since the 1960s. Moreover, the state's 17.6 percent growth rate was the slowest in more than 60 years. In 2010, Florida was the eighth fastest-growing state and dangerously close to falling out of the Top 10.

At the same time, the climate across the state has followed the national trend of becoming anti-immigrant. There have been state-level government actions and action taken by the general populace. One example of negative state government action was that Florida has considered anti-immigrant legislation like Arizona's Senate Bill (SB) 1070. The Support Our Law Enforcement and Safe Neighborhoods Act (introduced as Arizona SB 1070 and thus often referred to simply as Arizona SB 1070) was a legislative act in the state of Arizona that was the broadest and strictest anti-illegal immigration measure in recent U.S. history. U.S. federal law required certain immigrants to register with the U.S. government and to have registration documents in their possession at all times. The Arizona act additionally made it a state misdemeanor crime for a foreigner to be in Arizona without carrying the required documents, barred state or local officials or agencies from restricting enforcement of federal immigration laws, and cracked down on those sheltering, hiring, and transporting undocumented aliens. The paragraph on intent in the legislation says it embodies an "attrition through enforcement" doctrine. Florida is now following suit.

Additionally, eight Florida counties (Escambia, Leon, Orange, Osceola, Palm Beach, Polk, Sarasota, and Volusia) have successfully implemented a new information-sharing capability called Secure Communities, which was made available by U.S. Immigration and Customs Enforcement (ICE). Secure Communities was designed to help identify and remove criminal aliens from the United States. The program allows officers to check the criminal and immigration records of everyone arrested and booked into the local jails. Finally, Florida is an active partner in a federal program known as 287(g), which is one of ICE's top partnership initiatives. The program allows a state or local law enforcement entity to enter into a partnership with ICE, under a joint Memorandum of Agreement. The state or local entity receives delegated authority for immigration enforcement within their jurisdictions.

Alternatively, anti-immigrant and/or anti-diversity behaviors have received media attention across the state as well. For instance, in 2010, Rev. Terry Jones burned the Quran at his church in Gainesville, Florida, claiming it was guilty of crime. Another example is that of Dannie Baker. In the early hours of February 26, 2009, Dannie Baker, a 60-year-old Florida resident, left his townhouse armed with a rifle, walked across the complex to a neighboring unit, and opened fire on a quiet gathering of young, unsuspecting Latino residents in Miramar Beach. When the rampage ceased, two individuals were found dead, and three others were critically injured. All five victims were Chilean students participating in a foreign exchange program. Finally, according to a 2010 Southern Poverty Law Center report, Florida ranked third in terms of the number of anti-immigrant hate groups (with 51 groups), behind Texas (66) and California (60). These actions, taken together with those of Florida's government, create an uncomfortable (and potentially unsafe) environment for new immigrants and migrants—even those who would go to the state for short periods of time for tourism purposes. This opens up a series of questions: What will the future hold for the state given its economic foundations in immigrant-driven industries and the development of a relatively strong anti-immigrant atmosphere? How will Florida's state economy recover from the 2008–2009 U.S. recession in this context? Will the character of the state undergo significant and substantive change as a result of these events? Is it possible that Florida will return to its relatively pro-immigrant roots? How will immigrants already living in the state be affected by these events? The answers to these and other questions will inform Florida's path forward. In turn, Florida, as in the past, is leading the country in terms of immigration. Therefore, the lessons that can be learned from this case may be widely applicable to other states across the country over time.

TOPICAL ESSAYS

OTCs: Other than Cubans?

Florida's Latin population has diversified in contemporary times. There are clear historical ties to Cuba, and to a lesser extent Puerto Rico, but from 2000 to 2010 Florida witnessed growth among its Central and South American communities. Specifically, over the past decade, there has been 189.5 percent growth among Guatemalans, 183 percent growth among Hondurans, 170.3 percent growth for Venezuelans, 165.7 percent growth among Salvadorans, 120.5 percent growth among Colombians, and 69.7 percent growth among Nicaraguans. Taken together, these Latinos constitute more than 861,000 Florida residents or about 5 percent of the state's population and 20 percent of Hispanics in the state. Further, the population growth in Florida is approximately 18 percent, and clearly these populations are growing at a much faster pace. Here, we will focus on the groups with the largest growth rates: Guatemalans and Hondurans.

The average age for both groups is just above 27 years and they have low levels of educational attainment—with the majority having a high school diploma or less and median household incomes above $30,000. Just under a quarter of each community is married as well. But there are differences that distinguish these populations from one another beyond country of origin. For example, the Guatemalan population comprises more males than females, whereas the Honduran community has a more balanced gender distribution. Also, Guatemalans are the relative newcomers between the two communi-

A statue of Juan Ponce de Leon in downtown Miami, Florida. (Library of Congress)

ties. Almost 58 percent of Guatemalans in Florida arrived in or after 2000, in comparison to 43 percent of Hondurans. Just over 30 percent of Hondurans arrived between 1990 and 1999, and 27 percent arrived before 1990. As a result of these residency patterns, Hondurans were twice as likely to be naturalized citizens. Further, Hondurans have slightly higher rates of nativity, being U.S. born, than Guatemalans. These demographic changes are directly connected to the changing infrastructure, education, economic, and political needs of the state.

IMMIGRATION-RELATED POLICIES IN CONTEMPORARY TIMES

Despite the fact that immigration has been determined to be a federal issue, states have introduced a number of immigration-related bills, and Florida is no exception. For example, in 2005, the state agreed to provide child welfare services without regard to citizenship (SB 498), and a year later legislation was passed that requires proof of legal immigrant status or proof of pending adjustment to legal immigrant status of driver's license applicants (Section 322.08) and made human trafficking a crime.

In 2007, House Bill (HB) 7181 was signed. This law addressed immigrant survivors of human trafficking and other human rights violations, including domestic violence. It ensured that these trafficked persons were provided with state-funded support services. This law required that a sworn statement from the victim be sufficient evidence in receiving these services and provided for a public-awareness program. In the same year, SB 2114 limited the liability of a caseworker who signed an application for a driver's license for a minor who is in foster care. The bill requires all applicants to be U.S. citizens and provide documentation that proves that they are of a "nonimmigrant classification." HB 985–Act 196 places a $100 fine on vehicles that fail to show the sticker that certifies that they are allowed to transport migrant or seasonal farmworkers. While SB 2, which was signed on October 26, 2007, cut $36,644 from the state Refugee Assistance Trust Fund, the bill also cut $18,605,373 from the state Medical Care Trust Fund by limiting payment of claims for non-U.S. citizens/legal residents.

In 2008, legislation in Florida relating to the issue of immigration and immigrants increased, with 10 bills signed. Florida HB 601 revised the duties of farm labor contractors and eliminated the requirement of a farm labor contractor to submit a set of fingerprints. SB 1702 raised the annual license taxes for wholesale and retail saltwater product dealers; this bill differentiated among resident, nonresident, and alien dealers. Florida SB 1992 required all applicants for driver's licenses and ID cards to provide proof of identity, including a U.S. passport, an alien registration receipt card, an employment authorization card, all of which must be valid and unexpired, or a Consular Report of Birth Abroad provided by the U.S. State Department. Proof of nonimmigrant classification, for the purpose of proving identity, would include an unexpired foreign passport with an unexpired U.S. visa affixed, and accompanied by an approved I-94, beginning January 1, 2010. Applicants for driver's licenses must now provide proof of social security card number and of residential address satisfactory to the department.

Florida SB 2012 established that one must be a U.S. citizen or legal alien who possesses work authorization from the USCIS and is a resident of Florida to be qualified for a public adjuster apprentice license, and under Florida SB 948 the Department of Agriculture may only issue licenses to carry concealed weapons or firearms to U.S. citizens or permanent resident aliens as determined by USCIS. Further, SB 2102 mandated that the Agency for Health Care Administration oversees the Refugee Assistance Trust Fund, which uses federal grant funds under the Refugee Resettlement Program and the Cuban/Haitian Entrant Program to provide medical assistance to eligible individuals, and SB 2116 terminates the Refugee Assistance Trust Fund within the Department of Children and Family Services.

Florida HB 1193, which was passed by legislators and then vetoed, would have provided for the development of a plan to implement a statewide electronic benefits transfer program for the Special Supplemental Nutrition Program for Women, Infants, and Children (WIC).The program was structured to enable an individual who receives an electronic benefit transfer card for food stamp benefits and temporary assistance payments—including refugee cash assistance payments and asylum applicant payments—to also use that card for WIC benefits. HB 9023 was a resolution to recognize September 2008 as Nicaraguan American Heritage month celebrating the historical and cultural contributions of Nicaraguan Americans. Finally, Florida SB 2244 recognized Sheriff Don Hunter and the Collier County Sheriff's Office for completing the ICE cross-training program to improve immigration enforcement in Florida.

In 2009, Florida created a statewide task force and Rhode Island created an interagency task force. Illinois and Texas provided for assistance to crime victims. Washington required domestic employers of foreign workers to disclose certain information and required the Office of Crime Victims Advocacy to supply the health and social services regulatory bodies with information on methods of recognizing victims of human trafficking.

The year 2010 was another busy year for immigration-related immigration policy in Florida, but many of the proposals were symbolic in nature. For example, resolutions were passed to designate February 24, 2010, as the Day of the Cuban Exile; the career of Pedro J. Greer Jr., MD, was recognized for his work as a health professional working with poor undocumented immigrants in the Little Havana community; Holocaust survivors were honored; and the historical and cultural ties between Miami-Dade County and the Bahamas were acknowledged.

More substantive policies were enacted as well. Florida HB 5101 established funding formulas and guidelines for prekindergarten through grade 12 education in Florida, which included allocations for the transportation of migrant students. Along similar lines, Florida HB 2014 included funds for subsidized childcare, school readiness programs, child abuse, and neglect record access; Early Head Start grants; childcare grants; and transportation of children at risk for abuse and neglect. The law also targeted the children of migrant laborers for participation in school readiness programs. Florida HB 787 was another child-related policy that created the Child Abduction Prevention Act. It allowed the court to require written permission from both parents to take a child out of the country if there is substantial evidence that one parent intends to conceal the whereabouts of a child once abroad.

Regulations concerning sanitation requirements—migrant labor camps are included in the definition of a food service establishment—were enacted with the passage of HB 5311, and HB 971 required any agency contracted by state or local officials to immobilize vehicles to employ citizens, legal resident aliens, or those authorized to work in the United States.

According to the National Conference of State Legislatures, in the first half of 2011 state legislators introduced 1,592 bills and resolutions relating to immigrants and refugees in all 50 states and Puerto Rico. This number of bill introductions is an increase of 16 percent compared to the first half of 2010, when 46 states considered 1,374 bills and resolutions pertaining to immigrants. As of June 30, 2011, 40 state legislatures have enacted 162 laws and adopted 95 resolutions for a total of 257. There was a decrease of 18 percent in the total of laws and resolutions passed in 2011. Florida was among the states that were active on immigration legislation in 2011 and 2012.

Florida added an E-Verify requirement by executive order. Laws in the state generally address eligibility for healthcare benefits and licensing of healthcare professionals and interpreters. For example, Florida's Medicaid Program exempts foreigners eligible for emergency Medicaid from mandatory enrollment in the statewide Medicaid-managed care program. Also regulations were put in place regarding documentation and eligibility requirements for IDs and driver's licenses, professional licenses, and firearm and hunting/fishing licenses.

NOTABLE GROUP

AMERICANS FOR IMMIGRANT JUSTICES

Founded in 1996, Americans for Immigrant Justice is a Florida-based immigrant advocacy group dealing with immigration issues and would-be refugee issues, including the plight of post-1980s Cubans (who would have formerly been accepted as refugees but have since had a more indeterminate status) and Haitians, who are considered refugees but who are often blocked from landing on U.S. territory. This nonprofit group operates at policy and legal levels and provides direct services to immigrants, including helping women suffering from domestic abuse and unaccompanied minors. As the group's website notes, in the absence of constructive immigration legislation (rather than merely punitive policies), their services are needed now more than ever. To this end, this nonprofit group was formerly called the Florida Immigrant Advocacy Center but has changed its name and mission to work both locally and nationally.

BIBLIOGRAPHY

Americans for Immigrant Justice (formerly the Florida Immigrant Advocacy Center) Website. http://aijustice.org/. Accessed July 12, 2013.

Banks, Adelle. "Florida Pastor Oversees Quran burning." *USA Today*, March 21, 2011, http://www.usatoday.com/news/religion/2011–03–21-quran-burning-florida_N.htm. Accessed March 6, 2014.

Berthoff, Rowland. "Southern Attitudes toward Immigration, 1865–1914." *The Florida Historical Quarterly* 17, no. 3 (1951): 328–60.

Devine, Donald J. *In Defense of the West*. Lanham, MD: University Press of America, 2004.

Jones, Maxine D., Larry E. Rivers, David R. Colburn, and William W. Rogers. *Documented History of the Incident Which Occurred at Rosewood, Florida in January 1923*. 1993. http://www.displaysforschools.com/rosewoodrp.html. Accessed March 6, 2014.

Kunerth, Jeff. "Census: Florida's Population Grew by 2.8 Million in Past 10 Years." *Orlando Sentinel*, December 21, 2010. http://articles.orlandosentinel.com/2010-12-21/news /os-census-2010-demographics-sidebar-20101221_1_decade-state-demographer-population-decline. Accessed August 1, 2014.

Landers, Jane. "Gracia Real de Santa Teresa de Mose." *Encyclopedia of African-American Culture and History*. 2006. http://www.highbeam.com/doc/1G2–3444700540.html. Accessed March 6, 2014.

Mohl, Raymond. "Asian Immigration to Florida." *The Florida Historical Quarterly* 74, no. 3 (1996): 261–328.

Mohl, Raymond. "Review: Ethnic Transformations in Late-Twentieth-Century Florida." Reviewed work(s): *City on the Edge: The Transformation of Miami* by Alejandro Portes; Alex Stepick; *Miami Now! Immigration. Ethnicity and Social Change* by Guillermo J. Grenier; Alex Stepick; *The Exile: Cuba in the Heart of Miami* by David Rieff; *Maya in Exile; Guatemalans in Florida* by Allan F. Burns. *Journal of American Ethnic History* 15, no. 2 (1996): 60–78.

Pozzetta, George E. "Foreigners in Florida: A Study of Immigration Promotion, 1865–1910." *The Florida Historical Quarterly* 53, no. 2 (October 1974): 164–80.

Purdy, Barbara A. *Florida's People during the Last Ice Age*. Gainesville: University Press of Florida, 2008.

Rowland, Lawrence Sanders, Alexander Moore, and George C. Rogers. *The History of Beaufort County, South Carolina: 1514–1861*. Columbia: University of South Carolina Press, 1996.

Schafer, Daniel L. *St. Augustine's British Years, 1763—1784*. St. Augustine Historical Society, 2001: 38.

Schlakman, Mark. Presentation for the Center for the Advancement of Human Rights. 2011. Florida State University. http://www.flsenate.gov/UserContent/Committees/ 2010–2012/Immigration/historical percent20information-perspective.pdf. Accessed March 6, 2014.

Terrazas, Aaron. "Haitian Immigrants in the United States." Migration Immigration Source. 2010. http://www.migrationinformation.org/USfocus/display.cfm?id=770. Accessed March 6, 2014.

U.S. Bureau of the Census. Historical Census Browser, 1960. U.S. Census, University of Virginia. http://mapserver.lib.virginia.edu/. Accessed March 6, 2014.

U.S. Bureau of the Census. Thirteenth Census of the United States, 1910. Abstract with Supplement for Florida. Washington, 1913, 535.

Wasem, Ruth Ellen. "U.S. Immigration Policy on Haitian Migrants." CRS Report for Congress. 2005. http://trac.syr.edu/immigration/library/P960.pdf. Accessed March 6, 2014.

Weiss, Beth. "The Virtual Jewish History Tour: Florida." 2011. http://www.jewishvirtual library.org/jsource/vjw/florida.html. Accessed March 6, 2014.

10

GEORGIA

Carla R. Monroe

CHRONOLOGY

1526	San Miguel de Gualdape becomes the first European settlement in what is now U.S. territory. The colony was likely founded near Sapelo Island, Georgia.
18th and early 19th Centuries	The French presence grows as Huguenots, Acadians, colonists from Haiti, and refugees from the French Revolution relocate to North America.
1732	Georgia becomes a colony. Savannah is the first settlement.
1733	First Jewish immigrants land in Savannah. Of 42 individuals, 34 are Sephardim, having fled from Portugal to England before arriving in the New World.
1742	At the Battle of Bloody Marsh, Spanish and British forces fight to control parts of Georgia's coastline region; the British prevail.
1873	Approximately 200 Chinese laborers are brought to Augusta to work on the Augusta Canal.
1880	U.S. Census records identify 17 state residents as Chinese, 10 of whom live in Augusta.
1920s	Immigration from Italy and migration from the northern United States expand in Elbert County and help Elberton become a leading site for the granite industry.
1922 (July 26)	The American Hellenic Educational Progressive Association is founded in Atlanta to support Greek American people and causes. This group is initially concerned with addressing the Ku Klux Klan's attacks against Greek Americans and their businesses.

1927	The Chinese Consolidated Benevolent Association is formed in Augusta. It is one of the oldest Asian organizations in the Southeast.
1952	The McCarran Walter Act is passed, retaining racial quotas.
1965	The Hart-Celler Act equalizes quotas, removing the racial basis for immigration.
1970	Approximately 0.7 percent of the state population is foreign-born.
1980	According to census data, approximately 1 in 60 Georgians is foreign-born; Germany is the leading place of birth, followed by the United Kingdom, Canada, Korea, and Cuba.
1990	Mexico has become the top country of birth among foreign-born residents.
1994	The Immigration and Naturalization Service (INS) announces that 4,000 undocumented workers, largely individuals of Mexican heritage, were removed from U.S. jobs through Operation SouthPAW (PAW [Protecting America's Workers]). Although the effort encompassed several southern states, approximately one-third of affected workers were located in Georgia.
2000–2008	The percentage of foreign-born residents in metropolitan Atlanta rises from 11 to 15 percent.
2006	The Georgia General Assembly passes the Georgia Security and Immigration Compliance Act, which prohibits undocumented immigrants over the age of 18 from receiving public benefits, requires state agencies and private businesses with government contracts to use a federal verification system to ensure that all new hires are legally allowed to work, and mandates jail officials to check the legal status of all foreign-born people arrested for a felony or DUI charge and report anyone to the Department of Homeland Security who is not lawfully in the country. Two counties also participate in the 287(g) program, which requires a local police department in cooperation with Immigration and Customs Enforcement (ICE), to investigate inmates' legal status and begin deportation procedures for individuals who are in the United States without documents.
2009	Foreign-born individuals account for more than 9 percent of Georgia's population.
2011	Governor Nathan Deal (R) signs the Illegal Immigration Reform and Enforcement Act of 2011 (House Bill [HB] 87), which uses tighter employment rules to discourage undocumented employment in the state.
2012	The American Civil Liberties Union (ACLU) of Georgia releases the report "Prisoners of Profit: Immigrants and Detention in Georgia." The publication highlights concerns about the state's four immigrant detention centers, such as violations of detainees' due process rights, the quality of medical care provided, and abuses of power. One location, the Stewart Detention Center, is the largest immigration detention facility in the nation.

HISTORICAL OVERVIEW

Knowing when humans first settled the geographical space now known as the state of Georgia is, of course, impossible. Encounters between Native Americans inhabiting the region and foreign populations are dated as early as the sixteenth century when explorers and settlers began to occupy the region. According to many historical accounts, San Miguel de Gualdape was the first European settlement in the United States; the colony was probably near Sapelo Island, Georgia. The European presence in Georgia increased during the eighteenth and early nineteenth centuries as French immigrants, including Acadians, Huguenots, and individuals fleeing the French Revolution and Haitian slave rebellions, entered the area, particularly modern-day Savannah and Augusta. As the United States moved through the colonial period and toward the American Revolution, Georgia's population grew through the importation of Africans, who labored in the colony's slavery system as well as free blacks who worked as indentured servants.

Speaking during the first congressional session, James Madison (1751–1836) who went on to become the fourth U.S. president, declared:

> When we are considering the advantages that may result from an easy model of naturalization, we ought also to consider the cautions necessary to guard against abuse. It is no doubt very desirable that we should hold out as many inducements as possible for the worthy part of mankind to come and settle amongst us, and throw their fortunes into a common lot with ours. But why is this desirable? Not merely to swell the catalogue of people. No sir, it is to increase the wealth and strength of the community; and those who acquire the rights of citizenship, without adding to the strength or wealth of the community are not the people we are in want of. (First Congress Feb. 3)

Immigration is often cast as a modern-day concern, fraught with questions about the costs and benefits of whether and how to incorporate "new Americans" into U.S. society. Yet, Madison's words in 1790 are a powerful reminder that contemporary questions, in fact, have deep historical roots. Madison was perceptive to recognize that "the advantages" attached to allowing individuals to enter and live in the United States as naturalized citizens must be tempered against a sober consideration of investments that are returned to the nation at large. While Madison surely could not have anticipated the furor that frames immigration debates of the twenty-first century, his notation that "those who acquire the rights of citizenship, without adding to the strength or wealth of the community are not the people we are in want of" was prescient as the continuum of "what immigrants bring" in relation to "what they take" has become a defining juggernaut. Perceptions of where a given community falls on this continuum are often mediated by social forces ranging from political coalitions to economic climates, among other influences. Anecdotal evidence simultaneously offers immigrant narratives as historic accounts of resiliency and evidence of achieving the "American Dream" at the same time that contemporary stories of furtive border crossings are alleged to drain federal resources and endanger the nation's "legitimate" citizens.

The historical backdrop to immigration in Georgia provides support for both themes depending on where the balance of immigration leans. Most early immigration to Georgia proceeded from the West and functioned in support of drives to create a cohesive nation. Despite religious, linguistic, and other cultural differences the influx of populations from Spain, France, and other European countries did not galvanize national action such as the federal government's later steps to curtail Asian immigration through the Chinese Exclusion Act (1882) or the Gentlemen's Agreement of 1907, which were largely spurred by economic tensions in states like California.

Available statistics provide evidence that major waves of immigration in Georgia unfolded during the twentieth century, particularly between 1970 and 1990, as the state increasingly became home to many of the nation's immigrants. The population specifically increased by more than 875,000 people during the 1970s and over 1 million during the 1980s; there were statistical gains of 19.1 percent and 18.6 percent for each decade, respectively. The numbers were partially attributable to the approximately 81,100 legal immigrants who entered Georgia between 1970 and 1989. Entrance averages hovered around 2,700 per year during the 1970s and increased to about 5,450 annually during the 1980s. The U.S. Census Bureau estimated that 173,000 immigrants came to Georgia in 1990. Compared to national immigration averages, the state growth rate was four times faster than the U.S. average between 1970 and 1990.

When analyzing the primary countries of origin, the geographical foci have shifted considerably from the 1970s through the 1990s. In 1970, most legal immigrants arrived from Western societies, particularly Germany and the United Kingdom, which jointly accounted for one-third of immigrants, as well as Canada. Census data also documented the presence of 4,000 Asian-born individuals and 2,813 Cuban immigrants. Although immigrant stories in Georgia are not well documented during the 1970s, it is reasonable to attribute the state's Asian and Cuban presence to overarching sociopolitical movements. As Portes (1984), Masud-Piloto (1996), and others chronicled, the majority of Cubans who entered the United States in 1970 were members of the upper-and middle-class exodus fleeing the Castro regime. Furthermore, the passage of the Immigration and Nationality Act (also known as the Hart-Celler Act) in 1965 also facilitated significant Asian immigration as "national origin quotas" were equalized and family reunification provisions allowed entry without a numerical ceiling. Represented among these populations were Chinese ethnics from Hong Kong and Taiwan, as well as the Indian subcontinent. Mexicans, now the largest immigrant group, totaled a mere 294.

These trends continued into 1980. Germany continued to provide the largest share of immigrants as 13,589 new residents arrived from the European republic. The United Kingdom ranked second with 6,935 immigrants and 5,319 people arrived from Canada. Korean immigration considerably increased to 5,117; Cuban migrants numbered 3,431; and 1,452 immigrants were identified as being of Mexican heritage. Steady growth in Asian and Latino immigration during the decade likely resulted from legal provisions of the Hart-Cellar Act, which allowed for an unlimited number of family reunification visas.

By 1990, geographic trends involving Europe, Asia, and Latin America reversed as the movement of Mexican-born individuals into Georgia clearly signaled. At the time, over 20,000 foreign-born people of Mexican heritage relocated to the state, a figure that far surpassed the 13,268 individuals who came from Germany; 11,678 people from Korea; and 7,511 residents from India. Interestingly, Filipino/as who were represented among the first waves of Asian migration to the United States numbered less than 5,000. Despite mass immigration during the past 40 years, however, Georgia continued to be a state where most residents self-identified as native-born African Americans or whites.

Within Georgia, the immigrant distribution has been uneven, prompting diverse clusters of international communities to emerge in different regions of the state. Not surprisingly, locations with military outposts, such as Muscogee, Chattahoochee, and Hall Counties, are spotted with an international presence as U.S. military personnel often marry or adopt children from abroad. Additionally, military personnel may petition the government to allow a fiancé to enter the country, provided that specific conditions are met. Although foreign nationals who marry U.S. citizens may become Lawful Permanent Residents (LPRs) who have the right to live and work in the United States as they proceed toward naturalization, and U.S. residents who adopt foreign children may confer LPR or citizenship status on their new family members, the two groups comprise a relatively small percentage of the state's immigrants. As a result, local communities may not be aware of these individuals' foreignness.

In 1970, most immigrants in the City of Atlanta were Cuban, followed by Europeans and Asians. During the 1980s, the city's foreign-born population doubled and was primarily comprised of Latin and Central Americans, 1,967 of whom were Mexican. The 1980s were also the first decade when African immigration approximated other regions as 1,692 people emigrated from the continent to Georgia. During the 1990s, Latinos, specifically Mexicans, continued to be the largest immigrant group. Bouvier and Martin (1995) observed that "the 20,309 Mexican born [represent] almost 12 percent of all of Georgia's immigrant population. Other leading sources included Germany, Korea and the United Kingdom (each of which had 10,000 or more), India, Canada, Vietnam and Japan (each with over 5,000), and Cuba and the Philippines (with over 4,000 each)." Refugees are immigrants in the broadest sense, that is, they are individuals who are born abroad and move to the United States; these populations were also significant in analyzing Georgia's international presence. According to the Office of Refugee Resettlement of the U.S. Health and Human Services Department, 18,823 refugees came to the state between 1983 and 1993.

From 1970 to 1990, immigrants become increasingly visible by establishing civic organizations, such as the Korean American Chamber of Commerce and the Atlanta Hispanic Chamber of Commerce (now the Georgia Hispanic Chamber of Commerce); opening businesses that catered to specific ethnic markets; and establishing native-language churches among other initiatives. The "Latin Explosion" of the 1990s solidified Georgians' awareness of Latin American culture through the increased presence of Spanish language media (e.g., *La Voz Latina*), an Atlanta chapter of the National Society of Hispanic MBAs, and restaurants and other businesses. Gains in politics have proceeded at a slower pace. The first Asian judge, the honorable Alvin T. Wong, was elected to the State Court of DeKalb County in 1998, and the first Latino trial judge was appointed by former governor Sonny Perdue in 2010.

Although estimates can never be truly accurate, anecdotal accounts suggest that rural and suburban sections of the state are increasingly inhabited by undocumented workers and their families. A number of journalistic accounts and commentaries argue that the real and imagined perceptions of the impact of undocumented workers on the state have provoked actions to restrict immigration. (See, e.g., *Ledger-Enquirer* 2011.) For example, despite the small percentage of immigrants that undocumented individuals comprise, their alleged growth prompted state lawmakers to pass the Georgia Security and Immigration Compliance Act (Senate Bill [SB] 529) on July 1, 2007.

As the first piece of state-level legislation directed at immigrants, SB 529 set requirements for employment verification, eligibility for public benefits, human trafficking, tax withholdings, state enforcement of federal immigration laws, and ethics standards for the provision of immigration services. Additionally, the act required all employers that engaged in business transactions with the State of Georgia who employed more than 500 people to enroll in the federal government Basic Pilot Verification Program. All subcontractors with more than 500 employees were required to use the verification program as well. The act was significant largely because it crafted a legally grounded and economic means of addressing undocumented immigration—companies and individuals were prohibited from deducting business expenses above $600 from state income taxes for individuals who were not verified as being eligible to legally work in the United States. Lawmakers also authorized the state to withhold 6 percent of income tax for an individual using a non-U.S. resident taxpayer identification number. Furthermore, the bill created training to help law enforcement officers enforce federal immigration laws. Undocumented immigration was specifically targeted as officers were expected to act on national immigration laws and determine the legal status of felony suspects and people who were driving while intoxicated (DUI). Under SB 529, ICE must also be notified if an individual does not furnish proper documentation, such as a driver's license. Finally, SB 529 required verification of U.S. citizenship or residence status for adults who applied for state or local benefits.

Fortuny, Capps, and Passel (2007) have found that most undocumented workers entered the country during the 1990s and 2000s, based on U.S.–Mexican economic conditions. Anti-immigration advocate Steven Camarota (2007) also estimated that 7 percent of Georgia's workforce was undocumented in 2007. Most data suggest that industries with the largest percentage of undocumented workers are in construction, leisure, and hospitality. Other areas include professional and business services, wholesale and retail trade, and manufacturing.

Although undocumented immigrants are routinely criticized for their impact on the nation's citizens, researchers of the Federal Reserve Bank of Atlanta (Hotchkiss and Quizpe-Agnoli 2008) have documented impacts on legal immigrants as well. Using the state's administrative data on invalid social security numbers to measure the impact of undocumented workers on wages in Georgia, some researchers found that documented workers suffer financially when industries rely on undocumented immigrants as a labor source. On one level, it is claimed that undocumented workers drive real wages down because they accept lower remuneration levels and are more likely to remain in undesirable jobs due to limited employment options. Secondarily, undocumented immigrants may displace legal immigrants who may be more secure in requesting higher wages, better-working conditions, and job benefits. Many other studies show the opposite: that undocumented workers meet rural labor demands and occupy other positions; that they contribute more to the Social Security system and taxes without ever drawing on state or federal benefits; and that their contribution is, overall, positive. Nevertheless, the policies stated earlier reflect unresolved racial tensions in this region, combined with economic changes and a failure to appreciate the positive role of these immigrants. In the post-9/11 era, as the South has become a new immigrant gateway (particularly for low-tier laborers), it has enacted increasingly hostile policies even while providing employment: "southern politicians legislate against immigrant efforts to establish themselves in local communities. Through mechanisms from the curtailment of immigrant access to driver's licenses to the blurring of local and federal policing responsibilities, local, regional, and national borders are fusing, and simultaneously policed, in southern communities" (Winders 2007, 922). In turn, these policies produce an increasingly hostile context of reception that has discernible racial impacts at the enforcement level.

State efforts have also been supported by federal initiatives. Specifically, the INS intensified deportation efforts, such as through Operation SouthPAW, which resulted in the deportation of over 2,000 undocumented immigrants in the southeast, the majority of whom are detained in Georgia. The largest apprehension of undocumented immigrants was in Gainesville, Georgia, a suburban to rural community located northwest of Atlanta. Since this time, these harsher policies and raids have had a chilling effect on immigration to the state.

TOPICAL ESSAYS

INTRODUCTION

Similar to most southern states, scholarly attention on Georgia's population has traditionally revolved around race and what has been construed as a black–white divide. Demographic shifts during the twentieth century, however, exploded this binary as Georgia became a favored destination space for internal and external migration. Not surprisingly, much of the state's growth has unfolded around metropolitan Atlanta, which is home to the nation's busiest airport, several major corporations (e.g., Home Depot, Coca-Cola), prestigious institutions of higher education (e.g., Georgia Institute of Technology, Emory University), and popular activities such as the National Black Arts Festival and events at the Georgia Aquarium, the nation's largest aquarium.

According to the U.S. Census Bureau, more than 1.7 million people have moved to Georgia during the past 20 years and the percentage of foreign-born individuals has steadily increased, going from 2.7 percent in 1990 to 7.1 percent in 2000 to 9.4 percent in 2008. Latinos accounted for the largest share of immigrants, approximately 765,000 people in 2008, and the University of Georgia Business Outreach Services/Small Business Development Center (2003) estimated that Latinos accounted for at least 5 percent of the population in 30 Georgia counties. The percentage rose to at least 10 percent in seven counties (Atkinson, Chattahoochee, Colquitt, Echols, Gwinnet, Hall, and Whitfield). Individuals of Mexican heritage comprised the largest ethnic group and Dominican Republicans the smallest. Asians are the second-largest immigrant population. Moreover, the state and United Nations have established refugee resettlement sites that have facilitated growth from Eastern Europe, the Middle East, and Africa, including Bosnia, Iraq, Burma, Afghanistan, Sudan, and Somalia. Most refugees are concentrated in DeKalb County, a north Georgia suburban county where the local public school district serves over 11,000 students (or approximately 11 percent of the total student population) who speak a language other than English. Finally, alongside gains in legal immigration, the federal Department of Homeland Security's U.S. Citizenship and Immigration Services (USCIS) charts significant challenges in undocumented movement as well. USCIS statistics suggest that Georgia's 228,000 undocumented immigrants have positioned the state to have the seventh-largest undocumented immigrant population in the country.

The Illegal Immigration Reform and Enforcement Act of 2011

In April 2010, Arizona governor Jan Brewer (R) incited national controversy by signing what was widely viewed as one of the nation's toughest bills on undocumented immigration into law. One year later, Georgia lawmakers delivered the Illegal Immigration Reform and Enforcement Act of 2011, or HB 87, to Georgia Governor Nathan Deal (R). At its most basic level, HB 87 aimed to discourage an undocumented presence through employment rules, sanctions against individuals who transported or moved undocumented immigrants, and clauses that permitted peace officers to verify a suspect's immigration status. More specifically, the bill outlined several requirements for public businesses, including (a) verifying employment eligibility information for newly hired employees, pursuant to the Immigration Reform and Control Act of 1986, commonly known as E-Verify, and (b) procedures for local governments to submit such information to the Carl Vinson Institute of Government of the University of Georgia and make it publicly accessible through a website dedicated to local government audits and budget reports, among other policies. The bill also authorized tough punishments for identity fraud; a person under 21 may receive up to three-year prison sentence and/or a $5,000 fine. Persons over the age of 21 face 1 to 10 years in jail and/or a fine of up to $100,000. It should be noted that using a social security number to secure employment is not identity theft or identity fraud.

While activities in Georgia have failed to rouse the same level of national interest as events in Arizona, the "copycat" bill has incited controversy throughout the state as the intersection of law with power and demographic shifts capture how Georgia has become the latest battleground for competing interests in the immigration debate. Travis Kim, president of the state's Korean American Chamber of Commerce, has protested the legislation, stating, "We don't want to become another Arizona" (Redmon 2011). Representative Matt Ramsey (R), the bill's author, matter-of-factly defended his actions, claiming that, "We [legislators] have done the job that we were sent to do" (Valdes 2011, 1). Both stances reflect a certain logic.

Opposition to HB 87. From an employment perspective, HB 87 is somewhat of a paradox and is opposed by a number of leading organizations in the business world, including the Georgia Chamber of Commerce, the Georgia Restaurant Association, the Georgia Hotel and Hospitality Association, and the Georgia Farm Bureau. On one level, the bill "protects" Georgia jobs by embedding stringent hiring controls within the employment process. Confirming that social security numbers are valid through the federal E-Verify system, for instance, decreases the likelihood that undocumented immigrants will "take" jobs by using fraudulent social security numbers or identification cards. The ostensible result is that available positions of employment will be filled by U.S. citizens and other legal residents. Moreover, businesses and subcontractors that deliberately exploit the labor market by hiring undocumented immigrants will be harshly penalized. The bill even identifies a new offense: knowingly and intentionally inducing an undocumented immigrant to enter Georgia. Individuals found in violation of the bill could potentially spend five years in jail.

In spite of the mania surrounding "immigrant threats" to the U.S. labor force, a compelling body of research directly challenges such ideas. As in many states with a large agrarian economy (e.g., California, the Carolinas), major state agriculture companies largely depend on migrant workers who are oftentimes undocumented immigrants lacking valid work visas particularly for low-paying farm jobs. Some state estimates place the percentage of undocumented agricultural workers in Georgia as high as 40 percent; undocumented immigrants also represent at least 6.3 percent of the state workforce. Factions of the business community contend 40 percent is too conservative an estimate for undocumented Georgia agriculture workers and elevate the figures to 50 to 70 percent.

The large share of agricultural laborers that undocumented workers comprise has facilitated a long and hazy relationship among the law, business, and immigrant communities. For example, national recognition of undocumented workers' critical, albeit controversial, role in some industries has even been recognized through federal acts, namely the Immigration and Control Act (IRCA) of 1986 and the Illegal Immigration Reform and Immigrant Responsibility Act of 1996. IRCA, in particular, created two legalization programs for undocumented immigrants seeking a path to naturalization and a new classification group for seasonal agricultural workers, which allowed individuals who had worked for at least 90 days in certain agricultural jobs to apply for permanent residence. IRCA provisions eventually allowed about 2.7 million undocumented people to become legal U.S. residents. Journalistic accounts suggested that introducing HB 87's hiring measures would discourage immigrants (both legal and undocumented) from working in Georgia entirely.

Beyond possibly losing current and future workers, many business leaders believe that HB 87 creates an unfriendly environment for commerce in general. First, HB 87 is grounded in the mistaken notion that businesses always purposefully hire undocumented immigrants to exploit cheap labor and bolster corporate profits. On the contrary, according to researchers with the Federal Reserve Bank of Atlanta, "It is a common misconception that undocumented workers are all working 'off the books.' There is considerable evidence that employers do report, either knowingly or unknowingly, and pay tax taxes on the wages paid to undocumented workers" (Hotchkiss and Quizpe-Agnoli 2008, 11). In practice, a company may only become aware of a worker's undocumented status after tax discrepancies are noted at the state level. Because many companies already make use of E-Verify when hiring workers, tacking on additional punishments for immigration violations may make companies overly cautious when hiring legal immigrants. Officials with Wayne Farms LLC, the sixth-largest vertically integrated poultry producer in the nation and a Georgia-based company, released a press statement soon after the bill's passage that expressed this concern:

> Wayne Farms is of the belief this bill [HB 87] will negatively impact all immigrants as it could prompt documented workers to exit Georgia businesses and communities along with undocumented workers to avoid being subject to an anti-immigrant climate . . . . We understand this is a sensitive and serious issue, and we want to ensure our Georgia neighbors that we already play by the rules and work hard to keep our workforce free of ineligible or illegal workers. (Wayne Farms LLC 2011)

Second, some elements of the bill are identical to the Georgia Security and Immigration Compliance Act (SB 529) that was passed in 2007. Perhaps most obvious is the mandate that certain companies use the federal E-Verify system. As a

Adelina Nicholls with the Georgia Latino Alliance for Human Rights rolls a copy of the petition containing more than 23,000 signatures that activist groups delivered to Governor Nathan Deal on April 11, 2011. Activists urged the governor to veto proposed legislation that aimed to crack down on undocumented immigration in Atlanta, Georgia. (AP Photo/ David Goldman)

result, this element of HB 87 is largely symbolic, duplicating procedures that are already in place.

Third, potentially losing millions of dollars in tax revenue has also galvanized opposition from the business community and civic leaders. Existing estimates suggest that undocumented individuals account for $9.4 billion in a state economy of roughly $320 billion and $215 to $253 million in sale and property tax dollars. These revenues are generated through their work as well as sales tax. In light of the state's (and nation's) current deficit struggles, the state is likely to sustain a major financial hit if undocumented workers were to leave Georgia in large numbers.

Finally, Latinos in general have remained the state's largest immigrant group since the 1990s and will be disproportionately affected by the bill. Georgia Southern University professor Sally Brown has reminded Georgia lawmakers that 13,000 firms in Georgia are owned by Latinos, 8,000 of which are also female-owned. These businesses are an asset to the Georgia's economy because they collectively generate $253 million of sales, income, and property tax money; create jobs; limit reliance on public welfare (which is not available to any immigrants for the first five years of residency anyway), and reduce unemployment (a concern that is on the rise among immigrants), poverty, and teenage pregnancy.

Beyond an economic lens, the degree to which undocumented immigration has been racialized (against Latino/as) and criminalized in public and political debates leads many opponents to believe that HB 87 is incompatible with the aims of a democratic society. Examples in popular media notwithstanding (see, e.g., Gibson 2011), bill opponents argue that the legislation will invite an unwarranted level of racial profiling. Speaking at the University of Georgia in April 2011, Georgia congressman John Lewis (D) likened HB 87's severe punishments for using false documents to the Jim Crow era of discrimination against African Americans, even suggesting that he would willingly be jailed to fight the bill. Harkening back to the pluralistic message of the Civil Rights Movement, Representative Lewis spoke as follows during a protest outside of state capitol:

> We are all brothers and sisters. It doesn't matter whether we are black, white, Latino, Asian-American, Native American. We are one people. We are one family," Lewis said, eliciting cheers. "We all live in the same house. If any one of us is illegal, then we all are illegal. There are no illegal human beings." (Redmon 2011)

Lewis's sentiments found support among other liberal organizations during the bill's debate, including Rev. Joseph Lowery's Coalition for the People's Agenda and the Georgia State Conference of the National Association for the Advancement of Colored People. Moreover, the ACLU of Georgia urged lawmakers to reject the bill early on, as well as accompanying legislation (e.g., SB 40) which allowed state and local law enforcement officers to investigate a suspect's immigration status. In February 2011, Debbie Seagraves, the ACLU of Georgia executive director, declared, "The proposed bills are unconstitutional and violate core American values. The ACLU of Georgia will challenge such racial profiling legislation if passed in Georgia." Given litigation surrounding Arizona's recent immigration law, reasonable fears regarding expensive and lengthy challenges to HB 87 are well founded.

Support for HB 87. Profoundly misunderstanding the nature of the job market, in which it is commonly held one person's gain is perceived as another's loss, misguided questions can be posed, such as: Will Georgians become antagonistic to immigrants as employment options become scarce in challenging economic times? Does the state have the natural resources to meet the needs of a state whose population base is steadily growing? Do Georgia taxpayers have the capacity or political will to fund educational initiatives to meet immigrants' needs, such as special services for English Language Learners (ELLs)? Does Georgia have an infrastructure that can sustain demands on public utilities, healthcare agencies, and roadways? HB 87 supporters believe the answer to each of these questions is no. Clearly a thorough consideration of each of the previous questions is impossible. Therefore to review and analyze arguments that support HB 87, this essay offers a brief discussion and synopsis of ideas that are advanced in two areas—employment and public education.

Employment. On February 23, 2011, the *Atlanta Journal Constitution* published a commentary piece by state legislator Matt Ramsey, the HB 87 author ("YES: Taxpayers Shoulder the Costs of Undocumented Workers"). In the article, he tackled the business community's charge that HB 87 was antagonistic to Georgians' prosperity.

> Perhaps the most misleading rhetoric in this debate has been the attempt to discredit the use of the free, easy and effective employment eligibility verification system known as E-Verify. Statements have been made about the "inaccuracies" inherent in the system. Let me report the facts. Based on FY [Fiscal Year] 2009 data, E-Verify instantly verifies 97.4 percent of all employees as eligible to work. The very small percentage who are not instantly verified are given the right to appeal before an employer can take action. Further, the 16,000 Georgia employers already enrolled in this user-friendly system will tell you it takes a matter of minutes to enroll and adds less than a minute to the hiring process.
>
> Those who rely on illegal labor know that the use of E-Verify will deter illegal employment and they will stop at nothing to prevent its use. Critics of this measure continue to attempt to obscure the simple fact that E-Verify protects jobs for Georgians legally eligible to hold them and that there is absolutely nothing about the use of the program that will prevent a single employer in Georgia, in any industry, from employing a legal work force.

As a Republican lawmaker, Ramsey's concerns about corporate avarice and potentially ruthless drives to hire undocumented workers are an interesting departure from popular notions of a political party that is frequently tabbed as the political defender of "big business." Convinced that the "need" for undocumented workers in the state agriculture industry was fallacious, Ramsey asserted that the existing H-2A visa program offered a sufficient conduit for drawing in temporary foreign workers. Provisions of the H-2A visa, on the surface at least, do appear to strike a balance between importing foreign labor when needed and investing in the existing citizenry workforce. Employers who wish to hire outside U.S. borders must submit an application to the U.S. Department of Labor, indicating an insufficient number of possible workers exists and noting that employing immigrants will not adversely affect the wages and working conditions of U.S. workers holding analogous positions. An application must be approved by USCIS as well. Existing mandates to employ an active effort to recruit U.S. workers as well as give them preference in hiring decisions ostensibly builds a healthy labor force. Senator Judson Hill (R), who represented the 32nd District, sponsored similar legislation (SB 27) and was quoted as backing such actions because the "legislation is intended to protect our taxpayer dollars, public employers, and law abiding public contractors, but most importantly it will help insure that Georgians get the public works jobs. The bill provides real, enforceable penalties that are missing in current law" (Georgia Tea Party 2011).

Conceptually, the H-2A visa program appears to be a welcome compromise for business leaders and individuals seeking to control immigration, particularly as related to the agriculture industry. Unfortunately, it is difficult to assess whether Ramsey's argument is empirically robust because undocumented workers are notoriously difficult to track, making numerical comparisons to H-2A visa holders difficult. The program is also rife with human rights abuses because it places guest workers outside any constitutional protections, even those based on "personhood."

Education. In 2010, Jessica Colotl was stopped for a traffic violation. Normally such routine matters do not penetrate statewide news media. However, the fact that the Kennesaw State University student was an undocumented immigrant moved her case from obscurity to front page headlines. In short, Colotl, who was born in Mexico, came to the United States along with her parents as a child. She is one of 480,000 undocumented immigrants who live in Georgia. Beyond mainstream arguments related to undocumented immigration, Colotl's enrollment in a state-supported university incited fierce controversy about the role of immigrants in the state's educational system.

Within higher education circles, Colotl's case provoked two questions: Should individuals living in Georgia without documents be permitted to attend state institutions? And if so, should they be permitted to pay relatively low in-state tuition rates rather than elevated out-of-state rates? While the answers to these questions are as diverse as the number of respondents providing answers, anti-immigration activists maintain that students like Colotl constrain educational options for legal residents when they fill limited seats available in higher education. This ignores the fact that her parents brought her to the country thus her "illegal entry" must be contextualized, and she was already guaranteed access to public schools according to the Supreme Court decision *Plyler v. Doe* (1982). However, it is conventionally held that legal residents are essentially forced to subsidize higher education degrees for undocumented workers who do not legitimately meet established guidelines to be considered a state resident, if these immigrants' tax contributions are ignored. In a related vein, out-of-state residents who pay more to receive post-secondary degrees in Georgia are allegedly penalized for complying with these policies. The perceived losses that states stand to suffer from situations like Colotl's have led to public support for anti-immigration bills aimed at undocumented families, despite other facts that would challenge these simple assumptions. In fact, a bill (HB 59) to bar undocumented immigrants from all 35 institutions in the university system of Georgia has already cleared the House of Representatives. At the very least, it sends a message to children who have been raised in the state and have attended public schools: their presence is not welcome when they enter adulthood.

At the K-12 level, Georgia public school districts, of course, act in response to 1982 *Plyler v. Doe* decision rendered by the Supreme Court, the decision that settled a case originating in Texas. More specifically, in 1975 the state of Texas passed a law to prevent undocumented minors from receiving a public education. Under the law, elementary, junior, and high school education would be restricted to U.S. citizens and foreigners who are in the country legally. Lower courts ruled against the law, as well as against a related Tyler, Texas, policy that charged a $1,000 tuition fee for foreign children, a measure designed to offset per-pupil expenditures that were not collected through state-funding equations. *Plyler v. Doe* (1982) famously struck down both practices as illegal and sets precedents for educational rights afforded to undocumented children

Korean-born Pittsburgh Steelers wide receiver Hines Ward poses with the Pete Rozelle Trophy after receiving it at a news conference in Detroit on February 6, 2006. Ward's family moved from Korea to Atlanta, Georgia, and he was recruited by the Pittsburgh Steelers while playing at the University of Georgia. (AP Photo/Paul Sancya)

as attorneys for the children successfully argued that parental decisions to enter without inspection do not justify educational barriers against minors who had no meaningful say in their families' decision to enter the United States. In a 5–4 ruling, the Court found that the state and district policies would probably contribute to "the creation and perpetuation of a subclass of illiterates within our boundaries, surely adding to the problems and costs of unemployment, welfare, and crime." The minority dissented on the basis that schooling for undocumented children should be dealt with legislatively and that "[t]he Constitution does not provide a cure for every social ill, nor does it vest judges with a mandate to try to remedy every social problem" arguing that the majority is overstepping its bounds by seeking "to do Congress' job for it, compensating for congressional inaction."

The majority's decision not only opened the door for open educational access for undocumented children but also, in conjunction with other legal and social movements, pushed public school districts to be proactive in schooling students with limited English proficiency. Specific to HB 87, bill supporters claimed that public school resources are being drained by ELL students (both legal and undocumented) as local institutions must increasingly train and hire bilingual teachers, develop English for Speakers of Other Languages certification programs, translate school documents, and gather bilingual pedagogical materials that still address children's developmental, cognitive, social, and other needs. Others have argued that these changes are relatively minimal and that these families deserve to be treated with dignity.

NOTABLE FIGURES

HINES WARD (1976–)

The Atlanta metropolitan area is the center of a robust entertainment industry and has become the home of several well-known figures in popular culture. Hines Ward, a former wide receiver in the National Football League, is one of the most recognizable state residents. Ward was born in Seoul, South Korea, on March 8, 1976, to a Korean mother and an African American father and later moved to the Atlanta metro area, where he grew up. The Pittsburgh Steelers drafted him from the University of Georgia in 1998 as a third round pick. In his 14 seasons with the Steelers, Ward became the team's all-time leader in receptions and earned yardage. Most notably, he was voted most valuable player of Super Bowl XL, becoming the first Korean American to earn this distinction. During his career, he also made four Pro Bowl appearances, and won the television dance competition *Dancing with the Stars*. In 2006, Ward helped to establish the Hines Ward Helping Hands Foundation, an organization that is designed to improve literacy skills in the United States and help biracial children who experience discrimination, especially in Korea. He currently resides in Sandy Springs, a suburb of Atlanta.

BIBLIOGRAPHY

Bouvier, Leon F., and John L. Martin. *Shaping Georgia: The Effects of Immigration, 1970–2020*. Washington, DC: Center for Immigration Studies, 1995.

Camarota, Steven A. *Immigrants in the United States, 2007*. Washington, DC: Center for Immigration Studies, 2007.

Diamond, Laura. "Bill to Bar Undocumented Immigrants in Public Colleges Clears Panel." *Atlanta Journal Constitution*, 2011. http://www.ajc.com/news/georgia-politics-elections/bill-to-bar-illegal-839985.html. Accessed February 8, 2014.

Diamond, Laura, and A. Simmons. "Legal Struggles Continue for Immigrant Student." *Atlanta Journal Constitution*, 2011. http://www.ajc.com/news/legal-struggles-continue-for-839732.html. Accessed February 8, 2014.

Fortuny, K., R. Capps, and J.S. Passel. "The Characteristics of Unauthorized Immigrants in California, Los Angeles County, and the United States." *Mimeo*. Washington, DC: The Urban Institute, 2007.

Fry, R. *The Higher Dropout Rate of Foreign-Born Teens: The Role of Schooling Abroad*. Washington, DC: Pew Hispanic Center, 2005.

"Ga. Organized Walk to Spotlight Immigration Issue." *Ledger-Enquirer*, April 18, 2011. http://archive.13wmaz.com/news/story.aspx?storyid=125061. Accessed August 1, 2014.

Georgia Tea Party. "Georgia Tea Party Endorses Two Immigration Bills in General Assembly." 2011. http://www.thegeorgiateaparty.org/. Accessed February 8, 2014.

Gibson, Dave. "Gwinnett County, Georgia Is Experiencing an Undocumented Alien Crime Wave." 2011. http://www.examiner.com/immigration-reform-in-national/gwinnett-county-georgia-is-experiencing-an-illegal-alien-crime-wave. Accessed February 8, 2014.

Hotchkiss, J.L., and M. Quizpe-Agnoli. "The Labor Market Experience and Impact of Undocumented Workers." Working Paper 2008–7c. Atlanta: Federal Reserve Bank, 2011.

Johnson, Kevin R. "Race and Immigration Law and Enforcement: A Response to Is There a Plenary Power Doctrine?" *Geography Immigration* 289 (1999–2000): 289–305.

Joyner, T., and M.E. Kanell. "Immigrants a force in Georgia." *Atlanta Journal Constitution*, July 29, 2010. http://www.ajc.com/news/immigrants-a-force-in-580926.html. Accessed February 8, 2014.

Keber, M.L. "French Presence in Georgia." 2002. http://www.georgiaencyclopedia.org/nge/Article.jsp?id=h-638. Accessed March 6, 2014.

Kochhar, R. *Unemployment Rises Sharply among Latino Immigrants in 2008*. Washington, DC: Pew Hispanic Center, 2009.

Masud-Piloto, F.R. *From Welcomed Exiles to Illegal Immigrants: Cuban Migration to the U.S., 1959–1995*. Lanham, MD: Rowman and Littlefield, 1996.

McClain, Paula D., Niambi M. Carter, Victoria M. DeFrancesco Soto, Monique Lyle, Jeffrey D. Grynaviski, Shayla C. Nunnally, Thomas J. Scotto, J. Alan Kendrick, Gerald F. Lackey, and Kendra Davenport Cotton. "Racial Distancing in a Southern City: Latino Immigrants' Views of Black Americans." *Journal of Politics* 68 (2006): 571–84.

Morris, J. E., and Carla R. Monroe. "Why Study the U.S. South? The Nexus of Race and Place in Investigating Black Student Achievement." *Educational Researcher* 38 (2009): 21–36.

Pew Hispanic Center. *Statistical Portrait of Hispanics in the United States, 2006*. Washington, DC: Pew Hispanic Center, 2006.

Pew Hispanic Center/Kaiser Family Foundation. *National Survey of Latinos: Education*. Washington, DC: Pew Hispanic Center, 2004.

Pew Research Center. *Between Two Worlds: How Latinos Come of Age in America*. Washington, DC: Pew Hispanic Center, 2009.

Phelps, L. "Opposition to Crack Down on Georgia's Undocumented Aliens at Savannah Hearing." *Savannah Small Business Journal*, 2011. http://www.savannahbusiness journal.com/news/local-politics/1017-opposition-to-crack-down-on-georgias-illegal-aliens-at-savannah-hearing. Accessed February 8, 2014.

Plyler v. Doe (1982) 457 U.S. 202.

Portes, Alejandro. "The Rise of Ethnicity: Determinants of Ethnic Perceptions among Cuban Exiles in Miami." *American Sociological Review* 49 (1984): 383–97.

Redmon, J., "Thousands Protest Immigration Bills at State Capitol." 2011. http://www.ajc.com/news/georgia-politics-elections/thousands-protest-immigration-bills-884543.html. Accessed February 8, 2014.

Tully, Matthew B. "When You Marry or Adopt Overseas." *Army Times*, October 8, 2007. http://www.armytimes.com/community/ask_lawyer/military_askthelawyer_071008w/. Accessed February 8, 2014.

The University of Georgia Business Outreach Services/Small Business Development Center. *Hispanic Fact Sheet*. 2003.http://www.sbdc.uga.edu. Accessed February 8, 2014.

U.S. Census Bureau, Census. Washington, DC: Census Bureau, 2000.

U.S. Census. *Mobility for States and the Nation*. Washington, DC: Census Bureau, 1970.

Valdes, Gustavo. "Georgia Governor to Sign Law Targeting Illegal Immigration." April 15, 2011. http://articles.cnn.com/2011–04–15/politics/georgia.legislature_1_illegal-immigrants-immigration-status-sign-law?_s=PM:POLITICS. Accessed February 8, 2014.

Wayne Farms LLC. "Wayne Farms Responds to GA Immigration Bill." 2011. http://www.waynefarms.com/content/view/197/98/. Accessed February 8, 2014.

Weber, David. *The Spanish Frontier in North America*. New Haven, CT: Yale University Press, 1994.

Winders, Jamie. "Bringing Back the (B)order: Post-9/11 Politics of Immigration, Borders, and Belonging in the Contemporary US South." *Antipode* 39, no. 5 (2007): 920–42.

11

HAWAI'I

James Wren

CHRONOLOGY

2500 BCE	The earliest migration to Hawai'i may have been a Tahitian invasion or the arrival of the first Polynesians in the third century from the Marquesas, followed by Tahitian settlers some 1,000 years later.
100–500 CE	Polynesian settlers from the South Pacific migrate some 2,000 miles to Hawai'i in double-hulled voyaging canoes.
850	The main Hawaiian Islands (e.g., Hawai'i or the "Big Island," Kaua'i, Lana'i, Mau'i, Moloka'i, Ni'ihau, and O'ahu) are populated.
900–1100	Further immigration from Tahiti brings war-like people who enslave previous immigrants and rule by fear and violence for nearly 1,000 years.
1400	Social classes stratify and the islanders split into tribes.
1555	Juan Gaetano, captain of a Spanish galleon, comes across the islands while sailing from the Mexican Coast to the Spice Islands.
1758	Island astronomers predict a brilliant celestial star (likely, Halley's Comet), heralding the birth of Kamehameha the Great.
1770–1794	Kahekili, brother-in-law to his avowed enemy Kalani'opu'u rules Mau'i.
1778 (January 18)	Seeking the Northwest Passage, Captain James Cook comes upon the "Sandwich Islands." The indigenous people welcome him as *Lono*, their mythic god of peace, rain, and fertility. On February 13, a skirmish breaks out and Cook is murdered.
1794	Kamehameha reconquers Mau'i after uniting the island of Hawai'i under his rule.

1795	The area known as Ka Punahou falls in the battle to Kamehameha. Thereafter, he conquers Mau'i, Lana'i, Moloka'i, and O'ahu.
1798 (August 19)	A scroll of the Torah and *yad* ("pointer") are presented to the royal family, thereby establishing a bond between Hawaiians and the early Jewish community.
1810	Kamehameha unifies the Hawaiian Islands under a single ruler, moving from a feudal society toward a constitutional monarchy.
1810	Individual African Americans arrive.
1812	The War of 1812 leads Britain to blockade Hawai'i for two years.
1819	A French ship arrives at Kawaihae, and, in September, the first New England whalers arrive.
1819 (May 8)	Death of Kamehameha I.
1820 (March 30)	Protestant missionaries aboard the *Thaddeus* arrive at Kailua, Hawai'i, from New England to teach reading and writing, but they forbid *he'e nalu* (surfing).
1823	Skilled Chinese workers arrive to set up sugar mills.
1823 (November 24)	Kamehameha II and members of the royal family board the English whaler *L'Aigle* for England.
1824 (July)	Queen Kamāmalu contracts measles and dies. A week later, on July 14, Kamehameha II also succumbs to measles.
1826	The Hawaiian language is standardized as a written language by Protestant missionaries who transcribe the sounds they hear to produce the first Hawaiian-language Bible.
1827	Antonio Silva arrives from Portugal and plants the first commercial sugar crops. On July 7, the French ship *Comète* brings Roman Catholic missionaries to Honolulu.
1831 (December 31)	Catholic priests are expelled after discord breaks out between priests and local Protestants.
1832	Richard Armstrong (1805–1860), the son of a black minister, arrives and builds a church on Mau'i.
1832	Mexican *vaqueros*, contracted as expert horsemen with cattle experience, arrive; called *paniolo*, these skilled cowboys train local men in Waimea and North Kohala.
1834	Because *kānaka maoli*, "native Hawaiians," refuse to work for low wages, agricultural corporations import cheap labor under contract from Asia.
1840	The first Hawaiian with Hansen's disease ("lepromatous leprosy") is detected in Mau'i.
1840 (October 8)	Kamehameha III proclaims the First Hawaiian Constitution, subjecting himself and his heirs to the law, establishing the House of Nobles and an elected House of Representatives, and including provisions for freedom of worship.
1842	U.S. president John Tyler recognizes the Kingdom of Hawai'i, invoking the Monroe Doctrine to dissuade European intervention and agreeing in principle to Hawaiian independence.

1844	The United States recognizes Hawai'i and, within a year, California gold miners introduce influenza to the islands.
1850	Mormon missionaries arrive. In August, Hawai'i's Privy Council officially designates Honolulu as the kingdom's capital.
1852	The second group of Chinese arrives.
1864 (May 31)	Joseph De Veuster is ordained as Father Damien at the Cathedral of Our Lady of Peace in Honolulu and goes to Puna on the Big Island. The following year, patients with Hansen's disease are exiled to Kalawao, on the Kalaupapa Peninsula of Moloka'i.
1868	The emperor Meiji is restored and Japanese are now free to travel abroad as contract laborers.
1872	The Royal Hawaiian Hotel opens on Hotel Street and caters to wealthy clients.
1872	Mark Twain visits the Hawaiian Islands and writes 25 articles for the *Sacramento Union* newspaper.
1874 (February 12)	David Kalākaua (1836–1891), known as the "Merrie Monarch," is elected king by the legislature and the House of Kalākaua comes to power. He reigns until his death in 1891 and is revered for restoring extinct, cultural traditions of the Hawaiian people, including myths and legends. On November 17, Kalākaua embarks on a goodwill visit to the United States aboard the warship *Benicia*.
1875 (January 30)	The Hawai'i–United States Treaty (the "Reciprocity Treaty of 1875") is signed, creating an open market for Hawaiian exports. The treaty, while explicitly acknowledging Hawai'i as a sovereign nation, requires that Hawai'i cede Pearl Harbor to the United States, including Moku'ume'ume (Ford Island), together with its shore for four or five miles back *gratis*. Later that same year, Isabella Bird's travelogue, *The Hawaiian Archipelago*, establishes her as the most famous female traveler of her generation.
1879	The first Portuguese immigrants arrive at McGregor Point from Madeira and the Azores. They introduce a small Portuguese four-string guitar, what native Hawaiians would call *ukulele* ("leaping flea").
1881	As Germans arrive in the islands, Kalākaua travels around the world with Queen Kapi'olani.
1884–1886	Five shiploads of Portuguese laborers arrive.
1884	Princess Ke Ali'i Bernice Pauahi Paki Bishop (1831–1884), great-granddaughter and last royal descendant of Kamehameha the Great, establishes the Kamehameha School under the auspices of the Bishop Trust.
1885	The first major immigration from Japan begins, with approximately 2,000 workers finding positions on sugar plantations.
1887	A group of cabinet officials and advisors form an armed militia—collectively recognized as the All-White Hawaiian League—and force the king to modify the Hawaiian Constitution.

	Termed the "Bayonet Constitution," it strips the monarchy of much of its authority and denies citizenship to all Asians.
1889	British novelist and poet Robert Louis Stevenson (1850–1894) arrives in Honolulu and befriends Kalākaua. His friendship with the king's niece, Princess Victoria Ka'iulani, is recounted in his *In the South Seas*.
1894	President Grover Cleveland recognizes the Republic of Hawai'i. The following year, Queen Lili'uokalani agrees to absolute abdication.
1896	The government of the new Republic of Hawai'i immediately passes the English Language Law, making English the basis of all education in public and private schools.
1898 (May)	The Spanish-American War begins, and Hawai'i becomes the strategic U.S. base of operations against the Philippines. On July 7, President William McKinley signs the Treaty of Annexation, thereby creating the Territory of Hawai'i. By August 12, McKinley annexes the independent Republic of Hawai'i, its citizens receiving full American citizenship.
1900	Okinawan immigration begins.
1901 (January)	The first African Americans to work Hawai'i's plantations arrive from Tennessee, Alabama, and later from Mississippi and Louisiana. Thereafter, the Hebrew Benevolent Society establishes its first cemetery at Pearl City Junction. Almost immediately, the Japanese government lifts restrictions on emigration.
1902 (December 22)	The first group of 102 Korean immigrants (56 men, 21 women, and 25 children) sail across the Pacific to Hawai'i aboard the SS *Gaelic* in search of work.
1906	Immigration of Filipinos (termed *sakadas* or *Hawayanos*) begins.
1907	The University of Hawai'i at Mānoa is established.
1910	Sara Choe is the first of 951 "picture brides" to arrive from Korea.
1919	The first group of Samoan immigrants arrives; as Mormons, they settle on the windward coast of O'ahu.
1920	The first treatment option to relieve symptoms of Hansen's disease results from the work of Alice Ball at the University of Hawai'i; the first woman to graduate from the University of Hawai'i with a master's degree, she is a black woman from Seattle.
1920–1930	Anglo immigrants—members of the U.S. armed forces—increase sharply.
1930 (August 13)	Of Chinese, Hawaiian, Portuguese, Dutch, and German descent, Donald Tai Loy "Don" Ho (1930–2007) is born.
1941 (December 7)	Japan attacks Pearl Harbor, thus drawing the United States into World War II. Governor Poindexter declares martial law, suspends the writ of Habeas Corpus, closes the local courts, and hands the powers of government over to the military.

1943	Japanese American soldiers from Hawai'i join the 100th Infantry Battalion and fight in Europe. On December 4, Military Order No. 45 exempts Koreans in the United States from enemy alien status.
1944 (October 24)	Military rule ends in Hawai'i.
1945	Hawai'i reopens immigration; Samoans and a second wave of Filipinos follow. And while the War Brides Act allows non-Asian American military personnel to bring their foreign-born wives and underage children to the United States, Asian personnel are specifically excluded.
1947	Courtesies extended to non-Asians under the War Brides Act of 1945 are extended to Asian personnel.
1952 (June)	The McCarran-Walter Act provides all Asian immigrants, Japanese included, eligibility for naturalization.
1954	The Democratic Party comes into power, ending *haole* ("Caucasian") oligarchy.
1959 (August 21)	President Dwight D. Eisenhower proclaims Hawai'i the 50th state, and Democrat Daniel Ken Inouye (1924–) becomes the first Japanese American to serve in the U.S. House of Representatives. Inouye is elected to the U.S. Senate in 1962.
1960–1970s	Post-Korean War immigrants continue to arrive as Thai immigration begins.
1960–1999	As the Japanese economy improves, Japanese emigration decreases.
1961(August 4)	Barack Hussein Obama II is born in Kapi'olani Maternity and Gynecological Hospital (now Kapi'olani Medical Center for Women and Children) in Honolulu, Hawai'i.
1963	The Polynesian Culture Center opens at O'ahu to study and preserve Polynesian arts, crafts, and cultures.
1964	The Civil Rights Act safeguards employees from systemic racial discrimination.
1968 (September 20)	Shot on location, the series *Hawaii Five-O* airs, mirroring the ethnic richness of the region.
1970	Hawaiian land and native rights movements begin.
1976	Canoe voyages of *Hōkūle'a* confirm the ancestral ability to travel across the Pacific using only celestial signs as a "compass."
1980–1988	*Magnum, P.I.*, starring Tom Selleck as a private investigator living on O'ahu, begins. It introduces the *Aloha* shirt as standard attire.
1986	Marshallese and Chuukese immigration begins.
1986	Ellison Onizuka, astronaut from the Big Island, perishes in the *Challenger* disaster.
1987	Hawaiian language immersion schools open to promote culture.
1989	After the Tiananmen Massacre in China, President George H. W. Bush signs an executive order allowing Chinese foreign students and visiting scholars to become permanent residents. This same

	year, the Amerasian Homecoming Act is implemented, allowing children in Vietnam who were born of American fathers to emigrate.
1993	President William Jefferson "Bill" Clinton apologizes formally for the overthrow of Hawai'i's monarchy. That same year, native performer Israel "IZ" Ka'ano'i Kamakawiwo'ole achieves international fame outside of the Islands with the release of his medley of "Over the Rainbow" and "What a Wonderful World."
1993	About 100 Cambodians, 3,000 Laotians, and 8,000 Vietnamese reside in Hawai'i, with an annual increase of 600–800 people, most of whom are Vietnamese.
1997	Of Hawaiian and Korean ethnicity, Brook Lee, the reigning Miss Hawai'i, becomes Miss Universe.
1998 (January 21)	Much-beloved star of *Hawai'i Five-O*, Jack Lord dies. His estate funds 12e Hawaiian nonprofit educational, cultural, and medical institutions.
2000	In Old Waikīkī, the Queen's Banyan tree is felled.
2000–2003	Japanese migration doubles as a response to the sudden downturn of the Japanese "Economic Bubble."
2005	The National Academy of Recording Arts and Sciences introduces the *ki ho'ala* ("Hawaiian slack-key guitar") as a new awards category.
2006	The University of Hawai'i at Hilo establishes a PhD program in the Hawaiian language.
2009 (January 20)	Barack Obama, who was born in Hawai'i, is elected the 44th president of the United States and receives the Nobel Peace Prize.
2010 (September 19)	The remake of *Hawai'i Five-O* premieres.
2012	Hawai'i land leases become "fee-simple," thereby allowing individual homeowners to own the land upon which they dwell.

HISTORICAL OVERVIEW

Although small in total land area, the numerous islands and archipelagoes, with their startlingly diverse habitats and biomes, that comprise Oceania and Polynesia extend across a third of the globe and, as such, are the last major world region to be discovered by humans. Even so, during this relatively brief history, two recurrent issues have made themselves apparent: the exceptional environmental challenges and the demographic, economic, and political challenges facing the region. It is all the more remarkable, then, that while modern technology and media and waves of continental tourists are fast eroding island cultures, the continuing resilience of Pacific island populations remains strong. Perhaps nowhere is this strength toward survival and preservation of identities more apparent than in the state of Hawai'i.

However, this state also remains particularly rich precisely for its *differences*: they are products of interrelationships between culturally created meanings and specific contexts and explain why Hawai'i is so unique. These interrelationships demonstrate how cultural traditions are maintained, how traditional figures remain even today as context-bound articulations, and how the cultural traditions of Hawai'i result from interactions between diverse peoples. This perspective entails accounting for indigenous agency and that of newcomers. Furthermore, the diversity that gives definition to Hawai'i is never far removed from a complex set of interactions with *kānaka maoli*, the "native Hawaiians" who first inhabited and developed the islands. Broadly put, it is the *Aloha Spirit* that characterizes Hawai'i.

Still, there are those who insist that Hawai'i be viewed as an outgrowth of its past interconnections and mutual negotiations resulting from European and American colonialism. The result is an emphasis on the ostensibly shared com-

President Clinton presents the Medal of Honor to Senator Daniel K. Inouye, D-Hawaii, left, one of 22 Asian American soldiers receiving the Medal of Honor for service in World War II, on June 21, 2000, at the White House in Washington, D.C. Inouye, 1st Lt. of the 442nd Regimental Combat Team, crawled up a hill, despite multiple wounds, and used grenades and his submachine gun to knock out three German machine-gun nests, near Terenzo, Italy, on April 20, 1945. (AP Photo/Joe Marquette)

mercialized cultural experience which has been challenged by post-colonial studies and movements, most notably in the movements toward sovereignty and exclusion. The currently accepted system of historical division from this perspective, for example, falls neatly into four major periods: *antiquity* (ancient Hawai'i), *monarchy* (kingdom of Hawai'i), *territorial* (territory of Hawai'i), and *statehood* (state of Hawai'i).

But the imposition of a Eurocentric view effectively negates—if not erases in the Derridean sense—any history of native Hawaiians. If, for example, we examine how both a mythic understanding of Hawai'i and the material realities of the island's shared specific immigrant experiences, then and only then can we return to a more complete and accurate, not to mention inclusive, account of migration to Hawai'i.

To put it simply, the worlds of the Hawaiian Island and its original inhabitants and the world beyond, outside, collided, as two discordant understandings of life

Korean-born first-time novelist Nora Okja Keller, 31, talks about her book *Comfort Woman* in New York on May 2, 1997. Keller, who emigrated from Seoul, Korea, when she was three, and was formally educated in Honolulu, heard the lecture of a World War II Japanese sex camp survivor in 1993 and started having dreams about war and camps thereafter. "One of the only ways I could exorcise it from my dreams was to write it down," said Keller. (AP Photo/Bebeto Matthews)

and living come into contact. This contact often leads to conflict; matters of culture and diversity would be undermined or become reprioritized in such a manner as to become unrecognizable.

In the early nineteenth century, for example, as American and European missionaries arrived, they introduced new creeds and newer myths. The history of modern Hawai'i soon became one of how disparate peoples struggled to maintain their identity *and* live with one another in harmony, joined together to build America's strong and vital 50th state. The source of that strength and vitality was the interconnectedness of the many populations, native or immigrant, and in doing so, constructing a larger historical understanding of each group as each evolves from *race* to *ethnicity* to our various understandings of the island's culture(s).

A second point providing Hawai'i with its particular vitality and strength lies in the oft-heard motto: *E Ola Mau Ka 'Olelo Hawai'i!* That "the Hawaiian Language Lives Forever!" is a constant reminder that Hawai'i, unlike any of the other 50 states of the union, maintains two official state languages, Hawaiian and English. At least since the early 1990s, bilingualism has become the norm with Hawaiian language immersion schools and because instruction in Hawaiian is now commonly offered from kindergarten to the graduate level at university. Most Hawaiian residents can also speak a sort of Hawaiian Creole English, commonly referred to as *Pidgin*, a dialect of English created by children in the multilingual environment of Hawaiian plantation camps. In fact, Hawaiian Creole English now dominates Hawaiian fiction, poetry, and drama.

Compared to the other states of the union, the 50th state is also defined by the concept of "decentralization," due to the extensive chain of islands recognized as the Polynesian cultural region. Hawai'i, the Aloha State, lies some 3,682 kilometers away from and extends across the Northeast Pacific Ocean from the domestic

United States, the so-called mainland. A chain of 137 islands, shoals, and reefs, mostly uninhabited, 8 islands, however, are far better known for their size and their large populations, among them Hawai'i (the "Big Island"), Mau'i ("the Valley Isle"), O'ahu ("the Gathering Place"), Kaua'i ("the Garden Isle"), Moloka'i, Lana'i, Ni'ihau, and Kaho'olawe. These islands have served, perhaps for the past 5,000 years, as "points of transit" as Polynesian sailors crossed the vast Pacific between Oceania to the coast of South America. Thus, Hawai'i is the only state that was never led by a white majority. Even today, the 2000 and 2010 censuses underscore how a few islands isolated in the middle of the Pacific Ocean have become "home" to peoples from Polynesia and Asia, Europe and Africa, while there is no racial majority. In fact, its inhabitants claim ancestors from more than one country or race and the concepts of diversity and of multiethnic community appear to be the rule rather than the exception.

It is best to view the populations comprising contemporary Hawai'i as neither monolithic nor static. Instead, the islands are better understood in terms of dramatic transformations, in the complexities associated with recent immigration and associated settlement patterns and the multiethnic metropolis. In fact, the diversity and success that characterize Hawai'i indicate larger social, economic, political, and living patterns and maintenance of the nation's diversity rather than forced assimilation. This, in turn, strengthens the United States within an increasingly globalized, interrelated world.

The initial landing of Captain James Cook, the British explorer and navigator, at Waimea, on the island of Kaua'i, on January 20, 1778 represents a significant moment in Pacific history: the bridging moment between pre-contact and the arrival of the first European presence in the islands. This initial contact was followed by a period of intermittent contact with the West. In 1820, the first of 15 companies of New England missionaries arrived. After the arrival of missionaries, a small but powerful Anglo minority began to exert greater and greater power over the Hawaiian monarchy.

Hawaiian culture, doubtless, was irrevocably changed, as the contact would have a profound effect on indigenous islanders. Significantly, there was the introduction of diseases from both the East and the West against which the islanders, theretofore virtually disease-free, had no natural immunities. Venereal disease, cholera, measles, and tuberculosis all contributed to the decimation of the native peoples, whose population fell from approximately 300,000 to fewer than 40,000 by the 1890s, little more than a century later.

The collapse of the population, coupled with the impact of outside cultures, resulted in crisis, initiating dramatic social and political change. Even so, the issue of how the distant island kingdom of Hawaii became part of the United States has been obfuscated by a combination of a mainland American mythology and old-fashioned denial.

In 1893, only 2 percent of the population of the kingdom of Hawai'i was of American descent, but the complex interplay of missionaries, financiers, sugar growers, and politicians would soon see that this number increased dramatically. But the population of Hawai'i began to change with the arrival of outsiders. In short, as a U.S. territory, Hawai'i until 1940 was distinguished by a rapid growth in population, the development of a plantation economy based on the production of sugar and pineapples for consumption on the U.S. mainland, and the growth of transport and military links.

Movements for statehood, based in part on Hawai'i's obligation to pay U.S. taxes without having corresponding legislative representation, began to emerge. Concomitantly, the United States entered World War II with the Japanese bombing of Pearl Harbor. From this day forward, the population of Hawai'i would experience even more significant changes in immigration and growth patterns in the region.

The Japanese attack on the American Pacific Fleet at Pearl Harbor on December 7, 1941 lead to a declaration of martial law, a state that continued until October 24, 1944. The war brought a massive increase in American military personnel in Hawai'i, with numbers increasing from 28,000 in 1940 to 378,000 in 1944. The total population increased from 429,000 in 1940 to 858,000 in 1944, thereby substantially stimulating the demand for retail, restaurant, and other consumer services. An enormous construction program to house the new personnel was also undertaken in 1941 and 1942. However, the wartime interruption of commercial shipping reduced the tonnage of civilian cargo arriving in Hawai'i by more than 50 percent. Employees working in designated high-priority organizations, including sugar plantations, had their jobs and wages frozen in place by General Order 18 which also suspended union activity.

None of these changes led to an amorphous, multiracial mixing. Far more accurate, we must center on the accounts and degrees of acceptance and assimilation that these various groups encounter in Hawaiian society and culture up to the present day. Within this context, the term "local" has been deeply contested. Emerging in the 1930s to distinguish between the native-born people of Hawai'i and mainlanders, "local" increasingly represents something of a fictitious Hawaiian pan-ethnic identity underscoring a shared ethnic experience and rooted in the history of plantation economies, where indigenous Hawaiians and Asian immigrant groups are held subordinate to a *haole* (white) elite. However, with the growth of the indigenous Hawaiian sovereignty movement, many individuals have sought to critique the ideology underpinning this pan-ethnicity. Increasingly, scholars and activists have argued that the various ethnic groups in Hawai'i cannot be lumped together. Most obviously, their cultures were and remain distinct, and each of these groups has settled in Hawai'i under widely varying circumstances. As such, families living in the Hawai'i for several generations naturally resent being stereotyped as part of, say, a superminority (e.g., the disingenuous term "Asian American" within the Hawaiian context). Their long-rooted ties and hard work—they have often had to work harder to overcome the hurdles of racism and ethnic discrimination to varying degrees over the years—make them a distinct group, worthy of recognition.

Whereas the population of prewar Hawai'i by and large represented the immediate needs of behemoth corporate plantations—rural settlements scattered throughout the islands, in tiny fishing villages far off the main roads and larger coastal and upland villages, plantation, and ranch towns—the city of Honolulu, however much an exception, remains the epitome of picturesque "sleepy" island living, even as World War II came to an end.

The increase in tourism, for example, leads to the construction of new hotels and other hospitality-related facilities which, in turn, lead to an increasingly sprawling urban infrastructure. This building boom is particularly significant during the 1950s and 1960s; massive construction projects of 30- and 40-story buildings suddenly give the city a new, multileveled skyline. On O'ahu, agricultural lands fall before the development for housing, and rural towns become suburbs.

Further complicating the political scene of the time, the Hawai'i Statehood Commission proves itself strong enough to push its agenda in Washington. In contrast, the Big Five *haole* companies, which prewar had dominated the island's business, finance, shipping, and government, see statehood as a threat to their base of power. Adding to the social upheaval of the 1950s, Hawai'i finds itself in a strategic position in the U.S. defense system. As a result, more than 100,000 U.S. military personnel and their dependents are—and continue to be—stationed in or have their home port in Hawai'i. Their presence has exerted a significant and lasting influence on the local economy and social life.

As Hawaiian culture becomes more popular on the U.S. mainland, there is a massive immigration to the islands. The perception of a "secluded paradise," for example, was further and consciously promoted and finely honed in the 1950s as local filming increased dramatically. Such mainland box-office hits as *From Here to Eternity, The Caine Mutiny, Mister Roberts*, and *South Pacific* further reinforce such naïve perceptions among individuals on the mainland eager for a carefree lifestyle. Those who could not "escape" to the islands would find other means to sate their curiosity: pineapple production and canning, as a direct result, substantially increases over the decade, from 13,697,000 cases in 1949 to 18,613,000 cases in 1956.

But it was another "export" that captures and holds the imagination of non-islanders far and wide. The most influential of all such cinematic productions touting an exoticism akin to Orientalism, the very popular *Gidget*, in fact, introduces the wholly alien sport of surfing to masses of mainlanders. Shortly thereafter, the first Hawaiian television show intended for an audience beyond her shores, *Hawaii Five-O*, starring Jack Lord, begins broadcasting stateside to an audience hungry for all things Hawaiian.

In short, the post-1945 period in many ways mirrors Hawai'i's transition from a sugar oligarchy to a democratic society marked by further economic consolidation and a long constitutional path toward statehood. In 1959, Hawai'i holds a special election on June 27. An overwhelming number of Hawaiians vote in favor of it, and only the small island of Ni'ihau, populated exclusively by native Hawaiians, votes against it. Hawai'i officially becomes the 50th state on August 21, 1959. Statehood, in turn, brings more change: in 1959, 243,000 tourists visit Hawai'i, and it was the transition of status from territory to statehood behind the 1958–1973 economic boom, in which real per capita personal income increases at an annual rate of 4 percent.

In 1964, for instance, Japan eases travel restrictions and Hawai'i almost instantaneously undergoes yet another tourism boost. That same year, some 46,000 immigrant Japanese take their oaths of citizenship. In fact, officials overseeing tourism in Hawai'i would witness hundreds of thousands of new visitors each year.

The Immigration Act of 1965, for example, permitted residents of the Asia-Pacific Triangle to enter the United States as quota immigrants, resulting in heavy emigration from Korea, Taiwan, Hong Kong, and Indochina. And whereas this wave of Korean immigration was based on family and employment immigration, resulting in the development of large Korean immigrant communities in Los Angeles, New York and Chicago, for example, the result is entirely different in Hawai'i, where it is the Philippines that would fuel Hawaiian immigration. As a result, the number of Filipino/as multiplies manifold. Allowing for a new and different wave of Filipino/a migration, this new law encourages a "dual chain" system of immigration consisting of the "relative-selective" and "occupational" migration. Under "relative-selective immigration," Filipino/as came as petitioned relatives of previous migrants who have become U.S. citizens. Furthermore, the "occupational immigration" clause in the 1965 immigration law is in response to the need for more professionals, specifically in the medical field, in the United States. Thousands of Filipino/a professionals, mostly doctors and nurses, arrive in the United States as complete families. Most settle along the East Coast, thus creating a marked occupational distinction between Filipino/a communities on the mainland and in Hawai'i.

This growth in new arrivals once again accompanies growth in the construction industry, particularly from 1965 to 1975, fueling even greater movements of peoples onto the islands. The increase in tourism, for example, will in turn require an increased workforce to service the hospitality industry. Hence, more than 354,000 emigrants from India—many well educated and holding professional rank at home—arrive in the two-and-a-half decades from 1961 to 1986, in large part to meet just this need. In fact, this mass emigration from the Indian subcontinent is made possible only with the passage of the 1965 Act.

The end of the Vietnamese conflict also means an increased numbers of immigrants entering in unique circumstances. Ethnic communities commonly associated with the Indochinese War, be they Laotian, Cambodians, or Indo-Chinese (among them the Indo-Chinese Hmong, formerly a mountain-dwelling people of Vietnam and Laos), each holds fast to their own language and culture and prefer to live isolated from other groups. As a direct result, they rarely relocate to Hawai'i, preferring instead the promises of a better life on the mainland. Instead, this increased traffic from Asia is met with increased travel from Japan. And by 1970 there are more than 70,000 Koreans in the United States, their number having grown dramatically since 1965. At the very same time, it is estimated that there are more than 13,000 Samoans and part-Samoans living in Hawai'i. A majority of them reside on the island of O'ahu.

Similarly, a wave of emigration from the Federated States of Micronesia (FSM) is set in motion in 1986, when the Pacific Island state signs a Compact of Free Association with the United States. Within weeks, whole families of Micronesians and especially young, single men begin leaving the FSM for countries overseas, at first to Guam and the Commonwealth of the Northern Mariana Islands and later to Hawai'i.

By the end of the 1980s, the unemployment rate in Hawai'i is just 2–3 percent; employment has been steadily growing since 1983, and tourism and the economy in general appear to be strong. From 1991 to 1998, however, the island's economy suffers from several negative shocks. The 1990–1991 U.S. recession, the closure of California military bases and defense plants, and uncertainty over the safety of air travel during the 1991 Gulf War combine to reduce tourism and settlement in the early and mid-1990s. Volatile and slow growth in Japan throughout the 1990s led to declines in Japanese visitor arrivals in the late 1990s. The ongoing decline in sugar and pineapple production gathers steam in the 1990s, with only a handful of plantations still in business by 2001. As a direct result, the cumulative impact of these adverse shocks is so severe that real per capita personal income shows no change between 1991 and 1998.

The final decade of the twentieth century witnesses a fully developed renaissance of native Hawaiian culture, having sprung as it were from modest beginnings in the 1970s, most notably with the resurgence of the *hula*, the voyaging canoe, the art of tattooing, and its music and language. Most Hawaiian inhabitants know at least some Hawaiian words and observe cultural practices including the giving of the *lei*, a garland of flowers. The *Aloha Spirit*, however commercialized it has become, is reflective of the way many diverse groups live together on the small islands. Contemporary Hawaiian cultural identity has gone largely unnoticed by all but a few social activists, who have been left to tease out the complexities comprising tradition, culture, and institutional intervention.

As stated earlier, today the various ethnic groups—be they *haole*, *hapa haole*, or *kama'aina*—cannot not be lumped together because these cultures are distinct. Each of these ethnic groups came to the islands under widely varying circumstances. What ultimately will be the outcome of establishing a native Hawaiian governing body to negotiate with the state and federal governments on issues relating to land, assets, and natural resources? Ultimately, it is an internal matter, up to those residing in Hawai'i to come to terms with identity, self-definition and self-worth over this new millennium. What remains critical at this juncture is that residents, regardless of ethnic origin, not lose sight of community and interpersonal relationships. But the most salient point is that a particular sensitivity to the host and neighboring cultures is of the utmost importance, certainly.

That is, an island perspective requires that *everyone* give greater credence to mutual respect and to an overriding need to celebrate the ease of solutions arising from our differences, to peace through compassion and empathy, to the unbroken bonds of a timeless unity arising our overwhelming—and equally undeniable—sense of diversity.

NOTABLE FIGURES

Satoru Abe (1926–)

A painter and sculptor, Satoru Abe was born in the Mo'ili'ili area of Honolulu in 1926. He attended President William McKinley High School. In 1948, after spending his summer at the California School for Fine Arts, he moved to New York, where he attended the Art Students League of New York, studying with George Grosz, Louis Bouche, and Jon Carrol. Abe returned to Hawai'i in 1970.

Abe is a prolific member of the Metcalf Chateau, seven Asian American artists with ties to Honolulu who, gathering to promote modern abstract art in Hawai'i, flourished after World War II. Abe is perhaps best known for his sculptures of abstracted natural forms resembling trees, many of which are held in Honolulu among the public collections of The Contemporary Museum, The Honolulu Academy of Arts, and The Hawai'i State Art Museum. Representative of his depth and range are *Wheel* (a 1991 Indian red granite sculpture at Hawaii State Art Museum), *Aged Tree* (a 1976 copper, bronze and longan wood sculpture at the Kauikeaouli Hale Courthouse), *Five Trees* (a 1978 copper and bronze sculpture at The Contemporary Museum), *Inverted Tree* (a 1973 copper and bronze sculpture at The Contemporary Museum), and *The Man* (a 1979 copper and bronze sculpture at The Contemporary Museum).

George Ariyoshi (1926–)

As a Democrat, George Ryoichi Ariyoshi served as the fourth governor of Hawai'i from 1974 to 1986. Born to Japanese immigrant parents on March 12, 1926, in Honolulu, Hawai'i, he graduated in 1944 from McKinley High School. As World War II was ending, he served as an interpreter with the U.S. Army Military Intelligence Service in Japan. Upon returning stateside, he first attended the University of Hawai'i at Mānoa, then transferred to Michigan State University, where he graduated with his BA in 1949. He went on to receive his law degree from the University of Michigan Law School.

Ariyoshi's distinguished political career began in 1954 when he was elected to the territorial House of Representatives. In1970, he was elected lieutenant governor and in 1974, became the first American of Asian descent to be elected governor of any state in the nation. He was re-elected in 1978 and 1982. He currently serves as advisor at the law firm of Watanabe Ing LLP, a position he has held since retiring from public office in 1986.

Don Ho (1930–2007)

The most beloved entertainer in Hawai'i and one of the biggest draws in show business, Don Ho was born Donald Tai Loy Ho on August 13, 1930, in the hard-scrabble Honolulu neighborhood of Kaka'ako, but he grew up in Kāne'ohe on the windward side of the island of O'ahu. Of Chinese, Hawaiian, Portuguese, Dutch, and German descent, his early years were remarkable if only because of the poverty he overcame, settling in Kāne'ohe, and then boarding at Kamehameha School. Combining his musical gift, beachboy demeanor, and love of the islands, Ho was for nearly half-a-century synonymous with the Hawaiian Islands, from early shows at Duke Kahanamoku's to a tour and television career that carried the *Aloha Spirit* to audiences around the world, as his island charm invariably endeared him to millions.

Ho graduated from the Kamehameha Schools in 1949 and attended Springfield College on a football scholarship a year later. Not long separated from the islands, he returned home to earn his BA in sociology from the University of Hawai'i at Mānoa in 1953. In 1954, he entered the U.S. Air Force, doing his basic training at Keesler Air Force Base in Mississippi. Later, he spent time flying fighter jets in both Texas and Hawai'i.

Ho left the U.S. Air Force in 1959 after learning that his mother was ill and began singing Hawaiian and traditional pop music at her club in Kāne'ohe. Honey's quickly caught the attentions of local servicemen and became *the* hotspot for local entertainment. In 1963, he relocated the Kāne'ohe Honey's to Waikīkī, but he soon outgrew that venue and moved to Duke's, a local night club owned by

Duke Kahanamoku. There, between sessions, Ho made jokes about being sent to Mississippi in the 1950s and about being Hawaiian. He was also known for asking for all Pearl Harbor survivors to stand and be recognized. These unsuspecting veterans were then invited on stage to join the *hula* dancers.

Whether it was his musical talents, his dynamic personality, or his overall charisma, Ho quickly caught the attention of several record company officials and was signed to Reprise Records. Ho released his first album, *Do Ho Show*, in 1965, and cut the lilting ballad "Tiny Bubbles," his first big hit and his signature song until the end of his life, in 1966. He soon afterward conquered the mainland, appearing on the likes of *The Brady Bunch, Batman, Sanford and Son, Fantasy Island, I Dream of Jeannie*, and *Charlie's Angels*. He was by this time a Hawaiian icon.

Ho lived and conducted business at his Diamond Head residence. In 1995, at the age of 65, Ho's health began declining; by 2002, he developed an incurable heart condition. In 2005, he was diagnosed with cardiomyopathy and on December 6, 2005, had his own blood-derived stem cells injected into his heart by his surgeons in Thailand. Despite his poor health, Ho continued his routine of nightly performances. He died in Waikīkī from heart failure on April 14, 2007.

Daniel K. Inouye (1924–2012)

Inouye was born on September 7, 1924, in Honolulu, Hawai'i, the son of Kame (née Imanaga) and Hyotaro Inouye. As a Nisei, an American-born child of Japanese immigrants, he grew up in the Bingham Tract, a Chinese American enclave within the predominantly Japanese American community of Mo'ili'ili in Honolulu. He graduated from McKinley High School.

Inouye continuously represented Hawai'i in the U.S. Congress since it achieved statehood in 1959, serving as the first Japanese American in the U.S. House of Representatives and later the first in the U.S. Senate. The recipient of the U.S. Medal of Honor, Senator Inouye had, prior to his death on December 17, 2012, announced plans to run for a record 10th term in 2016, when he would have been 92 years old.

Duke Paoa Kahanamoku (1890–1968)

Hawai'i's ambassador of Aloha, Duke Paoa Kahanamoku, may forever be remembered for his Olympic medals and as the father of international modern surfing, but those who place assorted *lei* on his statue in Waikīkī equally honor him for his strength of character and the Hawaiian ideals of *Aloha* he so aptly represented.

Kahanamoku was born Duke Paoa Kahinu Mokoe Hulikohola Kahanamoku on August 24, 1890, in Waikīkī, at Hale'ākala, the home of Bernice Pauahi Bishop (later converted into the Arlington Hotel). The name "Duke" is not a title but a given name: he was named after his father, Duke Halapu Kahanamoku, who was christened "Duke" by Bernice Pauahi Bishop in honor of Prince Alfred, Duke of Edinburgh, who was visiting Hawai'i at the time of the elder man's birth in 1869. The younger "Duke," as eldest son, inherited the name. As a five-time Olympic medalist in swimming, Duke's name became widely known.

In 1893, the family moved to Kālia, Waikīkī (the present site of the Hilton Hawaiian Village) to be closer to his mother's parents and family. He attended the Waikīkī Grammar School, Kaahumanu School, and sometime later the Kamehameha Schools, although he never graduated because he was needed to help support the family.

Growing up on the outskirts of Waikīkī, Kahanamoku spent his youth as a "bronzed beach boy," and it is at Waikīkī Beach where he developed his surfing and swimming skills (Osmond 2010). He easily qualified for the U.S. Olympic swimming team and won a gold medal in the 100 meter freestyle in the 1912 Stockholm Olympics and a silver medal with the relay team. During the 1920 Olympics in Antwerp, he won gold medals both in the 100 meters and in the relay. And he finished the 100 meters with a silver medal during the 1924 Olympics in Paris, with the gold going to Johnny Weissmuller and the bronze to Duke's brother, Samuel Kahanamoku. Between Olympic competitions, and after retiring from the Olympics, Kahanamoku traveled internationally to give surfing exhibitions. Until then, he was known only in Hawai'i. A monument at Waikīkī Beach, showing Kahanamoku standing in front of his surfboard with his arms outstretched, was erected in his honor.

Kahanamoku died of a heart attack on January 22, 1968, at the age of 77. A long motorcade of mourners, accompanied by a 30-man police escort, carried his body across the town to Waikīkī Beach, as throngs of local surfers gathered along the beach. As everyone sang "Aloha Oe," his ashes were scattered across the ocean.

Israel "Iz" Kamakawiwo'ole (1959–1997)

A local Hawaiian who against all odds rose to unrivaled celebrity on the strength of his golden voice and a simple four-string 'ukulele, Israel "Iz" Ka'ano'i Kamakawiwo'ole became the undisputed voice of contemporary Hawai'i and the conscience of generations, young and old. He was born on May 20, 1959, at Kuakini Hospital in Honolulu. In his youth, he triumphed over untold adversity and his humble origins, overcoming drugs, youth gangs, and the loss of his parents and his only brother.

At the age of 11, Kamakawiwo'ole began playing music. 'Ukulele in hand, he melded the smooth sounds of the Hawaiian tenor with such seemingly unrelated genres as jazz and reggae to become the premiere influence and driving force in contemporary Hawaiian music and the hope of his people.

In his early teens, Kamakawiwo'ole studied at Upward Bound at the University of Hawai'i, Hilo, and his family moved to Mākaha. He recorded *No Kristo* in 1976 and released four more albums, including *Kahea O Keale*, *Keala*, *Mākaha Sons of Ni'ihau*, and *Mahalo Ke Akua*. In 1990, IZ released his first solo album, *Ka 'Ano'i*, and he won awards for Contemporary Album of the Year and Male Vocalist of the Year from the Hawai'i Academy of Recording Arts. At this time, he began to speak and stand up for his people at a critical junction in Hawaiian history and demand justice and sovereignty.

IZ's *Facing Future* was released in 1993, featuring his most popular song, the medley "Somewhere over the Rainbow/What a Wonderful World," along with "Hawai'i 78," "White Sandy Beach of Hawai'i," "Maui Hawaiian Sup'pa Man," and "Kaulana Kawaihae." The album debuted high on *Billboard* magazine's Top Pop chart, and his fame outside Hawai'i rose rapidly. His medley of "Somewhere over the Rainbow" and "What a Wonderful World," was subsequently featured in several films, in television programs, and in commercials. In 1994, Kamakawiwo'ole was named Favorite Entertainer of the Year by the Hawai'i Academy of Recording Arts. In 1995, he made a conscious turn toward issues of serious social and economic import and released *E Ala 'E*, featuring the political title song, together with "Kaleohano." In 1996, with his release of *N Dis Life*, which featured "In This Life" and "Starting All over Again," IZ found himself the unchallenged voice of a nation. Enduring several hospitalizations, he died at The Queen's Medical Center in Honolulu on June 26, 1997, at the youthful age of 38, from a weight-related respiratory illness.

NORA OKJA KELLER (1965–)

The highly acclaimed Korean American novelist Nora Okja Keller was born in Seoul, South Korea, on December 22, 1965. After graduating from the Punahou School in Honolulu, Keller matriculated at the University of Hawai'i, Mānoa, where she received her BA with a double major in psychology and English. She remained in Honolulu after graduation and found employment as a freelance writer, including at, among other locations, the *Honolulu Star-Bulletin*. She earned her MA and PhD in American Literature from the University of California at Santa Cruz.

Keller's 1997 breakthrough work of fiction, *Comfort Woman*, and the 2002 sequel, *Fox Girl*, focus on the multigenerational trauma arising from the experiences of Korean women conscripted as sex slaves, euphemistically called "comfort women" (in Japanese, *jungan ianfu*), for Japanese troops during World War II. Taken together, Keller's novels do, in fact, deconstruct complex ethnic identity as she relocates, then repositions herself within Hawaii's multiethnic society, recognizing as she did so that individuals of mixed race necessarily reflect the extremes of the strength and turbulence of their experiences.

BEATRICE KRAUSS (1904–1998)

Beatrice Krauss, respected and beloved by generations of students and admirers alike as "Auntie Bea," was born in Honolulu, Hawai'i, in 1904. A much-revered *kupuna* ("elder") within her community, she eschewed the absence of legal precedent for women in academia and organized community-wide activities, sharing as she always did her wealth of knowledge and expertise in native agricultural sciences and botany with all who had a need. By 1926, she had become the first woman to earn a degree in agriculture from the University of Hawai'i, Mānoa. She earned her MS in 1930.

In 1968, when retirement was upon her, Beatrice Krauss shifted her perspective and spent the next five years within the teaching faculty of the Botany Department at her *alma mater*. There, she developed the first course in Hawaiian ethnobotany, thereby contributing to a renewed interest in Hawaiian culture. Additionally, she spent 25 years teaching pro bono at the Lyon Arboretum, where she conducted informal classes in ethnobotany for young and old alike, and designed, then planted, the internationally recognized ethnobotanical garden. She was never paid for her services to the university and to the community but, in 1988, she was awarded an honorary doctorate by unanimous decree of her colleagues at the university. She remained with the arboretum as a distinguished research affiliate until her death in 1998.

ELLISON ONIZUKA (1946–1986)

A Japanese American astronaut from Kealakekua, in the Kona district of the Big Island, Ellison Shoji Onizuka became the first Asian American to reach space where he served aboard the Space Shuttle *Discovery*. In 1986, he—alongside pilot Michael J. Smith, mission-specialists Ronald McNair and Judith Resnik, and payload-specialists Gregory Jarvis and Christa McAuliffe—died in the destruction of the *Challenger*, onboard which he served as Mission Specialist.

Born on June 24, 1946, Onizuka was the elder son of Masamitsu and Mitsue Onizuka. He graduated from Konawaena High School in Kealakekua in 1964. He then left for the mainland and received his BS in aerospace engineering in June 1969, and his MS in that field in December 1969, from the University of Colorado at Boulder.

In January 1978, Onizuka was selected for the astronaut program and had completed one year of evaluation and training by August 1979. His first space mission took place from January 24 to January 27, 1985, aboard the *Discovery*, where he completed a total of 74 hours in space. He was then assigned to *Challenger* a year later on January 28, 1986. Just a minute into the launch, a leaking solid rocket booster ruptured the fuel tank. Everyone perished. His body was returned to the islands, where he was laid to rest at the National Memorial Cemetery of the Pacific in Honolulu. At the time of his death, Onizuka held the rank of lieutenant colonel. He was promoted, posthumously, to the rank of colonel. He was also awarded the Congressional Space Medal of Honor.

Akebono Tarō (1969–)

Akebono Tarō is perhaps the best known of several American-born Japanese sumo wrestlers. The son of Randolph and Janice Rowan, he was born in Waimānalo, Hawai'i, on May 8, 1969, as Chad Haakeo Rowan. He attended Kaiser High School before matriculating to Hawaii Pacific University on a basketball scholarship. Within the year, he joined the Azumazeki stable to train under the pioneering Hawaiian sumo wrestler Takamiyama. He flew to Japan in early 1988. Quickly accepted by the professional sport in Japan, he adopted the *shikona* of Akebono, meaning "new dawn," and made his professional debut in March 1988. He rose rapidly through the ranks and became the first foreign-born wrestler to reach the highest rank, *yokozuna*.

Charles Nainoa Thompson (1953–)

Charles Nainoa Thompson was born in O'ahu on March 11, 1953.He became the formidable captain of the *Hōkūle'a* voyaging canoe and a noted trustee of the University of Hawai'i and the Kamehameha Schools and the executive director of the Polynesian Voyaging Society. Thompson is best known, however, as the first Hawaiian to practice the ancient Polynesian art of navigation; he navigated two double-hulled canoes, the *Hōkūle'a* and the *Hawai'iloa*, from Hawai'i to other island nations in Polynesia without the aid of Western instrumentation. Given his prowess and ingenuity, Nainoa Thompson the navigator has become a cultural hero to Hawaiians.

A 1972 graduate of Punahou School, Nainoa Thompson earned his BA in Ocean Sciences in 1986 from the University of Hawai'i at Mānoa. Between high school and his graduation from university, he studied non-instrumental celestial navigation, or wayfinding, under master navigator Mau Piailug of Satawal, Micronesia. He became the first Hawaiian to practice the art of wayfinding on long-distance ocean voyages in some 600 years. His first long voyage took place in 1980, when he navigated the *Hōkūle'a* from Hawai'i to Tahiti and back. Then, in 1985–1987, he navigated it without instrumentation across Polynesia from Hawai'i to New Zealand and back, stopping at islands along the way. In 1995, the

Hawai'iloa made its maiden voyage from Hawai'i to Tahiti to Ra'iatea and back via Nuku Hiva. By doing so, Thompson confirmed that such a difficult journey across the Pacific—the same route believed to have been undertaken by the first people to the islands—was entirely plausible. In 1999, he undertook a solo voyage from Hawai'i to Tahiti. On March 18, 2007, Thompson and four other native Hawaiian navigators were inducted into Pwo as master navigators. The ceremony was conducted by Piailug on Satawal.

HAUNANI-KAY TRASK (1949–)

Haunani-Kay Trask is a professor of Hawaiian Studies at the University of Hawai'i, a political activist who staunchly supports the Sovereignty movement, and a fierce poet. She is descended from the Pi'ilani line of Mau'i and the Kahaku-makaliua line of Kaua'i. She was born in the San Francisco Bay area on October 3, 1949, and, after returning to her ancestral home, graduated from the Kamehameha Schools in 1967. She then attended the University of Wisconsin at Madison, earning her BA in 1972; her MA in 1975; and her PhD in political science in 1981, with a dissertation on Eros, power, and feminist theory. An active member of the *Ka Lahui Hawai'i*, a native Hawaiian initiative for self-government, she has earned a reputation for having represented indigenous rights before the United Nations and across various other global forums.

As a powerful writer and poet, Trask uses her art as a vehicle for change. *Light in the Crevice Never Seen*, the first volume of poetry ever published by an indigenous Hawaiian in the mainland United States, speaks directly about the racial issues that plague the islands and the social realities affecting native Hawaiians today, from youthful suicide and loss of language to verbal racism and physical violence. To restore balance, she establishes a deep reconnection to land and to the sustaining strengths of family and love.

Taken together, her anthologies of poetry equate the native Hawaiian experience in its historical context as no more than colonialism, initiated by military invasion and sustained through military and economic occupation and oppression. Uncompromising, she uses her poetry to link the rights of native peoples the world over.

LOIS-ANN YAMANAKA (1961–)

Critically acclaimed contemporary Japanese American poet and novelist Lois-Ann Yamanaka equates comfort with writing in Pidgin. Born in Ho'olehua, Moloka'i, on September 7, 1961, her writings primarily deal with controversial ethnic issues; she struggles with such notions as the Asian American family and the disintegration of the "local culture" of Hawai'i.

She received her bachelor's degree in 1983 and her master's degree in 1987 in Education from the University of Hawai'i at Mānoa. As descendants of Japanese immigrant laborers, her narrators remind us time and again of a process whereby we at first confront and, sometime later, find solace in the nature of our personal cultural identity. Her first book, written in 1993, would neither abandon poetry nor privilege narrative but would find life in the hybridity of her world. Narrated by a wholly typical group of working-class Hawaiian adolescents, *Saturday Night at the Pahala Theatre* comprises four verse novellas exploring such daunting subjects as ethnic identity, sexual awakening, drug use, and relationships built upon abuse. Thereafter, her *Father of the Four Passages* (2001), *The Heart's Language* (2005), *Behold the Many* (2006), and her short screenplay *Silent Years* (2004, later made into a film by James Sereno) would reflect a maturity of vision and voice, even as she dissected issues relevant to adolescent well-being, at times even survival, as they struggle with the complexities inherent to ethnicity.

In addition to grants from the National Endowment for the Humanities in 1990 and the National Endowment for the Arts in 1994, Yamanaka has been recognized for her literary accomplishments with the likes of back-to-back Pushcart Prizes for Poetry in 1993 and 1994, a Carnegie Foundation Grant, the 1996 Rona Jaffe Award for Women Writers, and both the Lannan Literary Award and the Asian American Literary Award in 1998.

BIBLIOGRAPHY

Abrahamson, Harold. "Assimilation and Pluralism." In Stephan Thernstrom, Ann Orlov, and Oscar Handlin, eds. *Harvard Encyclopedia of American Ethnic Groups*. Cambridge, MA: Harvard University Press, 1980, pp. 150–60.

Adamski, Mary. "Isles Bid Aloha, Not Goodbye, to 'Brudda Iz.'" *Honolulu Star-Bulletin*, July 10, 1997. http://archives.starbulletin.com/97/07/10/news/story3.html. Accessed July 1, 2013.

Agard, Keoni Kealoha. *A Call for Hawaiian Sovereignty*. Waipuhu, HI: Na Kane O Ka Malo Press, 1990.

Apio, Alani. *Kāmau*. Honolulu: Palila Books, 1994.

Apio, Alani. *Kāmau A'e*. Honolulu: Kumu Kahua Theater Co., 1998.

Arakawa, Linda. "First Asian in U.S. Senate Broke Barriers." *Honolulu Advertiser*, August 19, 2004. http://the.honoluluadvertiser.com/article/2004/Aug/19/ln/ln07a.html. Accessed July 1, 2013).

Ariyoshi, George R. *Hawaii: The Past Fifty Years, the Next Fifty Years*. New York: Watermark Publishing, 2009.

Ariyoshi, George R. *With Obligation to All*. Honolulu: University of Hawai'i Press, 1997.

Asahina, Robert. *Just Americans: How Japanese Americans Won a War at Home and Abroad*. New York: Gotham/Penguin, 2007.

Beckwith, M. *Hawaiian Mythology*. Honolulu: University of Hawai'i Press, 1970.

Beechert, Edward D. *Working in Hawaii: A Labor History*. Honolulu: University of Hawai'i Press, 1985.

Bird, Isabella L. *The Hawaiian Archipelago: Six Months among the Palm Groves, Coral Reefs, and Volcanoes of the Sandwich Islands*. London: Putman, 1886.

Black, Cobey, and Kathleen Mellen. *Princess Pauahi and Her Legacy*. Honolulu: Kamehameha Schools Press, 1965.

Blaisdell, R. K. *The Health of Native Hawaiians*. Vol. 32. Honolulu: University of Hawai'i Press, 1989.

Boylan, Dan. *John A. Burns: The Man and His Times*. Honolulu: University of Hawai'i Press, 2000.

Bray, D. K., and D. Low. *The Kahuna Religion of Hawaii*. Garberville, CA: Borderland Sciences Research Foundation, Inc., 1990.

Brittingham, Angela. *Ancestry 2000*. Census Brief. Washington, DC: U.S. Census Bureau, 2004.

Bushnell, Andrew F. "The 'Horror' Reconsidered: An Evaluation of the Historical Evidence for Population Decline in Hawai'i, 1778–1803." *Pacific Studies* 16 (1993): 115–61.

Calabresi, Massimo, and Perry Bacon Jr. "Daniel Akaka: Master of the Minor." *Time*, April 24, 2006, 30.

Carrigan, Anthony. *Postcolonial Tourism: Literature, Culture, and Environment*. Routledge Research in Postcolonial Literatures. New York: Routledge, 2010.

Carroll, Rick. *IZ: Voice of the People*. Honolulu: Bess Press, 2006.

Cataluna, Lee. *Folks You Meet in Longs and Other Stories*. Honolulu: Bamboo Ridge Press, 2005.

Cayetano, Benjamin J. *Ben: A Memoir, from Street Kid to Governor*. New York: Watermark Publishing, 2009.

Charr, Easurk Emsen, and Wayne Patterson. *The Golden Mountain: The Autobiography of a Korean Immigrant, 1895–1960*. Urbana-Champaign: University of Illinois Press, 1996.

Chinen, Nate. "Don Ho, Hawaiian Musician, Dies at 76." *New York Times*, April 15, 2007. http://www.nytimes.com/2007/04/15/arts/music/15ho.html?_r=0. Accessed August 2, 2014.

Chock, Eric, and Darrell H. Y. Lum, eds. *Poetry. Fiction. Pacific Island Studies*. Honolulu: Bamboo Ridge Press, 2011.

Choy, Bong Youn. *Koreans in America*. Chicago: Nelson-Hall, 1979.

Clarke, Joan, and Diane Dods. *Artists/Hawai'i*. Honolulu: University of Hawai'i Press, 1996.

Craighill-Handy, E. S., et al. *Ancient Hawaiian Civilization: A Series of Lectures Delivered at the Kamehameha Schools*. Tokyo: Charles E. Tuttle Company, Inc. 1976.

Crowe, Ellie. *Surfer of the Century: The Life of Duke Kahanamoku*. Honolulu: Bess Press, 2004.

Cummings, Bruce. *Korea's Place in the Sun*. New York: Norton Press, 1997.

Danico, Mary Yu. *The 1.5 Generation: Becoming Korean American in Hawai'i*. Honolulu: University of Hawai'i Press, 2004.

Daniels, Roger. *Asian America: Chinese and Japanese in the United States since 1850*. Seattle: University of Washington Press, 1988.

Daws, Gavan. *Holy Man: Father Damien of Molokai*. Honolulu: University of Hawai'i Press, 1984.

Daws, Gavan. *Shoal of Time: A History of the Hawaiian Islands*. Honolulu: University Press of Hawaii, 1968.

Diamond, Heather A. *Cultural Tourism and the Negotiation of Tradition*. Honolulu: University of Hawai'i Press, 2011.

Doherty, Jim. "Will the Real Charlie Chan Please Stand Up." In *Just the Facts: True Tales of Cops and Criminals*. New York: Deadly Serious Press, 2004, pp. 111–20.

Doi, Isami. "Letters to Satoru Abe, 1952–1965." *Bamboo Ridge: Journal of Hawai'i Literature and Arts* (Spring 1998): 57–64.

Dooley, Jim. "Kamehameha Schools Settled Lawsuit for $7M." *The Honolulu Advertiser*, February 8, 2008. http://the.honoluluadvertiser.com/article/2008/Feb/08/ln/hawaii802080371.html. Accessed August 2, 2014.

Dudley, M. K. *A Hawaiian Nation I: Man, Gods, and Nature*. Honolulu: Na Kane No Ka Malo Press, 1990.

"Duke Kahanamoku Dies at 77: Leading Swimmer of His Time. Olympic Swimming Champion of '12 and '20 in Freestyle. Best-Known Hawaiian." *New York Times*, January 23, 1968. http://solution-nine.com/kahanamoku. Accessed March 12, 2014.

Dye, Tom. "Population Trends in Hawai'i before 1778." *The Hawaiian Journal of History* 28 (1994): 1–20.

Edmond, Rod. *Leprosy and Empire: A Medical and Cultural History*. London: Cambridge University Press, 2006.

Emerson, N. B. *Pele and Hiiaka: A Myth from Hawaii*. Honolulu: Ai Pohaku Press, 1997.

Garrison, Jessica. "Samoan Americans at a Crossroads." *Los Angeles Times*, April 14, 2000. http://articles.latimes.com/2000/apr/14/local/me-19599. Accessed July 1, 2013.

Gleason, Philip. "American Identity and Americanization." In Stephan Thernstrom, Ann Orlov, and Oscar Handlin, eds. *Harvard Encyclopedia of American Ethnic Groups*. Cambridge, MA: Harvard University Press, 1980, pp. 31–57.

Goodman, Grant. *A Flood of Immigration: Japanese Immigration to the Philippines 1900–1941*. Lawrence: The University of Kansas Center for East Asian Studies, 2011.

Gordon, Larry. "Occidental Recalls 'Barry' Obama." *Los Angeles Times*, January 29, 2007. http://articles.latimes.com/2007/jan/29/local/me-oxy29. Accessed August 2, 2014.

Gordon, Mike, et al. "The Legacy: A Voice of Hawai'i and Hawaiians." *The Honolulu Advertiser*, August 19, 2008. http://the.honoluluadvertiser.com/iz/story_p2.html. Accessed July 1, 2013.

Gorenflo, Larry J., and Michael J. Levin. "Changing Migration Patterns in the Federated States of Micronesia." *ISLA: A Journal on Micronesian Studies* 3 (1995): 29–71.

Grant, Glen, and Dennis Ogawa. *Ellison Onizuka: A Remembrance*. Honolulu: Mutual Publishing, 1986.

Groseclose, David A., comp. *James A. Michener: A Bibliography*. Austin, TX: State House Press, 1996.

Haar, Francis, and Prithwish Neogy. *Artists of Hawaii: Nineteen Painters and Sculptors*. Honolulu: University of Hawai'i Press, 1974.

Haas, Michael, ed. *Barack Obama: The Aloha Zen President: How a Son of the 50th State May Revitalize America Based on 12 Multicultural Principles*. New York: Praeger, 2011.

Hall, Sandra Kimberly. *Duke: A Great Hawaiian*. Honolulu: Bess Press, 2004.

Handy, E. S., and M. K. Pukui. *The Polynesian System in Ka'u, Hawaii*. Tokyo: Charles E. Tuttle Co., 1972.

Hara, Mary, ed. *Intersecting Circles: The Voices of Hapa Women in Poetry and Prose*. Honolulu: Bamboo Ridge Press, 1997.

Hayden, Dolores. *The Power of Place: Urban Landscapes as Public History*. Cambridge, MA: MIT Press, 1995.

Hazama, Dorothy, and Ochiai Okamoto Komeiji. *Okage Sama De: The Japanese in Hawai'i, 1885–1895*. Honolulu: University of Hawai'i Press, 1986.

Heenan, David A., and Warren Bennis. *Co-Leaders: The Power of Great Leaders*. New York: John Wiley and Sons, Inc., 1999.

Helman, Scott. "Small College Awakened Future Senator to Service." *The Boston Globe*, August 25, 2008, 1A.

"Historian-Novelist Ozzie Bushnell Dies at 89." *Honolulu Advertiser*, August 23, 2002. http://the.honoluluadvertiser.com/article/2002/Aug/23/br/br03p.html. Accessed July 1, 2013.

Hitch, Thomas Kemper. *Islands in Transition: The Past, Present, and Future of Hawai'i's Economy*. Honolulu: First Hawaiian Bank, 1992.

Ho, Don, and Jerry Hopkins. *Don Ho: My Music, My Life*. New York: Watermark Publishing, 2007.

Hong, Terry. "The Dual Lives of Nora Okja Keller, an Interview." *The Bloomsbury Review* 22, no. 5 (2002). http://www.bloomsburyreview.com/Archives/2002/Norapercent20 Keller.pdf. Accessed March 12, 2014.

Hongo, Garrett. *Volcano: A Memoir of Hawai'i*. New York: Alfred A. Knopf, 1995.

Hope, B. E., and J. H. Hope. "Californian Journal of Health Promotion 2003." *Hawai'i*, 1 (2003): 1–9.

Hope, B.E.D., and G. Massey. "Hawaiian Materia Medica for Asthma." *Hawaii Medical Journal* 25, no. 6 (1993): 160–67.

I'i, J. P. *Fragments of Hawaiian History*. Honolulu: Bishop Museum Press, 1959.

Inglis, Kerri A. *Ma'i Lepera; a History of Leprosy in Nineteenth-Century Hawai'i*. Honolulu: University of Hawai'i Press, 2012.

Jackson, Miles M. *And They Came: A Brief History of Blacks in Hawaii*. Durham, NC: Four Gs Publishers, 2001.

Jarvis, F. Washington. "James Drummond Dole, 'The Pineapple King.'" In *Jamaica Plain Historical Society*. Boston: Roxbury Latin School, 2008. http://www.jphs.org /people/2005/4/14/james-drummond-dole-the-pineapple-king.html. Accessed August 2, 2014.

Johnson, Sarah Anne. "Lois-Ann Yamanaka: The Characters Know the Sound of Their Own Voice." In *Conversations with American Women Writers*. Hanover, NH: University Press of New England, 2004.

Jolly, Margaret, and Martha Macintyre. *Family and Gender in the Pacific: Domestic Contradictions and the Colonial Impact*. New York: Cambridge University Press, 1989.

Jones, Tim. "Barack Obama: Mother Not Just a Girl from Kansas; Stanley Ann Dunham Shaped a Future Senator." *Chicago Tribune*, March 27, 2007, 1.

Judd, C.S. "Leprosy in Hawaii, 1889–1976." *Hawaii Medical Journal* 43, no. 9 (1984): 328–34.

Ka'anoi, P. *The Need for Hawaii*. Jefferson, MO: Ka'ano'i Productions, 1992.

Kalākaua, David. *The Legends and Myths of Hawaii*. New York: Charles L. Webster and Co., 1888.

Kallen, Horace M. "Democracy versus the Melting Pot." *Nation*, February 18, 1915, 190–94.

Kamakau, S.M. *Ka po'e kahiko: The People of Old*. Honolulu: Bishop Museum Press, 1964.

Kame'eleihiwa, Lilikala. *Native Land and Foreign Desires: Pehea La E Pono Ai?* Honolulu: Bishop Museum Press, 1992.

Kamins, Robert M., and Robert E. Potter. *Mālamalama: A History of the University of Hawai'i*. Honolulu: University of Hawai'i Press, 1998.

Kanahele, George. *Pauahi: The Kamehameha Legacy*. Honolulu: Kamehameha Schools Press, 2002.

Kanahele, G.H. *Ku kanaka. Stand Tall*. Honolulu: University of Hawai'i Press, 1986.

Kawaharada, Denni. *Storied Landscapes: Hawaiian Literature and Place*. Honolulu: Kalamaku Press, 1999.

Kanahele, George S. *Pauahi, the Kamehameha Legacy*. Honolulu: Kamehameha Schools Press, 1986.

Keller, Nora Okja. *Comfort Women*. New York: Viking Press, 1997.

Keller, Nora Okja. *Fox Girl*. New York: Viking Press, 2003.

Kent, Harold W. *Charles Reed Bishop, Man of Hawaii*. Palo Alto, CA: Pacific Books, 1965.

Kim, Hyung-chan. *A Legal History of Asian Americans, 1790–1990*. Westport, CT: Greenwood Press, 1994.

Kimmich, R.A. "100 Years of Hawaiian Psychiatry." *Hawaii Medical Journal* 15 (1956): 345–47.

King, Samuel P., and Randall W. Roth. *"Broken Trust": Greed, Mismanagement, and Political Manipulation at America's Largest Charitable Trust*. Honolulu: University of Hawai'i Press, 2006.

Kirch, Patrick V. *Feathered Gods and Fishhooks: An Introduction to Hawaiian Archaeology and Prehistory*. Honolulu: University of Hawai'i Press, 1985.

Kirch, P.V. *How Chiefs Became Kings: Divine Kingship and the Rise of Archaic Hawai'i*. Berkeley: University of California Press, 2010.

Krauss, B.H. *Plants in Hawaiian Medicine*. Honolulu: Bess Press, 2001.

Kurashige, Lon. *Japanese American Celebration and Conflict: A History of Ethnic Identity and Festival in Los Angeles*. Berkeley: University of California Press, 2002.

Kuykendall, Ralph S. *A History of the Hawaiian Kingdom*. 3 Vols. Honolulu: University of Hawai'I Press, 1938–1967.

La Croix, Sumner, and J. Price Fishback. "Migration, Labor Market Dynamics, and Wage Differentials in Hawai'i's Sugar Industry." *Advances in Agricultural Economic History* 1 (2000): 31–72.

Lal, Brij V., and Kate Fortune. *The Pacific Islands*. Honolulu: University of Hawai'i Press, 2000.

Law, Anwei Shinsnes. *Kalaupapa: A Collective Memory*. Honolulu: University of Hawai'i Press, 2012.

Lee, Joann Faung Jean, ed. *Asian Americans in the Twenty-first Century*. New York: New Press, 2008.

Lee, R.K.C. "History of Public Health in Hawaii." *Hawaii Medical Journal* 15 (1956): 331–37.

Li, We. *The New Ethnic Community in Urban America*. Honolulu: University of Hawai'i Press, 2011.

London, Jack. *Stories of Hawaii*. New York: Appleton-Century Publishers, 1965.

Low, Sam. "Nainoa Thompson's Path to Knowledge: How *Hokulea*'s Navigator Finds His Way." In K. R. Howe, ed. *Vaka Moana: Voyages of the Ancestors*. Honolulu: University of Hawai'i Press, 2007.

Lum, Darrell H. Y. *Pass On, No Pass Back!* Honolulu: Bamboo Ridge Press, 1990.

Lum, Darrell H. Y. *Sun: Short Stories and Drama*. Honolulu: Bamboo Ridge Press, 1980.

Malo, D. *Hawaiian Antiquities*. Honolulu: Bishop Museum Press, 1951.

McBride, L. R. *The Kahuna: Versatile Masters of Old Hawaii*. Hilo, HI: Petroglyph Press, 2000.

McDermott, John F. Jr., et al., eds. *People and Cultures of Hawaii: A Psychocultural Profile*. Honolulu: University of Hawai'i Press, 1981.

McDermott, John F. Jr., and Naleen Naupaka Andrade, eds. *People and Cultures of Hawai'i: The Evolution and Ethnicity*. Honolulu: University of Hawai'i Press, 2011.

McKinney, Chris. *Bolohead Row*. Honolulu: Mutual Publishing, 2005.

McLellan, Dennis. "Don Ho, 76: Singer Was Best Known for '66 hit 'Tiny Bubbles.'" *Los Angeles Times*, April 15, 2007. http://articles.latimes.com/2007/apr/15/local/me-ho15. Accessed August 2, 2014.

Michaels, Barry. *Saint Damien de Veuster: Missionary of Moloka'i*. Boston: Pauline Books and Media, 2009.

Michener, James A. *Hawaii: A Novel*. New York: Random House, 1959.

Michener, James A. *Tales of the South Pacific*. New York: Fawcett Books, 1947.

Mills, G. H. "Hawaiians and Medicine." *Hawaii Medical Journal* 40, no. 10 (1981): 272–76.

Min, Pyong Gap. *Asian Americans: Contemporary Trends and Issues*. New York: Pine Forge Press, 2006.

Morgan, Theodore. *Hawaii: A Century of Economic Change: 1778–1876*. Cambridge, MA: Harvard University Press, 1948.

Mullaney, Marie Marma. *Biographical Dictionary of the Governors of the United States: 1988–1994*. Westport, CT: Greenwood Press, 1994.

Murayama, Milton. *All I Asking for Is My Body*. Honolulu: University of Hawai'i Press, 1975.

Nakaso, Dan. "Hiram Fong Dead at 97." *Honolulu Advertiser*, August 18, 2004. http://the.honoluluadvertiser.com/article/2004/Aug/18/br/br03p.html. Accessed August 2, 2014.

Nidel, Richard O. *World Music: The Basics*. New York: Routledge, 2004.

O'Brien, David J., and Stephen S. Fugita. *The Japanese American Experience*. Bloomington: Indiana University Press, 1991.

Office of Hawaiian Affairs. *Native Hawaiian Data Book*. Honolulu: Office of Hawaiian Affairs, 2002.

Osmond, Gary. "Duke Kahanamoku." PediaView.com. 2010. http://pediaview.com/openpedia/Duke_Kahanamoku. Accessed August 2, 2014.

Osmond, Gary. "Honolulu Maori': Racial Dimensions of Duke Kahanamoku's Tour of Australia and New Zealand." *New Zealand Journal of History* 44, no. 1 (2010): 22–34.

Patterson, Wayne. *The Ilse: First-Generation Korean Immigrants in Hawai'i, 1903–1973*. Honolulu: University of Hawai'i Press, 2000.

Patterson, Wayne. *The Korean Frontier in America: Immigration to Hawai'i, 1896–1910*. Honolulu: University of Hawai'i Press, 1994.

Rapaport, Moshe. *The Pacific Islands: Environment and Society*. Honolulu: University of Hawai'i Press, 2012.

Remnick, David. *The Bridge*. New York: Alfred A. Knopf. 2010, 98–112.

Remnick, David. *The Life and Rise of Barack Obama*. New York: Praeger, 2011.

Ripley, Amanda. "The Story of Barack Obama's Mother." *Time*, April 9, 2008. http://content.time.com/time/magazine/article/0,9171,1729685,00.html. Accessed August 2, 2014.

Sakamoto, Edward. *Aloha Las Vegas and Other Plays*. Honolulu: University of Hawai'i Press, 2000.

Sakamoto, Edward. *Hawai'i No Ka Oi: The Kamiya Family Trilogy*, edited by Franklin Oda. Honolulu: University of Hawai'i Press, 1995.

Schmitt, R. C. "Differential Mortality in Honolulu before 1900." *Hawaii Medical Journal* 26, no. 6 (1967): 537–41.

Schmitt, R. C. "Health Personnel in Hawaii, 1820–1974." *Hawaii Medical Journal* 34, no. 10 (1975): 53–55.

Schmitt, R. C. *Historical Statistics of Hawaii*. Honolulu: University of Hawai'i Press, 1977.

Serafin, Peter. "Punahou Grad Stirs Up Illinois Politics." *Honolulu Star-Bulletin*, March 21, 2004. http://archives.starbulletin.com/2004/03/21/news/story4.html. Accessed August 2, 2014.

Shu, Ramsay. "Kinship Systems and Migration Adaptation: Samoans in the United States." *Amerasia Journal* 12 (1985–1986): 23–47.

Spickard, Paul R. *Japanese Americans: The Formation and Transformations of an Ethnic Group*. New York: Twayne, 1996.

Spikard, Paul R., ed. "Pacific Island Peoples in Hawaii." *Social Process in Hawaii* 36 (1994). Stannard, D. E. *Before the Horror: The Population of Hawaii on the Eve of Western Contact*. Honolulu: University of Hawai'i Press, 1988.

Stevenson, Robert Louis. *Robert Lewis Stevenson: His Best Pacific Writings*. Honolulu: Bess Press, 2003.

Stewart, Richard. *Leper Priest of Moloka'i*. Honolulu: University of Hawai'i Press, 2000.

Takahashi, Jere. *Nisei/Sansei: Shifting Japanese American Identities and Politics*. Philadelphia: Temple University Press, 1997.

Takaki, Ronald. *Strangers from a Different Shore: A History of Asian Americans*. Rev. ed. Boston: Back Bay, 1998.

Tamura, Eileen H. *Americanization, Acculturation, and Ethnic Identity: The Nisei Generation in Hawai'i*. Urbana-Champaign: University of Illinois Press, 1994.

Tayman, John. *The Colony: The Harrowing True Story of the Exiles of Moloka'i*. New York: Simon and Schuster, 2007.

Tempski, Armine von. *Fire: A Novel of Hawai'i*. New York: F.A. Stokes, 1929.

Thomas, James A. *Some Trust in Chariots*. Honolulu: Xulon Press, 2006.

Tranquada, Jim, and John King. *The 'Ukulele: A History*. Honolulu: University of Hawai'i Press, 2012.

Trask, Haunani-Kay. *From a Native Daughter: Colonialism and Sovereignty in Hawai'i*. Honolulu: University of Hawai'i Press, 1999.

Trask, Haunani-Kay. *Light in the Crevice Never Seen*. New York: CALYX Books, 1999.

Trask, Haunani-Kay. "Night Is a Sharkskin Drum." In *Talanoa Contemporary Pacific Literature*. Honolulu: University of Hawai'i Press, 2002.

Trask, Haunani-Kay. "Settlers of Color and 'Immigrant' Hegemony: 'Locals' in Hawai'i." *Amerasia Journal* 26, no. 2 (2000): 1–24.

Tsai, Michael. "James Dole." *Honolulu Advertiser*, July 2, 2006. http://the.honoluluadver tiser.com/150/sesq6luahine. Accessed August 2, 2014.

Twain, Mark. *Sandwich Islands: Views of Mark Twain: A Characteristic Letter from the Humorist*. New York: New York Tribune, 1873.

U.S. Census Bureau. *1980 Census of Population*. Washington, DC: U.S. Census Bureau, 1983.

U.S. Census Bureau. *1990 Census of Population*. Washington, DC: U.S. Census Bureau, 1993.

U.S. Census Bureau. *Census 2000*. Washington, DC: U.S. Census Bureau, 2000.

Walters, Jerome. *Seeking the Sacred Raven: Politics and Extinction on a Hawaiian Island*. Honolulu: Island Press, 2006.

Wermager, Paul. "Healing the Sick." In *They Followed the Trade Winds: African Americans in Hawaii*. Honolulu: University of Hawai'i Press, 2004.

Wiarda, Iêda Siquera, et al. *Handbook of Portuguese Studies*. Philadelphia: Xlibris, 1999.

Williams, Jerry R. *In Pursuit of Their Dreams: A History of Azorean Immigration to the United States*. North Dartmouth: Center for Portuguese Studies and Culture, University of Massachusetts Dartmouth, 2005.

Williams, Julie Stewart. *Princess Bernice Pauahi Bishop*. Honolulu: Kamehameha Schools Press, 1997.

Wilson, Rob. *Reimagining the American Pacific: From South Pacific to Bamboo Ridge and Beyond*. Durham, NC: Duke University Press, 2000.

Wren, James A. "'Half Fish and Half F-o-u-l': Kibei Youth, Conflicting Iconographies, and Japanese American Internment Experiences." In Geoffrey Kain, ed. *Ideas of Home: Literature of Asian Migration*. East Lansing: Michigan State University Press, 1997, pp. 197–248.

Yamamoto, Eric. "The Significance of the Local." *Social Process in Hawai'i* 27 (1979), pp. 252–64.

Yoshihara, Lisa A. *Collective Visions, 1967–1997*. Honolulu: Hawai'i State Foundation on Culture and the Arts, 1997.

12

IDAHO

Kathleen R. Arnold

CHRONOLOGY

1800–1810	French Canadians, most of them fur traders, begin to arrive.
1830s	Although Idaho is still largely unsettled, Basques fleeing the war in Spain come to Idaho territory.
1860s	Some miners arrive, including a significant number of Basques, either coming back from the California gold rush or to mine in Idaho (e.g., silver mining). They establish small settlements. Many other groups also arrive because of the gold rush (coming from other states) or to mine in Idaho territory. Some Chinese arrive, also following the gold rush. French Canadians join the mining rush in Idaho. Silver miners establish settlements in Silver City in Owyhee County.
1860s and 1870s	Welsh individuals migrate to the territory because of a depression in their homeland. Wardner is one of the first mining towns and is populated mostly by Welsh miners. Irish individuals also come to work as miners or in other jobs in and near the mining settlements. Greeks and Chinese arrive with the gold rush and people of Germanic descent come to work as miners, brewers, and bakers. The latter group includes Jews from areas that are now Poland, Austria, and Hungary, who work as traders. Swiss Mormons begin to settle in Idaho and found Bern in 1873 and Geneva in 1879. Mexicans and individuals of Mexican descent also come to this territory with the gold rush and work as miners (including mining quartz in the Salmon River Mountains).

1870s–1880s	The population increases as more miners arrive and railroad workers settle in Idaho; cattle ranching also increases. The Irish now have a strong presence in the mines (one in four miners is Irish). Irish men outnumber Irish women significantly. Chinese individuals are also strongly represented in various types of employment, including mining and work related to mining camps, such as cooks, merchants, and launderers. Some Mexicans work as ranch hands and begin to buy their own farms.
1880s	The Irish still have a strong presence in mining (e.g., in the Woods River area) and many serve in the military. Because anti-Chinese feeling is strong, the Chinese population begins to decline. Germans begin to arrive in greater numbers, working in mines and on farms. They establish various religious institutions (Catholic, Lutheran, Methodist, and Mormon). Russian Germans also arrive in areas such as Aberdeen, Dubois, Tabor, and American Falls. Mexican individuals are employed by the railroads at this time, especially in places like Nampa and Pocatello.
1881–1919	Yiddish-speaking individuals who practice Conservative Judaism arrive from central and eastern Europe.
1882	The Oregon Short Line railroad project begins and over 3,000 Japanese workers are recruited.
1882	This is the year of highest German immigration to the United States, including to the territory of Idaho.
1890	Idaho becomes a state. The Idaho legislature prohibits Chinese from owning mining lands.
1890–1920	Finns come to settle in Idaho; the majority goes to Silber Valley and Long Valley. Italians also come in greater numbers during this time and work as farmers, ranch hands, miners, and on the railroads.
1892	Anti-Japanese sentiment is evident in news articles and localities.
1895	Basques become predominant as sheepherders and ranch hands for roughly five decades.
1896	Ahavath Beth Israel is established in Boise and, by the twenty-first century, becomes one of the oldest synagogues in the West that is still used for worship.
1897	The Idaho legislature increasingly constrains Chinese mining. Several violent and lethal acts are committed against Chinese at this time. Accordingly, the Chinese population begins to decline except in Boise. Increasing numbers of Mormons (many are Welsh and Scandinavians) settle in Idaho and hold festivals, play their traditional music, and retain their language and customs. Some Scandinavians work on the railroads.
1900	Scandinavians make up about a quarter of the foreign-born population; they include Danes, Finns, Norwegians, and Swedes. Finns in

	Long Valley become farmers and loggers (most Finns arrive between 1900 and 1925).
Early 1900s	Some desert areas are settled. A good part of the Idaho population is British, Scandinavian, or German. The German population increases in the next decade (1900–1910) by about 5,000 people. About 6,000 Basques live in and around Boise and there are some Japanese settlements throughout the state. Chinatown is established in Boise, although, in 1900, city authorities have the neighborhood moved to a new location, where it remains for the next 70 years.
1904	Turnverein Hall is designed and constructed by German American architect Charles Hummel in Boise but is sold when Germans become the target of discrimination during World War I (1916).
1907	Japanese workers are the majority of farm hands in the sugar beet fields.
1908	Three Dutch communities are founded in Idaho; they establish Christian Reformed and Dutch Reform churches in Grangeville.
1910	French Canadians have settled in Bonner, Kootenai, and Shoshone Counties. More Germanic people (broadly defined as people from Holland, Prussia, the Austrian Empire, Switzerland, and from German communities in Russia) arrive and settle in Idaho. Over 2,500 Italians have settled in places like Boners Ferry, Naples, and Lava Hot Springs; the largest group lives in Pocatello, many of whom work with the railroads in some capacity. Greeks are also a significant source of labor for railroad work. Japanese workers continue to be employed in sugar beet-processing, railroad construction, service work, and business.
1914	One of the most prominent Jewish immigrants, Moses Alexander (who arrives in Boise in 1891) is elected governor in 1914, despite a very small Jewish population. A group of Czechs move to Idaho (Castleford) soon after.
1920s	Basques become more dispersed and more Americanized.
1920	Approximately 1,000 individuals of Mexican descent live in Idaho.
1922	Many Italians and Greeks leave the state, some because of labor issues.
1923	Japanese-born residents (Issei) are barred from property ownership and naturalization; in Idaho, they are also barred from renting land (from 1923 to 1955).
1924–1942	United States policy excludes Japanese immigrants from the country entirely, but in Idaho a Japanese community still formed between 1882 and 1924. Compared to other immigrant groups, the Japanese group is remarkable because it has roughly equal numbers of women and men. They can better retain language, customs, and culture because of this.

1943	The Chinese Exclusion Act is repealed and naturalization is now possible. Idaho is a participant in the Bracero Program, which brings Mexican guest workers to the state to work in agricultural jobs. The Forest Service also hires Mexican workers to plant trees and help put out fires. Idaho is also one of the states that houses Japanese internees. There is prejudice against Japanese at this time.
1950s	Mexicans continue to settle in Idaho.
1952	Prejudice against the Japanese subsides and they gain more rights. They are allowed a path to naturalization and immigration is permitted again.
1955	Japanese Americans in Idaho demand that the Alien Land Law be abolished.
1960s	As the construction and food-processing industries grow, increasing numbers of Mexicans are hired. The Mexican American population nearly doubles at this time. A small number (200) of Filipinos come to Idaho and live in rural areas.
1962	Idaho amends the state constitution to abolish the section that barred Japanese from naturalization and full citizenship.
1967	Pete Cenarrusa, the son of a Basque immigrant, is elected Idaho's secretary of state.
1970s	A group of Dutch dairy farmers leaves California and comes to Idaho, settling in Jerome and Gooding.
1975–1988	Approximately 1,800 Southeast Asian refugees are resettled in Idaho, mostly in Boise and Twin Falls. Many work in the service industry, as agricultural workers, in food-processing, in electronics, and in fish hatcheries.
1976	Mexican Americans form an association to maintain customs and share food and holidays.
1980	There is a reunion of the descendants of the original French Canadian settlers in Nampa.
1990	The cities of Boise; Idaho; and Gernika, Spain, become sister cities. Basque individuals and culture continue to play a significant role in Idaho and especially in Boise. About 65,000 Latinos are employed in hops production, a labor-intensive job. When Pete Cenarrusa is reelected in 1990, he becomes the longest serving public official in Idaho history.
2001–present	Boise remains an important center for Basque culture and life. This area and surrounding areas have the highest number of Basques outside Europe. Idaho's culture of reception for immigrants can be described as conservative, although undocumented workers play a significant role in agriculture. Idaho's detention and deportation practices are criticized for not informing potential detainees of the dangers involved in pleading guilty in a trial.

2003	Former University of Idaho football star Abdullah al-Kidd is detained by federal authorities for 16 days as a material witness. He is not charged with a crime and never serves as a witness in any trial. Represented by the American Civil Liberties Union, he tries to sue Attorney General John Ashcroft for unfairly detaining him.
2003	The United States offers to resettle about 13,000 Somali Bantus in 1999. Actual resettlement occurs in 2003, when they become one of the largest groups from Africa ever resettled in the United States. Boise receives 250 refugees in 2003.
2012	Abdullah al-Kidd's case proceeds to the Supreme Court and the Court decides against him but warns that citizens' rights must be better protected in the future.

HISTORICAL OVERVIEW

This territory was largely unsettled between 1830 and 1860. Within this time period, a small number of settlers began to come for mining, to farm, and later, to work on railroads. Early settlers, particularly French Canadians, had become aware of this territory through the Lewis and Clark Expedition (1804–1806). Later, French Canadian fur trappers worked with the North West Company and the Hudson Bay Company. This early French Canadian influence is evidenced in the names of places, such as "Coeur d'Alene, Pend Oreille, Nez Perce, and Payette River" as well as Godin Valley (Link et al. n.d.). Some British also participated in the fur trade. Another important group that first arrived to this territory in the 1830s were the Basques, who were fleeing war in Spain. More arrived with the mining rush in the 1860s when settlement of this area really began. French Canadians also joined the mining rush, many settling in the Boise Basin. "One of these was Joseph Perrault, from Montreal, who went to California, Walla Walla, Lewiston, and finally to Boise, where he became assistant editor and part owner of the *Statesman*. Lafayette Cartee built the first sawmill and quartz mill at Rocky Bar, moved with his family to Boise in 1866, and was appointed the first surveyor general of Idaho Territory" (Link et al. n.d.). Some had gone to California and Oregon first and settled in Idaho territory when they were leaving these areas, as word spread of mining opportunities in Idaho, including "the gold fields of Idaho's northern panhandle" ("Idaho Emigration and Immigration" 2012). Others were attracted by silver mining and began to establish mining camps and towns around Silver City in Owyhee County.

Chinese individuals also came to settle in Idaho territory, many because of the gold rush in the 1860s. By 1870, over 4,000 Chinese were in Idaho, 60 percent of who were miners and many others worked in service positions, as business owners and as doctors.

In the 1870s and 1880s, their numbers increased and many began harvesting fruits and vegetables to support the mining camps. One community, Garden City, reflected the gardening activity of the Chinese during this time. Chinese food became common in towns like Lewiston, Boise, and St. Maries. However, this population began to decline after 1870 because of prejudice and by 1900, their numbers were halved. At the national level, the Chinese Exclusion Act of 1882 only fostered local prejudice and exclusion.

Irish, Cornish, and Welsh individuals also arrived in the 1860s to work as miners and business owners. The Welsh often worked in mines in north Idaho territory. They founded the town of Wardner (now a city) in the Bunker Hill area. The Cornish, in particular, were attracted to the gold mining industry, having left a dire economic situation in their region of Britain. Their religion (many were Methodists), music, sports (particularly wrestling), and food were all influential in areas where they settled. Their religious beliefs were also taken into account in the mines and setting labor standards because, among other things, they refused to work on Sunday. Two notable figures were Richard Tregaskis and Luke Williams, who became legislators.

Catholic Irish would often settle together as a reaction to anti-Catholic sentiment, which was pervasive at this time. Men outnumbered women, as many had come to work in mines in the 1870s and 1880s. Others served in the military, especially in the 1880s. One interesting figure was Robert Dempsey, an Irish glassblower. Among many of his achievements, he worked as a miner, an interpreter of Native American languages, and founded both a trading post (on the Snake River) and the town of Dempsey (later called Lava Hot Springs). The few Irish women who had migrated to this territory created various work opportunities for themselves. The Irish, in general, had a strong cultural tradition that they maintained and were ardent labor union supporters.

Some Mormon groups also began to settle in Idaho territory after first having traveled to Utah territory. These groups perceived themselves to be almost a distinct ethnicity because of the persecution they experienced in Europe and the United States, their shared history and traditions, and their in-group marriage practices. Many of these groups were British (especially Welsh) and Scandinavians. For example, about 400 Welsh Mormons settled in Malad Valley in 1890. Scandinavians (many from Denmark, Sweden, and Norway) came for railroad work as well as religious community. They comprised about a third of the Mormon population in the late 1800s. Yet another group was the Swiss, who arrived in the 1860s and 1870s and founded towns like Bern (1873) and Geneva (1879). Non-Mormon Scandinavians also began to arrive in the late 1800s (some via Missouri) and often settling in Long Valley.

Germans migrated in significant numbers to the United States and the year of the most significant immigration was 1882. Many had come for property ownership opportunities that were not possible in Europe. They worked in a variety of positions, including as miners, brewers, bakers, and farmers. Some established Methodist churches and other Catholic institutions. Some settled in Council Valley, Minidoka County, and/or in towns such as St. Maries and Moscow. Mormon Germans often settled around Blackfoot, Rexburg, Iona, Soda Springs, the Bear Lake Valley, and Teton County. Russians of Germanic descent often went to Aberdeen, Dubois, or Tabor.

Individuals from southern Europe also helped to settle this area from the 1860s on. For example, Greeks came in the 1860s to work on railroads and by 1910 they, with Italians, were a significant part of all facets of the railroad business. Greeks and Italians settled in places such as Boise, Orofino, Pocatello, and Rupert. Their respective churches—Greek Orthodox and the Roman Catholic Church—aided these immigrants when they first arrived. Some Portuguese, particularly from the Azores, Syrians, and Lebanese also settled.

Japanese individuals first began arriving in Idaho territory in the 1880s. Many performed labor-intensive work such as mining, railroad work and farming. Some individuals passed through Hawai'i first, having worked on sugar plantations. Recruiters from the Oregon Short Line, which began construction in 1882, hired Japanese men from other territories and "by 1892 there were about 3,500" (Link et al. n.d.). They worked for low pay and in subpar conditions. Unlike other immigrant groups, Japanese immigrants often came with some savings and as intact families. Nevertheless, due to prejudice, those who had been born in Japan (*Issei*) were prohibited from land ownership and naturalization. Newspapers like the *Idaho Daily* helped to foster local prejudice. Despite these prejudices and discriminatory laws, a community formed between 1882 and 1924.

Jewish immigrants from what are now Poland, Austria, and Hungary often arrived on the East Coast and eventually settled in Idaho in the 1860s and 1870s. Many were traders and peddlers. More came from these areas, as well as eastern Europe, between 1881 and 1919. Many spoke Yiddish and were conservative Jews. One of the most prominent of these immigrants was Moses Alexander who came to Boise in 1891. He was later elected governor in 1914 with only a numerically small Jewish constituency. One of the temples established at the turn of the century (1896, Boise) is "the oldest synagogue in continuous use west of the Mississippi" (Link et al. n.d.).

Individuals from Mexico and of Mexican descent came before the 1860s and more came to mine gold and quartz. One part of Boise was even called "Spanish Town" and some buildings remained even in 1972. Some Mexicans worked on ranches and eventually bought their own farms; others worked on the railroads and settled in areas like Nampa and Pocatello. As agriculture developed in Idaho, more recent arrivals performed physically intensive labor like picking fruits, thinning sugar beets, and harvesting other vegetables.

Idaho gained statehood in 1890. In the early 1900s, more settlers arrived to farm in desert areas and formed settlements in southern Idaho. Most of the population at this time was of British, German, or Scandinavian descent, but a small (6,000) and influential group of Basques were still in Idaho. By 1900, more Scandinavians had arrived and they made up about a quarter of the foreign-born in Idaho. They included Danes, Finns, Norwegians, and Swedes. Swedes formed the New Sweden Pioneer Association both to record their settlement in this area and to remember Swedish culture and traditions. Finns worked as miner and settled in Silber Valley and Long Valley. They were sympathetic to workers' rights, socialism, and the Industrial Workers of the World. Finns settling in Long Valley were often farmers and loggers. Men also were good at woodworking and construction while women wove rugs and made Finnish bread as well as serving as some of the area's only midwives.

In 1890, the Idaho legislature had barred Chinese from owning mining lands and in 1897 it restricted them from mining activity. After World War II, attitudes toward the Chinese softened and they were increasingly viewed positively. The Chinese Exclusion Act was repealed in 1943, which made naturalization possible. Anti-German sentiment also emerged during this time period. One example was when Turnverein Hall was built by the German American architect Charles Hummel in Boise in 1904. It was sold in 1916 as Germans were increasingly targeted in campaigns during World War I. There is still great German influence on music and architecture, especially in ski areas such as Sun Valley. While Italians and Greeks had previously settled in the state, quite a lot of individuals from both groups left in 1922 because of labor issues. After World War I, a group of 120 Czechs moved to Castleford. Basques remained there but became increasingly incorporated into American culture and more dispersed as a group in the 1920s.

United States policy had barred Japanese immigration but previous immigrants had formed a community. For example, "Bonneville County had from 200 to 250 Japanese throughout 1900, 1901, 1920, and 1930. By 1980, there were 2,066 persons claiming Japanese ancestry in Idaho" (Link et al. n.d.). In the early 1900s, many continued to work in sugar beet fields and, in 1910, many worked in railroad construction, service jobs, and business. By the 1920s, the Japanese had attained rough gender parity (in numbers) which made it easier for them to retain cultural practices and language. On the other hand, because of the gendered division of labor (men went out to work and women often stayed close to home), fewer women learned English. By the 1920s, Nisei outnumbered *Issei*. Japanese formed the Japanese American Citizen League to help with legal issues, naturalization, and other incorporation issues.

During World War II, Idaho was one of the sites for the Japanese internment. "[T]hese relocatees did not affect the permanent settlers in Idaho, but were nevertheless often subjected to prejudice, abuse, and hatred" (Link et al. n.d.). After

World War II, many of the internees stayed in Idaho; particularly in Nampa, Caldwell and Weiser. In the postwar period, Japanese were subjected to less prejudice and increasingly gained their rights. In 1952, they were allowed to naturalize and Japanese immigration was permitted again. In 1955, they lobbied the Idaho legislature to end the Alien Land Law. In 1962, "Idaho voters passed a constitutional amendment that deleted the section disqualifiying [sic] Japanese from full citizenship rights" (Link et al. n.d.).

During World War II, the Bracero Program was created, based on predictions of wartime labor shortages in agriculture. Idaho farms participated in this program, using Mexican workers as guest workers. The Forest Service also hired Mexicans to plant trees and fight fires at this time. In the postwar period, as construction and food-processing expanded in the 1950s and 1960s, more Mexicans were hired by these industries. By the 1960s, the number of individuals of Mexican descent had doubled. In 1976, the Association of Mexican Americans was formed to maintain customs, food, and holidays.

By the 1980s, all of these communities have produced successful individuals and contributed to the state. For example, prominent Basque politicians from Idaho have been: Secretary of State Pete T. Cenarrusa; his successor Ben Ysursa (both Republicans); Democrat David H. Bieter, Boise mayor; and Republican J. David Navarro, clerk, auditor and recorder of Ada County. The Basque Block in Idaho has restaurants, historical building, a museum, and a cultural center. They also have a number of organizations and language instructions. Because of their continued presence outside Europe, Boise and Gernika became sister cities in 1990. Although a less-visible group, descendants of French Canadian settlers held a reunion in Nampa in 1980.

The most numerous of newer immigrants have often come as refugees. From 1975 to 1988, about 1,800 Southeast Asians were resettled in Idaho. Most lived in Boise and Twin Falls and were employed in "fish hatcheries, food-processing plants, electronics factories, as tailors," in the service industry, and as agricultural workers (Link et al. n.d.). The Lao Association of Twin Falls has cultural events; assists immigrants; and is the site of different ceremonies, rites, and celebrations.

In the post-9/11 era, Idaho's immigration issues and policies have reflected both conservative and progressive tendencies. First, in the context of a nationwide immigration policy that now uses detention and deportation as a primary mechanism of social control, Idaho is one of the few states that does not require attorneys to advise their clients who have been charged in criminal cases to warn them that they will almost certainly be detained and deported if they do. This provides insight into the fact that there may be a more hostile context of reception toward certain immigrants. Second, some University of Idaho law professors charged in 2003 that the Immigration and Naturalization Service (INS) and the Federal Bureau of Investigation (FBI) unfairly questioned their students, violating their rights

Emiliano Napoles, 7, of Boise, Idaho, holds up a sign while sitting on the shoulders of his father, Jared, during an immigration rights rally on April 9, 2006. (AP Photo/Troy Maben)

and mixing agency aims inappropriately. Law professors Monica Schurtman and Elizabeth Brandt held that this unprecedented instance of the two agencies working together blended the criminal sphere (the FBI), in which the students have certain rights, and immigration practice (the INS), in which they have very few rights, thus jeopardizing the students' legal status. As Schurtman stated at the time, "The way that immigration law is written right now, if [international students] fail to cooperate with an INS agent and answer questions, which happened with several of our clients, then they can immediately charge [the students] with being in violation of [their] status for failing to talk to INS agents" (Thompson 2003).

Third, the policy proposals and rhetoric of certain politicians like Robert Vasquez establish a hostile context of reception for immigrants. Robert Vasquez, who was Republican county commissioner in 2005, called Mexican immigration an "invasion" and argued that "the newcomers overwhelm public services, bring gang violence and drugs, spread diseases like tuberculosis and insist on rights that should not be granted to noncitizens" (Egan 2005). These sorts of claims do not examine the actual percentage of the group attacked or the lack of evidence about diseases, among other of his claims. Furthermore, these sorts of assertions can be traced to less well-known groups that promote biological racism. Vasquez's positions were supported by some (including talk radio in Idaho: KBOI News Talk Radio) but criticized by the business community—especially agribusiness—for not understanding the degree to which undocumented immigrants sustain agriculture. Conservative Democrat Walter Minnick similarly criticized his opponent for Congress, Raul Labrador, for helping immigrants naturalize when he worked as a lawyer. Despite this assertion and the problematic assumption that helping immigrants to naturalize is negative, Labrador's politics also fall into the very conservative sphere. Labrador's conservative credentials have been certified by the endorsement of ultra-conservative (and even extremist) sheriff of Maricopa County, Arizona, Joe Arpaio. For both contestants, immigration is portrayed as a problem rather than a benefit for this area.

Nevertheless, there have been instances of more positive politics, starting with Idaho cities and rural areas helping to resettle refugees. Refugees have come from a wide range of countries, including Afghanistan, Bosnia, Eritrea, Iraq, Rwanda, and Somalia. For example, as Emily Smith discusses, Somali Bantus were brought to Idaho in 2003. The United States had decided to resettle about 13,000 Somali Bantus in 1999, but resettlement did not occur until 2003. Boise accepted 250 in 2003. As Smith (2011) recounts, they were the largest group ever resettled from Africa. Refugees were encouraged to find work as quickly as possible and many participated in an agricultural project—Global Gardens' Star Farm—in addition to their jobs. While this project did not lead to great profits, it demonstrated the organizational capacities of this refugee group and their desire to foster community. As one worker Smith spoke to noted, "they have [an] incredible community organizing mentality so they, more than any other group ethnic or national group have really cared for one another in the community and worked together in a self-supporting way" (Smith 2011, 30).This organizational capacity and political agency is also demonstrated in the example of immigrants' and citizens' participation in one the many 2006 nationwide rallies on behalf of immigrant rights. Idaho's rally occurred in Boise. In 2012, the state is perhaps divided in its welcoming of refugees and innovative programs dealing with refugees and its adoption of state laws and practices that are increasingly punitive toward the undocumented.

NOTABLE FIGURES/GROUPS

ABDULLAH AL-KIDD (CA. 1972–)

Abdullah Al-Kidd was born in Kansas and was a star football player at the University of Idaho. After graduating from college, he had been accepted to a doctoral program in Islamic Studies in Saudi Arabia. On his way there in 2003, he was detained by U.S. authorities at Dulles Airport in Washington, D.C., because he was targeted in what is now known as the "Idaho Probe" ("Indefensible detention" 2011). In detention, he states, " 'I was made to sit in a small cell for hours and hours and hours buck naked,' he said. 'I was treated worse than murderers'" (Liptak 2010). He was detained on the basis of the material witness statute but was never charged with a crime and never testified in a trial. An amicus brief (a friendly brief written for the Supreme Court) written by 31 former federal prosecutors stated that "the facts are that, without a claim he had broken any law and as one of four seized as part of the F.B.I.'s wider 'Idaho probe,' Mr. Kidd was arrested, strip-searched, shackled and jailed for 15 days-handled like a suspect, not a witness" ("Indefensible detention" 2011). Upon his release, Al-Kidd tried to sue Attorney General John Ashcroft because of this misuse of the statute. Al-Kidd was successful in trials at various levels and his case was heard by the Supreme Court beginning in March 2011. While they ultimately rejected Al-Kidd's claims, they warned that this case highlighted the problems with the use of this statute in the future. Although he was not a foreigner, Al-Kidd's part in the "Idaho Probe" and his record as a football star connect Idaho state issues to national ones concerning immigrant detention policies that ultimately apply to foreigners, including selectivity based on alienage and ideology (to the degree that Islam is viewed as based in the Middle East and is interpreted as a politico-religious affiliation). To put it more simply, despite the fact that he was born in the United States and was a U.S. citizen, his treatment essentially made him an outsider, signaling a disturbing trend for others with his profile.

BASQUES

For over a century, Idaho has had the largest population of Basques outside of Europe. Some Basques first came to Idaho in the decades following the war in Spain in the 1830s but many more began coming with the gold rush in the 1860s. Most of the Basques came from Bizkaia (Biscay) in the Basque region of Spain and worked as sheepherders, loggers, and miners. By the 1920s, Basques had become more Americanized and more dispersed as a group but Boise and other areas (like Twin Falls) still had important cultural institutions and events.

Prominent figures of Basque descent include the secretary of state, Republican Pete T. Cenarrusa; Ben Ysursa also a Republican; Democrat David H. Bieter, current long-standing Boise mayor; and Republican J. David Navarro, clerk, auditor and recorder of Ada County. Boise and Gernika, Basque Country, became sister cities in 1990, highlighting the political, cultural and linguistic ties these two regions continue to have. Bieter is the only Basque-speaking mayor in the United States (O'Connor 2012). There is a Basque Block in Idaho with restaurants, historical sites, a cultural center and museum, among many other things.

Today, there are a few remaining Basque sheepherders in Idaho—for example, in the Minidoka desert. However, Peruvian sheepherders are now the predominant group in sheepherding. As one reporter states, "Tens of thousands settled in Idaho, Nevada, California, Utah and Wyoming, many finding work in the sheep trade or establishing boardinghouses and restaurants catering to Basque herders. Though a precise tally is elusive, Basques once roamed Idaho's sheep ranges in formidable numbers. Today, just two or three remain" (O'Connor 2012). The continued influence of Basque institutions and politicians evidences Idaho's ties to its immigrant past and hopefully fosters a more welcoming context of reception for other immigrant and refugee groups.

Pete T. Cenarrusa (1917–2013)

Pete T. Cenarrusa was descended from Basque immigrants and was an Idaho politician who served in office for about 50 years. In 1990, he was elected secretary of state. Cenarrusa was born in Idaho in 1917 and studied at the University of Idaho. He taught math and served in the military in World War II as a marine pilot. In 1950, he became a Republican politician and "was elected to the Idaho House of Representatives, where he served nine consecutive terms including three as Speaker of the House. In 1967, he was appointed Secretary of State to fill the unexpired term of Edson Deal, who had died, and was elected in succeeding terms so that, by 1990, when he was reelected, he had served as a continuously elected state official for forty years—longer than any person in Idaho history" (Link et al. n.d.). His last term, which he completed, began in 1998. Cenarrusa was fluent in the Basque language (one of the most unique languages in the world) and was a long-time proponent of Basque rights in relation to the Spanish government. When fascist dictator Francisco Franco was still in power in Spain, Cenarrusa tried to block aid to that country. He also advocated greater autonomy for this region of Spain and argued for some leniency in the treatment

Former NASA astronauts Joe Engle, left, and Gene Cernan, center, look over a collection of 30-year-old photographs with Idaho's Secretary of State Pete Cenarrusa at the Craters of the Moon National Monument on May 22, 1999, in Pocatello, Idaho. Cenarrusa is the son of a Basque immigrant who has maintained ties to the Basque Country in Spain as well as holding public office continuously for longer than any other Idaho official in its history. (AP Photo/Bill Schaefer)

of Basque political prisoners. He established a foundation with his wife called the Cenarrusa Foundation for Basque Culture, aiding cultural events and education in Idaho and Oregon. He also supported the study of Basque culture at the university level in Idaho. He died on September 29, 2013.

ATTICUS HOFFMAN (1993–)

When 14 years old, Atticus Hoffman created "One World Soccer" for refugee children in Idaho. This soccer player had previously read about a refugee soccer team and decided he wanted to create one in Boise because "as a relocation center, Boise is home to more than 5,000 refugees who came here from strife-ridden areas such as Bosnia and Afghanistan, Sudan and the Congo" (Oland 2007). He began by asking various people for help: he asked families he knew to donate used clothing and equipment, and he requested help from the Parks and Recreation Department, the YMCA for help with transportation, and the refugee agency—Agency for New Americans—for help with communication with these children. His first camp was very successful and oversubscribed. Since then, he has continued to run these camps and help refugee children. The camp, according to his promotional video, is a means to build community and change children's lives. Soccer facilitates community and English language acquisition. As one participant who was born in a Russian refugee camp after fleeing Afghanistan, Sahim Fahim (10 years old) stated, "it doesn't matter what country you are, just play," he said. "Most kids are feeling that way. We're having fun, getting more energy, meeting new people and making friends. That's really good. It's good to know more people" (Oland 2007).

BIBLIOGRAPHY

American Civil Liberties Union. *Abdullah al-Kidd v. John Ashcroft*, et al. ACLU Website. September 27, 2012. http://www.aclu.org/immigrants-rights-national-security/abdullah-al-kidd-v-john-ashcroft-et-al. Accessed December 12, 2012.

American Civil Liberties Union. "Supreme Court Rules Ashcroft Cannot Be Held Responsible for Arrest and Detention of U.S. Citizen." ACLU Website. May 31, 2011. http://www.aclu.org/national-security/supreme-court-rules-ashcroft-cannot-be-held-responsible-arrest-and-detention-us. Accessed December 16, 2012.

"The Basque Community of Boise, Idaho USA." Boise Basques. n.d. http://boisebasques.com/. Accessed December 1, 2012.

Bearce, Sara M. "Justice before Deportation: Idaho Should Guarantee Non-Citizens the Right to Know the Immigration Consequences of Pleading Guilty." *Idaho Law Review* 42, no. 3 (2005): 853–81.

Egan, Timothy. "Mexican-American Fights Illegal Immigration." *New York Times*, May 31, 2005. http://www.nytimes.com/2005/05/30/world/americas/30iht-immigrant.html?_r=0. Accessed December 1, 2012.

"Idaho Emigration and Immigration." Family Search Website. 2012. https://www.family search.org/learn/wiki/en/Idaho_Emigration_and_Immigration.Accessed   December 1, 2012.

"Idaho Rush/Atticus Hoffman; Refugee Scholarships.mov." youtube.com. May 20, 2010. http://www.youtube.com/watch?v=QQ5PTQNHpoI. Accessed March 12, 2014.

"Indefensible Detention." *New York Times*, March, 2011. www.nytimes.com/2011/03/11 /opinion/11fri1.html?_r=0&pagewanted=print. Accessed December 1, 2012.

Kanstroom, Daniel. *Deportation Nation*. Cambridge, MA: Harvard University Press, 2007.

Link, Paul, John Welhan, Chuck Peterson, Stephen Sommer, Jim McNamara, and Tamara Schiappa. "Immigration and Emigration." In *Digital Atlas of Idaho: Idaho's Natural History Online*. n.d. imnh.isu.edu/digitalatlas/geog/imem/text/main.htm. Accessed December 1, 2012.

Liptak, Adam. "Justices to Hear Appear over Liability for Detention." *New York Times*, October 18, 2010. www.nytimes.com/2010/10/19/us/19schotus.html?pagewanted=print. Accessed December 1, 2012.

McFadden, Robert D. "Across the U.S., Growing Rallies for Immigration." *New York Times*, April 10, 2006. www.nytmes.com/2006/04/10/us/10protest.html?pagewanted=print. Accessed December 1, 2012.

O'Connor, John. "Herding Sheep in Basque Country (Idaho)." *New York Times*, August 24, 2012. www.nytimes.com/2012/08/26/travel/herding-sheep-in-basque-country-idaho .html? Accessed December 1, 2012.

Oland, Dana. "Idaho Teen Creates a Soccer Camp That Helps Refugee Kids." *The Idaho Statesman Knight Ridder/Tribune Business News*, 2007. http://www.active.com/soccer/ Articles/Teen_Creates_Camp_for_Refugees.htm (site reprinted the article). Accessed December 1, 2012.

"Pete Cenarrusa Biography." Cenarrusa Foundation for Basque Culture, n.d. http://cenar rusa.org/content.asp?id=3. Accessed December 15, 2012.

Sherman, Mark. "High Court Rules Out Damage Claim against Ashcroft." *Washington Times*, May 31, 2011. http://www.washingtontimes.com/news/2011/may/31/high-court-rules-out-damage-claim-against-ashcroft/. Accessed December 12, 2012.

Shifrin, Simon. "Untapped Potential: Boise-area Businesses, Refugee Community Work Together to Reap Benefits." *The Idaho Business Review*, 2009. http://search.proquest .com.ezproxy2.lib.depaul.edu/docview/219090948?accountid=10477. Accessed December 1, 2012.

Smith, Emily Rene. "Putting Down Roots: A Case Study of the Participation of Somali Bantu Refugees in the Global Gardens Refugee Farming Project in Boise, Idaho." M.A. Thesis. Presented to the Department of International Studies and the Graduate School of the University of Oregon, June 2011. https://scholarsbank.uoregon.edu /xmlui/handle/1794/11496. Accessed December 1, 2012.

"So Much for the Nativists." *New York Times*, October 26, 2011. www.nytimes.com /2011/10/27/opinion/so-much-for-the-nativists.html. Accessed December 1, 2012.

Thompson, Leif. "Lawyers Believe Agents May Have Violated Idaho Students' Rights." *New York Times*, March 4, 2003. www.nytimes.com/uwire/uwire_UMBK030420031355934. htttml?ei=5034&en=315. Accessed December 1, 2012.

Yardley, William. "A Democrat in Idaho Not Hindered by Incumbency." *New York Times*, October 25, 2010. www.nytimes.com/2010/10/26/us/politics/26minnick.html?_r=0& pagewanted=print. Accessed December 1, 2012.

Yardley, William. In Katharine Q. Seelye et al. "Immigration Law Debate Resonates Far From Border." *New York Times*, April 30, 2010. www.nytimes.com/2010/05/01/us /01states.html?pagewanted=print&_r=0. Accessed December 1, 2012.

13

ILLINOIS

Sarah Garding

CHRONOLOGY

1809	Illinois Territory is created.
1818	Illinois gains statehood.
1837	Chicago is incorporated as a city; it has a population of 4,000.
1848	Completion of the Illinois and Michigan Canal, which links the Great Lakes to the Mississippi River Valley and puts Chicago at the transportation juncture of the waterway connecting the Eastern Seaboard to the Gulf of Mexico, paving the way for its population boom and rise as an economic powerhouse.
1855	The nativist Know Nothing Party wins local elections.
1855	Mayor Levi Boone and the Chicago City Council pass measures to raise liquor licensing fees and enforcement. German and Irish immigrants riot against the initiatives and the next year they mobilize politically to throw the Known Nothings out of office.
1871	The Great Fire destroys a large portion of Chicago, leaving tens of thousands homeless.
1889	Jane Addams and Ellen Gates Starr open Chicago's first settlement house on the West Side, spurring the creation of dozens of other neighborhood immigrant institutions across the city that would provide social services to immigrants and lobby on their behalf.
1893	John Peter Altgeld becomes Illinois's first foreign-born governor.
1908	Native-born immigrant allies in Chicago form the Illinois Immigrants Protective League, of which Jane Addams is a founding member.

1914	World War I begins, mobilizing German, Czech, Croatian, Polish, and other immigrants and their descendants, and occasionally leading to conflict.
1917	The United States enters World War I; anti-German sentiment grows, prompting many German immigrant organizations and clubs to "Americanize" their names.
1919	Chicago Race Riot occurs, as Irish American gangs instigate violence against African Americans.
1920	Palmer raids are conducted in Illinois, arresting the members of several communist parties and organizations. Several hundred are arrested in Chicago, Rockford, East St. Louis, and other cities with a large immigrant working-class population. Many foreigners are turned over to immigration officials.
1931	Having successfully forged a cross-ethnic coalition of German, Irish, Polish, Jewish, and Czech voters, Czech immigrant Anton Cermak is elected mayor of Chicago, marking the beginning of Chicago's Democratic "Machine."
1942	Bracero Agreements are signed between the United States and Mexico, bringing millions of Mexican workers to the United States, of which roughly 15,000 go to Illinois.
1942	Approximately 30,000 Japanese Americans are interned in camps in the Chicago area during the course of the federal Japanese internment policy.
1965	Immigration Act of 1965 paves the way for new flows of immigrants from Asia and Latin America.
1983	Harold Washington, an African American, is elected mayor of Chicago with the strong backing of the Latino population.
1986	Chicago becomes one of the country's first sanctuary cities.
2003	Illinois becomes one of the first states to adopt legislation allowing in-state tuition for the children of undocumented immigrants, provided they graduate from an Illinois high school and have resided in the state for three or more years.
2005	The Illinois Department of Human Services partners with the Illinois Coalition for Immigrant and Refugee Rights (ICIRR) to launch the New Americans Citizenship Initiative.
2005	Illinois governor Rod Blagojevich issues the New American Executive Order, taking a step toward developing a comprehensive immigrant incorporation policy.
2006	Hundreds of thousands of immigrant rights advocates rally in Chicago as part of the nationwide March 10 campaign.
2007	Amendments to the Illinois Human Rights Act and the Illinois Right to Privacy in the Workplace Act bar use of the federal Basic Pilot/E-Verify Program in hiring decisions.

2007	About 300,000 people march from Union Park to Grant Park in support of immigration rights, the largest of the May 1 rallies held that day across the nation.
2011	Governor Pat Quinn notifies Immigration and Customs Enforcement (ICE) that Illinois will opt out of the Secure Communities Program.
2011	The Illinois Development, Relief, and Education for Alien Minors (DREAM) Act is passed.
2011	The Cook County Board of Commissioners adopts an ordinance demanding that Cook County Jail inmates held at the request of ICE be released unless ICE begins to pay per diem expenses for the additional jail time.

HISTORICAL OVERVIEW

ILLINOIS: IMMIGRANT HUB OF THE MIDWEST

Since its induction into statehood in 1818, immigration has been one of the key forces driving the economic, political, and demographic development of Illinois. In particular, Chicago has been the state's premiere immigrant destination and the city's rich, ever-evolving mosaic of ethnic communities has been part and parcel of its rise as an early industrial power and a postindustrial economic powerhouse. Although Chicago's traditional manufacturing-based economy has experienced profound changes since the end of World War II, the greater Chicago metropolitan area continues to be home to successive generations of immigrants from around the world and the area in which the vast majority of the state's foreign-born population lives. Today, Illinois has the sixth-largest immigrant population in the United States, with roughly 1.76 million foreign-born individuals comprising 13 percent of the state's population, and nearly a fifth of the population of the Chicago metropolitan area. While the overwhelming majority of pre-World War II immigrants to Illinois came from Europe, in the postwar period the immigrant stock has greatly diversified, with Mexicans constituting the largest share of the foreign-born population, and Poles, Asian Indians, and Filipinos the second-, third-, and fourth-largest communities, respectively.

Because immigrant settlement in Illinois is so strongly concentrated in the greater Chicago metropolitan region, the discussion is limited to state-level trends and urban migration to metropolitan Chicago. After briefly summarizing prewar European immigration to set the context, the chapter reviews immigration to Illinois after 1945, focusing in particular on the evolving composition of the foreign-born population and changes to employment and settlement patterns in light of Illinois's transformed postwar economy. It then provides overviews of Illinois's four largest foreign-born communities today: Mexican, Polish, Asian Indian, and Filipino/a immigrants. Nationwide, one of the most important trends in immigration policy during the 2000s has been the increasingly proactive role of state and local governments. Illinois's state and local governments have intervened in a number of policy areas affecting immigrants, with important implications for federal immigration policy prerogatives as well as the incorporation of immigrants in Illinois. As such, the second part of the chapter focuses on immigration policies at the state and local levels since 2000.

Immigration to Illinois: Structural Changes after 1945

From the mid-nineteenth century until the national origins quota system introduced by the immigration laws of the 1920s, immigration to Illinois was almost exclusively an urban and European affair. By 1920, 87 percent of immigrants lived in urban areas. Through the first several decades of the twentieth century, Germans were the largest group of immigrants, constituting over a third of the state's foreign-born population. Irish immigrants were the second-largest group during the nineteenth century, peaking at 124,498 in 1890. They subsequently remained a large subset of the foreign-born population through the first decades of the twentieth century and had considerable clout in city politics.

Around the turn of the twentieth century, the source countries shifted from northern and western Europe to eastern and southern Europe. Large waves of Poles, Russians, Italians, Czechs, and other immigrants from the region settled in Chicago, where they worked in stockyards, factories, transport, and steel mills. Polish immigrants comprised over 12 percent of the state's foreign-born population by 1910, and they were Chicago's largest foreign-born group in the 1920 Census.

Since the end of World War II, Illinois has experienced profound demographic and economic changes. The population of the city of Chicago, historically the state's densely packed demographic nucleus, grew far more diffuse as urbanites relocated to the suburbs and satellite cities in the collar counties surrounding Cook County. After more than a century of steady growth, the city of Chicago's population began to decrease after World War II. This trend was only briefly reversed in the 1990s, due to the arrival of immigrants. By contrast, the collar counties (Kane, McHenry, Lake, DuPage, and Will) grew by nearly 25 percent between 1970 and 1980. By the 2000s, an estimated 65 percent of the greater Chicago area's population resided in the suburbs, a trend likely to continue for the foreseeable future.

Likewise, jobs, factories, office complexes, and retail outlets also hemorrhaged from Chicago's urban core to the suburbs and satellite cities in the postwar period. In 1947, the city of Chicago's share of the metro area's manufacturing jobs was 78 percent. By 1982, just 37 percent of the metro area's manufacturing jobs were in the city of Chicago. By 2000, an estimated two-thirds of the Chicago area's jobs were located between 10 and 35 miles from the central financial district. While Chicago remained one of the nation's premiere industrial and manufacturing employer—even after the devastating decline of the steel mills in the 1980s and 1990s—its knowledge-based and service sectors expanded considerably. Many of the facilities of these new sectors were located in the suburbs, and immigrants—particularly the highly educated wave that followed the Immigration Act of 1965—settled accordingly.

The postwar economy, with expanding information technology, service, and healthcare sectors, attracted different kinds of immigrants from the rural and uneducated immigrants typical of the prewar era. After 1965, many newcomers were highly educated engineers, scientists, doctors, nurses, and academics. At the same time, the service sector and manufacturing base continued to attract immigrants with lower levels of education and skills. Immigrant labor's share in Chicago's workforce grew from 11.3 percent in 1980 to over 20 percent of the labor base in 2000. By 2000, the metro area's immigrant workforce included over 400,000 Mexicans; 100,000 Poles; 58,000 Asian Indians; 52,000 Filipinos; 38,000 Chinese; and 23,000 Koreans. There was a considerable amount of ethnic occupational clustering. Koval (2006) that Mexican men have high occupational clustering in food service, construction, janitorial work, and grounds maintenance. A high proportion of female Filipina workers were employed in the healthcare industry. Asian Indian immigrants were heavily recruited in the 1980s and 1990s for jobs in information technology and healthcare, but a large occupational clustering was also found in franchise convenience stores and taxi drivers. Polish men were clustered in carpentry, janitorial work, construction, machinery, and metal and plastic work. Approximately two-thirds of the more than 3,000 dry cleaning businesses in Chicago were owned or operated by Koreans.

Additionally, the racial composition of Illinois's population changed. In 1920, African Americans comprised only 2.8 percent of the population in Illinois and just over 4 percent of the population of Chicago. With more than 500,000 African Americans settling in Chicago during the Great Migration, African Americans comprised a third of the city's population by 1970, triggering white flight from many Chicago neighborhoods. The influx of Asian and Latin American immigrants since the 1960s has further diversified the city.

With the exception of the Bracero Program, which brought millions of Mexican workers to the United States during World War II and the 1948 Displaced Persons Act, which admitted refugees from Europe, immigration to the United States declined considerably from the 1920s until the 1965 Immigration Reform Act. Cosmopolitan Chicago's foreign-born community hit a low of 11 percent of the city's population in the 1970s. In 1960, 6.8 percent of the state's population was foreign-born, compared to 18.6 percent in 1920 and 12.3 percent in 1940. No longer based on an archaic national origins formula that heavily favored Northern and Western Europeans, the 1965 Act paved the way for a tide of immigrants from Latin America and Asia. In the 1960 Census, just before the act, the aging European immigrant population still dominated among the foreign-born. The Lithuanian immigrant community, for example, outnumbered the 25,000 foreign-born Mexicans. The Asian Indian immigrant population numbered fewer than 1,000, while the Chinese, Japanese, and Filipino/a populations were fewer than 4,000 apiece. A decade later, the 1970 Census counted 50,000 foreign-born Mexicans; 15,607 Cubans; 9,704 Filipinos; 4,334 Asian Indians; and 6,863 Chinese. The largest foreign-born groups, however, were still European. By 1980, however, the state's population of 167,924 Mexican immigrants was more than twice the size of the second-largest immigrant population—the 64,000 Poles. There were over 10,000 Chinese; 23,000 Asian Indians; 7,000 Japanese; 34,000 Filipino/as; and nearly 20,000 Koreans. Over 40 percent of the state's immigrants have arrived between 1970 and 1980.

These striking changes in immigration flows continued into the 1990s. The foreign-born share of the state's population increased from 8.3 percent in 1990 to 12.3 percent in 2000. By 2010, an estimated 1.76 million foreign-born individuals lived in Illinois, making it the state with the sixth-highest number of foreign-born after California, New York, Texas, Florida, and New Jersey. As of 2009, an estimated 44 percent of the foreign-born population was between the ages of 25 and 44, whereas 25 percent of the native-born population falls into this age range. About 46 percent of the foreign-born are of Latino origin. Immigrants and the second generation constituted a growing share of the electorate. By the mid-2000s, an estimated 10 percent of Illinois's registered voters were born abroad or were the children of immigrants. A fifth of Illinois's registered voters were of Latino or Asian origin.

TOPICAL ESSAYS

FILIPINO/A IMMIGRANT COMMUNITY

In several important ways, Filipino/a immigration to Illinois resembles Asian Indian immigration, discussed later. Levels of education and income among Illinois's Filipino/a immigrants are higher than the average across all immigrant groups. Filipino/a migration swelled through the family reunification provisions and HI-B visa program of the 1965 Immigration Act. Chicago hospitals and medical employment agencies heavily recruited nurses from the Philippines beginning in the 1970s. The Filipino/a population in Illinois surged from just under 10,000 in 1970 to 34,800 in 1980 and 49,000 in 1990. By 2010, there were estimated to be nearly 83,000 immigrants in Illinois born in the Philippines, making Filipino/as the fourth-largest foreign-born population in the state after Mexicans, Poles, and

Asian Indians. The city of Chicago has 22,000 Filipino/a immigrants, while most of the remainder live in suburbs and satellite cities, particularly Skokie, Bolingbrook, Glendale Heights, Waukegan, Morton Grove, and Des Plaines. The Filipino American Network of Chicago, the Filipino American Community Health Initiative, and the Quezon Association are several of the many Filipino/a American associations in the Chicago area.

ASIAN INDIAN IMMIGRANT COMMUNITY

Asian Indian immigrants, Illinois's third-largest foreign-born group, are a relatively recent arrival. In the 1960s, an estimated 350 Asian Indians lived in the greater Chicago area. Long-denied immigration access due to restrictive, national origins quotas, the 1965 Immigration Act allowed family reunification and gave easier admittance to professionals with skills or talents in demand. As recently as 1980, the Asian Indian population was relatively small, with just over 10,000. A decade later, there were nearly 41,000 Asian Indians in the state. By 2010, there were an estimated 124,000 Asian Indians in Illinois. An estimated 18,000 live in the city of Chicago, while the most of the remainder are clustered in the Northwestern Suburbs. Naperville, Schaumburg, Hoffmann Estates, Skokie, and Hanover Park have some of the largest Asian Indian immigrant populations.

The Asian Indian community in metropolitan Chicago is bifurcated. On the one hand, a large portion of the postwar immigrants are highly educated professionals. This, combined with their fluency in English, has paved the way to high salaries, careers as doctors, scientists, and academics, and a comfortable lifestyle in the wealthier suburbs. Asian Indians are particularly prominent in science and engineering; many are employed in information technology, research, upper management, and healthcare. At the same time, there are also many Asian Indian immigrants who lack the educational and professional background of their compatriots. Many of them work as cab drivers and own or manage convenience stores. Asian Indian Chicago has over 50 associations, a rich array of specialty retail outlets geared toward the community, and organizations based on the many ethnic, cultural, and linguistic cleavages within India, such as the Punjabi Cultural Society, the Bengali Association, and several Gujarati associations.

MEXICAN IMMIGRANT COMMUNITY

Mexican immigration to Illinois expanded in the early twentieth century, particularly after the Mexican Revolution. Men migrated from villages located in the Mexican interior states to the factories, stockyards, steel mills, sugar beet farms, and railroad jobs in the Chicago area. Until the postwar period, however, the Mexican immigrant community was considerably smaller than its Polish, German,

Irish, and other major European American counterparts in Illinois. The trickle of Mexican immigrants to Chicago became a stream in the 1920s. The 1920 Census recorded 1,200 native- and foreign-born Mexican Americans in Chicago. By the end of the decade, Illinois had nearly 30,000 foreign- and native-born Mexican Americans. Although the permanent Mexican immigrants in Chicago were similar to other immigrant groups in that they tended to cluster in neighborhoods close to the industrial worksites and have an array of cultural and social institutions, circular and seasonal migration were far more prevalent among Mexican immigrants. Mexicans in Illinois were subjected to more racism and anti-immigrant sentiment than were white European immigrants. Of the immigrant groups, they were among the first to experience native white backlash when economic times hardened in the 1930s. During the Great Depression, the U.S. government, sometimes in cooperation with community organizations, carried out the voluntary, quasi-voluntary and involuntary repatriation of nearly 500,000 foreign- and native-born Mexican Americans. In Chicago, the government collaborated with local organizations like the American Legion of East Chicago to round up people who "looked Mexican," including many who were U.S.-born or had U.S. citizenship. Through this process, up to 75 percent of the Mexican population in Chicago left during the Great Depression; by 1940, there were only 7,000 Mexican immigrants in the region.

By contrast, during World War II, labor shortages prompted the U.S. government to import labor from Mexico. The Bracero Program agreements signed in the 1940s brought an estimated 4.5 million Mexican workers (*braceros*) to the United States. The Chicago railroads alone hired 15,000 guest workers between 1943 and 1945. Many of the *braceros* stayed on or return to the city after the war's cessation. Mexican communities also sprouted in Joliet, Aurora, and other cities. The 1960 Census tallied 25,477 foreign-born Mexicans in Illinois, as well as an additional 37,586 native-born Mexican Americans. By 1970, there were over 50,000 foreign-born Mexicans in Illinois, and 67,000 native-born Mexican Americans. Just a decade later, the U.S. Census figure on foreign-born Mexicans in Illinois increased more than threefold, with 167,924 tallied. By 1990, there were over 280,000 Mexican immigrants in Illinois, just shy of 30 percent of the foreign-born population. By comparison, the community of Guatemalan immigrants, the state's second-largest Latin American immigrant population, numbered 12,500. Between 1990 and 2000, the Mexican foreign-born population increased by 115 percent, reaching over 580,000 by the turn of the millennium.

In the 1960s and 1970s, a wave of activism sprung forth from Chicago's Mexican community, particularly among second- and third-generation Mexican Americans in heavily Mexican neighborhoods like Pilsen. A generation of community activists and organizations came of age during this period, such as the Organization of Latin American Students, La Raza Unida, the Mexican American Legal

Defense Fund, and Casa Aztlán. These activists mobilized in support of migrant farmworkers and undocumented immigrants, and they pushed for stronger Latino studies curriculum in schools and universities. In the 1980s, the Latino community flexed its political muscle in city politics. In the early 1980s, Latino organizations in Chicago spearheaded redistricting battles to improve Latino representation in city, state, and national politics. With the election of Mayor Harold Washington in 1983, who the Latino community strongly backed, they had a stronger ally in city government. The mayor created a commission on Latino affairs to devise programs to better serve the community, and he appointed more Latinos to city boards than his predecessors in office. In 1986, after concerted pressure from the Latino community, Mayor Washington issued an order barring the city government's agencies from cooperating with the federal Immigration and Naturalization Service (INS), making Chicago one of the country's first sanctuary cities. A decentralized supervisory organization was created with local councils, and the number of Latino faculty and administrators increased considerably.

The community's activism continued in the 1990s and the 2000s. Between 1996 and 2007, the number of Illinois-elected officials with a Latino background more than doubled. By the 2000s, there were 25 elected politicians of Latino origin in Cook County. In 2006, Latino organizations played a major role in mobilizing the 100,000 strong immigrant rights marches held in tandem with nationwide mobilization.

In 2010, nearly 700,000 Mexican-born immigrants were estimated to live in Illinois, or 40 percent of the foreign-born population. There were large pockets of Mexican immigrants across the greater metro area. The city of Chicago had an estimated 265,000. There were large Mexican immigrant populations in Aurora (33,115), Cicero (32,746), Waukegan (21,241), and Berwyn (10,900), and the most recent surveys indicated large populations in Addison, Carpentersville, Hanover Park, Melrose Park, and Round Lake as well. About 20 percent of Chicago's population is Latino, of which roughly half are U.S.-born, and an estimated quarter are undocumented immigrants. Mexican immigrants in the greater metropolitan area have the lowest socioeconomic status of the region's immigrant groups. In 2000, just a third of Mexican immigrants had a high-school diploma. By contrast, 70 percent of the second-largest immigrant group, the Poles, had a high-school diploma. The median income of a Mexican immigrant household is nearly $20,000 below the median white household income, and 16 percent of Mexican immigrants live below the poverty level, as opposed to less than 10 percent among other immigrant groups. The issue of undocumented immigration has been a major, ongoing issue for the community. The INS estimates that by 2000, Illinois had a population of 400,000 undocumented immigrants, the fourth-highest in the country after California, Texas, and New York. With the increase in deportations under the Obama administration, this is likely to be a hot button issue for immigration reform advocates in Illinois.

POLISH IMMIGRANT COMMUNITY

While immigration to Illinois from most of the historical European sending states steadily declined from the 1920s, the Polish community is a major exception. Poles migrated en masse to Chicago beginning in the late nineteenth century. By 1920, Chicago's Poles numbered over 130,000, cementing Polish Chicago's status as the largest foreign-born group. By 1930, the more than 170,000 Poles in the state comprised 14.2 percent of the foreign-born population. Chicago's Poles formed dense, nearly institutionally complete neighborhoods providing services to its members from cradle to grave through mutual aid societies, nurseries, orphanages, schools, Polish newspapers, social clubs, political organizations, hospitals, retirement homes, and cemeteries. Unlike the German and Swedish communities, and to a lesser extent the Irish and Italian communities, Polish Chicago aged but was replenished by waves of immigration in the aftermath of World War II, during periods of martial law and repression in the 1980s, and particularly after the collapse of communism in 1989. Nevertheless, in the first decades after World War II the population declined. By 1980, the Polish-born community of Illinois dipped to 64,000. A decade later, thanks to renewed emigration from Poland after the crackdown on Solidarity, the population surged to 80,000. An estimated 65,000 Poles immigrated to the Chicago area during the 1990s.

The most recent population estimates indicate that over 145,000 Poles live in Illinois, and 99 percent of them are in the Chicago metropolitan region. This makes Poles the largest foreign-born group after Mexican immigrants. About 46,000 Polish immigrants live in the city of Chicago, and there are large concentrations in Prospect Heights, Burbank, Elmwood, Mt. Prospect, Des Plaines, Schaumburg, River Grove, and Norridge. In the broad socioeconomic spectrum of Chicago's diverse immigrant communities, Poles fall roughly at midpoint in terms of their income and educational levels. In the 2000 Census, 69 percent of Polish immigrants had a high-school diploma (slightly above the 62 percent level across all foreign-born persons), and 16 percent had a BA degree (lower than the 25 percent across immigrant groups). The Polish American Association, Polish National Alliance, and Polish Initiative of Chicago are just a few of the many organizations of Chicago Polonia. Local unions have been active in soliciting the participation of Polish immigrant workers, publishing information in Polish alongside Spanish.

2010 IMMIGRANT PROFILE

Together, immigrants of Mexican, Polish, Asian Indian, and Filipino origin make up 60 percent of the foreign-born population of Illinois. Other sizable immigrant groups include Chinese (68,500), Koreans (46,000), Guatemalans (23,000), Pakistanis (21,000), Vietnamese (18,000), and Ecuadorans (17,000). At the state level, of the new immigrants who have arrived since 2000, 30 percent come from Asia, 19 percent from Europe, and 45 percent from Latin America. As of 2010, an estimated 42 percent of the 2000–2010 immigrant cohort aged 25 and above has a BA or higher degree, considerably higher than the 27 percent average across the entire foreign-born population aged 25 and above. About 63 percent of the foreign-born reside in Cook County, and nearly 95 percent of the state's immigrants live in the Chicago metropolitan area.

Census data on language proficiency, income, and education further highlight the diversity among immigrants in Illinois. In 2010, an estimated 55 percent of immigrants aged five and above have limited proficiency in the English language. The percentage is higher among Mexican-born immigrants aged five and above, 74 percent of whom were reported having limited English proficiency, compared to 41 percent of Asian-born immigrants, and 45.3 percent of European-born immigrants. At the same time, an increasing number of Illinois immigrants aged 25 and above have a college degree. In 2010, an estimated 28 percent of immigrants have a BA degree or above, yet an even higher percentage—30 percent—have not completed high school. Here again, there is variation based on the region of origin. About 58.8 percent of Asian foreign-born immigrants aged 25 and above have a BA or higher degree, while 11 percent have not completed high school. About 31 percent of the European foreign-born have a BA or higher degree, while 15.7 have less than a high-school degree. Just 5.2 percent of Mexican immigrants have a BA or higher degree, while 54.8 percent have not completed high school. Poverty remains a persistent problem for many Illinois immigrants. Although Illinois has the country's fifth-highest volume of immigrants living in poverty in 2009, the state is ranked 39th out of 51 in terms of the share of the total foreign-born living in poverty in Illinois, which is 14.4 percent. Income and poverty rates vary by subgroups. Asian-born immigrants had the highest median household income in 2010, $70,634. About 11.4 percent of the population lives below the poverty line. The median household income for European-born immigrants is $54,292, and 8.6 percent live below the poverty line. For Mexican immigrants, the median household income is $44,443, and 18.2 percent of the population lives below the poverty line.

POLICYMAKING

Interethnic conflict, xenophobia, discrimination, and perennial currents of nativism have impeded immigrant incorporation and mobility in Illinois, as they have in other parts of the United States. However, the state—and the Chicago area in particular—has been a generally welcoming environment for the foreign-born.

State and local governments, through their rhetoric and their policy initiatives, have tended to be more supportive of the immigrant population than their counterparts in other U.S. states. Indeed, some of Illinois's immigration policies and programs have been pioneering, even directly challenging federal immigration prerogatives. This is in large part a reflection of immigrants' success in mobilizing and forming coalitions with business associations, progressives, unions, faith-based organizations, and other allies. This tradition of activism goes back to the nineteenth century.

In the 2000s, as the U.S. Congress failed to pass comprehensive immigration reform, a deluge of policy measures were enacted at the state and local levels nationwide. While many of these initiatives, most notoriously Arizona's Senate Bill (SB) 1070, were restrictive, state and local policies in Illinois have tended to be pro-immigrant. Through laws, budgetary allocations, and new public–private initiatives, the general trend of policy has been to enhance immigrant security and privacy in the workplace, expand higher education opportunities for immigrant

Illinois governor Pat Quinn celebrates with students and supporters after signing the Illinois Dream Act into law on August 1, 2011, at a Latino neighborhood high school in Chicago. The new Illinois law gives undocumented immigrants access to private scholarships for college. Students qualify if they attended an Illinois high school for at least three years, received a diploma, and have at least one parent who is an immigrant. Under these circumstances, immigrant children who are either documented or undocumented may apply. (AP Photo/M. Spencer Green)

youth, facilitate access to ID cards, provide funds for immigrant assistance programs, and at times take a stand against federal immigration policy prerogatives. Many of these state and local initiatives in Illinois are the product of concerted campaigns of immigrant activists and allied organizations.

Education has long been an area of immigrant activism. In 2003, Illinois is one of the earliest states to adopt legislation allowing in-state tuition rates for the children of undocumented immigrants if they graduate from an Illinois high school and have lived in the state for at least three years. The 2011 Illinois DREAM Act (SB 2185) created a commission to build a privately funded endowment for scholarships for immigrants' children if they graduate from Illinois high schools. The DREAM Act also provided for expanded training of guidance counselors in public schools to better equip them to help the children of immigrants. This initiative grew from the most recent 2010 failure of the U.S. Congress to pass the federal DREAM Act. A coalition of immigrant youth organizations, immigrant rights organizations, university presidents, and religious leaders in Illinois pushed for this state-level initiative, which it attained with bipartisan support. Another area of education reform in the 2000s addressed curriculum. A 2009 initiative (SB 1557) amended the Illinois School Code to ensure that high school history curriculum covers the forced deportation of Mexican American citizens during the Great Depression.

In other instances, Illinois has refrained from participating in federal programs. Through a pair of 2007 laws (House bill [HB] 1743 and HB 1744), it became the first state to repudiate the Basic Pilot/E-Verify Program, an online database for employers to check the employment eligibility of workers against Department of Homeland Security (DHS) and Social Security Administration records. Though the program is voluntary, some state and local governments, such as Arizona and Oklahoma, passed laws to sanction employers who did *not* use E-Verify. Illinois took a step in the opposite direction. The laws revised the Illinois Human Rights Act and the Illinois Right to Privacy in the Workplace Act by making it a civil liberties violation for employers to make hiring decisions on the basis of E-Verify data, banning discrimination in hiring on the basis of citizenship, and laying out procedures for workers affected by these hiring decisions to recover damages and other fees. The law also stated that employers cannot use the database until the federal government resolved 99 percent of the cases of preliminary nonconfirmation given to employers. The law prompted a backlash from the federal government, with DHS secretary Chertoff attacking the law as "about as bold an anti-enforcement measure as I've ever seen," and the Department of Justice filing suit against Illinois. The laws were backed by the Illinois Chamber of Commerce and the Illinois American Federation of Labor and Congress of Industrial Organizations (AFL-CIO).

More recently, the state government took a stand against the Secure Communities Program, a federal initiative intended to clamp down on criminal undocumented immigrants and strengthened federal cooperation with local law enforcement by sharing DHS records. In 2010, the program expanded in the greater Chicago area to include most suburbs. However, with analyses of ICE program data suggesting that a large portion of those detained through Secure Communities either have no prior criminal record or have committed misdemeanor offenses, the state government stepped in. Governor Pat Quinn notified DHS in May 2011 that the state government would withdraw from the Secure Communities Program. Suspending cooperation with ICE in the program in late 2010, Quinn wrote that "during the suspension [as of November 2010], we voiced our concerns to ICE and asked them to prove that Secure Communities can and will be implemented as agreed to. After review, we were not satisfied and determined that ICE's ongoing implementation of Secure Communities is flawed" (Olivo 2011). This issue was ongoing, with the DHS initially countering that state compliance with the federal program was not optional; however, more recently it has backpedaled from making the program mandatory.

Local governments in Illinois have also entered the immigration policymaking fray, including the Secure Communities Program. In September 2011, the Cook County Board of Commissioners passed an ordinance demanding that Cook County Jail release inmates who were being held for additional time pursuant to ICE investigations unless the latter began to pay per diem expenses for the additional jail time. In effect, the Cook County Jail stopped detaining immigrant inmates for additional time when requested to do so by ICE. The board justified this move on the grounds that "holding inmates for ICE violates due-process rights and erodes community trust in local police" (Mitchell 2011). The sheriffs of Chicago area Lake and Kane counties have also been vocal in their criticism of the Secure Communities Program.

State and local governments in Illinois have taken measures to support the immigrant population by creating new agencies and programs to facilitate incorporation, often in cooperation with nonprofit organizations. In 2000, the Department of Human Services (DHS) Bureau of Refugee and Immigrant Services partnered with the private sector to develop the Outreach and Interpretation Program, which helped inform immigrants in Illinois on the services and programs they were eligible for in light of the federal Welfare Reform of 1996, which laid out restrictive criteria for welfare eligibility. In 2003, the Illinois Department of Human Services launched a project to broaden the access of limited English proficient (LEP) persons to social services and improve the quality of those services. In 2005, the Illinois DHS partnered with the ICIRR to launch the New Americans Citizenship Initiative, a multiyear, coordinated project to directly provide legal permanent residents with the necessary information for them to begin the naturalization process, and help them become engaged in civic life. During the project's first three years, roughly 126,500 immigrants have applied for citizenship in Chicago. The initiative's strong results prompted the governor to issue the New Americans Executive Order in November 2005, requiring state agencies to improve their ability to reach LEP clients. The same order created the Office of New Americans Policy and Advocacy to play a coordinating role among policies and initiatives dealing with immigrant incorporation and public sector immigrant services and to begin the process of crafting a comprehensive policy on immigrant incorporation. This office opened its first immigrant Welcoming Center in 2007. In 2010, the Illinois New Americans Integration Initiative received the Migration Policy Institute's *E Pluribus Unum* national award for exceptional immigrant integration projects. In 2011, Mayor Rahm Emanuel notified the public of a new Office of New Americans to assist the immigrant population in Chicago in gaining access to city services and help the city reach its "long-term goal of making Chicago the world's most immigrant-friendly city" (Mayor's Press Office 2011).

Although on balance, state and local government initiatives in Illinois have gone against the grain of restrictive subnational policymaking in states like Arizona, Georgia, and Alabama, some local measures have been restrictive in nature. The federal government intervened after discriminatory housing policies were introduced in Cicero, while the city of Elgin got in trouble with the federal government for its early morning raids on homes suspected of overcrowding, prompting discrimination suits from several Latino families affected by the raids. Latinos made up a quarter of the city's population, but received roughly 65 percent of code violations from 1995 to 1998. More recently, in 2007, newly elected village trustees in the commuter city of Carpentersville tried to make good on their campaign pledges to pass ordinances that would punish landlords for renting units to undocumented immigrants and employers who hired them and made English the village's official language. Restrictive measures have been introduced in the state legislature as well. In 2010 and 2011, several bills were introduced by Republican lawmakers in the state legislature that would detain and punish undocumented immigrants who do not carry a residence permit and penalize employers who hire undocumented immigrants. Both initiatives failed, but they highlight the reality that Arizona-style immigration legislation is not impossible in Illinois.

The pro-immigrant policies and initiatives that have been introduced by state and local governments in Illinois are in large part a product of the vibrant network of immigrant advocacy organizations, activists, and their coalition partners. These coalitions have brought together unions, business groups, and immigrant advocacy organizations who have banded together to push for policies and practices that protect immigrants and enhance their integration and to oppose ordinances and initiatives that are restrictive in nature. The pro-immigrant stance of unions is a more recent development. In 2005, the AFL-CIO changed its policy to support the concerns of undocumented immigrants. Faith-based organizations have also played a prominent role. For instance, the Archdiocese of Chicago has an Office

Illinois Coalition for Immigrant and Refugee Rights supporters rally in the rotunda of the Illinois state capitol in Springfield, Illinois, on March 3, 2011. The rally had the aim of urging lawmakers to restore funding directed to immigrants and refugees in Illinois. (AP Photo/ Seth Perlman)

for Immigrant Affairs and Immigrant Education and has been active in supporting immigrant interests and protesting deportation of undocumented immigrants.

Although the immigrant source countries, the backgrounds of immigrants themselves, and the patterns of their settlement in Illinois have changed dramatically over the nearly two centuries of the state's existence, one thing remains constant: immigration has always been a vital part of Illinois's economic, political, and social fabric.

NOTABLE GROUPS

Illinois Coalition for Immigrant and Refugee Rights

ICIRR is a coalition of over 100 immigrant and refugee groups throughout the state. These groups include different religious and ethnic groups, immigrant public health advocates, and legally oriented groups. They sponsor projects; workshops; and other initiatives like citizenship preparation, a flag day festival, and family and health resources. They also oppose some legislation, with information about why (e.g., Secure Communities policies), and promote current (as of 2013) efforts to overhaul immigration at the federal level with an emphasis on helping more people to naturalize, including the children of undocumented immigrants. The group provides important information and research on current policies, resources and aid, and educational issues. ICIRR is an important part of local politics in Illinois.

BIBLIOGRAPHY

American Community Survey. "2006–2010 American Community Survey 5-Year Estimates." 2010. http://factfinder2.census.gov/faces/nav/jsf/pages/index.xhtml. Accessed March 13, 2014.

Año Nuevo Kerr, L. "Mexican Chicago: Chicano Assimilation Aborted, 1939–1954." In M.G. Hollis and P.D. Jones, eds. *Ethnic Chicago: A Multicultural Portrait*. Grand Rapids, MI: W.B. Eerdmans Publishing Company, 1984, pp 269–99.

Arredondo, G.F., and D. Vaillant. "Mexicans." In Janice L. Reiff, Ann Durkin Keating, and James R. Grossman, eds. *The Electronic Encyclopedia of Chicago*. Chicago: The Chicago Historical Society, 2005. http://encyclopedia.chicagohistory.org/. Accessed March 13, 2014.

Avila, O. "Immigration Crackdown for Illinois." *Chicago Tribune*, May 19, 2010. http://articles.chicagotribune.com/2010–05–19/news/ct-met-immigration-laws-chicago-20100519_1_illegal-immigration-immigration-paperwork-homeland-security. Accessed March 13, 2014.

Badillo, D.A. "From *La Lucha* to Latino: Ethnic Change, Political Identity, and Civil Rights in Chicago." In G. Cardenas, ed. *La Causa: Civil Rights, Social Justice and the Struggle for Equality in the Midwest*. Houston: Arte Público Press, 2004, pp. 37–53.

Biles, R. *Illinois: A History of the Land and Its People*. DeKalb: Northern Illinois University Press, 2005.

Born, M. "Controversial Legislation Reignites Immigration Debate in Illinois." *Medill News Service*, February 28, 2011. http://www.nwitimes.com/news/local/illinois/chicago/article_715f5716–73c7–526b-95ca-0224ff9f66d0.html. Accessed March 13, 2014.

Camacho, E. "Comments." In L.J. Joseph, ed. *Economic Development and Employment in Metropolitan Chicago*. Champaign: University of Illinois Press, 1990, pp. 125–28.

Cruz, W. *City of Dreams: Latino Immigration to Chicago*. Lanham, MD: University Press of America, 2007.

Erdmans, M.P. *Opposite Poles: Immigrants and Ethnics in Chicago*. University Park: Pennsylvania State University Press, 1998.

Fidel, K. "The Emergent Suburban Landscape." In John P. Koval, Larry Bennett, Michael I. J. Bennett, Fassil Demissie, Roberta Garner, and Kiljoong Kim, eds. *New Chicago: A Social and Cultural Analysis*. Philadelphia: Temple University Press, 2006, pp. 77–81.

Fuller, J. "Perez: Illegal Immigration Program a Sham." Illinois Coalition for Immigrant and Refugee Rights, May 25, 2011. http://icirr.org/content/perez-illegal-immigration-program-sham. Accessed March 13, 2014.

Funchion, M. F. "Irish Chicago: Church, Homeland, Politics and Class—the Shaping of an Ethnic Group, 1870–1900." In M. G. Hollis and P. D. Jones, eds. *Ethnic Chicago: A Multicultural Portrait*. Grand Rapids, MI: W.B. Eerdmans Publishing Company, 1984, pp. 57–92.

Gaouette, N. "U.S. Sues Illinois over Immigration." *The Los Angeles Times*, September 25, 2007. http://articles.latimes.com/2007/sep/25/nation/na-immig25. Accessed March 13, 2014.

Gavett, G. "Why Three Governors Challenged Secure Communities." *Frontline*, October 18, 2011. http://icirr.org/content/why-three-governors-challenged-secure-communities. Accessed March 13, 2014.

Grossman, J. "Great Migration." In Janice L. Reiff, Ann Durkin Keating, and James R. Grossman, eds. *The Electronic Encyclopedia of Chicago*. Chicago: The Chicago Historical Society, 2005. http://encyclopedia.chicagohistory.org/. Accessed March 13, 2014.

Illinois Department of Human Services. *New Americans Initiative: 6-Year Report*. 2009. www.dhs.state.il.us/page.aspx?item=48880. Accessed March 13, 2014.

Immigration Policy Center. "New Americans in the Prairie State." 2009. http://www.immigrationpolicy.org/just-facts/new-americans-prairie-state. Accessed March 13, 2014.

Kotlowitz, A. "Our Town." *New York Times*, August 5, 2009. http://www.nytimes.com/2007/08/05/magazine/05Immigration-t.html?pagewanted=all. Accessed March 13, 2014.

Koval, J. P. "Immigrants at Work." In John P. Koval, Larry Bennett, Michael I. J. Bennett, Fassil Demissie, Roberta Garner, and Kiljoong Kim, eds. *New Chicago: A Social and Cultural Analysis*. Philadelphia: Temple University Press, 2006, pp. 197–210.

Koval, J. P., and K. Fidel. "Chicago: The Immigrant Capital of the Heartland." In John P. Koval, Larry Bennett, Michael I. J. Bennett, Fassil Demissie, Roberta Garner, and Kiljoong Kim, eds. *New Chicago: A Social and Cultural Analysis*. Philadelphia: Temple University Press, 2006, pp. 97–104.

Lal, V. "Indians." In Janice L. Reiff Ann Durkin Keating, and James R. Grossman, eds. *The Electronic Encyclopedia of Chicago*. Chicago: The Chicago Historical Society, 2005. http://encyclopedia.chicagohistory.org/. Accessed March 13, 2014.

Lau, Y. M. "Re-Visioning Filipino American Communities: Evolving Identities, Issues, and Organizations." In John P. Koval, Larry Bennett, Michael I. J. Bennett, Fassil Demissie, Roberta Garner, and Kiljoong Kim, eds. *New Chicago: A Social and Cultural Analysis*. Philadelphia: Temple University Press, 2006, pp. 141–51.

Mayor's Press Office. "Mayor Emanuel Announces Creation of Office of New Americans to Support Chicago's Immigrant Communities and Enhance Their Contributions to Chicago's Economic, Civic, and Cultural Life." Office of the Mayor of the City of Chicago, 2011. http://www.cityofchicago.org/city/en/depts/mayor/press_room/press_releases/2011/july_2011/mayor_emanuel_announcescreationofnewamericanstosupportchicagosim.html. Accessed March 13, 2014.

Migration Policy Institute. "Illinois." 2010. http://www.migrationinformation.org/datahub/state.cfm?ID=IL. Accessed March 13, 2014.

Migration Policy Institute. "Unauthorized Immigration to the United States." *Migration Policy Facts*. October 2003. www.migrationpolicy.org/pubs/USImmigrationFacts2003.pdf. Accessed March 13, 2014.

Mihalopoulos, D. "Elgin Still Uses Early Raid on Home Crowding; Hispanics Say Practice Is Biased." *Chicago Tribune*, November 7, 1999. http://articles.chicagotribune.com/1999–11–07/news/9911110062_1_inspections-elgin-raids. Accessed March 13, 2014.

Mitchell, C. "Illinois County Defies Feds on Immigrant Detentions." *National Public Radio*. September 12, 2011. http://www.npr.org/2011/09/12/140407306/cook-county-ill-bucks-immigration-enforcement. Accessed March 13, 2014.

Moran, Tyler. "New Illinois Laws Create Important Protections against Flaws in Employment Eligibility Verification Basic Pilot." *Immigrants' Rights Update* 21, no. 8 (2007), http://www.nilc.org/07newil.html. Accessed August 3, 2014.

National Council of State Legislatures. "2009 State Laws Related to Immigrants and Immigration, January 1-December 31, 2009." 2010. http://www.ncls.org/immig/2009ImmigLaws.pdf and http://www.ncsl.org/default.aspx?TabId=19209. Accessed March 13, 2014.

National Immigration Law Center. http://www.nilc.org/immsemplymnt/ircaempverif/eev015.htm. Accessed March 13, 2014.

National Immigration Law Center. "Continuing the Pioneer Tradition: Illinois' Basic Pilot/E-Verify Laws as a Model Policy." October 29, 2008. http://www.nilc.org/Illinois-model-policy-2008–10–29-ri.html. Accessed March 13, 2014.

Olivo, Antonio. "Illinois Withdraws from Federal Immigration Program." *Chicago Tribune*, May 5, 2011. http://articles.chicagotribune.com/2011–05–05/news/ct-met-state-dream-act-0505–20110504_1_illegal-immigrants-numbersusa-dream-act. Accessed March 13, 2014.

Pacyga, D. A. "Poles." In Janice L. Reiff Ann Durkin Keating, and James R. Grossman, eds. *The Electronic Encyclopedia of Chicago*. Chicago: The Chicago Historical Society, 2005. http://encyclopedia.chicagohistory.org/. Accessed March 13, 2014.

Pacyga, D. A. *Chicago: A Biography*. Chicago: University of Chicago Press, 2009.

Pallares, A. "The Chicago Context." In A. Pallares and N. Flores-Gonzalez, eds. *¡Marcha! Latino Chicago and the Immigrant Rights Movement*. Champaign: University of Illinois Press, 2010, pp. 37–64.

Paral, R. "Latinos of the New Chicago." In John P. Koval, Larry Bennett, Michael I. J. Bennett, Fassil Demissie, Roberta Garner, and Kiljoong Kim, eds. *New Chicago: A Social and Cultural Analysis*. Philadelphia: Temple University Press, 2006, pp. 105–14.

Paral, R. "The Polish Community in Chicago. A Community Profile of Strengths and Needs." The Polish American Association, 2004. http://robparal.com/MidwestIL.html. Accessed March 13, 2014.

Portes, Alejandro, and Ruben G. Rumbaut. *Immigrant America: A Portrait*. Berkeley: University of California Press, 1996.

Rangaswamy, P. "Asian Indians in Chicago." In John P. Koval, Larry Bennett, Michael I. J. Bennett, Fassil Demissie, Roberta Garner, and Kiljoong Kim, eds. *New Chicago: A Social and Cultural Analysis*. Philadelphia: Temple University Press, 2006, pp. 128–40.

U.S. Census Bureau. *Census of Population and Housing. Volume 1: Characteristics of the Population: Illinois*. 1980. http://www.census.gov/prod/www/abs/decennial/1980cenpopv1.html. Accessed March 13, 2014.

U.S. Census Bureau. *Census of Population and Housing. Volume 1: Characteristics of the Population, Parts 1–57: Number of Inhabitants, General Population Characteristics, General Social and Economic Characteristics, and Detailed Characteristics: Illinois.* 1960. http://www.census.gov/prod/www/abs/decennial/1960cenpopv1.html. Accessed March 13, 2014.

U.S. Census Bureau. *Census of Population and Housing. Volume 3: Composition and Characteristics of the Population by States.* 1920. http://www.census.gov/prod/www/abs/decennial/1920.html. Accessed March 13, 2014.

U.S. Census Bureau. *Census of Population and Housing. Volume 3: Reports by States, Showing the Composition and Characteristics of the Population for Counties, Cities, and Townships or Other Minor Civil Divisions.* 1930. http://www.census.gov/prod/www/abs/decennial/1930.html. Accessed March 13, 2014.

U.S. Census Bureau. *Census of Population: Social and Economic Characteristics (CP-2): Illinois.* 1990. http://www.census.gov/prod/cen1990/cp2/cp-2.html. Accessed March 13, 2014.

U.S. Census Bureau. "The Newly Arrived Foreign-Born Population of the United States: 2010." *American Community Survey Briefs,* November, 2011.

Varsanyi, Monica W., ed. *Taking Local Control: Immigration Policy Activism in U.S. States and Cities.* Palo Alto, CA: Stanford University Press, 2010.

Yates, J. "Immigrants to Pay In-State Tuition." *Chicago Tribune,* May 19, 2003. http://articles.chicagotribune.com/2003–05–19/news/0305190174_1_illegal-immigrants-out-of-state-tuition-universities. Accessed March 13, 2014.

14

INDIANA

William P. Kladky

CHRONOLOGY

1614–1615	Samuel de Champlain, the governor of New France, explores the Maumee River region.
1671	Simon de Saint-Lusson claims most of the area for France. Using the Wabash River, French Canadian fur traders become the first Europeans to enter Indiana.
1728–1732	Vincennes is established on the Wabash River by France, becoming the first European settlement in the area.
1747	The British convince a Huron chief, King Nicolas, to attack French-owned Fort Miami.
1752–1753	A smallpox epidemic devastates the local American Indian population.
1763	Britain gains control of Vincennes and the Indiana area.
1768	After making a treaty with several British colonies, the Iroquois give up their land claims in the area and the "Indiana Land Company" is formed to manage the lands. This is the first recorded use of the word "Indiana."
1769	Because of British harassment, many French settlers leave Indiana, though some fur traders remain.
1772	General Gage orders the French to leave settlements in the Wabash Valley and demands land deeds.
1774	The British Parliament passes the Quebec Act; French settlements, including those in Indiana, become part of the province of Quebec.

1778	The expedition of U.S. colonel George Rogers Clark captures Fort Sackville at Vincennes; Indiana becomes part of Virginia.
1779	The British at Fort Sackville surrender to Colonel George Rogers Clark.
1783	The Treaty of Paris gives modern-day Indiana to the United States.
1787	The Continental Congress creates the Northwest Territory, which includes Indiana.
1794	Anthony Wayne defeats the Tecumseh-led Shawnee Indians near the Maumee River and establishes a military installation called Fort Wayne.
1800	Indiana Territory is established from the Northwest Territory; William Henry Harrison is the first governor and Vincennes the first capital.
1803	Several American Indian tribes sign treaties ceding their Indiana land; immigration quickens.
1805	The Michigan Territory is separated from Indiana Territory.
1809	The United States separates the Illinois Territory from the Indiana Territory.
1810s	Using the steamboat, many from Pennsylvania, the South, and New England migrate to Indiana, becoming part of the great national migration westward. A number of immigrants from Scotland, England, and Germany arrive.
1811	William Henry Harrison defeats an Indian alliance led by Chief Tecumseh at the Battle of Tippecanoe.
1813	Chief Tecumseh is killed at Battle of the Thames; the capital of Indiana Territory moves to Corydon.
1816	Indiana becomes the 19th U.S. state, with Jonathan Jennings as the first governor.
1818	Some American Indian tribes give up their claims to some of central Indiana, with the exchange called the "New Purchase." White settlers rush in for the land.
1825	The state capital moves to Indianapolis.
1835	The Wabash and Erie Canal opens from Fort Wayne to Huntington. Irish, German, and French Canadian laborers immigrate to Indiana to work on constructing the National Road and the Wabash and Erie Canal. Using the canals and the newly constructed railroads, many more migrants, including English farmers, move to Indiana.
1842	The University of Notre Dame is founded.
1851	Indiana adopts a state constitution that includes a provision protecting the property rights of married women.
1860	The U.S. Census discovers that Indiana has a population of 1,350,428, including 11,428 blacks and 118,284 foreign-born. Polish immigrants from Poznan settle near La Porte to work as farm laborers.

1882	Many immigrants from Hungary and Belgium are directly recruited by companies to work in the new industries in South Bend and Muncie.
1897	The tribal status of the Miami Indians is terminated.
1906	U.S. Steel Corporation builds a plant, and founds the town of Gary. Many immigrants soon arrive, including Serbs and Croats, as well as black migrants from southern states.
1910	Immigration to Indiana peaks, with many drawn to work in the state's expanding industries. The black population also rises, with many recruited by U.S. Steel Corporation.
1911	The first Indy 500 auto race is held.
1920s	Indiana's industrial boom attracts many Irish, Italian, and Polish immigrants to work the multitude of booming plants and factories.
1940s and 1950s	Charities and societies settle many European displaced persons, including Latvians and Estonians, in Indiana. Iranian and Japanese immigrants arrive.
1956	The Northern Indiana Toll Road is completed. Many Hungarian and Polish immigrants come to Indiana to escape political oppression in their home countries.
1974	A series of 148 tornadoes strikes the Midwestern and southern states (including Indiana); many are killed and property damage is severe.
1988	Indiana senator J. Danforth Quayle is elected U.S. vice president.
1990s	A steadily increasing number of Latino and Asian immigrants arrive in Indiana, attracted by the state's expanding economy.
2010	Immigrants constitute 5.6 percent of the state's workforce, with 2.3 percent being undocumented immigrants.

HISTORICAL OVERVIEW

COLONIAL PERIOD

In the 1670s, French fur traders from Canada came down the Wabash River and became the first Europeans to enter Indiana. Indiana was central to the communication and trade routes of New France. In 1673, the French established the first European outpost in Indiana at Tassinong, a trading post near the Kankakee River. French explorer René-Robert Cavelier, sieur de La Salle (1643–1687) claimed the area for Louis XIV (1638–1715) in 1679 (Allison 1986, 16). Father Ribourde, who traveled with La Salle, marked trees for their route. La Salle negotiated a common defense treaty between the Illinois and Miami Indian nations against the Iroquois in 1681.

The French then built a number of forts and outposts to trade with the American Indian tribes and to block the westward expansion of British colonies from the east. Fort Miami in the Miami town of Kekionga (modern Fort Wayne) was built during this time. In 1717, the French soldier François-Marie Picoté, sieur de Belestre (1716–1793) founded the post of Ouiatenon in Lafayette. In 1732, François-Marie Bissot, sieur de Vincennes (1700–1736), set up a post near the Piankeshaw Indians; known as Vincennes, the post became the only permanent European presence in the area. Jesuit priests accompanied French soldiers into Indiana, where they undertook a largely futile attempt to convert Native Americans to Christianity. The Jesuits did provide needed healthcare, education, and advocacy for the American Indians, helping to ease their eventual transition to other areas. Gabriel Marest (1662–1714), one of the first missionaries in Indiana, taught among the Kaskaskia in 1712.

As a result of the French and Indian War, the French lost control of Canada and the Indiana region. The 1763 Treaty of Paris gave Indiana to the British. After Britain made peace with the American Indian tribes, they abandoned most of the French outposts and forced the Jesuit priests to leave. Many French settlers then left, but some fur traders remained. The Iroquois later sold their land claims as part of a 1768 treaty with several British colonies. As a result, the Indiana Land Company was formed to manage the lands. This was the first recorded use of the word "Indiana."

In 1773, the British government transferred the territory of Indiana to the Province of Quebec to appease its French population. This move infuriated the Americans, and the Quebec Act, which authorized the transfer, became one of the "Intolerable Acts" that the Thirteen Colonies cited as the reasons for breaking with Britain. When the Revolutionary War ended in 1783, Britain ceded the entire Indiana region to the United States. The area was placed under the authority of the state of Virginia, which governed the region as Virginia territory until that state gifted it to the United States in 1784.

Indiana Territory

In 1795, the Treaty of Greenville was signed ending the Northwest Indian War. This treaty opened some of eastern Indiana for American settlement. Fort Miami at Kekionga was rebuilt as Fort Wayne. New settlers from eastern states flocked in. Indiana became part of the Northwest Territory, which was formed by the Congress of the Confederation on July 13, 1787. The territory included land between the Appalachian Mountains, the Mississippi River, the Great Lakes, and the Ohio River—the future states of Ohio, Michigan, Indiana, Illinois, Wisconsin, and part of eastern Minnesota. The two American settlements in Indiana were Vincennes and Clark's Grant. The population of the entire territory was 4,875, which included 298 blacks and an estimated 20,000 to 75,000 American Indians. Most transportation was by the many rivers and streams that blessed the area, and that aided development through the next century.

A group of Swiss surveyors immigrated to Indiana in 1796. In 1803, they were joined by other Swiss immigrants and established Vevay along the Ohio River in southeast Indiana. On July 4, 1800, the Indiana Territory was carved out of the Northwest Territory in preparation for congressional approval of Ohio statehood. The Indiana population had increased to 5,641. The name "Indiana" meant "Land of the Indians," which was very descriptive because American Indian tribes still occupied most of the area. The territory's first capital was Vincennes, but it was moved to Corydon in 1808. In the early 1800s, free blacks were among the settlers who arrived in the territory.

In 1809, the territory was granted permission to elect its own legislature. Although Article 6 of the Northwest Ordinance had outlawed slavery, the institution had been in Indiana since the arrival of the French. After much religious advocacy, slavery became a major political issue, and the anti-slavery party won a strong majority in the territory's first election. The new legislature then overturned the indenturing and pro-slavery laws.

Warfare with the American Indian tribes continued. In 1811, during Tecumseh's War, General William Henry Harrison led an army against Tecumseh's Indian tribal confederation. The Battle of Tippecanoe ended the war and earned Harrison national fame, as well as his "Old Tippecanoe" nickname, which became widely known when Harrison ran for president in 1840. In the War of 1812 with Britain, the battle at Fort Harrison, Indiana, catapulted Captain Zachary

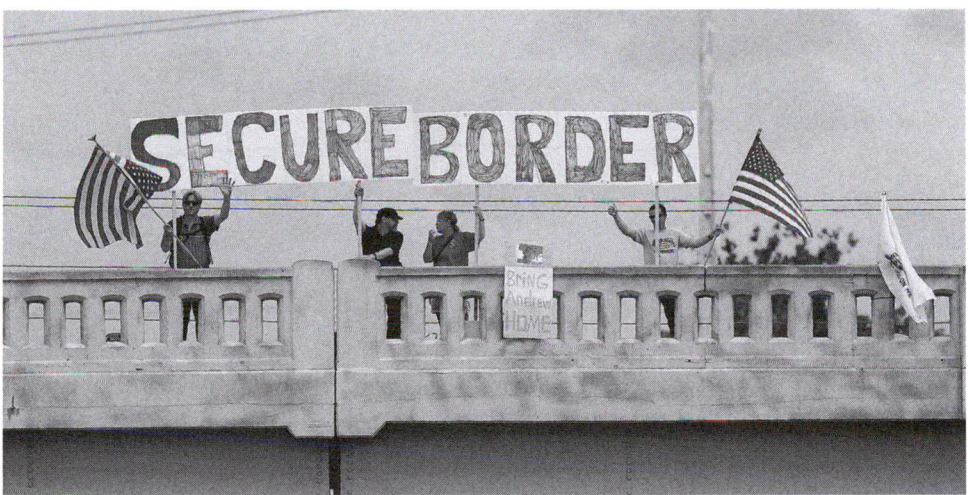

Demonstrators with signs on an overpass in Indianapolis protesting undocumented immigration on July 18, 2014. These protestors believe that there is an immigration crisis at the border and that White House officials will grant work permits to potentially millions of undocumented immigrants despite the recent history of mass detention and deportation. (AP Photo/Darron Cummings)

Taylor to fame and became a military career that brought him to the presidency in 1848. By ending the war, the 1814 Treaty of Ghent brought peace with the British and American Indian tribes and led to increased immigration into the territory.

STATEHOOD

In 1812, anti-slavery advocate Jonathan Jennings (1784–1834), the territory's first congressional representative, sponsored legislation calling for Indiana statehood. Technically, Indiana was not eligible for statehood because its population was below 25,000, and the subsequent outbreak of the War of 1812 postponed consideration of the legislation.

There was a large migration to Indiana during this period, part of the powerful national migration westward. Boats that took grain to Toledo would return with a load of new immigrants. Most were drawn by the low cost of land. Land in Lagrange sold for $1.25 an acre. Twelve Scottish immigrants from Pennsylvania came around 1813 to settle the land near Canaan in Jefferson County. English immigrants from Yorkshire went to Wayne County in 1800–1810 to get land for farming.

Some immigrants came to Indiana for religious freedom. George Rapp (1757–1847) and his followers came from Germany to create a religious center in Indiana. In 1814, they established a community based on Christian fellowship, calling it the "Harmony Society." They bought land on the Wabash River and built a brewery, a distillery, and mills that proved so successful that settlers established their own bank. This settlement was greatly facilitated by the wide usage of the steamboat, which made transportation quicker and easier. These new arrivals came mostly from Pennsylvania, the South, and New England. Twenty new counties were added to Indiana, as the state's population center pressed northward. The 1820 U.S. Census discovered that the state's population was almost 150,000.

In 1815, after Indiana's population was documented as 63,897, Congress passed the Enabling Act giving the territory permission to form a state government. At the 1816 constitutional convention, for which Jennings was elected president, delegates represented the 13 counties in the southern section; the central and north of the area was all Indian land. A ban on slavery was put in the state constitution. In November 1816, Congress approved Indiana statehood. Jonathan Jennings, whose motto was "No slavery in Indiana," was elected governor, defeating Thomas Posey (1750–1818) by a vote of 5,211 to 3,934. Upon election, Jennings declared Indiana a free state. In 1820, the Indiana Supreme Court, in the case of *Polly v. Lasselle*, freed the remaining slaves in the state. Jennings served two terms as governor and then was the state's congressional representative for 18 years.

Indiana is justifiably proud of the fact that Abraham Lincoln (1809–1865), the 16th president of the United States, spent his childhood in the state. The Lincoln

Boyhood National Memorial is a U.S. Presidential Memorial, and there is a National Historic Landmark District (designated in 1966) in Lincoln City, where Lincoln lived with his family from 1816 to 1830. His mother, Nancy Hanks Lincoln, and 27 other settlers are buried there.

Indiana's population rapidly increased at this time, especially in the northern section. Despite being a dense forest, Indianapolis was selected in 1821 to be the site of the new state capital. It is said that Jeremiah Sullivan (1794–1870), a justice of the Indiana Supreme Court, invented the name Indianapolis by joining "Indiana" with "polis," the Greek word for city, to create "Indiana City." Indianapolis became the seat of government in 1825.

Unfortunately, lavish spending on a new state capitol building put the new state into financial peril, and a recession followed. In the national financial Panic of 1819, the state's only two banks collapsed. Once the state's credit was re-established in the 1830s, Indiana funded many improvements, particularly with the Internal Improvements Act of 1836. This act funded three canals, two railroads, two roads, and removal of river obstructions. The state's prospects, like others, were saved by the influx of migrants and immigrants. With population growth came more revenues, and the state paid all its debts by 1846.

Migration to Indiana was facilitated by significant internal improvements in transportation. In earlier years, settlers followed the old Indian paths or trails. This was totally inadequate to cope with the increased population. In 1834, the federally funded National Road was constructed to Indianapolis. Stagecoach travel then became frequent. There also was a strong demand for a northern road to Michigan from migrants interested in settling in Indiana's north. After negotiating several treaties with American Indian tribes occupying the lands, the Michigan Road was built in 1826. In 1836, the U.S. Congress granted funds to Michigan City, the sole Indiana city bordering Lake Michigan, to construct a harbor.

Irish and German laborers immigrated to Indiana to work on constructing the National Road in the 1830s. Many remained in towns like Indianapolis and Terre Haute. Many canals were also built at this time, such as the state's longest, the Wabash and Erie Canal, which was constructed between 1832 and 1843. This canal covered 380 miles in Indiana and 88 miles in Ohio, and connected Toledo on Lake Erie with Evansville on the Mississippi. It made water transportation from New Orleans to Lake Erie a comparatively direct, internal route rather than sailing around the eastern United States and through Canada. Many immigrants came to work on building the canals. Thousands of Irish settlers, fleeing famine in Ireland, worked on the Wabash and Erie Canal.

Immigrants also were an essential part in the construction of railroads across Indiana at this time. French Canadians came to northwest Indiana to farm and to work on the New York Central. During this period, many railroads were built despite the strident opposition of the canal interests. The Madison to Indianapolis railroad was completed in 1847, and the capital became a railroad hub by the Civil War. Indiana was now firmly connected to the rest of the nation.

Unfortunately, the influx of immigrants to Indiana also stimulated protests, particularly around the always-sensitive issue of jobs. When Irish and German immigrant workers arrived to build the canals, many citizens joined "Know-Nothing" organizations that denounced immigrants. Also, Slovenes in Indianapolis were harassed by rock-throwing residents who thought their wages would be lowered because of the competition.

More immigrants were coming to work in the rapidly developing commercial and manufacturing sectors facilitated by the improved state transportation network. The railroad turned Madison into the "Porkopolis" of the West, second only to Cincinnati. A migration and immigration boom followed, and immigrants from England and from peasant villages in southwestern Germany arrived to work and to farm. The German-speaking arrivals mainly went to central and southern Indiana, and constituted over 5 percent of the state's population after 1850.

During the 1840s, population growth pressured the state to finish the relocation of American Indian tribes. Many were forced to leave for Kansas in the "Potawatomi Trail of Death," leaving only the Pokagon Band of Potawatomi Indians living in the Indiana area. The payment of subsidies and land grants in the west were given to the tribes as part of treaties that opened the land to settlers. In 1846, the state's population had grown to almost 700,000. New Albany was the largest city with a population of 4,000, and Indianapolis ranked third.

The state responded positively to its new immigrants, granting them political rights. The many Irish immigrants in the state were cited as the reason why the state constitutional convention in 1850–1851 made it easier for immigrants to qualify to vote. Before and during the war, the "Underground Railroad" was a part of Indiana life. Though the 1851 Constitution had prohibited blacks from entering the state, the race issue was hotly contested. As in a number of other northern states, anti-slavery advocates, aided by religious group, eventually succeeded in fighting back the pro-slavery forces.

Although most Polish immigrants settled in industrial parts of the state, Poles from Poznan settled near La Porte as early as 1860 to work as farm laborers to save money to afford their own homesteads. The 1860 U.S. Census found the state had a population of 1,350,428, including 11,428 blacks and 118,284 foreign-born. During the U.S. Civil War, Indiana stayed in the Union. The state had 208,367 men serving, with a casualty rate of about 35 percent. This was despite the fact that the state had so many recent migrants from southern states.

Post-Civil War Era

After the Civil War, many Blacks migrated from southern states to the Midwest (including Indiana) searching for employment and a better quality of life.

The state's African American population more than doubled in the 1860s. For example, Evansville's black population went from 96 in 1860 to 1,408 in 1870. The state's total population reached 1,680,637 in 1870 as new migrants continued to arrive. By 1880, Indiana had the sixth-highest population in the country. Many important new industries drew immigrants from many countries. The 1886 discovery of natural gas in the northern section of the state led to the rapid growth of Gas City, Hartford City, and Muncie. This gas boom lasted until 1900 when the supplies were exhausted. Subsidiary industries also prospered. Other important Indiana industries were the Ball Brothers glass plant, Eli Lilly and Company, and C.G. Conn Ltd.

Many immigrants came to Indiana to work in the new industries, often directly recruited by the companies. In 1882, one company's officials arranged for 32 from Sopron Country, Hungary, to come to work at the Studebaker wagon plant and the Oliver plow plant in South Bend. The state gained thousands of new residents from such immigration. The American glass industry also brought skilled Walloon Belgians from the Liege area to the Muncie region.

The industrial boom led to many immigrants arriving to work the expanding plants and factories. Among the most numerous were the Irish, who settled in the South Bend area during the 1865–1920 period. As the immigrants accumulated funds, they became entrepreneurial, often serving their own community's needs. Syrian immigrants opened 11 groceries in Terre Haute, and Slovak immigrants in Whiting bought a bank. In the 1920s, East Chicago Polish immigrants were only able to get loans to buy their homes because a building and loan association had been set up by two earlier Polish immigrants.

The immigrants' arrival was greatly enhanced by continuing technological advances. An electric interurban railway came to Lafayette in 1889. By 1920, some 2,400 miles of track had been built to connect 175 cities. The state then had a dependable, fast, and economical statewide transportation system. In 1890, Indiana's population had risen to 2,192,404. There were 45,215 blacks (or 2.1 percent) and 146,205 foreign-born.

BEGINNING OF THE TWENTIETH CENTURY

In 1900, Indiana's population was 2,516,462. Most of the state remained rural, with agriculture being the major export until after World War I. Most immigrants lived in the cities. In 1900, Fort Wayne was 80 percent German. Companies continued to recruit immigrants to work in their plants. Between 1906 and 1914, the U.S. Steel Corporation brought Croats, Slovaks, Lithuanians, and Poles to labor in its Gary works. In Indianapolis during 1895–1907, Jurij Lampert recruited fellow native Slovene workers to labor for the National Malleable Castings Company.

The surge in industrial development that began in the 1890s ultimately resulted in the state becoming an industrial powerhouse, which drew immigrants and migrants. In 1906, Gary was founded by the U.S. Steel Corporation as the home for its new plant. Many immigrants soon arrived. Serbs, Croats, and blacks mainly lived on the city's Southside. Many immigrants had come to work, save money, and then immediately return home. The lucky ones did, even at 17 cents per hour. But many were disabled by company negligence and the perils of the heavy industrial work.

Sicilians, Piedmontese, and Venetians immigrated to Vermillion County to work as coal miners. Many Italian immigrants ventured to Richmond, Logansport, Fort Wayne, and Elkhart to work for the Pennsylvania and New York Central railroads. In 1910, immigration and migration to Indiana peaked. Black population had especially risen, as a result of U.S. Steel's active recruitment of blacks to work in its Gary plants. Enabling this, *The Chicago Defender*, a leading black newspaper, advertised that jobs were readily available in Indiana. As a result, by end of World War I, Gary had almost 5,000 blacks.

Most immigrants, especially the first generation who arrived, lived in housing in separate neighborhoods in Indiana communities. In Fort Wayne, "Irish Town" was located in the southwestern part of the city. In New Albany, an Irish neighborhood called "Bog Hollow" was situated between the Southern Railroad tracks and the banks of the Ohio River. In the Calumet City region, Mexican Americans came for the jobs, and by 1927 had built a church, a grocery, and ran two tailor shops, four barbershops, nine restaurants, and eleven pool halls. All were in a distinct part of town.

Indianapolis had its own "Irish Hill." The Roman Catholic Church dominated life in this community: St. John's Church held lectures, cultural entertainment, card parties, and, of course, religious functions. Irish immigrants belonged to a number of ethnic organizations, such as the Knights of Father Matthew and the Catholic Knights of America. In the Haughville neighborhood, Slovene immigrants supported a church and over 20 bars, where they spoke their native language. In a degree of integration into the wider society, a Slovene football team played other teams in 1930s Indianapolis. Mishawaka's Italians lived in two neighborhoods depending upon their immigration origin: Calabrians north of the St. Joseph River and northern Italians south of the river.

THE 1920S AND THE GREAT DEPRESSION

As of 1920, Indiana's population was 2,930,390. Its white population was 2,849,071, with 80,810 blacks (2.8 percent), as well as 150,868 foreign-born. The war-time economy was a boom to Indiana's industry and agriculture. Combined with the growth from industrialization, the state became much more urbanized. In 1925, for the first time, more were employed in industrial (steel, iron, automobile, and railroad car manufacture) than agricultural work. Many immigrants had come to the state to work the increasing number of jobs.

The state's various immigrant communities usually worked assiduously to maintain both their ethnic and American identities. For example, in South Bend in the 1920s, Belgians could join the Belgian-American Club, the Belgian Bicycle Club, or the Belgian Archery Club. While Belgian Americans spoke their native languages through the 1960s, they also elected members of their community to the city council.

The Great Depression of the 1930s severely affected Indiana and decimated immigration. More needy migrants from the rural Midwest were driven to the state by the Dust Bowl. The southern part of the state was especially hard hit, with unemployment over 50 percent. In response, Indiana governor Paul V. McNutt (1891–1955) set up a helpful state-funded welfare system despite drastically reduced spending and taxes. The federal Works Progress Administration also put 74,708 Hoosiers to work by 1936. As a result of the federally funded programs, the state's roads, bridges, flood control projects, and water treatment plants were greatly improved.

Like in most states, the prosperity involved in the build-up to World War II brought an end to the prolonged economic decline. Peace-time industries were converted into war materials production, huge ordinance plants were constructed, and a number of training camps and depots were built in Indiana. Migrants and immigrants came to work the jobs, and many stayed.

Postwar Growth and Conflict

Indiana rapidly returned to pre-depression levels of production after the war, and migrants and immigrants trickled in to staff the jobs. National trends were typical: industry boomed, urbanization surged, immigration followed, and cities spiked in population. Manufacturing was the leading economic activity and industrial growth along the Ohio River increased. The auto, steel, and pharmaceutical industries were especially prosperous.

The further modernization and improvement of the state's transportation network facilitated this development. In 1956, the Indiana Toll Road was opened, and in 1961 the Indiana Port Commission was established to plan and develop new deepwater facilities on Lake Michigan. However, modernization had its price. As farming became increasingly mechanized and farm production increased, the number of farmworkers declined. Soon, the number of farms fell as the sector consolidated. Despite the decrease in farms, Indiana's population increased to 3,934,224 (3,758,512 whites and 174,168 blacks) by 1950. Most of the new state arrivals were migrants from other states looking for employment, and the number of foreign-born in Indiana actually decreased to 100,630.

During the 1940s and 1950s, numerous displaced persons who were politically unable to go back to their home countries immigrated to Indiana with the help of religious and secular charities. In 1949 and 1950, Latvian and Estonian immigrants came to Indianapolis because a Lutheran Church there assisted them in finding jobs and housing. After the 1956 Hungarian Revolution, Hungarians already in Indiana helped other Hungarians emigrate, as did a group in Indiana Harbor, which held bake sales and collected clothing and household goods. Not all of the immigrants were low-skilled. Many educated Iranians moved to Indiana during this time. Two Iranian engineers began an engineering company in Lafayette, and recruited additional immigrants from their homeland to help. In Gary, Polish Americans set up a club to help displaced Poles learn to speak, write, and read English. In Richmond, Earlham College enrolled young Japanese American students who had been held in detention camps during the war.

Indiana's 1960 population rose to 4,662,498. The increase of 728,274 persons since 1950 was the largest decade increase in the state's history. In 1970, the first Mexican immigrants began to arrive in the state, drawn by the Mexican recession and Indiana's many jobs in agriculture and manufacturing. Two of the earliest known Korean residents moved to Indianapolis in 1962 after finishing graduate degrees, and both became college teachers. In 1971, there were 179 members of the Indiana-Philippine Medical Association practicing across the state.

The state suffered during the national economic recessions of the 1970s and 1980s, with a sharp drop in heavy industrial production and migration. The 1973 oil crisis created a recession that hurt the automotive industry. The state's unemployment rate reached 12 percent in 1983, one of the nation's highest. Many farmers went deeply into debt and hundreds of farms closed. The state's general deindustrialization trend continued until the 1990s, when the national and regional economy slowly began to diversify and recover. The state began prospering as a service center, and the pharmaceutical and agricultural chemical industries expanded. The Indiana Port Commission developed the state's deepwater port on Lake Michigan and river ports in the southern part of the state, which handled much international and national traffic. More automobile manufacturing plants and a major airline maintenance facility at the Indianapolis International Airport were also built. The state's population increased by over 536,000 in the 1990s, as Indiana's strong economy generated record low unemployment rates.

The new growth was bolstered by additions of foreign-born, Latinos, and Asians. The foreign-born share of Indiana's population rose from 1.7 percent in 1990 to 3.1 percent in 2000 to 4.6 percent in 2010. Indiana's immigrant population reached 300,789 in 2010. The Latino share of population grew from 1.8 percent in 1990 to 3.5 percent in 2000 to 6 percent (389,437) in 2010. The Asian share grew from 0.7 percent in 1990 to 1.0 percent in 2000 to 1.6 percent (103,850) in 2010.

Hispanic immigrants were now the largest foreign-born group in the state, and there were 249,623 people speaking Spanish at home in 2009.

Recent statistics on immigrants in Indiana indicate that the population has increased and changed. In 2010, immigrants were 5.6 percent of the state's workforce (183,342), according to the U.S. Census Bureau. Recent Indiana immigrant population growth has occurred mainly in the suburbs. For example, 7 percent of the Indianapolis suburban population was foreign-born in 2010, compared to 5 percent of urban and 1 percent of rural residents. Also, a larger percentage of immigrants (58 percent) than U.S.-born residents (50 percent) were married in 2010. The total 3.4 household size of the foreign-born was larger than the native-born's 2.5 average. Educationally, immigrants in Indiana and the Midwest had both higher and lower levels of education than the native-born in 2010. They were both much more likely to have below a high-school diploma and more likely to have a graduate or professional degree. The children of immigrants in the state usually achieved higher levels of education than their parents. Some 2.3 percent of the workforce (70,000) was undocumented immigrants, according to a report by the Pew Hispanic Center.

The economic recession of 2007–2011 tested the state's resilience. With the rise and fall of automobiles and manufacturing, diversity saved the state's economy. Lumber-based and transportation-related industries, as well as industries based on metals, chemicals, and other products stayed relatively strong. The diversity of resources and employment maintained the state's population and attracted immigrants. Development was aided by the state's central location and natural resources. The U.S. Census Bureau projects that Indiana's population will grow by 8.0 percent between 2000 and 2025, to 6.5 million.

TOPICAL ESSAYS

Anti-Immigrant Tension

During the past few years, Indiana has had an extremely strong anti-immigration movement. It has not always been successful in its objectives. In 2011, anti-immigrant forces attempted to pass an Arizona-style stringent anti-immigration bill (Senate Bill [SB] 590), which would have authorized the police to make warrantless arrests using assumed immigration status and criminalized the use of the consular ID card. There was strong protest from community organizations, educational and religious leaders, the Indiana Farm Bureau, several judges, and the state attorney general. Despite this opposition, the bill passed an Indiana Senate Labor panel. The bill was supported by various groups, including Occidental Dissent, Hoosier Nation, the Vinlanders Social Club, and the Indiana Council of Conservative Citizens (or the Indiana Tea Party).

Jennifer Min, 13, photographs the stage where Myanmar democracy leader Aung San Suu Kyi will speak in Fort Wayne, Indiana, on September 25, 2012. Fort Wayne is home to one of the largest Burmese populations in the United States. (Michael Conroy/AP/Corbis)

After an emotional battle, the Indiana legislature enacted SB 590 in 2011. Some state legislators had opposed the law because they felt it would increase law enforcement costs and stop employers and employees from coming to Indiana. Indiana University opined that the law would lessen enrollment and academic participation, in that the university hosted many foreign national students, faculty members, and visitors. Immediately after the law's passage, the American Civil Liberties Union (ACLU) of Indiana, the National ACLU, the National Immigration Law Center filed a class action lawsuit challenging the law. In 2011, the U.S. District Court blocked part of the law shortly before it was to become active. The Indiana law's passage and court-ordered partial negation typified the experiences of several other states in 2011. Despite state legislators sponsoring a record number of immigration-related bills, the states enacted fewer than expected. Of those enacted, most were struck down or severely restricted.

It is probable that, at least in the short term, citizen advocacy will continue to oppose immigration in Indiana because of the strong level of public support. This is evidenced by the April 2012 brief filed in U.S. District Court in Indianapolis by the Indiana state attorney general's office that argued the ACLU and other plaintiffs in the suit against SB 590 exaggerated the powers the law would have given to local police. The state was arguing against a bid by the ACLU and the plaintiffs to make the injunction against the law permanent. In Indiana, the struggle between those who welcome and those who oppose new immigration will continue.

Gary

Founded in 1906 by the U.S. Steel Corporation as the home for its new plant, Gary is most famous as a steel town, but it is an immigration story in itself. Named after the founding chairman of the corporation, Elbert Henry Gary (1846–1927), Gary's location was selected because of its close proximity to Chicago, ready Great Lakes shipping, and easy railroad access to bring in ore from Minnesota and coal from the south and east.

Because the steel industry prospered and had so many jobs, Gary was the destination of many immigrants throughout most of the twentieth century. Gary's population was over 55,000 by 1920. The city was an ethnic melting pot as jobs in the mills attracted immigrants from various countries, particularly eastern Europe. Gary was known as "Magic City" and "City of the Century" because of this incredible growth. Many African Americans came for the unskilled labor jobs, and a quota system limited them to 15 percent. Since the housing in the region was strictly segregated, African Americans had to live in "the Patch," the neighborhood with the worst housing. When Mexican workers later were brought in as strike breakers, they were also forced to live in the Patch.

Immigrants and their American-born children were some 45 percent of Gary's population in 1930. At U.S. Steel, there was a strict ethnic divide. The mostly unskilled immigrant steelworkers came from southern and eastern Europe—Italy, Greece, Poland, Russia, and the Balkans—whereas skilled and managerial staffs were English, Irish, German, or American-born. When the company's supply of lower-skilled works was curtailed in the 1920s when national immigration restriction was made permanent, Mexican workers were brought in to fill the mill jobs. By 1930, over 9,000 Mexicans lived in Gary and adjacent East Chicago, Indiana.

For many decades, Gary had a wild reputation. It was labeled a "wide open town" by the American Social Hygiene Association in 1946 because of its seven brothels, widely available pornography, and high crime and divorce rates. Gary's ethnic and racial diversity may also have led to its negative appellation. This troublesome public persona was reinforced by several serious steel strikes during 1948 and 1949, some of which were so serious that the federal government intervened in the city.

Because it was a virtually planned city, Gary was a veritable testing ground for the assimilation and Americanization of immigrants. This was limited to white

European immigrants, because blacks and Mexicans were isolated behind walls of discrimination, segregation, and racism. Many of the city's American institutions consciously tried to socialize the chosen immigrant steelworkers and their families, with mixed results, of course. The city's nationally famous "work-study-play" or "platoon school" system was set up to Americanize immigrant children and ready them for their eventual work in the plants. Gary soon had a network of settlement houses and Protestant churches helping the new arrivals. Despite this, Gary's immigrants established their own networks and organizations so they could preserve their own language, culture, and customs.

It is a truism that Gary—the case study of a one-industry town—has risen and fallen with the steel industry. When steel was "Big Steel," prosperity was everywhere in the community. Immigrants flocked to the multitude of jobs, significant architecture was built, and fortunes were made. When the steel industry began to decline in the 1960s, so did Gary. The city continues to struggle in the twenty-first century. Its economic woes have resulted in the reduction of immigration to a trickle. By 2010, Gary's population, 1950s population, of 200,000 had fallen to 80,294. The city continues to be mostly racially black, with 84.0 percent, 11.9 percent white, and a negligible number from other races. About 4.9 percent were Hispanic or Latino of any race.

SIGNIFICANT CHANGES IN IMMIGRATION

Recent immigrants to Indiana have changed from those who arrived in the postwar period. Highly trained professionals who have come are more likely to settle in non-ethnic neighborhoods. The growth is unevenly distributed across Indiana's 92 counties, with almost 75 percent in 10 counties. In many parts of the state, immigration was the only reason the population has increased.

Since 1990, Indiana has been economically and demographically bolstered by a steady increase in Latino and Asian immigrants. This growth has occurred during a period of strikingly increasing immigration. Between 1990 and 2010, the state's foreign-born population leaped 219 percent. Studies indicate that these entrepreneurs and consumers have added wealth and thousands of jobs to the state's economy. The U.S. Census found the state's 8,756 Asian-owned businesses had sales and receipts of $3.4 billion and 24,730 employees in 2007. The 8,558 Latino-owned businesses had sales and receipts of $1.7 billion and employed 14,304 people.

Diversity characterizes the new immigrants. Since 2000, some 9,579 refugees from 39 countries have been resettled in the state. Most came from Burma (6,049), Thailand (595), the former Yugoslavia (590), Somalia (459), and the former Soviet Union (420). Approximately 112 asylees settle in the state annually. Recently, most of these have been Burmese, with a decline in arrivals from the former Yugoslavia and Soviet Union. Refugees were 2.8 percent of the state's total foreign-born population in 2010. The largest group of Burmese refugees in the United States lives in Fort Wayne, the state's second-largest city. Indianapolis has received a significant number of ethnic Karen, Karenni, and Chin Burmese refugees, who are now about 95 percent of the refugee population. It is expected that the refugee population increase will continue.

In the past 10 years, the state has been one of the destinations of undocumented immigrants. The Pew Hispanic Center estimates that the number of undocumented immigrants as a percentage of Indiana's total population increased 135 percent between 1990 and 2010. It also estimates that the proportion of undocumented persons remains very small. A 2009 study by the Sagamore Institute found that undocumented immigrants in Indiana have an "unambiguously positive impact on the state's economy." Undocumented immigrants in Indiana paid $121.6 million in state and local taxes in 2010, according to data from the Institute for Taxation and Economic Policy (Sagamore Institute 2009).

NOTABLE GROUP

Indiana Student Coalition for Immigrant Rights

In response to increasingly harsh legislation at the state and local levels, the Indiana Student Coalition for Immigrant Rights has been active, educating other students about the issue; urging politicians to vote on behalf of the undocumented, particularly undocumented students (DREAMers); and organizing and participating in protests. The group's mission is to challenge harsh and punitive laws, including the mass detention and deportation system that was established through the 1996 Anti-Terrorism and Effective Death Penalty Act. Established in 2010, the group also focuses on refugee issues. The group is based in Indianapolis but is a coalition of student groups throughout the state and their leaders are undocumented.

BIBLIOGRAPHY

ACLU.org. "ACLU and NILC File Lawsuit Challenging Indiana's Draconian Anti-Immigrant Law." May 25, 2011. http://www.aclu.org/immigrants-rights/aclu-and-nilc-file-lawsuit-challenging-indiana-s-draconian-anti-immigrant-law. Accessed March 13, 2014.

ACLU.org. "Court Blocks Implementation of Discriminatory Anti-Immigrant Law in Indiana." June 24, 2011. http://www.aclu.org/immigrants-rights/court-blocks-implementation-discriminatory-anti-immigrant-law-indiana. Accessed March 13, 2014.

Allison, Harold. *The Tragic Saga of the Indiana Indians.* Paducah, KY: Graphic Design of Indiana, Turner Publishing Company, 1986.

Associated Press. "State Asks Judge to Uphold Indiana Immigration Law." Associated Press, April 11, 2012. http://www.ibj.com/state-asks-judge-to-uphold-indiana-immigration-law/PARAMS/article/33770. Accessed March 13, 2014.

Baldos, Uris, Tani Lee, Delphine Simon, and Brigitte Waldorf. "Immigrants in Indiana: Where They Live, Who They Are, and What They Do." Purdue Agricultural Economics Report, April, 2009. http://www.agecon.purdue.edu/extension/pubs/paer/2009/february/waldorf.asp. Accessed March 13, 2014.

Barnhart, John D., and Dorothy L. Riker. *Indiana to 1816. The Colonial Period.* Indianapolis: Indiana Historical Society, 1971.

Bodnar, John. "Introduction: Ethnic History in America and Indiana." Indiana Historical Society Press, 1996. http://www.indianahistory.org/teachers-students/teacher-resources/classroom-tools/immigration-and-ethnic-heritage/introduction. Accessed March 13, 2014.

Dunn, Jacob Piatt. *Indiana and Indianans.* Chicago: The American Historical Society, 1919.

Fowler, William M. *Empires at War* New York: Walker & Company, 2005.

Fox, Cindy Aisen. "Hoosier State Led with Involuntary Sterilization Laws." Indiana University, 2007. http://indiamond6.ulib.iupui.edu/cdm/search/collection/Eugenics. Accessed March 13, 2014.

Fulton County Historical Society. "What Is the Trail of Death?" 2006. http://www.potawatomi-tda.org/. Accessed March 13, 2014.

Funk, Arville L. *A Sketchbook of Indiana History.* Rochester, IN: Christian Book Press, 1969.

Goodrich, De Witt C., and Charles Richard Tuttle. *An Illustrated History of the State of Indiana.* n.p.: R.S. Peale & Co., 1875. http://books.google.com/books?id=YDIUAAAAYAAJ&hl=en. Accessed March 13, 2014.

Guyett, Susan. "Judge Blocks Parts of Indiana Immigration Law." *Reuters,* June 24, 2011. http://www.reuters.com/article/2011/06/25/us-indiana-immigration-idUSTRE75O09R20110625. Accessed March 13, 2014.

Hicks, Michael J., and Kevin F. Kuhlman. *The Puzzle of Indiana's Economy through the Great Recession.* Sagamore Institute, 2011. http://www.sagamoreinstitute.org/article/the-puzzle-of-indianas-economy-through-the-great-recession/. Accessed March 13, 2014.

Immigration Policy Center. *New Americans in Indiana: The Political and Economic Power of Immigrants, Latinos, and Asians in the Hoosier State.* Washington, DC: Immigration Policy Center, 2012. http://www.immigrationpolicy.org/just-facts/new-americans-indiana. Accessed March 13, 2014.

Immigration Research/Study Taskforce of the Indiana Commission on Hispanic/Latino Affairs. "Immigration Facts for Indiana." Indianapolis: Sagamore Institute, 2009. http://www.sagamoreinstitute.org/article/immigration-facts-for-indiana/. Accessed March 13, 2014.

Indiana Historical Bureau. "Indiana Statehood." Indianapolis: Indiana Historical Bureau, 2011. http://www.in.gov/history/2475.htm. Accessed March 13, 2014.

Indiana Historical Bureau. "Introducing Indiana: Past and Present." Indianapolis: Indiana Historical Bureau, 2011. http://www.in.gov/history/files/introindiana.pdf. Accessed March 13, 2014.

Indiana Historical Bureau. "The State House Story." Indianapolis: Indiana Historical Bureau, 2011. http://www.in.gov/idoa/2431.htm. Accessed March 13, 2014.

Indiana Junior Historian. "Gentleman from Indiana: The Vice Presidents." Indianapolis: Indiana Historical Bureau, 1992. http://www.in.gov/history/files/7013.pdf. Accessed March 3, 2014.

Lane, James B. *"City of the Century": A History of Gary, Indiana*. Bloomington: University of Indiana Press, 1978.

Law, Judge. *A Colonial History of Vincennes*. Vincennes, IN: Harvey, Mason & Co., 1858.

Lockridge, Ross F. *The Story of Indiana*. Oklahoma City: Harlow Publishing Corporation, 1956.

O'Bright, Jill York. *"There I Grew Up . . . ," a History of the Administration of Abraham Lincoln's Boyhood Home*. Ann Arbor: University of Michigan Library, 1987. http://babel.hathitrust.org/cgi/pt?id=mdp.39015029893214. Accessed March 13, 2014.

OccidentalDissent.com. "Quiet Awakening." Occidental Dissent, 2011. http://www.occidentaldissent.com/2011/01/30/quiet-awakening. Accessed March 13, 2014.

Schneider, Mary Beth. "Indiana Immigration Bill Passes Senate Committee 8 to 1." *Indystar*, February 9, 2011. http://www.indystar.com/article/20110209/NEWS05/102090385/1001/NEWS03/Indiana-immigration-bill-passes-Senate-committee-8–1?odyssey=nav percent7Chead. Accessed March 13, 2014.

Selig Center for Economic Growth. *The Multicultural Economy 2012*. Athens: University of Georgia, 2012.

Shore, Elena. "A Trend toward Anti-Immigrant, Anti-Choice Laws." *New American Media*, April 5, 2012. http://newamericamedia.org/2012/04/a-trend-toward-anti-immigrant-anti-choice-laws.php. Accessed March 13, 2014.

U.S. Bureau of the Census. *Quick Links*. Washington, DC: U.S. Government Printing Office, 2012. http://quickfacts.census.gov/qfd/states/05000lk.html. Accessed March 13, 2014.

U.S. Bureau of the Census. *State & County QuickFacts*. Washington, DC: U.S. Government Printing Office, 2012. http://quickfacts.census.gov/qfd/states/05000.html. Accessed March 13, 2014.

U.S. Bureau of the Census. *Survey of Business Owners*. Washington, DC: U.S. Government Printing Office, 2011. http://www.census.gov/econ/sbo/. Accessed March 13, 2014.

U.S. District Court, Southern Indiana District, Indianapolis Division. 2011. INGRID BUQUER, *et al.*, Cause No. 1:11-cv-0708-SEB-MJD, Plaintiffs, CITY OF INDIANAPOLIS, *et al.*, Defendants. Case 1:11-cv-00708-SEB-MJD Document 79 Filed June 24, 2011. Signed by Judge Sarah Evans Barker.

USimmigrationsupport.org. "Immigration to Indiana." 2012. http://www.usimmigrationsupport.org/indiana.html. Accessed March 13, 2014.

Voyagesphotosmanu.org. "History of Indiana in the 20th Century." 2011. http://www.voyagesphotosmanu.com/20th_century_indiana.html. Accessed March 13, 2014.

Wilson, William E. *Indiana: A History*. Bloomington: University of Indiana Press, 1966.

15

IOWA

Julia Skinner

CHRONOLOGY

1838	Iowa is named a U.S. Territory.
1840	Iowa is admitted to the Union.
1847	Dutch immigrants arrive in the town of Pella.
1850	Hungarian refugees establish the colony of New Buta, which lasts until 1858.
1855	German immigrants who are part of the Inspirationist movement establish the Amana Colonies.
1860	The Iowa General Assembly passes a law establishing a commissioner of immigration, who works in New York City to encourage immigration to Iowa.
1862	The position of commissioner of immigration is abolished.
1862	The Homestead Act is passed; this federal law encourages settlers to move onto land and construct buildings, and the government, in turn, gives settlers the land for free after they live on it for five years. While much of Iowa has been surveyed and sold by this point, some land in north-central and northwest Iowa is eligible.
1862	The Pacific Railway Act is passed. The construction of railroads in Iowa provides jobs for immigrants and makes it easier to move around the country.
1868	Iowa integrates public schools after 12-year-old Susan Clark is denied admission because she is black. The Iowa Supreme Court rules that "separate" is not "equal" and orders that Clark be admitted to the Muscatine Public School, which had denied her admittance.

1869	The Iowa Board of Immigration is created. The board publishes booklets in English, German, Dutch, Danish, and Swedish to encourage European immigrants to settle in Iowa.
1870	*Iowa: The Home for Immigrants* is published in several languages.
1893	Czech composer Antonin Dvorak spends the summer in the Czech settlement of Spillville.
1918	The Iowa Council of National Defense sends a letter to Iowa libraries urging them to search for and remove "pro-German" books from their shelves.
1918	The "Babel Proclamation" is signed into law by Iowa's governor, making English the only language that can legally be used in public places, including churches and schools, and on telephones.
1924–1925	Height of Ku Klux Klan influence and activity in Iowa, especially in Des Moines. The Klan increases membership and influences several school board elections before its influence dies out in the late 1920s.
1934	The first mosque in North America is built in the town of Cedar Rapids.
1994	The German American Heritage Center is founded in Davenport.
2008	The Postville immigration raid is the largest in the nation's history.

HISTORICAL OVERVIEW

Iowa was a part of the Louisiana Purchase, a large transfer of land from France to the United States in 1803. Iowa became a territory in 1838 and a state on December 28, 1846. Iowa's first white settlers came from the eastern United States during the 1830s, and the population boomed as more families came west. Iowa's population rose almost continuously from the founding of the state through 1915. Early immigrants who arrived prior to 1900 came to Iowa largely for the purpose of economic betterment, although Iowa has continued to attract immigrants for a variety of reasons up through the present day.

Early immigrants included those from Bohemia (later part of the Czech Republic), Holland, Germany, Great Britain, and Scandinavia. After the Civil War, the state experienced a population boom as more and more settlers moved in from the East. While most prewar settlement was been done by native-born Americans, immigrants comprised a sizeable portion of the state's postwar settlers. In 1869, the state urged immigrants to move to Iowa by printing a 96-page booklet titled *Iowa: The Home of Immigrants*. In the interest of attracting a diverse population of European immigrants, the booklet was published in English, German, Dutch, Swedish, and Danish.

Germans were the largest immigrant group in Iowa, and they settled in every county in the state by the late nineteenth century and were the most diverse immigrant group in terms of occupation, geographical settlement, and religion. Many

Malieh Nassar, left, dishes up food for her son, Ossama Nassar, 6, as Dhuha Tawil, 14, right, fills her plate in the kitchen of the Mother Mosque as they end their day of fasting in observance of Ramadan on November 18, 2001, in Cedar Rapids, Iowa. Taha Tawil, the imam, or spiritual leader, of the mosque, said neighbors of the Muslim community were supportive in the wake of the September 11th terrorist attacks and the war in Afghanistan. (AP Photo/Kevin Wolf)

Germans became farmers, although they worked in a number of other professions as well. Members of other immigrant groups also farmed and it seems that there was some competition for resources between groups. For example, Norwegian immigration to Clayton County all but stopped by 1855, probably because Germans came to the state during this time and "soon occupied all the best land" (Flom 1909).

In the late 1800s, Syrian and Lebanese immigrants also came to the country in large numbers and some settle in Iowa. Lebanese immigrants came to the country fleeing oppression under the Ottoman Empire. While many immigrants stayed on the East Coast, some came to Iowa and formed a vibrant community in the town of Cedar Rapids. These immigrants constructed the first mosque in the United State, referred to as the Mother Mosque.

Some immigrant groups became associated with certain parts of the state. Winneshiek County was home to a number of towns where about half the population was of Norwegian heritage. Swedish settlers formed a community called Brush Creek (later New Sweden) in Jefferson County in 1845. Immigrants from Holland began moving to Iowa in 1847 and settled in the towns on Pella and Orange City. Even though immigrants from Holland were far fewer in number than immigrants from other countries, their communities were still proud of their Dutch heritage, celebrated in part by annual Tulip Festivals. Bohemian (or Czech) immigrants traveled directly from their home country to Iowa and many settled in the town of Cedar Rapids. Many of them were craftsmen and found work in Cedar Rapids' craft occupations. They also found a number of social clubs and a bank to help Czech immigrants borrow money and purchase homes.

While Germans and Scandinavians comprised the largest percentages of Iowa's immigrant population, members of other immigrant groups came to Iowa as well. After the Civil War, many Italians and Croats came to the state to work in coal mines. Italian immigration was different from other groups as it tended to be male-dominated (most immigrants groups were full families). Irish immigrants were prevalent enough during this time that they founded several Irish communities, including the towns of Keokuk, Emmetsburg, and Temple Hill, and formed their own neighborhood in the southern parts of Dubuque and Des Moines. While there were a number of French place-names in the state (including Des Moines and Dubuque), these were mostly left over from the time when the French controlled the territory; very few French immigrants settled in the state of Iowa.

Religion played an important part in the lives of Iowans and this was no different for immigrants living in the state. Dubuque, a town along the Mississippi, served as the center for Catholics in Iowa, and a French clergyman, Bishop Mathias Loras, was instrumental in starting churches in the state during the 1830s. Up until the Civil War, most of Iowa's Catholic clergy were immigrants from France, Ireland, and Germany. After the war, this changed and most clergy were native-born. A number of other Christian denominations were present throughout the state, including Quakers, Congregationalists, Presbyterians, and Methodists. Iowa was also home to a Utopian community called the Amana Colonies, founded by a group of German immigrants known as the Community of True Inspiration.

Another religious group that moved to Iowa before 1900 was the Amish. Iowa's Amish settlers came from Germany before settling in Pennsylvania and Ohio and then moving to Iowa in search of cheaper homes. They first settled in the southeast part of the state in 1840, before another settlement was created in eastern Iowa in the town of Kalona. The Old Order Amish community in Kalona still exists to this day, and while they do not use automobiles, telephones, or electricity, other non-Amish members of the Kalona community do have access to these modern amenities.

During World War I, German Americans throughout the country were the targets of suspicion and were ostracized and in some cases harmed because of their heritage. In Iowa, books suspected of being "pro-German" were removed from Iowa libraries during the first months of 1918. German-language newspapers, which flourished before the war, were increasingly scrutinized, and most were closed. This left only a handful of German-language publications in a state that used to host dozens. The implications of these actions were that German-speaking Iowans, who may not have understood English, would have been unable to access information or to participate in their communities.

During World War II, Iowa farmers were assisted in their duties by a variety of laborers. Starting in 1942, Mexican nationals learned of jobs in Iowa and began relocating to the state in 1942. They were joined by workers from Jamaica the following year. The United States captured thousands of German prisoners of war, and some of them stayed in camps in Algona and Clarinda, and other locations throughout the state, beginning in 1944. These prisoners were hired out by farmers who needed additional workers.

In 2000, 3.1 percent of the Iowa population was foreign-born, compared with 11.1 percent nationwide. The late twentieth and early twenty-first centuries saw an increase in immigrants from Mexico seeking work in agriculture and meatpacking. Both documented and undocumented workers travel to Iowa to work in meatpacking plants, and the industry relies heavily on this labor force to function. The hiring structure in several rural industries has influenced immigration to Iowa from Mexico. Some individuals, after emigrating from Mexico, find greater opportunities by moving from California to the Midwest to work in farm-related industries.

Meat and poultry plants, along with some in the construction and hospitality industries, would hire a migrant worker who is seeking year-round employment and affordable housing. After the employer finds their new hire to be a good worker, the employer would ask him or her to invite family and friends from Mexico to fill vacant jobs. The result is that some migrants have moved directly from rural Mexico to some Iowa towns, including to Storm Lake. Consequently, workers from particular Mexican villages dominate harvesting jobs and factory crews in some workplaces.

For example, the meatpacking plant in the town of Marshalltown employs 900 individuals, half of whom have come to Iowa from the town of Villachuato, Mexico. Other towns in Iowa have seen demographic changes, due in part to rising immigration and falling wages at meatpacking plants, which make those jobs less appealing to documented workers and citizens with other employment opportunities. These rural employers pay less than their counterparts in urban areas because there is less competition from other employers and thus less incentive to provide higher wages.

Naples (1996) wrote a study of the changing demographics of a rural Iowa town as more Mexicans and Mexican Americans began to move there for work and for the slow pace and affordability of small town life. She found that the increased presence of Latino residents in the town not only brought about dynamic shifts but also brought about resistance by long-term residents who felt that those newer to the area were undermining their sense of community. However, the community did adapt to include its new residents, even if some of the community members were resistant to change.

While many immigrants working in the state have legal status or have become citizens, some who come to Iowa to work do so at great risk because they are undocumented. Several immigration raids have been undertaken in the state to locate undocumented workers, including the May 2008 raid in the town of Postville, which was the largest such raid in U.S. history. Even though undocumented workers may not be listed as taxpayers, they do still contribute to the Iowa economy. In 2007, undocumented workers were estimated to have contributed $40 to $62 million in state taxes, as well as $50 to $77.8 million in federal Social Security and Medicare taxes paid both by the workers and their employers.

Today, Iowa still continues to attract workers from Mexico. In addition, Asian and Asian American workers have come to the state in the past several decades. Despite this, Iowa is still populated mostly by non-Hispanic whites who are American-born. The 2010 U.S. Census finds that 93.9 percent of Iowa residents are white (with 89.8 percent being non-Hispanic whites) and only 3.1 percent of the population is foreign-born. Latinos comprise the largest non-European racial group living in the state, making up 4.5 percent of the population. Although most Iowans were born in the United States and speak English, 5.8 percent of Iowans speak a language other than English in their homes.

While immigration from Europe has tapered off, there are still a number of communities that celebrate their immigrant heritage with museums and festivals. These include the Danish Windmill Museum and Danish Immigrant Museum in Elk Horn, the Czech and Slovak National Museum and Library in Cedar Rapids, and the Vesterheim Norwegian-American Museum in Decorah. Other sites include the villages of the Amana Colonies, Pella Historic Village, and the German American Heritage Center, a museum that documents German immigration to Iowa. Festivals include Pella Tulip Time, a celebration of Dutch heritage, Nordic Fest in Decorah, and Guttenberg German Fest.

TOPICAL ESSAYS

The Amana Colonies

The Amana Colonies are a cluster of communities in eastern Iowa, which are one of the country's longest-living communal societies. They were founded by a group of German immigrants known as the Community of True Inspiration. This religious group, founded in Germany in 1714, faced persecution and economic depression in Germany. In 1834, the community came to the United States and purchased land near Buffalo, New York. The community was about 1,200 strong, and as it continued to grow, the community required more farmland to meet its needs. Farmland in Iowa was inexpensive and they arrived in the state in 1855. Six villages were established, with another added near the railroad in 1861.

The group lived communally, which meant that members shared resources and property. Members were assigned jobs and everyone received meals, medical care, and shelter as a part of communal life. The community was supported by farming and the production of wool and calico, and their craftsmen were known for producing high-quality goods. The Amana Colonies stopped using the communal model in 1932. Today, the Amana Colonies are a National Historic Landmark and a popular tourist attraction. Although the site is a tourist destination, many of the residents still pass down family traditions from their German and religious heritage.

Cedar Rapids Mosque

In the 1860s, immigration to the United States from Syria and Lebanon increased, and immigration numbers continued to rise in the decades that follow. High immigration numbers were seen again after World War II, in response to economic and political constraints in Europe and the Middle East. The largest numbers of Middle Eastern immigrants settled in a handful of states, including Iowa. The first Middle Eastern immigrant arrived in Cedar Rapids in 1895, and a small community of less than 20 immigrants formed over the next twenty-five years. They worked as farmers, open shops, and their community continues to grow. One obstacle they faced was the lack of a regular space for worship, instead relying on rented buildings.

The mosque was designed and built in the late 1920s and early 1930s and was dedicated on June 16, 1934. It was the first mosque in the Western Hemisphere and came to be referred to as "America's Mother Mosque." The original building still stands in Cedar Rapids but is a historical structure rather than one that serves an active congregation. After the city's Muslim community outgrew the space, a new mosque was built in 1972 and has subsequently undergone several expansions.

English-Only Laws in Iowa

Iowa came under fire for English-Only laws twice in the twentieth century. The first time was in 1918, when Governor Harding passed a law forbidding the use of any non-English language in public spaces or over telephones. Harding went even farther by saying that "American" could be the only spoken language. He encouraged those who do not know English to worship in their homes so that foreign language services would not be held in Iowa churches. Harding's law, called the Babel Proclamation, was written mostly in response to Iowa's large German population, who came under suspicion during World War I. Although German Americans throughout the country were scrutinized, many around the country criticized Harding's proclamation and he became the laughingstock of the nation after a group of women were arrested for speaking German in a telephone conversation. Harding repealed the law in December 1918, although he still supported the idea of wartime language restrictions.

The second English-Only law was passed in April 2002. This law made English the state's official language, a move that was found unconstitutional elsewhere. Laws that favored use of the English language both in discourse and in official documents were supported by several groups nationwide, including English First, U.S. English Inc., and English for the Children. Each group argues that requiring immigrants to learn English is a way to help immigrants be successful in the United States. Opponents of the English-Only law call for Iowans to reconsider their positions on immigration and language. Many Iowans worry that English-Only laws will alienate immigrants or even demonize them. A number of groups seek to welcome immigrants, especially from Latin American countries, and to remind Iowans that their ancestors were once immigrants too.

Governor Vilsack wants to attract more immigrants to Iowa to fulfill the business and production needs of the state in a way that the current population, which is both aging and declining in size, would not be able to. Although he has been a strong proponent of immigration and diversity in the state, he still signed the English-Only bill into law. This law made English the state's official language and prevented public notices from being printed in any language other than English. Vilsack's critics argued that it was because he was up for re-election. Despite the move toward official English, many new immigrants still moved to Iowa to be with family and to find work.

LAFAYETTE YOUNG (1848–1926) AND ANTI-GERMAN SENTIMENT DURING WORLD WAR I

Lafayette Young was a senator and journalist who lived in Des Moines. He was the publisher of the *Des Moines Capital*, a local newspaper, early in the twentieth century. When World War I broke out, Young was eager to be involved after having been a war correspondent during other conflicts. On January 30, 1915, he boarded the *Lusitania* for a four-month tour of European countries engaged in the conflict.

During his stay in Germany, Young felt that the Germans strongly disliked Americans, in part because of the aid the United States had sent to Belgium. After his return Young stated, "I wish the American people generally realized that we have no friends in Germany and that even our naturalized fellow-citizens there are not our friends." His distrust of Germany and the German people increased through the war and helped fuel the discriminatory anti-German climate of World War I.

When the United States entered the war in 1917, Councils of Defense were formed in each state. Young served as chairman of the Iowa State Council of National Defense from its formation in 1917 through the end of the war. The council's primary purpose was to suppress treason and disloyalty in any form, whether by speech or action. Governor Harding promised the support of law enforcement for the council's actions, giving the group a great deal of strength and influence. The council also wanted to promote "active, aggressive" loyalty by providing every Iowan with patriotic activities in which to be involved (Brigham 1918).

Because the United States was at war with Germany, German Americans were often the target of council activities. For example, the council ordered Iowa libraries to search for and remove any materials that might be sympathetic to the German war effort. Young and other council members also encouraged Iowans to be vigilant for behavior they considered treasonous and many letters from around the state were written to inform the council of individuals whose behavior was considered suspicious.

During the war, German Americans became the target for suspicion and violence around the state due to the anti-German sentiment caused in part by organizations like Young's. In 1917, two men were nearly lynched and community groups went into churches and schools to confiscate books on pacifism or books written in the German language. Many German newspapers went out of business and, in at least one case, the offices of a German paper were vandalized. After the war, anti-German sentiment gradually died down and organizations like the State Council for National Defense faded into obscurity or were disbanded. Young continued as editor of the *Des Moines Capital* until his death in 1926.

Postville Immigration Raid

On May 12, 2008, the U.S. Immigration and Customs Enforcement (ICE) raided Agriprocessors, Inc., a kosher slaughterhouse in the town of Postville. About 389 workers (10 percent of Postville's population) were arrested, making it the largest immigration raid in the nation's history. The workers were held in a makeshift detention center that was normally used to hold cattle for livestock shows. The ICE also set up a makeshift courtroom to begin deportation proceedings and to charge arrested workers with document fraud and identity theft for using ID cards given to them that allegedly belonged to others. Only one social security number was found to be a match and the workers' use of these numbers did not constitute the normal criteria for "identity theft" which involves using documents in order to obtain something illegally. Work does not fall under this category. Nevertheless, these charges fell under anti-terror policy and therefore, they were subjected to immediate potential detention and deportation.

The raid sparked outrage among some in the state and served as the basis for discussions about immigrant laborers in the United States. McCarthy (2010) contends that Postville provides an example of how the human rights of workers are not protected and how undocumented immigrants often work in exploitative conditions. Allegations of human rights violations and labor violations surfaced immediately, because many workers were paid less than minimum wage, and in one instance an employee was said to have been abused physically by his supervisor but did not report the incident for fear of losing his job. There were also substantiated claims of sexual harassment and 9,000 child labor violations.

Fr. Paul Ouderkirk, of St. Bridget's Catholic Church, left, looks over utility bills with 18-year-old Geraldo Solovi-Perez on July 14, 2009, in Postville, Iowa. The church has been paying Solovi-Perez's utility bills since the immigration raid at the Agriprocessors slaughterhouse. Solovi-Perez, an undocumented immigrant from Guatemala, hoped to work again after the meat-processing plant reopened under new ownership. Its former owners faced charges for exploiting hundreds of vulnerable workers, many of whom were under the legal working age. (AP Photo/Nigel Duara)

Dozens of newspaper articles and blog posts appeared criticizing ICE for their strategies both in conducting the raid and in handling the detainees afterward. Catholic churches in Iowa also responded by hosting prayer services for immigration reform. These included the Immaculate Conception Parish in Cedar Rapids, which is heavily involved with the Latino immigrant community, and the St. Bridget Parish in Postville. Demonstrations by various groups were held throughout the state, including in Des Moines and Waterloo.

The raid's aftermath can be seen both in the community of Postville and in federal policy. The town of Postville faced a shrinking population and unemployment, as many of the arrested women were released to care for their children but not allowed to work. Nearly all of the men were deported. The devastation caused by the raid evoked criticism of immigration laws and enforcement. In response to this, the Obama administration created enforcement guidelines that focus more heavily on punishing employers rather than the workers themselves. The U.S. Supreme Court also ruled in *Flores-Figueroa v. United States* (2009) that federal prosecutors must prove that someone using a fake ID must know it belongs to a real person before they can be charged with identity theft.

Agriprocessors was opened in the late 1980s by Orthodox Jews who moved to the town to work as kosher butchers and created a rural Jewish community. They were followed by immigrants, mostly from Guatemala, who came to the town for work. The raid sparked controversy in the Jewish community as the irony of a kosher meat-processing facility was contrasted with the poor treatment of the workers, many of whom were potential refugees. Agriprocessors went into bankruptcy after the raid. The community is still recovering two years after the raid, although the purchase of the Agriprocessors facility by Agri Star in April 2010 has made residents hopeful that the town's employment situation will improve.

NOTABLE FIGURES

NICHOLAS J. RUSCH (1822–1864)

In March 1860, the Iowa legislature created the position of commissioner of Immigration. The purpose of this position was for the commissioner to reside in New York City and encourage immigrants to continue west to Iowa. In May, Nicholas J. Rusch, a former lieutenant governor, was appointed to the position. He was to stay in New York from May until December and provide immigrants information about the state, including soil and climate, cheapest travel routes to Iowa, and opportunities for business. Documents were printed in English, German, and several other languages. The position was short-lived, however, after Rusch's report to the governor in December 1861 suggested that a New York office was not effective for recruiting immigrants. As a result, the law creating the position was repealed in February 1862.

SANDRA SANCHEZ

Sandra Sanchez emigrated from Mexico and has lived in Iowa since 1991. She worked in business administration in Mexico City before coming to the United States. After this, her experiences as an immigrant led her to work with social justice issues and she now works in several capacities in Iowa. These include the Des Moines School District and the Des Moines Family Violence Center. She has also worked to provide immigration assistance through the Board of Immigration Appeals. In 1995, she became the director of Immigrants Voice Program for the American Friends Service Committee and will be serving a term as chair of the Iowa Commission on Latino Affairs through 2012.

As someone active in immigrant affairs, Sanchez has been interviewed by a variety of news outlets and she provides commentary on current events and their impact on immigrants. Sanchez has been interviewed by multiple sources to share her views on the anti-immigration law that was passed in Arizona in 2010. As director of the Immigrants Voice Program, she has also pressed for immigration reform, giving speeches on the topic in both English and Spanish. Sanchez is considered an innovator in the area of immigrant integration into U.S. society, and as a result she has spoken at the First Round Table on Migration in the European Union in 2003.

BIBLIOGRAPHY

Amana Colonies Convention and Visitors Bureau. "The Amana Colonies Story." 2011. http://www.amanacolonies.org/history.htm. Accessed March 14, 2014.

"America Is Hated by All Germans." *New York Times*, May 30, 1915. http://query.nytimes .com/gst/abstract.html?res=9801E6D81338E633A25753C3A9639C946496D6CF. Accessed August 2, 2014.

Aurner, C. R. *Leading Events in Johnson County Iowa History*. Cedar Rapids, IA: Western Historical Press, 2010.

Brigham, J. *Iowa: Its History and Foremost Citizens, Volume II*. Des Moines, IA: The S.J. Clarke Publishing Company, 1918.

Byrne, J. P., P. Coleman, and J. King. *Ireland and the Americas*. Santa Barbara, CA: ABC-CLIO, 2008.

Carr, P. J., and M. J. Kefalas. *Hollowing Out the Middle: The Rural Brain Drain and What It Means for America*. Boston: Beacon Press, 2009.

Cunningham, R. K. "The Western United States in World War One-Chronology of Events." 1997. https://netfiles.uiuc.edu/rcunning/www/westchr.htm. Accessed March 14, 2014.

Derr, N. "The Babel Proclamation." *Iowa Heritage Illustrated* 85 (2004): 128–44.

Executive Council of the State of Iowa. *Census of Iowa for the Year 1915*. Des Moines, IA: Robert Henderson, 1916.

Flom, G. T. "The Coming of the Norwegians to Iowa." *Iowa Journal of History and Politics* 3 no. 3 (1905): 347–83.

Flom, G. T. "The Early Swedish Immigration to Iowa." *Iowa Journal of History and Politics* 3 no. 4 (1905): 583–615.

Flom, G. T. *A History of Norwegian Immigration to the United States*. Iowa City, IA: Privately printed, 1909.

Frese, H. E. "German-American Journalism in the State of Iowa." Master's Thesis, Graduate College of the State University of Iowa, 1935.

German American Heritage Center. "History and Mission." 2011. http://gahc.org/?page_id=21. Accessed March 14, 2014.

Grey, M. A., and Anne C. Woodrick. "Unofficial Sister Cities: Meatpacking Labor Migration between Villachuato, Mexico, and Marshalltown, Iowa." *Human Organization* 61 no. 4 (2002): 364–76.

Guttenberg Germanfest Committee. "21st Annual Germanfest, Guttenberg, Iowa." 2010. http://www.germanfestinguttenberg.com/. Accessed March 14, 2014.

Henderson, O. K. "Postville Mayor Says Community Still Recovering from Immigration Raid." *Radio Iowa*, April 14, 2010.

Hoogeveen, L., and S. Putnam. *Images of America: Atlantic*. Chicago: Arcadia, 2010.

Iowa Division of Latino Affairs. "Commission of Latino Affairs." 2011. http://www.latinoaffairs.iowa.gov/Pages/Commission percent20Bio-Photo.htm. Accessed March 14, 2014.

Iowa Public Television. "Iowa History Timeline: Text Version." http://www.iptv.org/iowapathways/timeline_text.cfm? Accessed March 14, 2014.

Islamic Center of Cedar Rapids. "Islam in Iowa." http://crmosque.com/about-iccr/islam-in-iowa. Accessed March 14, 2014.

Janzen, R. A. "The Amana Colonies." 1988. http://www.kalonaiowa.org/amish/amana.html. Accessed March 14, 2014.

Janzen, R. A. "The Old Order Amish." 1988. http://www.kalonaiowa.org/amish/amish.html. Accessed March 14, 2014.

Marshall, B. *France and the Americas*. Santa Barbara, CA: ABC-CLIO, 2005.

Martin, P. L., M. Fix, and E. Taylor. *Agriculture & Immigration in California: The New Rural Poverty*. Washington, DC: The Urban Institute Press, 2006.

McCarthy, A. L. "The May 12, 2008 Postville, Iowa Immigration Raid: A Human Rights Perspective." *Transnational Law and Contemporary Problems* 19 (2010): 293–315.

Metcalf, H. J. "Papers, 1910–1919." Ms 74, State Historical Society of Iowa.

Morain, T. J. "To Whom Much Is Given: The Social Identity of an Iowa Small Town in the Early Twentieth Century. In Marvin Bergman, ed. *Iowa History Reader*. Ames: Iowa State University Press, 1996, pp. 291–326.

Naples, N. A. "The Case of Mexican American Immigrants in Rural Iowa." Presented at "Immigration and the Changing Face of Rural America Focus on the Midwestern States." Ames, Iowa, July 11–13, 1996.

Nordic Fest. "Nordic Fest." 2009. http://www.nordicfest.com/. Accessed March 14, 2014.

Norman, J. Jacobs, and T. Leys. "Claims of ID Fraud Lead to Largest Raid in State History." *Des Moines Register*. May 12, 2008. http://archive.desmoinesregister.com

/article/20080512/NEWS/80512012/Claims-ID-fraud-lead-largest-raid-state-history. Accessed August 2, 2014.

Olivo, Antonio "Immigration Raid Leaves Damaging Mark on Postville, Iowa." *Los Angeles Times*, May 19, 2009. http://articles.latimes.com/2009/may/12/nation/na-postville-iowa12. August 2, 2014.

Pella Historical Village. "Pella Tulip Time." 2011. http://www.pellatuliptime.com/. Accessed March 14, 2014.

Perez, W. *We Are Americans: Undocumented Students Pursuing the American Dream*. Sterling, VA: Stylus Publishing, 2009.

Printer's Ink. "Lafayette Young, at 66, War Correspondent." *Printer's Ink*, January 21, 1915, 82.

Ruthvin, M., and A. Nanji. *Historical Atlas of Islam*. Singapore: Cartographica, 2004.

Sanchez, S. "A Call for Iowa Immigration Reform." 2010. http://afsc.org/story/call-iowa-immigration-reform. Accessed March 14, 2014.

Schweider, D. *Iowa: The Middle Land*. Iowa City: University of Iowa Press, 1996.

Schweider, D. "Iowa Official Register: History of Iowa." 1999–2000. http://publications.iowa.gov/135/1/history/7–1.html. Accessed March 14, 2014.

Spolksy, B. *Language Policy*. New York: Cambridge University Press, 2004.

State of Iowa. "Regular Session of the Ninth General Assembly of the State of Iowa." Des Moines, IA: P.W. Palmer, 1862.

Union Historical Company. *The History of Polk County, Iowa*. Des Moines, IA: Birdsall, Williams, & Co., 1880.

United States Census Bureau. "State and County Quickfacts: Iowa." 2010. http://quickfacts.census.gov/qfd/states/19000.html. Accessed March 14, 2014.

University of Iowa. "UI String Faculty Will Present Second Annual Gala Concern Sept. 12." 2006. news-releases.uiowa.edu/2006/august/083106string-gala.html. Accessed March 14, 2014.

Waddington, L. "Postville Aftermath: Faith Community Prays for Reform." *The Iowa Independent*, May 23, 2008. http://iowaindependent.com/2366/postville-aftermath-302-detainees-charged-criminally-297-plead-guilty. Accessed August 2, 2014.

Wiegand, W. A. *An Active Instrument for Propaganda: the American Public Library during World War I*. New York: Greenwood Press, 1989.

16

KANSAS

William P. Kladky

CHRONOLOGY

1500 The most numerous indigenous peoples in Kansas are the Pawnee, Kansa, Wichita, and Apache. The state is named for the Kansa, which means People of the South Wind.

1541 While fruitlessly searching for the mythic "Seven Cities of Cibola (Gold)," the Spanish conquistador Francisco Vásquez de Coronado (1510–1554) travels around Kansas, including the Junction City area.

1650–1750 The Dismal River culture, which is related to the Plains Apache culture, establishes villages in territory that will become Kansas.

1719 In the first official French expedition to Kansas, Charles Claude du Tisne (1688–1730) explores the upper "Louisiana" territory. He visits Osage Indian villages near the Osage River's mouth and around Doniphan County, and then visits the Wichita and the Padoucas across Wilson County.

1724 The French commander at Fort Orleans, M. Étienne Veniard, sieur de Bourgmont (1679–1734), sets up a trading post near a large Kansa village at the mouth of the Kansas River. Around this time, the Otoe tribe of the Sioux settles in the northeast corner of Kansas.

1762 France cedes the province of "Louisiana" to Spain by the Treaty of Fontainebleau.

1780 The Kansa tribe moves its "Blue Earth Village" up the Kansas River to its junction with the Big Blue River, a site later to become Manhattan, Kansas.

1800	Spain cedes the province of "Louisiana" back to France by the Treaty of St. Ildefonso.
1803	As part of the Louisiana Purchase, the United States annexes Kansas as an unorganized territory.
1806–1807	While exploring the region, U.S. Army captain Zebulon M. Pike (1779–1813) negotiates a treaty between the Kansa and Osage Nations. His description of Kansas as a desert influenced the government's future settlement policy.
1819	On a scientific exploration, the 30-ton *Western Engineer* of U.S. Army major Stephen H. Long (1784–1864) becomes the first steamer to enter the Kansas River.
1820s	The Kansas area is designated as Indian territory (until 1854) by the U.S. government and closed to settlement by Anglos. Various eastern American Indian tribes—the Potawatomi, Kickapoo, and others—immigrate to reservations established as a result of the Indian removal policy. Nearly all these groups later move to Oklahoma.
1821	The Santa Fe Trail is established by trader William Becknell (1787–1856) to take freight from Kansas City to Santa Fe, New Mexico.
1825	U.S. surveyor George Sibley (1782–1863) negotiates an agreement with the Osage Indians to allow travelers through Kansas safe passage on the Santa Fe Trail.
1827	Cantonment Leavenworth or Fort Leavenworth—named in honor of American soldier Henry Leavenworth (1783–1834)—is built just inside Indian territory to guard travelers on the nation's Western frontier.
1829	The Reverend Thomas Johnson (1802–1865) establishes a Methodist mission and school for Shawnee Indians near Turner.
1831	Moses Grinter (1810–1878) sets up the first ferry that crosses the Kansas River in Kansas. The ferry crossing serves as a military link between Fort Leavenworth and Fort Scott.
1850s–1860s	Mexican workers come to Kansas during the construction of the railroads. French settlers continue to arrive in the state.
1854	The Massachusetts Emigrant Aid Company arranges to send anti-slavery settlers (known as "Free-Staters") to Kansas. Topeka is founded by five anti-slavery activists, one of them being Cyrus K. Holliday (1826–1900). At the same time, pro-slavery emigrants cross the Missouri border into Kansas. The Kansas-Nebraska Act becomes law, establishing the Nebraska Territory and the Kansas Territory. Swiss immigrants arrive in Kansas and settle in Potawatomie (Onage), Nemaha (Bern, Neuchatel), and Allen (Geneva) counties.

1857	Timothy and Sylvia Hersey establish Abilene ("city of the plains") as a stagecoach stop along the Mud Creek.
1859	A stageline bringing immigrants begins operating between Leavenworth and the gold fields near Denver.
1860	The foreign-born population of Kansas is about 12 percent, mostly coming from the British Isles or Germany.
1861	Kansas is admitted into the Union as a free state.
1867	Illinois-born Joseph G. McCoy (1837–1915) builds stockyards in Abilene and helps develop the Chisholm Trail, encouraging Texas cattlemen to undertake cattle drives to his stockyards and immigrants to come to Kansas to work.
1867–1930	The Orphan Train Movement welfare program transports children from the crowded cities of the United States to foster homes across the country, many in Kansas.
1870	An economic depression in Britain and Ireland stimulates Irish immigration to Kansas. The depression ironically results in part from the cheaper and better grain being imported from the United States, much of which was grown by Irish Americans.
1870s–1890s	Homesteaders flock to the state.
1871	The first railway in the state begins operation in Lawrence.
1873	Mennonite immigration to Kansas from Russia begins; these Russian immigrants introduce Turkey Red wheat to Kansas.
1877	Nicodemus, the first all-black town in Kansas, is founded by African American migrants from Kentucky.
1880s	Slavs, Balts, Italians, and Iberians begin to arrive.
1893	Thousands from Caldwell, Arkansas City, and other Kansas border towns race for lands in the Cherokee Strip, a stretch of land in southern Kansas.
1910	Mexicans immigrate to take agricultural work.
1922–1927	As the result of legal battles between the state and the Ku Klux Klan, the Klan is ejected from Kansas.
1936	New oil fields are developed in western Kansas.
1942	A prisoner–of–war camp is built in Concordia.
1970s	Some of the Hmong who fled Laos after the Vietnam War settle in the state's southwest and other areas. Over 1,000 Jewish Soviet immigrants come to Kansas City.
1990	The population of the state jumps to 2,477,000.
1990–2010	Immigrants surge from 2.5 percent of the state's total population, to 5 percent in 2000, and to 6.5 percent in 2010. Many Vietnamese, Laotians, Cambodians, and, most recently, Mexicans come to southwest Kansas to work in the meatpacking plants in Garden City and Dodge City.
2000–2010	The state's foreign-born population increases 38.7 percent, with many coming from Latin America and the Caribbean.

HISTORICAL OVERVIEW

Pre-1850

Kansas has always been a crossroads. In the late eighteenth century, the Kansa and Osage Nations dominated the eastern part of the state, with the Kansa on the Kansas River to the north, and the Osage on the Arkansas River to the south. The Pawnees were mostly on the plains to the west and north of the Kansa and Osages. U.S. Army captain Zebulon M. Pike (1779–1813) was the first governmental explorer of the area. Because Pike called Kansas a desert in his report, the government subsequently utilized the area largely as a reservation for the American Indian tribes that were subsequently relocated from the East.

Slowly, it became less difficult to get around. The keelboat era finally ended around 1830 when steamers on the Kansas River hauled people and goods from Kansas City to Lawrence, to Topeka, and to Fort Riley through the territorial period and early statehood. Most of Kansas's population at this time was the American Indian tribes who were moved to the area from the nation's East and Great

Somali refugee Abdikarim Jimale loads cuts of meat into a vat at a Tyson meatpacking plant in Emporia, Kansas, on December 21, 2007. (AP Photo/Charlie Riedel)

Lakes area via the Indian Removal Act of 1830, which moved over 10,000 American Indians to the territory. During the 1840s, migrants on the California Trail and Oregon Trail used the 800 miles of the Santa Fe Trail that snaked through Kansas.

THE 1850S: "BLEEDING" KANSAS

Kansas did not attract settlers of European descent until the 1850s, when migration was allowed. The early settlers generally arrived from the states of Ohio, Missouri, Illinois, and Indiana. A significant number came from the New England states in 1854 and 1855, aided by the New England Emigrant Aid Company. Other families immigrated from the British Isles and Germany. Many who settled came for land and business opportunities. A significant number were driven out of the territory after the bitter winter of 1856.

Already living in the area when the Kansas Nebraska Act opened Kansas Territory for settlement in 1854 were several tribes of Native Americans. Plains Indian tribes, the Kansas, Pawnees, and Osages, lived in and moved across Kansas, depending on the season. French settlers continued to settle in the state. In 1852, Ernest Valeton de Boissière, a former French army engineer, founded Silkville as an experimental Utopian community in Franklin County. Most Silkville residents were French, and the community did well initially. After its silk and dairy production declined, members left to other parts of Kansas to find employment.

By 1855, the various tribes had ceded most of their land to the federal government through various treaties. The Otoe and Missourian Indians ceded all except a small strip on the Big Blue River, the Delawareans ceded all theirs except a reservation, the Shawnees ceded over 6 million acres, the Iowans kept only a small reservation, the Kickapoos ceded everything except 150,000 acres in the western part of the territory, and lands were also ceded by the Sacs and Foxes.

The slavery issue—"bleeding Kansas"—influenced most new settlements in the 1850s. By 1854, the New England Emigrant Aid Society (later Company) and other groups had formed to promote and support anti-slavery settlement. The Society sent out a total of 1,240 settlers under agents such as Charles Robinson. Pro-slavery Missourians also migrated to Kansas. The first New Englanders arrived that year when the Society founded Lawrence, named to honor one of their major benefactors, Amos A. Lawrence (1814–1886). Wabaunsee was founded in 1855 by 100 emigrants from Connecticut inspired by a sermon given by well-known abolitionist Henry Ward Beecher (1813–1887). Beecher's money purchased Sharps rifles for the migrants' self-defense. Reputedly, the rifles were smuggled across pro-slavery states in crates marked "books" or "bibles," and rapidly became known as "Beecher's Bibles."

Most of frontier Kansas's new settlers were seeking land and opportunity. The first came from Missouri, but were soon followed by migrants from the Ohio valley, mid-Atlantic, upper South, and New England. In 1859, Kansas became a free state and outlawed slavery. The first governor was Charles L. Robinson (1818–1894), the principal agent for the New England Emigrant Aid Company and the founder of several anti-slavery towns.

Kansas after the Civil War, 1860–1900

Of the territory's 1860 population of 107,209, 16 percent were from the states north of the Mason-Dixon line, 13.5 percent from the lower South, and 59.4 percent from the border states. The primary birthplaces of the 1860 population were Ohio (11,617), eastern Missouri (11,356), Indiana (9,945), and Illinois (9,367), as well as Kentucky, Pennsylvania, and New York. The foreign-born population was about 12 percent, most from the British Isles or Germany. The population was mostly rural and individuals were of European descent, with only two slaves and 625 "Free Colored" residents. One hundred and eighty-nine Native Americans were listed in the U.S. Census, with 141 in Wyandotte County. The only cities were Leavenworth (5,000 population) and Atchison (2,500). Lawrence's population was 2,000, and seven other towns had over 500.

When Kansas became a state, the government tried to encourage immigrants and migrants. Some 30,000 copies of a pamphlet *The State of Kansas, a Home for Immigrants* was released by the third governor, Samuel J. Crawford (1835–1913), and was distributed widely. Crawford also appointed a state immigration agent in 1866. The enabling legislation set up two commissioners, appointed by the governor with the consent of the senate, and the governor was an ex-officio member. Section 1 of the legislation stated that the commissioners had the "power to appoint one or more agents to visit Europe for the purpose of encouraging and directing immigration to this State" (*Laws of the State of Kansas*, 1864, Ch. 75, sec. 1, 143–44). Individual towns sought to attract new businesses and settlers with their own promotional information; some competed to be on the routes of railroads, which were just starting to be built.

Resolution of the Indian-settler conflict greatly facilitated the upcoming surge in migration and immigration. By 1870, most American Indian tribes had been moved to Oklahoma, although Potawatomi, Sauk, Fox, and Kickapoo Indians still lived on small reservations.

The population of Kansas then surged by the greatest amount in its history. Generally, settlement of the state progressed from east to west. More than 1 million came. Many purchased land for farms or businesses in the new emerging towns. Most of the farmland acquired by the first settlers in Kansas Territory was claimed under the national Preemption Act of 1841—also known as the Distributive Preemption Act (27 Cong., Ch. 16; 5 Stat. 453). The act permitted anyone to claim up to 160 acres and pay $1.25 per acre. More free and cheap land provided by the 1862 Homestead Act (settlers also could claim 160 acres of public land) and the railroads attracted many settlers. Settling in Kansas also were Union war veterans, mostly from the Ohio River Valley, the Middle Atlantic, and New England states. Over 70 percent of the immigrants arriving during 1860–1880 worked in agriculture, which was the main occupation of residents until the 1920s.

The 1870 Census found that 5,972 ethnic Germans had arrived in Kansas during the 1860s or represented 3.9 percent of the state's population of 135,792 in 1870. While the Kansas Territory never had many slaves, the population of "free" blacks grew steadily. Many used the "Underground Railroad," and during the Civil War hundreds fled Missouri for freedom in Kansas. After the war ended, many African Americans moved from the South in search of better lives. Promoters encouraged black families to move to Graham County in western Kansas. As a result, the state's black population rose from 17,108 in 1870 to 43,107 in 1880.

In the boom, more towns were founded, schools established, businesses and small industries started, and railroad track was extending to the West. In 1869, the Kansas (now Union) Pacific reached the Colorado boundary line, as had the Santa Fe 1873. This led to the era of the great cattle drives. Abilene became a shipping center for Texas cattle in 1867 as the extended Chisholm Trail was used to bring the herds to the Union Pacific. Along the tracks, the towns of Eastern Division, Newton, Ellsworth, Caldwell, Wichita, and Dodge City grew quickly. Religious groups also established some of the early settlements in Kansas. These included Quakers, River Brethren, Dunkards and German Baptists, and German Russian Catholics who lived near Hayes.

Several organizations in Kansas (e.g., the National Kansas Committee) and in northern states raised funds and collected clothing and supplies for the many needy Kansas settlers. Children without parents—some recent European immigrants, some abandoned or homeless—were given special help to come to Kansas. The Children's Aid Society of New York operated orphan trains between 1854 and 1929. Of the 150,000 children who left New York, nearly 5,000 were adopted by families in Kansas.

In 1870, many immigrants came from Great Britain, especially Ireland. Many immigrants were stimulated by an economic depression in Britain and Ireland during 1873–1896. The depression ironically resulted in part from the cheaper and better grain being imported from the United States that was probably grown by Irish Americans.

This coincided with a major campaign by railroads, newspapers, and businesses to recruit even more new settlers to Kansas. By 1882, the state had 3,855 miles of railroad track, and immigrants and migrants used it heavily. The railroads especially attempted to court European immigrants, leading to significant ethnic diversity in the state. In 1872, two railroads funded large advertising campaigns to sell their land along their railways. The Kansas Pacific and the Atchison, Topeka and Santa Fe printed circulars in the German language and sent agents to Russia to encourage farmers to settle and ship grain on the railroad lines. Because Russian Germans were experienced at dry-land (prairie) farming, they were especially prized. Some railroads offered free sleeping cars on express trains leaving Kansas City for the farmlands, granted land for churches and schools, supplied some farmers with seed wheat for their crop, and sometimes provided temporary housing until the new arrivals could purchase land. Resultantly, about one-third of all Russian Germans left Russia, with many heading to Kansas.

By 1879, about 12,000 Russian Germans had arrived. The two main concentrations of Russian German settlement were 400 Mennonite families in Marion, Harvey, and McPherson counties, as well as Volga Germans in Ellis, Russell, and Rush counties. Following were other Mennonites, with many Dutch Mennonites who had previously migrated from the Netherlands to Polish Prussia and then to Russia in 1820. They left Russia after the Czar introduced compulsory military training, thus violating their pacifist religious beliefs. The rush of German immigration during the 1870s pushed their population up to 14,551, or 4.2 percent of the state. Some left because of political oppression, economic downturns, inheritance laws, and ethnic strife.

The arrival of these Russian Germans and Mennonites revived a distressed state, just recovering after severe drought, grasshopper infestation, and economic depression. Their farming expertise helped turn Kansas into a major grain exporter. Mennonites are credited, however correctly or not, with introducing Turkey red wheat to the state around 1875–1880, which then flourished on the plains. The state changed from corn to wheat production.

The Swedish immigrants who moved to central Kansas in the mid-1800s called their new home *framtidslandet*, "the land of the future." Many left Sweden when famine threatened starvation. Because land in Illinois and Iowa was too costly, they came to Kansas. The Swedes encouraged their friends and family to join them, and formed a colony south of Salina. In the 1865 Census, there were 204 Swedes in Kansas, which grew to 17,096 in 1890. Mexican workers also came to Kansas during the construction of the railroads. They worked in sugar-beet production and manufacturing, and mostly settled in the southwestern part of the state.

About 7,000 African Americans from Tennessee came to Cherokee County after 1873, joined by several thousands from the lower Mississippi Valley states to Kansas City in the "Great Exodus" of 1879 and 1880. In 1877, during Reconstruction, 300 African Americans established a new town, Nicodemus, in Graham County. Several other African American settlements also were established in other parts of the state.

The western part of the state had conflicts with Native Americans until their last raid in Decatur County in 1878. By 1880, most Native Americans in the state had been moved to Oklahoma.

Kansas also received immigrants from southern and eastern Europe—Slavs, Balts, Italians, and Iberians—at this time. Smaller groups of Czechs and French joined them. The Czechs tended to settle west of Ellsworth. One group of Czechs named their original settlement in Rawlins County "Prag" for Prague, and another near Herndon called it "Pest" for Budapest.

In 1890, all areas in Kansas had been settled. The state's population was 934,300, with 38,566 ethnic Germans (4.1 percent), who were about a third of all immigrants. The number of foreign-born had reached a high of 147,630 or 10.3 percent of the state's population. In 1895, there were 188,000 Kansans (about 14 percent) using a language other than English.

There was another wave of immigration to Kansas between 1895 and 1915. Small groups arrived from Mexico, Italy, Greece, and Yugoslavia. Most overseas immigrants came via East Coast ports, particularly New York, and then by railroad to Kansas. Earlier immigrants tended to land at the port of New Orleans and then steamboat to the state.

Kansas in the Early Twentieth Century, 1900–1945

Additional migrants and immigrants arrived to work the oil fields and towns that sprung to life when the state's oil industry began booming. The state drew large groups of English-speaking immigrants from Ireland, Wales, and Scotland. Southeastern Kansas attracted more such immigrants than any other Midwestern state during this time.

A sizable Mexican immigration started around 1900 in response to the growth of railroads and a need for labor around World War I. Agricultural mechanization and wartime food demands created a temporary boom but grain prices fell afterward.

Most of the 8,429 Mexicans in Kansas in 1910 worked on railroad section gangs, construction, or in roundhouses. Until 1940, many Mexican immigrants worked on railroads or in the salt mining, sugar beet-processing, or meatpacking industries. Mexicans constituted almost all of the workers in the sugar beet industry of western Kansas, and lived together in colonies, outside the settled community and without basic services. Most Mexican immigrants came from the Central Mesa region, northwest of Mexico City, driven by poverty and the Mexican Revolution. By the late 1920s, the depression and immigration laws effectively ended migration from Mexico.

From 1920 to 1930, the state experienced for the first time a net loss from interstate migration. By 1930, some 39.2 percent of native Kansans lived elsewhere in the United States, and the state's population included 36.3 percent born in states other than Kansas. In 1920, the U.S. Census that found 54.7 percent were born in Kansas, 38.5 percent in other states, and 6.8 percent in foreign countries and places not identified.

The population peak point for the western part of Kansas was 1930, when it had almost 200,000. The decline set in soon afterward. The Great Depression made the farmers' problems worse, leading to more decline. The population of western Kansas fell almost 17 percent during the dust bowl years of the 1930s. A prolonged drought produced huge dust storms, especially in the state's southwestern corner. The population consequently declined.

During World War II agriculture thrived and industry expanded rapidly. The food-processing industry grew substantially, the cement industry enjoyed a major revival, and the aircraft industry boomed. Even the population of western Kansas increased 9.6 percent during the 1940s.

Kansas in the Late Twentieth Century, 1945–1990s

From 1945 to 1990, the state's population increased from 1.79 to 2.36 million, some 32 percent. Most growth was in the eastern one-third, such as in Kansas City. Those counties in the western two-thirds of Kansas declined during this period. Around the midpoint of the twentieth century, about one-half of the people of Kansas had grandparents or great grandparents born in Europe.

The state's agricultural sector declined when it was hit by a severe drought and grasshopper invasion in 1948. Immigration and migration flattened. Prosperity returned briefly during the Korean War (1950–1953), but in the mid-1950s farm surpluses and competitive world markets combined to depress the state's farm sector and to force some to migrate elsewhere.

In the 1960s, another recession prompted even more Kansans to move. The popularity of the automobile at this time did help to break down the social isolation of German farmers in the western part of the state. During the period from 1965 to 1969, annual immigration admissions averaged about 926 persons. During the most recent five years, annual admissions averaged about 4,917 persons.

Subsequently, immigration became more diverse, with most still driven by political and economic recession. Some of the Hmong who fled Laos after the Vietnam War settled in the state's southwest and other areas in the 1970s. During 1970–1999, the 1,000-plus Jewish Soviet immigrants to Kansas City were provided with furnished apartments, job assistance, and Jewish educational opportunities.

Many Vietnamese, Laotians, and Cambodians have come to southwest Kansas to work in the meatpacking plants in Garden City and Dodge City since the 1980s. The number of Asian immigrants has also grown, primarily in the cities. Over 60,000 of Asian descent were counted in the 2010 U.S. Census.

Since 1990, the state has had a relatively modest immigrant increase from 2.5 percent of Kansas's total population to 5 percent in 2000 and 6.5 percent in 2010. Between 1996 and 2005, some 21,145 immigrated to Kansas. The leading countries of origin were Mexico (2,748), India (2,175), China (1,792), Soviet Union (1,258), and the Philippines (884).

Even sparsely settled western Kansas added population. Between 1985 and 1990, it gained 651 foreign-born. Changing economics was the major cause, as well as internal migration. Kansas, more than any other in the region, had many young, U.S.-born workers migrate from its rural to urban areas. This has led to worker shortages in many rural industries. Layoffs in its meatpacking and aircraft plants, a national recession, and changing federal policies pushed many Vietnamese and Laotians from Wichita to migrate to Garden City, in the state's southwest, to take meatpacking jobs. Because they pay comparatively well and do not require specific skills or English proficiency, Kansas's meat plants have been a magnet for immigrant labor. Chain migration and recruiting incentives also drew other Southeast Asians from Alaska and Hawai'i to move to Garden City. By the mid-1980s, over 2,000 Southeast Asians, primarily Vietnamese, had settled there. When no more arrived, the packers instead tried to recruit Mexicans.

This demand for Mexican workers was magnified when in the mid-1990s large dairy operations arrived. By 2012, there were over 20 large dairies with more than 70,000 milk cows. Most of these dairies have been extremely reliant on Latino/a workers—including citizens, documented workers from Mexico and Central America, and undocumented immigrants. Resultantly, in 2000, some 9,865 (34.7 percent) of Garden City's 28,451 residents were of Mexican origin, with about half foreign-born. Most Hispanics traced their ancestry to Mexico, followed by El Salvador and Guatemala.

In the period between 1999 and 2001, there were 24,000 people eligible for naturalization and 46,000 or 65 percent of the eligible were naturalized. Some 15,000 were soon-to-be-eligible for naturalization. This is in line with a national increase in naturalization prior to 9/11.

KANSAS IN THE TWENTY-FIRST CENTURY

The state's immigration increases continued in the new century. The foreign-born share of Kansas's population rose from 2.5 percent in 1990 to 5.0 percent in 2000 and to 6.9 percent in 2011. The Latino share grew from 3.8 percent in 1990 to 7.0 percent in 2000 and then to 10.7 percent (or 306,806) in 2011. Similarly, the Asian proportion of the state's population grew from 1.2 percent in 1990 to 2.3 percent (or 67,235 people) in 2011. In 2000, there were 46,000 Asian Americans in Kansas, with 1,679 in Shawnee County.

Mexican immigration has continued because of the expanding meatpacking and dairy industries in Garden City, Dodge City, and Liberal in southwest Kansas and Emporia in eastern Kansas. Companies also began turning to the arriving Myanmar and Somalia refugees when immigration enforcement strengthened after 2001, and regular immigration (whether documented or undocumented) has decline significantly.

In 2007, Kansas was identified as one of the 22 "growth states" in terms of naturalization. Most immigrants are linked to networks created by decades of migration from the same regions (Aguilar 2008, 1, 4).The cumulative total of immigrant admissions to Kansas between 1965 and 2010 was 129,578. As of 2010, there were 186,942 foreign-born of the state's 2,853,118 population (6.6 percent). Kansas has the third-highest percentage of foreign-born in the 12 Midwestern states, though it is about one-half of the nation's 12.7 percent in 2010.

Twelve percent of the population in Wichita and Kansas City suburbs was foreign-born in 2010, compared to 8 percent of urban and 3 percent of rural residents. Between 2000 and 2010, the population increased more in rural areas. Some 68 percent of immigrants living in metropolitan areas in the state live in Kansas City. Other major metropolitan areas had little change in the proportion of foreign-born residents during 2000–2010. In 2010, a larger percentage of immigrants (61 percent) than U.S.-born residents (52 percent) were married and the total household size was larger (3.4 individuals compared to 2.5 for American-born).

Between 2000 and 2011, there was an average annual rate of change in the state's foreign-born population of about 5,692 people, compared to the state's population gain of 16,251. Combining the average increase in the foreign-born and estimated immigrant births indicates that immigration accounts for about 11,227 persons added to the state's population annually: 69.1 percent of the population increase. In 2011, 44.9 percent of Kansas's foreign-born population had arrived in the state since 2000. This compares with the national average of 35.7 percent. In 2000, 55.1 percent of the state's foreign-born population had arrived since the previous census.

The foreign-born population increased 38.7 percent between 2000 and 2010. The share of that population from Latin America and the Caribbean went up 44.0 percent. That region's share of the state's total immigrant population grew from 54.7 to 56.8 percent in 2010. The Census Bureau estimated that between 2000 and 2011, the change in Kansas's population resulting from net international migration has been about 4,450 people. It was 30.7 percent of total change (not including the children born to the immigrants after their arrival in the United States). The remainder was due to net domestic migration and natural change (births minus deaths), according to the anti-immigration group, Federation for American Immigration Reform (FAIR).

Kansas had a slow increase in the number of legal immigrants (i.e., persons obtaining legal permanent resident status) during 2002–2011 from 4,500 to 5,086. Recent 2012 green-card recipients who intend to reside in Kansas were 431.2 percent of the level of admissions after adoption of the immigration system in 1965. The 2011 U.S. Census Bureau data found that 67,411 (33.9 percent) of the foreign-born population in Kansas were naturalized U.S. citizens, compared to 44,763 residents (33.2 percent) in 2000.

In 2011–2012, 4,980 persons living in Kansas obtained legal permanent resident status from the federal government. Some 54.0 percent were female, 64.6 percent were married, and 49.7 percent were immediate relatives of U.S. citizens. They mainly came from Mexico (1,298), Burma (347), India (306), China (300), Vietnam (250), and the Philippines (207).

As of 2012, 6.9 percent of Kansans are foreign-born, with 13.0 percent Latinos or Asians. About 33.9 percent of immigrants in the state are naturalized U.S. citizens. About 87.9 percent of children with immigrant parents are U.S. citizens, and 83.4 percent of children with immigrant parents are English-proficient and 73.8 percent of naturalized citizens have a high-school diploma or higher.

Immigrants also have a significant economic impact on Kansas. Its 9,277 foreign students contribute $204 million to the state's economy and make up 8.6 percent of the workforce. Latino-owned businesses had sales and receipts of $1.3 billion and employed 7,935 people. Asian-owned businesses had sales and receipts of $1.4 billion and employed 12,676 people. The purchasing power of Latinos is $6.7 billion. Asian buying power totaled $3.1 billion.

TOPICAL ESSAYS

Recent Anti-Immigrant Controversies

Like other states with relatively low immigrant numbers, Kansas has had strong debates over various immigration proposals. Depending upon the political wind, Kansas has fluctuated in how it has dealt with immigrants and the undocumented. In 2004, a bill offering some undocumented immigrants (DREAMers) a tuition break at Kansas's public colleges and universities was enacted.

On the other hand, current Kansas secretary of state Kris Kobach has been advocating both in Kansas and nationally for restrictive immigration policies. He has proposed repealing the state's awarding of in-state college tuition for undocumented children of immigrants, a bill to require businesses to verify their workers' immigration status; and one to give police the right to check the immigration status of people they suspect are undocumented. Reaction to his advocacy has been strong. In 2010, there was a silent vigil of more than 350 people in Kansas City against an anti-immigrant rally/fundraiser "Illegal means Illegal" with Kobach and Maricopa County sheriff Joe Arpaio. Almost 1,000 attended the actual event.

In the 2012 state legislative session, a state-sponsored program that would allow businesses with a proven labor shortage to recruit undocumented immigrants was proposed. However, in 2013, some anti-immigration legislation has also been proposed.

Any anti-immigrant movement is somewhat surprising given that Kansas has increasingly come to rely on immigrants for economic growth. In the past 10 years, the state's population has grown by only 20,000. Native Kansans have been leaving the state (77,890 in 2000–2011) at a faster rate than in-immigration (57,951). Immigrants constituted 8.3 percent of the state's workforce in 2010 (or 124,253 workers). Undocumented immigrants were about 3.3 percent of the workforce (or 45,000 workers) in 2010. A recent study found that if all undocumented immigrants were removed from Kansas, the state would lose $1.8 billion in economic activity, $807.2 million in gross state product, and approximately 11,879 jobs.

REFUGEES

Kansas received 1,996 refugees over the most recent 10 fiscal years (FYs) including 402 refugees in FY 2009. Refugee settlement is the only immigration program that requires consent of the state government. Since FY 2000, Kansas has become home to 2,378 refugees from 30 different countries. The majority of these refugees came from Burma (623), Bhutan (367), Somalia (213), Iraq (193), and Vietnam (184). Additionally, roughly 31 asylees settle in Kansas each year. Similar to most states in the region, refugees from Burma and Bhutan are the fastest-growing core groups. Though in much smaller numbers, arrivals from countries like Somalia and Iran have also been steady over the past decade. Arrivals from Vietnam (a historically important refugee group), meanwhile, are steadily decreasing.

In 2012, Kansas had a low number of refugees and asylees compared to national averages. Kansas hosts fewer refugees than any other state in the Midwest. In FY 2010, refugees constituted 1.1 percent of the state's total foreign-born population. The meatpacking industry, especially in Garden City and vicinity, has attracted much secondary migration.

UNDOCUMENTED POPULATION

The proportion of undocumented immigrants of the total population of Kansas increased 233 percent during 1990–2010 (granted that any statistics on the undocumented population can only be speculative). In 2002, there were an estimated 50,000–75,000 undocumented individuals in Kansas. This ranked below 21 and above 29 other states. In 2009, Kansas had 87,000 children of immigrants (i.e., children with foreign-born parents), or about 13 percent of all children. The state's 2009 status represented a significant increase from 1990s, 33,000 children or 5 percent.

Undocumented immigrants were approximately 2.4 percent of the state's population (65,000 people) in 2010, according to a report by the Pew Hispanic Center. The anti-immigration group FAIR estimated the undocumented foreign population of Kansas in 2010 to be 70,000 persons, but their estimates tend to be inflated given the bias of this group.

The estimated economic impact of undocumented immigrants in Kansas is substantial. They paid $57.3 million in state and local taxes in 2010, which included $10.3 million in state income taxes, $3.9 million in property taxes, and $43.1 million in sales taxes. About 3.3 percent of the state's workforce is undocumented.

NOTABLE FIGURES

SAM BROWNBACK (1956–)

Perhaps a typical modern Kansan regarding immigration is Samuel Dale "Sam" Brownback, the 46th governor of Kansas. A Republican, he served as a representative for Kansas's Second Congressional District in the U.S. House of Representatives from 1995 to 1996. From 1996 to 2011, he was a U.S. senator from Kansas and was subsequently elected governor in 2010, beginning his term in January 2011.

As a religious man, Brownback has said that he supports immigration reform because the Bible says to welcome the stranger. His Senate voting record basically supports higher legal immigration levels and strong refugee protections. While in the Senate, for example, he was a cosponsor of Ted Kennedy and John McCain's 2005 bill that would have created a legal path to citizenship for undocumented

Kansas governor-elect Sam Brownback announces appointments to his cabinet, including Dale Rodman, left, his nominee for agriculture secretary, and Deb Miller, center, his nominee for transportation secretary, during a news conference on December 7, 2010, at the statehouse in Topeka, Kansas. Although Brownback is a Republican, he supports legal paths to immigration and strong refugee protections. (AP Photo/John Hanna)

immigrants already living in the United States. In 2007, Brownback voted in favor of SB 1639, the Comprehensive Immigration Reform Act.

However, he has staked out a position that is considered moderate on immigration: he advocates legal immigration, supports increasing numbers of legal immigrants, building a fence on Mexican border, and the reform bill. For instance, he initially supported giving guest workers a path to citizenship, but then voted against it.

BIBLIOGRAPHY

Aguilar, Daniel. "Adaptation as a Process of Acquisition of Cultural Capital: The Case of Mexican Immigrants in Meatpacking Areas in Kansas." *Journal of Latino-Latin American Studies* 3 (2008): 1–25.

Broadway, Michael. "Meatpacking and the Transformation of Rural Communities: A Comparison of Brooks, Alberta and Garden City, Kansas." *Rural Sociology* 72 (2007): 560–82.

Church, Michael. "Irish Immigration." Kansas Memory Blog, 2010. http://www.kansas memory.org/blog/post/74315032. Accessed July 6, 2013.

Dickenson, James R. *Home on the Range: A Century on the High Plains*. New York: Scribner, 1995.

"Emigrant Aid Company." *Columbia Electronic Encyclopedia*, 6th ed., 2013. http://www .infoplease.com/encyclopedia/history/emigrant-aid-company.html. Accessed July 2, 2013.

Federal Writers Project. *Kansas: A Guide to the Sunflower State*. Work Projects Administration, State of Kansas. New York: Hastings House, 1939.

Federation for American Immigration Reform (FAIR). "Immigration Facts: Kansas." FAIR, 2012. http://www.fairus.org/states/kansas. Accessed July 8, 2013.

Fix, Michael, Jeffrey S. Passel, and Kenneth Sucher. *Trends in Naturalization*. Brief No. 3. Washington, DC: Urban Institute, 2003.

Fortuny, Karina, and Ajay Chaudry. *Children of Immigrants: Growing National and State Diversity*. Brief No. 5. Washington, DC: Urban Institute, 2011.

Harrington, Lisa M., B. Lu, and David E. Kromm. "Milking the Plains: Movement of Large Dairy Operations into Southwestern Kansas." *Geographical Review* 100 (2010): 538–58.

Immigration Policy Center. *Bad for Business: How Anti-Immigrant Laws Can Hurt the Kansas Economy*. Washington, DC: American Immigration Council, 2012.

Immigration Policy Center. "New Americans in Kansas: The Political and Economic Power of Immigrants, Latinos, and Asians in the Sunflower State." Washington, DC: American Immigration Council, 2013.

Jewish Federation of Greater Kansas City. "History." 2012. http://www.jewishkansascity .org/About-Us/History. Accessed July 9, 2013.

Jiménez, Tomás R. "Weighing the Costs and Benefits of Mexican Immigration: The Mexican-American Perspective." *Social Science Quarterly* 88 (2007): 599–618.

Kansas Hispanic and Latino American Affairs Commission. "History of Kansas Hispanic Community." 2012. http://www.khlaac.ks.gov/about-us/history/history-of-kansas-hispanic-community. Accessed July 12, 2013.

Kansas Historical Society. "Asian Americans in Kansas." Kansapedia, 2011. http://www.kshs.org/kansapedia/asian-americans-in-kansas/17046. Accessed July 12, 2013.

Kansas Historical Society. "Beecher Bibles." Kansapedia, 2011. http://www.kshs.org/kansapedia/beecher-bibles/11977. Accessed July 12, 2013.

Kansas Historical Society. "French Settlers in Kansas." Kansapedia, 2011. http://www.kshs.org/kansapedia/french-settlers-in-kansas/12203. Accessed July 12, 2013.

Kansas Historical Society. "Germans from Russia in Kansas." Kansapedia, 2011. http://www.kshs.org/kansapedia/germans-from-russia-in-Kansas/12231. Accessed July 12, 2013.

Kansas Historical Society. "Settlement in Kansas." Kansapedia, 2011. http://www.kshs.org/kansapedia/settlement-in-kansas/14546. Accessed July 12, 2013.

Kansas State Historical Society and University of Kansas. "Immigration and Early Settlement." Territorial Kansas Online, 2012. http://www.territorialkansasonline.org/~imlskto/cgi-bin/index.php?SCREEN=immigration&option=more.Accessed July 10, 2013.

"Kansas, State, United States." *Columbia Electronic Encyclopedia*, 6th ed., 1 (2012). http://www.answers.com/topic/Kansas. Accessed July 11, 2013.

Lindquist, Emory. "Kansas: A Centennial Portrait, Part One." *Kansas History* 33 (2010): 116–35.

Lindquist, Emory. "The Swedish Immigrant and Life in Kansas." *Kansas Historical Quarterly* xxix (Spring 1963): 1–24.

Luo, Michael. "On the Road: A Week with 'Values' Voters." *The New York Times*, October 28, 2007. http://thecaucus.blogs.nytimes.com/2007/10/28/on-the-road-a-week-with-values-voters/. Accessed July 12, 2013.

Martin, Daniel C., and James E. Yankay. *Refugees and Asylees: 2012*. Office of Immigration Statistics, U.S. Department of Homeland Security, Annual Flow Report. Washington, DC: U.S. Government Printing Office, 2013.

NumbersUSA. "Immigration-Reduction Grades." 2012. https://www.numbersusa.com/content/my/tools/grades/testgrades.php3?District=KS&VIPID=317. Accessed July 12, 2013.

Office of Immigration Statistics. *2011 Yearbook of Immigration Statistics*. U.S. Department of Homeland Security. Washington, DC: U.S. Government Printing Office, 2012.

Passel, Jeffrey S., Randy Capps, and Michael Fix. *Undocumented Immigrants: Facts and Figures*. Urban Institute Immigration Studies Program. Washington, DC: Urban Institute, 2004.

The Perryman Group. "An Essential Resource: An Analysis of the Economic Impact of Undocumented Workers on Business Activity in the US with Estimated Effects by State and by Industry." Waco, TX: The Perryman Group, 2008.

Piedra, Jessica. "Kansas City Supports Protest against Arpaio." *Guild Notes* 35 (2010): 21.

Plummer, Mark A. *Frontier Governor: Samuel J. Crawford of Kansas*. Lawrence: University Press of Kansas, 1971.

Richardson, Gary. "The Origins of Anti-Immigrant Sentiments: Evidence from the Heartland in the Age of Mass Migration." *B. E. Journal of Economic Analysis & Policy: Topics in Economic Analysis & Policy* 5 (2005): 1–48.

Task Force on Immigration and U.S. Economic Competitiveness. "A View from Kansas." Chicago Council on Global Affairs, 2012. http://midwestimmigration.org/in-your-state/overview/state/Kansas. Accessed July 9, 2013.

Turk, Eleanor L. "Germans in Kansas." *Kansas History* 28 (2005): 44–71.

Turk, Eleanor L. "Getting Together: German-American Social Organizations on the Kansas Frontier." *Kansas Quarterly* 25 (1993): 57–67.

United States Senate. *U.S. Senate Roll Call Votes 110th Congress—1st Session*. 2007. http://www.senate.gov/legislative/LIS/roll_call_lists/roll_call_vote_cfm.cfm?congress=110&session=1&vote=00235. Accessed July 12, 2013.

USA Today. "Kansas Passes Tuition Bill Aiding Illegal Immigrants." *USA Today*, May 5, 2004.

U.S. Census Bureau. *Census of Population Social and Economic Characteristics*. CP-2–18, Kansas. Washington DC: U.S. Government Printing Office, 1993.

U.S. Department of Homeland Security. *Profiles on Legal Permanent Residents: 2012—State of Residence*. Washington, DC: U.S. Government Printing Office, 2013.

White, Jeremy. "Kansas Immigration Law Would Authorize Illegal Workers, Bucking National Trend." *International Business Times*, February 3, 2012. http://www.ibtimes.com/kansas-immigration-law-would-authorize-illegal-workers-bucking-national-trend-405290. Accessed July 12, 2013.

White, Stephen E. "Migration Trends in the Kansas Ogallala Region and the Internal Colonial Dependency Model." *Rural Sociology* 63 (1998): 253–71.

Winckler, Suzanne. *The Smithsonian Guide to Historic America: The Plains States*. New York: Stewart, Tabori & Chang, 1990.

Wulfkuhle, Virginia. "Kansas Archeology Basics." Kansas Historical Society, 2012. http://www.kshs.org/p/kansas-archeology-basics/14588. Accessed July 12, 2013.

Yale, B. "Congress Fails to Reform Immigration: How That Changes the Law for Dairy Farmers." In *Proceedings, 2008 High Plains Dairy Conference*. Albuquerque, NM, 2008, pp. 49–56.

17

KENTUCKY

Kathleen R. Arnold

CHRONOLOGY

1739	Big Bone Lick is discovered.
1750	The Cumberland Gap is explored by Europeans.
1751	The Ohio River is explored by Europeans and a map is drawn.
1763	England receives territory from France, part of which is Kentucky.
1767	Daniel Boone and fellow hunters explore and hunt in parts of the area now known as Kentucky.
1769	Boone and other hunters return to this territory, finding a trail through the Cumberland Gap. Tensions arise with Native American groups.
1774	First permanent settlement in Kentucky is established at Harrod's Town. Skirmishes occur with Native Americans.
1775	Daniel Boone establishes Boonesboro. Boone and his colleagues clear a trail through Central Kentucky (the Wilderness Road). Lexington, Kentucky, is established.
1776	Kentucky County is created.
1779	Elizabethtown becomes the site of the first Baptist Church in this region.
1784	Negotiations are held to separate Kentucky from Virginia.
1792	Kentucky becomes the 15th state. Isaac Shelby is the governor and the capital is first established at Lexington.
1798	The Kentucky legislature passes the Kentucky Resolutions, which oppose the Alien and Sedition Acts, which seek to exclude or remove foreigners based on ideology and alienage.

1818	Increase in Kentucky territory after the Chickasaw Indians cede land to the United States.
1819	First commercial oil well in this area is established on the Cumberland River.
1833	Kentucky strengthens its slavery laws even while anti-slavery activity (particularly the Underground Railroad) is also active in the state.
1849	Kentucky resident Zachary Taylor is elected president of the United States.
1850	First official count of the foreign-born finds there are 31,400 foreigners in Kentucky, which was about 4 percent of the entire population.
1861	As Civil War breaks out, Kentucky attempts to declare its neutrality but an unsuccessful attempt is made to take the state out of the Union and thereafter pro-Union forces control the state government. Nevertheless, the state supplies troops to both the North and the South. Fort Jefferson is seized by Union troops after Confederates first occupy this area.
1862	Several important battles, including the Battle of Middle Creek, the Battle of Lucas Bend, the Battle in Prestonsburg, and the Battle of Perryville, are fought in Kentucky.
1862	Jews are expelled from Tennessee, Mississippi, and Kentucky.
1865	The University of Kentucky is established. While the Thirteenth Amendment (abolishing slavery and involuntary servitude) is passed in the United States, Kentucky refuses to ratify it until 1976. The governor issues official message calling for immigrants to come to the state while encouraging African Americans to leave the state.
1867	The governor again publicly declares that (white) immigrants should come to the state to fill labor shortages.
1869	The governor proposes open recruitment of European immigrants. This year and 1870 mark the greatest percentage and number of foreign-born individuals in the state.
1871	The governor calls for foreign investment in the state and more immigrants to take open positions.
1875	The first Kentucky Derby is held. The Geologic Survey proposes that railroads pass through Kentucky to attract more immigrants.
1883	Out-migration of African Americans and other Kentucky residents leads to the Geologic Survey's call for foreign immigrants. The governor recognizes seven European immigrant colonies in the state, including colonies of Austrians, Germans/Prussians, Swedish, and Swiss.
1885	A state pamphlet is published, attempting to attract immigrants to the state.
1896	In keeping with national sentiment and responding to an economic depression, the governor publicly denounces immigrants.

1904–1909	The Black Patch War marks the end of the tobacco monopoly.
1933	Dam projects begin in Kentucky.
1950s	Because the state is less industrialized than other states, Kentucky sees considerable out-migration.
1966	Kentucky introduces a civil rights law, becoming the first state in the region to do so.
1974	The Equal Education Opportunities Act of 1974 stipulates that the state must provide equal educational opportunities to children who speak limited English.
1986	From this year on, the H-2A visa program, an agricultural guest worker program, is expanded in Kentucky.
1989	The Kentucky Supreme Court holds (per Section 183 of the Kentucky Constitution) that state schools are required to provide free education that is "substantially uniform and offers equal opportunities to all Kentucky children." This provision affects all children attending schools, regardless of legal status.
1990	The legislature passes the Kentucky Education Reform Act. Immigration to Kentucky begins to increase. Vietnamese immigrants have the highest growth rate of any immigrant group in the state.
Late 1990s	Mexican immigration to Kentucky increases, as agricultural jobs increase (particularly in tobacco).
2000	Immigrants to Kentucky make up about 2.5 percent of the population.
2001	Stricter driver's license requirements are passed, aiming at immigrants. Approximately 3,000 H-2A workers are authorized and mostly work in tobacco production.
2006	Kentucky's Latino population increases. Some estimates hold that this population has tripled since 1990. *Padilla v. Commonwealth of Kentucky* (2006) is filed; this important case deals with criminal defense lawyers who do not advise their clients of the consequences of pleading guilty or who give the incorrect advice regarding immigration consequences (particularly, detention and deportation).
2010	The *Padilla* case is decided by the Supreme Court of the United States. The Court holds that criminal lawyers must warn noncitizen clients about immigration consequences of a guilty plea. If they do not, the lawyer can be held responsible. In particular, they cannot remain silent regarding the possibility of removal proceedings.

HISTORICAL OVERVIEW

Eighteenth and Nineteenth Centuries

Kentucky territory was explored by the British and French in the early 1700s. In the 1750s, the Cumberland Gap was discovered and the Ohio River was surveyed. Part of what is now Kentucky was controlled by the French but was handed to the British in 1763. Daniel Boone explored this territory in the 1760s, hunting and surveying the land. Throughout this time period, there were tensions with Native American groups. In the 1770s, some permanent settlements were established, including Lexington, and Kentucky County which was part of Virginia. In 1784, leaders began proposing that Kentucky should become a separate state and in 1792, it became the 15th state. While the state defended basic freedoms of speech and political opinion in its opposition to the Alien and Sedition Acts (1798), it also upheld slavery laws in the early 1800s. Nevertheless, the Underground Railroad was also active in the pre-Civil War era. During the Civil War, the state's attempt to remain neutral did not last long and it became a Confederate state by the end of 1861. The state supplied troops to both sides in the war but remained under Confederate control until 1862, when Union troops took over parts of the state.

Despite the war, the cotton trade continued between the North and South. As part of Kentucky was controlled by the Union in 1862, General Ulysses S. Grant issued General Order No. 11, seeking to expel all Jews from the southern region he controlled to be rid of unscrupulous cotton trading, including a black market (Sarna 2012). While the aim was allegedly to purge enemies of the free market, this order did not specify individuals in the cotton trade but rather all Jews, who were viewed as perpetual migrants. Grant lumped them together with vagrants and others lacking morals, undermining the notion of the United States as a haven of religious liberty: "though they formed less than 1 percent of the population at that time, Jews were by far the most significant non-Christian immigrant group in the nation" at that time (Sarna 2012). While there were immediate protests and the order was rescinded in the beginning of 1863, it still constructed the figure of a migrant as an outsider and criminal, not to mention crystallizing the anti-Semitism of that time period. This order was indicative of the blending of national and regional prejudices, even as civil libertarians protested against the order.

In 1865, with the end of the war, Kentucky (along with some other states) refused to ratify the Thirteenth Amendment. It did not do so until 1976. At this time, the governor began urging African Americans to leave the state (offering to pay a sum if they did leave) and issuing calls for immigrants to fill jobs. In the next few years (1867 and 1869), the governor continues to invite white European immigrants to come to work in the state. By 1870, the state experienced its highest immigration levels. Throughout the 1870s, there were continuous efforts to recruit racially desirable immigrants to the state. In the meantime, there was continuous out-migration of African Americans and others, who were seeking work and a less hostile context. In 1883, the governor of Kentucky recognized seven European immigrant colonies in the state, including colonies of Austrians, Germans/Prussians, Swedish, and Swiss.

TWENTIETH CENTURY

By the 1890s, the United States was dealing with several national issues: an economic depression, the emergence of pseudoscientific racism (which would become eugenics), and the greater predominance of openly racist discourse in newspaper and public policy. Following this national trend, the governor of Kentucky officially denounced immigrants in 1896. While the state continued to develop its resources, its agricultural-based economy (particularly the growth of tobacco) led many to seek work in more industrialized states at the turn of the century. This was true even though urban centers had played an important industrial role during World War II. By the 1950s, the state's population declined, even as temporary seasonal labor was hired for tobacco and other crops. Cities experienced decline and out-migration to the suburbs while also serving as key sites for civil rights activism and debates. While the state remained segregated up through the 1970s, civil rights activists and Black Power advocates were also very active at this time. As a gesture to civil rights, the state introduced a civil rights law in 1966 and was the first state in the region to do so. The Equal Education Opportunities Act of 1974 helped to remedy (in theory, at least) the continued history of racial segregation and provided a policy that would increasingly establish the rights of children born to foreign residents. This act stipulated that the state must provide equal opportunities to students with limited English (Anderson et al. 2002). In 1975, the state moved toward desegregating its schools. In 1989, the Kentucky Supreme Court rules that state schools must be relatively uniform, allowing for "equal opportunities" for all school-aged children resident in the state, regardless of legal status (Anderson et al. 2002). Nevertheless, immigration to the state is fairly minimal at this time.

With the passage of the Immigration Reform and Control Act of 1986, the United States' guest worker program was revitalized with the creation of special agricultural workers (SAWs). Growers in Kentucky took advantage of this program, particularly in tobacco-processing. For various reasons, by the 1990s, immigration to Kentucky had increased slightly. Asian immigrants and immigrants from Eastern Europe began arriving from the 1990s on. Both of these broad categories of immigrants made up about 49 percent of all new immigrants to Kentucky from 1990 to 1998. Many immigrants were also from China and Cuba. Vietnamese immigrants were one of the largest groups settling in the state and by the end of the 1990s, increasing numbers of Mexican immigrants arrived as agricultural jobs became more available.

TWENTY-FIRST CENTURY

Like other states in the South, parts of Kentucky became a new gateway for immigrants, even while more traditional sites of immigration experienced slight

Alonzo Morales, right, and Steve Lathery cut tobacco on September 11, 1997, in Sulphur Well, Kentucky. Immigrant workers are primarily hired by tobacco farmers in this region. (AP Photo/Breck Smither)

declines in immigrants number (particularly after stricter immigration controls after September 11, 2001). While various people in the state recruited immigrants to work in agricultural employment, for example, there was also a backlash against these new arrivals. For example, in 2001, stricter ID and driver's license requirements was are passed, with a longer waiting period than before. Policymakers have address many of the fears in the state, attempting to reassure constituents that immigration numbers are relatively low, that immigrants are merely seeking work, and that they often contribute quite a lot to the state, including revitalizing relatively depopulated areas and helping to sustain declining agricultural enterprises. Nevertheless, the state is now dealing with a number of unresolved issues from the past involving race and racism together with newer concerns about national security in the post-9/11 era. As Winders argues, "Post 9/11, debates about borders, immigration, and belonging have reached a new intensity in the U.S. South. The temporal overlap of growing immigration to the South since the late 1990s and growing nativist sentiment across the U.S. since 9/11 has led southern communities to fuse new *regional* racial demographics to new *national* border anxieties" (Winders 2007, 920, her emphasis).

As stated above, Kentucky has become a new destination for immigrants since the 1990s, despite stricter immigration controls and despite the fact that much

Senate Minority Leader Mitch McConnell of Kentucky, left, and Senator Rand Paul, R-Kentucky speak with reporters following their appearance at the 50th annual Kentucky Country Ham Breakfast at the Kentucky State Fairgrounds in Louisville, Kentucky, on August 22, 2013. McConnell recently waged a campaign against his Democratic opponent, arguing she is soft on immigration. (AP Photo/Timothy D. Easley)

of the South has unresolved issues regarding racism and segregation. This increase is still not significant, compared to more traditional destinations for immigrants—numbers have (roughly) tripled since 1990—but this population still makes up just about 2.5 percent of the entire population. In this way, "the state ranked third highest among all states in immigration increases in the 1990s" (Anderson et al. 2002, ix). The average age of these immigrants is younger than that of U.S.-born residents, which arguably aids an aging population but means that public schools are the key institutions for integrating immigrants in this region. Since the year 2000, immigrants to the state come from Bosnia, Central and Latin America, China, Cuba, India, and Vietnam. Of all of these groups, Vietnamese immigrants are coming in the greatest numbers. Many of these immigrants are employed in high-tier (professional) positions or low-tier (agricultural) positions, reflecting general trends in this job market. At the highest tiers, these immigrants tend to be better educated (even if only slightly) and better paid than residents born in this area. Indeed, "well-educated legal immigrants are raising the average education levels of the overall population. Legal immigrants in the southeast region appear to be slightly better educated than immigrants nationally in 2000" (Anderson et al. 2002, 20). Immigrants with high educational attainment are often from India, China, Iran, Russia, and Italy.

Although low-tier workers are often paid less well (compared to salaries for professional positions) and work in labor-intensive positions, they are coming to this state because wages are relatively higher for this region, home ownership is possible, and people do not show overt hostility to workers, even if they are not particularly welcoming either. "Following the West, the South is now home to the second largest number of Latinos in the United States, with Mexicans comprising the largest single group" (Shultz 2008, 204). Many of these workers arrived between 2004 and 2006, defying national trends in the post-9/11 era of reduced immigration and initiating new immigration paths to cities and areas that were and are not traditional places of immigration. While the reception has been mixed to this much-needed labor force, in one study, workers described their treatment as "tranquilo" (calm) as they did not perceive the overt hatred or racism they expected (Shultz 2008, 211). Nevertheless, the reality may be more that these workers are isolated in rural areas, have limited opportunities to interact with others, have difficulty in getting groceries, and have little to no access to transportation. In this way, there is not so much openness to this needed workforce as much as they are in a "gilded cage" (Shultz 2008). Defying images of single young men coming to work and leaving, many of these immigrants are bringing their families, indicating a desire to settle in this area for the long term. The speed with which these immigrants have arrived, even despite their relatively low numbers, has evoked a mixed reaction: on the one hand, they are being hired and are settling into communities, sometimes turning to religious institutions for help and information (see Ehrkamp and Nagel 2012). On the other hand, policymakers' fears of higher crime rates, language barriers, and educational burdens indicate resistance to this immigration pathway (see Anderson et al. 2002). In some of these communities, gendered hiring practices (hiring men but not women) may reinforce older patterns of gendered and racial stratification (see Shultz 2008; Winders 2007).

H-2A workers are also part of this increase in immigration, occupying about 3,000 jobs in agriculture (mostly tobacco production). Immigrant workers also make up a significant part of thoroughbred workers—roughly 80–90 percent of all workers are immigrants (mostly Latinos). Many of these jobs are in the central part of Kentucky (e.g., Fayette, Woodford, Scott, Bourbon, Madison, Jessamine and Harrison Counties). These workers are recruited directly or by word-of-mouth recruitment.

The tobacco industry—another major source of employment—has undergone recent changes including increased mechanization (for some crops), unifying smaller farms into a larger enterprise, and greater diversity in crops. Since the

1990s, there has been "unprecedented economic growth" (Anderson et al. 2002, 39). Many of these workers were recruited using the H-2A visa program in the early 1990s, establishing a pattern of immigration (including social networks and fostering word-of-mouth recruitment) to this region. Today, farms are fewer in number, involving less family and unpaid employment, and important shifts in demand for labor that lead to more seasonal (i.e., irregular or temporary) hiring. Some crops, like burley tobacco, must be handpicked and therefore labor demands are different than for more modernized farms. The largest farms have steadier employment needs and high harvest rates; many continue to hire H-2A workers for employment. Some studies suggest that smaller and more medium-sized farms are turning to undocumented, seasonal workers to avoid the bureaucracy of the H-2A visa program. Regardless of legal status, this temporary labor is often viewed in terms of post-9/11 national security concerns: "The combination of this visa program, designed to regulate local work spaces and communities by making immigrants always temporary, and a militarized border designed to regulate the hyperflexibility of workers in specific southern locales was maintained through heightened border policing from new fences at the US-Mexico border to new visa programs at the local workplace. Through such legislation, the temporary 'place' of Latino/as in the South would keep them beyond the boundaries of local communities, at times quite literally, giving official backing to informal employer practices" (Winders 2007, 928).

While some immigrant workers stay in agricultural positions, others use these jobs to establish a base and then take service or construction positions later, because they are steadier and slightly better paid. SAWs have done this after residing in the state for 2 to 4 years, after attaining residency papers. Labor in factories is physically intensive and can include janitorial services, working on a production line, and processing work. Those who move up to supervisory positions often speak English well. Interestingly, because of requirements from the Immigration Act of 1990 which requires the filling of Form I-9 for anyone hired after November 1986, some employment agencies now screen and hire immigrant workers before they are hired by individual firms. Some employers help foreign workers by offering free English classes and others help to get medical tests necessary for establishing residency or filing for refugee status. Because growers and thoroughbred industry owners are aware that workers want the steadier pay in factories or service, they are beginning to offer housing and benefits to keep workers.

TOPICAL ESSAYS

9/11 AND *PADILLA V. COMMONWEALTH OF KENTUCKY* (2006)

In the post-9/11 era, the southern region has become an interesting locus of national and regional immigration concerns. This is partly due to its unresolved racial tensions and the fact that many of these states were the site of important labor battles for workers' rights. It is also due to the fact that this region has become a new gateway for immigrants and refugees. Various moves to disempower these new arrivals have been cast as national security concerns. In this way, these proposals—from limiting day laborers' hiring sites to imposing English only rules in places that have few language attainment issues—have symbolically extended the border to the South. In some of these states, criminal lawyers have not been required to tell their clients of the immigration consequences of pleading guilty. Kentucky was one of these states and a key Supreme Court case emerged from this failure to inform clients that any plea of guilty entered on the record—even if no jail time was served—would most likely lead to removal proceedings (aka deportation). While Kentucky's policy that lawyers did not need to inform their clients of these clients demonstrated an indifference to foreigners' rights, several efforts in this state to correct the situation also indicate that some wanted a closer adherence to constitutional provisions for effective counsel and a broader understanding of political rights held by all "persons" resident in the state (see Benson and Palmieri 2007). At this time (1996–2010), lawyers who were sympathetic to immigrants argued that even if criminal lawyers were not legally required to inform their clients of these consequences, that ethical reasoning would hold that they should inform them anyway. This was because the immigration consequences of pleading guilty were often far greater than the consequences of the often minor crimes that these immigrants had committed. A second issue was not remaining silent on the immigration consequences of pleading guilty but giving incorrect advice. *Padilla v. Commonwealth* (July 2006) brought these debates to the Kentucky Court of Appeals, which "determined that giving wrong advice regarding immigration consequences that result from plea agreements could constitute ineffective assistance of counsel" (Benson and Palmieri 2007, 553).

Padilla was from Honduras and was a long-term legal resident as well as a military veteran of the Vietnam War. He was arrested for transporting marijuana but was advised by his lawyer that pleading guilty would not result in any major penalties or other consequences. Even without the immigration consequences for criminal activity, an individual could lose his/her professional license, be temporarily disenfranchised, and/or be ineligible for some government benefits and employment. Before this case was heard, the high possibility of deportation was considered merely "collateral" and, therefore, a criminal lawyer was not negligent if he or she neglected to warn a client about these consequences (Benson and Palmieri 2007). The case moved to the U.S. Supreme Court and was decided in 2010. Today, criminal defense attorneys are obligated to advise citizens about the risk of deportation if they plead guilty. This case is considered a landmark in expanding lawyers' accountability.

Nevertheless, the fact that even a minor crime for which no jail time was required can lead to possible detention and definite removal demonstrates how ordinary crimes, immigration, and national security concerns have become linked together. Thus, the South has become a new site of these struggles. Older elements of racism mix together with the racialization of immigrants from Mexico and Central America, particularly as they are viewed as not merely undocumented but also criminals and national security threats. On the one hand, it needs young, able-bodied workers willing to take certain positions. But on the other hand, "southern politicians legislate against immigrant efforts to establish themselves in local communities. Through mechanisms from the curtailment of immigrant access to driver's licenses to the blurring of local and federal policing responsibilities, local, regional, and national borders are fusing, and simultaneously policed, in southern communities" (Winders 2007, 922). These debates are evident in Kentucky in discussions about undocumented immigration, despite lack of clear empirical evidence, language barriers in schools, and the delays in processing state IDs and driver's licenses. Interestingly, despite the diversity of immigrants arriving in this state, there is a significant focus on Latino/a immigrants more than others. While this focus is not always racist per se, it can involve "slippages" between "patriotism" and anti-immigrant sentiment that draws on racist imagery (Winders 2007, 934). Undocumented immigrants, even as they are a key part of the agricultural labor force and seem to be relatively small in numbers in this state, can then serve as "vectors of disease," but "extreme nativism has [also] 'served to engender sympathy, rather than competition, between African Americans and Latinos'" (Winders 2007, 935). Indeed exclusionary acts are not always decisive and there are a range of individuals and groups who hire and/or welcome these new arrivals. In this way, "the *Nuevo* South is a contradictory space for new immigrants, who face exclusion at the state level through restrictive legislation and inclusion at the local through grassroots campaigns" (Winders 2007, 935). The state document produced soon after 9/11 "Immigration in Kentucky: A Preliminary Description," is indicative of these worries but in a very balanced (if not perfect) response to various fears. Indeed, the authors note that new immigrants contribute more to social security and taxes than they utilize; that they are more often the victims of crimes than the perpetrators, and that employers interviewed in this report have almost uniformly recorded their satisfaction with immigrant workers.

REFUGEES

Refugees to Kentucky include individuals and families from Bosnia, Vietnam, and Russia. Cubans and Haitians have also applied for refugee status in this state, although far more Cubans have been admitted than Haitians. Interestingly, refugee agencies, charitable organizations, and other intermediaries (like employment agencies that specifically deal with immigrants and refugees) are perhaps responsible for shifting patterns of immigration to new cities, that is, nontraditional sites for immigration settlement. Refugee centers and organizations (often religious organizations) work with the federal government to locate a suitable area for resettlement and employment. These organizations help refugee applicants in filling out an I-94 document that will aid them in obtaining legal work and in receiving a social security number.

These organizations help to fill out requests for family reunifications, provide information about any necessary documentation needed during this process, and can provide links to sponsor families that aid integration as well as employers that hire refugees. As noted earlier, employers who regularly hire immigrants and refugees often make provisions for them in exchange for their hard work and loyalty to the company. These provisions include helping the immigrants to regularize their legal status; providing English classes; and helping to get water, electricity, and phone connections when they first arrive. Most employers now know that when immigrants take a vacation to see their family, their vacations will be lengthy because of airline costs and long-term connections to their country of origin, so they have begun working around these sorts of extended absences. As these groups aid refugees, they foster links between long-term residents and new arrivals, increasing civic education and perhaps civic solidarity, even despite anti-immigration sentiment.

NOTABLE GROUPS

Kentucky Groups That Assist Immigrants and Refugees

Several notable groups in Kentucky aid immigrants and refugees at the state and local levels. The Migrant Network Coalition, which was formed in Lexington in 1994, is a group of roughly 45 organizations. The Coalition helps migrant workers, particularly those who are employed in tobacco production and on thoroughbred horse farms. They help immigrant workers find resources and information, as their needs arise. A smaller umbrella group, the Hispanic Initiative Network is composed of four social service agencies and directly targets Latino/as. Among services they provide, some of these organizations teach English to immigrants, provide employment information and help to others, and help others with bilingual resources and interpretation. The Kentucky Consortium for Hispanics and Latinos serves broader state interests and is more oriented toward policy making. Smaller groups like the Hispanic-Latino Community Coalition and (separately) the Bluegrass Farmworkers Health Center provide health information and services at the local level, including attending to migrant workers. For foreign students and tourists, the Louisville Office of International and Cultural Affairs provides information about resources and events for this more privileged demographic.

As discussed more broadly by Ehrkamp and Nagel (2012), religious organizations have provided civic support for immigrants and refugees. According to these authors, religious ties in this context should be viewed as important democratic and democratizing activity, fostering civic solidarity. The Migrant Network Coalition, a group of 15 religious organizations, offers services in Spanish and conducts English classes and cultural events. Some, like the Catholic Hispanic Ministry in Lexington, have emergency housing for immigrants in need as well as providing transportation in areas that have few resources. Catholic Social Services provides financial assistance and assists with negotiating rent and utilities. Centro Latino, also affiliated with the Catholic Church, helps workers—particularly farmworkers and poultry workers—to find housing, translation services, and transportation. The Kentucky Refugee Ministries provide similar services to refugees. The strong presence of these groups helps to explain why and how Kentucky has become a place of permanent settlement for many new immigrants, despite stricter laws nationally and regionally since the events of September 11, 2001.

BIBLIOGRAPHY

Anderson, Lauren, Lowell Atchley, Lynn Aubrey, Evelyn Gibson, Margaret Hurst, and Perry Nutt. "Legislative Research Commission 'Immigration in Kentucky: A Preliminary Description.'" Research Report No. 305, Frankfort, Kentucky, March, 2002. http://www.lrc.ky.gov/lrcpubs/Rr305.pdf. Accessed November 11, 2013.

Arnold, Kathleen R. *American Immigration after 1996: The Shifting Ground of Political Inclusion*. College Station, PA: Penn State University Press, 2011.

Benson, Mathew L., Marisa N. Palmieri. "I Got a Great Please Agreement for My Client but He Ended Up Being Deported-Immigration Considerations for the Kentucky Criminal Practitioner." *North Kentucky Law Review* 34, no. 3 (2007): 547–74.

Brown, Lawrence A., Tamar E. Mott, and Edward J. Malecki. "Immigrant Profiles of U.S. Urban Areas and Agents of Resettlement." *The Professional Geographer* 59, no. 1 (2007): 56–73.

Ehrkamp, Patricia, and Caroline Nagel. "Immigration, Place of Worship and the Politics of Citizenship in the US South." *Transactions of the Institute of British Geographers* 37, no. 4 (2012): 624–38.

Kanstroom, Daniel. *Deportation Nation*. Cambridge, MA: Harvard University Press, 2007.

Kentucky Historical Society. "Comings and Goings: Kentucky's Immigration and Emigration History." Kentucky Historical Society website. n.d. http://www.lfpl.org/pdf/Hollingsworth.pdf. Accessed January 27, 2014.

Sarna, Jonathan D. "When Gen. Grant Expelled the Jews." *Slate*, March 13, 2012. http://www.slate.com/articles/news_and_politics/history/2012/03/ulysses_s_grant_and_general_orders_no_11_how_the_infamous_order_changed_the_lives_of_jews_in_america_.html. Accessed March 15, 2014.

Shackel, Paul A., and Matthew M. Palus. "The Gilded Age and Working-Class Industrial Communities." *American Anthropologist* 108, no. 4 (2006): 828–41.

Shultz, Benjamin J. "Inside the Gilded Cage: The Lives of Latino Immigrant Males in Rural Central Kentucky." *Southeastern Geographer* 48, no. 2 (2008): 201–18.

Varsanyi, Monica. "Rescaling the 'Alien,' Rescaling Personhood: Neoliberalism, Immigration and the State." *Annals of the Association of American Geographers* 98, no. 4 (2008): 877–96.

Winders, Jamie. "Bringing Back the (B)order: Post-9/11 Politics of Immigration, Borders, and Belonging in the Contemporary US South." *Antipode* 39, no. 5 (2007): 920–42.

18

LOUISIANA

William P. Kladky

CHRONOLOGY

1519	Alonso Álvarez de Piñeda (1494–1520), a Spanish explorer and cartographer, discovers the mouth of the Mississippi River.
1541–1542	The Spanish explorer and conquistador Hernando de Soto (1496–1542) discovers the Mississippi River.
1682	The explorer René-Robert Cavelier, sieur de La Salle (1643–1687), erects a cross at the mouth of the Mississippi River and claims the territory for Louis XIV (1638–1715) of France, after whom Louisiana is named.
1715	Louis Juchereau de St. Denis (1676–1744) establishes Fort St. Jean Baptiste (Natchitoches), which is the first permanent settlement in the Mississippi Valley.
1718	New Orleans is founded and named after Philippe I, Duc D'Orléans (1640–1701), the youngest son of Louis XIII of France and known as "the grandfather of Europe."
1718	The Cathedral-Basilica of St. Louis King of France is built in New Orleans; it is the oldest operating Catholic cathedral in the United States.
1723	New Orleans becomes the capital of Louisiana, replacing Biloxi.
1736	Charity Hospital (originally the Hospital of St. John or L'Hôpital des Pauvres de la Charité—Hospital for the Poor) is founded on May 10, 1736, by a grant from the French sailor and shipbuilder Jean Louis.
1751	Sugarcane is first introduced into Louisiana.

1762	Louis XV gives the "Island of New Orleann" and all of Louisiana west of the Mississippi to his cousin, Charles III of Spain.
1763	The Treaty of Paris ends the Seven Years' War, resulting in the transfer of Louisiana to Spain. In the settlement, the Florida Parishes are ceded to England, and Baton Rouge is renamed New Richmond.
1764	The initial four Acadian families arrive in Louisiana from New York.
1796	While some hold that opera is first performed in the United States at New Orleans, others claim "The Beggars Opera" runs in New York in 1750.
1803	The United States purchases the Louisiana Territory from Napoleon I of France for $15 million.
1804	Louisiana is divided into the Territory of New Orleans (south of 33° latitude) and the District of Louisiana (north of 33° latitude). W.C.C. Claiborne (1775–1817) is appointed governor of the Territory of Orleans.
1808	The first parish to establish public schools in Louisiana is Pointe Coupée Parish, near Baton Rouge.
1811	The first institution of higher learning in Louisiana opens in New Orleans (College of Orleans).
1812	Louisiana is admitted to the Union as the 18th state.
1812	The first steamboat to navigate the Mississippi River, *The New Orleans*, arrives at New Orleans from Pittsburgh on January 10, 1812.
1815	The Battle of New Orleans, the final major battle of the War of 1812, is won by General Andrew Jackson (1767–1845).
1823	The first natural gas field is discovered in Louisiana, at a depth of 400 feet.
1837	Shreveport is founded.
1838	The first Mardi Gras parade is held in New Orleans. The city's first parade with floats is held in 1857.
1838	Myrthee Bedeau, a free quadroon woman (i.e., a person of mixed race, generally of African and Caucasian ancestry), who was sold into slavery, successfully sues for her freedom.
1840	World-renowned Antoine's in New Orleans, the state's oldest continuously operating restaurant, is established.
1849	Baton Rouge becomes the capital of Louisiana.
1861	Louisiana becomes the sixth state to secede from the Union.
1861	For six weeks after secession, Louisiana is a republic, before joining the Confederacy.
1862	The first salt mine is discovered at Avery Island. It is the oldest in the United States.
1867	Shrimp is first canned commercially at Grand Terre Island.
1868	Louisiana is readmitted to the Union.
1869	The first sulfur produced in the United States is produced in Louisiana.
1872	Rex, king of Carnival, parades for the initial time during Mardi Gras in New Orleans.

1915	The name "Jazz" is given to any music of New Orleans origin.
1917	Dr. Linda Coleman becomes the first woman to graduate from a medical school in Louisiana.
1926	Louisiana's first public airport is built in Mansfield.
1928	The Grand Isle Tarpon Rodeo is established; it is now the oldest fishing tournament in the United States.
1932	The new state capitol building is completed in Baton Rouge at a cost of $5 million.
1935	Senator Huey P. Long (1893–1935) is assassinated in the state capitol.
1935	The first Sugar Bowl football game is played at Tulane Stadium in New Orleans, with Tulane beating Temple 20–14.
1935	Louise Simon Davis (1880–1974) founds Magnolia School, the first school for the mentally disabled in New Orleans.
1947	The Kerr-McGee Corporation, with its offshore operations based in Morgan City, drills the first commercial producing oil well out of sight of land in the United States.
1963	Tulane University racially integrates, accepting 11 black students.
1973	A team of surgeons performs Louisiana's first heart transplant.
1975	The Super Dome in New Orleans is completed, with a final cost of $163 million for its building and grounds.
1977	Ernest N. Morial (1929–1989) is elected mayor of New Orleans, becoming the city's first black mayor.
1979	David C. Treen Sr. (1928–2009) is elected governor, the first Republican to hold the office since Reconstruction.
1983	Edwin W. Edwards (b. 1927) becomes the state's first three-term governor.
1984	The successful Louisiana World Exposition is held in New Orleans.
1987	Louisiana celebrates the 175th anniversary of its admission into the Union. The Louisiana State Archives Building opens in Baton Rouge.
1991	The renovation of Louisiana's Old State Capitol begins to provide a home for the Louisiana Center for Political and Governmental History.
1992	Edwin W. Edwards is inaugurated to an unprecedented fourth term as governor of the state.
2005	Hurricanes Katrina and Rita devastate Louisiana and the Gulf Coast region.

HISTORICAL OVERVIEW

EARLY SETTLEMENT

Many American Indian groups inhabited Louisiana when Europeans began colonization, including the Atakapa in southwestern Louisiana; the Caddo nation in the central, west, and northwest; and several others. Numerous Louisiana town and place names, such as Atchafalaya, Natchitouches (now Natchitoches), and Caddo, were transliterations of those in Native American languages.

In 1528, the first Europeans came in a Spanish expedition led by Pánfilo de Narváez (1478–1528), which discovered the mouth of the Mississippi River. In 1542, Hernando de Soto (1496–1542) roamed Louisiana's north and west before going down the Mississippi River to the Gulf of Mexico. The French explorer René-Robert Cavelier, sieur de La Salle (1643–1687) named the region Louisiana to honor France's king Louis XIV in 1682. In 1699, the first permanent settlement, Fort Maurepas (now Ocean Springs, Mississippi), was founded by a French military officer Pierre Le Moyne d'Iberville (1661–1702). France's colony of Louisiana (ruled 1682–1764 and 1802–1804) originally claimed all the land on each side of the Mississippi River, north to far northeastern and northwestern Canada. Some 15 states were part of the then vast tract of Louisiana.

French and Canadian colonists began to settle in significant numbers by the end of the seventeenth century, where they encountered Native Americans as well as traders and settlers from Spanish colonies. The oldest permanent settlement in Louisiana was Natchitoches (along the Red River in northwest Louisiana), established in 1714 by Louis Juchereau de St. Denis (1676–1744). The French settlement had two purposes: to establish trade with the Spanish in Texas and to deter

Populist governor Huey P. Long in January 1935. (Library of Congress)

Spanish advances into Louisiana. It became a prosperous river port, supporting the many cotton plantations and homes. Louisiana's French settlements were concentrated along the Mississippi and its major tributaries, from Louisiana to Illinois and Missouri.

THE ARRIVAL OF SLAVES

Slaves began to be transported to Louisiana around 1716 by ships directly from Africa or via the French Caribbean. In the eighteenth century, thousands of African slaves were transported to Louisiana from the Senegambian coast, the interior of Benin, and Angola. Some 2,000 came from the upper West African slave ports from Saint-Louis, Senegal to Cap Appolonia (*Côte d'Ivoire*), 2,000 were from Whydah in Benin, and 300 were from Cabinda. Almost 70 percent of the slaves brought to the state came from Senegambia.

Under French and Spanish colonial rule, slaves were allowed to purchase their own or their families manumission. Resultantly, freed slaves became their own community, so that in antebellum Louisiana, and particularly New Orleans, free people of color (*gens de couleur libres*) made up a third social class that had a higher status than enslaved African Americans but lower than white Louisianans.

The reason for New Orleans's location was because a lieutenant in the French Navy, Jean-Baptiste Le Moyne, sieur de Bienville (1680–1767)—the younger brother of a naval hero—recommended establishing France's first agricultural settlement there. He recognized the site's strategic importance, at the mouth of the major river, but it also was, as many have said since, an "impossible but inevitable city." Because of its location, and despite being usually flooded and full of mosquitoes (Powell 2012, 2), Bienville and his partners acquired land and cleared it in 1718 near New Orleans, seeing the capital as the key to their prosperity. New Orleans would have been established at a remote bend in small 18-mile-long Bayou Manchac River linking Baton Rouge to Lake Pontchartrain and the Gulf, via Lake Maurepas and the Amite River.

Initially Mobile, Alabama, and Biloxi, Mississippi, were the first two capitals of the colony. In 1722, recognizing the importance of the Mississippi River to trade and military interests, France made New Orleans the location of civilian and military authority.

Settlement in the Louisiana colony was not exclusively French. In the 1720s, German immigrants settled along the Mississippi River in a region called the German Coast. The climate and terrain of Louisiana were inhospitable to early French traders and the colony had difficulty in attracting French citizens to immigrate. In the 1720s, facing the fact that the colony would fail without more people to sustain trade, the colony deliberately lured many struggling Germans with grandiose promises of enrichment.

By the mid-eighteenth century, the French colony included Indians, French, Canadians, Africans, and Germans, as well as Spanish and Caribbeans. Isolated from other colonies, these communities were forced to work together. Resultantly, languages and traditions intertwine, as well as men and women. From this volatile combination emerged the Louisiana Creole—a black, white, or mixed-race person born in Louisiana, with French, Spanish, or possibly German (or possibly something else) ancestry. The term "Creole" usually was utilized to refer to southern Louisianans, with French Catholic heritage, distinguishing them from the Protestant, white settlers who soon arrived in waves after the nation's Louisiana Purchase. Largely a military outpost, the Louisiana Territory initially was populated primarily by men.

IMMIGRANTS FINALLY ARRIVE

As discussed earlier, compared with many other American territories, Louisiana was settled by an unusually diverse assortment of immigrants. Because few colonists were willing to come when the territory was new, the Company of the Indies (which administered Louisiana during 1717–1731) imported French convicts, vagrants, and prostitutes. In 1721, there were so few women that the French government shipped 25 prostitutes to the colony, trying to lure the Canadian settlers away from their Indian mistresses. Needing more settlers, the company then turned to struggling farmers in Germany and Switzerland, who became more productive settlers.

France's defeat by Great Britain in the French and Indian War (1754–1763) resulted in the loss of most of the Louisiana Territory located east of the Mississippi River to Spain. The sole exceptions were the area around New Orleans and parishes surrounding Lake Pontchartrain.

As a result of land grants, French-speaking immigration then increased significantly. Some 10,000 Acadians, or Cajuns—French descendents exiled from Nova Scotia (Acadia) in the 1740s—came to Lafayette and Breaux Bridge, as well as to the area along Bayou Lafourche and the Mississippi River. These settlements later attracted additional Acadian migrants, after the British forced them out of their homes beginning in 1755. Some of these new Acadians went to the bayous of southern Louisiana and intermarried with other ethnic groups. A Cajun was a descendant of the Acadians.

With Spanish administrative control, some Spanish-speaking immigrants then arrived. These were mainly Canary Islanders, called Isleños, who came between 1778 and 1783 mostly to the southwestern area around Lake Charles. The Isleños have been able to preserve their language. Today in St. Bernard Parish, the Amerindian Nathualt dialect is still spoken (Din 1988). The area's population surged as the new settlers and Creoles imported large numbers of black slaves to work on plantations. Most slaves came directly from Africa. This increase resulted in "the re-Africanization" of southern Louisiana (Hall 1992, 279).

According to the 1800 Census, there were 19,852 free persons and 24,264 slaves in Lower Louisiana (including western Florida). Nonetheless, the second-largest group to come to Louisiana in the late eighteenth century was from the British colonies and after 1776 from other parts of the United States.

After 1800, significant political changes affected migration. A Napoleon-pressured Spain yielded its part of Louisiana to France in the Third Treaty of San Ildefonso of 1800. But with Napoleon's fortunes changing, France soon sold Louisiana to the United States in the Louisiana Purchase of 1803. Subsequently, the United States divided it into the Territory of Orleans, which became the state of Louisiana in 1812, and the remainder was designated the District of Louisiana.

During this period, the settlement of northern Louisiana by French-speaking immigrants continued. In the southern part of the area, some Canary Islanders and Spaniards from Málaga settled. The 1791 slave insurrection on Hispaniola (now Haiti and the Dominican Republic) caused many French-speaking immigrants to flee to the territory.

New Orleans was the major destination for many of these French-speaking immigrants. Crop failures brought some, but many came because of the Haitian Revolution of 1804. These new settlers included free people of color, whites, and enslaved Africans. More Cuban immigrants arrived in 1809. In the 1830s, the slave trade resulted in a number of black slaves being sold to plantations in Florida. During the 1840s and 1850s, there was a major Irish and German influx to New Orleans.

The territory continued to gain population. However, some black slaves fled to freedom. The slaves went north into the Indian Territory, west toward the frontier, or, increasingly, south to Mexico. As of 1850, the state's population was 517,762, with 49.3 percent white and 50.7 percent African American. Of the African Americans, 3.4 percent were free and 47.3 percent were slaves, with a large number unclassified.

THE CIVIL WAR ERA

As a Deep South state, Louisiana was affected significantly by the Civil War and Reconstruction. In some ways, Reconstruction began in Louisiana in 1862, when Union armies seized New Orleans and the state's southeastern sugar parishes. Hoping to save their plantations and slaves, many planters quickly swore allegiance to the Union. It appeared as if Louisiana might be able to smoothly be readmitted. This was supported by the fact that with 11,000 of its 144,000 total population, New Orleans had the largest free black community in the Deep

South. Many, the descendants of French settlers' union with black women or rich mulatto emigrants from Haiti, used French as their primary language.

Thus seeing Louisiana as a possible best first step model for easing Confederate states back into the Union, President Abraham Lincoln proposed a moderate plan that granted amnesty to those who took a loyalty oath and readmission if 10 percent took the oath. African American free workers were tied to labor on plantations for one year at $10 a month pay. The state also was required to abolish slavery in its new constitution. Later that year, a Louisiana constitutional convention passed a sweeping overhaul, allowing African Americans the voting rights and various freedoms.

In local practice, the resistance to change coupled with widespread prejudice meant that discrimination against African Americans continued. The state might have been defeated militarily, but was still overwhelmingly pro-Confederate in sentiment. Lincoln's moderate plan was frustrated on the national level as well. When, in 1864, the Louisiana legislature sent two senators and five representatives to Washington, the Radical-led Congress refused to count their votes. They instead passed the Wade–Davis Bill, which would have required a majority of the voters to take the loyalty oath, but Lincoln pocket-vetoed it. As a result, the divide widened between the Radicals and the Southerners, de facto prolonging the Civil War.

Following the Civil War, much of the South, including Louisiana, was placed under the supervision of military governors under northern command. Louisiana was in the Fifth Military District (with Texas). During Reconstruction, Louisiana had the same pestilential influx of shady northern entrepreneurs as other southern states. This was unfortunately abetted by the military leader Gen. Nathaniel P. Banks who pushed the continuation of the plantation system as the best means to stabilize the state. Many "entrepreneurs" then came to grab the quick profits available from running plantations while severely exploiting the black workers. Louisiana's labor legislation proved inadequate, and most emancipated slaves simply remained exploited plantation laborers.

By 1870, violence against blacks and Republicans increased. In 1872, emblematic of the problem's severity, the Louisiana gubernatorial election was settled by martial law. Both Republican and Democratic candidates held inaugural balls while returns were reviewed and each certified their own candidates for many parish offices. Only with federal intervention was the Republican declared governor. But immediately afterward in 1873, the Democrat Samuel D. McEnery used his own militia to control the capitol, then New Orleans.

Violence was frequent. In rural Grant Parish in the Red River Valley, freedmen fearing a Democratic attempt to take over the parish government decided to defend the Colfax courthouse. In 1873, the whites attacked the defenders' courthouse, killing three whites and 120–150 blacks. Historians called this the Colfax

Massacre rather than the Colfax Riot, as it was known locally. This began a period of violence against Republican officeholders.

In the 1873 elections, Louisiana was one of the only four southern states to remain under Republican control (along with Arkansas, Mississippi, and South Carolina). White militias transformed into dangerous paramilitary organizations in 1874. The most prominent was the White League, which began in the Red River Valley. The league, which operated in the open, had the goals of the violent overthrow of Republican rule and suppression of all black voting. Funded by some wealthy men, White League chapters were formed in many rural parishes. In 1874, the White League killed six white Republican officeholders and several black witnesses near Coushatta. Later that year, the White League sent 5,000 troops to New Orleans to fight the Metropolitan Police and state militia in an attempt to force Republican governor William P. Kellogg out of office and seat their candidate. They succeeded in temporarily taking over the state house and city hall. When federal troops arrived, the league retreated.

With the end of Reconstruction in 1876, the white Democrats regained control of Louisiana. President Rutherford B. Hayes removed troops from the capitals of the remaining Reconstruction states, Louisiana and South Carolina, allowing the Redeemers to have full control. In 1879, however, "Kansas fever" struck blacks from the cotton country of Louisiana and Mississippi, and many migrated to the Wheat State; many later returned to their home states. Through the 1880s, white Democrats reduced voter registration of African Americans and poor whites by making registration and elections more complicated.

In the late 1880s, many Midwestern farmers migrated to southwestern Louisiana to become rice farmers. Louisiana did not have a significant number of African American out-migrants after the Civil War. Blacks mainly moved to state's cities in search of work. In 1870, there were 57,000 urbanized African Americans in Louisiana. This grew to 117,000 in 1900; to 190,400 in 1920; to 314,100 in 1940; and to 421,700 in 1950.

The state had a major role in the landmark 1896 U.S. Supreme Court decision *Plessy v. Ferguson*, which found segregation was legal as long as it did not deliberately result in inequality. The case stemmed from a lawsuit by the New Orleans Comité des Citoyens (Committee of Citizens), which had arranged for the arrest of Homer Plessy (1862–1925) who challenged Louisiana's strict segregation law.

As a result of this legal disenfranchisement, African Americans in Louisiana essentially had no political representation. Consequently, black-dominant areas had inadequate funding for schools and services; lack of representation on juries; no representation in local, state, or federal governments; and lack of attention to their interests.

Additionally, there were continual efforts to limit African American political power during the Postbellum period. In 1898, the white Democratic legislature enacted a new disenfranchising constitution. The constitution's restrictive provisions for voter registration, such as poll taxes, residency requirements, and literacy tests, were aimed at limiting black voter registration. In 1896, there were 130,334 black voters on the rolls and about the same number of white voters, in proportion to the state population, which was evenly divided.

The state actively tried to draw migrants and immigrants in the hope of stimulating and developing the economy. However, the state's "rigid rural economy, natural impediments, and uncongenial social and political conditions" frustrated the boosterism (Shanabruch 1997).

EARLY TWENTIETH CENTURY

In 1900, Louisiana's population was 1,381,625, with 52.8 percent whites and 47.1 percent African Americans. Many in New Orleans were descendants of Creoles of color, mostly free before the Civil War. Due to the legislature's efforts, only 5,320 black voters were registered to vote. This declined in 1910 to 730, below 0.5 percent of eligible men, despite advances in education and literacy among blacks and people of color. In effect, white Democrats established one-party political rule.

Tim Nguyen ties up his shrimp boat to a dock while performing maintenance in Grand Isle, Louisiana, on August 4, 2010. Nguyen, his father, brother, and an uncle captain four shrimp boats. "My father, my uncle, they have done this all their lives," Nguyen said. "But if I have a son, I don't what him to be a shrimper. I don't think the business will last anyway, not the way things are now." (AP Photo/Patrick Semansky)

In the early decades of the new century, thousands of African Americans left Louisiana in the Great Migration north to industrial cities. The state's serious boll weevil infestation and ongoing agricultural problems eliminated many of the jobs of cost sharecroppers and farmers. Furthermore, the mechanization of agriculture had dropped the need for laborers. They sought skilled jobs in the defense industry in California, better education for their children, and living opportunities in communities where they can vote, as well as an escape from southern violence.

During the early part of the Great Depression, the populist governor Huey P. Long (1893–1935) dominated Louisiana political life. Everything about Long was extreme. Long's many public work projects transformed the state. His administration provided many jobs, significantly increased the level of public education, and increased suffrage for poor whites. However, Long received much local and national criticism for his allegedly demagogic and autocratic style. His assassination in 1935 curtailed his budding national career.

While mobilization for World War II created some jobs in the state, the Second Great Migration during 1940–1970 resulted in significant population loss for Louisiana (Berlin 2010, 155). During the 1960s, Louisiana had a net out-migration of 15 percent of its black population, but the trend had slowed somewhat by 1975. Thousands of workers migrated to California for better jobs in the defense industry. The Great Migration was stimulated by the mechanization of agriculture which had decimated the need for laborers. Beginning in World War II, large numbers of both black and white farmworkers left Louisiana and migrated north and west.

Between 1940 and 1960, Louisiana had an economic and demographic revolution. Agriculture was mechanized, the natural assets of the region were developed, and industry grew rapidly. Many left the farms and went to the cities (52 percent in 1960). There were also substantial increases in the rural nonfarm areas. The age and sex distribution were warped, especially below age 30, slowing down the early marriage rate and the crude birth rate.

CIVIL RIGHTS PERIOD TO 2000

In 1950, Louisiana's 2,683,516 population was 67.0 percent white, 32.9 percent African American with a negligible percentage of other races. After World War II, Louisiana state legislators created other ways to suppress black voting, which had crept up to 5.0 percent of those eligible from 1948 to 1952. Civil rights organizations in New Orleans and southern parishes, where there had been a long tradition of free people of color before the Civil War, worked hard to register black voters.

In the 1950s, under federal pressure, Louisiana instituted a less-restrictive requirement for a citizenship test for voter registration. Despite opposition by the States' Rights Party, African American voters began to increase their rate of registration, also showing the growth of the African American middle classes. Black voter registration and turnout increased to 20 percent. In 1964, African American registration was still only 32 percent.

At this time, the percentage of black voters varied widely by section of the state, from a high 93.8 percent in Evangeline Parish to a miniscule 1.7 percent in Tensas Parish. After the passage of the Civil Rights Act of 1964 and Voting Rights Act of 1965, almost 59 percent of eligible-aged African Americans had registered to vote in Louisiana by 1968.

The civil rights changes happened during a period when the state's population was growing fairly rapidly, over 20 percent during the 1960s. During the late 1960s, African Americans continued to migrate from Louisiana. There was a net loss of African Americans of over 37,000. However, as the 1970s began, some began to migrate to cities of the New South to take advantage of emerging opportunities.

In 1980, Louisiana's 4,203,972 population ranked 19th among the 50 states. This had increased over 15 percent in the 1970s. Like many other states, Louisiana's rural areas grew slightly during this time. From 1980 to 1990, the state's urban population fell from 68.6 to 68.1 percent. Louisiana continued to lose migrants during the 1980s. Louisiana's net loss of 250,654 was the third-largest change during 1985–1990. Overall, Louisiana suffered a net loss from migration of about 368,000 from 1940 to 1990.

This out-migration continued in the 1990s, but at a slower pace. Demographically, the state's population was comparatively stable during the period, as the state had the seventh-lowest percentage of movers. Between 1990 and 1998, the state had a net loss of 117,000 in domestic migration and a net gain of 25,000 in international migration. In 1998, 2,193 foreign immigrants arrived in Louisiana. Between 1990 and 1998, the state's overall population increased by 3.5 percent. During 1995–2000, 253,520 people moved into the state and 329,279 moved out, for a net loss of 75,759, many of whom moved to Texas. Some 90.1 percent of immigrants to the state were from other states in the South. About 75.3 percent out-migrated to other southern states, and 22.3 percent went to western states (U.S. Bureau of the Census 2000, Table 21). Ominously, Louisiana was one of the few southern states to actually lose its over-65 population by net migration in 1995–2000, a 4.8 percent decline.

The state's population increase slowed to a virtual standstill during the 1980s. In 1990, the U.S. Census found the population to be 4,219,973—a negligible increase of 0.3 percent. The population density in 2000 was 102.6 persons per square mile.

TWENTY-FIRST CENTURY

Since 2000, some long-standing population trends have reversed whereas others have strengthened. In 2000, Louisiana's median age was 34 years. Those under 18 years consisted of 27.3 percent of the population, and 11.6 percent were aged 65 or older. In 2002, Louisiana ranked 24th in population with an estimated total of 4,482,646, an increase of 48 percent since 2000. Between 1990 and 2000, Louisiana's population grew from 4,219,973 to 4,468,976, an increase of 5.9 percent. The population was projected to reach 4,535,000 by 2005 and 5.1 million by 2025.

In 2009, New Orleans was the largest city, with an estimated 2002 population of 354,850, followed by Baton Rouge, 225,702 and Shreveport, 199,242. Baton Rouge, the capital, had grown greatly since 1940, when its population was 34,719. Since 1980, the capital's population had been decreasing. The state's largest metropolitan areas were New Orleans, with an estimated 1,305,479 in 1999, and Baton Rouge, with 578,946.

Since the late twentieth century, political refugees from Southeast Asia (Laos, Vietnam, and Cambodia, among others) brought their families, cultures, and languages to the area and contributed significantly to its fishing industry. Recent migration within Louisiana generally has been from north to south, and from rural to urban areas, especially to Shreveport, Baton Rouge, and the suburbs of New Orleans.

In 2010, Louisiana had a population of 4,544,228, the 24th-largest. The state had the highest proportion born in the state of 78.8 percent, indicating the slowdown in migration and immigration. Only 3.8 percent were foreign-born, one of the lowest proportions in the country. These were typical for west-southern states. The state had a very low percentage of same-sex couple households in 2010, between 0.29 and 0.66 percent (U.S. Bureau of the Census 2010).

Compared to most of the South, Louisiana has a high percentage of the foreign-born who are naturalized. In 2009, some 44.1 percent of the state's 4,492 foreign-born were naturalized, roughly the nation's average. Like many states, the number of naturalized citizens increased significantly between 2006 and 2010.

AFTER HURRICANE KATRINA (2005 TO THE PRESENT)

In August 2005, New Orleans and other parts of Louisiana were devastated by Hurricane Katrina. It was the worst Atlantic hurricane of that year, as well as the costliest natural disaster and one of the five deadliest hurricanes in nation's history. Katrina killed over 1,836 with a total estimated property damage of $81 billion.

With the failure of the levee system, many deaths occurred in New Orleans. Eventually 80 percent of New Orleans and many parts of adjacent parishes were flooded. Experts considered the hurricane surge protection failures in New Orleans the worst civil engineering disaster in U.S. history. Because of this, lawsuits are still pending against the U.S. Army Corps of Engineers, the designers and builders of the levee system as mandated by the Flood Control Act of 1965. All levels of government failed to prepare Louisiana and the Gulf Coast adequately despite severe hurricane warnings, and emergency responses were absurdly slow.

As a result, Louisiana faced a humanitarian crisis and a large tide of refugees, especially from New Orleans. With the extremely slow recovery of much of the city, the population of New Orleans has plummeted. Katrina's destruction has exacerbated trends already established of out-migration from the state.

SUMMARY

Louisiana had the national reputation of being "the human gumbo mix of cultures, nationalities, races, personalities, and talents in fascinating detail." From Mardi Gras to Hurricane Katrina, the many conventions in New Orleans, and the oil rigs, the state is characterized by diversity and a touch of the exotic. The resurgence of New Orleans evidenced this, as the city has emerged as a major national tourist and convention center that continues to bolster its economy (Wilds, Dufour, and Cowan 1996). It remains to be seen whether the state's citizens will choose to embrace this diversity or restrict immigration and the state's welcome mat.

TOPICAL ESSAYS

ACADIANS AND ACADIANA

Many Acadians left France (under the influence of Henri Peyroux de la Coudreniere), to settle in Louisiana, then a Spanish colony. The transfer of Louisiana to the Spanish government was done in 1762. Good relations between the two nations, and their common Catholic religion resulted in many Acadians choosing to take oaths of allegiance to the Spanish government.

The Acadians became the largest ethnic group in Louisiana. Acadians initially settled along the Mississippi River, then later in the Atchafalaya Basin and in the prairie lands to the west, a region later renamed Acadiana. During the nineteenth century, as Acadians reestablished their culture, "Acadian" elided locally into "Cajun." Today, Acadiana consisted of 22 of the state's 64 parishes. In 1971, the Louisiana state legislature officially recognized 22 Louisiana parishes and "other parishes of similar cultural environment" for their "strong French Acadian cultural aspects" (House Concurrent Resolution No. 496, June 6, 1971), and made *The Heart of Acadiana* the official name of the region.

German settlers found their way to Acadiana as early as 1721, preceding the Acadians. Several Native American tribes, including the Chitimacha, Tunica-Biloxi, Attakapas, and Coushatta, lived in Acadiana. It also had a large Creole population—black, white, or mixed-race persons (Creole meaning "native to Louisiana"). Other ethnic groups also resided in the area, including

Anglo-Americans, who came in increasing numbers after the 1803 Louisiana Purchase. In recent years (after Hurricane Katrina and Hurricane Rita in 2005), a significant number of Latinos/as had moved into the region.

THE GERMAN COAST

The four German settlements along the coast were Karlstein, Hoffen, Meriental, and Augsburg. The area's name was derived from the large population of German pioneers who were settled there in 1721 by John Law (1671–1729), controller general of finances of France under King Louis XV, and his Mississippi Company or Company of the Indies. After a wild speculation scheme produced a frenzy, Law was dismissed from his position in 1720 by Philippe d'Orléans, regent of France for Louis XV.

Despite periodic flooding, hurricanes, and the rigors of frontier life, the German pioneers made a success of their settlements. Their farming endeavors provided food not only for themselves but also for New Orleans's residents. Some historians credited these German farmers with the survival of early New Orleans. In 1768, they joined with Acadians from the Cabannocé Post area to overthrow the Spanish colonial governor in New Orleans. The German and Acadian settlers united again, under Spanish colonial governor Bernardo de Gálvez (1746–1786), to fight the British during the American Revolution.

Many Germans came from the German-speaking region of Alsace-Lorraine in France, and some from Switzerland and Belgium (German-Acadian Coast Historical and Genealogical Society 2012). As soon as they arrived, the Germans began speaking French and intermarried with the French settlers. German settlers introduced the diatonic accordion into music, which by 1900 became the main instrument in Cajun music.

The German Coast was the site of the largest slave revolt in U.S. history, the 1811 German Coast Uprising. Charles Deslondes, a free person of color who emigrated from Haiti, gathered over 200 slaves and marched to New Orleans. They killed two whites, but 95 slaves were killed by the militia or in executions after summary trials.

During World War I, in a reaction against Germany as the enemy, the Louisiana state legislature passed Act 114 which made all expressions of German culture and heritage, especially the printed or spoken use of the German language, illegal in the state.

RECENT IMMIGRATION CONTROVERSIES

Louisiana has not escaped the developing protest movement against undocumented immigration. Two Louisiana groups were formed to agitate for the state to adopt a law similar to Arizona's strict statute Senate Bill (SB) 1070. These groups are Louisiana Citizens for the New Arizona Immigration Law and Stand with Louisiana (against Illegal Immigration).

Bills have been introduced in the Louisiana House to curb undocumented immigration. In 2010, Representative Joe Harrison of District 51 introduced House Bill (HB) 1205, the "Louisiana Taxpayer and Citizen Protection Act of 2010." A similar bill was defeated in 2008. Harrison's 2010 bill was intended to "discourage undocumented workers from even thinking about crossing the state line into Louisiana" (Tyler 2010).

Rep. Ernest Wooton's (I-Belle Chasse) introduced a bill in 2011 that was similar. His "Louisiana Citizens Protection Act" (HB 411), introduced to the Louisiana House on April 25, would require law enforcement officers to conduct lawful stops to determine the citizenship status of detainees, where reasonable suspicion existed.

In 2011, two E-Verify bills were passed by the Louisiana legislature with support from organized labor and the Democratic leader of the House of Representatives. Louisiana's governor signed the E-Verify bills into law. Despite promises of "wait till next year," no immigration enforcement bills were introduced during the 2012 session. For the future of anti-immigrant bills in Louisiana, much depended on the interpretation of the U.S. Supreme Court's ruling on Arizona's SB 1070.

NOTABLE GROUPS

Immigration Advocates Network

The Immigration Advocates Network provides two overall services: it serves as a consulting resource for nonprofits and it offers assistance to lawyers who work pro bono with immigrants and refugees in the state. The group does this by providing no cost web information and computer tools for immigration advocates and service providers. They have an online library, with numerous legal references and information (such as legal referrals), and the group has produced webinars, training videos, and podcasts. They also provide an online service called CitizenshipWorks, to aid immigrants with applying for citizenship, and "Own the Dream" ("Únete al Sueño"), which aids children who are eligible for Deferred Action for Childhood Arrivals provision to apply and obtain legal authorization to work (Immigration Advocates Network n.d.).

BIBLIOGRAPHY

Adegbile, Debo P. "Voting Rights in Louisiana: 1982–2006." Renew the VRA Website. March 6–7, 2006. www.protectcivilrights.org/pdf/voting/LouisianaVRA.pdf. Accessed March 17, 2014.

Alexander, Danielle. "Forty Acres and a Mule: The Ruined Hope of Reconstruction." *Humanities* 25, no. 1 (January/February 2004). http://www.neh.gov/humanities/2004/januaryfebruary/feature/forty-acres-and-mule. Accessed February 8, 2014.

Anderson, Ed. "House Passes Bill Requiring Companies to Verify Workers Are Not Illegal Immigrants." *The Times-Picayune*, June 22, 2011. http://www.nola.com/politics/index.ssf/2011/06/house_passes_bill_requiring_co.html. Accessed February 8, 2014.

Arsenault, Bona, and Alain Pascal. *Histoire des Acadiens*. Saint-Laurent, Québec: Éditions Fides, 2004.

Berlin, Ira. *The Making of African America: The Four Great Migrations*. New York: Viking, 2010.

Blum, Edward, and Abigail Thernstrom. "Executive Summary of the Bullock-Gaddie Expert Report on Louisiana." American Enterprise Institute, Washington, DC, 2006.

Brasseaux, Carl A. *Founding of New Acadia: The Beginnings of Acadian Life in Louisiana, 1765–1803*. Baton Rouge: Louisiana State University Press, 1996.

Caron, Peter. "'Of a Nation the Others Do Not Understand': Bambara Slaves and African Ethnicity in Colonial Louisiana, 1718–60." *Slavery and Abolition* 18, no. 1 (1997): 99.

Din, Gilbert C. *The Canary Islanders of Louisiana*. Baton Rouge: Louisiana State University Press, 1988.

Doughty, Arthur G. *The Acadian Exiles. A Chronicle of the Land of Evangeline*. Toronto: Glasgow, Brook & Co., 1916.

Faragher, John Mack. *A Great and Noble Scheme: The Tragic Story of the Expulsion of the French Acadians from their American Homeland*. New York: W.W. Norton, 2005.

Foner, Eric. *Reconstruction: America's Unfinished Revolution 1863–1877*. New York: HarperCollins, 1988.

Frey, William H. "The New Great Migration: Black Americans' Return to the South, 1965–2000." Brookings Institution, Washington, DC, 2004. http://www.brookings.edu/research/reports/2004/05/demographics-frey. Accessed March 17, 2014.

German-Acadian Coast Historical and Genealogical Society, Inc. *The German Coast*. 2012. http://germanacadiancoast.com/. Accessed March 17, 2014.

Hall, Gwendolyn Midlo. *Africans in Colonial Louisiana: The Development of Afro-Creole Culture in the Eighteenth Century*. Baton Rouge: Louisiana State University, 1992.

Hori, M., M. Schafer, and D. Bowman. "Displacement Dynamics in Southern Louisiana After Hurricanes Katrina and Rita." *Population Research & Policy Review* 28 (February 2009): 45–65.

Immigration Advocates Network. Immigration Advocates Network Web Page. n.d. http://www.immigrationadvocates.org. Accessed February 8, 2014.

Johnson, Sally. "The Cajun Kingdom of the Bayou." *New York Times*, January 27, 1991. http://www.nytimes.com/1991/01/27/travel/the-cajun-kingdom-of-the-bayou.html. Accessed March 17, 2014.

Kanstroom, Daniel. *Deportation Nation*. Cambridge, MA: Harvard University Press, 2007.

Knabb, Richard D., Jamie R. Rhome, and Daniel P. Brown. "Tropical Cyclone Report: Hurricane Katrina. August 23–30, 2005." National Hurricane Center. http://www.nhc.noaa.gov/pdf/TCR-AL122005_Katrina.pdf. Accessed March 17, 2014.

Kuznets, Simon Smith. "Negro Population in Rural Areas, by States, 1870–1950." In *Population Redistribution and Economic Growth: United States, 1870–1950*. Whitefish, MT: Literary Licensing LLC, 2011. Ann Arbor, MI: Inter-university Consortium for Political and Social Research [distributor], 1982. http://doi.org/10.3886/ICPSR07753 .v2. http://doi.org/10.3886/ICPSR07753.v2.

Louisiana Citizens for the New Arizona Immigration Law. http://www.facebook.com/pages /Louisiana-Citizens-for-The-New-Arizona-Immigration-Law/126752434001631. Accessed March 17, 2014.

McCarthy, Kevin F., D.J. Peterson, and Narayan Sastry. *Repopulation of New Orleans after Hurricane Katrina*. Santa Monica, CA: RAND Corporation, 2006.

Medley, Keith Weldon. *We as Freeman*: Plessy v. Ferguson: *The Fight against Legal Segregation*. Gretna, LA: Pelican Publishing Company, 2003.

Mitford, Nancy. *The Sun King*. London: Penguin Publishing, 1966.

Moen, John. "John Law and the Mississippi Bubble: 1718–1720." *Mississippi History Now* (October 2011). http://mshistory.k12.ms.us/articles/70/john-law-and-the-mississippi-bubble-1718–1720. Accessed March 17, 2014.

New York Public Library. Schomberg Center for Research in Black Culture. *In Motion: The African-American Migration Experience*. 2011. http://www.inmotionaame.org/home .cfm. Accessed March 17, 2014.

Pildes, Richard H. "Democracy, Anti-Democracy, and the Canon." *Constitutional Commentary* 17 (2000): 295, 297.

Powell, Lawrence N. *The Accidental City: Improvising New Orleans*. Cambridge, MA: Harvard University Press, 2012.

Ross, Robert. "Louisiana Next in Line for Arizona Illegal Immigration Bill, and Its Consequences." *The Pelican Post*, May 12, 2011. http://www.thepelicanpost.org/2011/05/12 /louisiana-next-in-line-for-arizona-illegal-immigration-bill-and-its-consequences/. Accessed March 17, 2014.

Schomberg Center for Research in Black Culture, New York Public Library. "The Second Great Migration." 2005. http://www.inmotionaame.org/migrations/landing.cfm; jsessionid=f83023773813427808371004?migration=9&bhcp=1. Accessed March 17, 2014.

Shanabruch, Charles. "The Louisiana Immigration Movement, 1891–1907: An Analysis of Efforts, Attitudes, and Opportunities." *Louisiana History: The Journal of the Louisiana Historical Association* 18, no. 2 (Spring 1977): 203–26.

Stand with Louisiana (against Illegal Immigration). http://www.facebook.com/pages /Stand-With-Louisiana-Against-Illegal-Immigration/138724599543445. Accessed March 17, 2014.

State of Louisiana. *Acts Passed by the General Assembly of the State of Louisiana at the Regular Session Begun and Held in the City of Baton Rouge on the Thirteenth Day of May 1918*. Baton Rouge, LA: Ramires-Jones Printing Co., 1918.

State of Louisiana. "The Louisiana State Capitol Building." 2012. http://www.crt.state.la.us /tourism/capitol/capitol.htm. Accessed March 17, 2014.

Stlouiscathedral.org. "Welcome to the St. Louis Cathedral." 2012. http://stlouiscathedral .org/. Accessed March 17, 2014.

Sturdevent, William C. "Early Indian Tribes, Cultures, and Linguistic Stocks, Smithsonian Institution Map (Eastern United States)." 1967. http://www.lib.utexas.edu/maps/united_states/early_indian_east.jpg. Accessed March 17, 2014.

Sublette, Neal. *The World That Made New Orleans: From Spanish Silver to Congo Square.* Chicago: Chicago Review Press, 2008.

Tyler, Lori. "Arizona Copy Cat Immigration Law Pending in Louisiana." *Jambalaya News,* June 21, 2010. http://newamericamedia.org/2010/06/louisiana-hb1205-to-protect-or-scare.php. Accessed February 8, 2014.

U.S. Bureau of the Census. *Geographic Mobility: 1995 to 2000.* Washington, DC: U.S. Government Printing Office, 2003.

U.S. Bureau of the Census. *Selected Place of Birth and Migration Statistics: 1990.* Washington, DC: U.S. Government Printing Office, 1995.

U.S. Bureau of the Census. *1850: Summary Population and Housing Characteristics.* Washington, DC: U.S. Government Printing Office, 1850.

U.S. Bureau of the Census. *2000: Summary Population and Housing Characteristics.* Washington, DC: U.S. Government Printing Office, 2000.

U. S. Census Bureau, Census 2000, special tabulation. 2000 Census: PHC-T-22, "Migration for the Population 5 Years and Over for the United States, Regions, States, Counties, New England Minor Civil Divisions, Metropolitan Areas, and Puerto Rico: 2000." Prepared by: State Library of Iowa, State Data Center Program, 800-248-4483, http://www.silo.lib.ia.us/specialized-services/datacenter/.

U.S. Bureau of the Census. *2010: Summary Population and Housing Characteristics.* Washington, DC: U.S. Government Printing Office, 2010.

U.S. Census Bureau, 2010 American Community Survey, as cited in Daphne Lofquist, "Same-Sex Couple Households," American Community Survey Briefs ACSBR/10-03, Issued September, 2011 (Washington, DC: U.S. Department of Commerce, Economics and Statistics Administration, U.S. Census Bureau), 2.

U.S. Bureau of the Census. *1900 U.S. Census.* Washington, DC: U.S. Government Printing Office, 1900.

Wilds, John, Charles L. Dufour, and Walter G. Cowan. *Louisiana, Yesterday and Today: A Historical Guide to the State.* Baton Rouge: Louisiana State University Press, 1996.

Winzerling, Oscar William. *Acadian Odyssey.* Baton Rouge, LA: Claitors Publishing Division, 1955.

Woofter, T. J. "Migration in the Southeast." *Demography* 4, no. 2 (1967): 532–52.

Wright, John, ed. *The New York Times Almanac 2002.* New York: Routledge/Psychology Press, 2001.

19

MAINE

Katherine M. O'Flaherty

CHRONOLOGY

1000 CE	It is believed that a band of Norse sailors, including Leif Erikson, reached Newfoundland and Nova Scotia in eastern Canada. The Norse sailors may also have reached Maine.
1524	Esteban Gómez, a Portuguese explorer, is the first to map the coast of Maine.
1604	The first European colony in present-day Maine is founded at the mouth of the St. Croix River by French explorer Pierre du Gua, sieur de Monts.
1609	A French Jesuit mission is established on Penobscot Bay.
1607	The first English settlement, the Popham Colony, is established by the Plymouth Company. The colony does not survive the harsh winter.
1613	A French Jesuit mission is established on Mount Desert Island.
1652	Massachusetts annexes the territory that forms much of present-day Maine.
1675	Beginning of King Phillip's War and continued struggle between English settlers, French settlers, and native peoples for control of territory that includes Maine.
1775	Battle of the *Margaretta* and the *Unity* off the coast of Machias. This is the first naval battle of the Revolutionary War.
1820	Maine becomes a state as a result of the Missouri Compromise.
1838–1839	The Aroostook War, a noncombative confrontation between England and the United States erupts; the conflict concerns the boundary between New Brunswick and northern Maine.

1842	The signing of the Webster–Ashburton Treaty settles the boundary dispute between New Brunswick and northern Maine.
1853	Portland is linked to Montreal via the Atlantic and St. Lawrence (Grand Trunk) Railway.
1860	Maine-native Hannibal Hamlin is elected vice president on the Republican ticket under Abraham Lincoln.
1860	The first Latinos are recorded in Maine census data.
1866	Fire destroys much of the Old Port section of Portland, Maine.
1866	The Fenian Brotherhood, an Irish American organization, invades Canada from Eastport, Maine.
1870	Fifty-one Swedish settlers arrive in Maine. Over the next few years, more than 550 Swedish migrants relocate to Maine and settle in rural Aroostook County towns, including New Sweden, Stockholm, Perham, and Westmanland.
1870	Asian immigrants first appear in census records for Maine.
1880	Portland Longshoremen's Benevolent Society (PLSBS) is incorporated.
1895	A Chinese New Year celebration is mentioned in Portland newspapers.
1904	The Congregation Shaarey Tphiloh begins construction of a new synagogue in Portland.
1915	A small group of Albanian and Turkish immigrants establish a mosque at the Pepperell Counting House, part of a textile mill in Biddeford where they are employed.
1920	About 20 Chinese laundries are in operation in Portland.
1924	The Ku Klux Klan (KKK) boasts 50,000 members in Maine.
1947	Baron Vladimir von Poushental settles in Maine.
1948	Maine-native Margaret Chase Smith is elected to the U.S. Senate; she is the first women to serve in both houses of Congress.
1952	Immigration and Naturalization Act is passed.
1952	Toy Len Goon, a native of Canton, China, is named Maine Mother of the Year and later American Mother of the Year.
1953	Thirty-five Russian settlers arrive in Richmond.
1953	Loring Air Force Base in Limestone, Aroostook County, is opened.
1980	Maine-native senator Edmund Muskie becomes President Jimmy Carter's secretary of state.
1980	Indian Land Claims agreement is signed by President Jimmy Carter.
1980	Portland begins a multilingual program teaching English to 50 students.
1990s	Amish families begin settling in rural Maine towns, including Smyrna, Easton, Unity, and Thorndike.
1994	Loring Air Force Base in Limestone, Aroostook County, is closed.
1997	Maine-native senator William Cohen becomes President Bill Clinton's secretary of defense.

2001	The first Somali refugees move from Atlanta, Georgia, to Portland and Lewiston.
2002	Mayor Laurier T. Raymond writes an open letter to Lewiston's Somali community discouraging future Somali migration to the city.
2002	Fourteen migrant workers from Guatemala and Honduras are killed in the Allagash Wilderness Waterway when the van they were riding in swerved off a bridge.
2003	A rally by a white supremacist organization and one by a pro-diversity coalition are held simultaneously in Lewiston.
2004	The first Somali Bantus are resettled in Maine.
2010	The *Lewiston Sun Journal* reports that Somali entrepreneurs had opened shops in many previously closed storefronts, thus helping to reinvigorate the economy of downtown Lewiston.

HISTORICAL OVERVIEW

Over the past half century, Maine has attracted a diverse array of immigrants, albeit in small numbers when compared to other states. Those immigrants who have moved into the state have settled in Maine's few metropolitan areas, including Portland, Lewiston, Auburn, and Bangor. This pattern continues broad population trends from the nineteenth and early twentieth century when many thousands of Canadians and northern and western Europeans were attracted to Maine to work in industries such as textiles, mining, and lumbering. Maine's immigrant demographics have shifted since World War II. Recent immigrants to Maine still come from Canada, and to a lesser degree Europe, but also come from Asia, especially China, and Latin America. Maine also has a growing population of African immigrants, especially Somalis, who are contributing greatly to the diversity of the state.

The New England Public Policy Center estimated that more than 1.6 million immigrants lived in New England by 2006. Of these immigrants, 92 percent lived in Massachusetts, Connecticut, and Rhode Island. The remaining 8 percent were distributed across Maine, Vermont, and New Hampshire. In 2006, the U.S. Census Bureau estimated that the foreign-born population of Maine stand at only about 42,000 (a little over 3 percent of the 1.3 million total population). In fact, The Michigan Policy Institute estimated that between 2000 and 2006 the foreign-born population of Maine rose by only about 14 percent, one of the lowest growth rates in the country. The great majority of these immigrants lived in Maine's few urban areas, especially Portland, yet, unlike other states, Maine continued to lack large ethnic centers that attract additional immigrants. Maine's overall population and immigrant population have grown slowly over the past several years.

Maine has a unique demographic profile. According to the 2010 U.S. Census, the population of Maine was 1,327,567. Of those, the foreign-born population

Community advocate Nimo Yonis leads a protest chant against the mayor of Lewiston, Maine, on October 4, 2012. Critics of the mayor delivered petitions asking for his resignation because of comments he made about Somali refugees in his city. (AP Photo/Robert F. Bukaty)

was 45,666. Maine's population is overwhelmingly white. The 2010 Census figures indicated that Maine, long identified as the "whitest" state in the union, remained 95.22 percent white (Vermont is currently the whitest state at 95.29 percent). Native American, African American, Latino, Asian, and those of biracial heritage made up only about 5 percent of the current Maine population—a 37 percent increase over previous census data. Maine also holds the distinction of being the oldest state in the union. The 2010 Census found that Maine had the oldest population in the country with a median age of 42. In addition, less than 5 percent of the Maine population was under five years of age. These demographic factors continue to have a profound impact on the Maine workforce.

The majority of Maine's population lives in the southern third of the state and along the I-95 corridor between Kittery and Bangor. Geographically, Maine is about the same size as the rest of New England combined, yet the state's population is quite small, ranking 41st out of the 50 states. Maine's rural and isolated counties in the north and east continue to lose population and neither area has drawn large numbers of immigrants.

Maine's geography has and continues to have an influence on immigration to the state. In the late nineteenth and early twentieth centuries, Maine's geographic proximity attracted immigrants from Canada and Europe. In the late twentieth century, Maine's geographical remoteness from industrial areas and population centers across the United States as well as its distance from immigrant-generating countries resulted in few immigrants relocating to the state. Yet, Maine has a rich immigrant past and continues to attract diverse immigrants, albeit in small numbers.

In the nineteenth century, immigration to Maine consisted of a diverse group of Europeans and Canadians. Because of Maine's unique geographical location, bordered on the west by Quebec and on the east by New Brunswick, European immigrants who arrived at Canadian seaports routinely entered the United State by way of Maine. Many passed through Maine on their way to larger urban centers on the East Coast. Natives of the Canadian Maritime Provinces and Quebec also moved regularly across the Maine border in search of economic opportunity. The Canadian population stood at about 100,000 in the 1760s and by 1851 had increased to 2.5 million. The population was predominantly composed of French, British, and Amerindians but became increasingly diverse as Scottish, German, and both Protestant and Catholic Irish arrived in Canada. Members of the growing Canadian population moved easily back and forth into Maine and other border states. Even though the Webster–Ashburton treaty finally clarified the Maine–New Brunswick border in 1842, it would not be until the mid-twentieth century that virtually unrestricted access ended.

Maine's population remained small into the twentieth century and immigrants from Canada and Europe found work in various industries. As more Canadian and European immigrants arrived, competition for jobs increased. Maine was not spared ethnic tension. By the 1920s, Maine's demographics had clearly shifted, straining the social system. Immigrants to Maine lived largely in Maine's few urban areas increasing their visibility to urban residents. By the 1920s, more than one-third of Maine residents were first- or second-generation Americans and almost a quarter had at least one foreign-born parent. Cultural and linguistic differences as well as the Roman Catholicism of French Canadian and Irish immigrants put them at odds with the Maine population. By 1924, the KKK boasted a membership of 50,000 in the state. While the true number of members was difficult to estimate, suspicion of foreigners particularly Franco-Americans was evident across the state.

In 1970, Maine's population was still under 1 million. Population growth had been relatively flat since the 1860s, despite continued immigration to the state by Canadians and northern Europeans. Maine had long suffered from the out-migration of young, educated workers seeking economic opportunity. Between 1970 and 1980, Maine's population did increase by about 13 percent but this was generally not a result of immigration by foreign-born immigrants. Instead, the population of Maine increased as a result of returning Maine natives and relocation of residents from other states in the northeast. These new Maine residents were almost all white.

TOPICAL ESSAYS

Historically, Canadian and European immigrants were attracted to Maine. French Canadians arrived in large numbers throughout the period to work in the mill towns in the southern parts of Maine as well as to cut timber in the north. Irish immigrants also worked in the industrial centers and on the Portland docks. Finnish and Swedish immigrants began arriving in Maine in the 1870s and cleared and settled rural agricultural regions of Aroostook County. Although the majority of Canadian and European immigrants arrived before the mid-twentieth century their impact on Maine can still be felt.

Geographic factors had an important impact on the growth of certain regions of the state, such as Portland, and the attraction of those areas to immigrants. For example between the mid-nineteenth and early twentieth centuries, many Irish immigrants settled in Portland, Maine, working at various low-skill professions, including as longshoremen on Portland's waterfront. In fact, membership in the longshoremen's union, the PLSBS was predominantly Irish until well into the twentieth century. Employment opportunities for immigrants boomed on Portland's docks in the 1850s when the city became linked to Montreal by rail. From April to November, while the St. Lawrence River was frozen, legions of Irish immigrant dock workers loaded Canadian grain onto ships in Portland harbor. As historian Michael C. Connolly notes, Portland became, in essence, Canada's main winter port as Montreal and Quebec were virtually "landlocked" until spring. By the 1920s, the Canadian government had invested in the ports of Halifax, Nova Scotia, and St. John, New Brunswick, so Canadian goods processed through Portland steadily declined. This decline in work coincided with calls for immigration restriction during the 1920s reducing the number of Irish immigrants to Portland.

Perhaps no immigrant group has had as deep an impact on Maine as the Franco-Americans. Although most arrived prior to the mid-twentieth century, the Franco population continued to influence Maine's social, political, and economic system. Franco-American immigrants had an important and well-documented place in Maine's history.

Maine's Franco-American heritage has roots leading back to early French settlers and explorers. In the nineteenth century, many French Canadians came to Maine from Quebec to work in the growing textile industry centered in cities such as Lewiston, Brunswick, Topsham, Auburn, Biddeford, and Waterville. Franco immigration to Maine remained strong through World War I. As James P. Allen argues, at the beginning of the twentieth century, Franco-American settlement occurred in phases. The cumulative effects of which were an uneven distribution of Franco-Americans around the state. Franco-American settlement of Maine involved an expansion of settlement along the upper St. John River; permanent settlement of seasonal workers in the Kennebec and Penobscot River Valleys; and intensive settlement of Franco-Americans in towns, such as Lewiston, where textile manufacturing was a dominant industry and settlement in areas where pulp and paper manufacturing were prevalent. These same population centers attracted a much smaller but more diverse immigrant population in the late twentieth century.

Reed Ueda noted that between the 1920s and 1950s, upward of 1.4 million Canadians arrived in the United States. About a quarter came from French-speaking areas of Canada. These immigrants generally settled near the U.S. border in the Great Lakes region and in New England because of its proximity to Quebec, Nova Scotia, New Brunswick, and Prince Edward Island. Maine's location, adjacent to Quebec and the Canadian Maritime Provinces, proved attractive for immigrants.

The Maine textile industry declined by the mid-twentieth century and therefore Franco-American immigration to the state decreased. Franco-Americans, many of whom were upwardly mobile and several generations removed from their immigrant roots, often found it difficult to preserve their language and culture. Those of Franco-American heritage were no longer concentrated solely in the few urban areas of the state and by mid-century have moved into suburbs and small towns across the state. Yet, in the early twenty-first century, Franco-Americans still represented Maine's largest ethnic group.

Franco-Americans struggled to preserve their language and culture in the latter half of the twentieth century. In 1940, Maine had 138,260 people who identified French as their mother tongue. By 1970, 141,489 identified French as their mother tongue. In both cases, Maine ranked second only to Massachusetts among New England states. The difference between 1940 and 1970 has less to do with migration from Canada and more to do with internal migration within the region, according to James P. Allen. The Franco-American population in southern sections of the state shifted dramatically between 1908 and 1970. For example, in Androscoggin County, the French population grew by 20,000 between 1908 and 1970. The stronger economy in the southern section of Maine was an important factor in attracting Franco-American workers.

In the second half of the twentieth century, Franco-American settlement patterns shifted, as those immigrants drawn to mill towns and suburban areas were diffused outward into towns they had not previously inhabited. This cultural and social assimilation along with demographic shifts in the past 30 years resulted in the large-scale decline of the French language in Maine. Franco-Americans retained their Catholic identity to a greater extent than their language. Allen notes that, in 1970, three-quarters of the state's Catholics were Franco-American even though only one-fifth of the Maine population was identified as Franco-American.

Canadian immigrants also came to Maine to work seasonally in the remote northern areas of the state. In some cases they brought their families, but in most cases they came alone for the winter months. Beginning in the mid-nineteenth century, workers from Quebec and New Brunswick came seasonally to Maine to harvest timber. From the beginning there were tensions between American and Canadian workers as native workers complained that Canadian workers depressed wages. Despite the unrest, Canadian woods workers continued to migrate to Maine in fairly large numbers into the mid-1970s.

Bill Parenteau argues that geographic proximity was a major attraction for these woods workers. Quebec and New Brunswick workers lived closer to Maine's remote, northern forests than did Maine or other American workers; therefore, it was easier for American companies to attract Canadian rather than American workers to Maine's remote north. Cutting timber was an attractive option for Canadian farmers and agricultural workers who crossed the border into Maine to spend the winter cutting timber. The cutting season ran from mid-October to early January. By late January, crews comprised mainly of Canadian workers would haul the cut timber to river banks where it would sit until the spring thaw in April or May. Most of the Canadian workers would leave at the thaw to return home for the planting season. As a result, the river driving was done by Maine woods workers.

The migration of Canadian woods workers to Maine remained largely unchanged into the twentieth century. Few Canadian workers cut wood in Maine during the depression years as pulpwood production was drastically reduced. In addition, poor, native Maine workers were willing to cut timber for lower wages and traveled hundreds of miles north. The World War II labor shortages in the United States meant that Canadian woods workers again returned to the Maine north woods at pre-Depression levels (e.g., 8,000 in 1942). By the early 1950s, a formalized system of recruiting and admitting Canadian labor emerged. The U.S. Immigration and Naturalization Act of 1952 sought to protect domestic workers by giving them preference. Yet, despite federal regulations and labor laws, little changed in Canadian migration to the Maine north woods, Parenteau argues. Traditional seasonal patterns of migration from New Brunswick and Quebec continued due largely to the clout of the paper industry but also because the geographic isolation of the logging camps, especially in winter, made it virtually impossible for federal monitoring. Woods workers could make more money in Maine during the harvesting season and the powerful paper industry was able to manipulate restrictive immigration practices to control workers. Woods work was dangerous and living conditions were miserable, especially during the harshest parts of winter.

In addition to Canadian and northern European immigrants, Maine attracted small numbers of southern and eastern European immigrants. Records indicate that Albanian and Turkish immigrants worked as weavers in the mills of Biddeford, Maine, in the first few decades of the twentieth century. Some of these men died as a result of Spanish Flu around 1918 and were buried in a local cemetery. Although the population of Albanian and Turkish weavers was undoubtedly small, evidence suggests that they established a small mosque or prayer space in the Pepperell Counting House.

Other Eastern European groups were more visible and their history is easier to trace. Two important examples are Maine's Eastern European Jewish population and a small colony of Russian refugees who moved to Richmond Maine in the 1950s. Maine's Jewish population was quite small when compared with other states. Much research has been done on Jews living in urban areas especially on the East Coast but few studies have incorporated smaller cities and rural parts of the northeast. There were a handful of Jews living in Maine as far back as the Colonial era. The first rudimentary synagogue was built in Bangor in 1849, when the Jewish community was only about six families. The first synagogue in Portland was built in the 1860s.

Jewish communities were thriving in other east coast cities by the 1860s; however, Portland's Jewish community was quite small, temporary, and comprised "itinerant peddlers and merchants" (Cohen 2009, 175). By 1878, the Jewish population of Portland stood at only 185, some of whom were Eastern Europeans who began arriving in 1866. Over the next 20 years, the population had grown to about 60 families. Some of these families were merchants attracted to Portland in the wake of the Portland fire of 1866. By the turn of the twentieth century, the number had grown to about 1,500 Jews in Portland, about 700 in Bangor, and about 250 in the Lewiston-Auburn area. The Jews of Bangor like the Jews of Portland were immigrants from German-speaking areas of Europe.

It is unclear if Maine Jews in the late nineteenth and early twentieth centuries faced persecution in Maine as much of the local hostility toward religious minorities was directed toward Roman Catholics. In the 1920, the KKK experienced a resurgence across the United States and in Maine. There were very few African Americans in Maine during this era so the KKK directed its efforts toward white Roman Catholics, most of whom were Franco-Americans or Irish, between the 1920 and 1940s.

Religious leaders in Portland recognized that the meeting houses in use at the turn of the century were simply not capable of holding the growing congregation. Leaders secured land and support for the construction of Shaarey Tphiloh which combined two Orthodox communities and incorporated the majority of Portland's Jews. Construction began in 1904 and the synagogue would be the largest constructed in the city to that point.

Portland's Jewish community remained relatively small and congregants wrestled with the difficulties of commitment to an Orthodox Jewish life while also valuing integration into Portland's Anglo-American culture. After World War II, upwardly mobile members of the community moved out of Portland to surrounding suburbs. By 1942, about half the Jewish population of Portland lived in Woodfords, a suburb of Portland. Diminished numbers of Jews in Portland made it very difficult for the Orthodox congregation who struggled to maintain faith and culture. Between1966 and 1974, membership at Shaarey Tphiloh dropped from 466 to 373.

In the 1950s, the largest rural Russian-speaking population in the United States lived in Richmond, Maine, a small town with a population of about 1,600 residents on the banks of the Kennebec River. The Russian population totaled about 500 immigrants, including Russian, Cossack, Ukrainian, and Byelorussian emigrants. Many of the immigrants who settled in Richmond arrived directly from Displaced Persons camps in Europe. Others were secondary migrants, moving to Maine from other parts of the United States. The settlers shared a language, common faith, and customs. The community thrived, and within a few years a Russian Orthodox Church, St. Alexamde Nevsky, was constructed in the town of Richmond. It was Maine's first Russian Orthodox Church.

The Russian settlers come to Maine at the behest of Baron Vladimir von Poushental who immigrated to the United States in the 1920s and eventually settled in Maine in 1947. Poushental first came to Maine some years earlier. An avid hunter, Poushental was impressed with the rustic Kennebec Valley and settled in the area. He also saw potential for real estate development. In the late 1940s, as many as two-thirds of the area's dairy farms were abandoned. Hundreds of area residents had simply left the valley and moved to Portland and Bath, Maine, in search of work in the burgeoning war-related industries, especially shipbuilding. Poushental began purchasing tracts of cheap cutover timberland (some of which was sold for as little as a dollar an acre) and abandoned farms. He then marketed the property in Russian language newspapers throughout the United States. Poushental touted the similarity of Maine's climate and land to that of Russia as well as the inexpensive nature of property. Poushental's goal was to establish a settlement of Russians in Richmond, Maine, where Russian families could live and work peacefully among others of similar faith and language.

In 1952, Robert S. Jaster argued, about 1,000 veterans of the "Russkii Corpus" or White Russian Army who had been living in Yugoslavia with their families, arrived in the United States. Poushental was especially interested in attracting members of this community to Maine, in part because he felt a "special kinship with these aging warriors" who, like Poushental, had fought the Bolsheviks and were forced to leave Russia in the 1920s. Poushental went to New York to meet leaders of the group and invited them to visit Richmond, Maine. The veterans and their families had no money to purchase the land in Maine, so Poushental donated it to those who wished to move to Maine.

In May 1952, members of the Corpus met with Maine governor Frederick G. Payne and announced ambitions to establish Richmond as "the world headquarters" of Corpus veterans, of whom about 1,000 lived in the United States. The leadership also planned to establish a veteran's home in Richmond. By August 1953, 35 Russian settlers were living in Richmond and the first chapel had been constructed. Poushental continued to advertise land in Richmond and Russian language newspapers followed the colonies' development with interest. By the mid-1960s, there were about 130 Russian households in the area, a stark increase from zero in 1950.

The Russian colony in and around Richmond, Maine, thrived for a few decades despite its geographic distance from larger centers of Russian life. The arrivals in the 1950s were not wealthy and few spoke any English. The settlers came from various regions across Russia and Eastern Europe and were united by past experience of fighting together, language, and faith. In addition, they were united by strong anti-Communist sentiments. By the 1970s, many of the older settlers had died and the Russian American children of the original settlers were largely assimilated into American culture, Jaster argues. They had attended Maine public schools, spoke English, and had acquired skills and trades their mainly agrarian parents had not. The colony in Richmond remained small so many in the second generation married outside their ethnicity and outside the Russian Orthodox faith.

In the latter half of the twentieth century, Maine attracted a small but growing population of Asian, Latino, and African immigrants. As with earlier immigrant groups, these populations have remained in Maine's few urban centers. As their numbers have increased, Asian, Latino, and to a lesser degree African immigrants can now be found in all Maine counties.

Maine's Asian immigrants are few but have added a rich layer to life in the state. Census records indicate Asian immigrants living in Maine as far back as 1870. Over the next 100 years, fewer than 200 Asian immigrants were recorded on each of the decennial censuses. It was not until 1960 that the number began to increase. By 2009, there were about 12,500 Asian's living in Maine representing about 1 percent of the state's population.

Although numbers are hard to estimate, there were enough Chinese living in Portland that a celebration of the Chinese New Year was noted in Portland newspapers in 1895. Chinese immigrants in Portland during the late nineteenth and early twentieth centuries were likely all young men, many of whom joined Christian churches and attended Christian Sunday schools in an effort to acquire language skills and socialize. These early Chinese immigrants were generally self-employed and owned small laundries, restaurants, or shops. By 1920, there were about 20 Chinese laundries in Portland. For example, Dogan Goon and his wife Toy Len Goon, a native of Canton, operated a laundry in Portland. After

Dogan died in 1940, his wife continued the business and raised their eight children. Toy Len Goon was named Maine Mother of the Year in 1952 and later that year she was chosen as American Mother of the Year.

There was little documentary evidence about Asians other than the Chinese in Maine in the nineteenth and early twentieth centuries. It can safely be assumed that the numbers of Asians who were not Chinese in Maine were only in the hundreds and likely the bulk of this population lived in and around Portland, Lewiston-Auburn, and to a lesser degree in Bangor. During the 1970s and 1980s, some Asian refugees were resettled in Maine. Following the Vietnam War, Vietnamese, Laotian, and Cambodian refugees were settled mainly in Portland. According to U.S. Census data, the population of Asians in Maine rose from 185 in 1950 to 6,450 in 1990.

The Maine Center for Economic Policy (MECEP) estimated that the primary countries of origin for Maine's Asian residents in the early twenty-first century were China, the Philippines, and India. In addition, MECEP identified a 44 percent decrease in the number of Vietnamese immigrants in Maine, many of whom had arrived as refugees in the 1970s and 1980s. A population of 909 Vietnamese lived in Maine in 2000, but by 2006, the number dropped to 503.

Like Maine's Asian population, Maine's Latino population was quite small. U.S. Census records indicate that 25 Latinos (from Mexico, Cuba, and South America) lived in Maine in 1860. By 2007, there were 15,656 Latinos in Maine representing a little over 1 percent of the state's population. This represented a 67 percent increase in population between 2000 and 2007. In 2010, about half Maine's Latino residents were Puerto Rican and Mexican. The MECEP notes that Latinos, unlike Maine's other immigrant groups, were dispersed further from Maine's population centers, although the majority do still live in Maine's urban and suburban locations. Maine, unlike other states does not have large ethnic communities in its urban centers. Latino immigrants, like Asian immigrants, work at a variety of jobs and professions. Maine has a migrant workforce comprising largely of workers from South and Central America in addition to Latino business owners and other professionals.

Latinos in Maine have been dispersed throughout the state to a greater degree than Asian immigrants, but census estimates indicated that more than half live in the southern third of the state. The MECEP notes that employment opportunities in diverse industries have attracted Latino workers to small Maine towns. For example, Topsham in Sagadahoc County in the southern part of the state had a population of 9,100 in 2000. Of that population, about 113 were Latinos. The entire Latino population of Sagadahoc County was just 391. In 2000, rural Washington County was home to a Latino population of about 274. Of those, 84 lived in Milbridge, a town with an overall population of just 1,200. Latino workers were likely attracted to Topsham to work at the Naval

Air Station and to rural Washington County to work in blueberry harvests and fish-processing and wreath-making industries.

Aroostook County, in far northern Maine had seen a decline in the Latino population according to MECEP estimates. In 1953, Loring Air Force Base opened in Limestone in Aroostook County, Maine. The facility was located in the rural northern section of Maine because of its proximity to the Soviet Union—an important Cold War consideration. The facility was designed to accommodate B-36 bombers. The 1990 U.S. Census recorded 554 Latinos in Aroostook County, many living and working at the Air Force base. By 2000, the number had dropped 15 percent to 441, making Aroostook County the only county in Maine that recorded a drop in Latino population during the 1990s.

Maine also has a migrant workforce that comes each year to harvest crops. Some migrant workers enter on visas arranged by employers, while others migrate within the state or between states. It is difficult to determine how many undocumented migrates live and work in Maine. Immigrant advocates estimate that prior to 2007 about 5,000 undocumented immigrants lived in Maine. Because of Maine's geographic location, the growing season is short and migrant workers who might otherwise be attracted to agricultural work do not make the long journey.

The MECEP estimates that between 10,000 and 12,000 migrant workers are employed seasonally in Maine. Migrant workers harvest apples from late summer through fall in Androscoggin, Cumberland, Kennebec, and Oxford counties. In recent years, the numbers of seasonal workers has declined and as much as one-third of Maine crops went unharvested in 2007. Migrant workers also harvest broccoli and blueberries, work in the egg and seafood industry, and grow Christmas trees. Maine is the largest producer of wild blueberries in the United States and much of the harvest is done by migrant workers from South and Central America. It is important to note that this is a relatively new phenomenon in Maine. Prior to the late 1980s, Maine blueberries were harvested by Native Americans, primarily Micmac, Penobscot, and Passamaquoddy laborers from Maine and Canada. While Native Americans can still be found working in the blueberry industry, they have largely been replaced by Latino workers.

Seasonal workers were also employed in remote northern sections of Maine to thin and harvest trees, work done a few decades earlier by Canadian woods workers. This work remains dangerous and workers are subject to difficult conditions and low wages. In 2002, 14 workers from Honduras and Guatemala died when a van in which they were commuting swerved off a bridge on a private road into the water in the remote Allagash Wilderness Waterway. The men commuted two-and-a-half hours between where they lived and worked and were paid $84 a week to ride in the van. The men, many of whom were on H-2B visas (guest worker visas) were employed by Evergreen Forestry Services of Idaho to thin trees at $75 an acre. They were guaranteed the prevailing wage of $8.27 an hour to plant trees and $10.13 an hour to clear brush and thin woodlands. Evergreen had 340 of Maine's 5,800 H-2B workers in 2002.

Maine's Latino population is quite diverse and many are year-round residents of the state. Latino immigrants to Maine work in diverse fields and many are business owners. In 1987, U.S. Department of Commerce estimated that there were only 139 Latino-owned businesses in Maine but, by 2002, the number had increased to 731.

According to the U.S. Department of Education, the primary language spoken by English Language Learners (ELLs) in Maine in 2009 was not Spanish, as is the case in most other states, but was Somali. This makes Maine one of only seven states where Spanish is not the primary language spoken by ELLs. Over a third of Maine's 4,562 ELLs speak Somali and represent part of a new and very important immigrant group to Maine.

Maine's Somali population is still relatively new and quite small when compared to other states. The migration of Somalis to Maine is of particular importance because it represents the first large migration of Africans to the state. As one of the whitest states in the country with a tiny Muslim population, Maine seems an unlikely destination for Somali immigrants.

Between 1981 and 2004, about 5,000 refugees were settled in Maine. They came from a number of countries, including Cambodia, Vietnam, Bosnia, Sudan, Russia, Somalia, Poland, Afghanistan, Iran, and Ethiopia. Maine resettled the smallest number of refugees of any state in the union. For example, in 2007, the state of Maine resettled only 118 refugees: 94 from Somalia and the rest from Sudan, Iran, Democratic Republic of Congo, Ethiopia, Burma, and Vietnam. This number continued to fall.

The first Somalis in Maine were resettled by The Catholic Charities of Maine (CCM) Office of Refugee and Immigration Services in the Portland area. Between 1982 and 2000, CCM resettled 315 Somalis in Maine (Nadeau 2011, 53–57). Maine has a tiny refugee population when compared to other states. Refugees from Asia and Africa tend to stand out in an overwhelmingly white state like Maine, especially when they are centered primarily in a few locations. Most refugees who reside in Maine in the early twenty-first century are not initially resettled in the state but moved to Maine after initial settlement in other areas of the country.

Most of the Somali population in Maine comprises secondary migrants. About 1,000 secondary Somali migrants arrived in Portland between 2001 and 2002, many moving from the Atlanta, Georgia region. By 2008, there were about 6,000 Somalis living in Maine and over half of that population lived in the Lewiston-Auburn area. Lewiston, which is about 40 miles from Portland, is up to that point most closely associated with Franco-American immigrants who had come to work in the textile-manufacturing industry.

By the late 1990s and early 2000s, Lewiston was a depressed city with few opportunities for employment and a high vacancy rate in homes and apartments as many residents left the city to look for work. In the 1950s, Lewiston was still a prosperous city and major textile-manufacturing center of the state. For example, in the 1950s, Bates Manufacturing of Maine, a Lewiston cotton mill was one of the largest employers in the state, employing about 6,000 people. Auburn, on the other side of the river was a center of shoe-manufacturing and, like Lewiston, attracted thousands of workers. Over the past half century all of the textile mills, manufacturing plants, and shoe-manufacturing plants in the Lewiston Auburn area had closed, devastating the local economy.

Initially, Somali refugees were settled in Portland, yet a shortage of available housing forced resettlement agencies to seek other locations. In 2001, as Lewiston had a high vacancy rate, Somalis were settled in the city. This resettlement represented just a few hundred people but over the next decade thousands of ethnic Somalis and more recently Somali Bantus had relocated to the city.

The integration of Somalis into Maine has not been easy. Many native Mainers have reacted with suspicion to the newcomers who are different racially and religiously. In October 2002, Lewiston mayor Laurier T. Raymond made national headlines when he wrote an open letter to the elders of the Lewiston Somali community. Raymond discouraged Somalis from further migration to Lewiston and noted that continued Somali migration will have a negative impact on the city. He asked Lewiston's Somali community to discourage family and friends from relocating to the city.

Maine lacks a large minority population. In 2000, only 1 in 29 Maine residents was non-white or Latino (as compared to one in three in the U.S. population). Maine has had few large, sustained employment centers around the state. As a result, the thousands of African Americans who moved north and west throughout the mid-twentieth century do not come as far north as Maine. A similar trend was evident in recent years as Latino immigrants have not come to Maine in large numbers.

Those immigrants who had come to Maine were found around the state, albeit in small numbers. Maine's immigrant population had attained significant levels of education. By 2006, over a third of Maine's foreign-born population had a college degree (in contrast to about one-quarter of the native-born population). Cities such as Portland Maine have undertaken impressive English language programs as the student body diversified. In 1980, Portland began a multilingual program teaching English to about 50 students from Southeast Asia. By 2008, the program had grown to incorporate 1,500 students which represented a fifth of the Portland School district's enrolment. Adult education programs, which had begun to aid Southeast Asian refugees in the 1970s, in Portland also blossomed, increasing from an enrolment of 400 in 1995 to over 1,000 in 2007. The New England Public

Policy Center found that New England's immigrants are better educated than immigrants nationwide. In addition, they have higher income levels and lower poverty rates when compared to national populations.

Immigrants to Maine own a number of small businesses around the state. Latino immigrants owned about 731 businesses in 2002. The MECEP estimates that Latina women owned about 45 percent of those businesses. This was substantially higher than the state average of 25 percent. Latino/as operate a diverse array of professional, healthcare-related and sales-related businesses in Maine. The state's Asian immigrants also operate a number of small businesses but, according to MECEP estimates, most are in accommodations and food services. In 2007, there were 252 Asian-owned accommodation and food service businesses in Maine accounting for 22.1 percent of all Asian-owned businesses. African immigrants are also making headway in the business community in Maine although many are recent arrivals. In Portland and Lewiston, Maine Somali immigrants and other African immigrants have opened some small shops, restaurants, and other businesses. In Lewiston, vacant storefronts are now home to Somali businesses. Additionally, Somali immigrants, many of whom have now become U.S. citizens have entered politics. In 2010, Mohammed Dini, a Democratic, ran in Portland's District 119 race and Badr Sharif, a Republican, ran in District 116. Although both candidates were defeated in the primaries, this marked an important new era for Maine.

In 1960, most immigrants to the United States were still European and Canadian. Maine has a larger proportion of immigrants from these parts of the world than does the United States as a whole. In part, this is a result of geographic proximity. By 2000, 1 in 35 Maine residents was an immigrant (as compared to one in nine U.S. residents). The national demographic profile of the U.S. immigrant population had also changed by 2000 when the majority of immigrants were from Asia and Latin America. Maine had difficulty attracting immigrants and continues to lag behind other New England states and the United States in general.

NOTABLE GROUPS

Catholic Charities of Maine

CCM is Maine's only refugee resettlement group and aims at helping a primarily those who have faced war and genocide, particularly refugees from Iraq, Somalia, and the Sudan. This organization oversees case management of refugees who have come to Maine as a secondary entry point or who have just arrived. They work in cooperation with other organizations and some businesses to provide a wide range of services—from housing to employment to medical care—as well as referrals and information. Its mentoring program links individuals or families from Maine to refugees, in order to provide additional social support and resources for newly arrived families. This includes a mentoring program for young adults who want to further their education or who are seeking work. Because the organization is Catholic, it supports international human rights norms and is working with the government to screen and identify any victims of human trafficking. The organization provides information and referrals for all clients who need legal services and serves as a vital link to the Maine community.

BIBLIOGRAPHY

Allen, James P. "Franco-Americans in Maine: A Geographical Perspective." *Acadiensis* 4, no. 1 (Autumn 1974): 32–66.

"Asians in the Maine Economy: Opportunities for Growth." Maine Center for Economic Policy, Augusta, 2011.

Band, Benjamin. *Portland Jewry, Its Growth and Development*. Portland, ME: Jewish Historical Society, 1955.

Barringer, Richard, ed. *Changing Maine: 1960–2010*. Gardiner, ME: Tilbury House, 2004.

Brault, Gerard J. *The French-Canadian Heritage in New England*. Hanover, NH: University of New England Press, 1986.

Bucklin, Kate. "Somali Immigrants Eye Portland Legislative Seats." *The Forecaster*, April 20, 2010. http://www.theforecaster.net/node/54789. Accessed August 4, 2014.

Catholic Charities. Catholic Charities home page, n.d. http://www.ccmaine.org /refugee-immigration-services. Accessed February 9, 2014.

Cohen, Michael R. "Adapting Orthodoxy to American Life: Shaarey Tphiloh and the Development of Modern Orthodox Judaism in Portland, Maine, 1904–1976." *Maine History* 44 (2009): 172–95.

Conkling, Philip. *Islands in Time: A Natural and Cultural History of the Islands of the Gulf of Maine*. Camden, ME: Down East Books, 1999.

Connolly, Michael C. *They Change Their Sky: The Irish in Maine*. Orono: University of Maine Press, 2004.

Connolly, Michael C. *Seated by the Sea: The Maritime History of Portland, Maine, and Its Irish Longshoremen*. Gainesville: University Press of Florida, 2010.

Dryden-Peterson, Sarah. "Bridging Home: Building Relationships between Immigrant and Long-Time Resident Youth." *Teachers College Record* 112, no. 9 (September 2010): 2320–351.

Finnegan, William. "New in Town: The Somalis of Lewiston." *New Yorker*, December 11, 2006, 46–58.

Freidenreich, David M. "The Jews of Maine." Maine History Online. *Maine Memory Network*. 2010. http://www.mainememory.net/sitebuilder/site/1888/page/3104/display? use_mmn=. Accessed March 18, 2014.

"The Growing Latin American Influence, Opportunities for Maine's Economy." Maine Center for Economic Policy, Augusta, 2009.

Huisman, Kimberly A., Mazie Hough, Kristin M. Langellier, and Carol Nordstrom Toner, eds. *Somalis in Maine: Crossing Cultural Currents*. Berkeley, CA: North Atlantic Books, 2011.

Jaster, Robert S. *Russian Voices on the Kennebec: The Story of Maine's Unlikely Colony.* Orono: University of Maine Press, 1999.

Judd, Richard W., Edwin A. Churchill, and Joel W. Eastman, eds. *Maine: The Pine Tree State from Prehistory to the Present.* Orono: University of Maine Press, 1995.

Libby, Gary. "Chinese in Maine." Maine History Online. *Maine Memory Network.* 2010. http://www.mainememory.net/sitebuilder/site/165/page/424/display?use_mmn=. Accessed March 18, 2014.

Madore, Nelson, and Barry Rodrigue, eds. *Voyages: A Maine Franco-American Reader.* Gardiner, ME: Tilbury House, 2007.

"Maine H-2B Tragedy." *Rural Migration News* 8, no.4 (October 2002). http://migration.ucdavis.edu/rmn/more.php?id=619_0_3_0. Accessed March 18, 2014.

Miller, Rachel. "Twenty Nationalities, But All American." Maine History Online. *Maine Memory Network.* 2010. http://www.mainememory.net/sitebuilder/site/1718/slideshow/864/display?use_mmn=&format=slideshow&prev_object_id=2729&prev_object=page&slide_num=1&amp=&amp=. Accessed March 18, 2014.

"Multicultural Resources Introduction to Immigration." Office Multicultural Affairs, Office of the Maine Department of Health and Human Services. 2010. http://www.maine.gov/dhhs/oma/ MulticulturalResource/intro.html. Accessed March 18, 2014.

Mundy, James H. *Hard Times, Hard Men: Maine and the Irish, 1830–1860.* Scarborough, ME: Harp Publishing, 1990.

Nadeau, Phil. "A Work in Progress: Lewiston Responds to the Rapid Migration of Somali Refugees." In Kimberly A. Huisman, Mazie Hough, Kristin M. Langellier, and Carol Nordstrom Toner, eds. *Somalis in Maine: Crossing Cultural Currents.* Berkeley, CA: North Atlantic Books, 2011, pp. 53–72.

Owens, Antoniya. *A Portrait of New England's Immigrants.* New England Public Policy Center, Research Report 08–2. November 2008. http://www.bos.frb.org/economic/neppc/research reports/2008/rr0802.pdf. Accessed March 18, 2014.

Parenteau, Bill. "Bonded Labor: Canadian Woods Workers in the Maine Pulpwood Industry, 1940–55." *Forest & Conservation History* 37, no. 3 (July 1993): 108–19.

Peck, Abraham J., and Jean M. Peck. *Images of America: Maine's Jewish Heritage.* Charleston, SC: Arcadia Publishing, 2007.

"Peopling Maine." Maine History Online. *Maine Memory Network.* 2010. http://www.mainememory.net/sitebuilder/site/879/page/1290/print?popup=1. Accessed March 18, 2014.

Ploch, Louis A. *Immigration to Maine 1975–1983.* Bulletin 820. Orono: Maine Agricultural Experiment Station University of Maine, 1988.

Raymond, Laurier T. Jr. "Somalis in Lewiston." *Portland Press Herald,* October 1, 2002. http://www.immigrationshumancost.org/text/raymond.html. Accessed August 4, 2014.

Richard, Mark Paul. "From Franco-American to American: The Case of Sainte-Famille, An Assimilating Parish of Lewiston, Maine." *Histoire Sociale: Social History* 31, no. 61 (1998): 71–93.

Richard, Mark Paul. "'This Is Not a Catholic Nation': The Ku Klux Klan Confronts Franco-Americans in Maine." *The New England Quarterly* 82, no.2 (June 2009): 285–303.

Sandweiss, Maria D. "Five Modules on Immigration for Third-Year College Level and AP Spanish Classes: A Model for Other Languages and Multiculturalism." MA Thesis, University of Maine, 2010.

See, Scott. *The History of Canada*. Westport, CT: Greenwood Press, 2001.

Sherwood, Richard, and Destiny-Deirdre Mageean. "Demography as Destiny." In Richard Barringer, ed. *Changing Maine*. Gardiner, ME: Tillbury House Press, 2004.

"Somali, Sudanese and Cambodian Refugee Parents' Perspectives." *New Americans Child Care Choices of Parents of English Language Learners*. Edmund S. Muskie School of Public Service, University of Southern Maine. http://muskie.usm.maine.edu /newamericans/assets/maine.pdf. Accessed March 18, 2014.

Stewart, Alice R. "The Franco-Americans of Maine: A Historiographical Essay." *Maine Historical Society Quarterly* 26, no. 3 (1987): 160–79.

Tierney, James A. *Diversity in Maine: An Opportunity*. Distinguished Honors Graduate Lecture, University of Maine, April 22, 2002. http://www.umehon.maine.edu /documents/tierney.htm. Accessed March 18, 2014.

"Top Languages Spoken by English Language Learners Nationally and by State." *ELL Information Center Fact Sheet Series*. Migration Policy Institute, National Center on Immigrant Integration Policy, no.3. 2010. http://www.migrationinformation.org/ellinfo /FactSheet _ELL3.pdf. Accessed March 18, 2014.

Ueda, Reed. *Postwar Immigrant America: A Social History*. Boston: Bedford/St. Martin's, 1994.

Voorst van Beest, Jan, Pieter van Pat Nyhan, and Reza Jalali. *New Mainers Portraits of Our Immigrant Neighbors*. Gardiner ME: Tilbury House, 2009.

Waldron, Florencemae. "The Battle over Female (In)Dependence: Women in New England Quebecois Migrant Communities, 1870–1930." *Frontiers: A Journal of Women Studies* 26, no. 2 (2005): 158–205.

"Woodlawn Cemetery-Muslim Burial Ground." *The Pluralism Project at Harvard University*. 2012. http://www.pluralism.org/profiles/view/73366. Accessed March 14, 2014.

20
MARYLAND

Catherine Morrisey-Ribeiro

CHRONOLOGY

1200	Permanent Native American villages are established in the Maryland area.
1498	John Cabot sails along the Eastern Shore off present-day Worcester County.
1634/35 (February 26)	The first general assembly (law-making assembly of freemen) meets at St. Mary's City.
1649	The Maryland Act of Toleration is passed, allowing freedom of conscience for all Christians.
1655 (March 25)	Puritans from Virginia defeat Governor William Stone's forces at the Battle of the Severn.
1663	Augustine Herrman becomes the first naturalized citizen of Maryland.
1664	Slavery is sanctioned by law; slaves are to serve for life.
1670	Voting is restricted by the governor to planters with a 50-acre freehold or property worth 40 pounds; holding office is restricted to owners of 1,000 acres.
1698	The Royal African Company's monopoly of the slave trade is abolished by the Parliament; slave imports markedly increase.
1727 (September)	The *Maryland Gazette*, first newspaper in the Chesapeake area, is published by William Parks at Annapolis (until 1734).
1744 (June 30)	Native American chiefs of the Six Nations relinquish by treaty all claims to land in the colony. The assembly purchases the last Indian land claims in Maryland.
1747	A tobacco inspection law enables Maryland to control quality of exports.

1754	Fort Cumberland is constructed by militiamen.
1755	General Edward Braddock leads an expedition through Maryland to the West. French and American Indians defeat Braddock's forces near Fort Duquesne. American Indians attack Western settlers.
1774 (June 22)	The First Provincial Convention (an extralegal body) meets at Annapolis and sends delegates to the First Continental Congress.
1776 (July 6)	Two days after the Declaration of Independence, the Maryland Convention declares independence from Great Britain.
1776 (August 14–November 11)	The meeting of the Maryland Constitutional Convention is held.
1776 (November 3)	The Declaration of Rights (Maryland's Bill of Rights) is adopted by the Ninth Provincial Convention. The Church of England is disestablished.
1776 (November 8)	The First State Constitution is adopted by the Ninth Provincial Convention.
1777 (February 5)	The first general assembly is elected under the State Constitution of 1776 and meets at Annapolis.
1783	The German Society of Maryland is established to help German immigrants to the state.
1788 (April 28)	The Maryland Convention ratifies the U.S. Constitution, making Maryland the seventh state to do so.
1789 (December 19)	Maryland ratifies the federal Bill of Rights.
1793	Refugees from the Haitian slave uprising arrive in Baltimore. Residents help these refugees.
1794	The first of many yellow fever epidemics strikes Baltimore.
1796	Maryland law forbids the importation of slaves for sale and permits voluntary slave emancipation.
1802	Property qualifications for voting are removed by constitutional amendment in local and state elections (granting suffrage to adult white males).
1803	Irish immigrants are assisted by the newly established Ancient Order of Hibernians.
1807 (December 18)	The University of Maryland is chartered at Baltimore as the College of Medicine of Maryland.
1810	Adult white male suffrage is extended by constitutional amendment to federal elections; property qualifications are ended in voting for electors for president, vice president, and congressmen.
1821	Significant number of foreigners arrive to the state. From 1821 to 1914, Baltimore is one of the top three ports of entry for immigrants in the country.
1830	Baltimore establishes a fixed trade with Liverpool and Bremen.
1833 (November)	The first settlers sail for Cape Palmas, Liberia.
1860	The Irish-born population of Baltimore City peaks at 15,536 of 212,418.

1860(November)	Maryland voters give John C. Breckinridge (Southern rights Democrat) 42,482 votes; John Bell (Constitutional Union) 41,760 votes; Stephen A. Douglas (popular sovereignty Democrat) 5,966 votes; and Abraham Lincoln (Republican) 2,294 votes in the presidential election.
1864 (November 1)	Maryland slaves are emancipated by the State Constitution of 1864.
1867	The Baltimore and Ohio (B&O) Railroad and the North German Lloyd Company agree to build an immigration port and facilitate European immigration. The port opens in 1868.
1882	Anti-immigration sentiment becomes stronger at state and national levels. Concerns about mental hygiene and ideology emerge.
1890	The German-born population of Baltimore City peaks at 41,930 of 365,863.
1893	The Women's College of Frederick is founded; it later becomes Hood College.
1894	The first child labor law is passed.
1902	Regulations for miners' work conditions are enacted. Child labor under age 12 is forbidden by law and a workmen's compensation law is enacted (but later overturned in courts); it is the first such law in the United States.
1904	An Immigrant House is built to house immigrants and sailors; it is run by the German Evangelical United Church of Christ.
1907	This is a peak year of immigration to the nation and to Maryland (Baltimore, in particular).
1910	The workmen's compensation law is redrafted and enacted.
1910	Pure food and drug laws and anti-prostitution measures are enacted.
1910	The Russian-born population of Baltimore (including Eastern European) peaks at 24,798 of 558,485.
1913	The Baltimore Chapter of the National Association for the Advancement of Colored People (NAACP) is formed; it is now the second oldest in country.
1914	Baltimore terminates its role as an immigration port with the outbreak of World War I.
1920 (November 2)	Women vote for the first time in Maryland.
1924	With increasingly restrictive immigration through 1965, immigrant arrivals to the state decrease.
1930	The Italian-born population of Baltimore peaks at 9,022 of 804,874.
1938 (June)	The National Institutes of Health is established in Bethesda.
1941 (December 7)	The USS *Maryland* is among naval ships attacked at Pearl Harbor in Hawai'i.
1949	The Department of Mental Hygiene is established for mentally ill residents.

1950	A lawsuit opens the University of Maryland School of Nursing to blacks.
1954	Public housing in Baltimore is integrated.
1954	The first black is elected to Maryland House of Delegates, from Baltimore.
1954	The Baltimore-Washington Expressway is opened.
1954 (May)	Thurgood Marshall and the NAACP win the *Brown v. Board of Education* decision.
1968	Marshall W. Nirenberg, National Institutes of Health scientist, wins a Nobel Prize.
1968 (April)	Riots in Baltimore and Washington, DC, follow the assassination of Dr. Martin Luther King Jr., in Memphis.
1969 (October 5)	Maryland Public Television is first broadcasted.
1972	The first general election is held in Maryland following the lowering of the voting age to 18.
1974	Both houses of the general assembly are elected, for first time, on the basis of equal representation by population.
1998 (October 15–19)	The Wye Summit is held. Middle East peace talks between Israel and the Palestine Liberation Organization are held at the Aspen Institute's Wye River Conference Centers, Queen Anne's County. The Wye River Memorandum, resulting from the talks, is signed in Washington, DC, on October 23, 1998.
2009	*Padilla v. Commonwealth of Kentucky* is decided by the Supreme Court and influences Maryland state immigration cases.
2011	The Maryland Development, Relief, and Education for Alien Minors (DREAM) Act is passed.

HISTORICAL OVERVIEW

Similar to the other 13 original colonies that came to form the current United States, Maryland's territories were settled by American Indian tribes centuries before English settlers arrived. When John Cabot arrived in 1498 with other English explorers, new trends in immigration began to emerge in the territories that now make up Maryland. These early immigration trends include European settlers arriving in the New World and African slaves trafficked out of Western African for forced labor.

Maryland was not exempt from the slave trade that took place during these times. European colonies in Africa exported slaves to the new lands in record numbers. Maryland received a number of slaves and was even known as a slave state until after the Civil War. However, because of its proximity to other Northern states and more democratic ideas, Maryland always maintained a less-rigid stance on slavery than its southern counterparts. Many slaves had been freed for 20 years prior to the Civil War being declared in the 1860s.

Europeans began settling along the East Coast in large numbers in 1642, each laying claim to the plots of land before them. English and French citizens were primarily among the populations to explore the areas around current-day Maryland. These Puritans landed in an area of Maryland that was originally called Providence. After localized religious battles took place between Catholics and Anglicans in the region, the territory quickly saw disagreement and war amongst the new settlers. Eventually, the Catholic settlers gained control of the land and renamed the state after their holy figure, Mary. Mary's Land was soon shortened and known as Maryland.

Maryland's immigration is defined by the events that occurred very early in its formation until the 1940s and beyond. The voluntary migration of European colonists (primarily French, Irish, and English) and the forced migration of slaves out of West Africa show the ways in which immigration impacted the landscape, politically, ethnically, racially, socially, and economically. German immigrants began arriving in the early 1700s and settled throughout the area, but mostly in Baltimore. By the pre-Civil War period, many of the German migrants and their descendants opposed slavery. German Jews arrived later in the nineteenth century, establishing several cultural institutions. The 1840s and 1850s were a key period of Irish immigration, particularly to Baltimore as British repression and the Irish Potato Famine drove survivors out of their country. Many of the new arrivals worked for the B&O Railroad (Maryland State Archives 2001–2005). Others worked in domestic service, as miners, and as small farmers. Most lived in overcrowded conditions and were paid very little. Up to 1890, German and Irish immigrants were the two predominant foreign groups settling in the state.

During this time period, the Know-Nothing Movement arose, triggered by the nativist American political factions and was characterized by political xenophobia, anti-Catholic sentiment, and occasional instances of violence against the groups the nativists targeted. This group played on popular fears that German and Irish Catholic immigrants—who were viewed as backward—were going to take over the country and these claims were elaborated by yellow press journalism. Mainly active from 1854 to 1856, the Know-Nothing group identified themselves as the American party and strove to stop immigration and naturalization, though its efforts met with little success. Membership of the party was primarily represented by Protestant males of British American lineage. There were few prominent leaders, but they managed to fragment the traditional political party lines and created additional fears surrounding immigrants in Maryland. The group was also responsible for violence and uprisings that happened at voting locations during local elections. In Baltimore, the Know-Nothings caused violence and ballot-rigging specifically, which created fears of additional backlash for three election cycles. Despite being poorly organized, the Know-Nothing candidate Thomas Swann was successfully elected as mayor of Baltimore in 1856 amid violence and a heavily disputed ballot. In 1857, fearing similar violence at the upcoming elections, Governor Thomas W. Ligon ordered the First Light Division, Maryland Volunteers to readiness. However, Mayor Thomas Swann successfully argued for a compromise measure involving special police forces to prevent disorder, and the governor's efforts were stood down. This time, although there was less violence than in 1856, the results of the vote were again compromised, and Swann was reelected in a heavily disputed ballot. By 1860, the Know-Nothing Party was less popular and the Republican Party (the party of Abraham Lincoln) was able to reclaim a number of seats in local and federal governments.

After 1890, the primary migrant-sending countries changed and greater numbers of Eastern Europeans (particularly Jewish immigrants), Poles, Italians, and Greeks either arrived directly or used Maryland as a secondary site of migration, after arriving in other states first. Baltimore, in particular, reflected these new groups as ethnic neighborhoods developed.

The end of the nineteenth century was a period in which there were still significant waves of immigration, but other dynamics were set in motion that would lead to much more restrictive controls. First, the country experienced a severe economic recession at the end of the 1800s. Second, now discredited "scientific" findings began to develop into eugenic racism and groups like the Chinese and later, Eastern Europeans, were targeted as racially inferior despite their long-standing presence in the country and their significant contributions to building the infrastructure of the country. These eugenic concerns led to some of the first federal policies at the turn of the century. Third, anti-communist sentiment was broadly expressed against immigrants who tried to unionize and others from countries viewed as socialist or communist. The combination of these factors led not merely to more restrictive controls but to highly eugenic (racist) federal controls, culminating in prewar country quotas. As a result, immigration to the country and this state, decreased. In the mid-1930s, the United States continued its policy of isolationism. As fascism arose in Spain, Germany, and Italy, however, the United States government became weary of Europe's overall intent and began to argue the benefits of increased military powers to aid France and England.

With this military expansionism came the responsibility to assist nations falling to extreme leaders in Europe and elsewhere around the globe. Fighting during World War II was not just reserved for European lands, but it also took place in Asia, South America, and Africa as a result of European colonialism. As the United States committed itself to England and France during the war, it also committed itself to postwar reconstruction around the globe, which brought some immigrants from diverse communities and backgrounds despite strict controls.

The 1950s were largely characterized by the United States' fears of communism and Soviet takeover; this is known as the second Red Scare. In 1952, the

Immigration and Nationality Act, also known as the McCarran–Walter Act, maintained the eugenic quotas but justified this continuation for reasons related to the Cold War. This legislation accomplished the task of housing a number of immigration laws within one body of text. This legislation also outlined the following immigration practices: it changed the language of certain racial restrictions found in earlier immigration statutes; it retained a quota system for nationalities and regions; and eventually, the act established a preference system that determined which ethnic groups were politically desirable immigrants for the United States, placing greater importance on labor qualifications. Additionally, the act formally identified three types of immigrants: immigrants with special skills or relatives of U.S. citizens who were exempt from quotas and who would be admitted without restrictions; average immigrants whose numbers were not supposed to exceed 270,000 per year; and refugees, or individuals seeking asylum in the United States for a number of internationally recognized reasons (most importantly for the United States, political persecution by communist or fascist states).

Because threats of the Cold War were perceived as significant to American foreign policy at the time, the act also allowed the government to deport immigrants or denationalize citizens engaged in uncertain or questionable acts, and allowed the government to ban allegedly high-risk individuals from reentering the country. President Truman vetoed the measure and called it un-American (because it maintained its eugenic basis), but Congress proceeded to pass the measure with a two-thirds majority vote, and it became law in late 1952.

Even with these restrictive new policies in effect, immigrants from Latin American and Asia continued to arrive in Maryland for a new life. While these families and individuals hardly had an easy life, much of Maryland's political efforts of the 1960s and 1970s were wrapped up in outcomes of the forced migration of Africans two centuries earlier. The Civil Rights Movement characterized efforts of Maryland's politicians, educational establishments, police protocols, churches, and virtually every other facet of life at the time. While the Chicano Rights Movement did make its way through parts of Maryland, its Latino immigrants were far less mobilized and coordinated than members of the black Civil Rights Movements of the time.

Once President John Kennedy placed troops in Vietnam in 1963, American's occupation of the Asian country only grew for the next 15 years. President Lyndon Johnson took office in 1963 after Kennedy's assassination and intensified the fighting, leading to significant refugee flows, particularly of Vietnamese refugees from both the southern and northern regions of the country. Families from Cambodia, Laos, and Thailand also filed for refugee status as fighting spilled over international borders in Southeast Asia. Maryland experienced an increased number of Asian immigrants as a result of these conflicts during the war and immediately after the United States withdrew troops in 1975. Cambodian refugees came to the state in higher numbers as the violent Khmer Rouge regime took power and killed nearly 2 million Cambodians in several months.

The state's population doubled between 1940 and 1970. It also increased an estimated 7.5 percent between 1970 and 1980. The expansion of the federal government and exodus of people from Washington, DC, to surrounding suburbs contributed to the rapid growth seen in Maryland by 1980, with 4,216,446 residents. There was an increase of 13.4 percent between 1980 and 1990 alone, with 4,781,468 people. Almost all the growth since World War II has occurred in the four suburban counties around Washington, DC, and Baltimore. Metropolitan Baltimore, embracing Carroll, Howard, Hartford, Anne Arundel, and Baltimore counties, expanded from 2,244,700 to 2,491,254 between 1984 and 2000.

Maryland continues its history of hosting individuals and families from around the world through several programs. Universities are more willing and are able to accept international students, and Maryland has been in the top 20 states for the number of international students hosted each year (roughly 8.5 percent of the overall college populations) since 1995. Maryland also has a high number of immigrants with high-educational attainment, roughly 43 percent in 2002. In many professions, educated immigrants actually outnumber native Marylanders because they hold higher degrees, including in the fields of medicine and science.

Immigrant populations in Maryland now represent every major geographical region of the world, including Africa, the Middle East, Asia, Europe, and South America. Twelve percent of Maryland's overall state population is born outside of the United States, and accounts for half of the state's population growth from 2000 to 2006 because of the growing economic developments. Despite representing 12 percent of the overall state's growth, Maryland immigrants make up 15 percent of the hard labor market, suggesting that immigrants are more likely to take up blue collar, labor-intensive work. It should be noted that while Maryland sees immigrants from a diverse background of cultures and communities, most immigrants come from Central and South America, the Caribbean, and Asia. Currently, El Salvador makes up 10 percent of the state's overall legal immigrant population.

Undocumented residents are also reflected in these statistics, though the precise numbers cannot be determined. The state of Maryland estimated, in 2009, that roughly 330,000 of its overall immigrant population remained undocumented, placing the state at the 10th-highest of all states in the country for undocumented migrants. The peak of undocumented immigrants came in 2007 and has decreased steadily each year, most likely due to the shrinking economy and harsher immigration policies at the federal level.

The issue is complicated further when looking at split-residency families, or families with at least one immigrant parent (mixed-status families), who may have children born in the United States, and who are therefore legal citizens, while parents and extended family do not have legal documentation. The number of children born to immigrant parents also increased 110 percent between 1990 and 2000. Immigrant children are estimated to represent 19 percent of the overall child population in Maryland, though it is unknown how many of these children come from mixed-status households.

Because immigrants are so diverse in their standings in Maryland—from residency status to educational attainment to number of children—income ranges are very wide among immigrant groups. According to some, the national origins of immigrants also contribute to income attainment in Maryland. The state published in 2009 that more than two-third of immigrants from Europe and Asia together earned $75,000 or more a year, a figure that aligns with the state's median income for American-born residents. The state admitted that immigrants from Africa, Central and South America are considerably less likely to reach high levels of educational attainment, and therefore make considerably less than other immigrant populations.

Median household income in Maryland for 2006–2008 totaled $70,300 for the native-born population and $67,700 for the foreign-born population. Naturalized citizens had a median household income of $78,900; whereas, noncitizens had a median household income of $58,100. For immigrants who entered the United States since 2000, the median household income totaled only $52,700 or approximately one-fourth less than the amount for native-born Marylanders.

The unemployment rate for foreign-born residents in Maryland for 2006–2008 was slightly lower than the rate for native-born residents due primarily to the high educational and skill levels of naturalized citizens. Naturalized citizens in Maryland had a 2.4 percent unemployment rate in 2006–2008 compared to a 3.7 percent unemployment rate for native-born residents. In Anne Arundel and Baltimore counties, the unemployment rate in 2006–2008 for naturalized citizens was below 2 percent. For recently arrived immigrants (those arriving in the United States since 2000), the unemployment rate was significantly higher at 5.3 percent.

While the statewide educational attainment levels for the foreign-born population are relatively high, wide disparities exist within several Maryland counties between the native- and foreign-born populations, particularly for populations without a high-school diploma or GED. The disparities are most pronounced in Montgomery and Prince George's counties. In Montgomery County, only 3.8 percent of the native-born population has not graduated from high school compared to 17.5 percent of the foreign-born population. Among the county's foreign-born population, 11.6 percent of naturalized citizens and 23.6 percent of noncitizens have not graduated from high school. Furthermore, 62.9 percent of the native-born population in Montgomery County has a bachelor's degree or higher compared to only 45.6 percent of the foreign-born population. Among the county's foreign-born population, 50.6 percent of naturalized citizens and 40.2 percent of noncitizens have at least a bachelor's degree.

Ricky Campos, 23 (left), and Katye Hernandez, 22 (second from left), both undocumented immigrants originally from El Salvador who live in Silver Spring, Maryland, hold signs saying "Thank You President Obama," along with others from the group Casa de Maryland during a rally outside the White House in Washington, D.C., on June 15, 2012. The rally supported the president's announcement that the U.S. government will stop deporting and begin granting work permits to younger undocumented immigrants who came to the United States as children and have since led law-abiding lives. (AP Photo/ Jacquelyn Martin)

In Prince George's County, 40.1 percent of noncitizens have not graduated from high school, compared to 8.9 percent of the native-born population. Naturalized citizens in Baltimore City and Anne Arundel, Baltimore, and Prince George's counties tend to have higher-educational levels than the native-born populations.

TOPICAL ESSAYS

Maryland DREAM Act

The controversial act was introduced in 2011 as state legislators reviewed a bill that would give some undocumented residents the right to in-state tuition rates at all public universities and colleges. The bill was passed by both the state House and Senate, and was signed into law by Democratic governor Martin O'Malley. Opposition created such dramatic backlash that a petition was started to move the measure to the voters' ballot in 2012. Petitioners were able to gather over 100,000 signatures to move the bill away from represented officials and toward the individual voter. Because the bill was signed into law by the governor O'Malley, questions remained regarding the repeal process of bills. The bill would reduce tuition fees for undocumented students from the out-of-state rate of $24,831 to the in-state rate of $8,416. Currently, federal immigration policy does not allow schools to question the immigration status of students. Despite the controversy, this act has now "boosted" state graduation rates, placing the state above national averages.

Padilla v. Commonwealth of Kentucky (2009)

This court case originated in Kentucky but as it was reviewed by the Supreme Court, this decision now affects how all lawyers advise foreign-resident clients when faced with criminal charges. This case had a profound impact on the state of Maryland. The Supreme Court decided that criminal defense attorneys must advise noncitizen clients about the deportation risks of a guilty plea. The case extended the Supreme Court's prior decisions in criminal defendants' Sixth Amendment right to counsel context. The duties of the counsel recognized in *Padilla* were broad and included where the law is unambiguous, the provision that attorneys must advise their criminal clients that deportation "will" result from a conviction. Second, where the immigration consequences of a conviction were unclear or uncertain, attorneys must advise that deportation "may" result. Finally, attorneys must give their clients some advice about deportation-counsel cannot remain silent about immigration. The decisions of this court case inspired the work completed by students and faculty affiliated with the University of Maryland's Francis King Carey School of Law's Immigration Clinic. This clinic allows students to gain international and immigration law experience by assisting the legal needs of allegedly undocumented individuals and families. The clinic is also the home of the Immigration Consequences of Maryland Convictions Project. The project strives to educate and train criminal defense lawyers about the severe immigration consequences of criminal convictions under Maryland criminal law. The project utilizes the Maryland Immigration Consequences of Convictions chart, which analyzes the likeliness of certain outcomes depending on convictions and Maryland state laws.

U.S. Refugee Act of 1980

This federal law attempted to synthesize the growing needs for immigration reform while noting that many international populations have extensive needs to migrate to the United States. Given Maryland's diverse immigrant population, it has obviously had considerable impact on the state's overall population demographics, social policies, educational structures, and funding decisions. The law

Hundreds of immigrants line up to get help with documents and filing for the Deferred Action for Childhood Arrivals applications at Casa de Maryland in Langley Park, Maryland, on August 15, 2012. Under DACA, they can become legal residents and pursue post-secondary education. (AP Photo/Jose Luis Magana).

was created to provide a permanent and systematic procedure for the admission to the United States of refugees of special humanitarian concern and to provide more consistent provisions for the effective resettlement and absorption of those refugees who are admitted. The act was passed on March 3, 1980, was signed by President Jimmy Carter on March 17, 1980, and became effective on April 1, 1980. This was the first comprehensive amendment of U.S. general immigration laws since 1965, designed to acknowledge the realities of modern refugee situations establishing precise national policy and flexible mechanisms to meet the always changing needs of the world's populations.

NOTABLE GROUPS

MARYLAND IMMIGRATION RIGHTS COALITION

The Maryland Immigration Rights Coalition (MIRC) is a nonprofit organization providing legal support for immigrants, refugees, and lawyers helping this clientele. This organization was established in 2008 to provide legal support for lawyers working pro bono with immigration and refugee clients, to advocate on behalf of immigrants and to provide education on this subject. They work to help with young immigrants who are eligible for Deferred Action for Childhood Arrivals and want their record expunged and work closely with the University of Maryland's School of Law to provide pro bono training, advising immigration lawyers about collateral consequences of criminal procedures, and has set up (within the office of the Maryland Office of the Public Defender) a Deportation Defense Project. Finally, this group supports would-be DREAMers, children who want to attend public universities as residents of the state.

BIBLIOGRAPHY

Baltimore Immigration Memorial (BIM) Foundation. BIM Foundation webpage, n.d. http://www.immigrationbaltimore.org/quick_facts.htm. Accessed February 9, 2014.

Brugger, Robert. "From Province to Colony (1634–1689)." In *Maryland: A Middle Temperament*. Baltimore: The Johns Hopkins University Press in association with the Maryland Historical Society, 1988.

Clemens, Mark. "Frederick Douglass." *Cobblestone* 31, no. 1 (2010): 46.

"Dashing the Dream Act." *The Washington Post*, 2011, A12.

Dauphine, Durand de. *A Huguenot Exile in Virginia; or Voyages of a Frenchman exiled for his Religion with a Description of Virginia and Maryland* (1687). New York: The Press of the Pioneers, Inc., 1934.

Everstine, Carl N. "Maryland's Toleration Act: An Appraisal." *Maryland Historical Magazine* 79, no. 2 (Summer 1984): 99–116.

Fausz, J. Frederick. *By Warre upon Our Enemies and Kinde Usage of Our Friends: The Secular Context of Religious Toleration in Maryland, 1620–1660*. Published privately by the author, 1983.

Kohn, Margaret. "Frederick Douglass's Master-Slave Dialectic." *The Journal of Politics* 67, no. 2: 497–514.

Krug, Elisabeth. *Thurgood Marshall: Champion of Civil Rights*. New York: Fawcett Columbine, 1993.

Krugler, John D. "With Promise of Liberty in Religion: The Catholic Lords Baltimore and Toleration in Seventeenth-Century Maryland, 1634–1692." *Maryland Historical Magazine* 79, no. 1 (Spring 1984): 21–43.

Maryland Immigration Rights Coalition (MIRC). MIRC website, n.d. http://marylandimmigrantrightscoalition.org/. Accessed February 9, 2014.

Maryland State Archives. "Irish Immigrants in Baltimore." Teaching American History in Maryland website. Maryland State Archives, 2001–2005. http://teaching.msa.maryland.gov/000001/000000/000131/html/t131.html. Accessed February 9, 2014.

O'Neill, Peter. "Frederick Douglass and the Irish." *Foilsiú* 5, no. 1 (2006): 57.

Pearson v. Murray. Minnesota Law Review 20 (1935): 673.

Pearson v. Murray. Yale Law Journal 45, no. 7 (1936): 1296.

"Refugee Act of 1980: An Act to Amend the Immigration and Nationality Act to Revise the Procedures for the Admission of Refugees." no. 96–212. Washington, 1980.

Ryan-Kessler, Michael. "A Complex Relationship: Lincoln and Frederick Douglass." *OAH Magazine of History* 21, no. 4 (2007): 42–48.

Schmeckebier, Laurence F. *History of the Know Nothing Party in Maryland*. New York: Johnson Reprint Corp., 1973.

Simmonds, Yussuf J. "Frederick Douglass," *Sentinel*, 2007, A12.

Simmonds, Yussuf J. "Thurgood Marshall." *Sentinel*, 2007, A12.

Swann, Thomas. "Rights of American Citizenship-Ireland and the Irish." Speeches of Hon. Thomas Swann, of Maryland, in the House of Representatives, February 2 and 15, 1870.

Wood, P. "O'Malley Signs 'DREAM Act' Measure: Immigrant Tuition Bill Becomes Law—for Now." *The Capital*, Annapolis, 2011, A.1.

Wood, Skip. "Daybreak Daily: Dream Act Boosts Maryland Graduation Rate." ABC 7 (TV) website, January 29, 2014. http://www.wjla.com/articles/2014/01/daybreak-daily-dream-act-boosts-maryland-graduation-rate-99697.html. Accessed February 14, 2014.

Zwerdling, Daniel. "Thurgood Marshall." NPR website. Weekend: All Things Considered, October 31, 1998. http://www.highbeam.com/doc/1P1–28937935.html. Accessed March 18, 2014.

21

MASSACHUSETTS

Julia Skinner

CHRONOLOGY

1620	Immigration to New England begins.
1628–1629	Charles I sends letters to the Massachusetts Bay Company regarding the colony and states that the company is permitted to transport British subjects (and foreign subjects loyal to the British Crown) to New England.
1629–1640	The Great Migration causes Massachusetts's population to skyrocket.
1640s and 1650s	Colonial government passes laws against Quakers and Jesuits.
1645	Massachusetts passes the first law against "public charges" in an attempt to keep impoverished and/or disabled persons, who might come to rely on public assistance from settling in the colony.
1661	Jacques Pepin submits a petition asking permission for himself and other French Protestants to settle in the area. The magistrates turn him down but allow Pepin to remain in the colony as long as he does not violate trade laws.
1691	William and Mary decree religious tolerance for all groups in the colonies except Catholics.
1700	The colonial government passes a law to exclude disabled passengers from immigrating by ship unless they, or the ship captain, could provide a deposit.
1747	Shakerism, later an American Utopian movement, is founded in England by a group of dissenting Quakers.
1774 (May 19)	Mother Ann and her Shaker followers board a ship in England and immigrate to the United States.

1800	Irish immigrants build their first Roman Catholic Church in Boston.
1809	The Massachusetts legislature passes a law exempting pacifist Shaker and Quaker church members from military service, provided they each pay a $6 fine.
1810	Samuel Slater builds 61 of his water-powered textile mills throughout Massachusetts and the Northeast by this year.
1820–1845	Immigration from England and Ireland increases steadily.
1820	Customs officials in the state and nationwide begin keeping records of new immigrants, including age, gender, and country of origin.
1821	Francis Cabot Lowell builds a textile factory based on his new industrial model in the town of East Chelmsford.
1848 (January)	Massachusetts officials begin recording the names of immigrants as they arrive in the port by ship. These names are recorded in passenger manifests, which can still be found in the state archives.
1859 (February)	Irish women lead a strike in Lowell, cementing their place in the labor leadership of Massachusetts.
1886 (April)	Pemberton Mills in Lawrence catches fire, the second disaster at the factory in 25 years.
1891 (July)	Federal authorities take over recordkeeping for passenger manifests.
1894	The Immigrant Restriction League is founded by a group of Harvard graduates.
1905	A report from the Massachusetts State Board of Health indicates that the textile industry employs more Massachusetts residents than any other.
1912	About 25,000 textile laborers, many of them immigrant women, go on strike in what becomes known as the "Bread and Roses Affair" in Lawrence.
1917	The Massachusetts Bureau of Education is founded.
1919 (February)	Another strike takes place in Lawrence textile mills after workers walk out in protest of pay cuts agreed to by union representatives and employers.
1920s	Immigrants in the state ally themselves with the Democratic Party and influence politics through their votes and through campaigning for Democratic candidates such as Al Smith.
1980s	Debates take place over the value of bilingual education. Rosalie Porter, a Massachusetts teacher, is an outspoken opponent of the model during this time.
2010 (May)	The Massachusetts legislature passes strict measures to discourage undocumented immigration to the state.
2011 (June 6)	Governor Deval Patrick announces that he will not participate in the Department of Homeland Security's (DHS) Secure Communities Program.
2012 (May)	The Obama administration announces that Secure Communities Program would be activated in Massachusetts despite the state's 2011 decision not to participate in the program.

2013 (May)   The foreign-born comprise roughly one-seventh of the state's total population in 2013, with more than half of these immigrants being naturalized U.S. citizens eligible to vote.

HISTORICAL OVERVIEW

Immigration to Massachusetts led to some of the earliest white settlement in U.S. history, with immigration to New England beginning in 1620. When Charles I of England wrote his 1629 letters patents to the Massachusetts Bay Company, he indicated that the prime objectives of the new colony were the progress of religion, good order, and the conversion of Native Americans to Christianity. The Massachusetts Bay Company, in a 1628 Charter, was permitted to transport British subjects to New England. Transport companies during this time were also allowed to bring non-British passengers, so long as they swore allegiance to the British Crown.

Immigration to the new colony was sparse until the period from 1629 to 1640, when Charles I sought to rule without Parliament. This period, known as the Great Migration, saw over 21,000 new immigrants come to New England as a result of economic oppression and religious persecution. The wave of immigration ended in 1640 after Charles I was forced to reinstate Parliament and the king's oppression of his subjects was mitigated.

The Puritans who founded the colony of Massachusetts had come to the new land in order to worship, in keeping with their beliefs. They were very critical of the English monarchy and the Church of England, even though they were still under English rule. However, until 1691, not all immigrants enjoyed such protections. If one was not a member of the recognized Massachusetts church, which was Puritan, that person might be deprived of political and civil rights. In the 1640s and 1650s, the legislature passed laws against Jesuits and Quakers, whose beliefs were seen as dangerous and subversive. Religious persecution decreased when William and Mary wrote a charter in 1691, granting religious tolerance for everyone in the colonies except Roman Catholics.

In addition to religious freedom, many people immigrated to New England to obtain land. In the same charter, William and Mary gave the General Court of Massachusetts power to grant land to settlers who came to the state. In addition to granting land to new settlers, Massachusetts officials created other laws throughout the eighteenth century that regulated immigration. For the most part, these excluded immigrants whose financial resources were considered insufficient for beginning life in the colony without the assistance of those already settled there. The admission of new settlers was also regulated to ensure that they would help ensure the preservation of the government's religious and moral qualities.

This was seen in a number of laws created early on in the colony's history that discouraged the presence of "public charges" (or those requiring state assistance). The earliest public charge law in New England was passed in Massachusetts in 1645, in an attempt to discourage immigration by impoverished British subjects seeking a new life. This was enforced through the mandatory reporting and screening of ships' passengers, and the exclusion of "undesirables" upon their arrival in the New World. In 1700, the colony enacted a law to exclude disabled passengers who have "no security against their becoming public charges." Ship captains had to post bonds for these passengers, or were required to carry them back to Europe (Loucky, Armstrong, and Estrada 2006, 265).

Because of the colony's strict and exclusive stance on immigration, by the 1770s, Massachusetts was the most culturally "British" of all the colonies, while the other colonies had assimilated some practices from other European settlers. Despite the state's exclusivity and large British population, other groups had also settled there. In 1661, Jacques Pepin submits a petition asking permission for himself and other French Protestants to settle in the area. The magistrates did not consent but allowed Pepin to remain in the jurisdiction as long as he did not violate trade laws. Others who were brought over to the New World were not free: slaves from Africa came into Massachusetts from its settlement in the 1600s up until the late 1700s, when slavery was abolished in the state.

During the period between 1783 and 1820, immigration to the United States was low, with only about 225,000 immigrants estimated to have arrived during this time. In 1819, around the time immigration numbers began to increase, the U.S. Congress declared that customs officials were required to create detailed records of immigrants' arrivals, allowing for more accurate information on immigration. The collection of data was further assisted by the Steerage Act, which helped to more tightly regulate the number of passengers aboard a ship. Immigration steadily increased in Massachusetts from 1820 to 1845. During this time, many of the people who came to the state chose to settle there, while in later years they were more likely to move to other parts of the country. Many of these individuals came from the England and Ireland, although a few others came from Scotland, France, and Germany. Around this time, the Steerage Act, along with The Passenger Acts (1847 and 1855), had the effect of raising the price of passage on a ship, which reduced the ability of poor immigrants to come to the United States.

Like other parts of the Northeast, Massachusetts saw many immigrants in the nineteenth century come into its cities by ship. Immigrants arrived at numerous ports in the state, but the records kept today by the Massachusetts Archives are only for the town of Boston. Massachusetts only kept records of arrivals by ship, or passenger manifests, for about 40 years, starting in 1848. In 1891, federal officials took over the recording of passenger manifests, but during that time over 1 million immigrants landed in the Port of Boston.

The second half of the nineteenth century was a time when immigrants faced discrimination and barriers to full participation in American life. In the 1850s, the Know-Nothing Party, a highly anti-immigrant political group, seized power of the legislation and enacted a two-year delay on voting rights for naturalized citizens residing in the state, although it was overturned by the next Republican administration. Other Know-Nothing proposals to lengthen the naturalization process and outlaw Catholic convents failed. In 1894, a group of Harvard alumni founded the Immigrant Restriction League. It soon was led by Senator Henry Cabot Lodge, and its purpose was to require that new immigrants must pass a literacy test upon arrival in the United States.

The nineteenth century also became a time when western Massachusetts saw an influx of immigrants. This was especially true near the end of the century. In 1850, there was a small foreign-born population consisting mostly of immigrants from England, Ireland, Scotland, and Wales. However, by 1900, more than 60 percent of the region's population had been born in an increasingly varied number of foreign lands or were second-generation immigrants (or the children of immigrants.)In the early twentieth century, Italians became the largest nationality to enter the state, although they were still outnumbered in the population as a whole by those with English and Irish ancestries. Many of the immigrants during this period came to work in factories (see Eric Arnesen 2007, 111, 459, 486) in a state that was at the forefront of the American Industrial Revolution. These immigrants also faced discrimination and ill treatment in the workplace, and it takes years of striking, labor-organizing, and struggle before laborers began to have their demands met.

Despite these victories, some immigrants still had trouble settling in the United States because of laws that excluded Asian immigrants from coming to the states. In May 1918, Congress streamlined the naturalization process for foreign soldiers, and a federal judge in Massachusetts allowed Filipino veterans to become naturalized citizens because "their military service was more important than the racial test for citizenship" (Ueda 2011). Immigrants also had an impact on politics in the state. In the 1920s, many immigrants began to move away from the Republican Party that had dominated state politics for decades and opted instead to vote for Democratic candidates. Much of this had to do with the GOP's identification with anti-immigration sentiment, such as 100 percent Americanism, the Ku Klux Klan, and immigration restriction. A number of immigrant groups, spurred by the Democratic nomination of Al Smith, organized to support his campaign. These included eastern and southern Europeans, who the campaign organizers contacted directly by translating pamphlets into about a dozen languages, and the "Smith Italian League of Massachusetts," headquartered in Boston's North End. At the onset of the Great Depression, many more immigrants, including French Canadians, aligned themselves with the Democrats.

During the Depression, immigration slowed to a trickle due to economic hardship and President Roosevelt's refusal to aid refugees. As a result, only 528,000 immigrants came to the United States in the 1930s. After the Nazis came to power, many wanted to help German children escape. Edith Rogers, a Massachusetts politician, and Robert Wagner of New York introduced a bill to Congress to bring 20,000 German children to the United States. The discussion surrounding the bill generated sympathy for the refugees but also revealed a strong opposition to immigration. Immigration continued to be slow during World War II, both because the U.S. government was hesitant to divert resources toward amnesty and away from winning the war and because the United States government had placed strict control on immigration by this time.

In the second half of the twentieth century, more immigrants began to arrive from Spanish-speaking countries, including Puerto Rico, the Dominican Republic, and Cuba. As in the past, immigrants continued to play a pivotal role in the state's manufacturing economy. In the 1990s, despite a loss of many manufacturing jobs, half-a-million workers were still employed in the industry. Immigrant Americans were nearly twice as likely as native-born citizens to hold manufacturing jobs, and while conditions were much improved, immigrants still had to contend with inequality. During this time, immigrants could only expect to make wages equal to 75 percent of those received by their native-born counterparts. Immigrants and native-born Bay State residents wishing to develop their language skills also encountered obstacles during debates on bilingual education. One of the most outspoken opponents of such instruction was Rosalie Porter, a teacher in the state, who felt such programs were wasteful and spoke out against them in the 1980s.

Today, the state's relationship with immigration issues remains complex. The state government has been criticized for 2010 legislation targeted at immigrants. Seen as a response to Arizona's harsh stance on immigration, the Massachusetts proposal seeks to increase punishments for employing undocumented immigrants while also reducing eligibility for public assistance. It also requires public housing agencies to give priority for subsidized housing to legal residents and the state attorney general's office to set up a hotline for callers to report businesses employing undocumented immigrants. Critics call the legislation "the most anti-immigrant bill we've seen in Massachusetts in years" (Goodnough May 2010). That same year, the state legislature tried to close a loophole that allowed people to register their vehicles legally even if they did not have a driver's license. The reasoning behind the proposed changes was to create a more secure environment for all drivers through registration.

On the other hand, Governor Deval Patrick denied the federal government use of immigrants' fingerprints for the Secure Communities Program. He also vowed to adopt the recommendations of an advisory panel on immigration, which included a push for providing in-state tuition for undocumented immigrant students in Massachusetts. The move was heralded by immigrant advocacy groups as a triumph for immigrants' rights. Others, including conservative talk-show hosts, criticized the recommendations. The governor's desire to promote immigrant education also faced obstacles because of a state law that bars undocumented immigrants from qualifying for in-state tuition. In 2012, the Obama administration declared that it would, despite the state's opposition, extend the Secure Communities Program into Massachusetts.

There were a number of groups currently advocating for immigrants in the state of Massachusetts. These included the Massachusetts Immigrant and Refugee Advocacy Coalition , which was an umbrella group comprising about 130 organizations. It was created to advance and preserve the rights of foreign-born residents through policy analysis, grassroots organizing, and training. A smaller group is the Immigrant and Worker Rights Coalition, which is based in western Massachusetts that seeks to protect the rights of workers in communities throughout that region. These and other groups work to protect and provide assistance to a thriving Bay State immigrant population.

The state's immigrant heritage can still be seen in U.S. Census data. In 2000, 26 percent of residents were of Irish heritage, while 15 percent were of English descent, which spoke to the large waves of immigrants from these countries in the seventeenth through the nineteenth centuries. About 14 percent of the population can trace their ancestry back to Italy, as a result of high Italian immigration that took place in the early twentieth century. About 7 percent of residents claimed Latino ancestry, as a result of more recent immigration from Spanish-speaking countries. Other Massachusetts residents can trace their ancestry to places all over the globe, including Canada, Syria, France, Germany, China, Greece, and Southeast Asia. Today, Massachusetts's legacy of immigration continues, as the state with the seventh-largest immigrant population in the country.

TOPICAL ESSAYS

MASSACHUSETTS AND THE SECURE COMMUNITIES PROGRAM

On June 6, 2011, Governor Deval Patrick announced that his state would not participate in the Secure Communities Program, which had been implemented by the U.S. government's DHS. The program automatically runs fingerprints of those apprehended by law enforcement to check their immigration status, and immigration advocates say that this could result in the deportation of individuals based on racial profiling, even if they have not committed a crime. Patrick became the third governor to reject the program, although the issue became complicated because it has already been implemented in Suffolk County, which included Boston.

Guards block the approach to the Lawrence textile mills during a strike in Lawrence, Massachusetts, on January 12, 1912. This strike, along with the motto "Bread and Roses," is considered one of the most important in immigrant labor history in the United States. (Library of Congress)

Despite Patrick's desire to keep the program out of the state, he faced some resistance from other elected officials. Marlborough city councilor Matt Elder, with the support of the Greater Boston Tea Party, wanted his city to opt in to the program, suggesting that it would help remove violent criminals from the area. Opponents of Secure Communities say it encourages racial profiling and discourages immigrants who are victims of crimes to report them to the police. The Marlborough police chief indicated that joining was not possible because the state as a whole was not a part of the program. However, the DHS indicated that they would continue to use fingerprints from Massachusetts, since the program was nationwide and could only be amended at the federal level. The Secure Communities Program currently includes over 1,300 cities and towns in the United States, with the goal of having complete nationwide coverage by 2013. On May 15, 2012, the Secure Communities Program took effect in Massachusetts, with the Obama administration announcing that it would implement the program in Massachusetts despite the state's objections to it.

Immigrants and the Industrial Revolution in Massachusetts

Immigrants have been a part of the labor force in the state since before the Civil War. The first 100 years of the textile-manufacturing industry in the state, from approximately 1810 to 1920, were a time of innovation, exploitation, and struggle for immigrants and native-born laborers alike. Many immigrants worked in manufacturing in the state as the demand for readymade clothing and textiles boomed in the nineteenth century. In fact, the town of Lowell, Massachusetts, had been referred to as "the birthplace of the American Industrial Revolution" (Lowell.com 2011). Industrial centers were established around the state during this time, with Boston and New Bedford adding new factories for clothing manufacture, along with textile mills in Lawrence. The American textile industry became centered in the state, after Samuel Slater developed the first water-powered textile mills that mechanized the carding and spinning processes, building 61 throughout the Northeast by 1810. Twenty years later, Francis Cabot Lowell introduced a workable power loom as well as the concept of an integrated factory, where every step of the manufacturing process took place under one roof.

The rural town of East Chelmsford became the site of Lowell's textile manufacturing. In 1821, Lowell and a group of financial backers began the "Lowell experiment" to capitalize on Lowell's visions for building looms and operating factories. By 1826, Lowell had attracted enough new residents to the area (about 2,000) to declare Lowell as a separate town. Ten years later, as manufacturing overtook farms and rural landscape in the area, the town of Lowell had swelled to a city of 20,000. Factories became a common site in Massachusetts, and many of those built in the middle of the century last for decades. By 1900, Massachusetts had reached a level of nonagricultural employment that the rest of the country would not reach until after World War II. By 1905, the textile industry employed more Massachusetts' residents than any other industry.

Immigrants faced difficult labor conditions in Massachusetts. The town of Lawrence was a center for industry and had a large immigrant population, and so contained many examples of labor conditions in the late nineteenth and early twentieth century. At the turn of the century, textiles were the town's most important industry, and there were many textile mills operating in the town. Many buildings were poorly built or dangerous to work in, such as the Pemberton Mill, which caught fire in April 1886 and collapsed into ruins, killing hundreds of workers, 25 years earlier. Laborers also faced health hazards associated with the textile industry. A 1905 report from the Massachusetts State Board of Health found that dust from the textiles was irritating to the respiratory system and made workers vulnerable to respiratory illnesses, such as tuberculosis.

Immigrant laborers often lived in cramped quarters as well. In 1914, the Massachusetts Immigration Commission studied the living conditions of immigrants and found the following examples: "In a mill town which has one of the largest Greek colonies in Massachusetts, in the downstairs tenement of a two-story house, is a group of eight people. . . . A Lithuanian girl has lived four years in a family of three who have four rooms and eight lodgers. . . . The girl works as a stitcher in a tailor shop. She started to go to night school when she first came, but the landlady objected, as she wanted her to help out with the housework in the evening. . . . A Polish girl of eighteen is lodging with a family of four who live in four rooms with five lodgers . . . [she] is working seven days a week washing cars in the railroad yards in Boston" (Massachusetts Immigration Commission 1914, 60–61).

Laborers throughout the state began to organize against difficult and dangerous labor conditions. In 1912, the "Bread and Roses Affair" garnered national attention, as tens of thousands of women went on strike against unfair labor practices in Lawrence. Another strike took place in Lawrence in 1919, after a group of workers walked out on strike in response to pay cuts agreed upon by employers and unions. The resulting strike was participated in by 15,000–30,000 laborers. The Industrial Workers of the World (IWW), which was founded in 1903, assisted in uniting immigrant laborers during the 1912 strikes. The IWW helped bring

Bristol County sheriff Thomas Hodgson gestures during a news conference in regard to the Secure Communities program, or S Comm, held by Massachusetts County sheriffs at the statehouse in Boston on September 28, 2011. The program was designed to immediately check the immigration status of those arrested for crimes. There have since been problems with this program, leading to charges of racial profiling and selective enforcement. (AP Photo/Charles Krupa).

together workers who had come from a variety of countries, including Italians, Irish, and French Canadians. French Canadian laborers made up a large percentage of these workers, comprising one-third of all textile laborers in the state.

During World War I, the Americanization movement sought to further its cause by teaching English classes to foreign-born factory workers. The Massachusetts Bureau of Immigration began working with industrial executives to promote such classes, arguing that "Speaking English will win the War!" (Leiserson 1924, 122). The bureau, founded in 1917, sought to protect immigrants from mistreatment and to promote their assimilation into American culture. While its mission did not change, it was later made a division of the Massachusetts Department of Education.

In 1919, the Massachusetts Bureau of Immigration published a statement that outlined the potentially tense relationship between immigrants and their employers. The statement indicated that "industrial unrest" and the difficulty of creating an understanding between employers and workers was caused by the indifference of employers and the exploitation of employees by their supervisors (Massachusetts Bureau of Immigration 1919, 21). Immigrants and native-born laborers continued to work in factories around the Bay State, and factories had continued to open and operate throughout the area. These included the Zildjian Cymbal Company, which opened its factory doors in Norwell in 1973, and rubber-maker Quabaug, which had a factory in the state since 1916.

IRISH IMMIGRANTS IN MASSACHUSETTS

Irish immigrants came to Massachusetts along with other immigrants from the British Isles during the Great Migration of the 1630s to 1640s. Throughout most of U.S. history, they faced discrimination and hardship. In one instance, they were targeted after the passage of The Naturalization Act, Aliens Act, and Enemies Act (or Alien and Sedition Acts) of 1798. These laws were meant to reduce the influence of radicals and revolutionaries from France by increasing the residency requirements for citizenship. The president also authorized the apprehension and deportation of enemy aliens during wartime. Those who fought against Irish and Jacobin immigrants passed the Alien Friends Act, which made every noncitizen in the U.S. liable to arrest and deportation at any time. This act was allowed to expire when Thomas Jefferson became president.

Irish immigration to the state saw an upward trend in the first half of the nineteenth century. In 1820–1825, the increase was only about 100 new immigrants (from 125 people to 252), but by 1835, 2,381 Irish immigrants arrived in the state. Irish immigrants began to build Roman Catholic churches, including one in Boston in 1800. After 1823, the population increased so rapidly that two more parishes were established in the city between 1834 and 1835. The number of Irish residents increased in many towns during the 1830s and 1840s, including Quincy, Worcester, and Lowell.

Irish immigrants worked in quarries and mills and on the railroads and canals that were being built at the time. Irish laborers faced discrimination from their fellow laborers and from decisionmakers, who were nativist and anti-Irish. A number of anti-Catholic policies were put into place, including those that caused the deportation of the most impoverished Irish immigrants back to their homeland.

Irish workers began to resist nativist policies and organize. While they may have participated in the labor unrest of the 1850s (when there are record numbers of strikes), they often found themselves a target of violence. In 1852, mill workers in Amesbury and Salisbury went on strike. The native-born workers became angry with Irish workers who were "scabbing," or brought in to work during a strike, which was often an act of desperation done to curry favor with employers. Several years later, however, Irish immigrants were in the picket lines participating in strikes.

In February 1859, a strike took place in the town of Lowell. The strike was spearheaded by Irish women and marked their entrance into labor leadership. Prior to this, labor-organizing, like labor itself, had been divided along gender lines, where men did most of the mule spinning (a vital component of textile production taking place early in manufacture) while women worked in other areas of the factory. The mule spinners, mostly immigrants from Lancashire, England, were a powerful group because of the importance of their jobs, and kept their unions exclusive in order to perpetuate an all-male labor movement.

A number of prominent labor leaders were of Irish descent, including Elizabeth Gurley Flynn, who helped organize 25,000 striking textile laborers (most of whom are women) in the 1912 "Bread and Roses Affair" in Lawrence, and ultimately had their demands met. George Edwin McNeill, son of a Scotch Irish immigrant, was from Amesbury, and worked in factories as a teenager before becoming an organizer for labor rights in Boston. These individuals, and many other immigrants from Ireland, helped to shape the labor movement in the state and ensure workers' rights for future generations.

NOTABLE GROUPS

IMMIGRATION RESTRICTION LEAGUE

The Immigration Restriction League was formed in 1894 by three Harvard graduates named Charles Warren, Robert DeCourcy Ward, and Prescott Farnsworth Hall. They formed the group after becoming concerned that new immigrants would not be assimilated into U.S. life, and that newly arrived groups of "undesirable" immigrants would be unable to participate in society or adopt American values (Harvard University Library Open Collections Program 2011). The League drew considerable interest, sending out about 150,000 flyers and pamphlets by 1900. In a 1900 article, Hall indicated that one of their primary concerns had to do with the nationalities of immigrants arriving in the country. He argued that in the mid-nineteenth century, people "from our kindred races" (the United Kingdom, France, Germany, and Scandinavia) were arriving and this was acceptable, but the decline in immigration from these countries and an increase of Jewish and Italian immigrants was a cause for alarm (Hall 1900, 307–08).

Members of this group felt that society could be improved by restricting immigration to the United States, and they introduced legislation to Congress in order to make it more difficult for immigrants to settle in the United States or even move to exclude whole groups (such as illiterate individuals) entirely. While they did manage to pass some legislation, most of it was rejected, even though the group claims that there were hundreds of U.S. constituents who had signed petitions indicating that they wished to see the proposed changes.

The Shakers in Massachusetts

The United Society of Believers, or "Shakers" as they are more commonly known, was a Utopian religious movement centered in the Northeast in the eighteenth and nineteenth centuries. The founder of the movement, named Mother Ann Lee, traveled throughout the state of Massachusetts providing religious counsel and attracting followers. The Shakers got their name from their dances and from their Quaker heritage, which caused them to popularly be called the "shaking Quakers" (Stein 1992, 14). Shakerism was founded in Manchester, England, in 1747, by those wishing to break apart from the Quaker Church. Ann Lee, and her Shaker followers, believed in communal life and common ownership of property and practiced celibacy and the confession of sins. Because they did not believe in procreation, Shakers would adopt children, giving them the choice once they became adults whether or not they wished to remain in Shaker society.

Shakers had very progressive ideas of gender and race equality and were abolitionists. They believed that gender equality was inherent in the natural order of things, as every aspect of nature was created with male and female elements. They believed that community members should have access to activities to promote artistic and intellectual development and encouraged simple dress, speech, and mannerisms. Their communities were always in rural areas, in order to be far away from potentially corrupting influences found in cities. For a time, Shaker communities became prosperous and came to be respected by individuals throughout U.S. society.

Ann Lee was an illiterate Englishwoman when she had a vision in which she discovered the way of life that she feels would be the "Heaven on Earth" so long sought-after. She received financial backing from a follower named John Hocknell, and on May 19, 1774, she and a small group of followers left England for New York. In 1776, the group moved to land in the settlement of Watervliet, New York. Shakerism began to spread in the United States via missionaries traveling around the northeast during the 1780s. In May 1781, Ann Lee and five others left for a long missionary tour. They headed to the town of Harvard and took to engaging in evangelical work throughout the region northwest of Boston and in central Massachusetts.

The movement took hold largely in New York and Massachusetts, and a contemporary account left behind by minister Valentine Rathbun in 1781. Rathbun felt there were inconsistencies in the Shaker doctrine, and described the group's beliefs and practices as "new and strange" (Stein 1992, 15). Ann Lee and her followers would travel frequently, but most frequently made stops in the town of Harvard, Massachusetts, where they stayed with an early convert named Isaac Willard, later moving to a large house constructed by a Baptist group, known as the Square House.

In the 1780s, Shakers began to live communally, combining their possessions and wealth in order to construct communities and share responsibilities. Shakers, like Quakers, are pacifists, which meant that they did not participate in wars or military training and were opposed to violence. Because of this, the Shakers of Massachusetts were subjected to fines, after the Federalists in the state passed a bill in 1809 that Shakers and Quakers were exempt from service, provided that each pays $6.

The Shakers were harassed for their beliefs in a variety of ways, although they were resistant toward suggestions that they brought their complaints to the magistrate or other officials. During their evangelical missions of the 1780s, Ann Lee and her followers frequently encountered mob violence and abuse. After hearing of the Shakers' mistreatment, Henry Van Schaak from Richmond, Massachusetts, stepped forward to advocate for the Shakers in an attempt to alleviate their mistreatment. Van Schaak insisted that the Shakers endured "hear[ing] Gods name profaned on Sundays in their places of worship, themselves abused, their women treated with obscenity" (Stein 1992, 34). They also faced violent opposition in Petersham and a mob in Harvard.

Early Shaker converts were scattered throughout the state, including the towns of Shelburne and Shirley in the north, and Norton Rehoboth near Boston. A number of Shaker villages were established in the state, including those in Shirley, Hancock, Harvard, and Tyringham. In a time when the rest of the state was rapidly embracing industrialization, Shaker communities still operated on large farms, which gave them a romantic appeal. By the 1820s, westward expansion brought many more people to areas where Shakers inhabited, and their varied backgrounds and traditions were different from those in which the Shakers had traditionally found converts. The size of the communities fluctuated as members joined and left, and tension and weakening of Shaker society grew by the 1840s.

By the 1920s, many of the Shaker villages in Massachusetts and elsewhere closed, unable to support themselves financially or to operate with a dwindling membership. The remaining societies lacked effective oversight and leadership, but members still felt a strong connection to their traditions. Modern-day Shaker brother Arnold Hadd stated that Shakerdom was never made up of 18 larger villages, but instead the 60 families who comprised those communities. That connection to family and to other community members had been part of Shakerism's enduring appeal.

While the number of Shakers has lessened considerably, Shakerism is still practiced today in one active Shaker community, called Sabbathday Lake, in Maine. Other Shaker buildings and villages, including Hancock Shaker Village in Massachusetts, have been preserved as museums. Those still practicing Shakerism insist that it was not a failed Utopian experiment. Instead, they believe that "Shakerism has a message for this present age—a message as valid today as when it was first expressed. It teaches above all else that God is Love and that our most solemn duty is to show forth that God who is love in the World" (National Register of Historic Places 2011).

Massachusetts Immigrant and Refugee Advocacy Coalition

This broad-based statewide coalition's main office is in Boston and it was established in 1987, first aiming to help newly legalized immigrants who had been granted legal status through the 1986 Immigration and Reform Control Act (IRCA). Its founder and long-term director (until 2000) was Muriel Heiberger and the coalition has since expanded at the local level—increasingly including more community groups—as well as its lobbying efforts in Washington, DC , and connections to other state advocacy groups throughout the nation. Originally focused on policy (particularly in response to IRCA's stricter delineation of political status, both in positive and negative terms), the organization now deals with a host of issues, ranging from public health to education to refugee advocacy. The coalition's activities are similarly multifaceted, from grassroots organizing to public education and informational texts. This organization serves a vital function in the state, identifying a broad range of immigrants' needs and helping to foster links to politicians and the community in order to build a more open and democratic civic environment.

BIBLIOGRAPHY

Arnesen, Eric, ed. *Encyclopedia of U.S. Labor and Working-Class History*. Volume 1: A-F. New York: Taylor and Francis Group, 2007. "The Fall of Pemberton Mill." *New York Times*

Arnesen, Eric, Julie Greene, and Bruce Laurie. *Labor Histories: Class, Politics, and the Working Class Experience*. Champaign: University of Illinois Press, 1998.

Associated Press. "Massachusetts Governor's Second Term Will Push Tuition for Illegal Immigrants." *The Herald News*, June 7, 2011. http://www.heraldnews.com/article/20101116/News/311169246. Accessed August 4, 2014.

Barenblat, Rachel. "Massachusetts: The Bay State." World Almanac Library, Milwaukee, 2002.

Beaudet, Mike. "Illegal Aliens Able to Register Cars in MA." Fox News Boston. November 16, 2010.

Bierman, Noah, and Maria Sacchetti. "Mass. Senate Passes Crackdown on Illegal Immigrants." *Boston Globe*, May 27, 2010. http://www.boston.com/news/local/breaking_news/2010/05/mass_senate_pas.html. Accessed August 4, 2014.

Bischoff, Henry. *Immigration Issues*. Westport, CT: Greenwood Press, 2002.

Des, Mitra Des, and Shirley Kolack. *Technology, Values, and Society: Social Forces in Technological Change*. New York: Peter Lang Publishing, 2008.

"The Fall of Pemberton Mill." *New York Times*, April 18, 1886. http://www.nytimes.com/1860/02/16/news/the-fall-of-the-pemberton-mill.html. Accessed August 4, 2014.

Foley, Elise. "Massachusetts Rejects Secure Communities Immigration Enforcement Program." *Huffington Post*, June 6, 2011. http://www.huffingtonpost.com/2011/06/06/massachusetts-rejects-immgration-enforcement-program_n_871970.html. Accessed March 24, 2014.

Golden, Hilda H. *Immigrant and Native Families: The Impact of Immigration on the Demographic Transformation of Western Massachusetts, 1850–1900*. Lanham, MD: University Press of America, 1994.

Goodnough, Abby. "A Massachusetts Move on Immigration Law." *New York Times*, May 27, 2010. http://www.fosterquan.com/news/ma_imm_law052710.pdf. Accessed August 4, 2014.

Goodnough, Abby. "Surprising Immigration Crackdown Advances." *New York Times*, June 10, 2010. http://www.nytimes.com/2010/06/11/us/11boston.html?_r=0. Accessed August 4, 2014.

Hall, Prescott F. "Present Status of Immigration Restriction." *Gunton's Magazine* XVIII (January–June 1900). http://www.archive.org/stream/cu31924064104254/cu31924064104254_djvu.txt. Accessed August 4, 2014.

Hancock Shaker Village. "Hancock Shaker Village." 2011. http://www.hancockshakervillage.org/index.php. Accessed March 24, 2014.

Harvard University Library Open Collections Program. "Immigration Restriction League." 2011. http://ocp.hul.harvard.edu/immigration/restrictionleague.html. Accessed March 24, 2014.

Hillstrom, Kevin, and Laurie Collier Hillstrom. *The Industrial Revolution in America: Automobiles*. Santa Barbara: ABC-CLIO, 2006.

Homeland Security Newswire. "Massachusetts Defies Feds, Rejects Secure Communities." June 10, 2011. http://www.homelandsecuritynewswire.com/massachusetts-defies-feds-rejects-secure-communities. Accessed March 24, 2014.

Immigrant and Worker Rights Coalition. "Immigrant and Worker Rights Coalition." 2011. http://wmciwr.blogspot.com/. Accessed March 24, 2014.

Karow, Edna Cornelia. "The Immigration Policies of Colonial Massachusetts, Pennsylvania, and Virginia." Master's Thesis, University of Wisconsin, 1922.

Koven, Steven G., and Frank Gotzke. *American Immigration Policy: Confronting the Nation's Challenges*. New York: Springer, 2010.

Leiserson, William M. *Adjusting Immigrant and Industry*. New York: Harper and Brothers, 1924.

Loucky, James, Jeanne Armstrong, and Lawrence J. Estrada. *Immigration in America Today: An Encyclopedia*. Westport, CT: Greenwood Press, 2006.

Lowell.com. "Lowell, Massachusetts History." 2011. http://www.lowell.com/city-of-lowell/lowell-history/. Accessed March 24, 2014.

"Made in Massachusetts: The Globe 100." *Boston Globe*, 2009. http://www.boston.com/business/globe/globe100/globe_100_2009/madeinmass09/. Accessed March 24, 2014.

Massachusetts Archives. "Massachusetts Archives Collection (1629–1799) Search Detail: Volume 15A, Page 009." 2011. http://www.sec.state.ma.us/ArchivesSearch/RevolutionarySearch.aspx. Accessed March 24, 2014.

Massachusetts Archives. 2011. "Passenger Manifest (1848–1891) Contents." http://www.sec.state.ma.us/arc/arcsrch/PassengerManifestSearchContents.html. Accessed March 24, 2014.

Massachusetts Bureau of Immigration. *First Annual Report*. Boston: Wright & Potter Printing Company, 1919.

Massachusetts Immigrant and Refugee Advocacy Coalition. 2011. "About Us: What Is MIRA?" http://www.miracoalition.org/en/roknav-what-is-mira. Accessed March 24, 2014.

Massachusetts Immigration Commission. *Report of the Massachusetts Immigration Commission: The Problem of Immigration in Massachusetts*. Boston: Wright & Potter Printing Company, 1914.

Massachusetts State Board of Health. *Annual Report of the State Board of Health of Massachusetts*. Vol. 36. Boston: Wright and Potter Co. 1905.

MetroWest Daily. "Marlborough Councilor Wants City to Join Secure Communities." July 11, 2011. http://www.metrowestdailynews.com/news/x1850043079/Marlborough-councilor-wants-city-to-join-Secure-Communities. Accessed March 24, 2014.

National Register of Historic Places. "Essay on Shaker History." 2011. http://www.nps.gov/nr/travel/shaker/shakers.htm. Accessed March 24, 2014.

Paterwic, Stephen J. *Historical Dictionary of the Shakers*. Lanham, MD: Scarecrow Press, 2008.

Perreira, Krista A. "Immigration Timeline." 2011. http://www.unc.edu/~perreira/198timeline.html. Accessed March 24, 2014.

Petrin, Ronald Arthur. *French Canadians in Massachusetts Politics, 1885–1915*. Cranbury, NJ: Associated University Presses, 1990.

Powell, John. *Encyclopedia of North American Immigration*. New York: Facts on File, 2005.

Proper, Emberson Edward. "Colonial Immigration Laws." Doctoral Thesis, Columbia University, Department of Political Science, 1900.

Reimers, David M. *Unwelcome Strangers: American Identity and the Turn against Immigration*. New York: Columbia University Press, 1998.

Stein, Stephen J. *The Shaker Experience in America*. Westford, MA: Courier Westford, Inc., 1992.

Turvill, Helen. "Immigration into Massachusetts, 1820–1900." Bachelor's Thesis, University of Wisconsin, 1906.

Ueda, Reed ed. *A Companion to Immigration*. Hoboken, NJ: Wiley Blackwell, 2011.

22

MICHIGAN

William P. Kladky

CHRONOLOGY

Pre-European Settlement	The Chippewa and Dakota or Sesseton Sioux are the major American Indian tribes in the interior northwest.
1620	Etienne Brule, under assignment from the colony of New France's Samuel de Champlain, explores the Sault Ste. Marie area.
1680s	The French fortify the area around Port Huron and set up a permanent military establishment at Fort St. Joseph in the mid-1690s.
1701	Sieur Antoine de La Mothe Cadillac founds Detroit as "La Ville d'Étroit," which is translated as city of the strait; he also builds Fort Pontchartrain. Detroit is the state's oldest permanent settlement.
1795	Government-owned and -operated stores are established in Mackinac, and the like to develop the area and deal in fur trade with the American Indian tribes.
1796	American settlement begins in Michigan.
1796	Detroit and all other British posts in Michigan are turned over to the United States under terms of the Jay Treaty between the United States and Great Britain; the treaty resolves issues arising since the Treaty of Paris of 1783, which ended the American Revolution. Wayne County, containing Detroit, is established as an administrative division of the Northwest Territory.
1803	Boundary disputes begin with Ohio over the mouth of the Maumee River.
1805 (July 1)	Territorial authority is granted to Michigan. About 80 percent of the population is of "French extraction." The name Michigan is the

	French form of the Ojibwe/Chippewa word *mishigamaa*, meaning "large water" or "large lake."
1805	The first Supreme Court of Michigan is established.
1818	The United States gains control of the Upper Peninsula and the St. Clair River islands from the British through border negotiations arising from the Treaty of Ghent (1814), which ended the War of 1812.
1820	Detroit's population reaches 1,422, and is mostly French-speaking.
1823	Expedition begins to settle the international boundary with British Canada.
1832	Great chief Black Hawk makes the last attempt to drive whites away, but the combined effort of his Sauk and Fox nations fails.
1835	After armed clashes, including hostage-taking, Congress restores order and settles the Michigan–Ohio boundary dispute. In the compromise, Michigan gives up claim to Toledo and the Maumee and receives the Upper Peninsula.
1837	Michigan gains statehood, having spent the longest period as a territory for any state east of the Mississippi. It enters as a free state.
1837	Detroit becomes capital of the state, until Lansing is designated in 1847.
1842	Noticeable declines in the number of fur-bearing animals lead to decline of fur trade.
1844	The first mining of Keweenaw copper begins. By 1850, Michigan-mined copper represents 88 percent of total U.S. production.
1845	Michigan appoints a special office to entice new settlers from other countries.
1848	The Illinois and Michigan Canal opens, linking Chicago to the Mississippi, permitting boat transportation from the Great Lakes to the Mississippi River and the Gulf of Mexico.
1855	The opening of the Soo Canal further spurs the mining industry, as does the establishment of the first railroad to state mining regions in 1857. Rapid population growth accompanies this development.
1860s and 1870s	Lumbering is at its height—drawing lumberjacks, swampers, camp crews, and overseers to Michigan.
1879	The new state capitol is dedicated in Lansing.
1887	Montana surpasses Michigan in mining.
1896	The manufacturing of American automobiles begins in Detroit.
1909	Michigan prohibits the issuance of a barber's license to any foreigner.
1926	A U.S. Supreme Court decision settles the Michigan–Wisconsin dispute over the Montreal River and islands in Green Bay.
1929	The Ambassador Bridge is opened between Detroit and Windsor, Ontario—it is the longest bridge in the world when completed.
1930	The Detroit-Windsor Tunnel opens.
1957	The Mackinac Straits Bridge opens.

1959	The St. Lawrence Seaway opens, permitting ocean-going ships to access the Great Lakes and Detroit.
1967	Race riots in Detroit devastate the city.
1974	Gerald R. Ford of Grand Rapids, Michigan, becomes the 38th president of the United States.
2001	The emigration rate for Michigan first exceeds the state's immigration rate, resulting in a population loss.
2002	The state elects its first female governor, Jennifer Granholm (D).
2008 (September 19)	Kwame Kilpatrick resigns as Detroit mayor after pleading guilty to two counts of obstruction of justice and no contest to one count of assaulting and obstructing a police officer.
2013	The foreign-born comprise about 6.1 percent of Michigan's total population.

HISTORICAL OVERVIEW

Bordering on four of the five Great Lakes, Michigan is divided into Upper and Lower peninsulas by the Straits of Mackinac, which link Lakes Michigan and Huron. The two parts of the state are connected by the Mackinac Bridge. Before the European settlement of Michigan, the northerly Chippewa mostly lived peacefully near good fishing on Lake Superior and other river areas. The southern Sioux were more agricultural, with corn and hunted animals. The early European fur traders, such as the American Fur Company, dealt with them, hunting the plentiful bison, deer, beaver, otter, muskrat, mink, and the like.

EIGHTEENTH CENTURY

Originally, Detroit was founded during the British-French rivalry. Two Indian trails met between two water bodies, and the site had been an Indian town, Teuchsagondie. The 1787 Northwest Ordinance set up government for the Northwest Territory, later the states of Michigan, Ohio, Indiana, Illinois, and Wisconsin. Several states had claims on the territory. To get ratification of the Articles of Confederation, these states ceded their claims on the territory to the federal government in return for payment of their war debt. Michigan's central-southern section was ceded by Massachusetts and Virginia in 1784–1786. What became Michigan, therefore, was public land owned by the U.S. government. The territory existed until March 1, 1803, when its southeastern section was admitted as the state of Ohio.

NINETEENTH CENTURY

The French primarily thought of Michigan as a large game preserve to be exploited for its furs. As the British replaced the French settlers, they brought a

The Mackinac Bridge as seen from St. Ignace, Michigan, on July 18, 1999. (AP Photo/Carlos Osorio)

monopolistic market orientation to the fur trade that dominated the Michigan area. John Jacob Astor was the major American who bought into the fur trade, eventually controlling the industry and encouraging American settlement.

The name Michigan first was utilized in 1805 in the various organizations of the old Northwest Territory by Congress. The 1787 Act initially separated Ohio, leaving the rest as a territory. After repeated petitions from Michigan, Congress then created Michigan. Originally, the fledgling territory had much more land in the south and much less in the north than when it finally became a state. The territorial capital was Detroit.

The first governor of the Michigan territory after 1805 was Lewis Cass, who encouraged American settlement by getting title for the lands from the American Indians as well as preparing the land for settlement. This was facilitated by the beginning of a policy by Congress in 1785 to make it easier for settlers to purchase federal land. Before land could be bought, however, all American Indian claims had to be settled. The American Indian population of Michigan was 4,672 in 1810, mostly concentrated in the southeast.

During the War of 1812, Britain regained the strategic fort at Detroit, but retreated after the war concluded. For the American Indians, this was a severe setback. The British had not been interested in land, but the Americans—being mostly farmers—certainly were. Following the war, the federal government built forts, encouraged settlers, and in 1816 Congress made certain that only Americans could engage in the lucrative fur trade. Travelers came by stagecoach and by wagon, destined for the rich farmland of southern Michigan, now part of the Midwestern farm belt.

In 1820, most of the state's population lived within a short distance from the Detroit River. Agriculture dominated employment, and property divisions were measured in arpents, or one-tenth of a mile distances. Regarding the northern peninsula, according to the *Cleveland Herald*, "No part of the United States is less well known" (March 21, 1820, quoted in Brown 1948, 291). Most of Michigan's non–American Indian population had a French background.

Detroit, with its 1,450 population, was a frontier town, a connecting link between the civilized East and the primitive heartland. A large population floated in and out, using the town as a seasonal or temporary resting spot: emigrants, fur traders, adventurers, American Indians of Northern tribes. This included visitors coming just across the river from Canada. The opening of the Erie Canal was in 1825, making Detroit's and Michigan's farm produce accessible to the Eastern markets. A rush of immigration then occurred. Land-office business boomed. In 1824, less than 62,000 acres had been sold. By 1826, almost one-and-one-half million acres had been sold, just around Detroit. Detroit grew as a half-way station for goods being shipped from the Upper Lakes' furs, peltry, and salt to the Ohio, Pennsylvania, and New York ports by other vessels. The opening of the Erie Canal, new roads, many steamboats on Lake Erie, and the opening of a land office were factors in Detroit's growth beginning in the 1820s. Between 1821 and 1920, Detroit was a frequent destination for immigrant Poles, Russians, Italians, Bohemians, and others mostly from eastern and southern Europe.

Before 1830, it was mostly pioneers from the American South who subdued the wilderness and built log cabins, kept livestock, and farmed. Kalamazoo County was settled in 1829 by Kentuckians, and southerners were reported as dominant on all the county's major prairies by 1831. Stimulated by the 1832 Black Hawk War, the federal government put in a military road, and this was utilized for the rush of emigrants coming from the East.

In the 1830s, the state's population grew sevenfold, as so-called Michigan fever gripped the East (May 1987, 50). This rapid growth, of course, drew some for exploitative reasons, and developments like Port Sheldon and White Rock City were purchased by speculators who hoped to turn a vast profit. While the national Panic of 1837 curtailed some of this boom, this activity did continue. This was greatly aided by the development of railroads, which were not supported by everybody. Farmers near the tracks initially were infuriated by frequent livestock accidents and by the loss of the open range. In 1849, a number of mostly Leoni Township farmers sabotaged the Michigan Central's tracks, by greasing or placing obstructions on the tracks, burning woodpiles, and so on. Some 79 percent of those subsequently arrested were originally from New York and New England, and 71 percent were below 40 years. Most arrested farmers produced noncommercial crops and were in the process of being financially squeezed by the developing new economy. The railroads kept coming, however, and commercial farming boomed.

The state's population finally reached approximately 60,000 in 1833, the statehood minimum established by the Northwest Ordinance. Following admission as a state in 1837, aid poured in for river improvements, railroad lines, and roads. The state's population hit 175,000. This was assisted greatly by a grant from the federal government. There were about 400 sawmills in the state in 1837, mostly small mills serving agricultural areas. As the forests in the East were exhausted, Michigan's plentiful timber was enticing. The center of the industry began and was in the Saginaw Valley in central Michigan off Lake Huron. Michigan was the third-most lumber-producing state in 1860, and became the leading state in the 1880s. Lumbermen flocked to the state and the number of millionaires grew. This industry faded as the forests became exhausted by the end of the century.

At the same time, New Englanders migrated west via the National Road (opened in 1818) and rivers to states like Michigan. Boston money had always been involved in the region's development and was in control of the major mines early. While farming was the main occupation, other trades and employment were pursued. The largest number of migrants had been born in the western section of New York and they were called "York Staters." The significant number of New England newcomers of course was "Yankees," such as the first governor Lewis Cass (May 1987, 51–52). Natives of Vermont and Maine were settled in the St. Joseph Valley as early as 1827. There were vestiges of the New England town meeting heritage in the form of the government of rural townships, as well as the architecture in many buildings.

Often, Yankee settler groups saw their migration as an extension of their religious mission. For example, the 10 families from Addison County, Vermont, who founded Vermontville (in south-central Michigan) signed a written compact modeled on the Mayflower Compact. In 1836, the Reverend Sylvester Cochrane, a Congregational minister from East Poultney, Vermont, and the Union Colony organized the town, which had 789 residents in 2010. The village was incorporated on March 11, 1867. Other religious denominations appeared with these migrants: Congregationalists, Methodists, Presbyterians, Baptists, and Episcopalians (May 1987, 53). Colleges were started to continue the New England Yankee culture, such as Olivet College in Olivet.

They were joined by migrants from Pennsylvania and Ohio in search of good land, or "mixed vegetation areas" like prairie for farming—on the fringes rather than in forestlands (Jordan 1974, 56–57). These were the first (and costliest) geographical choices for settlement, chosen by the Yankees and easterners before foreign immigrants arrived. In the 1840s and 1850s, the state actively sought settlers, selling school and university lands cheaply. All American Indian land claims had been concluded by 1842. The American Indians received cash, as well as medical, practical, and other services. The prime reason for the ease of land transfer was that the American traders had kept their exploitation of the American Indians comparatively mild. This was in contrast to the British and French traders, who ruthlessly swindled for huge profits. German-speaking immigrants settled in the area, for example, in Frankenlust, Saginaw County. The southern third of the state still constituted about 90 percent of the total population.

Before the railroads arrived, the opening of two canals greatly promoted the state's development and immigration growth. The Illinois and Michigan Canal was finished in 1848, and in 1855 the Soo Canal linked Lake Superior to Lake Michigan. Soon, the lake trade flourished and migration from the East quickened.

With the mining ore discoveries, even the remote Upper Peninsula was explored. Attracted by the copper and iron mining boom in the Keweenaw Peninsula (the northern part of the state's Upper Peninsula), many miners from England's southwestern Cornwall district arrived and became naturalized citizens. The federal government assisted this settlement by negotiating treaties with the American Indians in 1842 and 1854, surveying the land, and selling it at low prices to those interested in mining. Later, though, when the government asserted and enforced its right to a 6–10 percent royalty for ore found on public lands, the copper frenzy dampened. Some disgruntled miners went to California for the gold rush of 1849.

In the 1850s, the Polish influx to the rural farmlands began but quickened considerably in the early twentieth century in search of manufacturing employment. In 1860, less than 20 percent of the state's population was foreign-born. The most came from Britain (61,497), some 38,878 come from Germany, 36,482 from Canada, and there were 6,335 Dutch. There also were 6,799 blacks, drawn by the cheap fertile farmland.

During the Civil War, about one-eighth of Michigan's 1860s' total population served in the North's cause. Some 15,000 of the 90,000 died. The Civil War greatly stimulated the use of labor-saving machinery on the farms, then facing a dire labor shortage. With the war demand, farming prosperity hit a new high. Immigrants could solve the labor need, and 90,000 came in the 1860s alone. The national Homestead Act of 1862, which gave free public lands to foreigners intending to become citizens, did diminish the supply of cheap labor. However, the 1864 contract labor law allowed companies to bring foreigners to the United States if they paid their labor, and immigration increased.

In 1868, artist Albert Bierstadt portrayed Hiawatha—undoubtedly Michigan's most famous Indian—departing from the shores of Lake Superior ("Gitchee Gumee"). Henry Wadsworth Longfellow's 1855 poem "Song of Hiawatha" identified Hiawatha with the Upper Peninsula. The real Hiawatha was an Iroquois who resided in central New York, though today there is a large Hiawatha National Forest.

In 1870, the most numerous foreign-born grouping was from Canada, with some English and many French Canadians. As usual, most migrants came to the state in search of economic opportunity. This was true of both the migrants from other parts of the nation and foreign immigrants. Some also came for other reasons, like the Dutch who were searching for religious freedom. Canadians in the 1830s and the Germans in mid-century came to Michigan as refugees of political fighting. There was a boom in the 1880s from the exploration of iron ore in the third and last of the Upper Peninsula's iron ranges, powerfully aided by the openings of the Soo Canal and the growing railroad network.

In 1881, the state began to actively court settlers, both domestic and foreign. The active marketing campaign, however, was halted in 1885 when the new governor declared that the immigration bureau's actions had undermined native employment. This criticism turned to outright discouragement of immigration in 1887, when another governor said there is a large percentage of foreign-born among residents of state asylums, poorhouses, prisons, and jails. The state, he claimed, also was threatened by "a horde of Chinese Pagans" and needed to halt Mormon polygamy (Catton 1976, 155).

Despite this alarmism, rapid immigration continued. People came from many countries. In the mines, the Irish were the norm, joined by some Swedes. In the lumber camps around the Straits, Finns (by the 1870s), French Canadians, Swedes, and Norwegians came to work. The southern and central farmland was the home of the Dutch. Irish came to Detroit and worked in the lumber camps, sawmills, and railroads. The factories and shops in southern towns were staffed by Italians and Germans. Many Finns, for example, utilized their lumber earnings to purchase farms, especially in the Upper Peninsula. As these various other nationalities entered, the predominant French ethnic culture of the state changed into the modern polyglot.

The state's rapid population growth slowed considerably in the 1890s, as the rich resources in the West drew settlers and workers. Poles were about 15 percent of Detroit's population by the 1890s, plagued by some of the same political problems they had encountered in Europe. Violence erupted in 1885 because of simmering tensions between Poles and Germans, and 1894 labor riot also stemmed from Irish German tensions with the Poles.

This era also was the beginning of Michigan's slow development of a vibrant industrial economy in its southern third. In 1860, there were 3,500 manufacturing companies in the state. This grew to 16,000 by 1900. Automobile manufacturing began in Detroit in 1896, as Charles B. King, Henry Ford, and Ransom E. Olds experimented with "horseless carriages" (May 1987, 118). The Olds Motor Works formally began in 1899, and produced the runabout in 1900. Henry Ford's company came up with the Model T in 1908, and the car boom was on. Detroit mainly benefited, hitting a population of over 250,000 in 1900. In 1900, it was the nation's 13th most-populous city.

TWENTIETH CENTURY

In the new century, the state's agricultural areas no longer could support significant increases in population. By the 1920s, the halcyon days of the copper, iron ore, and timber resources of the state were over. More costly underground mines were required to reach the remaining deposits, which rendered the state simply not competitive with other sources.

The manufacturing industry arrived in time to provide employment for the state's workers and to draw new migrants and immigrants. Immigration reached a new high. Different industries flourished. The chemical industry took advantage of the southern part of the state's salt and brine deposits, which also led to the Dow Chemical Company's founding in 1897. The state's northern limestone deposits stimulated the development of the state's Portland cement industry. Also, the paper industry emerged, utilizing rags, straw, and other materials in their mills, as well as the wood pulp from the Upper Peninsula. The furniture industry attained national prominence in the late nineteenth century, mostly around Grand Rapids.

In addition, Battle Creek became the "breakfast food city" soon thereafter, not because of using the local grains from southern Michigan's rich farmland but due to the decision of the Seventh Day Adventists to headquarter in that city. The various cold breakfast products were developed at the Battle Creek Sanitarium, established to promote and support the church's healthcare regimen.

By World War I, there were over 200 workers born in Palestine employed in a Lansing plant. The first mosque was built in Highland Park in 1920. That year, Detroit's population hit 1 million, and then 1.5 million in 1930. Migrants from the farms of southern Michigan and the formerly booming Upper Peninsula mines had flocked to Detroit. They were joined by a rush of Germans in the 1920s.

By 1930, manufacturing was 43 percent of Michigan's total workforce. Just 13 percent were in farming and 2 percent in lumbering, mining, and fishing. Some 68 percent of the population lived in urban areas, higher than any state other than Illinois and California. Most of this growth was in southern Michigan, particularly in those cities, like Flint, that had transitioned from agricultural to manufacturing centers. Flint's population soared from 13,103 in 1900 to 156,492 in 1930, as the completion of what was called the largest automobile factory in 1908–1909 had attracted workers and their families. New arrivals lived in tents until housing was built. Dearborn, Highland Park, and Hamtramck also saw their population skyrocket, after large car-manufacturing plants were built there.

Michigan was extremely diverse. Many Germans came for manufacturing employment, the Dutch staffed Grand Rapids's furniture industry, and Canadians grabbed jobs in the various southern Michigan auto plants. Immigrants from other countries also came in large numbers, including a couple of thousand from Asia and the Near East. Many of the immigrants were from southern and eastern Europe, with the most from Poland (119,228). There were 43,000 Italians and 34,000 Russians in the state in 1930, more than the Dutch, Swedish, or Irish. There also were roughly 10,000–20,000 from Czechoslovakia, Hungary, Yugoslavia, Greece, and Romania. Many were from a rural, peasant background and were low-skilled.

The predominant migratory route to Michigan from the nation's Eastern states slowed considerably by 1916 to be replaced by a wave from the South. The number of Southern-born Anglos—primarily from Arkansas, Kentucky, Missouri, and Tennessee—grew to 165,926 by 1930.

The prosperity in auto sales and the related population explosion led to a building boom during the 1920s that produces symphonies, libraries, infrastructure, and the other aspects of modernity. An all-weather statewide highway system replaced the dirt roads. This economic surge was aided by financial institution's extension of easy credit.

The Great Depression in 1929 resulted partially from the high consumer debt levels that had accumulated from buying automobiles on installment. Michigan's non-farm unemployment reached 50 percent, with the hardest hit areas in the auto-manufacturing cities and the Upper Peninsula.

During World War II, the state was truly "the arsenal of democracy" as the automobile plants were converted into building war material—including the B-24 bomber, tanks, bombs, and guns. Some 350,000 people came to the city of Detroit during 1941–1942 to work in these defense plants. Former automobile plants built everything from tanks to bombs to guns.

In 1957, the five-mile Mackinac Straits Bridge (3,800 feet/1,158 meters long) was opened, linking St. Ignace with Mackinaw City. The bridge had aided economic development of the state's Upper Peninsula for tourists and vacationers. The bridge was familiarly known as "Big Mac" and "Mighty Mac," and was the world's third-longest suspension bridge.

The national post–World War II surge in Mexican and other Latino immigration helped reverse a long-standing state trend. In 1900, 34 percent of Detroit's population was foreign-born, but fell by 1970 to 7.1 percent. Southern-born Latinos outnumbered the foreign-born by 1970 (Gregory 2005, 35). By the 1970s, Detroit had become the second city for Arab Americans with over 70,000, which was the largest Arabic population in the continent.

Michigan's economy plummeted in the late 1970s, and its 17 percent unemployment rate was the highest in the nation in the early 1980s. Mechanization had reduced employment in the mining industries and the auto industry was in freefall. One sign of this decline was that Detroit was among those cities who sued the federal government alleging that its population was significantly undercounted in the 1980 U.S. Census.

In the late 1980s, the state's economy rebounded. Western Michigan had developed many diversified industries beyond automobile manufacturing and gained population. Dearborn also did well, becoming a tourist attraction for Arabic food and Arabic products. For the tourism surge in the 1980s, the northern part of the Lower Peninsula was the primary beneficiary, as the Upper Peninsula's long-term population decline continued unabated.

With a significant public–private partnership, Detroit experienced another revival in the 1990s. One Detroit Center (1993) opened, drawing young professionals. The city's three casino resort hotels—MGM Grand Detroit, MotorCity Casino, and Greektown Casino—were built to serve one of the larger gaming industry markets in the nation. New downtown sports stadiums were constructed, along with major renovations. Tourism was stimulated further by the development of the International Riverfront, the River Walk, and a renovation of the Renaissance Center.

TWENTY-FIRST CENTURY

With few exceptions, the decline in Michigan's automobile industry has continued in the new century. While the state's economy has moved into a diversified and high-tech direction, off-setting some of the job losses, this has not been sufficient to halt the population exodus. In the 2006–2010 period, Michigan had the worst unemployment rate of any state, with a high 14.2 percent in August 2009. Major factors included the great decline in the automobile industry and the global financial crisis.

The state's population exodus accelerated with the continuing decline of its traditional industries and resultant persistently high unemployment rate. The 2008s net migration loss, with 109,000 more people leaving than moving in, was one of the worst rates in the nation, four times the 2000 loss. In 2010, the state's population fell to 9,876,187, and was the only state to show a net loss since 2000. Florida, Texas, and Nevada were the most popular destinations for out-migrants. Detroit's population plummeted 25 percent to 713,777—its lowest since 1910. That decline made Detroit, once the nation's fourth most-populous city, now 18th-down from 10th in 2000.

Detroit's various problems have not been helped by political shenanigans. Kwame M. Kilpatrick, mayor from 2002 to 2008, was sentenced to four months in jail after pleading guilty of charges of perjury and obstruction of justice, was released on probation after serving 99 days, was sentenced to 18 months to 5 years for violating probation, and then served time at the Federal Correctional Institution in Milan, Michigan. In 2012, he was also indicted on 38 additional corruption charges, in what a federal prosecutor called a "pattern of extortion, bribery and fraud" by some of Detroit's prominent officials (Martin and Hill 2010).

Not all parts of the state lost population. The population of the seven counties around Grand Rapids in the western part of the state increased 6.2 percent, and the northwest part of the Lower Peninsula around Traverse City went up 5.8 percent. The significant national Latino population increases had also impacted Michigan. While the state's white population decreased 2 percent and the black population fell 1 percent, the Latino population soared by 35 percent.

The number of Asians also rose about 35 percent. A bright sign was that the unemployment rate has declined from 2009s high to 8.5 percent in March 2012. It is not unreasonable to expect this economic upsurge to attract workers and families back to Michigan in the future.

TOPICAL ESSAYS

GLOBAL DETROIT AND GLOBAL MICHIGAN

In response to Michigan's population decline and probably also to the anti-immigrant rumblings, there has been a governmental push to welcome and encourage immigration. The New Economy Initiative of Southeast Michigan, the Detroit Chamber of Commerce and The Skillman Foundation funded Global Detroit. Its Global Detroit Study documented immigrants' positive contributions, dispelling the "fears and myths surrounding the role of immigrants in the regional economy," and advocating a strategic plan to help Michigan attain economic prosperity (New Economy Initiative of Southeast Michigan 2012).

Its first statewide summit on immigration and the economy was held in 2011 and highlighted: how immigrants have run 33 percent of all high-tech startups, making the state third in the nation in producing new high-tech jobs; how the purchasing power of Michigan Asians and Latinos is $17.5 billion in 2009, up 300 percent since 1990; how immigrants are three times more likely to start a business in Michigan than native-born residents; and how foreign students spend $592 million in tuition, fees, and living expenses in 2008–2009.

Michigan's governor Rick Snyder (R) began Global Michigan, an initiative to attract more foreign investors and entrepreneurs to help the state's economy. The plan hoped to attract highly skilled immigrants and investors, and focused on talent attraction, international student retention, and easing visas for foreign nationals who invested in state businesses (Kozlowski 2011). It is hoped that these efforts will help Michigan rebuild its economy and again become a magnet for immigrants.

STATE LEGISLATION REGARDING IMMIGRATION, 2007–2012

Michigan has had recent controversies over undocumented immigration. New state laws have both encouraged and discouraged such immigration. In 2007, state legislators passed an unprecedented amount of legislation about immigration law enforcement. Many were friendly to immigrants: Michigan Senate Bill (SB) 773 allocated funds to school districts for serving migrant children, Michigan House Bill (HB) 4207 extended licensure as a registered professional nurse for Canadians, Michigan SB 232 made foreigners and refugees eligible for state disability assistance, Michigan HB 4348 appropriated money for a federal-state criminal alien assistance program, and Michigan SB 222 budgeted to build housing for migrant farmworkers.

Other 2007 state laws were not so friendly. Michigan SB 229 directed state agencies to consider the immigration and residency status of employees of a prospective contractor to determine if using noncitizen workers was detrimental to state residents or the state economy. Michigan HB 4344 prohibited funds for multicultural services from going to undocumented immigrants, except in emergency medical situations. While legal resolutions both supporting and opposing Arizona's restrictive 2010 law were introduced in the Michigan House during 2010, none were passed.

Many of Michigan's 2011 new laws were directed at limiting state benefits for undocumented immigrants. SB 189 set up a sex-offender registry requiring proof of citizenship or immigration documents; HB 4408 made undocumented immigrants ineligible for employment benefits; and HB 803 forbade licenses, unless legality was documented. SB 4305 required checking the immigration status of possible offenders, and verifying the status of public benefit applicants.

Reflecting the nationwide concerns on one side about an "immigration problem" and racism and economic exploitation on the other side, families in Detroit

Michigan Republican governor Rick Snyder speaks during an interview before signing legislation to provide state funding for Detroit municipal pensions in Detroit on June 20, 2014. Snyder has advocated for immigration for foreigners with professional skills necessary for the state and is against "Arizona-style" immigration bills that allow for broad, anti-immigration measures. (AP Photo)

marched against harassment and racial profiling by the Border Patrol and Immigration and Customs Enforcement (ICE) in April 2011. The immigration agency had been criticized for targeting a school where immigrant parents were transporting their children. There were also arrests of undocumented immigrants in Kalamazoo by U.S. ICE agents. The Hispanic American Council of Kalamazoo stated that the raids had triggered fear in the local Latino community, with many afraid to open their businesses or send their children to school.

Despite the activity in the legislature, Michigan governor Rick Snyder (R) had said that the state should not have an Arizona-type law, and he might resist any attempt to pass one by the Michigan legislature, even if the Arizona law was approved by the U.S. Supreme Court. In light of the strong feelings, pros and cons, the only thing certain is that the undocumented immigration issue will not be settled soon.

NOTABLE GROUPS

Migrant and Immigrants Rights Advocacy Group

The Migrant and Immigrants Rights Advocacy Group is a student organization at the University of Michigan that was established in 2005. This group wants to foster constructive debate on immigration and help to educate University of Michigan students about this topic. The group works with other immigrant, human rights, and fair trade advocacy groups on campus, recognizing that immigration issues demand an intersectional approach. They also work with the Washtenaw County Workers' Center, aiding immigrants and poorer workers in Washtenaw County.

BIBLIOGRAPHY

Antone, N. Peter, Justin D. Casagrande, and Ryan J. Adwers. "Immigration Blog." 2011. http://www.immigrationusablog.com/. Accessed March 24, 2014.

Bailey, Ruby L. "The D Is a Draw: Most Suburbanites Are Repeat Visitors." *Detroit Free Press*, August 22, 2007.

Brown, Ralph H. *Historical Geography of the United States*. New York: Harcourt, Brace and Co., 1948.

Bunkley, Nick. "Prison Term for Ex-Mayor of Detroit." *New York Times*, May 25, 2010. http://www.nytimes.com/2010/05/26/us/26detroit.html. Accessed March 24, 2014.

Catton, Bruce. *Michigan: A Bicentennial History*. New York: W. W. Norton & Company, 1976.

Chandler, Anne B. "Why Is the Policeman Asking for My Visa? The Future of Federalism and Immigration Enforcement." *Tulsa Journal of Comparative and International Law* 15, no. 2 (2008): 209–42.

Chardavoyne, David G. "The Northwest Ordinance and Michigan's Territorial Heritage." In P. Finkelman, and M. J. Hershock, eds. *The History of Michigan Law*. Athens: Ohio University Press, 2006, pp. 13–36.

Daniels, Roger. *Coming to America: A History of Immigration and Ethnicity in American Life*. 2nd ed. New York: HarperCollins Publishers, 2002.

Devine, T. M. *To the Ends of the Earth: Scotland's Global Diaspora 1750–2010*. London: Smithsonian Books, 2011.

Dunbar, Willis F., and George S. May. *Michigan: A History of the Wolverine State*. Rev. ed. Grand Rapids, MI: William B. Eerdmans Publishing Company, 1980.

"Education, Not Deportation." *Progressive* 75, no. 11 (November 2011): 10.

Fassia, Anika. "Immigration and Michigan's Economy." Michigan League for Human Services, 2011. http://www.milhs.org/immigration-and-michigans-economy. Accessed March 24, 2014.

Foote, Margaret D. "History of Vermontville's Churches." Village of Vermontville, Michigan, 1978. http://www.vermontville-mi.gov/churches/churches.htm. Accessed March 24, 2014.

French, Ron, and Mike Wilkinson. "Leaving Michigan Behind: Eight-Year Population Exodus Staggers State." *The Detroit News*, April 2, 2009. http://www.detroitnews.com/article/20090402/METRO/904020403/. Accessed August 10, 2013.

Gregory, James N. *The Southern Diaspora: How the Great Migrations of Black and White Southerners Transformed America*. Chapel Hill: University of North Carolina Press, 2005.

Hershock, Martin J. "Blood on the Tracks: Law, Railroad Accidents, the Economy, and the Michigan Frontier." In P. Finkelman, and M. J. Hershock, eds. *The History of Michigan Law*. Athens: Ohio University Press, 2006, pp. 37–60.

Infrastructure Canada, Government of Canada. "History of the Saint Lawrence Seaway." 2012. http://web.archive.org/web/20080625044719/http://www.infrastructure.gc.ca/research-recherche/result/alt_formats/pdf/hm05_e.pdf. Accessed March 24, 2014.

John Higham, *Strangers in the Land: Patterns of American Nativism 1860–1925*. New Brunswick, NJ: Rutgers University Press, 1988.

Jordan, Terry G. "Between the Forest and the Prairie." In D. Ward, ed. *Geographic Perspectives on America's Past: Readings on the Historical Geography of the United States*. New York: Oxford University Press, 1979, pp. 50–60.

Kozlowski, Kim. "High-Skilled Immigrants Pursued to Boost Michigan Economy." *The Detroit News*, June 7, 2011. http://detnews.com/article/20110607/POLITICS02/106070372&template=printart. Accessed March 24, 2014.

Library of Michigan. "Michigan in Brief: Information about the State of Michigan." 2012. http://www.michigan.gov/documents/hal_lm_MiB_156795_7.pdf. Accessed March 24, 2014.

Llorente, Elizabeth. "Michigan Bill Requires Police and State Agencies to Check Immigration Status." FoxNews Latino, March 6, 2011.

Mackinac Bridge Authority. "About the Bridge." 2012. http://mackinacbridge.org/about-the-bridge-8/. Accessed March 24, 2014.

Martin, Elizabeth Anne. *Detroit and the Great Migration 1916–1929*. Lansing: University of Michigan, 1992.

Martin, Michel, and Lee Hill. "New Charges for Disgraced Detroit Ex-Mayor Kilpatrick." NPR.org transcript, December 17, 2010. http://www.npr.org/2010/12/17/132139281

/New-Charges-For-Disgraced-Detroit-Ex-Mayor-Kilpatrick. Accessed March 24, 2014.

May, George S. *Michigan: An Illustrated History of the Great Lakes State*. Northridge, CA: Windsor Publications, 1987.

McDougall, Walter A. *Freedom Just Around the Corner: A New American History 1585–1828*. New York: HarperCollins Publishers, 2004.

McDougall, Walter A. *Throes of Democracy: The American Civil War Era 1829–1877*. New York: HarperCollins Publishers, 2008.

McHugh, Kevin E. "Black Migration Reversal in the United States." *Geographical Review* 77, no. 2 (1987): 171–82.

McKether, Willie. "Roots of Civil Rights Politics in Northern Churches: Black Migration to Saginaw, Michigan 1915 to 1960." *Critical Sociology* 37, no. 5 (2011): 689–707.

Morse, Ann. "Down to the Details." A Special Report: Immigration and the States: March 2011. http://www.ncsl.org/issues-research/immig/a-special-report-immigration-and-the-states.aspx. Accessed March 24, 2014.

National Conference of State Legislatures, Immigrant Policy Project. *Enacted State Legislation Related to Immigrants and Immigration*. NCSL 1, 2007, 20.

National Conference of State Legislatures, Immigrant Policy Project. *2011 Immigration-Related Laws and Resolutions in the States (Jan. 1–Dec. 7, 2011)*. 2012. http://www.ncsl.org/issues-research/immig/state-immigration-legislation-report-dec-2011.aspx. Accessed March 24, 2014.

New Economy Initiative of Southeast Michigan. *Global Detroit Study*. 2012. http://new economyinitiative.cfsem.org/resources/research-library/global-detroit-study. Accessed March 24, 2014.

Nolan, Jenny. "Willow Run and the Arsenal of Democracy: Michigan History." *The Detroit News*, January 28, 1997. http://www.clanfowler.com/articles/Willow%20Run%20 and%20the%20Arsenal%20of%20Democracy.htm. Accessed March 24, 2014.

Parker, William N. "From Northwest to Midwest: Social Bases of a Regional History." In D. Ward, ed. *Geographic Perspectives on America's Past: Readings on the Historical Geography of the United States*. New York: Oxford University Press, 1975, pp. 167–78.

Parris, Terry Jr. "Can Immigration Loosen Our Rustbelt?" *Metromode*, May 14, 2009. http://www.metromodemedia.com/features/Immigration0116.aspx. Accessed March 24, 2014.

Saunders, Roger. "Black Migration to Detroit, Michigan." 2008. http://roger-saunders .suite101.com/black-migration-to-detroit-a46035. Accessed March 24, 2014.

Shelley, F. M., J. C. Archer, F. M. Davidson, and S. S. Brunn. *Political Geography of the United States*. New York: Guilford Press, 1996.

Tavernise, Sabrina, and Robert Gebeloff. "Many U.S. Blacks Moving to South, Reversing Trend." *New York Times*, March 24, 2011. http://www.nytimes.com/2011/03/25 /us/25south.html?pagewanted=all. Accessed March 24, 2014.

U.S. Census Bureau. "Annual Estimates of the Resident Population for the United States, Regions, States, and Puerto Rico: April 1, 2010 to July 1, 2011." *2011 Population Estimates*. Washington, DC: U.S. Census Bureau, Population Division, 2011.

U.S. Department of Labor, Bureau of Labor Statistics. "Economy at a Glance: Michigan." Series LASST26000003. 2012. http://www.bls.gov/eag/eag.mi.htm. Accessed March 24, 2014.

U.S. Department of Labor, Bureau of Labor Statistics. "Local Area Unemployment Statistics." Databases, Tables & Calculators by Subject, Series LASST26000003. 2012. http://data.bls.gov/timeseries/LASST26000003?data_tool=XGtable. Accessed March 24, 2014.

VanZandt, F. K. " 'Massachusetts.' Boundaries of the United States and the Several States." *USGS Bulletin* 1212 (1966): 95–106.

Washington, Forrester B. *The Negro in Detroit: A Survey of the Conditions of a Negro Group in a Northern Industrial Center during the War Prosperity Period.* Detroit: Associated Charities of Detroit, 1920.

Wisely, John, and Todd Spangler. "Motor City's Population Declines 25 Percent." *USA Today*, March 24, 2011. http://usatoday30.usatoday.com/news/nation/census/2011–03–22-michigan-census_N.htm. Accessed August 10, 2013.

Woodard, Colin. *American Nations: A History of the Eleven Regional Cultures of North America.* New York: Viking, 2011.

Young, Coleman, and Lonnie Wheeler. *Hard Stuff: The Autobiography of Mayor Coleman Young.* New York: Viking Adult, 1994.

Yung, K. "Immigration Start-ups Seen as Key to Reinventing Michigan." *Detroit Free Press*, January 21, 2011.

23

MINNESOTA

Candice Quinn and Anduin Wilhide

CHRONOLOGY

Pre-European Settlement	The earliest immigrants are Minnesota's two principal American Indian tribes, the Dakota and the Ojibwe. They are well-established hunting and gathering societies prior to the arrival of European traders. In the early 1800s, the area that would become Minnesota has an economy based on the fur trade.
1821	Beginning of Norwegian immigration to this area.
1825	Quaker and Haugean Norwegian immigrants travel to this area (via other routes), seeking religious toleration.
1849	Minnesota Territory is established.
1850s–1860s	The first sizeable wave of settlement occurs as town developers, timber magnets, and others head to Minnesota. While some of these people are from Sweden, Norway, Great Britain, and French Canada, many of these people are New England Yankees. The Minnesota Territory, established in 1849, offers great potential, and many hope to make it the New England of the West. After the Civil War, many free African Americans also come to the state.
1858	Minnesota becomes the 32nd state.
1862	The Homestead Act becomes law. In Minnesota, nearly 10,000 homestead entries draw immigrants. Tensions between the U.S. Army and the Dakota erupt in the U.S.-Dakota War. The conflict ends in the violent and brutal repression of the Dakota.
1867	The Minnesota legislature creates the State Board of Immigration to promote settlement to Minnesota abroad. Under the

	Immigration Act of 1891, the federal government assumes control of immigration.
1868	The Fourteenth Amendment provides for citizenship of all persons born on U.S. soil, thus ensuring that all children of immigrants are given citizenship.
1870	About 65 percent of Minnesota residents are either immigrants or first-generation Americans, with the majority of them originally from Britain, Germany, and Scandinavia.
1880s	Increased numbers of Norwegians and Swedes come to the state; most settle in Minneapolis.
1896	Election instructions are in nine languages: Czech, English, German, Norwegian, Swedish, Finnish, French, Italian, and Polish.
1900	First significant wave of immigration to the state is reported, particularly from Germany, Norway, and Sweden. Minnesota has the seventh-highest rank of foreign-born residents.
1910–1930s	The Mexican Revolution and its aftermath, combined with American labor shortages during World War I, spur Mexican immigration as people move seeking agricultural work opportunities.
1950s	The destruction caused by World War II and the rise of communism in Eastern Europe forces many Eastern Europeans to flee; many immigrate to Minnesota.
1980s	Starting after the Vietnam War and lasting into the 1980s, Southeast Asians start immigrating in larger numbers to Minnesota.
1990	The outbreak of Civil War in Somalia forces many Somalis to flee their home country and leave East Africa. By 2003, Minnesota is receiving more Somali immigrants than any other state.
1994	The Dalai Lama allows the only Dharma Monastery outside of Tibet or India to be built in Minneapolis.
1999	The first Somali mall in the United States opens in Minneapolis. The Karmel Mall serves as a community hub and a place to shop for familiar items for the Somali population.
2002	More than 13,000 people, coming from approximately 150 countries immigrate to Minnesota. In 2009, 18,020 people immigrate to Minnesota. About 1,000 Tibetans live in Minnesota, which is the second-largest Tibetan community in the United States after New York.
2002	Mee Moua becomes the first Hmong American to be elected to the Minnesota legislature after immigrating to the state as a refugee in 1978. She is reelected in 2006.
2006	A large Hindu temple opens in Maple Grove, Minnesota.
2008	According to the U.S. Census, 46,000 Hmong live in Minnesota, second only to California. About 29,000 Asian Indians and 27,000 Somalis call Minnesota home.
2013	The foreign-born comprise about 7.3 percent of the state's population.

HISTORICAL OVERVIEW

The popular image of Minnesota characterizes the state as ethnically homogeneous, a white agricultural land with one major metropolitan area that is only slightly more culturally diverse. To a certain extent, this is a simplified, but somewhat accurate portrayal. The largest ethnic groups in Minnesota are Germans, Swedes, and Norwegians, with large portions of the population descendant from French Canadians. In 2006, Minnesota's foreign-born population comprised 6.3 percent of the general population, which was less than half the national average. However, the story of Minnesota's post–World War II immigration is an interesting one, as the state has been trending toward greater diversity and is leading the country in the acceptance of refugees.

Minnesota territory was primarily settled by two Native American tribes, the Dakota and the Ojibwe. Some early European arrivals in this area initiated a fur trade between European traders and Native Americans. This continued into the early 1800s before more Europeans came to settle in the area in the next few decades. Norwegians were one of the primary groups that arrived in Minnesota Territory, with some early exploration in 1821 and more established settlements appearing in 1825 as some Norwegians fled religious persecution in their home country. Quakers and Haugeans particularly sought religious toleration.

In 1849, the Minnesota Territory was formally established and in the next two decades, more sizeable European settlement began. This included immigrants and residents from the East Coast who had decided to move to this territory for new opportunities. Immigrants also came from Germany, England, Canada, Norway, and Sweden. Minnesota became the 32nd state in 1858.

During the Civil War, Minnesota drew a significant number of immigrants because of the passage of the Homestead Act (1862). Unfortunately, there were also violent conflicts between settlers, the U.S. military, and the Dakota. Hundreds of settlers and Dakota were killed in the U.S.-Dakota War of 1862, which led to the brutal repression of the remaining Dakota residents in Minnesota. Many Dakota residents were forcibly removed from Minnesota and sent to reservations in other states.

In 1867, the Minnesota legislature decided to establish a State Board of Immigration to promote settlement to Minnesota from abroad. By 1870, 65 percent of Minnesota residents were foreign-born or first-generation Americans. The majority of them were originally from Britain, Germany, and Scandinavia. Norwegian immigration particularly increased in the 1880s, with most settling in Minneapolis. By 1896, there was such diversity in the state that election instructions were given in nine languages.

The year 1900 marked a peak wave of immigration to the state and Minnesota had the seventh-highest rank of foreign-born residents by this point. From the turn of the century through the postwar period, Supreme Court decisions and increasingly narrow numerical ceilings were established, based on eugenic understandings of immigrants. However, some Mexican individuals came to the state seeking temporary agricultural work in the interwar and postwar period. Some Eastern European refugees also arrived in the postwar period and settled in Minnesota.

From the Vietnam War period on, Southeast Asian refugees and other refugees (in smaller numbers) began to arrive in the state. In the 1990s, Somali refugees began arriving and by 2003, Minnesota became the primary destination of these refugee flows. In 1999, the first Somali mall opens in Minnesota: the first in the country. At the turn of this century, new immigrants come to the state, including a large group of Tibetans. Mee Moua, a refugee Hmong American, became the first Hmong American to be elected to the legislature in 2002 and was reelected in 2006. By 2008, the number of Hmong was about 46,000; Somalis 27,000; and Asian Indians 29,000.

Community Coordinator Fatima Jama and Director Sabah Yusuf of the Aishah Center for Women pose inside one of the booths at a Somali Mall in south Minneapolis on March 19, 2008. The two women coordinated an effort to open a 10,000– to 15,000-square-foot cooperative department store in Minneapolis owned and operated by Somali women. The store sells African imports, caters to a broader audience, and allows many Somali women shopkeepers to expand their businesses. (AP Photo/Dawn Villella)

TOPICAL ESSAYS

The topical essays explore who the people are that chose Minnesota as their new homes. It is important not only to understand the reasons why they come to this state, but the challenges they faced and how they became a part of Minnesotan society. While it would be tempting to categorize immigrants by the geographical areas they come from, experiences and reasons for migration vary greatly within geographical starting points. Instead it is more revealing to discuss immigrants in terms of their situations when they first arrived. The first category of immigrants this chapter shall discuss came to Minnesota either as university students or educated people looking for professional or other well-paying employment. A second category first came to Minnesota as migrant workers and later established their roots in the state. The last group this chapter shall discuss came to Minnesota as refugees, seeking to escape dangerous situations in their homelands.

PROFESSIONALS

Most of the immediate post–World War II immigration was made up of displaced persons coming over as refugees. However, some European professionals and intellectuals decided to immigrate during this time as they were drawn to the better employment opportunities that the United States provided. After the war, greater numbers of university students from the Middle East, Asia, and Africa began studying in Minnesota, a trend that still continues. Students from several different Middle Eastern groups, including large numbers of Iranians and Arabs chose to attend Minnesota universities in larger numbers specifically at the start of the 1980s. Interestingly, most did not plan to stay. While some did return to their native countries, many changed their minds, as they either desired more advanced studies, have formed strong bonds with American citizens, or simply enjoyed the American lifestyle and wanted to make this their new home. Other Middle Easterners came to Minnesota with the intentions of staying. In 1965, the United States and Egypt reached an agreement, allowing educated Egyptians to immigrate. In the following years, over 1,000 Egyptians came to Minnesota under this agreement, with almost all of them finding homes in the metro Twin Cities area.

Filipino immigration to Minnesota has included professionally trained men and women in search of greater professional opportunities since 1965. This movement of people was part of the great Asian "brain drain" as the United States admitted a significant number of professionals in various fields. In particular, Minnesota saw an influx of Filipino doctors and nurses during the early 1970s. Minnesota was a choice location within the United States for Asian medical professionals, as the state was known throughout Asia as an important medical center and a good place to acquire specialized training.

In 1969, Korea provided the second-highest number of immigrants per year to Minnesota, surpassed only by Canada, and by 1971, Koreans were the largest group. This community was made up of mostly students and intellectuals until the mid-1970s when it became more diversified and blue-collar workers outnumbered professionals. By 1981, the Korean population included servicemen's wives, adopted children, students, professionals, and blue-collar workers. Unlike most immigrant communities, Koreans usually formed no separate community and rarely isolated themselves geographically from larger society. However, one exception to this statement is the large community of Korean elders who live in Cedar-Riverside in Minneapolis.

Migrant Workers

The United States, and in particular its agricultural states, experienced labor shortages during World War II as men mobilized for deployment. The Bracero Program attempted to relieve predicted labor shortages by allowing temporary foreign workers into the country. Under this program, Mexican agricultural field workers came to the United States by the hundreds of thousands between 1942 and 1964. From 1944 until 1946, an estimated 4,000 Mexican workers came to Minnesota, with the 13 canneries requesting another 2,255 workers in 1947, and the next year Clay County alone received almost 2,000 more migrants. These workers lived (and worked) in deplorable conditions, but sadly, the Mexican migrants deemed these housing conditions better than those available to them in other states in the country. Living conditions were poor enough that they contributed to frequent cases of tuberculosis among Mexican immigrants, which occurred both in rural areas and continued when many moved to urban areas. Among Mexican Americans, Minnesota earned a reputation of offering a high level of services for residents.

During the late 1940s, the Mexican population in Minnesota began to shift from mostly rurally based to a more urban population. Despite being a community characterized by poverty for decades, Mexican American communities have had a low incidence of crime. By 2000, 42,000 Mexican immigrants lived in the state, making it the largest foreign-born group in the state.

Since the 1980s, the issue of undocumented immigrants has become part of a national political debate, with Mexican Americans often being the main focus. It is difficult to estimate the number of undocumented people living in Minnesota. The Pew Hispanic Research estimated in 2006 that approximately 55,000–85,000 undocumented immigrants may be in Minnesota. Much of the undocumented labor force is concentrated in the service, agricultural, construction, and manufacturing sectors, and is often composed of Latino/a peoples. While the face of the undocumented labor debate is usually Latino/a, it is worth noting that some experts suggest that Canadians make up the second-largest group of undocumented immigrants, who do not have to sneak across dangerous boarders, but simply overstay their visas. As many of these undocumented immigrants from Canada visibly blend in with the rest of the Minnesota population, they rarely face any of the scrutiny of Latino population. A 2000 report by HACER-MN estimated that undocumented labor is worth almost $1.6 billion a year to the Minnesota economy, and if all undocumented laborers were suddenly removed, Minnesota's economic growth would decline by 40 percent.

REFUGEES

Following World War II, Minnesota was one of the first states to act under the federal refugee policy outlined in the Displaced Persons Act of 1948. By establishing a Citizen's Committee, Minnesota began a tradition of accepting refugees. In the 1990s, the proportion of immigrants who were refugees ranged from 24 to 46 percent in Minnesota, as compared to 6 to 16 percent nationwide. On average during the past decade, 25 to 50 percent of Minnesota's immigrants were refugees, an impressive number compared to 8 percent nationally. Once in Minnesota, immigrants in general and refugees in particular enjoyed one of the highest rates of employment in the country, and high levels of social benefits were readily available in the state.

Immediately following World War II, huge numbers of political refugees who had been displaced by the war arrived. Not surprisingly, many who fled Eastern Europe did not want to return home now that the areas were under Soviet control. Baltic people who left Europe after the war included Estonians, Latvians, Lithuanians, Hungarians, Ukrainians, Jews, Czechs, Slovaks, Poles, and South Slavs. Approximately 7,000 people of these displaced persons landed in Minnesota between 1948 and 1952. While a few people from all these groups were represented, slightly under half were Polish. The largest group of Baltic immigrants to Minnesota was the Latvians, with 1,300 people coming to Minnesota between 1940 and 1952. While Latvians chose areas through the state to eventually settle down, most began their new life in Minneapolis. Only a few hundred Estonians and Lithuanian people immigrated during the same period, but all these Baltic groups shared key characteristics: staunch anti-communist beliefs and a well-defined ethnic and political consciousness.

Another wave of Slavic immigration also came after the war, when 530 Yugoslavian immigrants moved to Minnesota between 1949 and 1952. The pre-existing Ukrainian community was not hostile toward new immigrants the way the older Polish community was toward their new community members. Established Ukrainian families sponsored and helped newer immigrants, who mostly moved to the Twin Cities. During the 1950s, 2,780 Polish displaced persons chose Minnesota as their new home, altering the culture of the preexisting Polish community in the Twin Cities. In general, the newer immigrants were more highly educated and from a higher social class than earlier settlers. Two different groups of Hungarians immigrated to Minnesota during the second half of the twentieth century. These fourth and fifth waves of Hungarian refugees (with earlier waves arriving before World War II) were displaced persons and freedom fighters. Freedom fighters needed to escape after the Hungarian revolt against Soviet dominance. These two groups were culturally different from Hungarians already in Minnesota. The displaced persons were educated, urban, and from the middle and upper classes. Social clashes with the more rural farmers of early immigration groups occurred as the new immigrants were often right-wing nationalists, constituting the very group that earlier immigrants attempted to escape.

In more recent decades, Minnesota has kept up its commitment to helping refugees start a new life, with the Minnesota Department of Human Services estimating that more than 70,500 refugees lived in Minnesota as of 2006. However, the ethnic composition of refugee groups has changed dramatically.

State senator Foung Hawj, D-St. Paul, center behind a young boy, looks around to make sure all his family members gather for a photograph, after a mock swearing-in at the state capitol in St. Paul, Minnesota, on January 8, 2013. Hawj is the third Hmong to serve in the Minnesota Senate. (AP Photo/Jim Mone)

Since the 1990s, refugees have come to Minnesota mostly from the former Soviet Union, Bosnia, Somalia, Sudan, Ethiopia, Eritrea, Liberia, Vietnam, Laos, and Cambodia.

Indochinese refugees include Vietnamese, Laos, Cambodians, and ethnic Chinese, but by far, the largest group is the Hmong. The Hmong first arrived in 1976, but the most dramatic increase took place in 1980 when the Hmong population quadrupled to 10,000, with most choosing to live in the Twin Cities. By 2000, it was estimated that 42,863 Hmong lived in Minnesota. Many are still suffering from the consequences of war, but adapt well to life in the Twin Cities. The state is now home to the second-largest Hmong refugee community in the United States, after California.

Minnesota is home to the largest Somali population in the United States and has the ninth-largest African immigrant population in the country. In 2008, one in five immigrants to Minnesota was from an African country, when the number of African immigrants reached between 70,000 and 80,000. The largest single group of African immigrants comes from Somalia, with an estimated 29,000 Somalis arriving in Minnesota between 1992 and 1999. Almost all Somali immigrants, and in fact most African immigrants, are refugees. As of 2000, almost a third of Minnesota Somali residents came directly from refugee camps. Most Somali immigration occurred between 1990 and 2000, but after the attacks of September 11, 2001, and the subsequent economic downturn, refugee arrivals dropped sharply. However, some African immigrants continued to arrive under family reunification plans and from other states (Remington 2008). Most African immigrants choose to live in the Twin Cities; however, in more recent years more African immigrants have chosen more rural parts of the state, including Rochester, Faribault, Owatonna, Pelican Rapids, and Wilmar, where they are primarily employed in the meat-processing plants. No major problems have been recorded, but these rural areas had little prior ethnic diversification, and some cultural clashes have arisen.

SOMALI MIGRATION AND SETTLEMENT IN MINNESOTA

In 2006, 11 percent of all refugees admitted to the United States were resettled in Minnesota. The largest refugee communities are from East Africa, Southeast Asia, and Eastern Europe. While many refugees have settled in the Twin Cities where they can access diverse opportunities for employment, services, education, and housing, others have chosen to live in small towns across Minnesota, which offer employment in agricultural and meat-processing industries.

Minnesota has become an important site for refugee resettlement because of a distinctive blend of social service organizations, governmental policies , and the choices of individuals, who pursued the best interests of their families with the help of their own social networks.

Since 1991, when Civil War broke out in Somalia, thousands of Somalis have fled their homes because of political conflict, clan-based violence, and devastating famine. Many Somalis have resettled in Minnesota. Some Somalis came as refugees, while others arrived as immigrants through the sponsorship of family members. Somalis have also relocated to Minnesota from other parts of the United States to seek employment and educational opportunities and to join a thriving Somali community.

Minnesota now hosts one of the largest Somali communities in the Somali diaspora. The exact number of Somalis living in the state is difficult to determine, but estimates range from 30,000 (American Community Survey 2009 and Minnesota Compass 2012) to 60,000 (World Relief Minnesota 2012) to 100,000. The majority of Somalis in Minnesota live in the Twin Cities Metropolitan area, while others have settled in smaller towns throughout the state. Many Somalis have chosen Minnesota because of their social networks, for educational and employment opportunities, and for accessing an array of services. Somalis also cite Minnesota's high standard of living and a reputation for hospitality as reasons why they have chosen to stay in Minnesota.

The Somali experience of refugee resettlement can be viewed as a case study for understanding recent immigration in Minnesota. Somalis like many immigrants before them, arrived in Minnesota with social and cultural resources to help them adapt their lives to a new place. They have built extensive social and professional networks which have helped them find housing, employment, and educational opportunities. Like earlier immigrant communities, Somalis have struggled to figure out where they belonged and how to maintain cultural and social traditions as they adjusted to living in a new place. The challenges include dealing with the separation of family and friends ; learning English while preserving their native language; maintaining cultural and religious practices in a multicultural society; finding housing that meets their needs, and jobs that meet their skill levels; and achieving success in secondary and higher education systems.

Somalis have faced unique challenges as well. They are African Muslims living in an historical moment (post-9/11) when their religion is being scrutinized and their home country exists without an effective central government. Somalia is most often in the news for instances of Islamic terrorism and piracy. Somalis face discrimination both as Africans in America and as Muslims in America. They are also trying to figure out how to unify and rebuild Somalia after decades of civil unrest and famine and to maintain connections to Somalis around the world. In spite of these challenging conditions, Somalis have forged livelihoods and have created a thriving community in Minnesota for more than 20 years.

The Somali Experience in Minnesota. Oral history plays a vital role in telling the history of the Somalis in Minnesota not only because Somali society is an oral society but also because the Somalis in Minnesota did not arrive with many historical artifacts. Their stories and memories depend on their vibrant oral tradition. These stories show the everyday experiences, individual agency, and decision-making processes of Somalis as they have adjusted to living in Minnesota. The journey out of Somalia was often a dangerous one, as one Somali refugee recounted:

> We were living in a city called Kismayo. . . . One morning, . . . some bandits came to our home. And then they killed my father. I woke up and my mom was crying over there, outside the apartment. . . . We left that place the same evening. When it became dark, like midnight, my mom took us and we come all the way down to the border of Kenya. . . . And I remember some nights there were some bandits coming, even at the border, killing people, taking their foods out, raping the women. It was difficult.—Shamarke (Minnesota Council of Churches 2011)

The United States began issuing visas to Somali refugees in 1992. For those who received a visa, the decision to leave their families and homes in East Africa was painful but many did leave and resettled in the United States. Refugee resettlement agencies like the International Institute of Minnesota and World Relief Minnesota, nonprofit social service organizations like Lutheran Social Services and Catholic Charities, Somali-led organizations like Somali Family Services and the Confederation of the Somali Community in Minnesota, and Somali individuals and families, helped facilitate the migration and resettlement of Somalis in Minnesota.

The Somalis in Minnesota represent a cross-section of Somali society: they are teachers, civil servants, nomads, farmers, entrepreneurs, students, professors, and merchants. They represent all regions of Somalia. Abdisalam Adam came with a student visa and lived in Washington, DC, before deciding to move to Minnesota.

> I used to hear about Minnesota as a very cold state, the snow and the ice. . . . But, also, I heard that it's a state that's very welcoming. Its people are friendly. It has good education. It has very understanding people who, you know, are tolerant of other cultures and values and so on. When I came here, I did find all that to be true.—Abdisalam Adam (Minnesota Historical Society 2004)

Most Somalis settled in the Twin Cities because they offered opportunities for housing, employment, services, and education. Somalis eventually spread out into adjoining suburbs such as Eden Prairie and into smaller towns such as Rochester, Owatonna, Pelican Rapids, Worthington, and St. Cloud. They were drawn by employment opportunities in a number of agricultural and meat-processing industries, many of which did not require English proficiency, a major concern for some Somalis. Some of the first Somalis in Minnesota settled in Marshall to pursue employment at a meat-processing plant.

The Cedar-Riverside neighborhood in Minneapolis has become a hub for the Somali community and continues to host the largest concentration of Somalis in Minnesota. Cedar-Riverside provided residential relocation for Somalis through affordable housing structures. Many community-building institutions, including the Confederation of the Somali Community in Minnesota, the Brian Coyle Community Center, the East African Women's Center, and the African Development Center, emerged in Cedar-Riverside. There are several mosques in the neighborhood which provide spaces for religious worship as well as community gatherings. Cedar-Riverside is also home to many educational institutions such as the University of Minnesota and Augsburg College which Somali students have attended in growing numbers.

Maryan Del reflects on how her experience in Cedar-Riverside influenced her decision to leave Virginia and move to Minnesota.

> I came here for vacation in summer time. I wasn't planning to stay here. But when I came in, I realized there was a bunch of Somali people here. . . . [W]hen you come to Cedar Riverside, there's a bunch of Somalis, the Coyle Community Center. So I figured maybe this is the right place for me to stay, because I have a lot of my people where I can observe my culture, my religion, and my traditions. . . . I went back, got my stuff, got my school changed, and I moved here, and Minnesota has been good to me.—Maryan Del (Minnesota Historical Society 2004)

Leaving their homes in East Africa, traveling thousands of miles, and arriving in Midwestern America could be a bewildering experience as one young refugee explained:

> It was hard for me to come here, and when I stepped off the plane into America I knew that everything was gonna change, I knew that nothing was gonna be the same. It was hard for me, you know, seeing all these different people, seeing people that I'd never saw, just looking at people.—Saida Hassan (Minnesota Historical Society 2004)

Somalis faced language and cultural barriers when they first arrived.

> We first came to New York and then Chicago. We are being helped by the immigration officers who were with us all the time in every airport that we came. We did not need that much help for language, but when I came to Minneapolis, then was a little bit difficult. . . . Everything you need you have to ask for. . . . You have to ask someone to translate, so it was kind of like you cannot do anything. You are like a little kid that cannot even speak.—Hared Mah (Minnesota Historical Society 2004)

Many Somali refugees have faced a different adjustment process than previous immigrants in Minnesota because they have dealt with multiple traumas; they have survived a Civil War, life in refugee camps, and now face resettlement in a country with very different cultural and religious traditions. Somalis came to the United States because they were forced out of their country and some still hope for the day when they can return to their homeland. The chaotic situation in Somalia has affected their approach to adjusting to American society. The top causes of immigration-related stress for Somalis in the Twin Cities included separation from family and friends, homesickness/isolation, and language barriers.

Language. Many Somalis arrived in Minnesota with proficiency in multiple languages: Somali; Arabic; and sometimes Swahili, French, or Italian, but gaining English proficiency was an obstacle. Some had arrived with a knowledge of English others arrived without any English language skills. A survey conducted with Somalis in the Twin Cities reported that a majority of Somalis had some confidence in their English-speaking skills but more than half continued to take English language classes.

> I remember when I went to the school first day, I'd be sitting there . . . literally, you are deaf. That's how I felt, because you'd be seeing teachers talking, doing math or ESL [English as a Second Language] classes. Can you imagine just sitting there without . . . knowing what they are talking about?—Maryan Del (Minnesota Historical Society 2004)

Somali elders have had more difficulties learning English than Somali youth who are exposed to English at school and through popular media. Because of this language barrier, many Somali elders struggle with isolation, which can be a major obstacle to social interaction and adjusting to a new culture. In many ways, the Cedar-Riverside area has become a refuge for Somalis, in particular elders of the community, struggling to understand the new society they live in. They are surrounded by people who speak their language, stores that cater to the Somali community, and can take care of many necessities within the neighborhood.

It has been difficult for Somali parents who struggle with English to participate in their children's education and this has sometimes led to conflicting expectations about their role. As the Somali community liaison for St. Paul Public Schools, Abdisalam Adam, explains:

> It has been a real challenge, parental involvement in the schools. The assumption was the teacher is responsible for everything. So once I send my child to school, it's the teacher's and the school's responsibility. This was the mindset that the parents came with, and us teachers continue to . . . tell them about how they need to be in the building. They need to know the teacher. Of course, I don't blame the parents

who do not speak the language, who are not used to the educational system, who feel intimidated by this huge system. But, gradually, I think the younger parents are beginning to be more involved and more outgoing in knowing about their child's education. This also is a huge adjustment that parents need to make.—Abdisalam Adam (Minnesota Historical Society 2004)

Many Somalis are concerned that Somali youth are losing their Somali language skills but understand that they are surrounded by English in American society. One of the ways that Somali families have addressed this concern has been the creation of charter schools that cater specifically to the Somali community.

Being Muslim in Minnesota. Somalis are one of the largest Muslim communities in Minnesota, a state that has been mostly comprised of Lutheran, Catholic, and Jewish communities for most of its history. When Somalis arrived in the 1990s, many in Minnesota were not familiar with Islam or the religious practices of Muslims. There has been a long period of adjustment as Somalis have sought to educate Minnesotans about Islam and as Minnesotans have gained more familiarity with Muslim religious practices.

Many Somalis see their Islamic faith as an integral part of Somali identity. However, Somalis have faced challenges to the practice of their faith in Minnesota. The Islamic faith has certain practices that Muslims are expected to follow which can be hard to maintain in the United States. For example, Muslims are expected to pray five times a day and to fast from sunrise to sundown during the holy month of Ramadan. Muslims have certain dietary restrictions and are expected to avoid pork and alcohol and to eat foods processed according to Islamic law. Muslim women are expected to dress modestly and to wear the *hijab*, or head covering.

For many Somalis, finding space for the daily prayers while at school or at work is a recurring challenge. One of the basic tenets of Islam is ablution, the ritual of cleansing one's hands and feet before the daily prayers. Many Somalis finds it difficult to practice this ritual in a society that is not used to accommodating prayer in schools or workplaces.

Abdisalam Adam highlights this as one of the hardships he faced adjusting to life in Minnesota.

Of course, the main ones were the religious practices, like where do you pray? You're driving or you have a meeting or you're somewhere or you're in a classroom and the time of the prayer comes, that was the biggest challenge we had to struggle with. A lot of times, before leaving home, I have to plan ahead to go with my ablution or I'll do it before I leave home. A lot of times, I'll step out of where I am and have to look for a small corner to be able to pray. That, of course, required a lot of commitment and patience.—Abdisalam Adam (Minnesota Historical Society 2004)

Many Somali women have continued to wear the *hijab* while living in the United States and they become more visible as Muslims than men are. Young Somali women have faced religious discrimination at school. Other Somali women have decided not to wear the *hijab*. The decision to wear the *hijab* in the United States can be a complicated as one young Somali woman explains,

> I sometimes wear it but I've been living here for like eleven years. I feel like I've been Americanized but really I'm not it's just I'm just trying to fit in with Americans and I just caught up with them and I just kind of stopped wearing it. I sometimes wear it though to try and fit in with everyone else that's Muslim and all the other Somali girls. But then I feel like I shouldn't do that because I feel like I should just follow my heart and do what I think I should even though that's against my religion to not wear it.—Hibo Mohamed (Minnesota Historical Society and TV By Girls 2004)

Increasingly, Minnesotans have tried to accommodate the needs of Somalis in schools and in the workplace. Many public schools have removed pork from their food menus or have provided options for those students who cannot have pork products. Many schools and workplaces have tried to accommodate the practice of daily prayers by providing space for students and employees to pray during the day. The number of mosques has grown to accommodate the growing Somali population, as well as other Muslim communities in Minnesota.

The events of September 11, 2001, impacted people around the world, including Somalis in Minnesota. The fear of terrorism led the U.S. government to scrutinize anything that they believed had connections to the terrorist network known as Al-Qaeda. Money-wiring businesses in the Twin Cities were closed because of suspicions that they were connected to terrorist groups in Somalia. Many Somalis used these wire transfer businesses to send funds to family members still living in Somalia and in Kenyan refugee camps and did not know about any links to a terrorist network. A possible connection of a wire service to Al-Qaeda in a *Minneapolis Star-Tribune* article might have even spurred attacks on a few Somali in Minneapolis. The Somali community was outraged at these allegations and was quick to assure the Minnesota community that it did not in any way support the mission of Al-Qaeda.

> Of course, immediately after 9–11, there were major challenges. There was a lot of fear in the community that there would be a backlash from mainstream Americans, ... But, luckily, that did not happen much in Minnesota; Minnesota was one of the states that there wasn't much of a backlash. Of course, the public officials made it very clear right from the beginning. The governor and the state officials spoke out that these are not mainstream Muslims that are doing this. So that kind of helped ease the tension. But on the general level, of course, there are a lot of pressures. There's a lot of focus and there's a lot of always tying what's happening in the Middle

> East or in East Africa, always making a link, that maybe the people here could have a link to people there.–Abdisalam Adam (Minnesota Historical Society 2004)

The U.S. government has continued to investigate possible links between Somalis in Minnesota and the Islamic terrorist group, Al-Shabaab. From 2007 to 2008, approximately 20 young Somali men left Minnesota and returned to Somalia. The reasons they left remain unclear, but many were forced to join Al-Shabaab and have participated in acts of Islamic terrorism as suicide bombers. The families and friends of these young men did not even know that they had left for Somalia until long after they were gone. This is an ongoing tragedy for many Somalis in Minnesota as they struggle with the loss of sons, nephews, and friends at the same time that the FBI investigates the situation (Yuen and Aslanian 2012). Most Somalis do not have any connection to Islamic terrorist networks and they strongly disagree with the ideas and practices of groups like Al-Shabaab and Al-Qaeda.

Adapting to Life in Minnesota and Balancing Cultures. Somalis have used a wide array of social service resources made available by state, county, and community organizations to help them navigate their way in Minnesota. They have created their own organizations and networks to help each other through the process of immigration and adjusting to a new society.

Many Somalis have begun to purchase homes as they decide to settle in Minnesota. However, Islamic law restricts Muslims from paying interest on loans, a major obstacle for Somalis who need financial assistance to buy a house. The Somali-led organization, the African Development Center, has stepped in and has created an innovative program to provide interest-free loans for Somalis and other Muslims in Minnesota.

Many Somalis were not able to transfer their degrees or professional training to jobs in the Minnesota economy. However, Somalis have been active in the education and health fields and they have been important in the transportation sector. The Somali business community has earned an international reputation for successful small-business entrepreneurship.

> We have a lot of businesses. We have a great economic impact on Minnesota with our businesses. We're people with ambitions. If you go around, you'll see a lot of Somali stores, malls. We have a very rich culture, people should learn about us like we're willing to learn about them.—Maryan Del (Minnesota Historical Society 2004)

Somali youth are pursuing educational opportunities in many higher education institutions. The Somali Student Association at the University of Minnesota, Twin Cities serves over 500 Somali students on campus. Many Somali youth see education as a way to achieving a better quality of life.

Now I'm a senior and I will be graduating this year. I'm planning to go to the University of Minnesota. I'm accepted there. . . . I think I will study electrical engineering. I think the future is bright now for me.—Hared Mah (Minnesota Historical Society 2004)

Balancing Cultures

As Somalis adjust to their lives in Minnesota, many are concerned about what parts of Somali culture they will hold on to and what parts of American culture they will adopt. Many Somalis find themselves balancing two cultures.

I have two homes-my American home and my Somali home. I have two cultures, two languages. This is part of my life because I grew up having my life here.—Maryan Del (Minnesota Historical Society 2004)

There is a lot of concern about a growing divide between Somali elders and Somali youth. Many of the young people arrived in Minnesota when they were teenagers or even younger. Scholars in the United States tend to label such persons the 1.5 generation, since much of their socialization has occurred abroad after being born in Somalia or East Africa. As a result, youth are more likely than their elders to speak English, to be exposed to mainstream American culture, and to have more social interaction with Americans from diverse backgrounds.

Many Somalis are concerned that Somali youth will abandon their Somali cultural traditions as they continue to live in the United States. However, both Somali elders and Somali youth recognize the importance of Somali cultural preservation as a young Somali woman Sumaya Yusuf explains,

We have to keep that part of our traditions very important to us. I'll be the first to admit that I can't speak Somali as well as I would like to. I would love to learn.—Sumaya Yusuf (Minnesota Historical Society 2004)

In fact, many Somali youth feel like they are combining both American culture and Somali culture. According to Mohamed Jama, "Most of our young people are not losing culture, but they are entwining with the culture" (Minnesota Historical Society 2004).

Staying Connected to Somalia. As Somalis focus on their lives in Minnesota, they also maintain transnational connections to Somalis living in Somalia and in other parts of the world. Many send remittances to family members still living in Somalia. Remittances play an important role in Somalia's economy. Somalis also travel around the world to visit relatives who have been displaced due to the war.

It is important to maintain these connections with other Somalis in the diaspora as they try to reunite with their families and help each other in places such as Europe, North America, and Australia.

Somalis in Minnesota are also deeply concerned with questions of how to unify and rebuild Somalia after decades of chaos and political, social, and economic instability. Some have returned to help, while others have participated in rebuilding the political, social, and economic infrastructure of Somalia. For example, the Minnesota-based Somali organization, Somali Family Services, built the Puntland Library and Resource Center in northern Somalia. The library is used by thousands of people who live in the region and Somali Family Services (SFS) uses the space to provide trainings and workshops for civil society organizations. There are plans to build sports and recreation facilities too.

Even as they build new lives in Minnesota, many Somalis stay connected to Somalia. They hope that peace will return to Somalia and some plan to return home. As of 2012, however, the Somali federal government still struggles to establish a safe and secure Somalia. The desperate social, political, and economic conditions in Somalia prevent many Somalis from returning home and many have tried to bring family members to Minnesota.

> People are settling here. They're buying houses; some are buying houses. People are investing in businesses. Because Somalia is not a safe place to be in right now because there's no government, there's no bank, there's nothing stable right now. . . . So I think people are willing to invest their life here. They want their kids to be educated, to be somebody. I think going back to Somalia, it doesn't offer a lot of opportunities Minnesota offers you. I think Minnesota is a good state to invest . . . so we're all of us moving here, you see?—Maryan Del (Minnesota Historical Society 2004)

Sometimes not even people from the same country arriving in Minnesota during the same time fall into the same category. Chinese immigrants to Minnesota are a case in point. During the late 1940s and early 1950s, Chinese immigrants to this state included wives and children of earlier settlers, students, professionals, political refugees, and wives of servicemen. By the 1960s, Minnesota's Chinese population doubled to approximately 1,270. By the 1960s, sharp divisions existed in the Chinese population between southern Chinese businessmen and northern Chinese intellectuals.

In 2000, Minnesota's foreign-born population numbers 113,039, or approximately 5 percent of the state population. Minnesota does not have much ethnic diversity compared to many states, but does have a history of welcoming refugees who mostly choose to live in the Twin Cities, making the urban center of the state fairly ethnically diverse.

NOTABLE GROUPS

Immigration Law Center of Minnesota

The Immigration Law Center of Minnesota is a group founded in 1976 but was called at the time *Oficina Legal*. This group provides immigration legal services to immigrants and refugees. The group tries to raise public awareness about issues related to immigration and refugees and helps to foster good public policy on these issues. Among other services, this group helps clients pro bono and has a detainee assistance program. The New Beginnings Project helps immigrants and children who are victims of domestic violence or a related crime, particularly targeting those eligible for a T or U Visa. Although this group is urban-based, it also recognizes the need to help immigrants in rural communities, particularly those experiencing domestic violence or who could be or are in detention.

BIBLIOGRAPHY

Aamot, Greg. *The New Minnesotans: Stories of Immigrants and Refugees*. n.p.: Syren, 2006.

Abdi, Cawo M. "The Newest African-Americans?: Somali Struggles for Belonging." *Bildhaan: An International Journal of Somali Studies* 11 (2011): 90–107.

Advocates for Human Rights. "The Facts: Immigration in Minnesota." 2006. www.threadvocatesforhumanrights.org. Accessed March 24, 2014.

Ali, Ihotu. "Staying off the Bottom of the Melting Pot: Somali Refugees Respond to a Changing U.S. Immigration Climate." *Bildhaan: An International Journal of Somali Studies* 9 (2011): 82–114.

Amherst H. Wilder Foundation. *Speaking for Themselves: A Survey of Hispanic, Hmong, Russian and Somali Immigrants*. St Paul, MN: Wilder Foundation, 2000.

"Becoming Minnesotan: Stories of Recent Immigrants and Refugees." Minnesota Historical Society. 2004. http://education.mnhs.org/immigration/. Accessed July 12, 2013.

Brons, Maria. *Society, Security, Sovereignty and the State: From Statelessness to Statelessness*. Ann Arbor: University of Michigan, International Books, 2001.

Bryd, Erika, and Anne Gadwa. "Working Effectively with Somali Residents through the Arts: Collective Wisdom from the Cedar-Riverside Neighborhood." Unpublished Master's Thesis, University of Minnesota, Hubert H. Humphrey Institute, 2008.

Cameron, Linda. "Common Threads: The Minnesota Immigrant Experience." *Minnesota History* 62, no. 3 (2010): 96–106.

Cassanelli, Lee. *The Shaping of Somali Society: Reconstructing the History of a Pastoral People, 1600–1900*. Philadelphia: University of Pennsylvania Press, 1982.

Diebold, Susan. "The Mexican Americans." In June Drenning Holmquist, ed. *They Chose Minnesota: A Survey of the State's Ethnic Groups*. St. Paul: Minnesota Historical Press, 1981, pp. 92–110.

Dyrud, Keith. "The East Slavs—Rusins, Ukrainians, Russians, and Belorussians." In June Drenning Holmquist, ed. *They Chose Minnesota: A Survey of the State's Ethnic Groups*. St. Paul: Minnesota Historical Press, 1981, pp. 405–22.

Fennelly, Katherine. "Latinos, Africans, and Asians in the North Start State: Immigrant Communities in Minnesota." In Elzbieta M. Gozdziak, and Susan Forbes Martin, eds. *Beyond the Gateway: Immigrants in a Changing America.* Lanham, MD: Lexington Books, 2006, pp. 111–36.

Farah, Nuruddin. *Yesterday, Tomorrow: Voices from the Somali Diaspora.* New York: Cassell, 2000.

Gabaccia, Donna. "The Minnesota School of Immigration and Refugee Studies." http://www.ihrc.umn.edu/publications/pdf/winterwebminnesotaschool1.pdf. Accessed July 12, 2013.

Gelfand, Lou. "Readers Say Sunday Article Spurred Unfair Attacks on Local Somalis." *Minneapolis StarTribune*, October 21, 2001.

Gordon, Greg, Joy Powell, and Kimberly Hayes Taylor. "Terror Group May Have Received Local Funds; Some Minnesota Somalis Thought Al-Itihaad Was a Charity." *Minneapolis StarTribune*, October 13, 2001. http://www.startribune.com/world/11615521.html. Accessed August 5, 2014.

Holmquist, June Drenning, ed. *They Chose Minnesota: A Survey of the State's Ethnic Groups.* St Paul: Minnesota Historical Society Press, 1981.

Immigration Law Center of Minnesota. Immigration Law Center of Minnesota website. http://ilcm.org/index.php?option=com_content&view=category&layout=blog&id=95&Itemid=247. Accessed February 21, 2014.

"International Immigration and Foreign-born Population." Minnesota Department of Administration. www.demography.state.mn.us/immigration. Accessed March 24, 2014.

Kirchner, Paul, and Anne Kaplan. "The Hungarians." In June Drenning Holmquist, ed. *They Chose Minnesota: A Survey of the State's Ethnic Groups.* St. Paul: Minnesota Historical Press, 1981, pp. 423–39.

Kleist, Nauja. "Nomads, Sailors and Refugees: A Century of Somali Migration." Sussex Migration Working Paper No. 23, University of Sussex, 2004.

Lewis, I. M. *Peoples of the Horn of Africa: Somali, Afar and Saho.* n.p.: The Red Sea Press, Inc., 1998.

Maimbo, Samuel Munzele, ed. "Remittances and Economic Development in Somalia: An Overview." *Social Development Papers: Conflict Prevention and Reconstructions* 38. New York: World Bank, 2006.

Mason, Sarah. "The Chinese." In June Drenning Holmquist, ed. *They Chose Minnesota: A Survey of the State's Ethnic Groups.* St. Paul: Minnesota Historical Press, 1981, pp. 531–45.

Mason, Sarah. "The Filipinos." In June Drenning Holmquist, ed. *They Chose Minnesota: A Survey of the State's Ethnic Groups.* St. Paul: Minnesota Historical Press, 1981, pp. 546–57.

Mason, Sarah. "The Indochinese—Vietnamese, Ethnic Chinese, Hmong, Lao, Cambodians." In June Drenning Holmquist, ed. *They Chose Minnesota: A Survey of the State's Ethnic Groups.* St. Paul: Minnesota Historical Press, 1981, pp. 580–92.

Mason, Sarah. "The Koreans." In June Drenning Holmquist ed. *They Chose Minnesota: A Survey of the State's Ethnic Groups.* St. Paul: Minnesota Historical Press, 1981, pp. 580–92.

Miller, Deborah. "Middle Easterners—Syrians, Lebanese, Armenians, Egyptians, Iranians, Palestinians, Turks, Afghans." In June Drenning Holmquist, ed. *They Chose Minnesota: A Survey of the State's Ethnic Groups.* St. Paul: Minnesota Historical Press, 1981, pp. 511–30.

Minnesota Compass. "Immigration." 2012. http://www.mncompass.org/immigration/index.php. Accessed July 12, 2013.

Minnesota Council of Churches Refugee Services. *This Much I Can Tell You: Stories of Courage and Hope from Refugees in Minnesota.* Minneapolis: Minnesota Council of Churches Refugee Services, 2011.

Minneapolis Foundation. *Immigration in Minnesota: Discovering Common Ground.* Minneapolis Foundation. 2004. http://www.minneapolisfoundation.org/uploads/cuteeditor/publications/community/immigrationbrochure.pdf. Accessed July 12, 2013.

"Minnesota 2.0: Digital Archive." Immigration History Research Center, University of Minnesota. 2010. https://sites.google.com/a/umn.edu/mn20/. Accessed July 12, 2013.

Minnesota Historical Society. *Two Homes, One Dream: The Somalis in Minnesota* (45 min), 2004.

Minnesota Historical Society and TV by Girls. *What's with the Hijab?* (8 min), 2004.

O'Donnell, Kelly, and Jeanne Batalova. "US in Focus: Spotlight on Refugees and Asylees in the United States." Migration Policy Institute, 2007. http://www.migrationinformation.org/USFocus/display.cfm?ID=664#7. Accessed July 12, 2013.

Putman, Diana Briton, and Mohamood Cabdi Noor. *The Somalis: Their History and Culture.* Refugee Fact Sheet No.9. Center for Applied Linguistics, 1993. http://www.theirc.org/where/united_states_salt_lake_city_ut/the-somalis-a-cultural-profile.pdf. Accessed July 12, 2013.

Remington, Neal. "African Immigrants in Minnesota." The Institute for Agriculture and Trade Policy. 2008. www.iatp.org/documents/african-immigrants-in-minnesota. Accessed March 24, 2014.

Renkiewicz, Frank. "The Poles." In June Drenning Holmquist, ed. *They Chose Minnesota: A Survey of the State's Ethnic Groups.* St. Paul: Minnesota Historical Press, 1981, pp. 362–80.

Riippa, Timo. "The Baltic Peoples—Estonians, Latvians, and Lithuanians." In June Drenning Holmquist, ed. *They Chose Minnesota: A Survey of the State's Ethnic Groups.* St. Paul: Minnesota Historical Press, 1981, pp. 325–34.

Robillos, Mia U. "Somali Community Needs Assessment Project: A Report Prepared for the Somali Resource Center." Center for Urban and Regional Affairs, University of Minnesota, 2001.

Roble, Abdi, and Doug Rutledge. *The Somali Diaspora: A Journey Away.* Minneapolis: University of Minnesota Press, 2008.

Samatar, Hussein M. "Experiences of Somali Entrepreneurs in the Twin Cities." *Bildhaan: An International Journal of Somali Studies* 4 (2004): 78–91.

Shah, Allie. "Swedes Eye Somali Success." *Minneapolis Star Tribune*, October 19, 2010. http://www.startribune.com/local/minneapolis/105314968.html. Accessed August 5, 2014.

"Sheeko: Somali Youth Oral Histories." Immigration History Research Center, University of Minnesota. 2011. http://blog.lib.umn.edu/ihrc/sheeko/. Accessed July 12, 2013.

"Somalia." United Nations High Commissioner for Refugees (UNHCR). http://www.unhcr.org/pages/49e483ad6.html. Accessed May 6, 2014.

Vang, Chia. *Hmong in Minnesota*. Minneapolis: Minnesota Historical Society Press, 2008.

Yue, Laura, and Sasha Aslanian. "The Missing Somali Men." Minnesota Public Radio. 2012. http://minnesota.publicradio.org/projects/ongoing/somali_timeline/. Accessed July 12, 2013.

Yusuf, Ahmed Ismail. *Somalis in Minnesota*. Minneapolis: Minnesota Historical Society Press, 2012.

24

MISSISSIPPI

Amy Lively

CHRONOLOGY

1699	The European settlement of Fort Maurepas, also known as Old Biloxi, begins at present-day Ocean Springs, Mississippi. The settlement is under the direction of French explorer Pierre Le Moyne d'Iberville, who comes to the New World to establish a French colony.
1763 (February 10)	Following Great Britain's victory over France and Spain in the Seven Years' War, France relinquishes Louisiana to the British. The terms include the region now known as Mississippi. The area remains under British control until the end of the Revolutionary War.
1798 (April 7)	The Mississippi Territory is open for settlement by Congress, sparking the first phase of the Great Migration. European immigration stalls when the War of 1812 begins, but resumes following the war and peaks in 1818 and 1819.
1815	Irish immigrants begin to move to Mississippi from the North. Still heavily influenced by England, many northern states do not welcome the Irish, leading many to migrate the South where there is greater tolerance and more economic opportunity.
1865	The first Chinese immigrants arrive in Mississippi during Reconstruction. Planters begin to recruit Chinese laborers in anticipation of needing to replace slave labor.
1919	Italian immigrant William Cruso opens the CC Company in Biloxi. Penniless when he arrives in the United States, Cruso begins buying fresh seafood from Gulf Coast fisherman and selling it to

restaurants. By the 1960s, the Cruso seafood-packing plant is one of the largest of its kind in the South.

1927 (November 21)   The U.S. Supreme Court rules in *Lum v. Rice* that segregation in schools does not violate the Fourteenth Amendment. Gong Lum files the lawsuit after his nine-year-old daughter is denied the right to attend an all-white school in Rosedale.

1942 (July 23)   President Franklin D. Roosevelt signs an executive order legalizing a temporary guest worker program that brings Mexican field laborers to the United States. Mississippi growers, facing a labor shortage due to World War II, hire Mexican *braceros* to work in fields harvesting rice and cotton. The federal government ends the Bracero Program in 1964.

1975 (April)   The Fall of Saigon brings an end to the Vietnam War and leads thousands of Vietnamese refugees to migrate to the United States. Many settle in the South, where they can find work in the seafood industry. Between 1980 and 1990, the Vietnamese population in Mississippi doubles.

1978   The Hibernia Marching Society is formed in Biloxi to provide a place of fellowship for Irish Americans in Mississippi. Development of the group stems from informal meetings and parties held at Mary Mahoney's Old French Restaurant beginning in the 1960s.

1990   As the state's poultry-processing business grows, Latino immigrants enter the state in search of employment. The majority of Latino poultry workers make minimum wage at the processing plants, which gain a reputation for having unpleasant working conditions.

1992 (August)   Isle of Capri begins riverboat gambling in Biloxi, marking the beginning of the state's multi-billion dollar casino gaming industry. The growth of gaming in the state leads to an influx of immigrants seeking jobs in casinos.

2000   The Mississippi Immigrants Rights Alliance (MIRA) is formed to assist the growing immigrant population with advocacy, education, and union organizing. Within six years, MIRA helps immigrants recover over $1 million in wages that were either not paid or were wrongly withheld.

2008 (March 17)   Governor Haley Barbour signs Senate Bill (SB) 2988, the Mississippi Employment Protection Act. The bill makes it a felony for undocumented immigrants to work in the state and for employers in the state to hire undocumented workers.

2008 (August 25)   Howard Industries in Laurel is subjected to the largest federal immigration raid in American labor history. Nearly 500 undocumented immigrant workers are deported and the company pleads guilty to conspiracy to violate federal immigration laws, resulting in a $2.5 million fine.

2010	The state's population of Latinos reaches 74,000. While only representative of 2 percent of the state's population, it marks a 106 percent increase in Latino residents of Mississippi since 2000. Over a third of the Latino immigrants live in poverty and nearly half lack health insurance.
2012 (April 3)	House Bill (HB) 488, Mississippi's strong illegal immigration bill, dies in the Senate after passing in the state House earlier in the year. The bill would have required law enforcement to check the immigration status of people they arrest and have a "reasonable suspicion" of being in the country illegally.
2012 (August 23)	Governor Phil Bryant issues an executive order prohibiting undocumented immigrants from receiving public benefits, including driver's licenses and food stamps.

HISTORICAL OVERVIEW

Post–World War II Mississippi had little to offer immigrants. Certainly the civil rights struggles of African Americans seeking to eliminate Jim Crow's grip on the South did not present Mississippi as a welcoming environment for people who were not white. Even the *Clarion-Ledger*, the newspaper in the capital city of Jackson, was suspected of aligning with local segregationists and was given the dubious nickname, the *Klan-Ledger*.

At its most practical level, a state had to offer employment opportunities if it was to attract any type of migration, regardless of ethnicity. The state remained dangerously dependent on the cotton industry up until the end of World War II. With little diversity in the economy and a volatile political climate, Mississippi simply did not have the jobs to attract workers. Industries seeking a prime location to open new factories and offices bypassed Mississippi until the social turmoil subsided near the end of the 1960s. At this point, part of the attraction to the state was inexpensive labor and little threat from unions.

The immigrants who were in Mississippi after World War II had been there for decades. They were there primarily for the waters of the Gulf of Mexico, which yielded enough shrimp and oysters to give Biloxi the title of "Seafood Capital of the World" by 1903. Slavs and Cajuns mixed freely in those years, bound by their ties as fishermen. In the late 1970s, refugees from war-torn Vietnam began to arrive in Biloxi. The state's proximity to the port city of New Orleans, Louisiana, was a factor, as was the state's climate. Mississippi's subtropical weather was similar to that of Vietnam. The biggest draw was the seafood industry, which was a natural fit for the Vietnamese immigrants who were accustomed to making their living on the water. Fishing and shrimping became a niche industry for them.

Soletai Arellano, left, and Bill Chandler, executive director of the Mississippi Immigrants Rights Alliance call for unity during a news conference and rally at the capitol in Jackson, Mississippi, on January 12, 2011. The rally opposed a bill that would allow law officers to check for immigration status if they stopped people for traffic offenses or other reasons. (AP Photo/Rogelio V. Solis)

However, the Vietnamese immigrants had a difficult transition as they tried to settle into the communities of Point Cadet and Back Bay, just as the Slavs did a century before. They were viewed as competition and competition that was receiving government aid at that. Rumors began to spread that the government was providing free boats to the immigrants. These rumors, combined with the ill feelings about the Vietnam War and the different customs and culture of the Vietnamese, alienated them from the rest of the community. Some in the state did what they could to help the immigrants integrate. The assistance of those that sponsored their move to the United States helped the Vietnamese to locate housing and to enroll their children in schools. A prominent local boat builder also rented space in his boatyard to Vietnamese builders and some in Biloxi complained that the press was overblowing accusations of discrimination.

While the inability to speak English had little impact on the women who worked in the seafood-processing plants, primarily with Vietnamese coworkers, fishermen who could not understand the Coast Guard had a more difficult time. However, as generations passed and descendants of the first Vietnamese immigrants learned English, some of the barriers that made life in Mississippi more challenging for the Vietnamese began to break down. Some evidence of the Vietnamese culture's influence on Mississippi emerged, such as Biloxi's annual Autumn Moon Festival, a traditional day of celebration of the year's harvest every September.

Similarly, one needs to look no further than the rather odd marriage between the Mississippi Delta and the tamale to understand that Mexican influence in the state predated World War II. Some say that the Mississippi "hot tamale" has its origins in the arrival of Mexican cotton pickers, who took them into the fields for lunch as far back as the 1900s. Mexican workers continued to be a common sight in the Mississippi cotton fields after the war, largely due to Franklin Delano Roosevelt's Bracero Program. The treaty between the United States and Mexico encouraged Mexican workers to cross the border into the United States to fill the labor shortage caused by the war. Even though the processing centers were in the southwestern United States, *braceros* were shipped across the country to serve as guest workers for growers in need of labor. It was backbreaking work for low pay for most of the workers, but it was also more than they could make in Mexico and the jobs were highly coveted. Growers continued to hire Mexican labor long after the Bracero Program was terminated in 1964.

While agriculture continued to be a mainstay of the Mississippi economy into the 1960s and 1970s, advances in automation all but eliminated the need for Latino labor. Growers that did hire Latinos workers tended to hire *Tejanos*, families of Mexicans or Mexican Americans from Texas. Latinos who did go to Mississippi into the 1980s were there to go to college, especially the University of Southern Mississippi's English Language Institute in Hattiesburg. Other Latinos arrived via the military and remained in the state when their service ended, although they tended to integrate into the community rather than to form separate Latino communities. However, the Latino population in Mississippi remained small.

On a small scale, Mississippi began to see more Latino professionals settle in the state but overall, low wage Latinos arrived in the 1990s to find work in Mississippi's top agricultural commodity: poultry. As the country's demand for chicken grew, so did the need for workers in the poultry-processing plants. For many years, the labor force in chicken-processing plants was primarily made up of poor whites and African Americans. However, Latino immigrants began to take these jobs in the 1990s because they were willing to work for less and are not likely to complain about the working conditions. It is no secret that throughout American history, jobs in processing plants are among the least pleasant and most dangerous. The slaughter of live animals for minimum wage is a job that few would hope for but that many need for their own survival. Many have responded to advertisements in border towns that promise steady jobs, free transportation, and two weeks free rent. Critics contend that Latinos were and are the most vulnerable of the poultry workers because they have fewer job opportunities, overall, and fear retaliation if they complain.

By the 1990s, the state was mired in an economic recession, coupled with high unemployment. Those who found work often worked for low wages with few benefits. Almost out of desperation, the state authorized casino gaming in 1992 with the hope that it would provide a jolt to the state's economy. Few in Mississippi could have predicted how important casino gaming would become to the state. Riverboats became the equivalent to floating nightclubs as gamblers lined up for a chance to drop their money into slot machines or trade in cash for poker chips. The casinos eventually generated over $3 billion in annual revenue and contributed over $330 million in state taxes. The majority of Mississippi's gamblers were from other states, which also provided a boost to the local tourism industry.

Seafood plants began to close as business owners sold their property for top dollar to casino builders. This marked a transition for Vietnamese workers who were forced out of the seafood business and into the casino business. Many Mexicans also found work in the casinos following the signing of the North American Free Trade Agreement (NAFTA) in 1994. The United States, Canada, and Mexico all signed the NAFTA, which eliminated tariffs between the three nations. As a result, Mexico's agriculture industry was destabilized and many farms went bankrupt, leaving Mexican workers to seek employment in the United States.

Soon after the casinos opened, Bill Chandler moved to Mississippi to help casino workers organize. Chandler was an established advocate for immigration rights with experience in helping farmworkers organize. As he met with casino workers, he heard stories about immigrant workers being mistreated by employers and while the non-Latino workers were concerned, they feared retaliation if they protest. This led to the creation of the Mississippi Immigrants Rights Alliance (MIRA), which educated immigrants on their rights and provided services that included legal advocacy.

Mexicans were not the only Latinos finding work in the casinos. Immigrants from Costa Rica and Honduras were also contracted to work in them. These immigrants have tended to be middle class and some have college educations. There was already an established community of Honduran immigrants who have ties to the area from the banana trade and the new immigrants have gravitated toward them.

By 2000, a neighborhood in Laurel was dubbed "Hispanic City" because it was filled with immigrants from Mexico and Central America. They were attracted to Laurel because pine plantations, poultry-processing jobs, and Howard Industries were in close proximity. Howard Industries, which produced electrical products, was the largest employer in the small town. In 2008, it became the scene of the largest immigration raid in American labor history. Howard Industries ultimately was fined for not only knowingly hiring undocumented workers but for instructing undocumented workers on how to obtain false identification. Nearly 500 of the detained immigrants were eventually deported.

It took one of the worst natural disasters in American history to lure Latino immigrants on a broader scale. In late August 2005, Hurricane Katrina devastated the Gulf Coast. In desperate need of labor to help with clean up, to repair damaged buildings, and to rebuild where buildings had been swept away, contractors hired Latino laborers. These immigrants tended to be from rural Mexico and represented a different social class than the Latino casino workers. They were also more visible due to their large numbers.

Katrina also had a significant impact on the Vietnamese community in Mississippi. East Biloxi has been home to many Vietnamese immigrants because it was close to the docks and seafood-processing plants. The storm surge from Katrina wiped houses and businesses off their foundations and many Vietnamese families were permanently displaced from the region. In 2007, the non-profit group Asian Americans for Change was formed to assist the Vietnamese in the state still struggling to recover from the hurricane's damage.

Even though the immigrant population of Mississippi was just over 2 percent in 2010, immigration evolved into a high-profile political issue with the election of Governor Phil Bryant in 2011. The Republican governor ran on a platform of immigration reform, riding a wave of anti-immigration sentiment from conservatives who insisted that the federal government was not doing enough to secure the international borders. Citing the high cost of the presence of undocumented workers in the state, which he said was $25 million per year, Bryant called for strong immigration reform in the state.

In 2012, soon after Bryant took office, Representative Anne Currie sponsored HB 488, informally called the "Support Our Law Enforcement and Safe Neighborhoods Act." The bill would prohibit business transactions with undocumented immigrants, such as the issuing of driver's licenses or business licenses, as well as require local law enforcement to verify the immigration status of anyone who is under "reasonable suspicion" of being in the state illegally. Immigration advocates immediately protested and questioned how "reasonable suspicion" could be interpreted other than by skin color, which would amount to racial profiling. When local economists and business organizations pointed out the costs of losing a significant portion of the state's labor force and when local law enforcement argued that they have neither the funding nor the training to enforce these new laws, the bill died on the Senate floor in April 2012.

Bryant, who claimed to not understand the opposition to HB 488, joined a lawsuit against the Barack Obama administration in October 2012. The lawsuit was filed on behalf of federal immigration workers who stated that Obama's decision to delay deportation of children of undocumented immigrants prevented them from doing their jobs. Earlier in the year, Obama signed an executive order stating that minors who were eligible for the Development, Relief, and Education for Alien Minors (DREAM) Act, which could provide a pathway to citizenship for immigrant children who get a college degree or serve in the military, could apply for a renewable two-year work permit. Bryant called the order "irresponsible" and vowed to not ignore "the problem of illegal immigration in Mississippi."

TOPICAL ESSAYS

Defeat of HB 488 (2012)

HB 488, sponsored by Republican representative Beckie Currie, was passed by the Mississippi House of Representatives on March 12, 2012. The bill, informally called the "Support Our Law Enforcement and Safe Neighborhood Act," required law enforcement to check the immigration status of anyone arrested in the state if there is "reasonable suspicion" that the individual was in the state illegally. It also banned any business transactions with undocumented immigrants, including issuing library cards, driver's licenses, or business licenses. Governor Phil Bryant was a strong supporter of the bill, saying that it was time that Mississippi took action against illegal immigration.

The bill was immediately met with criticism by immigration rights advocates, who claimed that the term "reasonable suspicion" would lead to racial profiling since there was no way to determine an individual's potential citizenship status simply by looking at that person. Critics claim that it is more likely that the color of a person's skin will determine if immigration status is checked or not. They also point out that the opening section of the bill clearly states the intention of the bill, which is to make "enforcement through attrition the public policy." In other words, by making life so uncomfortable for undocumented immigrants, they will simply leave.

In March 2012, a week before HB 488 was due to be heard by the Republican-controlled Senate, Mississippi farmworkers groups, including the Sweet Potato Council and Mississippi Farm Bureau Federation, sent a letter to state lawmakers urging them to oppose the bill. They pointed to Alabama's harsh anti-immigration bill, HB 56, and how it has led to rotting crops, lawsuits, lost revenue, and economic harm to small businesses. That same week, local law enforcement groups joined in opposition to the bill. The Mississippi Association of Chiefs of Police, the Mississippi Sheriffs Association, the Mississippi Municipal League, and the Mississippi Association of Supervisors all wrote to state lawmakers that the bill was an "unfunded mandate." They questioned how the state would pay for enforcement and expressed concern that they have neither the training to enforce the law nor the money to pay for the lawsuits that were sure to follow.

Local economists, also referring to Alabama's HB 56, said that Mississippi could face billions of dollars in lost revenue if HB 488 is passed. They told lawmakers that such extreme restrictions on immigration would cause the state sales tax, income tax, and gross domestic product to plummet. They urged lawmakers to also consider the impact on tourism, foreign investment, and the potential damage to the economic development of the state if those who opposed the bill chose to take their business to a state without such harsh anti-immigration laws.

Democrat Hob Bryan, a representative of a rural area of the state, was the chairman of the Senate committee assigned for the bill. On the final day that the bill could be heard, April 3, 2012, Hoy declined to bring the bill up for a vote, citing concerns that it did not allow law enforcement to do their jobs without micromanagement. HB 488 died on the Senate floor, although Tea Party supporters and other anti-immigration advocates vowed to revive it in the future.

DREAM ACT IN MISSISSIPPI

The DREAM was first proposed introduced to the U.S. Senate in 2001. The intent of the bill was to provide permanent residency in the United States for minors who have been brought to the country by undocumented immigrant parents, provided they entered the United States before the age of 16, graduated from high school or earned a GED, have no criminal record, and lived in the United States for at least five consecutive years. This would then provide a six-year period to complete college or military service, at which time the immigrant would be granted permanent residency status.

On June 15, 2012, President Barack Obama signed an executive order stating that through DREAM Act eligible youth would have their deportation deferred and they would be granted work permits for up to two years, with the opportunity to renew. It was expected that more than 800,000 children of undocumented immigrants would be impacted by the president's order, which may provide a pathway to citizenship and the opportunity to work and earn an education.

Although some states have enacted their own versions of the DREAM Act, it has continued to face opposition from critics who claim that it amounts to an amnesty program. Among those critics are Nebraska governor Dave Heineman, Arizona governor Jan Brewer, Texas governor Rick Perry, and Mississippi governor Phil Bryant. In August 2012, Bryant joined his fellow Republican governors in refusing to allow the children eligible for the DREAM Act to receive public benefits, including unemployment and Supplemental Nutrition Assistance Program benefits, more commonly referred to as food stamps. Bryant also barred state agencies from granting driver's licenses to the immigrant youth.

On October 12, 2012, Bryant announced that the state of Mississippi was joining a lawsuit against the Obama administration. The lawsuit was filed in August in Texas federal court by Kansas secretary of state Kris Kobach on behalf of James D. Doebler and nine other employees for the Immigration and Customs Enforcement (ICE) Agency. The lawsuit alleged that Obama's executive order, officially called Deferred Action for Childhood Arrivals, required immigration officials to violate federal immigration laws, violated the U.S. Constitution by encroaching on the separation of powers, and prohibited Congress from regulating immigration.

Bryant said that Mississippi joined the lawsuit because undocumented workers are a financial burden to the state and that benefits should only go to those who are "lawfully eligible." In a written statement, Bryant accused the federal government of ignoring the nation's problems with border protection and he called the law "irresponsible." Bryant pointed out that joining the lawsuit came at no cost to Mississippi taxpayers as lawyers already involved with the case represented the state. The American Civil Liberties Union responded to Bryant's announcement with a statement reading "Shame on you."

HOWARD INDUSTRIES RAID (2008)

Howard Industries is a transformer-manufacturing plant based in Laurel, Mississippi. It was the largest employer in the town of less than 20,000 people. Following Hurricane Katrina in 2005, the population of Laurel grew somewhat and included Latino workers contracted to help complete construction projects along the Gulf Coast. Howard Industries eventually hired hundreds of Latino workers, many of whom had experience in machinery and welding from their home countries.

On August 25, 2008, Howard Industries became the setting of the largest federal immigration raid in American labor history (at that time). Acting on a tip from a union worker, immigration officials began investigating Howard Industries years before the raid. When officials from ICE finally acted on their information, nearly 600 immigrants were removed from the factory in a scene that was so chaotic that some workers thought there had been a bomb threat.

About 100 of the workers, primarily women with young children, were fitted with ankle bracelets and were allowed to go home under house arrest. Approximately 475 other workers were sent to the ICE facility in Jena, Louisiana. Nine workers under the age of 18 were placed in the custody of the Office of Refugee Resettlement. The detained workers came primarily from Mexico, although there were also workers from Peru, El Salvador, Germany, Brazil, Panama, the Honduras, and Guatemala.

Advocates for the arrested workers claimed that many of the detainees were not allowed to communicate with their families. Several of the families were so frightened that they did not permit their children to attend school the next day out of fear that they would be detained and deported. Female workers who were allowed to go home were left with no idea what had happened to their husbands, yet they were afraid to ask or could not do so because they did not speak English. The majority of the detained workers were eventually deported, although a few were sent to prison on federal charges of identity theft, stemming from the use of false social security numbers.

While Howard Industries officials claimed that they did not realize that they had hired undocumented workers because the immigrants used falsified documents to secure employment, further investigation revealed that the company provided instructions on how to obtain false identities. Prosecutors also charged that the company told its immigrant workers that they would be warned in the event of a raid. Howard Industries went so far as to offer jobs to immigrants even after being advised that some social security numbers were not valid.

The only official from the company who was charged with a crime was Jose Humberto Gonzalez, the human resources manager. After indictment on 6 of 25 charges of conspiracy and employee fraud, Gonzalez paid a $4,000 fine and was sentenced to six months of house arrest and probation for five years. Howard Industries pled guilty in February 2011 of conspiracy to violate immigration laws. Immigration officials stated that the company encouraged and enticed undocumented immigrants to live in the United States and then, by knowing that the immigrants were in the United States in violation of federal law yet not reporting it, concealed and harbored undocumented immigrants from federal authorities. In addition to waiving indictment and pleading guilty, the company agreed to pay a $2.5 million fine.

There were other legal consequences for Howard Industries following a class action lawsuit filed by four African American plaintiffs who accused the company of employment discrimination. Charlyn Dozier claims that she was repeatedly rejected as a job applicant in the years leading up to the raid and was only offered a job after the raid. She and the other plaintiffs claim that Howard Industries did not hire them because they were not Latino. Her lawyer, Lisa Ross, says that the company preferred to hire undocumented workers. In 2012, the company was ordered to pay $1.3 million into a settlement fund to be distributed to approximately 5,000 rejected job applicants.

Immigrant rights advocates, including Mississippi Immigrant Rights Alliance executive director Bill Chandler, claimed that the timing of the raid was suspicious. In 2008, white, African American, and Latino workers were part of the International Brotherhood of Electrical Workers. Their union contract expired on August 30, 2008, just five days after the immigration raid. Chandler and Jim Evans of the American Federation of Labor and Congress of Industrial Organizations charge that Howard Industries actually helped orchestrate the raid to break down the solidarity between the workers, which were gaining strength through the union and to force immigrants out of Mississippi. Chandler charged that the tactics were the same that have been used against African Americans in the past and the entire incident was an attempt to "demonize Latinos."

NOTABLE FIGURES

BILL CHANDLER (1941–)

California-native Bill Chandler is the executive director of MIRA, which has been in operation since 2000. Chandler's interest in immigrant rights dates back to his childhood in Los Angeles in the 1950s. With Orange County schools desegregated by the *Menendez v. Westminster* in 1946, Chandler's classmates and friends were a diverse group. On a trip to a movie theater, Chandler was an eyewitness to President Dwight D. Eisenhower's "Operation Wetback," the broad-sweeping anti-immigration program that deported between 2 and 4 million Mexicans. Not all of the Mexicans caught in the immigration sweeps were undocumented workers. Many were U.S. citizens of Mexican descent.

As Chandler and his friends watched a movie in a downtown Los Angeles, chaperoned by Latino parents, Border Patrol agents raided the theater. Anyone appearing to be Latino was forced by the armed agents to leave the theater while the non-Latino children were left behind. Chandler and his white friends were traumatized by the incident and this led to a broader discussion with his friends on civil rights. Chandler recalled a friend's mother showing him a photo in *Jet* magazine of Emmett Till, a Mississippi teenager who was brutally murdered after allegedly flirting with a white woman. Chandler began to follow news of the Civil Rights Movement with intense interest and volunteered to help with voter registration drives.

When Cesar Chavez led thousands of grape harvesters in California on a strike due to poor pay and working conditions in 1965, Chandler was recruited to help in the efforts to organize the workers. In 1966, Chandler moved to South Texas and helped workers in that state organize. By 1976, he traveled throughout the South advocating for farmworkers and their right to organize. In 1989, Chandler went to Mississippi to help state workers organize and when that was accomplished, he shifted his efforts to the state's new casino workers, many of whom were Latino immigrants.

Almost immediately after the casino workers began to organize, stories of abuse began to surface. However, white workers who witnessed the mistreatment were afraid to report it out of fear of retaliation. Meanwhile, Mississippi schools refused to enroll children of immigrants. These events led to the creation of MIRA as union, religious, and other civic leaders formed an alliance in an effort to protect the rights of the immigrant workers. Among the services that MIRA provided was education about immigrant rights and legal assistance in cases of workers not receiving wages due to them. MIRA has recovered over $1 million in stolen wages for immigrant workers, many from contractors who refused to pay without pressure from MIRA.

Chandler said that he has been a vocal opponent to the myriad of anti-immigration bills that have been created in Mississippi because he views them simply as harassment. Trying to scare immigrants away from the state seems no better than ethnic cleansing and reminds him of the violence that African Americans in the state were subjected to after Reconstruction. He also viewed it as a poor economic decision, pointing out that suddenly losing tens of thousands of workers would have a devastating impact on Mississippi's revenue.

In 2009, Chandler was awarded the 2009 Purpose Prize Fellowship. The prize was awarded to entrepreneurs over the age of 60 who used their experience and expertise to tackle some of society's most-pressing problems. The award was issued by Civic Ventures, a nonprofit organization that supported Baby Boomers as they pursued new careers.

BIBLIOGRAPHY

Aguilar, Julian. "Twenty Years Later, NAFTA Remains a Source of Tension." *The New York Times*, December 7, 2012. http://www.nytimes.com/2012/12/07/us/twenty-years-later-nafta-remains-a-source-of-tension.html?_r=0. Accessed April 30, 2013.

Bacon, David. "How Mississippi's Black/Brown Strategy Beat the South's Anti-Immigration." *The Nation*, April 20, 2012. http://www.thenation.com/article/167465/how-mississippis-blackbrown-strategy-beat-souths-anti-immigrant-wave#. Accessed April 30, 2013.

Bounds, Jaime. "Vietnamese in Mississippi." *Mississippi History Now*, June 2011. http://mshistorynow.mdah.state.ms.us/articles/372/vietnamese-in-mississippi. Accessed April 30, 2013.

Brignac, Kelly. "Bill Chandler." *Jackson Free Press*, November 5, 2009. http://www.jackson freepress.com/news/2009/nov/05/bill-chandler/. Accessed April 30, 2013.

Fox News Latino. "Mississippi Governor Is the Latest to Bar Benefits from Undocumented Immigrants." August 24, 2012. http://latino.foxnews.com/latino/politics/2012/08/24/miss-bars-benefits-for-deferred-status-immigrants/. Accessed April 30, 2013.

Hampton, David. "Bill Chandler Executive Director, MIRA, Miss. Immigrants Rights Alliance, 71, Jackson." *Clarion-Ledger*, March 30, 2012. http://www.clarionledger.com/article/20120401/OPINION03/204010317/Bill-Chandler-Executive-Director-MIRA-Miss-Immigrants-Rights-Alliance-71-Jackson. Accessed April 30, 2013.

"Mississippi Immigration Bill Faces Opposition from Agriculture Groups, Builders." *The Times-Picayune*, March 27, 2012. http://www.nola.com/politics/index.ssf/2012/03/mississippi_immigration_bill_f.html. Accessed April 30, 2013.

Nave, R. L. "Promised Land: Are Mississippi's Anti-Immigration Efforts Bad for Business?" *Jackson Free Press*, March 28, 2012. http://www.jacksonfreepress.com/news/2012/mar/28/promised-land-are-mississippis-anti-immigrant/. Accessed April 30, 2013.

"Nearly 600 Detained in Mississippi Immigration Raid." *USA Today*, August 26, 2008. http://usatoday30.usatoday.com/news/nation/2008-08-26-raid-miss_N.htm. Accessed April 30, 2013.

"New Americans in Mississippi." Immigration Policy Center, January 11 2012. http://www.immigrationpolicy.org/just-facts/new-americans-mississippi. Accessed April 30, 2013.

Nuwer, Deanne Stephens. "The Seafood Industry in Biloxi: Its Early History, 1848–1930." *Mississippi History Now*, June 2006. http://mshistory.k12.ms.us/articles/209/the-seafood-industry-in-biloxi-its-early-history-1848–1930. Accessed April 30, 2013.

Pender, Geoff. "Bryant Joins Mississippi Lawsuit; ACLU Responds." *The Clarion Ledger*, October 10, 2012. http://blogs.clarionledger.com/politics/2012/10/10/bryant-joins-immigration-lawsuit/. Accessed April 30, 2013.

Pettus, Emily Wagster. "Groups Oppose Mississippi Immigration Bill." New England Cable News, March 26, 2012. http://www.necn.com/03/26/12/APNewsBreak-Groups-oppose-Miss-immigrati/landing.html?&apID=253dec24a1414a6cab8ccc06e2e82047. Accessed April 30, 2013.

"Settlement Reached in Discrimination Suit over Howard Industries Hiring Practices." Gulf Live, August 21, 2012. http://blog.gulflive.com/mississippi-press-news/2012/08/settlement_reached_in_discrimi.html. Accessed April 30, 2013.

Sutton, Joe. "Mississippi Lawmakers Pass Controversial Immigration Bill." CNN, March 16, 2012. http://www.cnn.com/2012/03/16/us/mississippi-immigration-law. Accessed April 30, 2013.

von Herrmann, Denise. *Resorting to Casinos: The Mississippi Gambling Industry*. Oxford: University Press of Mississippi, 2006.

Walton, Shana, and Barbara Carpenter. *Ethnic Heritage Mississippi: The Twentieth Century*. Oxford: University Press of Mississippi, 2012.

WLOX. "Howard Industries Pleads Guilty to Immigration Conspiracy." February, 24, 2011. http://www.wlox.com/story/14138038/howard-industries-pleads-guilty-to-immigration-conspiracy. Accessed April 30, 2013.

25

MISSOURI

William P. Kladky

CHRONOLOGY

Pre-1540	The Native American nations of the Caddo, Dakota, Delaware, Fox, Illinois, Iowa, Kickapoo, Missouri, Omaha, Osage, Oto, Sauk, and Shawnee live in the Missouri area.
1540–1541	The Spanish explorer Hernando de Soto (1500–1542), the first European to enter Missouri discovers the Mississippi River.
1673	The Jesuit priest Jacques Marquette (1637–1675) and the French explorer and fur trader Louis Jolliet (1645–1700) explore the Mississippi.
1682	The explorer René-Robert Cavelier, sieur de La Salle (1643–1687), navigates the Mississippi River and claims it for France.
1714	The Frenchman Étienne de Véniard, sieur de Bourgmont (1679–1730), builds a fort on the Missouri River.
1719	Pierre Duque de Boisbriand (1675–1736), acting for the French king, and Marc Antoine de Is Loire des Ursins, acting for the India Company, establish St. Philippe. A company of the Indies crew led by Marc Antoine de La Loere Des Ursins begins digging for lead and silver in the Mine La Motte area, utilizing black slaves to work in the mines.
1724	Étienne de Véniard, sieur de Bourgmont, builds Fort Orleans on the Missouri River in Carroll County.
1750	The French establish Sainte Genevieve as a trading post, the first permanent white settlement.
1756–1763	The Seven Years' War (French and Indian War) is won by Great Britain. France gives England all French territory east of the Mississippi

	River, except New Orleans. The Spanish surrender east and west Florida to the English in return for Cuba.
1762	By the Treaty of Fontainebleau, Spain gains control of the Louisiana Territory from France.
1764	Pierre Laclede Liguest (1729–1778) and Rene Auguste Chouteau (ca.1749–ca.1825) found the city of St. Louis.
1769	Louis Blanchette (1739–1793) establishes the city of St. Charles as a trading post.
1770	The Spanish government officially assumes control of the territory of Louisiana.
1789	Colonel George Morgan (1743–1810) establishes the city of New Madrid.
1793	Louis Lorimier (1748–1812) receives trading privileges and authority to set up a post at Cape Girardeau.
1796	Daniel Boone (1734–1820) builds a cabin near the mouth of Femme Osage Creek in St. Charles County.
1800	Spain surrenders the Louisiana Territory to France by the Treaty of San Ildefonso.
1803	The United States buys the Louisiana Territory from France for $15 million.
1805	The territory of Louisiana is established with the seat of government at St. Louis. The Lewis and Clark expedition, led by Meriwether Lewis (1774–1809) and William Clark (1770–1838), explores the area.
1808	The city of Sainte Genevieve incorporates. Fort Osage is built on the Missouri River under William Clark's leadership as part of the federally controlled fur trade system.
1812	A part of the territory of Louisiana becomes the territory of Missouri. The first general assembly of the territory of Missouri meets.
1817	Zebulon M. Pike (1779–1813), coming from New Jersey, reaches St. Louis on the first steamboat to navigate the Mississippi River above the mouth of the Ohio River.
1818	The Speaker of the U.S. House of Representatives presents a petition to Congress from Missouri requesting statehood. At this time, 10,000 slaves live in Missouri.
1820	The slavery debate dominates Missouri's application for statehood.
1821	The U.S. Congress admits Missouri as the 24th state, with the state capitol temporarily located in St. Charles. The Santa Fe Trail opens with the successful trading expeditions of William Becknell (1787–1856) to Santa Fe. Governor Alexander McNair signs a bill setting the site for the city of Jefferson.
1826	Jefferson City is designated as Missouri's permanent capitol.
1831	Mormon leader Joseph Smith Jr. (1810–1844) settles with his followers in Independence.

1837	President Martin Van Buren (1782–1862) issues a proclamation finalizing the annexation of the Platte Purchase area by Missouri, which sets the state's northwestern border.
1838	Governor Lilburn Boggs (1796–1860) issues the "Extermination Order" against Mormons living in Missouri, which demands that Mormon church members leave the state.
1842	The national depression hits Missouri, bringing falling prices and many foreclosures and bankruptcies. The town of Carthage (named for the ancient Tunisian city) is established. Joseph Robidoux (1783–1868) founds the town of St. Joseph.
1844	Missouri bans free blacks from settling in the state.
1847	St. Louis connects to the East Coast by telegraph.
1850	The town of Kansas (later Kansas City) is incorporated.
1851	Groundbreaking ceremonies for the construction of the Pacific Railroad are held in St. Louis.
1860	The Pony Express starts its first run from St. Joseph to Sacramento, California.
1861	President Abraham Lincoln (1809–1865) revokes the emancipation proclamation issued by abolitionist John C. Frémont (1813–1890) for Missouri. Missouri's "Rebel Legislature" adopts an Act of Secession.
1862	In the Pea Ridge battle, the Union Army forces the Confederates to retreat, ending the possibility of Confederate military control of Missouri.
1865	Slavery is abolished in Missouri by an ordinance of immediate emancipation, making Missouri the first slave state to emancipate its slaves before the adoption of the Thirteenth Amendment in the U.S. Constitution.
1873	The Eads Bridge, spanning the Mississippi River, opens in St. Louis.
1921	The Centennial Road Law, funding a modern system of state highways, is signed into law.
1944	Missouri U.S. senator Harry S. Truman (1884–1972) of Independence is elected vice president.
1945	U.S. vice president Harry S. Truman becomes resident upon the death of Franklin D. Roosevelt (1882–1945).
1948	Voters reelect President Harry S. Truman to the presidency.
1965	The Gateway Arch (part of the Jefferson National Expansion Memorial) designed by Eero Saarinen (1910–1961) is completed. Located on the original settlement site of St. Louis, it symbolizes the city's importance in the development of the West.
1980	The population center of the United States moves into Missouri to DeSoto.
2009	The Pew Hispanic Center estimates that there are about 60,000 undocumented immigrants in Missouri.

| 2012 | Missouri religious leaders call upon the legislature to end consideration of Senate Bill (SB) 580, which would allow police officers to check the immigration status of an individual if the officers believed there was probable cause. |
| 2013 | The foreign-born are estimated to comprise about 4 percent of the state's population. |

HISTORICAL OVERVIEW

Pre-1800

Before European settlement, the Native American nations of the Missouri, Osage, Delaware, and the Shawnee, lived in the Missouri area. Probably the first Europeans to enter Missouri were a Spanish army under the explorer Hernando de Soto. In 1673, a Jesuit priest Jacques Marquette and the French explorer and fur trader Louis Jolliet explored the Mississippi. Supported by the French king Louis XIV, explorer René-Robert Cavelier, sieur de La Salle continued this Mississippi exploration and formally claimed the area for France in 1682. The 1680s saw unlicensed fur traders plying the region, and there were over 100 traders along the Mississippi and Missouri by 1690.

It was not until 1714 did a Frenchman, Étienne de Véniard, sieur de Bourgmont, built a fort on the Missouri River, and in 1719, Pierre Duque de Boisbriand and Marc Antoine de Is Loire des Ursins set up St. Philippe. While the fur trade was the first impetus for this settlement, the discovery of lead and silver in the Mine La Motte area rapidly led to mining using African slaves. While some of the lead was traded to the Native Americans, most was flatboated to New Orleans along the Mississippi and then exported to Europe.

The Spanish, from their colony at Santa Fe in the Southwest, tried to challenge the French dominance in the Missouri Valley in 1720. Because the Spanish and the French were cooperating with Native American tribes as a means to further their settlement aims, the American Indians joined them in warfare. At a crucial battle in 1721 in Missouri, the Spanish and their Indian allies were soundly defeated by the French and theirs.

The first permanent settlement in Missouri was Sainte Genevieve, established in 1750 by French Canadian farmers who utilized slaves as their field workers. The town was near salt springs, and exportation of salt soon had begun via New Orleans. St. Louis became the next permanent settlement in 1764, founded by Pierre Laclede Liguest as a base for his fur trading. Along with the French, the small town included some Irish settlers. St. Louis grew slowly and, by 1770, the population had reached 500. Most of its first settlers were from French towns in Illinois. When St. Louis's population was approximately 800 in 1780, it had 100 stone buildings and most of its inhabitants were involved in fur trading.

The main immigrants at this time were the French, Germans, and the Irish. In 1764, an Irish regiment of the British Army patrolled the area around Cahokia and other villages of the east bank. Irish men began migrating to Missouri from the East Coast and their friends and family joined them. When the Treaty of Paris was signed in 1783, the population of Sainte Genevieve was 949, St. Louis 925, St. Charles 875, and New Madrid 782. An army census in 1799 found 6,028 people in the area.

More immigration came after trader and American Indian agent Pierre Louis Lorimier acquired a vast area of land. Most of those who settled in his plots in the Cape Girardeau district on the White River were German and Swiss German. Major John Bollinger also brought settlers from North Carolina, Virginia, and Tennessee, including the first Protestant preacher.

1800–1850

When rule of Louisiana passed from Napoleon to Jefferson in 1803, St. Louis was largely composed of French colonists. Streets and people had French names. English began arriving in the early decades of the nineteenth century. Many land claims were filed in the early 1800s as Missouri residents attempted to transfer their claims that were granted by the French and Spanish during their power over the region. In 1805, Congress appointed a Board of Commissioners to determine if the grants were legal.

The other earliest arrivals in Missouri were Americans moving west. St. Louis was a major assembly point for those migrating from the Carolinas and Tennessee as well as from New England, Ohio, and Indiana. The fur trade drew many. Early traders confirmed that there were many animal pelts in the region. This stimulated the Missouri Fur Company's organization in St. Louis in 1809, as well as many other ventures like John Jacob Astor's Columbia Fur Company. The Missouri Fur Company's first venture consisted of 172 men as trappers and hunters. Some tribes, like the Arikara, traded with them, but others like the Blackfeet were always ready to engage in warfare. Native Americans were used as labor for the fur trade by the Americans. Astor eventually triumphed, pushing out all competitors and setting up the Missouri River as his private domain.

The territory of Missouri was established in 1812, with little population except for a few French towns like St. Louis and Sainte Genevieve consisting of miners and traders. When settlers began to arrive, they pushed the American Indians westward to the Great Plains. In 1808, the Osage nation surrendered its Missouri and Arkansas lands, opening the area to American settlement.

In Missouri, the War of 1812 was mainly fought with the Native Americans. Missourians were angry with the British for giving firearms to the American Indians and urging them to harass American settlers and traders. The governor used the Missouri Militia to hold the Native Americans west of the Mississippi and stop the British from uniting their allies.

After the war, settlement of Missouri quickened. More migration was stimulated by the traders' and miners' exaggerated claims about the richness of the Missouri farmland. In addition, federal public land in Arkansas, Illinois, and Missouri was given to soldiers who served in the War of 1812. During 1815–1819, 30–50 wagons daily crossed the Mississippi River at St. Louis. Many from Tennessee went to the Ozarks region in south-central Missouri and northern Arkansas. Kentucky arrivals set up farms along the Missouri River, and plats in Franklin and Boonville were established in 1817. In 1817, the first steamboat reached St. Louis. By 1820, roughly an 80-mile strip along the Mississippi and Missouri Rivers was settled. Between 1818 and 1922, public land was surveyed and sold through eight federal land offices.

With the population surge came interest in statehood. The Missouri Territorial Legislature submitted a petition for statehood in 1818 to the U.S. Congress. Normally, statehood applications were routine, but this was before the Civil War. If Missouri's application had been accepted, it would have entered as a slave state and upset the fragile balance in the U.S. Senate. After great national debate, the "Missouri Compromise" allowed Missouri to enter the Union as a slave state and Maine as a free state in 1821, thus maintaining the balance of slave and free states in Congress. The rest of the Louisiana Purchase area north of the 36°30' line was to be free of slavery. After its constitution was adopted, Missouri held its initial state elections. Alexander McNair (1775–1826) was elected the first governor and the first general assembly began the initial legislative session at the Missouri Hotel in St. Louis.

Immigration to Missouri quickened in the 1830s when many Germans settled in farms west of St. Louis and south of the Missouri River. The area came to be called the "Missouri Rhineland." Beginning in the 1840s, other Germans and a growing number of Irish immigrants arrived in the state's towns and cities.

In 1831, the Mormons reached western Missouri, and selected Independence as their "City of Zion." By 1833, one-third of its 4,000 population were Mormons. This surge—as well as the Mormons' curious beliefs and practices—sparked local hostility, and led to protests, demands, and finally a mob invading and destroying the Mormons' printing office as well as tar-and-feathering two Mormon leaders. After the Mormons publicly announced their intention to stay, another infuriated mob whipped Mormon men, drove women and children from their homes, and destroyed a dozen buildings. When the Mormons tried armed resistance, a few skirmishes proved they were no match for the mass of anti-Mormons, and they left the county. Similar conflict happened in several other counties, with the violence provoking the governor to send in troops to restore order. In 1838, Joseph Smith and six other Mormon leaders were arrested, tried, and convicted. They escaped to Illinois, later to be killed by another mob incensed by their beliefs and actions.

The 1830–1850 period was a time of great growth for St. Louis, and it was transformed from a sleepy river town into perhaps the West's major metropolis. Its population grew from 5,000 in 1820 to 16,489 in 1840, to 77,860 in 1850s. St. Louis continued to double its population in the 1850s, reaching 160,773 in 1860. With this remarkable growth, unfortunately, came severe overcrowding and disease, and in 1849 the second and most serious cholera epidemic struck St. Louis with over 4,000 fatalities.

Before the Civil War and the development of a complete railroad network, the Ohio-Mississippi-Missouri river system was the major migration route to the state. Many German immigrants came via New Orleans. The coming of the steamboat along the rivers also made it easier for disease to spread, and the fur trade somehow continued to prosper despite a horrible smallpox epidemic in 1837–1838 that killed many traders and Native Americans.

Missouri was a central axis for the westward movement, as both the Santa Fe and the Oregon Trails began at Independence. In 1849, St. Louis, Independence, Westport, and St. Joseph became major points of departure for migrants to the California gold mines, making Missouri the "Gateway to the West." Migrants even had a guidebook: Lansford Hastings's *The Emigrants' Guide to Oregon and California* was published in 1845 and described routes to the Pacific Coast, including one from Independence to Idaho. Missouri became the temporary home of gold-rush emigrants, who occasionally came back to settle. Westport Landing, Kansas City, and Independence grew to serve the wagons, river boats, and stragglers who passed through.

The Osage, Sac, Fox, Shawnee, and Delaware Indian nations were still present in Missouri until they were forced to move west across state lines and eventually to Indian Territory. While most were glad the American Indians were forced to leave, Father De Smet from Belgium, assigned to the Florissant novitiate, worked positively and supportively with the Indians during the 1830s and 1840s.

Missouri was also a crossroads for the railroads that were constructed to serve the travelers. This development was greatly facilitated by significant state financial aid, beginning in 1851 when the legislature voted $1.5 million in bonds for the Hannibal and St. Joseph Railroad to build a line across the state. The aim was to bolster the state's competition with Chicago for Western trade. By 1865, Missouri had 928 miles of track running on eight lines.

There were more German and Irish than any other immigrants in Missouri during this time. Germans comprised the largest immigrant, non-English-speaking group. Between 1830 and 1850, large numbers of Germans immigrated to the Missouri and Mississippi River Valleys, as well as the nearby areas. Expert German immigrants worked as wagon-makers, constructing the famed Murphy covered wagon in the 1830s. It is estimated that 200,000 Murphy wagons were utilized during the Western settlement era. German Catholics settled primarily in Westphalia, Taos, Rich Fountain, Loose Creek, Lustown, and Frankenstein. The Protestant separatists went to Wittenberg, Altenburg, and Frohna. Above all, they were attracted because of the low cost of land, easy river accessibility, and fertile soil.

Fleeing the terrible 1840s famine in their home country, the Irish usually arrived in New Orleans and then took a steamboat to St. Louis. They were helped by the emerging charitable organizations, and they worked loading steamboats, in railroad construction, mining the clay pits, and later in the manufacturing industry.

1850–1900

Missouri's population soared from 682,044 in 1850 to 1,182,012 in 1860, making it the eighth most-populous state. Much of this growth was due to foreign-born arrivals. In 1860, German immigrants composed half of Jefferson City's population and about 25 percent of Boonville. Over 15 percent of the state's population was foreign-born in 1861. With even more growth following in the early 1860s, Missouri became the fifth most-populous state by the end of the Civil War.

During the war, St. Louis was a strategic military location, and under firm Union control due to the strongly loyal Germans. Unfortunately, the state's economic boom ended because of the wartime halt of all railroad construction. This, combined with the heavy track damage during the conflict, led to severe financial problems for the railroad companies. Only one could pay its interest payments for the bonds, and a financial crisis snared the state, which originally had issued the bonds. When Missouri's debts reached $31,375,340 by 1866, it was forced to foreclose on many railroads.

After the war, most settlers came to Missouri by railroad through the lower Midwestern states. Although the state was not a major destination for the millions of eastern and southern European immigrants who came to America during the late 1800s, many did arrive. Italians and Croats came first to St. Louis, followed by Sicilians, Lombards, Piedmontese, Tuscans, and Calabrians (southern Italians) during the late 1800s. Most settled in a neighborhood formerly housing the German, Irish, and Jewish immigrants. In this segregated "little Italy," the Italian immigrants sold fruit and labored in the railroads, pits, factories, and brickyards. Later some opened restaurants.

St. Louis began getting Croat immigrants in 1862, primarily marines who sailed up the Mississippi and were temporary residents. In the 1880s, some Croats settled permanently, and the population grew until the early 1900s. Most Croat immigrants were unskilled laborers, and worked digging ditches, in mining, doing road construction, and in factories. Some prosperous ones opened small retail stores. Most immigrants lived in urban neighborhoods with others who shared their language and cultural traditions.

Immigrants also were attracted to Kansas City, which developed into a major industrial center. The construction of a railroad bridge across the Missouri River facilitated the development of the city's major industry, the Kansas City stockyards, which had started in 1871 as a slaughterhouse. The city's population rapidly grew from 32,000 in 1870 to over 132,000 in 1890, and it became the largest city between St. Louis and the West and one of the largest banking centers by 1900.

During the 1860s and 1870s, a small number of other southern and eastern European immigrants—Serbians, Lebanese, Syrians, and Greeks—immigrated to Missouri. Most were unskilled factory or railroad workers, living in ethnic neighborhoods in the least-expensive, substandard housing. Some Italians, Greeks, Poles, and East European Jews also moved to St. Louis and Kansas City at this time.

After the Civil War, St. Louis continued to expand rapidly. City boosters such as Logan Reavis, the owner of the *St. Louis Daily Press*, even campaigned to move the nation's capital to St. Louis. The city drew industries because of its regional dominance, the easily accessible rail and water transportation, and its central national location. The 1874 construction of the Eads Bridge made St. Louis an important link in transcontinental rail travel. The national and regional expansion of factories at this time increased the demand for firebrick, and that meant prosperity for those manufacturers in St. Louis. The resultant need for factory workers spurred additional immigration. By 1870, people of German birth or parentage composed more than 20 percent of the population of Osage, Franklin, Warren, St. Charles, and St. Louis Counties.

By the 1890s, St. Louis was the nation's fourth-largest city and mostly because of immigration. Of the city's 1870 population of 310,864, over one-third (112,294) were foreign-born, the majority from Germany (59,040) and Ireland (32,239). Foreign-born decreased slightly during the 1870s to 105,013 of the city's 350,518. By 1890, the 114,876 foreign-born were 25.4 percent of the city's 451,770. Most immigrants lived in ethnic neighborhoods in the north and south sections by the river and around the business district. The 170 Chinese immigrants lived in the city's south in their commercial, residential, and recreational center called "Hop Alley."

With these numbers, several mutual benefit organizations were formed in St. Louis to help the immigrants adjust, with some offering death and disability benefits. German and Czech immigrants lived in Southside apartments and had jobs in nearby foundries, cotton factories, and breweries. When the Czechs began to arrive early in the 1850s, the Germans welcomed them because of their shared culture. Coming from Bohemia where German was the official language, many could speak German. Additionally, many Czechs were Catholic and worshipped at the new German church; most were literate and middle class.

In the 1890s, a surge in demand for terra-cotta and firebrick stimulated a large influx of Italian immigrants to St. Louis from the Illinois coal fields. They replaced the German and African American clay miners and farmers in the Fairmount area. They settled north of the city on "The Hill," which actually grew the most during the 1900–1920 period.

TwENTIETH CENTURY

By 1900, St. Louis had become a major manufacturing center, with significant German and Irish, as well as Italian, Greek, Polish, and Eastern European Jewish immigrant communities. Most were segregated ethnic neighborhoods with poor housing. The International Institute was a point of entry for many in the city. Founded in 1919 to help World War I refugees, the Institute provided English classes, job search skill education, and transition services. In 1920, it sponsored its first International Folk Festival. In 1910, the Chinese immigrant population reached its zenith with 423. They started hand laundries, grocery stores, restaurants, tea shops, and opium shops.

Steady Italian immigration to St. Louis's "The Hill" increased the population from 700 in 1900 to 2,651 by 1920. While most of the new immigrants came directly from Italy, there were a number of miners who migrated from southern Illinois. World War I halted further Italian immigration, as well as the bitter 1917 brickyard strike. There was a final burst of Italian immigration during 1920–1923, partly composed of Lombards leaving southern Illinois's nativist hostility, frequent mining accidents, and continuing economic exploitation.

Until the 1920s, new immigrants continued to arrive. Jews were the largest new immigrant group in St. Louis during this time, surging from 10,000 to over 50,000 in population. Many eastern and southern European immigrants also came. The young women often labored in the garment industry, tobacco factories, or nut-processing plants. Also, there were almost 2,800 Greeks in St. Louis by 1910, mostly young men whose intentions were to work, save money, and then return to Greece. Similarly, almost all Italian immigrants to the Hill during this time were under 50.

There was also immigration to other parts of the state. In the West, many Mexican immigrants, mostly men, came to Kansas City in the early 1900s to work on the railroads or in meatpacking. During the 1902–1914 period, approximately 4,000 Bohemian, Czech, and Slovak immigrants arrived. They were joined by many from Croatia, Greece, and Sicily. Kansas City had about 27,000 foreign-born residents by 1920. In non-urban Missouri, immigrants primarily came to work in the mines and quarries. For instance, many arrived in 1901 to work in the Atlas Portland Cement Company's rich deposits of limestone and shale near Hannibal.

In truth, immigration to St. Louis had peaked in the nineteenth century, especially compared to other American cities. The 1910 U.S. Census found that only 18.3 percent of the city's 687,029 residents were foreign-born, which was one of the lowest figures for all large cities. While many Italians and Greeks had come in the 1910s, increasing by 19 and 56 percent, respectively, St. Louis was just not attracting the great numbers it had in the past. A large part of the reason was that manufacturers were locating in Illinois and other parts of Missouri.

Immigration to the United States and Missouri was curtailed by federal legislation in the 1920s that severely restricted new immigration. Some came, but in much smaller numbers. Missouri experienced a drastic reduction in immigration during the next few decades.

During the 1920s and 1930s, St. Louis's economic decline accelerated. Many factories relocated or constructed plants in either Illinois or in rural, less-expensive parts of Missouri. Many of the clay mines were exhausted, and the number of brick and tile factories shrunk. St. Louis also suffered during Prohibition, but recovered somewhat after the Volstead Act was repealed in 1933.

The major influx of new residents during this period was due to migration between states. During the between-war period's Great Migration, many African Americans moved to St. Louis. This helped swell the city's 1940 population to over 800,000. Like in most states, World War II closed immigration to Missouri.

After World War II, Missouri slowly began to draw people from different parts of the world. Although some African Americans from the South and southeast Missourians moved to St. Louis after the War, the earlier immigrants moved to suburbia and the cities' populations dropped. Immigration to the state did not increase again in any numbers until after the Immigration Act of 1965, when new immigrants arrived from Latin America, the Caribbean, and Asia.

In the early 1950s, Missouri seemed to have many dividing lines. St. Louis on the east and Kansas City on the west were rivals, and very different than the rural areas between them. Northern Missouri, rural with rolling hills, was like southern Iowa. The Ozarks, south of the Missouri River, was its own distinctive section.

Since the 1960s, more immigrants have been refugees, primarily because of changes in laws governing immigration and refugee status. Most have come from southeastern Asia, Haiti and the Caribbean, and Latin America. Most Southeast Asian arrivals are political refugees. Some have come to Missouri via the International Institute's refugee resettlement contracts with the U.S. State Department. Others have come from China and Africa to attend college and have stayed. They have been assisted by mutual aid societies, neighborhood groups, churches, and businesses. The Vietnamese, Thai, Laotian, and Filipinos have opened restaurants, groceries, bakeries, and other businesses.

The state's great rural population decline of 40 percent between 1900 and 1970 was caused more by out-state migration than urbanization. The populations of St. Louis and Kansas City both also fell during this same time. St. Louis's population fell from 857,000 in 1950 to 453,000 in 1980, a 47 percent drop—the largest decline of any major American city. The city had fallen victim to the car-driven suburban and Sunbelt exodus. This was exacerbated by the fact that St. Louis had not expanded its borders since 1876 and contained only 61 square miles, a very small amount compared to most large American cities.

In 1990, immigrants constituted 2 percent of Missouri's total population. The number of Latino/a residents almost doubled from 61,702 in 1990 to 118,592 in 2000. This increase was caused by job availability in the state's beef- and poultry-processing plants. Additionally, driven by the Balkan War in the former Yugoslav Republic in the 1990s, many Bosnian refugees came to Missouri. By the war's end in 1995, there were an estimated 40,000 to 60,000 Bosnians living in the state.

There was increased Latino/a immigration to Kansas City during the 1990s, with its population increasing from 17,017 in 1990s to 30,604 in 2000. The city's Latino/a percentage rose from 3.9 to 6.9 percent, respectively. The 2000 U.S. Census indicated that Missouri's population was growing more diverse especially in urban areas. The state had 25,076 American Indians and Alaska natives, 61,595 Asians, 3,178 native Hawaiian and other Pacific Islanders, and 118,592 Latino/as. The largest concentration of Asians was in St. Louis County, with 22,606. St. Louis city had 6,891 Asians, Boone County had 4,015, and Greene County had 2,728. Some 41,754 Latino/as lived in the Kansas City—area counties of Jackson and Clay, 14,577 in St. Louis County, St. Louis city had 7,022, and 4,434 in Greene County. There were few minorities in most rural counties. In 2000, the town of Edgar Springs, population 190, was the hypothetical center of the U.S. population.

TWENTY-FIRST CENTURY

Immigration to Missouri continued to be more diverse in the new millennium. The foreign-born population grew by 70,396 (or 178 percent) between 1990 and 2010. Most immigrants live in St. Louis (44 percent) and Kansas City (54 percent). The state's foreign-born population increased from 83,633 to 151,196, or 80.8 percent, in the 1990s.

The foreign-born population of the state increased by 53.8 percent between 2000 and 2010, representing a decline from the increase in the 1990s. During 2000–2010, Latino/as immigrants, mostly from Mexico, began arriving in the state. St. Louis had a substantial growth in the Latino population, up 28 percent between 2000 and 2005. Resultantly, Latino/as have become the second-largest immigrant group, after Asians. The Asian population is very diverse, with large foreign-born Asian Indian and Vietnamese communities, primarily in St. Louis and Kansas City.

Regarding the foreign-born in 2010, Missouri compared with other states as follows: size:26th out of 51; percentage of foreign-born in the total population: 41st out of 51; numeric change in the foreign-born: 24th out of 51; and percentage of change in the foreign-born population, from 2000 to 2010: 16 out of 51. Relatively few immigrants are moving once they arrive in the state. Of the 21,334 immigrants who moved to Missouri between 2009 and 2010, 47.8 percent (or 10,190) came from abroad and 52.2 percent (or 11,144) from another state. A total of 11,233 immigrants moved out of Missouri to somewhere within the United States, while 181,031 immigrants continued residing in the same house and 30,103 immigrants moved within Missouri.

In 2010, Missouri had one of the lowest proportions of foreign-born in the Midwest, ranking 10th of the 12 states with 3.9 percent. This is a slight increase from previous decades, as 2.7 percent were foreign-born in 2000 and 1.6 percent in 1990. This compares to a 2010 national average of 12.7 percent. Of the total immigrant population in Missouri in 2010, some 28.1 percent entered the state during the 1990s, and 44.9 percent entered in 2000 or later. About 15.5 percent entered the country before 1980, 11.5 percent in the 1980s, 28.1 percent in the 1990s, and 44.9 percent in 2000 or later.

Some 35.4 percent of the 2010 foreign-born population in Missouri was from Asia, 7.0 percent was from Africa, 22.0 percent was from Europe, 30.8 percent was from Latin America, 3.0 percent was from northern America, and 1.9 percent was from Oceania. The top three countries of birth of the foreign-born were Mexico, China, and India. Of all immigrants in 2010, 19.2 percent were born in Mexico, 6.7 percent China, and 6.5 percent in India. In contrast, the top three countries of birth in 1990 were Germany (10.5 percent), the United Kingdom (6.3 percent), and Mexico (5.6 percent).

The 2010 American Community Survey found that 100,144, or 43.1 percent, of the foreign-born population in Missouri were citizens. This was an increase since 61,786, or 40.9 percent, in 2000. This represents a change of 62.1 percent in the size of the foreign-born citizen population between 2000 and 2010. Some 80.9 percent of the immigrants who entered before 1980 were citizens, compared to 18.8 percent of those who entered in 2000 or later.

More foreign-born were male and were married, in large households, compared to the United States. In 2010, 59 percent of immigrants were married compared to 50 percent in the United States. The household size of the foreign-born was 3 compared with 2.45 for the native-born. Some 49.5 percent of the immigrant population was female in 2010 compared to 51.2 percent for the native-born. Immigrants were a tiny 0.5 percent of young children in

Missouri, 2.2 percent of youths, 5.4 percent of 18- to 54-year-old adults, and 2.9 percent of those over 55.

TOPICAL ESSAYS

REFUGEES

Since 2000, Missouri has had 13,814 refugees from 48 countries. During 2000–2011, most refugees came from: the former Yugoslavia (3,725), Somalia (1,900), Burma (1,198), Iraq (1,067), Cuba (823), and from the former Soviet Union (814). The fastest-growing refugee countries recently have been Burma and Bhutan. Refugees have continued to come from Cuba, Somalia, and Sudan, but arrivals from the former Yugoslavia, Soviet Union, and Vietnam have declined. Between 2006 and 2009, an annual average of 55 asylees has also come to Missouri.

In 2010, refugees were about 5.5 percent of the state's total foreign-born population. This is more than triple the national proportion of refugee arrivals in the past 10 years as a percentage of total foreign-born (1.7 percent). The number of

Mirha Avdagic, left, talks with her daughter Selma, 22, while cooking dinner at their home in O'Fallon, Missouri, on October 21, 2013. Mirha Avdagic was a doctor back home before being forced to leave a war-ravaged former Yugoslavia with her family in the 1990. She worked a succession of low-wage jobs in the St. Louis suburbs until she could obtain a U.S. medical license. Now her daughter, Selma, has taken part in the Bosnian Memory Project, a historical preservation effort at Fontbonne University outside St. Louis, to help keep her family's immigration story alive. (AP Photo/Jeff Roberson)

refugees is small compared with the total number of foreign-born. For most of the 1980s, St. Louis's foreign-born population declined, but this changed in the 1990s largely because of an influx of Bosnian refugees. Although St. Louis and Kansas City have served as the primary resettlement hubs for refugees arriving in Missouri, a growing number are resettling in other parts of the state. Many refugee families do a "secondary migration" from metropolitan areas to smaller cities and towns.

UNDOCUMENTED IMMIGRANTS

Estimates of the number of undocumented immigrants in Missouri vary considerably. For 2010, the U.S. Department of Homeland Security estimated 22,000 undocumented immigrants in Missouri, while the anti-immigration group Federation for American Immigration Reform (FAIR) estimated 50,000, with an estimated 70 percent from Mexico (although FAIR is considered biased). The Kansas City police chief reported to the Missouri House of Representatives that 60,000 undocumented immigrants lived in that city, also mostly from Mexico; this estimate is over double the 35,000 estimated to be living in the rest of the state. The Pew Hispanic Center estimated that there were 60,000 "unauthorized immigrants" in Missouri in 2009; 45,000 in 2008; 30,000 in 2000; and 10,000 in 1990. Whatever the number, it is still a relatively small part of Missouri's population. The Pew Hispanic Center estimates that the proportion of undocumented immigrants in Missouri almost quadrupled during 1990–2010 but adds that the proportion remains very small. The anti-immigration group FAIR's most-recent 2012 estimate is 60,000, but again, they are considered prejudiced.

The International Institute identified 100 ethnic groups in the St. Louis area, with most having arrived after World War II. One St. Louis neighborhood—"the Hill"—is still predominantly Italian, with about three-quarters of its city population. A statue of "The Italian Immigrants" in front of the church recognizes the bond between the immigrants and their religion (Mancuso 2010).

RECENT IMMIGRATION CONTROVERSIES

Anti-immigrant agitation in Missouri was considerable in the 2006–2009 period. As a result, Missouri has some of the most restrictive policies toward immigrants in the Midwest. The state requires employers to use the employment eligibility verification system E-Verify, and forbids state funds from cities that enact "sanctuary city" policies. This is ironic because the state has one of the lowest proportions of undocumented immigrants as a percentage of the total population in the region. Immigrant workers are 5 percent of the labor force compared to 16 percent nationwide. The anti-immigrant agitation probably was stimulated by the comparatively large increase between 2000 and 2009 in the percentage of foreign-born workers in the state—50 percent.

Missouri's current law strictly penalizes businesses that hire undocumented workers. The state requires public employers and businesses (with state tax credits or loans over $5,000 in government contracts) to use the federal E-verify system to check new employees' legal status. Between 2007 and 2010, the Missouri State Highway Patrol found that 583 people under arrest were in the United States without documents. The State Attorney General's Office has investigated and found 10 valid complaints about businesses hiring undocumented workers.

Anti-immigration activity in Missouri continued after 2010, but at a slower pace and with fewer legislative victories. In the 2011–2012 state legislative session, two proposed strict immigration laws failed to pass. Additional controversy may be stimulated by the enactment of the Department of Homeland Security's Deferred Action for Childhood Arrivals initiative. Some estimate that 1,000 to 10,000 Missouri immigrants may be eligible. It remains to be seen if Missouri will be as friendly to immigrants in the future as it mostly has been in the state's long history.

NOTABLE GROUPS

Missouri Immigrant and Refugee Advocates

The Missouri Immigrant and Refugee Advocates (MIRA) is a coalition of immigrant advocacy groups that was established in 2006. This coalition was preceded by the Immigrants Rights Action Task Force, part of Jobs with Justice (JwJ). When JwJ convened a 2006 meeting, in response to immigration proposals, this coalition was created. The coalition is made up of 40 organizations statewide and considers itself the leader in public interest groups related to immigration. This coalition opposes legislation against immigrants that creates a hostile legal context, as well as on the ground examples of bias. In 2013, they have established 10 "Fights," including advocating for immigration reform that helps immigrant families, strengthens all foreigners' rights, and allows for a realistic path to citizenship. They are also concerned about keeping families intact. These efforts—particularly to preserve families and communities—are particularly salient in Jefferson County. The coalition also advocates for fair housing legislation, access to higher education, and workers' rights. The group promotes public education, participates in protests, and provides referrals and help to immigrants and refugees.

BIBLIOGRAPHY

Benjamin-Alvarado, Jonathan, Louis DeSipio, and Celeste Montoya. "Latino Mobilization in New Immigrant Destinations: The Anti–H.R. 4437 Protest in Nebraska's Cities." *Urban Affairs Review* 44, no. 5 (2009): 718–35.

Billington, Ray Allen, and Martin Ridge. *Westward Expansion: A History of the American Frontier*. 5th ed. New York: Macmillan Publishing, 1982.

Burnett, Robyn, and Ken Luebbering. *Immigrant Women in the Settlement of Missouri*. Columbia: University of Missouri Press, 2005.

City of St. Louis. "A Brief History of the City of St. Louis." 2012. http://stlouis-mo.gov /visit-play/stlouis-history.cfm. Accessed March 24, 2014.

Culver, Leigh. "The Impact of New Immigration Patterns on the Provision of Police Services in Midwestern Communities." *Journal of Criminal Justice* 32 (2004): 329–44.

Dolin, Eric Jay. *Fur, Fortune, and Empire: The Epic History of the Fur Trade in America*. New York: W.W. Norton & Company, 2010.

Donna, Walter. "Immigration Decision May Have Some Impact In Missouri." *Missouri Lawyers Media Regional Business News*. 2012. EBSCO*host*. Accessed March 24, 2014.

Federation for American Immigration Reform. "Distribution of the Illegal Population." 2006. http://www.faims.org/site/PageServer?pagename=iicJmmigrationissuecentersdfe9. Accessed March 24, 2014.

Federation for American Immigration Reform. "Immigration Facts: Missouri." 2012. http:// www.fairus.org/states/Missouri?A=SearchResult&SearchID=2610449&ObjectID= 5121341&ObjectType=35. Accessed March 24, 2014.

Fennelly, Katherine. "History of Immigration in Missouri." Midwest Coalition of Immigration and the Region's Future, 2010. http://chicago.dpdev.cla.umn.edu/missouri /history. Accessed March 24, 2014.

Foley, William. *A History of Missouri, 1673 to 1820*. Columbia: University of Missouri Press, 2000.

Huping, Ling. "'Hop Alley': Myth and Reality of the St. Louis Chinatown, 1860's-1930's." *Journal of Urban History* 28 (January 2002): 184–219.

Kelly, Wiese. "Fight May Come to Missouri Next: Far-Reaching Law Targeted at Illegal Immigration." *Missouri Lawyers Media Regional Business News*, 2007. EBSCO*host*. Accessed March 24, 2014.

Larsen, Lawrence H. *A History of Missouri: 1953–2003*. Vol. VI. Columbia: University of Missouri Press, 2004.

Lazzerini, Rickie. *Missouri History*." Kindredtrails.com, 2005. http://www.kindredtrails .com/Missouri-History-3.html. Accessed March 24, 2014.

Mancuso, Janice Therese. "Little Italy—Italian Immigrants Influence America." *La Gazzetta Italiana*. Cleveland: PAS Publishing, 2010. http://www.lagazzettaitaliana.com/little italypart2.aspx. Accessed March 24, 2014.

Mannies, J. "Missouri Starts to Join the Big Debate over Immigration." *The St. Louis Post-Dispatch*, 2006. http://domino.stltoday.com:80/stltoday/emaf.nsf/Popup? ReadForm&db=stltoday percent5Cnews percent5Ccolumnists.nsf&docid=A3C25AB C3E3FO91B862571A3001355F7. Accessed March 24, 2014.

McReynolds, Edwin C. *Missouri: A History of the Crossroads State*. Norman: University of Oklahoma Press, 1962.

Migration Policy Institute. "Missouri: Social & Demographic Characteristics." MPI Data Hub, 2012. http://www.migrationinformation.org/datahub/state.cfm?ID=mo. Accessed March 24, 2014.

Missouri Immigrant and Refugee Advocates. Missouri Immigrant and Refugee Advocates Webpage. http://www.mira-mo.org/wordpress/?page_id=4. Accessed February 21, 2014.

Missouri Immigration and Refugee Advocates. "SB 590 Is Bad for Families and Bad for Missouri." 2012. http://www.mira-mo.org/wordpress/?paged=2. Accessed March 24, 2014.

Mormino, Gary Ross. *Immigrants on the Hill: Italian-Americans in St. Louis, 1882–1982.* Urbana: University of Illinois Press, 1986.

Mullen-Dominguez, Sarah E. "Alienating the Unalienable: Equal Protection and Valley Park, Missouri's Illegal Immigration Ordinance." *Saint Louis University Law Journal* 52 (2008): 1317.

Passel, Jeffrey S., and D'Vera Cohn. *U.S. Unauthorized Immigration Flows Are Down Sharply Since Mid-Decade.* Washington, DC: Pew Research Center, 2010.

Primm, James Neal. *Lion of the Valley: St. Louis, Missouri.* Boulder, CO: Pruett Publishing Company, 1981.

Segal, Uma A. "Mexican Migration to the United States: A Focus on Missouri." *Journal of Immigrant & Refugee Studies* 6, no. 3 (2008): 451–62.

Smith, Jeffrey E. "A Preservation Plan for St. Louis." 1995. http://stlouis-mo.gov/government/departments/planning/cultural-resources/preservation-plan/Part-I-St-Louis-Historic-Contexts.cfm. Accessed March 24, 2014.

U.S. Census Bureau. 2010 American Community Survey. "Selected Characteristics of the Native and Foreign-Born Populations: 2010 American Community Survey 1-Year Estimates." SO501, 2011. http://factfinder2.census.gov/faces/tableservices/jsf/pages/productview.xhtml?pid=ACS_10_1YR_S0501&prodType=table. Accessed March 24, 2014.